Lecture Notes in Computer Science 16091

Founding Editors

Gerhard Goos
Juris Hartmanis

Editorial Board Members

Elisa Bertino, *Purdue University, West Lafayette, IN, USA*
Wen Gao, *Peking University, Beijing, China*
Bernhard Steffen ⓘ, *TU Dortmund University, Dortmund, Germany*
Moti Yung ⓘ, *Columbia University, New York, NY, USA*

The series Lecture Notes in Computer Science (LNCS), including its subseries Lecture Notes in Artificial Intelligence (LNAI) and Lecture Notes in Bioinformatics (LNBI), has established itself as a medium for the publication of new developments in computer science and information technology research, teaching, and education.

LNCS enjoys close cooperation with the computer science R & D community, the series counts many renowned academics among its volume editors and paper authors, and collaborates with prestigious societies. Its mission is to serve this international community by providing an invaluable service, mainly focused on the publication of conference and workshop proceedings and postproceedings. LNCS commenced publication in 1973.

Sarah Neuwirth · Arnab Kumar Paul ·
Tobias Weinzierl · Erin Claire Carson
Editors

High Performance Computing

ISC High Performance 2025 International Workshops
Hamburg, Germany, June 10–13, 2025
Revised Selected Papers

 Springer

Editors
Sarah Neuwirth
Johannes Gutenberg University Mainz
Mainz, Germany

Arnab Kumar Paul
Birla Institute of Technology and Science
Pilani, Rajasthan, India

Tobias Weinzierl
Durham University
Durham, UK

Erin Claire Carson
Charles University
Prague, Czech Republic

ISSN 0302-9743 ISSN 1611-3349 (electronic)
Lecture Notes in Computer Science
ISBN 978-3-032-07611-3 ISBN 978-3-032-07612-0 (eBook)
https://doi.org/10.1007/978-3-032-07612-0

© The Editor(s) (if applicable) and The Author(s), under exclusive license
to Springer Nature Switzerland AG 2026

This work is subject to copyright. All rights are solely and exclusively licensed by the Publisher, whether the whole or part of the material is concerned, specifically the rights of translation, reprinting, reuse of illustrations, recitation, broadcasting, reproduction on microfilms or in any other physical way, and transmission or information storage and retrieval, electronic adaptation, computer software, or by similar or dissimilar methodology now known or hereafter developed.
The use of general descriptive names, registered names, trademarks, service marks, etc. in this publication does not imply, even in the absence of a specific statement, that such names are exempt from the relevant protective laws and regulations and therefore free for general use.
The publisher, the authors and the editors are safe to assume that the advice and information in this book are believed to be true and accurate at the date of publication. Neither the publisher nor the authors or the editors give a warranty, expressed or implied, with respect to the material contained herein or for any errors or omissions that may have been made. The publisher remains neutral with regard to jurisdictional claims in published maps and institutional affiliations.

This Springer imprint is published by the registered company Springer Nature Switzerland AG
The registered company address is: Gewerbestrasse 11, 6330 Cham, Switzerland

If disposing of this product, please recycle the paper.

Preface

The 40th edition of the ISC High Performance conference (ISC-HPC 2025) was held in Hamburg, Germany.

The in-person conference spanned the period from June 10 to June 13, 2025, and the HPC community responded enthusiastically, as manifested by over 3,500 attendees. Like in previous years, ISC 2025 was accompanied by the ISC High Performance workshop series. Due to a public bank holiday in Germany, ISC however started on a Tuesday, and the workshops hence moved to the Friday.

Out of the 24 workshops, ten chose the option to contribute papers to this proceedings volume:

- 6th ISC HPC International Workshop on Monitoring & Operational Data Analytics (MODA)
- 9th International Workshop on In Situ Visualization (WOIV)
- 5th International Workshop on Computational Aspects of Deep Learning (CADL)
- Energy Efficiency with Sustainable Performance: Techniques, Tools, and Best Practices (EESP)
- Fifth Workshop on Compiler-assisted Correctness Checking and Performance Optimization for HPC (C3PO)
- Fifth Workshop on Interactive and Urgent HPC (WIUHPC)
- Fifth Workshop on Communication, I/O, and Storage at Scale on Next-Generation Platforms – Scalable Infrastructures (IXPUG)
- HPC on Heterogeneous Hardware (H3)
- International Workshop on RISC-V for HPC at ISC
- The First International Workshop on Foundational Large Language Models Advances for HPC (LLM4HPC)

Besides the workshops represented by papers, we decided to give the organizers of 14 additional workshops without proceedings the opportunity to summarize their insights and outcomes in this volume.

In total, 49 workshop papers plus 5 state-of-the-art review/summary papers outlining the key findings of workshops were accepted for publication, from 70 submissions. Each paper underwent a thorough review by their respective workshops' Program Committee or the Proceedings team, respectively. With on average of three reviewers per paper, single-blind reviews, and the opportunity for the authors to revise their contribution after acceptance, the printed papers are of outstanding quality.

We will gather next year in Hamburg, Germany, for another successful ISC High Performance workshops series and continue connecting the dots—this year's conference theme. Until then, we want to thank our workshop committee members, workshop organizers, and all contributors and attendees of the ISC 2025 workshops, and we are proud to present the latest findings on the topics related to the research, development, and applications of large-scale, high-performance systems.

July 2025

Sarah Neuwirth
Arnab Paul
Tobias Weinzierl
Erin Claire Carson

Organization

Workshop Committee

Sarah Neuwirth (Chair)	Johannes Gutenberg University Mainz, Germany
Arnab Paul (Deputy Chair)	BITS Pilani, K. K. Birla Goa Campus, India
Tobias Weinzierl (Proceedings Chair)	Durham University, UK
Erin Claire Carson (Proceedings Deputy Chair)	Charles University, Czech Republic
Nick Brown	Edinburgh Parallel Computing Centre, University of Edinburgh, UK
Suren Byna	Ohio State University, Lawrence Berkeley National Laboratory, USA
Stefano Corda	Huawei Technologies AG, Switzerland
Jaap Dijkshoorn	SURF, Netherlands
Rafael Ferreira da Silva	Oak Ridge National Laboratory, USA
Marc Joos	CEA, France
Julian Kunkel	Georg-August-Universität Göttingen, GWDG, Germany
Sanmukh Kuppannagari	Case Western Reserve University, USA
Jay Lofstead	Sandia National Laboratories, University of New Mexico, USA
Ivy Peng	KTH Royal Institute of Technology, Sweden
André Pereira	University of Minho, INESC TEC, Portugal
Jonas Posner	University of Kassel, Germany
Nelson Ruwa	Zimbabwe Centre for High Performance Computing, University of Zimbabwe, Zimbabwe
Harisankar Sadasivan	AMD, University of Washington, Seattle, USA
Naw Safrin Sattar	Oak Ridge National Laboratory, USA
Sougata Sen	BITS Pilani KK Birla Goa Campus, India
Filippo Spiga	Nvidia Corporation, UK
Tom St. John	Meta, USA
Suyash Tandon	AMD, University of Michigan, USA
François Tessier	Inria, France
Andy Turner	Edinburgh Parallel Computing Centre, UK
Chen Wang	Lawrence Livermore National Laboratory, USA

Contents

6th ISC HPC International Workshop on Monitoring and Operational Data Analytics (MODA25)

Duration-Informed Workload Scheduler 3
   Daniela Loreti, Davide Leone, and Andrea Borghesi

Monitoring Energy Consumption of Workloads on HPC Vega 15
   Teo Prica and Aleš Zamuda

A Unified I/O Monitoring Framework Using eBPF 28
   Mahendra Paipuri

Supporting HPC Users with LLview 40
   Filipe Souza Mendes Guimarães, Aravind Sankaran, and Wolfgang Frings

What Time Taught Us: Monitoring a Computing Technology Testbed Across Multiple Years 52
   Eva Siegmann, David Carlson, Nikolay A. Simakov, Anthony Curtis, Alan Calder, and Robert J. Harrison

9th International Workshop on In Situ Visualization (WOIV'25)

Enabling Modular In-Situ Workflows Through *CatalystMaestro* and *CatalystComposer* 67
   Marcel Krüger, Torsten W. Kuhlen, and Tim Gerrits

Updating Inshimtu with Catalyst2 and Integrating an HPC MiniApp: Lessons Learned 81
   James Kress and Thomas Theußl

Issues and Challenges of Deploying in-Situ Visualization for SPH Codes 95
   Jean M. Favre and Jean-Guillaume Piccinali

5th International Workshop on Computational Aspects of Deep Learning (CADL)

Direct Feedback Alignment for Recurrent Neural Networks 111
   Sara Folchini, Andrea Cossu, Andrea Ceni, Vincenzo Lomonaco, Davide Bacciu, and Claudio Gallicchio

Assessing Tenstorrent's RISC-V MatMul Acceleration Capabilities 123
   Hiari Pizzini Cavagna, Daniele Cesarini, and Andrea Bartolini

Automatically Parallelizing Batch Inference on Deep Neural Networks
Using Fiats and Fortran 2023 "Do Concurrent" 135
   Damian Rouson, Zhe Bai, Dan Bonachea, Kareem Ergawy, Ethan Gutmann, Michael Klemm, Katherine Rasmussen, Brad Richardson, Sameer Shende, David Torres, and Yunhao Zhang

Optimizing Edge AI Models on HPC Systems with the Edge in the Loop 148
   Marcel Aach, Cyril Blanc, Andreas Lintermann, and Kurt De Grave

Evaluation of Distributed Asynchronous Checkpointing
in High-Performance Computing 162
   Riccardo Scheda, Domitilla Brandoni, Laura Cavalli, and Laura Morselli

Energy Efficiency with Sustainable Performance: Techniques, Tools, and Best Practices (EESP)

Characterizing GPU Energy Usage in Exascale-Ready Portable Science
Applications 177
   William F. Godoy, Oscar Hernandez, Paul R. C. Kent, Maria Patrou, Kazi Asifuzzaman, Narasinga Rao Miniskar, Pedro Valero-Lara, Jeffrey S. Vetter, Matthew D. Sinclair, Jason Lowe-Power, and Bobby R. Bruce

What A Waste 191
   Shaina Smith, Jordan M. Abt, and Ryan E. Grant

Pinpointing Idle-Power Regressions in Linux 205
   Hannes Tröpgen, Till Smejkal, Thomas Ilsche, Robert Schöne, and Horst Schirmeier

DARE-ML: Democratized Accessible Resource Environment for Machine
Learning in the SUPERCOM Platform 219
   Matteo Mendula, Caterina Leonelli, Marco Miozzo, and Paolo Dini

Power-Capping Metric Evaluation for Improving Energy Efficiency
in HPC Applications 231
   Maria Patrou, Thomas Wang, Wael Elwasif, Markus Eisenbach,
   Ross Miller, William Godoy, and Oscar Hernandez

Experience on Clock Rate Adjustment for Energy-Efficient
GPU-Accelerated Real-World Codes 245
   Giorgio Amati, Matteo Turisini, Andrea Monterubbiano,
   Mattia Paladino, Elisabetta Boella, Daniele Gregori, and Danilo Croce

Running Energy-Efficient HPL on APUs: Strategies and Best Practices 258
   Jean-Yves Vet and Gabriel Hautreux

Analysis of Application Power Characteristics Using Performance
Counters on A64FX 271
   Ryoma Ohara, Keiji Yamamoto, and Toshihiro Hanawa

Fifth Workshop on Compiler-Assisted Correctness Checking and Performance Optimization for HPC (C3PO'25)

CGPatch: Streamlining Static Call Graph Validation Using Selective
Instrumentation 287
   Sebastian Kreutzer, Silas Martens, Peter Arzt, Tim Heldmann,
   and Christian Bischof

Speculative Recursion Unrolling 300
   Tim Heldmann, Tim Ziegler, Peter Arzt, and Christian Bischof

From C to Rust: Evaluating LLM Capabilities in Transpilation Through
Compilation Errors 311
   Andrea Valenzuela, Marta Gonzalez-Mallo, Cristian Gutierrez,
   Dario Garcia-Gasulla, Gokcen Kestor, and Sara Royuela

CompilerGPT: Leveraging Large Language Models for Analyzing
and Acting on Compiler Optimization Reports 325
   Peter Pirkelbauer and Chunhua Liao

Improving Compiler Support for SIMD Offload Using Arm Streaming SVE ... 339
   Mohamed Husain Noor Mohamed, Adarsh Patil, Latchesar Ionkov,
   and Eric Van Hensbergen

Fifth Workshop on Interactive and Urgent HPC (WIUHPC)

Dynamic Resource Management Framework for Elastic Computing 351
   Arjun Parab, Amir Raoofy, and Josef Weidendorfer

Enabling Seamless Transitions from Experimental to Production HPC
for Interactive Workflows 363
   *Brian D. Etz, David M. Rogers, Michael J. Brim, Ketan Maheshwari,
Kellen Leland, Tyler J. Skluzacek, Jack Lange, Daniel Pelfrey,
Jordan Webb, Patrick Widener, Ryan Adamson, Christopher Zimmer,
Verónica G. Melesse Vergara, Mallikarjun Shankar, Sarp Oral,
and Rafael Ferreira da Silva*

A Novel Approach to Dynamic Computing Using Slurm 376
   *Leonardo Sala, Ivano Talamo, Borys Sharapov, Greta Assmann,
and Alvise Dorigo*

Fifth Workshop on Communication, I/O, and Storage at Scale on Next-Generation Platforms – Scalable Infrastructures (ixpug-comm-io-storage)

Combining Malleability and Distributed Control Mechanisms to Reduce
I/O Contention 387
   *Paula Sanchez-Checa, Javier Garcia-Blas, Jesus Carretero,
and David E. Singh*

DOCA UROM: A Vehicle for Offloading HPC and AI to DPUs 401
   *Ferrol Aderholdt, Zach Tiffany, Rohit Zambre,
Manjunath Gorentla Venkata, Yuri Shatsman, Muhammad Abu Saleh,
and Gil Bloch*

Accelerating I/O in Scientific Workflows with the Impact of Apache
Ignite's In-Memory File System 416
   *Vijayalakshmi Saravanan, Sai Karthik Navuluru, Lakshman Tamil,
and Khaled Ibrahim*

HPC on Heterogeneous Hardware (H3)

Generation of Mixed-Precision Kernels for Quantized Transformer
Encoders with EXO 431
   *Adrián Castelló, Héctor Martínez, Francisco D. Igual,
and Enrique S. Quintana-Ortí*

Training an Image Classification Model on a Supercomputer with AMD
Genoa Compute Nodes 444
    Maram Hesham Badawi and Mohsin Ahmed Shaikh

Exploring QUBO on LPUs for Engineering 456
    Johannes Gebert, Dan Glück, Chene Tradonsky, and Jonathan Schäfer

Investigating Matrix Repartitioning to Address the Over
and Undersubscription Challenge for a GPU-Based CFD Solver
.... 468
    Gregor Olenik, Marcel Koch, and Hartwig Anzt

Stream-K++: Adaptive GPU GEMM Kernel Selection and Scheduling
for AI Using Bloom Filters 480
    Harisankar Sadasivan, Muhammed Emin Ozturk, Muhammad Osama,
    Chris Millette, Astha Rai, Maksim Podkorytov, John Afaganis,
    Carlus Huang, Jing Zhang, and Jun Liu

Accelerating Electrostatics Simulations with GPUs 494
    Amir Bouslama, Pratik Nayak, Andreas Blaszczyk, Carsten Trinitis,
    and Hartwig Anzt

International Workshop on RISC-V for HPC at ISC

Streamlining Fedora Linux Distributions for RISC-V: A Scalable
and Automated Approach 509
    Surendra Billa, Arif Badar, Rushikesh Jadhav, Yogeshwar Sonawane,
    and Sanjay Wandhekar

Evaluating RISC-V Processor as an Alternative for High Performance
Computing 521
    Aniket P. Garade, Ashish Bisht, H. V. Deepika, P. Haribabu,
    S. A. Kumar, and S. D. Sudarsan

Evaluation of RVV-Enabled COTS Platforms with Matrix Multiplication
and Exo 534
    Adrián Castelló, Héctor Martínez, Sandra Catalán, Francisco D. Igual,
    and Enrique S. Quintana-Ortí

Advancing the RISC-V Performance Simulation Ecosystem with Data
Prefetching 548
    Luís Crespo, Nuno Neves, Pedro Tomas, and Nuno Roma

RISC-V in HPC: a Look Into Tools for Performance Monitoring 562
  *Fabio Banchelli, Rafel Albert Bros Esqueu, Tiago Rocha, Nuno Roma,
  Pedro Tomás, Nuno Neves, and Filippo Mantovani*

Monte Cimone v2: HPC RISC-V Cluster Evaluation and Optimization 576
  *Emanuele Venieri, Simone Manoni, Gabriele Ceccolini,
  Giacomo Madella, Federico Ficarelli, Daniele Gregori,
  Andrea Acquaviva, Luca Benini, and Andrea Bartolini*

Parallel FFTW on RISC-V: A Comparative Study Including OpenMP,
MPI, and HPX 586
  Alexander Strack, Christopher Taylor, and Dirk Pflüger

Exploring Fast Fourier Transforms on the Tenstorrent Wormhole 598
  Nick Brown, Jake Davies, and Felix Le Clair

The First International Workshop on Foundational Large Language Models Advances for HPC (LLM4HPC)

Leveraging AI for Productive and Trustworthy HPC Software: Challenges
and Research Directions 615
  *Keita Teranishi, Harshitha Menon, William F. Godoy,
  Prasanna Balaprakash, David Bau, Tal Ben-Nun, Abhinav Bhatele,
  Franz Franchetti, Michael Franusich, Todd Gamblin,
  Giorgis Georgakoudis, Tom Goldstein, Arjun Guha, Steven E. Hahn,
  Costin Iancu, Zheming Jin, Terry Jones, Tze-Meng Low, Het Mankad,
  Narasinga Rao Miniskar, Mohammad Alaul Haque Monil,
  Daniel Nichols, Konstantinos Parasyris, Swaroop Pophale,
  Pedro Valero-Lara, Jeffrey S. Vetter, Samuel Williams, and Aaron Young*

LLM & HPC: Benchmarking DeepSeek's Performance
in High-Performance Computing Tasks 626
  Noujoud Nader, Patrick Diehl, Steve Brandt, and Hartmut Kaiser

Analysis of MPI Parallel Code Generated by GPT-4o 639
  Rin Tanaka, Hayato Yamaki, Shinobu Miwa, and Hiroki Honda

Workshop Review Contributions

QRUCH Workshop Summary 655
  Philippe Deniel, Suzanne Talon, Venkatesh Kannan, and Ariana Torres

State of the Art in High-Performance Containerization: Insights
from the 11th HPC Container Workshop at ISC 2025 660
   Abdulrahman Azab, Christian Kniep, Barbara Krašovec,
   Holger Gantikow, and David Brayford

A2SD: Accelerating Scientific Innovation Through Autonomous
Discovery Systems 668
   Michela Taufer, Rafael Ferreira da Silva, Benjamin Mintz,
   Milad Abolhasani, Rosa M. Badia, Ewa Deelman, Robert G. Moore,
   and John Shalf

The Future of Benchmarks in Supercomputing 675
   Sreenivas Rangan Sukumar, Jack C. Wells, and Roy Varghese

RSEHPC@ISC25: Tools and Techniques for Continuous Integration
and Benchmarking 683
   René Caspart, Robert Speck, and Michele Mesiti

Author Index 693

6th ISC HPC International Workshop on Monitoring and Operational Data Analytics (MODA25)

MODA 2025 Preface

Objectives/Topics

The 6th Monitoring and Operational Data Analytics (MODA 2025) Workshop provided insights into the current state and trends of monitoring and analyzing operational data in High Performance Computing (HPC) systems and data centers. The focus of the MODA 2025 workshop was on ways to collect, store, visualize, interpret, and leverage large-scale system data, as well as the use of machine learning and artificial intelligence (AI) techniques to enable proactive system control and optimization. MODA 2025 also included contributions on energy efficiency, providing a forum for HPC operators, administrators, and researchers to share best practices and motivate users toward sustainable resource usage.

The MODA workshop has three goals. First, to establish common frameworks and standards to guide more consistent and effective MODA practices, and encourage work that closes the gap between simply collecting data and using it effectively to achieve real improvements in HPC operations. Second, to bring together experts to share practical solutions, discuss challenges, and explore new ideas for improving how we gather, analyze, and leverage operational data. Third, to identify current trends, highlight critical gaps, and shape the evolution of MODA, influencing the design, planning, and procurement of future HPC systems as we move into the post-Exascale computing era.

Workshop Organization

Organizers

Jim Brandt	Sandia National Laboratories, USA
Ann Gentile	Sandia National Laboratories, USA
Thomas Jakobsche	University of Basel, Switzerland
Torsten Wilde	Hewlett Packard Enterprise, Germany

Steering Board

Florina Ciorba	University of Basel, Switzerland
Utz-Uwe Haus	HPE EMEA Research Lab, Switzerland
Martin Schulz	Technische Universität München, Germany

Duration-Informed Workload Scheduler

Daniela Loreti, Davide Leone, and Andrea Borghesi[✉]

DISI, University of Bologna, Viale Risorgimento 2, Bologna, Italy
{daniela.loreti,andrea.borghesi3}@unibo.it,
davide.leone@studio.unibo.it

Abstract. High-performance computing systems are complex machines whose behaviour is governed by the correct functioning of its many subsystems. Among these, the workload scheduler has a crucial impact on the timely execution of the jobs continuously submitted to the computing resources. Making high-quality scheduling decisions is contingent on knowing the duration of submitted jobs before their execution–a non-trivial task for users that can be tackled with Machine Learning.

In this work, we devise a workload scheduler enhanced with a duration prediction module built via Machine Learning. We evaluate its effectiveness and show its performance using workload traces from a Tier-0 supercomputer, demonstrating a decrease in mean waiting time across all jobs of around 11%. Lower waiting times are directly connected to better quality of service from the users' point of view and higher turnaround from the system's perspective.

Keywords: High-Performance Computing · Duration Prediction · Machine Learning

1 Introduction

The ever-increasing capabilities of modern High-Performance Computing (HPC) facilities are already going beyond the exascale. Despite this impressive growth, the increase in service demand due to emerging fields of science makes the computing power offered by HPC infrastructures a coveted resource. By now, techniques to improve the efficient usage of HPC resources are a pressing need.

Workload schedulers are among the mechanisms that have the greatest impact on HPC facilities' efficiency (as they have on computing systems of any scale). Besides, the quality of the scheduling choices has a direct effect on HPC users' experience because it influences the turnaround time of the launched jobs. The ability of these systems to make high-quality scheduling decisions depends on a variety of factors, not least the availability of reliable estimations of the execution time for each job before it is submitted. Unfortunately, the ever-growing complexity of parallel HPC software makes performance prediction harder and harder with traditional methods (e.g., with techniques based on code analysis).

Over the last decades, Machine Learning models have been applied to almost any scientific field in order to improve the quality of predictions and help manage the complexity of domains characterized by many input features. In particular, although ML techniques have proven successful in the runtime estimation of specific tasks [11], the efficacy of integrating their predictive power in HPC scheduling systems still needs to be explored.

In this work, we focus on ML techniques as a means to manage the complexity of the runtime prediction task for HPC jobs, and we explore the advantages and drawbacks of integrating ML-based runtime estimations into an HPC scheduling policy.

In detail, the contribution of this paper is two-fold:

- Revealing how ML models can be used to predict the duration of the workload in modern, production supercomputers; a thorough analysis of the quality of the estimate is provided using a real supercomputer, Marconi100, as a case study.
- Developing an HPC workload scheduler that is informed by the predictions made by the ML models. The scheduler has been validated using an off-the-shelf HPC simulator, demonstrating significant improvements in terms of waiting time (a decrease of 11.21% with respect to using the standard duration estimate provided by users), mean turnaround time (decreased by 4.35%) and average job slowdown (decreased by 94.96%).

Therefore, the rest of the paper is structured as follows. Section 2 presents an overview of the state of the arts of runtime estimation as well as workload scheduling with a particular focus on HPC environments. Section 3 evaluates the performance of four different ML methods in predicting the duration of HPC jobs given only features that can be available at submission time as input. The logic of the proposed Duration-Informed Workload Scheduler (DIWS) is then presented in Sect. 4 along with a comparison of its performance with a widely employed scheduling policy. Conclusion and future work follow.

2 Related Works

2.1 Runtime Prediction

In recent literature, various machine learning techniques have been used to estimate application workflows, such as decision trees [13] and neural networks [14]. A comprehensive survey on resource provisioning prediction models is provided in [1]. It must be noted that the majority of existing works do not explicitly focus on the duration of HPC application as a prediction target. While most studies focus on lightweight algorithms on standard hardware, runtime prediction for HPC workloads remains under-explored; see [8,15] for some preliminary results.

2.2 HPC Workload Scheduling

First-Come First-Served (FCFS) and Earliest Available Start Time Yielding (EASY) backfilling are still the most widely used scheduling policies in production HPC systems as they are easy to implement and known to produce good results. EASY backfilling allows smaller jobs to skip ahead of larger jobs, as long as this does not delay the job at the head of the queue. As such, this policy strongly relies on user-provided runtime estimates, which are known to be significantly inaccurate on average [7]. Therefore, some recent works focused on improving EASY backfilling with ML-enhanced runtime predictions [12,16]. These works are limited as they do not consider full Tier-0 systems (but rather focus on smaller-scale datacenters), with a more diverse distribution of job durations.

3 Runtime Prediction

In this section, we start by introducing the ML models used to estimate the workload duration on the target supercomputer. Then, we report their performance in terms of prediction accuracy.

3.1 Prediction Models

The ML models selected are the following: *(i)* Decision Tree Regressor (DT) [6] – a supervised learning algorithm that constructs a tree-structured model to represent decisions and their consequences. Regression trees partition the input feature space recursively into smaller regions, assigning a numerical value as the output for each region. *(ii)* Random Forest (RF) [5] – an extension of the DT model designed for regression tasks, where the target is a continuous numeric value. It combines predictions from an ensemble of decision trees to improve robustness and accuracy. *(iii)* Gradient Boosting (GB) [10] – an ensemble learning technique that incrementally builds a strong predictive model by combining multiple weak learners, often decision or regression trees. Each new model corrects the errors of the previous ones, enhancing predictive performance. *(iv)* Fully Connected Neural Network (FCNN) [3] – a machine learning model inspired by biological neural networks. It consists of interconnected layers of nodes (neurons), where each layer processes and transforms input data into output predictions. Each neuron's input aggregates outputs from the previous layer, followed by a non-linear transformation to generate the layer's output. In particular, we employed a network with three hidden layers and dropout to prevent overfitting and used the Huber loss, which is less sensitive to outliers. The number of layers and the number of neurons in each layer are the result of a non-exhaustive naïve grid-like search, in which we trained a total of 15 networks varying only these two parameters to find the best combination.

3.2 Empirical Results

We evaluate the performance of the aforementioned ML techniques in predicting the runtimes from PM100 [2], a large dataset of real-life job runs, derived from

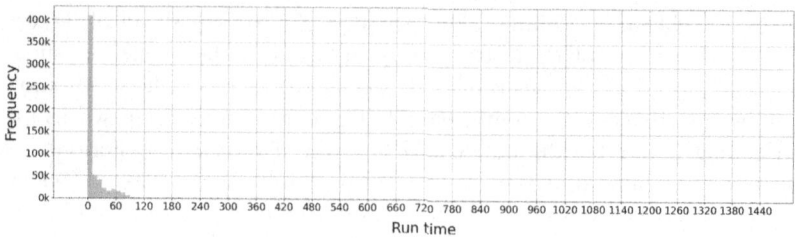

Fig. 1. Histogram of the target variable *run_time*

an accurate elaboration of a two-years-long data collection [4] from a production supercomputer: MARCONI100 hosted by the HPC center CINECA[1]. The considered dataset consists of 628.977 elements and a set of submission time features for each job, which are described in Table 1. In Table 2, the features are shown together with the target variable *run_time* and a statistical description of each field. We have selected a subset of the whole PM100 dataset (comprising more than one million jobs), as the removed entries contain missing values. The impact of missing data on the accuracy of ML models is an interesting problem by itself, but we leave it for future research, as in this work we want to focus on the base problem of predicting workload duration.

The analysis of the data reveals several significant characteristics. A particularly striking feature is the high variability observed in the *cpu* and *mem(GB)* metrics, as indicated by their large standard deviations and the substantial range between the minimum and maximum values. This variability highlights the heterogeneous nature of the dataset in these dimensions. Additionally, the data exhibits pronounced skewness across most variables. This skewness is primarily driven by the presence of a few extreme outliers, which have a notable impact on the mean values. Such outliers inflate the averages, creating a substantial gap between the mean and the more representative median values. The consistently lower median values across most variables suggest that the majority of the dataset is concentrated around lower values, while a small number of high-value entries significantly raise the mean. These trends are further corroborated by the visual analysis of histograms (as the one showed in Fig. 1), where the skewness and the influence of outliers are clearly discernible. The histograms provide a compelling illustration of how the distribution of values deviates from symmetry, emphasizing the predominance of lower values juxtaposed with infrequent but extremely high values. To summarize, we are dealing with a dataset coming from a real Tier-0, production supercomputer; this entails, that the workload we are considering is complex and non-trivial to handle.

The performance of four ML models—Decision Tree, Random Forest, Gradient Boosting, and Neural Network (see Sect. 3.1) – was evaluated based on their predictive accuracy and error characteristics. The following metrics were used for comparison: Mean Absolute Error (MAE), Mean Squared Error (MSE), Root Mean Squared Error (RMSE), the coefficient of determination (R^2), and the 95%

---

[1] https://www.hpc.cineca.it/systems/hardware/marconi100/.

Table 1. Brief description of the features.

Feature Name	Description
cpu	Number of CPU cores requested by the job
mem (GB)	Amount of memory requested by the hob
node	Number of nodes requested for the job
gres/gpu	GPU resources requested by the job
user_id	Identifier of the user submitting the job
qos	Quality of Service level associated with the job
time_limit	Maximum runtime allowed for the job

Table 2. Brief statistical description of the dataset.

	CPU	mem(GB)	nodes	GRES/GPU	user_id	QoS	time_limit	run_time
mean	121.379	236.068	1.693	5.630	110.895	0.051	1038.069	43.433
std	246.657	1008.594	6.961	27.927	118.594	0.368	506.318	168.719
min	1.000	0.098	1.000	1.000	0.000	0.000	1.000	0.017
25%	4.000	7.813	1.000	1.000	2.000	0.000	720.000	0.017
50%	80.000	230.000	1.000	4.000	93.000	0.000	1440.000	0.83
75%	128.000	237.5000	1.000	4.000	191.000	0.000	1440.000	22.700
max	32768.000	61500.000	256.000	1024.000	387.000	3.000	1440.000	1439.912

confidence interval for prediction errors. Furthermore, the analysis included an investigation of error characteristics categorized as overestimations, underestimations, and exact estimations (down to half a second).

Furthermore, we compute the *effectiveness* of the four considered models by measuring the improvements in approximating the actual run time with respect to the *time_limit* column, which reports the user-provided estimation. As the consequences of an underestimation are–in general–more problematic than overestimation, we also consider *valid predictions* the ones not lower than the actual run time. Table 3 shows the performance of the four considered models; the data has been normalized using the MinMax scaler algorithm implemented in Scikit-learn for the sake of the neural network (these models are notoriously better performing with normalized data). The dataset was randomly split between training and testing sets, with a split ratio of 70%/30%.

From the results RF appears to be the best model, followed at short distances by DT and FCNN, while GB yields the lowest performance. The Neural Network model had the lowest MAE, while RF achieved the lowest MSE, closely followed by DT. Decision Tree and Random Forest models achieved the highest R^2 values, indicating better explanatory power compared to the other models. All models predominantly overestimated predictions, with GB showing the highest proportion of overestimations and NN the lowest. Most overestimation errors (above 92%) were within 60 min across models. GB had the lowest proportion of underestimations – but the overall performance of GB is lowered by the higher number of overestimates. Exact predictions were rare, with Decision Tree and Random Forest achieving the highest proportion, while GB and FCNN had almost negligible exact predictions (0.02%).

Table 3. Performance of the four considered ML models

	Decision Tree	Random Forest	Gradient Boosting	Neural Network
MAE	23.51	23.53	40.11	21.95
MSE	8001.99	7968.58	13060.00	9202.41
RMSE	89.45	89.27	114.28	95.93
R^2	0.72	0.72	0.54	0.68
Confidence interval (95%)	[0.00, 326.70]	[0.00, 325.60]	[0.00, 227.48]	[0.00, 344.92]
OVERESTIMATION				
Total cases	79.49%	79.59%	82.07%	80.79%
min error	0.01	0.01	0.01	0.01
max error	1431.00	1303.47	806.34	1624.70
avg error	14.76	14.72	24.35	12.39
error < **60 min**	96.30%	96.26%	92.38%	97.98%
UNDERESTIMATION				
Total cases	20.02%	19.95%	17.93%	19.18%
min error	0.01	0.01	0.01	0.01
max error	1425.53	1425.54	1418.82	1427.30
avg error	58.85	59.23	112.26	62.23
error < **60 min**	86.67%	86.34%	73.95%	83.33%
EXACT ESTIMATION				
Total cases	0.50%	0.47%	0.02%	0.02%
EFFECTIVENESS				
General	78.09%	78.23%	74.16%	78.72%
Valid prediction	97.94%	97.96%	92.79%	97.63%

Data Augmentation. We conducted another experiment to explore the possibility of improving the quality of the predictions. Namely, we performed a data augmentation step before training by adding the average resource requested by each user, i.e., the mean values for the requested number of CPUs, memory, physical nodes, GPUs and time limit. As aspected, the results (shown in Table 4) sightly improve with data augmentation.

Time-Consecutive Split Setting. Finally, we performed a last experimental evaluation with a different splitting strategy for training and testing sets to simulate a real-life situation better. Since in practice the scheduler typically works on subsequent job submissions, it is requested to estimate the runtime of future jobs given the jobs arrived in the past as training examples. Therefore, randomly splitting the dataset into training and testing sets may not represent a real-life case. In the following, we repeat the evaluations using a consecutive split over time, i.e., all jobs before a certain date are used for training and all those after are used for testing. We chose the date such that the test set contains exactly the same number of jobs as the one with the random split. Table 5 shows that the quality of the results is comparable to those of the previous experiment. In particular, all the error values are better but R^2 is worse, indicating that the quality of the models has decreased despite an average better predictive capacity. These results can be explained by the fact that, using the consecutive split, in the test set there are much lower average runtime values than in the training set. Furthermore, the standard deviation of all the test set columns is smaller than that of the training set columns.

Table 4. Performance of the four considered ML models with data augmentation.

	Decision Tree	Random Forest	Gradient Boosting	Neural Network
MAE	22.24	22.26	26.01	20.53
MSE	7312.82	7275.61	8406.57	8623.19
RMSE	85.52	85.30	91.69	92.86
R^2	0.71	0.72	0.67	0.66
Confidence interval (95%)	[0.00, 307.77]	[0.00, 306.92]	[0.00, 291.46]	[0.00, 319.62]
OVERESTIMATION				
Total cases	79.90%	79.98%	80.57%	79.34%
min error	0.01	0.01	0.01	0.01
max error	1425.65	1425.66	1118.25	1470.79
avg error	13.97	13.97	16.20	12.26
error < **60 min**	96.20%	96.15%	95.64%	97.93%
UNDERESTIMATION				
Total cases	19.69%	19.63%	19.41%	20.63%
min error	0.01	0.01	0.01	0.01
max error	1425.42	1425.41	1424.76	1427.48
avg error	56.25	56.48	66.72	55.36
error < **60 min**	87.46%	87.29%	83.63%	86.07%
EXACT ESTIMATION				
Total cases	0.41%	0.39%	0.02%	0.03%
EFFECTIVENESS				
General	78.81%	78.81%	78.81%	78.81%
Valid prediction	98.51%	98.51%	98.51%	98.51%

Table 5. Performance of the four considered ML models with a consecutive split of train and test sets.

	Decision Tree	Random Forest	Gradient Boosting	Neural Network
MAE	8.33	8.35	22.90	8.22
MSE	3438.32	3432.47	5086.70	3674.63
RMSE	58.64	58.59	71.32	60.62
R^2	0.62	0.62	0.44	0.60
Confidence interval (95%)	[0.00, 155.35]	[152.11]	[0.00, 104.60]	[0.00, 165.33]
OVERESTIMATION				
Total cases	94.40%	94.86%	95.99%	94.49%
min error	0.01	0.01	0.02	0.02
max error	1196.12	1184.39	722.10	1311.46
avg error	4.18	4.08	16.96	4.18
error < **60 min**	99.44%	99.13%	98.90%	99.36%
UNDERESTIMATION				
Total cases	5.25%	5.13%	4.00%	5.50%
min error	0.01	0.01	0.02	0.02
max error	1425.71	1425.71	1399.33	1424.30
avg error	83.43	87.44	165.44	77.58
error < **60 min**	81.69%	80.87%	67.75%	82.63%
EXACT ESTIMATION				
Total cases	0.35%	0.01%	0.00%	0.01%
EFFECTIVENESS				
General	94.22%	94.27%	93.40%	93.42%
Valid prediction	99.45%	99.37%	97.79%	98.90%

Discussion. We notice how in all the tested cases, the values predicted by the models are better at approximating the runtime than the *time_limit* value provided by the user. In particular, when the models overestimate the runtime (on average around 80% of total cases), this results in almost a 98% improvement (on average). On the contrary, the models underestimate the runtime on average around 20% of total cases, while the *time_limit* value does so in just 1.4% of cases. In about 85% of these "underestimation" cases, a simple solution could be to add 60 min to the predicted runtime, reducing the number of jobs that would be interrupted before finishing to less than 3% of the total (which is still a lot but more in line with the original value of 1.4%). Using this "safe" prediction, we have that the models overestimate the runtime 97% of the time (obviously with higher average error). However, we still have a more than 91% improvement (on average).

4 DIWS Scheduler

In this section, we start by briefly describing the logic of the scheduling algorithm built on top of the previous analysis; then we evaluate its performance w.r.t. a widely adopted workload scheduler.

4.1 The Scheduling Algorithm

Given the results of the previous section, we propose to enrich the scheduling decisions of an EASY backfilling algorithm with the runtime estimations derived through ML. In practice, the DIWS algorithm prioritizes the jobs with shorter predicted execution times by operating in the following way:

1. It starts by loading historical job data and training a runtime prediction model consisting of a Decision Tree Regressor. This is done only once at the beginning of the algorithm execution.
2. The runtime of each job is then predicted upon submission, and the time requested by each job is set to this value.
3. The submitted jobs are sorted based on the requested time and those with smaller predicted runtimes are given higher priority.

We implemented the aforementioned steps into Batsim [9], an infrastructure simulator that allows the development and testing of resource management policies. The code of our Batsim-based DIWS implementation is publicly available on GitHub[2]. The repository also includes all the tests reported in this paper and the setups to reproduce the experiments.

4.2 Experimental Evaluation

In order to evaluate the performance of DIWS, we start from the dataset of job runs used in Sect. 3.2, which consists of almost 630'000 rows, and we divide it into two parts: *(i) df_sched*, which contains the data relative to the last 24 h stored in the original dataset (a total of 4'407 jobs), and is used to instruct

---
[2] URL redacted due to blind policy - it will be made public in case of acceptance.

Batsim about the amount of resources and execution time that each job will need at simulation time; *(ii) df_train*, which contains the rest of the data, and is used to train the regressor.

For our experimental evaluation, we wanted to maximally highlight the contribution obtainable by incorporating the duration prediction into the scheduling policy. Hence, we opted for the classical EASY backfilling algorithm [17], which we will dub EASYBF from now on, as the baseline. As previously underlined, EASYBF is a relatively simple, but still widely used.

The simulation was first carried out on a Batsim platform with a total of 15,680 computing resources, i.e., equivalent to what is available on the MARCONI100 infrastructure (980 physical nodes with 16 cores each). In the following, we refer to this configuration with *Setup A*. Then, aiming to test the schedulers' performance in stressing conditions, we repeat the experiments with a more constrained platform, consisting of just 512 computing resources (*Setup B*).

We compare DIWS and EASYBF based on the following values emerging from the simulations:

(i) makespan, is the completion time of the last job; *(ii) scheduling time* is the time (in seconds) spent in the scheduler; *(iii) mean waiting time* is the average waiting time observed on jobs, intending it as the time between job submission and its actual start time. It corresponds to the amount of time a job spends waiting in the queue before it starts executing. *(iv) mean turnaround time* is the average turnaround time observed on jobs, intending it as the difference between the time instant in which the job ends and the submission instant. Hence, the turnaround time includes both the time spent waiting in the queue and the execution. It reflects the efficiency of the system in handling jobs. *(v) mean slowdown* is the average slowdown observed on jobs. The slowdown of a job is useful for understanding how scheduling affects the performance of individual jobs because it measures how much longer a job takes to complete compared to its actual execution time. It is computed as: $slowdown = \frac{turnaround\_time}{execution\_time}$; *(vi) maximum waiting time* is the maximum waiting time observed on a job; *(vii) maximum turnaround time* is the maximum turnaround time observed on a job; *(viii) maximum slowdown* is the maximum slowdown observed on a job.

Table 6 refers to *Setup A* and reports the values of these metrics for both DIWS and EASYBF schedulers.

Observing these results, we can highlight that DIWS brings some clear improvements over EASYBF scheduler. The most relevant is the fact that with DIWS the mean waiting time of a job is more than 11% lower. Also, the mean slowdown is significantly improved (-94.96%).

On the other hand, using the DIWS scheduler, the maximum waiting time is higher than that obtained using the EASYBF scheduler by a significant margin (almost 35%). Indeed, as DIWS is better at estimating the jobs' duration beforehand, it is also able to identify how a few jobs are extremely more time-consuming than others and, accordingly, it changes their position further down the queue.

Table 6. Comparison of DIWS and EasyBF performance when scheduling jobs on a large HPC system (*Setup A*). Negative values in the "Improvement" column highlight desirable situations where DIWS brings a decrease in the corresponding metric.

	DIWS	EasyBF	Improvement
makespan	86272.0068	86272.0024	+0.00%
scheduling time	37.8449	240.7396	−84.28%
mean waiting time	846.5391	953.3813	−11.21%
mean turnaround time	2351.1828	2458.0250	−4.35%
mean slowdown	2.3089	45.8519	−94.96%
max waiting time	17003.0928	12608.0384	+34.88%
max turnaround time	64657.0068	00657.0024	+0.00%
max slowdown	261.0818	12156.04.06	−97.85%

It is worth noticing that when using DIWS, the waiting time is very low (less than 1 min) for 4.28% more jobs. Observing these results, we can highlight that DIWS brings some clear improvements over EasyBF scheduler. Besides testing DIWS on a Batsim, large infrastructure, we want to analyse how it performs on an extremely constrained system such as the one in *Setup B*, where a limited amount of computing resources is made available to jobs. Table 7 reports the metrics values for this case.

Table 7. Comparison of DIWS and EasyBF performance when scheduling jobs on a constrained HPC system (*Setup B*).

	DIWS	EasyBF	Improvement
makespan	1029198.2116	1090869.2938	−5.99%
scheduling time	210.3460	194.5042	+7.53%
mean waiting time	127474.5570	163846.3107	−28.54%
mean turnaround time	128979.2008	165350.9545	−28.21%
mean slowdown	22785.2399	20097.1711	+11.80%
max waiting time	994211.2116	1026349.2598	−3.21%
max turnaround time	1024094.2116	1027933.2894	−0.37%
max slowdown	450511.6491	1026350.2601	-=128.09%

The histograms in Fig. 2 show a comparison of the percentage of jobs that wait less than arbitrarily chosen time intervals (one minute, ten minutes, one hour and six hours), for the *Setup A* and *Setup B*.

DIWS shows the best performance in this constrained setup too. In particular, (from Table 7) the total time required to go through all jobs in the workload is almost 6% lower with DIWS to EasyBF, the mean waiting time of a job is more than 28% lower, and (as shown in Fig. 2b) the waiting time is less than 10 min for almost 8 times more jobs (going from 2.06% of EasyBF to 22.76% of DIWS).

On the other hand, when using the DIWS, the waiting time is very high (more than 1 day) for almost 5% more jobs than when using the EasyBF

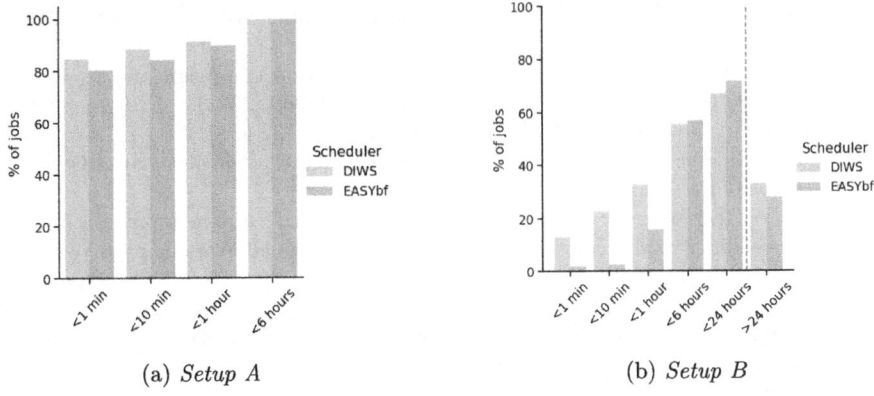

Fig. 2. Scheduling performance comparison

scheduler (1457 vs 1241). This is a direct consequence of the very constrained testing environment and–as already pointed out for *Setup A*–the better capacity of DIWS to estimate the durations, highlighting the huge difference existing between jobs.

5 Conclusion

As ML techniques have shown promising results in several scientific fields, we propose to apply analogous methods to the HPC scheduling too. Our preliminary analysis takes into consideration four different ML techniques and analyses their ability to predict the execution time of HPC jobs before their submission. The tests, conducted on an extensive real-life dataset of job runs, clearly show the enhancement that ML can bring to runtime prediction provided by users. Furthermore, we employ a well-known HPC workload simulator to evaluate the efficacy of a duration-informed scheduler by comparing it with a widely used alternative. The proposed solution's clear superiority when aiming to reduce the average waiting time.

Acknowledgements. This work has been partially supported by European Project HORIZON-EUROHPC-JU-SEANERGYS (g.a. 101177590).

References

1. Amiri, M., Mohammad-Khanli, L.: Survey on prediction models of applications for resources provisioning in cloud. J. Netw. Comput. Appl. **82**, 93–113 (2017)
2. Antici, F., Ardebili, M.S., et al.: PM100: A job power consumption dataset of a large-scale production HPC system. In: Proceedings of the SC '23 Workshops of The International Conference on High Performance Computing, Network, Storage, and Analysis, SC-W 2023, Denver, CO, USA, 12–17 November 2023, pp. 1812–1819. ACM (2023)

3. Bengio, Y., Goodfellow, I., Courville, A.: Deep Learning, vol. 1. MIT press, Boston (2017)
4. Borghesi, A., et al.: M100 exadata: a data collection campaign on the cineca's marconi100 tier-0 supercomputer. Sci. Data **10**(1), 288 (2023)
5. Breiman, L.: Random forests. Mach. Learn. **45**(1), 5–32 (2001)
6. Breiman, L., Friedman, J., Stone, C.J., Olshen, R.A.: Classification and Regression Trees. CRC Press, Boca Raton (1984)
7. Cirne, W., Berman, F.: A comprehensive model of the supercomputer workload. In: Proceedings of the Fourth Annual IEEE International Workshop on Workload Characterization. WWC-4 (Cat. No.01EX538), pp. 140–148 (2001). https://doi.org/10.1109/WWC.2001.990753
8. De Filippo, A., Di Giacomo, E., Borghesi, A.: Machine learning approaches to predict the execution time of the meteorological simulation software cosmo. J. Intell. Inf. Syst. 1–25 (2024)
9. Dutot, P.F., Mercier, M., et al.: Batsim: a realistic language-independent resources and jobs management systems simulator. In: 20th Workshop on Job Scheduling Strategies for Parallel Processing, Chicago, United States (2016)
10. Friedman, J.H.: Greedy function approximation: a gradient boosting machine. Ann. Stat. 1189–1232 (2001)
11. Hutter, F., Xu, L., Hoos, H.H., Leyton-Brown, K.: Algorithm runtime prediction: methods & evaluation. Artif. Intell. **206**, 79–111 (2014)
12. Li, J., Zhang, X., Han, L., Ji, Z., Dong, X., Hu, C.: OKCM: improving parallel task scheduling in high-performance computing systems using online learning. J. Supercomput. **77**(6), 5960–5983 (2021). https://doi.org/10.1007/S11227-020-03506-5
13. Miu, T., Missier, P.: Predicting the execution time of workflow activities based on their input features. In: 2012 SC Companion: High Performance Computing, Networking Storage and Analysis, pp. 64–72. IEEE (2012)
14. Nadeem, F., Alghazzawi, D., et al.: Modeling and predicting execution time of scientific workflows in the grid using radial basis function neural network. Clust. Comput. **20**(3), 2805–2819 (2017)
15. Pittino, F., Bonfà, P., Bartolini, A., Affinito, F., Benini, L., Cavazzoni, C.: Prediction of time-to-solution in material science simulations using deep learning. In: Proceedings of the Platform for Advanced Scientific Computing Conference, pp. 1–9 (2019)
16. Tanash, M., Dunn, B., ry al.: Improving HPC system performance by predicting job resources via supervised machine learning. In: Furlani, T.R. (ed.) Proceedings of the Practice and Experience in Advanced Research Computing on Rise of the Machines (learning), PEARC 2019, Chicago, IL, USA, 28 July–01 August 2019, pp. 69:1–69:8. ACM (2019)
17. Wong, A.K., Goscinski, A.M.: Evaluating the easy-backfill job scheduling of static workloads on clusters. In: 2007 IEEE International Conference on Cluster Computing, pp. 64–73. IEEE (2007)

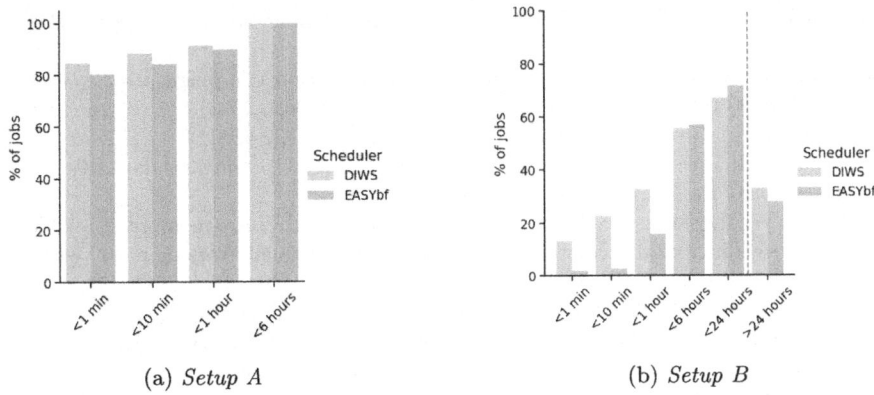

Monitoring Energy Consumption of Workloads on HPC Vega

Teo Prica[1,2](✉) and Aleš Zamuda[2]

[1] IZUM - Institute of Information Science, Prešernova ulica 17, Maribor, Slovenia
teo.prica@izum.si
[2] FERI, UM - University of Maribor, Koroška cesta 46, Maribor, Slovenia

Abstract. This paper presents management and monitoring of energy consumption within High-Performance Computing (HPC) Artificial Intelligence (AI) workloads and insight of the first launched EuroHPC JU system, EuroHPC Vega. The Vega entered its fourth year of operation, as it provides essential infrastructure for the Slovenian scientific community, and projects within scientific sphere. It is necessary to curb the latter and introduce effective and essential mechanisms for energy sustainability, leading to high energy consumption and carbon emissions in Data Centers (DC). Novel approaches within AI domain and workloads grow in size and the complexity requires a considerable amount of computational resources. Due to the different architectures between DCs, introducing different mechanisms with the tendency towards reducing power consumption, and more efficient approaches can be used. Differences in systems and their architectures lead to different end solutions, without a unified framework to govern such systems. The current setup, energy-efficient concepts, technologies, and mechanisms are presented, including configuration adjustments made to improve energy consumption management and monitoring on a case of HPC Vega.

Keywords: High-Performance Computing · Artificial Intelligence · Workloads · Monitoring · Energy Consumption

1 Introduction

Emergence and interest from various scientific domains, industry, mostly from small and medium-sized enterprises (SMEs), and collaboration projects within Europe are increasing innovations from the research within the Artificial Intelligence (AI) domain, taking advantage of exploiting convergence of cloud and High-Performance Computing (HPC), leveraging tailored workloads with the reachability and multitenancy environments of the state-of-the-art supercomputing systems and AI factories [25]. This paper presents management and monitoring of energy consumption within HPC AI workloads of first launched EuroHPC JU petascale system EuroHPC Vega, entering its fourth year of operation, as it provides essential infrastructure for the Slovenian scientific community, and projects within scientific sphere [1,29]. In addition to innovation, computer power and talent also contribute to a strong AI ecosystem within the European

Union [25]. Novel approaches within AI workloads grow in size and the complexity requires a considerable amount of computational resources, demands on data lakes with geographical data distribution and scalability, resulting in convergence from petascale to post-exascale computing era. Procurement of future AI-optimised HPC systems consequently increases the energy consumption and carbon emissions [32,43]. Driven by increasing awareness within the scientific community as a result and the needs for project reporting with a focus toward the acquisition of energy consumption data. It is necessary to curb the latter and introduce effective and essential mechanisms for energy sustainability as leading to high energy consumption through last years, where Data Centers (DC) rank among the highest consumers and carbon missions [21,43]. Due to the different architectures between DCs, DCs introduce different mechanisms with the tendency towards reducing power consumption and more efficient approaches can be used to lower the Power Usage Effectiveness (PUE), which result in reducing the global footprint [21]. New systems play a key role to provide a proper infrastructure for scientific community, as part of a powerful, efficient, economical, and Europe's world-class supercomputing ecosystem, revealed from the system ranking on TOP500 list [3]. Differences in systems and their architectures lead to different end solutions, methods, and policies, so there is no single framework to govern such systems [14]. Users with varying expertise across different domains often lack prior knowledge of HPC and may not prioritize the efficient use and optimal operation of their workloads. Their results can be evaluated using metrics like time-to-solution or power-to-solution, depending on the optimization approach, including commonly used frameworks. As a result, system administrators and Application Support Teams (AST) need to continuously broaden their expertise to provide high-level support across multidisciplinary areas, focus on efficient code, utilization, optimization, refactoring, performance analysis, and even awareness among users in HPC with efficient management of acquired computational resources [29]. The EuroHPC Federation Platform (EFP) project was launched with the goal of integrating and connecting current and future systems including, quantum systems, supporting services and data infrastructure [27], aiming to create a federated and unified access with job submission, software, and beyond [27]. However, this posed a significant challenge for EFP users, as there is no unified framework for monitoring and managing energy consumption, as the configurations and technologies used differ per each system [14,27]. While best practices and guidelines are also available to assist in efficient and optimal use of systems [14], monitoring and reporting of consumed energy, from both user and administration point of view, and leveraging the available mechanisms to reduce energy consumption without performance degradation, was shown to be feasible [1].

The following sections of this paper are organized as follows. Section 2 provides an overview of related work and methods. Section 3 describes the energy monitoring methodology details. Section 4 provides experimental results. Section 5 presents conclusions and future work.

2 Related Work and Methods

The research on energy efficient HPC involves researching and implementing mechanisms with focus on supporting pillars framework [41], including infrastructure, hardware, software, optimization, and enhancing energy efficiency within HPC facilities, while prioritizing sustainable energy consumption without sacrificing performance and achieving their balance [41]. Despite advancements in such research, there are challenges to maintaining performance considering efficiency trade-offs, scalability issues, infrastructure limitations and bottlenecks, and beyond [41]. The following paragraphs cover and briefly presents the concepts, technologies, and mechanisms available within our environment and beyond, some of which have been deployed within HPC Vega [1].

Power Capping. It ensures controlled and limited operation of the system environment [7]. There are a few approaches, such as monitoring and extending consumption according to requirements. This can be implemented at the hardware or software level maintained by system administrators or even a dynamical approach can be adjusted according to demand [16,43]. This brings advantages such as effective or preventive constraints due to the possibility of hardware failures, reducing high operating costs in higher peaks, operating on a smaller scale, lower priority tasks, or partially turning off the compute nodes for optimal and efficient execution of workloads, and bringing reliability in scope of extending the life of components, which enables distributed loads to prevent unexpected loads and failures that lead to downtime partially or completely [7,16,43].

This significantly affects performance, especially upon large or aggressive reductions of complexity of workloads. There is no single recipe, as adjustments are needed to achieve optimal efficiency and complexity of the control, monitoring, and alerting system, which provides the necessary functionality for real-time energy management [7,43]. In the last resort, jobs may still be killed [5,16].

Power Constraint. A tailored solution for HPC Vega is provided by an automatic overheating prevention solution and was implemented for sustaining the lifetime of the components [1]. To achieve this, appropriate temperature and load on compute racks need to be maintained. The solution is a Supervisory Control and Data Acquisition (SCADA) based system, where readings are retrieved from heating, ventilation, air conditioning (HVAC), and Direct Liquid Cooling (DLC) sensors from compute racks [28]. If the latter fail to cool due to heat, or due to an increased humidity or if humidifier is in a failed state, an alert is triggered, which results in reduction or increase of consumed power. The triggers are picked by the management system, taking advantage of Slurm [16] commands like `suspend` and `release` of the running jobs [16].

Baseboard Management Controller (BMC). BMC is a microcontroller integrated into the motherboard of servers [35]. It is reachable via Out-of-Band (OOB) network that enables remote and power management, monitoring, troubleshooting, system administration of server systems, independent of the Operating System (OS) [35].

Intelligent Platform Management Interface (IPMI). IPMI is a set of standard specifications and components which provides managing and monitoring functionalities of targeted sub-systems [15]. A commonly used utility is ipmitool [15], as it supports IPMI and is intended for system administration to preform remote tasks via OOB network. Main features are controlling computer subsystems including Basic Input/Output System (BIOS), Central Processing Unit (CPU), and OS, as well as monitoring, logging, recovery, retrieving data from sensors which are mapped to specific record ID and name within Sensor Data Pepository (SDR), including energy sensors [15].

Running Average Power Limit (RAPL). RAPL is an interface feature introduced by Intel's Sandy Bridge architecture and provides access to real-time measurements of hardware counters based on CPU sockets and DRAM. RAPL is suitable for measurements of power consumption of various hardware setups. [11]

System Management Interface (SMI). SMI is a command utility used for managing and monitoring NVIDIA devices, based on NVIDIA Management Library (NVML) which provides monitoring and management of NVIDIA Graphics Processing Units (GPUs) devices via C-based Application Programming Interface (API) [10]. NVML is included within NVIDIA display driver and allows direct access and management via nvidia-smi command [10]. Generic Resources (GRES) such as NVML are available within an additional configuration file (gres.conf) [16].

NVIDIA Data Center GPU Manager (DCGM). DCGM is managing and monitoring for GPUs and allows reducing the power consumption of GPUs clock speed in DCs. NVIDIA Multi-Instance GPU (MIG) provides up to seven independent slices per each GPU. This feature allows even smaller workloads, but is not limited to them. [38]

Frequency throttling. Is adjustment of the workload frequency and performance, which reduces the number of instructions inside the processor, with a goal and result to save consumed energy, while not affecting or compromising the performance [20]. The latter is possible within a heterogeneous system, namely on the CPU where the frequency is manipulated and on the GPU level, it is possible to adjust the core or memory frequency [22]. Solutions have been developed to automatically adjust frequencies depending on the workload [34] and dynamic adjustment without affecting the performance as an efficient operation on both CPU and GPU, while newer processors enable performance autonomous scalability on OS level [22].

Checkpoints and Restart (CR). CR mechanisms save states of jobs as checkpoints that are restored from these checkpoints upon restart after failure [12]. To ensure the possibility of continuing the execution after interruption, several checkpoints could be established per workload [12]. CR mechanism is adopted for fault tolerance in HPC workloads and is also used for power management to reduce cost, if potential crashes occur due to system complexity or even by interconnect errors caused by network congestion [19]. CR is beneficial when

there are short queues and demands on offloading a larger workload, which can be achieved on both CPU and GPU architectures, although energy management and their savings may be different on both architectures [17]. Due to different technologies and systems, there is not a single solution for CR, therefore adjustment have to be made depending on the workload and architecture [37]. Commonly used CR mechanism on CPUs is Distributed MultiThreader Check-Pointing (DMTCP) with Message Passing Interface (MPI) support or Berkeley Lab Checkpoint/Restart (BLCR) [12]. For GPU workloads there are additional mechanisms, like Checkpoint/Restore In Userspace (CRIU) or recent state-of-the-art CR on the OS level [13].

Software in HPC. The various application domains require meeting different needs, resulting in different workflows, workloads, and their requirements [1]. Software can be prepared differently and optimized per architecture, such as custom-builds from source, deployed through environment modules, or even containers, which includes preparation of definition files that users may modify and build themselves [1]. Containerization is increasingly popular due to various beneficial advantages such as reproducibility, portability, consistent environment, resource efficiency, scalability, and isolation, which also improves security [18,24]. Energy consumption within a containerized environment was presented in [30]. Software from various sources, repositories, and registers could be accessible from multiple clusters via CernVM-FS [1,6]. The importance of efficient code, code optimization, and performance analysis, is crucial for DC sustainability [29,32]. Solutions which support the myriad of different workloads could be integrated as a pipeline, with interactive platforms, libraries, monitoring, logging, and visualization [26]. Furthermore, there are some power management tools with capabilities within the supercomputing ecosystem such as APM, AMD ROCm, LIKWID, Perf, PAPI, EAR, LLview, MERIC, and beyond [14].

Slurm Workload Manager. Slurm [16] takes care of resources, job scheduling, measuring, and retrieving data from its database. It offers a wide range of plugins, which can be tailored to meet specific needs. In Slurm, power management is already integrated through a plugin, which enables power capping for nodes [16]. This may be also used to redistribute the load or even, add burden to some nodes, consequently applying saving mode on some nodes [16]. Load may be evenly distributed across the nodes to prevent hardware issues. In doing so, it enables interval lowering of required consumption of nodes to a specified value in a preferable unit (kW or watts) [16]. It could be used either to prevent overload or increase the utilization or consumption [16]. For these purposes, commands such as suspend or hold may be used to temporarily hold a running job, or resume to resume a previously suspended job [16]. The Slurm suspend command suspends the racks, and the unsuspend operation resumes the racks in reverse sequence of how they were suspended, through resume command [16]. The accounting is done through a Slurm Energy Accounting Plugin and a prerequisite is an installed client for Slurm Daemon (slurmd) on the clients, which are either worker nodes, login nodes, or edge virtual machines [16]. A daemon collects the data of the consumed energy for each job and by default, energy consumption monitoring is not enabled within Slurm [16]. The plugin can be enabled within Slurm using configuration parameters of AcctGatherEnergyType, with available values GPU management library, IPMI, PM_Counters, RAPL, and XCC, set in a configuration file (acct_gather.conf) [16]. The parameters related to Slurm Energy Accounting Plugin are related to profile (AcctGatherProfileType), energy (AcctGatherEnergyType), file system (AcctGatherFilesystemType), and interconnection (AcctGatherInterconnectType) types, respectively [16].

Due to the inconsistent subroutines such as Remote Procedure Calls (RPC) that may flood the network, log and service, an error message may appear from Slurm step manager (slurmstepd), which is even visible for end users [16]:

slurmstepd: error: _get_joules_task: can't get info from slurmd

This may cause the missing data for certain tasks or even jobs, resulting in incorrect reporting of energy consumption [16]. Alternatively, Slurm provides a fairly simple way to integrate new additional custom plugins [16]. Those are mainly within limited environments, which is understandable, since there is not yet a set of common solutions available and each cluster has a different architecture and setup [14], mostly targeted to collect and analyse the data of single node jobs on CPU architecture, without focusing on multi node jobs nor GPUs [4]. Interesting solutions have emerged in this direction, covered in papers [9,33,40]. Data is fetched from a Slurm database through sacct command [16]. A Lua script is used, where users are warned about incorrect configurations in submitted jobs to Slurm, such as incorrect number of tasks, memory per core, GPU allocations, and beyond, thus preventing unnecessary computing resources and energy [16]. Additionally, a custom script for total energy consumption is stored in a dedicated Slurm archive, where users may track their resource consumption on HPC Vega [1].

Monitoring and Metrics Visualization. In the facilities such as DC, supply infrastructure, system-wide overview of the cluster monitoring and metrics implementations are commonly used within HPC ecosystem [1,36]. These metrics are captured, collected, stored, and visualized using a variety of tailored solutions to the specific equipment, devices, hardware, and software being monitored. The major cost of operating a system is the electricity consumption, which fluctuates between 700 kW and 1 MW [1].

Grafana. It is an open-source solution for the visualization of metrics obtained from various databases and stored into Time Series Database (TSDB), upon which queries could be executed, for targeted equipment, and systems, which could then be visualized and monitored using prepared dashboards [8].

Prometheus. It is a standalone open-source used to collect various metrics, monitoring and alerting and can be added as a source within Grafana. Node exporter is a tool used to monitor, collect and export various metrics from a client and is commonly used within the Prometheus setup. [8]

Victoria Metrics. It is an open-source high performance time series database with capabilities to monitor and control the system, added as an additional source to Grafana [8].

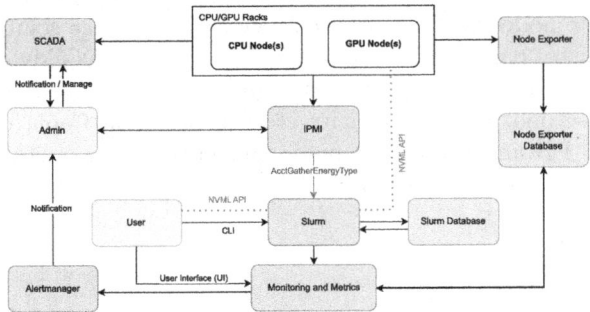

Fig. 1. Overview of measurement, monitoring, and metrics within HPC Vega. Reconfiguration is marked in red. (Color figure online)

2.1 Current Setup of HPC Vega

In HPC Vega (Fig. 1), energy consumption is retrieved through IPMI sensors, which report all monitored data from a node and the entries are assigned to parameters within Slurm configuration [15,16]. The data retrieval interval must match the settings from a Slurm controller (slurmctld) configuration, as well as on the Slurm clients to retrieve data (slurmd) [16]. Power constraint is managed through various physical sensors in a DC, and the tailored solution based on SCADA also includes other solutions such as Data Center Infrastructure Management (DCIM), and Local Management Interfaces (LMI) for management by system administrators [28]. An alert is triggered after deviations of events from given thresholds, which notifies all necessary system maintainers and those responsible for a specific service or system. A signal is sent to Slurm through snmptrap, which uses a static list of racks to reduce power consumption. The jobs of the entire rack are suspended through the Slurm abilities with **suspend** command and an unsuspend operation resumes the racks in reverse sequence of how they were suspended, through **resume** command. The entire implementation is cluster tailored and is executed synchronously rack-by-rack, as this is not part of Bull Energy Optimizer (BEO), provided and maintained by the vendor, and was initially meant to be used for capping capabilities [31]. Due to the recent activities and technical preparation, BEO is currently disabled on HPC Vega [31]. In addition to that, BEO covers power monitoring and management of the DC through OOB network and is managed via a Command Line Interface (CLI) or a Graphical User Interface (GUI) [31], with plans underway for an upgrade to Smart Energy Monitors (SEMS). Deployment and post installation, including configuration distribution cluster-wide, is managed through automation engine Ansible [23]. Compute nodes are divided into five partitions cpu, gpu, dev, largemem, and longcpu, covering the entire set of 1028 nodes [1]. Development partition allows users to prepare and compile the code and run it via Slurm, up to 30 min. Cluster-wide nodes have Red Hat Enterprise Linux (RHEL) 8.10 OS, Slurm 24.05.5, custom kernel build, MOFED 5.8, NVIDIA drivers 565.57.01, and CUDA Toolkit 12.7 [1]. To ensure smooth operation, resource waste, and detection of software or hardware failures, periodic checks are in place and ensured by the installed Node Health Check (NHC) on the compute nodes [2]. The cluster provides two storage solutions. The first utilizes the Lustre parallel file system (DDN Exascaler), NVMe disks of usable capacity of 1 PB, used as a scratch for highly intensive jobs that demand high I/O [1]. The second, a large capacity storage based on Ceph, offers a usable capacity of 19 PB and is used for home and project directories, data storage, environment preparation, and beyond [1].

3 Methodology

This section presents the required adjustments within the system and adjustments of Slurm and Generic Resources (GRES) Scheduling configuration.

First, the minor complications and challenges were encountered and had to be tackled when enabling the power measurement of consumption through Slurm configuration. Both frequencies had to be adjusted accordingly, and as the node frequency is set with `AcctGatherNodeFreq` parameter, this was adjusted from 25 to 60 and as job frequency is set with `JobAcctGatherFrequency` parameter, it was changed from 10 to 60 [16]. The configuration on Slurm controller was configured as follows:

```
AcctGatherEnergyType=acct_gather_energy/ipmi
AcctGatherNodeFreq=60
JobAcctGatherFrequency=60
JobAcctGatherType=jobacct_gather/cgroup
```

Then, the modifications to the configuration were made cluster-wide (in the file `acct_gather.conf`), by changing the last line with value for nodes only with a CPU mapped to the IPMI energy power sensor at position 13 and configuration value for the nodes with GPUs was set to 20 [16].

```
EnergyIPMIFrequency=60
EnergyIPMICalcAdjustment=yes
EnergyIPMITimeout=60
EnergyIPMIPowerSensors=Node=value
```

The modification was also made to the GRES configuration file (`gres.conf`). The line commented below represents the state before switching to NVML [16]:

```
AutoDetect=nvml
Name=gpu Type=ampere File=/dev/nvidia[0-3]
#NodeName=gn[01-60] Name=gpu Type=ampere File=/dev/nvidia[0-3]
```

To retrieve consumed resources of finished jobs from Slurm, the following `sacct` command was then used:

```
sacct -u $USER -X -j $jobids --format=JobID,State,ConsumedEnergy, \
    Elapsed,TresUsageOutAve%40,NNodes --parsable2 --delimiter=";"
```

Similarly, to retrieve consumed resources of finished Slurm jobs with `sacct` command and parameter `TRESUsageInAve` with enabled NVIDIA NVML [16]:

```
sacct -j $%jobid$ -u $%USER$ -Pno TRESUsageInAve
```

Monitoring of the GPU utilization, memory, and power consumption was then possible via `nvidia-smi` command:

```
nvidia-smi -l 1 --query-gpu=index,utilization.gpu, \
    utilization.memory,power.draw --format=csv,nounits > output &
```

4 Experimental Results

This section presents the consumed resources of the conducted experiment. Retrieved data from `ipmi-sensors` command was executed on GPU compute node.

```
ID | Name            | Type         | Reading | Units | Event
12 | CWG_LM5066I_IIN | Current      | 16.71   | A     | 'OK'
13 | LM5066_IIN      | Current      | 4.38    | A     | 'OK'
20 | CWG_LM5066I_PIN | Power Unit   | 915.00  | W     | 'OK'
```

Then, power management signal is received and visible within Slurm for rack with GPU nodes:

`NHC:_received_power_management_signal_at_Jul_10_10:19:31 gn[31-60]`

The retrieved consumed resources of finished jobs from Slurm with disabled NVML were obtained as:

```
cpu=10:00,energy=47340,fs/disk=158664, \
    mem=1136584K,pages=0,vmem=1179592K
```

The retrieved consumed resources of finished jobs from Slurm with enabled NVML were obtained as:

```
cpu=10:00,energy=74032,fs/disk=158791,gres/gpumem=19882M,\
    gres/gpuutil=100,mem=1136576K,pages=0,vmem=1146816K
```

In our experiments, TensorFlow, PyTorch, and NVIDIA NeMo frameworks were used as HPC AI workloads, from official and optimized Singularity containers, built from the public NVIDIA NGC catalog Evaluation benchmarks, like GLUE, SuperGLUE and wikitext-2, executed on single node with up to four GPUs per each workload. While taking into account the limitation of available amount of memory per GPU (node), iterations were set to 20 epochs, and batch size to 32. Loaded models are available within the `Transformers` package [39], and datasets within the `Datasets` package [42]. Our obtained monitoring results are presented in Table 1, where each entry lists number of nodes and GPUs, elapsed time (minutes), and consumed energy (joules), as obtained through IPMI, which is used for tracking the energy consumption within Vega. The results are gathered from Slurm via the `sacct` command. The fastest workload was by NVIDIA NeMo on the `super_glue (rte)` dataset with 4 GPUs, with elapsed time of 10 min and 52 s, while the longest was by PyTorch on the

Table 1. Obtained and measured results from High-performance AI workloads.

Framework	Model	Dataset	Nodes/GPUs	Counter	Elapsed Time (M)	Consumed Energy (J)
TensorFlow	distilbert-base-uncased	glue (mrpc)	1/1	IPMI	00:36:04	360.48K
TensorFlow	distilbert-base-uncased	glue (mrpc)	1/4	IPMI	00:17:28	284.36K
PyTorch	gpt2-medium	wikitext-2	1/1	IPMI	00:40:45	1.63M
PyTorch	gpt2-medium	wikitext-2	1/4	IPMI	00:25:11	1.43M
NVIDIA NeMo	distilbert-base-uncased	super_glue (rte)	1/1	IPMI	00:13:04	18.45?[a]
NVIDIA NeMo	distilbert-base-uncased	super_glue (rte)	1/1	IPMI	00:12:50	226.84K
NVIDIA NeMo	distilbert-base-uncased	super_glue (rte)	1/4	IPMI	00:10:52	123.59K

[a] Incorrect reporting on consumed energy was detected

wikitext-2 dataset with single GPU, with 40 min and 45 s. While the lowest energy consumption was by NVIDIA NeMo on `super_glue (rte)` with 4 GPUs, consuming 123.59K. The highest energy consumption was by PyTorch on `wikitext-2` with single GPU, with 1.63M. Discrepancies were detected within NVIDIA NeMo framework on the single GPU job. Although these values are not directly comparable due to the different models and datasets used, the results demonstrate a successful analytical data monitoring on HPC Vega.

5 Conclusion and Future Work

This paper presented management and monitoring of the consumed energy of HPC Vega workloads. Initially, power management was configured and utilized through BEO and RAPL. However, due to technical issues, we encountered bugs, data reporting limitations, and security concerns, RAPL was disabled. In addition, BEO was disabled, and a cluster-specific solution was then used to manage power constraints. Resource consumption is finally recorded and logged through Slurm and IPMI and consumption data on the GPU partition through NVML. This setup gained the capability to monitor and track resources and energy consumption of HPC Vega workloads from the project allocations.

Recent activities towards emphasizing energy efficiency and sustainability uncovered several possibilities for further evaluation of these essential mechanisms. To ensure more efficient management and measurement of consumption, a transition from BEO to SEMS could take place. Furthermore, RAPL assessment could be conducted in the future. An additional calibration with a professional power meter could be performed, to cross-check and validate the data gathered from IPMI sensors. The logged data could be made available for users through a portal based on monitoring and metrics gathering solutions.

Acknowledgments. The authors acknowledge the EuroHPC JU, HPC-RIVR and SLING consortium for providing allocation of computing resources on the national share of EuroHPC Vega within Development project (S24R08-01), which is hosted at Institute of Information Science (IZUM). This research was conducted within Individual Research Work 2 (55D007) unit of doctoral programme Computer Science and Informatics at University of Maribor. The tuition for study enrollment is financed by IZUM (17-2375-2024/01-ab).

Disclosure of Interests. The authors have no competing interests to declare that are relevant to the content of this article.

References

1. EuroHPC Vega Documentation. https://doc.vega.izum.si/. Accessed 25 July 2024
2. Node Health Check (NHC). https://github.com/mej/nhc. Accessed 25 Oct 2024
3. TOP500 Methodology 2.0rc1 (2025). https://www.top500.org/static/media/uploads/methodology-2.0rc1.pdf. Accessed 19 Jan 2024

4. Aaen Springborg, A., Albano, M., Xavier-de Souza, S.: Automatic energy-efficient job scheduling in HPC: a novel SLURM plugin approach. In: SC-W '23: Proceedings of the SC '23 Workshops of the International Conference on High Performance Computing, Network, Storage, and Analysis, pp. 1831–1838. ACM (2023)
5. Angelelli, L., Carastan-Santos, D., Dutot, P.F.: Run your HPC jobs in eco-mode: revealing the potential of user-assisted power capping in supercomputing systems. In: Workshop on Job Scheduling Strategies for Parallel Processing, pp. 181–196. Springer, Heidelberg (2024). https://doi.org/10.1007/978-3-031-74430-3_10
6. Blomer, J., et al.: New directions in the CernVM file system. In: Journal of Physics: Conference Series, vol. 898 (2017). https://doi.org/10.1088/1742-6596/898/6/062031
7. Cabrera, A., Almeida, F., Castellanos-Nieves, D., Oleksiak, A., Blanco, V.: Energy efficient power cap configurations through Pareto front analysis and machine learning categorization. Clust. Comput. **27**, 3433–3449 (2023)
8. Chapman, R., et al.: Observability with Grafana: Monitor, control, and visualize your Kubernetes and cloud platforms. Packt Publishing Ltd. (2024)
9. Corbalan, J., et al.: Energy optimization and analysis with EAR. In: 2020 IEEE International Conference on Cluster Computing, pp. 464–472. IEEE (2020)
10. Czarnul, P., Proficz, J., Krzywaniak, A.: Energy-aware high-performance computing: survey of state-of-the-art tools, techniques, and environments. Sci. Program. (2019). https://doi.org/10.1155/2019/8348791
11. David, H., et al.: RAPL: memory power estimation and capping. In: 2010 ACM International Symposium on Low-Power Electronics and Design, pp. 189–194 (2010). https://doi.org/10.1145/1840845.1840883
12. Egwutuoha, I.P., Levy, D., Selic, B., Chen, S.: A survey of fault tolerance mechanisms and checkpoint/restart implementations for high performance computing systems. J. Supercomput. **65**(3), 1302–1326 (2013). https://doi.org/10.1007/s11227-013-0884-0
13. Huang, Z., et al.: A concurrent OS-level GPU checkpoint and restore system using validated speculation (2024). https://doi.org/10.48550/arXiv.2405.12079
14. Iakymchuk, R., et al.: Best Practice Guide - Harvesting energy consumption on European HPC systems: Sharing Experience from the CEEC project (2024). https://doi.org/10.5281/zenodo.13306639
15. IPMI Working Group: IPMI Specification (2006). Accessed 25 Oct 2024
16. Jette, M.A., et al.: SLURM: simple linux utility for resource management. In: Proceedings of the 9th International Workshop on Job Scheduling Strategies for Parallel Processing (JSSPP) (2002). https://doi.org/10.1007/10968987_3
17. Jiao, Y., et al.: Power and performance characterization of computational kernels on the GPU. In: International Conference on Green Computing and Communications, pp. 221–228 (2010). https://doi.org/10.1109/GreenCom-CPSCom.2010.143
18. Krašovec, B., Prica, T.: Secure usage of containers in the HPC environment. In: Nordic e-Infrastructure Tomorrow, pp. 96–112. Springer, Heidelberg (2025)
19. Kumar, M., et al.: Study of interconnect errors, network congestion, and applications characteristics for throttle prediction on a large scale HPC system. J. Parallel Distrib. Comput. **153**, 29–43 (2021)
20. Liu, C., Chakraborty, A., Chawla, N., Roggel, N.: Frequency throttling side-channel attack. In: Proceedings of the 2022 ACM SIGSAC Conference on Computer and Communications Security, pp. 1977–1991. ACM (2022)
21. Liu, Y., et al.: Energy consumption and emission mitigation prediction based on data center traffic and PUE for global data centers. In: Global Energy Interconnection, pp. 272–282 (2020). https://doi.org/10.1016/j.gloei.2020.07.008

22. Ma, K., Bai, Y., Wang, X., Chen, W., Li, X.: Energy conservation for GPU–CPU architectures with dynamic workload division and frequency scaling. In: Sustainable Computing: Informatics and Systems, pp. 21–33 (2016)
23. Meijer, B., et al.: Ansible: Up and Running. O'Reilly Media, Inc., Newton (2022)
24. Mujkanovic, N., Durillo, J.J., Hammer, N., Müller, T.: Survey of adaptive containerization architectures for HPC. In: Proceedings of the SC '23 Workshops of the International Conference on High Performance Computing, Network, Storage, and Analysis, pp. 165–176 (2023)
25. Narasimhamurthy, S., et al.: ETP4HPC's SRA 6 - Strategic Research Agenda for High Performance Computing in Europe. ETP4HPC Strategic Research Agenda, Zenodo (2024). https://doi.org/10.5281/zenodo.14268783
26. Nguyen, G., et al.: Machine learning and deep learning frameworks and libraries for large-scale data mining: a survey. Artif. Intell. Rev. **52**(1), 77–124 (2019). https://doi.org/10.1007/s10462-018-09679-z
27. Nortamo, H.: EuroHPC FP: A Federated Platform for HPC Infrastructure in Europe (2025). https://fosdem.org/
28. Popescu, V.F., et al.: Supervisory control and data acquisition (SCADA) traffic simulation for controlling industrial processes and infrastructures. Land Forces Acad. Rev. **27** (2022). https://doi.org/10.1007/978-3-030-92188-0_16
29. Prica, T.: Development and supporting activities on EuroHPC Vega. In: Austrian-Slovenian HPC Meeting 2024 — ASHPC24, p. 14 (2024)
30. Santos, E.A., et al.: How does Docker affect energy consumption? Evaluating workloads in and out of Docker containers. J. Syst. Softw. **146**
31. Sauge, L.: PRACE at SC17: Bull Energy Optimizer (2017). https://prace-ri.eu/wp-content/uploads/PRACE-at-SC17-Ludovic-Sauge.pdf. Accessed 25 Oct 2024
32. Silva, C., Vilaça, R., Pereira, A., Bessa, R.: A review on the decarbonization of high-performance computing centers. Renew. Sustain. Energy **189** (2024)
33. Simsek, O.S., Piccinali, J.G., Ciorba, F.M.: Accurate measurement of application-level energy consumption for energy-aware large-scale simulations. In: Workshops of The International Conference on High Performance Computing, Network, Storage, and Analysis (SC-W 2023), Denver, CO, USA, 12–17 November 2023, pp. 1881–1884. ACM, New York (2023)
34. Sundriyal, V., et al.: Automatic runtime frequency-scaling system for energy savings in parallel applications. J. Supercomput. **68**, 777–797 (2013)
35. Super Micro Computer, Inc.: BMC: Baseboard Management Controller, Revision 1.0a, p. 270 (2022)
36. Terai, M., et al.: An operational data collecting and monitoring platform for fugaku: system overviews and case studies in the prelaunch service period. In: High Performance Computing, pp. 365–377 (2021)
37. Timalsina, M., et al.: Optimizing Checkpoint-Restart Mechanisms for HPC with DMTCP in Containers at NERSC (2024). https://doi.org/10.48550/arXiv.2407.19117
38. Vamja, T., Ray, K., George, F., Devi, U.C.: On the Partitioning of GPU Power among Multi-Instances (2025). https://doi.org/10.48550/arXiv.2501.17752
39. Vaswani, A., et al.: Attention is all you need (2023). https://doi.org/10.48550/arXiv.1706.03762
40. White, J.P., et al.: Monitoring and analysis of power consumption on HPC clusters using XDMoD. In: PEARC '20 (2020). https://doi.org/10.1145/3311790.3396624
41. Wilde, T., Auweter, A., Shoukourian, H.: The 4 Pillar Framework for energy efficient HPC data centers. In: Computer Science - Research and Development, vol. 29 (2013)

42. Wolf, T., et al.: HuggingFace's Transformers: State-of-the-art Natural Language Processing (2020). https://doi.org/10.48550/arXiv.1910.03771
43. Zhao, D., et al.: Sustainable supercomputing for AI: GPU power capping at HPC scale. In: 2023 ACM Symposium on Cloud Computing. ACM (2024)

A Unified I/O Monitoring Framework Using eBPF

Mahendra Paipuri(✉)

Institut du Développement et des Ressources en Informatique Scientifique (IDRIS),
CNRS, Orsay, France
mahendra.paipuri@cnrs.fr
http://www.idris.fr/

Abstract. I/O monitoring and profiling tools in the High Performance Computing (HPC) ecosystem are traditionally limited to MPI workloads and adding support to the non-MPI applications proved to be non-trivial for the existing tools. Widely adopted monitoring tools often lack the temporal information of the I/O activity which is often required to understand the I/O behavior of the applications. The increasing diversity of scientific applications and computing platforms demands greater flexibility and scope in I/O characterization. This work proposes a framework for monitoring I/O activity using extended Berkley Packet Filter (eBPF) technology which has gained much traction in observability and cloud-native landscape. By tracing the kernel's Virtual File System (VFS) functions with eBPF, it is possible to monitor the I/O activity on different types of platforms like HPC, cloud hypervisors or Kubernetes. By storing the metrics traced by eBPF programs in a high performance time series database like Prometheus, it is possible to perform system-wide monitoring of computing platforms that use different types of local or remote file systems in a unified manner. The current work presents the basics of eBPF and discusses the framework that is used to monitor I/O activity in a file system and application agnostic way. It also presents the experimental results of quantifying the overhead and accuracy of the proposed framework using IOR benchmark results as the reference. The results indicate that there is negligible overhead in using the framework and bandwidths reported by the proposed methodology are in a very good agreement with the ones from IOR tests. Finally, results from a production HPC platform that uses the proposed framework to monitor I/O activity on the LUSTRE file system are presented.

Keywords: eBPF · I/O · Unified Monitoring · IOR · MPI · Linux Kernel · Prometheus · Time Series

1 Introduction

With the rapid increase in the usage of more compute-intensive hardware like Graphics Processing Units (GPUs) in the context of Artificial Intelligence (AI) applications, the ever-existing performance gap between compute and storage is increasing rapidly. As GPUs have limited memory, they need to be continuously fed with the data at very high rates to keep them busy. Failing to do so will not only affect the application performance but also drive the operational costs due to the high power requirements of GPUs. Even in the traditional High Performance Computing (HPC) landscape, storage performance has always been a bottleneck for data-intensive applications like climate science. Although the performance gap between compute and storage has improved through 2010's due to the introduction of NVMe disks that provide very high bandwidths, the usage of GPUs in single precision mode for AI applications has widened this gap further [4].

In many cases, poor I/O performance is a result of applications using inefficient IO access patterns. To fix these issues, the step first is to detect them. Monitoring techniques and tools can be used to monitor the applications' I/O access patterns and tune them accordingly to extract the maximum performance from the underlying storage system. Typically, large-scale HPC platforms use remote shared Parallel File Systems (PFS) like LUSTRE [6], Spectrum Scale [19] or BeeGFS [5] to name a few. Different file systems present the I/O monitoring metrics in different ways and most of the time the telemetry data is available at the node level. Thus to monitor the application I/O behavior, HPC platform operators must impose the exclusive usage of compute nodes which have a negative impact on resource utilization and energy consumption of the platforms. When multiple jobs are running on the same compute host, node-level telemetry data is not sufficient to effectively monitor the application's I/O behavior.

There have been numerous tools to monitor and profile I/O statistics on HPC platforms. Tools like Darshan [21], Tau [20] intercept I/O requests, store raw metrics and compute aggregated metrics at the end of the application life cycle. Although the computational overhead is small, the application must exit cleanly for these tools to be able to process the raw data and generate compact reports. The other less desired consequence of this approach is that the temporal aspect of the I/O events is lost in the end report. This is addressed in tracing tools like DarshanXT [22] which provides the temporal data of I/O events, albeit, it generates a lot of data that can be cumbersome to process for the end users. In any case, the data is only available after the job terminates and not in real-time. Tools like Darshan and DarshanXT do not need any instrumentation of the application code which is a key reason for their wide adoption. However, end users still need to compile their application codes with Darshan support. Besides, Darshan offers only limited support for non-MPI applications.

The current work proposes monitoring the I/O activity of the applications using extended Berkley Packet Filter (eBPF) in an application and file system agnostic manner. The extended version of the Berkeley Packet Filter (BPF) is an abstract virtual machine (VM) with its own instruction set that can execute user-defined programs inside a sandbox in Linux. eBPF enables programs to run in the kernel of the host operating system and to instrument the kernel without changing the kernel source code [17]. This technology enables the injection of arbitrary user code into kernel space at runtime without requiring a reboot. eBPF programs are verified at load time to prevent kernel crashes and they run to completion. These sandbox programs are then triggered by kernel events, receiving pointers to the kernel or user space memory. Maps allow sharing of information between the kernel and user space as well as exchanging data between eBPF programs in the kernel. By hooking eBPF programs to kernel's Virtual File System (VFS) [18], it is possible to monitor the I/O statistics of any application using any type of backend file system in a unified manner. Moreover, by grouping all the processes on a given node by their cgroups, it is possible to report I/O statistics per job even when the node is being shared by multiple jobs.

To address the shortcomings of tools like Darshan, it is desirable to store this data in a central high performance database where real-time access to the data is possible. Prometheus [8] proved to be an effective and efficient solution to store the time series data for cloud-native applications. Prometheus works by scrapping its targets at a pre-configured interval of time and storing the metrics in its database. Using this approach it is possible to do system-wide monitoring of the I/O statistics of all jobs in a systematic way which does not require any modifications of the application codes either at compile time or at run time. For the current work, CEEMS Exporter [16] has been used. Originally CEEMS [15] has been created to measure the energy consumption and carbon footprint of compute workloads like HPC batch jobs, Openstack VMs, *etc*. However, later it has been extended to monitor performance, I/O and network metrics. It uses eBPF to monitor I/O and network metrics at a granularity of cgroups.

The objective of the current work is to propose a file system and application-agnostic way to monitor I/O activity on the HPC platforms. This real-time temporal monitoring data can be retrieved with a negligible overhead which can be used to understand the I/O patterns of the applications. This will give the developers and end users a preliminary idea of their applications' I/O performance in real-time with hints on whether they need to perform more detailed analysis using profiling tools. The fact that this monitoring approach can be used for any file systems ranging from classic Network File System (NFS) to parallel file systems like LUSTRE is a novelty of the work.

This paper has the following structure. Section 2 presents eBPF basics, Sect. 3 introduces the framework, Sect. 4 discusses the experimental setup and results and Sect. 5 presents the conclusions.

2   eBPF Basics

eBPF has three main components: eBPF programs, user space programs and BPF maps. eBPF programs are the ones that run in kernel space and react to events. User space programs are used to load eBPF programs into the kernel and manage their life cycle. Finally, BPF maps are the interface between eBPF kernel space and user space programs that allow data sharing. Typically in a development cycle shown in Fig. 1, an eBPF code written in C is compiled in the form of bytecode, expected by Linux kernel, using compiler suite like clang/LLVM.

The bytecode contains the BPF maps definitions and eBPF programs that refer to these maps. This compiled bytecode is loaded into the kernel using libraries like Cilium Go eBPF [7], BCC [10], *etc..*, using BPF system calls. All the BPF maps that eBPF programs refer to are created first in the kernel space so that programs can use the maps to share and retrieve the data. BPF maps act as a shared resource between user and kernel spaces where data can be transferred from user to kernel space and *vice-versa*. Hash tables, Arrays, Least Recently Used (LRU), Ring Buffer and Stack Trace are examples of maps supported in the kernel space.

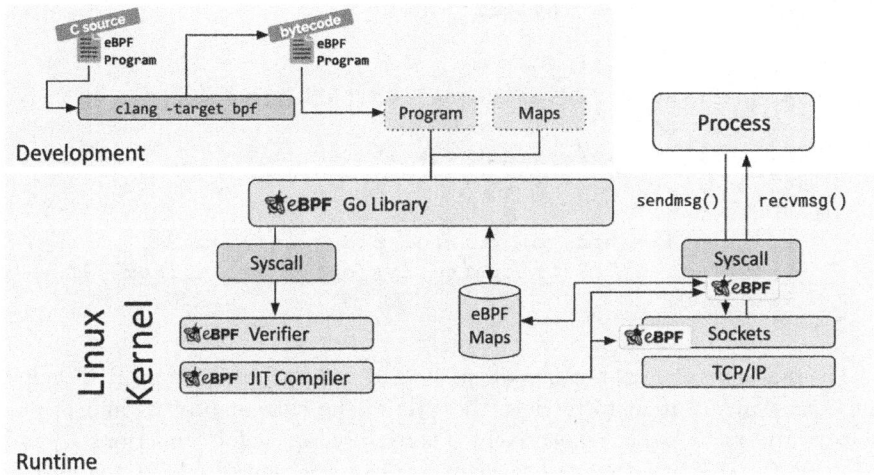

Fig. 1. eBPF framework [9].

The loaded eBPF programs will go through a verifier that will ensure that the programs will run to completion and not hang or crash the kernel. The verifier will also ensure that all memory access is legal and if it finds any illegal memory access, it refuses to load the eBPF program. Once the verifier passes all the tests on eBPF programs, they will be compiled into native instructions using Just-In-Time (JIT) compiler. Finally, the eBPF programs are attached to the selected kernel events where their execution is triggered by the event occurrence. For instance, in the Fig. 1, eBPF programs are hooked to sendmsg and recvmsg socket events. Every time a process calls these syscalls, the eBPF programs hooked to these functions will be executed thus, allowing users to add custom code into kernel space. eBPF programs can be hooked to syscalls, function entry/exit, kernel tracepoints, *etc..* If a predefined hook does not exist for a given use case, it is possible to instrument function calls, using kprobes for kernel space functions and uprobes for user space functions, and attach eBPF programs almost anywhere in the kernel or user applications. This means it is possible to monitor user space functions like MPI IO, netCDF, HDF5, *etc.*, using eBPF for monitoring I/O activity.

A sample eBPF program is shown in 1.1. The program attaches a function handle_tp to sys_enter_write tracepoint in the kernel using SEC macro.

Listing 1.1. Sample eBPF program

```
#define BPF_NO_GLOBAL_DATA
#include <linux/bpf.h>
#include <bpf/bpf_helpers.h>
#include <bpf/bpf_tracing.h>

typedef unsigned int u32;
typedef int pid_t;

char LICENSE[] SEC("license") = "GPL";

SEC("tp/syscalls/sys_enter_write")
int handle_tp(void *ctx)
{
   pid_t pid = bpf_get_current_pid_tgid() >> 32;
   bpf_printk("BPF triggered sys_enter_write from PID
   return 0;
}
```

The functions bpf_get_current_pid_tgid and bpf_printk are BPF helper functions that are used to retrieve the PID of the current process and print a message to trace_pipe, respectively. There are more helper functions [2] provided by libbpf [3] that can be used to retrieve information about the current process. This simple eBPF program prints a message to trace_pipe every time a process enters the syscall write. This very simple example, which is not very useful *per se*, can demonstrate the power of the eBPF framework in observability and monitoring.

3 I/O Monitoring Methodology Using eBPF

This section explains the methodology used to monitor the I/O activity on remote parallel file systems using eBPF. Whenever a process wants to access a file of any type of file system: local or remote, it invokes the syscalls read or write which in turn calls VFS layer [18] of the kernel as shown in Fig. 2.

VFS is essentially an interface that each client must implement to access the underlying storage hardware. At runtime, VFS will inspect the file descriptor and delegate the I/O to the correct client library which can be LUSTRE, BeeGFS, *etc.* In the current methodology, eBPF programs will be hooked into the VFS functions shown in Table 1 to monitor the I/O activity.

As discussed in the Sect. 1, tracing each syscall to the file system can generate exorbitant which is very hard to process and in some cases might not have real value. Thus, the activity is aggregated per cgroup [14] which is effectively per

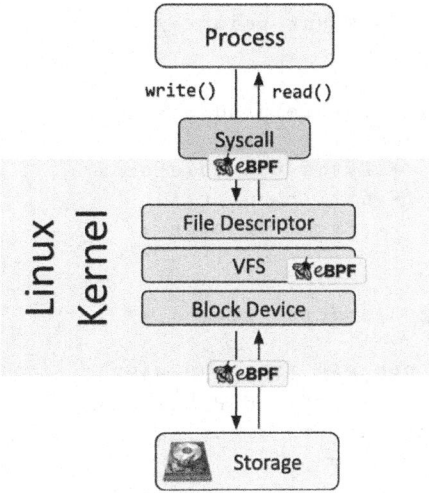

Fig. 2. Attaching eBPF programs to VFS functions [9].

Table 1. eBPF programs hooked to following kernel VFS functions.

Function name	Description
vfs_read	Read a file
vfs_write	Write a file
vfs_open	Open a file
vfs_create	Create a file
vfs_mkdir	Make a directory inode
vfs_unlink	Remove a file
vfs_rmdir	Remove a directory inode

HPC job on a given node. The data is further aggregated per mount point on the node which means I/O statistics are monitored per job on a given node and given class of storage at a given time t. The class of storage in this context can be high-performance low latency scratch storage, medium-performance work or project storage, low-performance long retention store or archive storage, *etc.*, which are classically used on the HPC platforms. Thus, the metrics are aggregated for each combination of the cgroup ID and mount point of the file system on a given node. Consequently, BPF maps are defined using a struct containing these two parameters as keys and I/O statistics like number of bytes, requests and errors as value. List. 1.2 shows the definitions of key, value and BPF map *per se*.

Listing 1.2. BPF maps definitions

```
/* vfs related event key struct */
struct vfs_event_key {
    __u32 cid; /* cgroup ID */
```

```
    __u8 mnt[64]; /* Mount point */
};

/* Any vfs read/write related event */
struct vfs_rw_event {
    __u64 bytes; /* Bytes accumulator */
    __u64 calls; /* Call counter */
    __u64 errors; /* Error counter */
};

/* Map to track vfs_write events */
struct {
    __uint(type, BPF_MAP_TYPE_LRU_HASH);
    __uint(max_entries, MAX_MAP_ENTRIES);
    __type(key, struct vfs_event_key); /* Key is the
    vfs_event_key struct */
    __type(value, struct vfs_rw_event);
    __uint(map_flags, BPF_F_NO_COMMON_LRU);
} write_accumulator SEC(".maps");
```

vfs_event_key is the key to the BPF map that contains the cgroup ID and mount point information of a given file operation. Similarly, vfs_rw_event stores the number of bytes read/written, number of requests and number of errors for a given vfs_event_key. Finally, write_accumulator stores the data in an LRU hash so that older data will be automatically evicted to add newer data. The maximum entries of the map can be configured either at the compile time or at the runtime.

Thus, the first challenge is to determine the cgroup ID and the mount point of each file operation inside the eBPF programs. libbpf already provides a helper function bpf_get_current_cgroup_id to get the cgroup ID of cgroups v2. However, an equivalent helper function does not exist for cgroups v1 and the fact that a lot of HPC platforms still rely on cgroups v1, there is a need to add support for cgroups v1 as well. This has been implemented by retrieving the task ID using the bpf helper function bpf_get_current_task of the current PID which contains a list of cgroups attached to this task. As in the cgroups v1, there are multiple subsystems [14], this approach requires the operators to configure the active subsystem that is being used by the resource manager. In the example of SLURM, it uses memory, cpuacct and cpuset controllers and by fetching the cgroup path of any of these controllers, it is possible to obtain the cgroup ID.

Similarly, to retrieve the mount point of the current path file object [1], which is one of the arguments to vfs_read and vfs_write functions, can be inspected. It contains an embedded struct file_path, where there are two members mnt_mountpoint and mnt_parent which contain the mount point and parent mount points of the current path. By iteratively, walking to the root of this current file path it is possible to build a mount path of a given file object. More details on finding the cgroup IDs and mount points from the current process and given file object can be found in the source code [16].

Both vfs_read and vfs_write functions return the number of bytes read or written on a successful I/O operation or an error code. Thus, by hooking the eBPF programs at the function that exists (fexit), it is possible to record the number of bytes, number of requests and number of errors. These maps that are being filled with the data will be read from user space programs. Reading the maps from user space programs too often can induce a non-negligible overhead as the kernel needs to wait to update the maps while user space programs reading them. Thus, the data is typically read for every few seconds from the user space which does not affect the performance of the applications. In the current methodology, whenever Prometheus makes a scrape request to the exporter running on a given node, the exporter will read maps and send the data to Prometheus. The data is accumulated in the kernel space in the maps during the duration of the job and this accumulated data is read from the user space at each scrape request. Thus, there is no loss of data between two scrape requests.

3.1 Technical Details

CEEMS exporter [16] supports monitoring I/O activity using eBPF and it has been used in the current work for the experiments. The way eBPF programs access the arguments to the kernel functions is by unpacking the register values. Thus, when the function signature changes, it means the registers that needs to be read to fetch a function argument must be a different one as well. The function signatures for vfs_read and vfs_write have changed in kernel versions v5 and v6. This is handled by compiling multiple eBPF programs based on the kernel version at the build time and loading the correct eBPF program at runtime based on the kernel version of the host. Similarly, the unpacking of registers is highly architecture-dependent. This can be handled by Compile Once - Run Everywhere (CO-RE) [11] approach. CEEMS exporter that is used in the current work supports kernel versions starting from 5.8 for AMD, ARM and MIPS architectures using CO-RE approach. The exporter has been implemented in Golang and Cilium eBPF [7] library has been used to manage the life cycle of the eBPF programs and maps.

4 Experiments

IOR [13] has been chosen for the experiments on a server Intel Xeon Gold 6130, 2.10 GHz with 192 GiB of DRAM. The server has a secondary SSD disk and a NFS server has been created on this disk. The NFS server is mounted on the same server as a client to emulate a remote file system on the loop-back interface. Although this mounting is not necessary for the current monitoring framework to work, it has been done to mimic the production setup. Moreover this setup eliminates network communication, thus providing reliable benchmark results. The server has been exclusively used for current tests to eliminate any noise due to other activity.

All the IOR tests have been configured to remove any cache effects as described in its documentation. For the write tests, flag O_DIRECT has been used to ensure the data is being written to the underlying storage disk. Similarly, to eliminate reading from the cache, the memory of the server is hogged up to 90% and a block size of 50 GiB is used in all tests. The tests are conducted with both POSIX and MPIIO APIs to demonstrate that the current framework works for any type of I/O. To keep the tests simple, all the tests have been run only with a single process writing the data onto the client mount point of the NFS server. Transfer sizes of 1,2,4,8 and 16 MiB have been chosen to study the accuracy and overhead of monitoring framework for different sizes. All the tests have been repeated 8 times. The mean values of I/O bandwidth for the tests *without* monitoring have been chosen as reference values in the comparison. Prometheus is configured to scrape the exporter at a frequency of 2 s which means the user space eBPF program will read the BPF maps every 2 s. On production systems, this scrape frequency is normally configured to be in the order of 10 s and the current scrape frequency of 2 s is chosen intentionally in an attempt to measure the overhead. It is worth emphasizing here that the proposed framework is to monitor I/O activity on HPC systems rather than to profile it. Hence, 2 s is considered a small enough interval in the context of monitoring.

Two different metrics have been chosen for the present analysis namely, relative overhead and relative error. Relative overhead is the ratio of observed bandwidth without monitoring enabled to the observed bandwidth with monitoring enabled. The observed bandwidth here refers to the bandwidth values reported by the IOR benchmark. Higher values indicate a noticeable overhead of the current monitoring framework. Similarly, the relative error is estimated as the observed bandwidth reported by IOR and the mean of the instantaneous bandwidths reported by the CEEMS exporter during the benchmark tests.

Figure 3 presents the results of experiments on NFS server using POSIX and MPIIO APIs using different transfer sizes of IOR benchmark. The first observable conclusion from the results of relative overhead is the median values are very close to 1. Moreover, values less than 1 are observed for certain cases (like MPIIO with a transfer size of 1024 KiB) which means the observed bandwidth with monitoring enabled is higher which cannot be true. Thus, the variability in the results is merely a transient effect and the overhead of monitoring is negligible or nonmeasurable with the current configuration. Generally, the overhead of eBPF programs is measured in nanoseconds and the current eBPF programs take around 150–200 ns for each execution which is measured by enabling `kernel.bpf_stats_enabled` kernel configuration parameter. Thus, the overhead of these eBPF functions is barely noticeable in the present results.

Now that it has been established that the framework induces negligible to no overhead, it is equally important to verify if the framework estimates the I/O activity accurately. Looking at the relative error plots, the median values stay very close to 1 confirming very good accuracy. It is worth noting that the comparison is made between the static value of the bandwidth reported by IOR at the end of each test with the instantaneous bandwidth reported by the

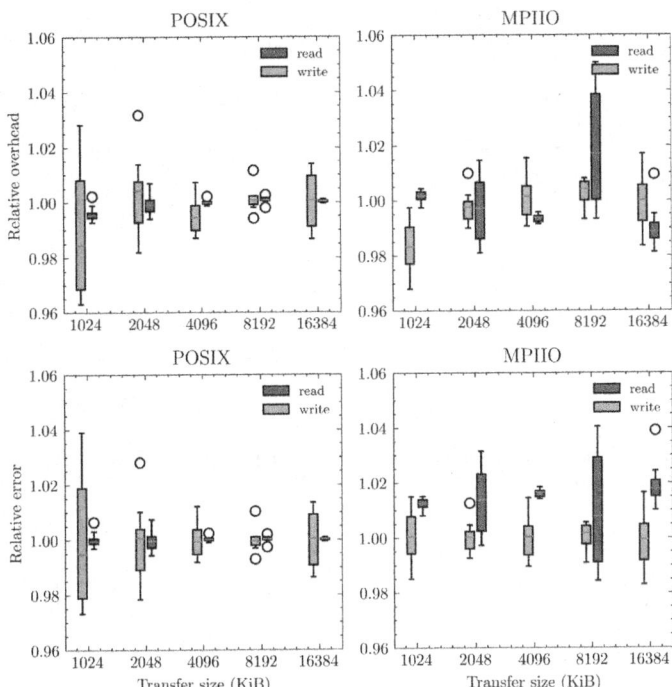

Fig. 3. Relative overhead and errors of eBPF based monitoring for POSIX and MPIIO APIs on a NFS server.

CEEMS exporter for every 2 s averaged over the duration of each benchmark test. Thus, it can be concluded that the bandwidths reported by the current monitoring approach are indeed what is observed from the remote file system clients.

This section is concluded by presenting the results from Jean Zay HPC platform [12] which uses the LUSTRE file system. IOR benchmark has been run with POSIX and MPIIO APIs using 16 MPI processes on 4 nodes with a transfer size of 1 MiB (which corresponds to the stripe size on the LUSTRE file system) and a block size of 25 GiB for each MPI process. To validate the current framework, Darshan has been used for this test and results between two frameworks have been compared. Figure 4 shows the instantaneous bandwidth estimated by the current monitoring framework and Darshan. In the plot, the legends $n[0-3]$ correspond to different nodes. The instantaneous bandwidth for Darshan has been estimated based on the heat map values that Darshan reported with a bin interval of 51.4 s where as the CEEMS exporter monitors with a frequency of 10 sec. Results reported by the CEEMS exporter (eBPF) agree very well with the ones from the Darshan for both POSIX and MPIIO. Thus, it can be

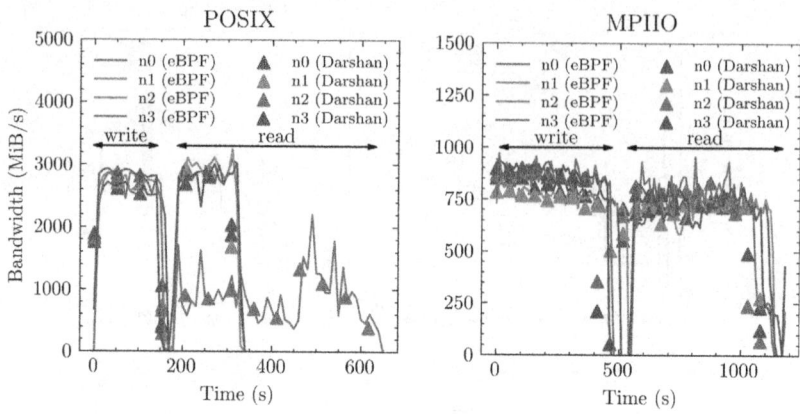

Fig. 4. Instantaneous bandwidth estimated by CEEMS (eBPF) exporter and Darshan on LUSTRE file system.

concluded that the temporal aspect of the I/O activity has been well captured by the CEEMS exporter which uses the proposed eBPF monitoring framework.

5 Conclusion

The paper proposes a monitoring framework based on eBPF to describe I/O activity on HPC platforms. The overhead and accuracy of the proposed method have been studied using the IOR benchmark on a NFS server. It has been shown that the proposed framework does not show any measurable overhead for the chosen test cases and configuration and at the same time, the reported I/O bandwidths agree very well with the ones from IOR tests. The results from the eBPF monitoring framework have been compared against Darshan results for multi node tests and a very good agreement between the results has been noticed. The proposed methodology is being used on the Jean Zay supercomputer for several months now which demonstrates the production readiness of the framework. Although the scope of the current work is only monitoring of the I/O activity, eBPF-based observability can be extended to profiling of I/O metrics by exporting traces in a format understandable by tracing tools like DarshanXT. Besides, it is possible to trace user space functions like MPIIO, and HDF5 using eBPF, albeit, with a slightly bigger overhead (a few hundred nanoseconds) penalty, which allows monitoring of I/O activity across user and kernel spaces in a unified manner.

Acknowledgments. Experiments presented in this paper were carried out using the Grid'5000 testbed, supported by a scientific interest group hosted by Inria and including CNRS, RENATER and several Universities as well as other organizations (see https://www.grid5000.fr).

Disclosure of Interests. The author has no competing interests to declare that are relevant to the content of this article

References

1. Authors, K.: BPF CO-RE (2025). https://docs.ebpf.io/concepts/core/. Accessed 24 Feb 2025
2. eBPF Docs.: bpf-helpers(7) — Linux manual page (2025). https://man7.org/linux/man-pages/man7/bpf-helpers.7.html. Accessed 24 Feb 2025
3. Authors, K.: Libbpf overview (2025). https://docs.kernel.org/bpf/libbpf/libbpf_overview.html
4. Bandet, A.: Characterization and monitoring of I/O for HPC workloads. Ph.D. thesis, Université de Bordeaux (2024)
5. BeeGFS: Documentation (2025). https://doc.beegfs.io/latest/overview/overview.html
6. Braam, P.: The lustre storage architecture (2019). https://arxiv.org/abs/1903.01955
7. Cilium: The ebpf library for go (2025). https://ebpf-go.dev/
8. Community: Prometheus (2024). https://github.com/prometheus/prometheus
9. eBPF Community: ebpf documentation (2025). https://ebpf.io/what-is-ebpf/
10. Contributors, B.: Bpf compiler collection (bcc) (2025). https://github.com/iovisor/bcc
11. eBPF Docs: bpf-helpers(7)—linux manual page (2025). https://man7.org/linux/man-pages/man7/bpf-helpers.7.html
12. GENCI: Jean zay (2025). https://www.genci.fr/en/institut-du-developpement-et-des-ressources-en-informatique-scientifique-idris
13. IOR: Ior documentation (2025). https://ior.readthedocs.io/en/latest/index.html
14. Linux Kernel Community: Control Groups (2024). https://docs.kernel.org/admin-guide/cgroup-v1/cgroups.html, version 6.11.0
15. Paipuri, M.: CEEMS: a resource manager agnostic energy and emissions monitoring stack. In: SC24-W: Workshops of the International Conference for High Performance Computing, Networking, Storage and Analysis, pp. 1862–1866. IEEE (2024). https://doi.org/10.1109/scw63240.2024.00233
16. Paipuri, M.: Compute Energy & Emissions Monitoring Stack (CEEMS) (2024). https://github.com/mahendrapaipuri/ceems
17. Rice, L.: Learning eBPF. O'Reilly Media (2023). https://books.google.fr/books?id=dW-yEAAAQBAJ
18. Richard Gooch, P.E.: Overview of the linux virtual file system (2005). https://www.kernel.org/doc/html/v6.3/filesystems/vfs.html
19. Schmuck, F., Haskin, R.: GPFS: a shared-disk file system for large computing clusters. In: Proceedings of the 1st USENIX Conference on File and Storage Technologies, FAST '02, p. 19–es. USENIX Association (2002)
20. Shende, S.S., Malony, A.D.: The tau parallel performance system. Int. J. High Perform. Comput. Appl. **20**(2), 287–311 (2006)
21. Snyder, S., Carns, P., Harms, K., Ross, R., Lockwood, G.K., Wright, N.J.: Modular hpc I/O characterization with darshan. In: 2016 5th Workshop on Extreme-Scale Programming Tools (ESPT), pp. 9–17 (2016).https://doi.org/10.1109/ESPT.2016.006
22. Xu, C., et al.: DXT: darshan extended tracing (2019). https://api.semanticscholar.org/CorpusID:32477133

Supporting HPC Users with LLview

Filipe Souza Mendes Guimarães[✉], Aravind Sankaran, and Wolfgang Frings

Jülich Supercomputing Centre, Forschungszentrum Jülich, Jülich, Germany
{f.guimaraes,a.sankaran,w.frings}@fz-juelich.de

Abstract. Diagnosing and reporting operational issues to optimise system usage and performance is challenging on large-scale HPC systems due to their sheer complexity. At the Jülich Supercomputing Centre (JSC), we address this challenge with LLview, an open-source system and job reporting framework. LLview provides near real-time metrics for analysis through a web portal with role-based access for users, administrators, and support staff. In this paper, we present a series of use cases demonstrating how LLview enables efficient diagnosis and resolution of system and application issues, enhancing both reactive and proactive support for HPC users.

Keywords: High performance computing (HPC) · Resource management · Monitoring · Operational Data Analytics

1 Introduction

High-Performance Computing (HPC) systems are continuously evolving, achieving unprecedented computational capabilities. As machines grow in size, the number of users and the scale of their computational simulations also increase, creating operational challenges in supporting users with their issues, keeping them informed about the system status, helping them adapt their codes to changing computing environments, and enabling them in achieving the best performance from the systems. To address these challenges, the LLview framework has been developed at the Jülich Supercomputing Centre (JSC), which leverages data from system daemons and various monitoring tools to reports on system and application behaviour. In this paper, we demonstrate how visualisations and reports from LLview assist in diagnosing issues within user applications.

LLview is a reporting framework that can be configured to work with input data from any given monitoring infrastructure. At JSC, the monitoring infrastructure collects data from the Slurm workload manager, various daemons running on compute nodes, and sensors that either log information to files or interface with the Prometheus monitoring system. LLview then aggregates and reorganises the monitoring data, stores the information necessary for reporting in

---

This work was supported by the State of North Rhine-Westphalia for application support of the JUWELS Cluster and Booster (SiVeGCS) and by the European Union's Horizon 2020 research and innovation program under grant agreement No. 101033975 (EUPEX).

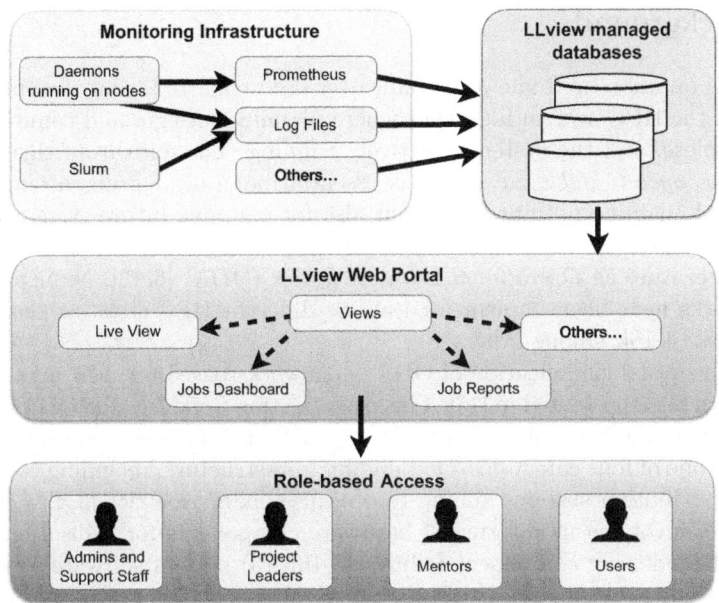

Fig. 1. Information flow through the LLview framework.

separate SQLite databases, and presents them to the user through a web-based front-end portal. The databases are updated every one minute, which enables near real-time reporting of the systems. The web portal has multiple views to enable different kinds of investigation into system and application behaviour. Access to the reporting interface is available to administrators, support staff, and all users having an account on the HPC systems at JSC, with role-based permissions defining their level of information access. At JSC, an additional "Mentor" role is defined, allowing mentors to assist project leaders by monitoring their jobs. This hierarchical access structure enables leaders to manage their projects more effectively, mentors to oversee the jobs of projects they advise, and support staff to proactively detect and address misconfigurations or inefficiencies. The role-based access enables the HPC centre to provide proactive support, helping users continuously and efficiently adapt to the ever-evolving HPC landscape. A schematic overview of information flow through the LLview framework is shown in Fig. 1.

LLview is open source, and the components of the framework are available online [12,15]. The implementation details are self-contained in [12] and are beyond the scope of this paper. In this work, we first position the analytics framework of JSC with LLview in relation to frameworks developed at other HPC centres (Sect. 2). Then, we focus on three views of the LLview web portal that are predominantly used to support HPC users—Live View, Jobs Dashboard, and Job Reports—and present the main analytic use cases of each (Sect. 3).

2 Background

We focus on analytic frameworks built over data collected from the operational phase of the HPC system lifecycle—where planning, design, and commissioning are complete, and the system is actively running. The data from this phase is known as *operational data* and it is essential not only for diagnosing system issues and enabling prompt action but also for planning future system developments. Analytics methods developed over operational data have been referred to in the literature as *Operational Data Analytics* (ODA) [5,13]. Numerous ODA frameworks have been implemented across different HPC sites, as described in Refs. [3,8,14,18], among others.

A conceptual classification of ODA frameworks based on their area of application has been presented in [13]. This classification organises the ODA activities within a two dimensional 4×4 grid. Along the first dimension, the analytic focus falls into one of four categories: (1) building infrastructure, including cooling and power distribution systems aiming to optimise energy metrics [3,4]; (2) system hardware, involving monitoring of hardware components for utilisation estimation and predicting component failures [3,16]; (3) system software, comprising workload manager and site-level software components, to improve resource utilisation [14,18]; and (4) application-level frameworks, focusing on reporting and diagnosing code-level issues [6,8]. At JSC, LLview is used for ODA that include parts from all the four areas, with more focus on the application level. The second dimension categorises each framework based on one of four data analytics methods applied: (a) Descriptive, addressing the question 'What has happened?'—this includes dashboards and system reports; (b) Diagnostic, which seeks to answer 'Why did it happen?'—focusing on anomaly detection and root cause analysis; (c) Predictive, which asks 'What will happen?'—involving HPC system simulations and job resource usage predictions; and (d) Prescriptive, which determines 'What should be done?'—such as job configuration recommendations and intelligent task and thread placement. LLview falls into the Descriptive and Diagnostic categories. Figure 2 shows the positioning of LLview within the 4 × 4 ODA grid alongside other tools indicated in Ref. [13].

Several frameworks provide functionalities comparable to LLview. One example is ExaMon [2], that has been designed to ingest over 70 GB/day of telemetry data, making it suitable for HPC centers managing large-scale systems. It facilitates the development of tools that leverage this data for ODA. Open XDMoD [14], primarily developed at the University of Buffalo, focuses on supporting the management of HPC centres and improving service quality. It features role-based access control, aggregates metrics at the project level, and also has provisions to generate job-focused reports. Frameworks such as ClusterCockpit [8] and PIKA [6] generate detailed job-specific reports by synthesising multiple hardware metrics with minimal overhead. All existing tools apply various analytical methods to monitored data. A key aspect of LLview lies in its carefully engineered user interface that is designed to be simple and intuitive, facilitating the investigation of user issues and providing a safe level of transparency into system operations. Another distinct feature is LLview's near real-time reporting

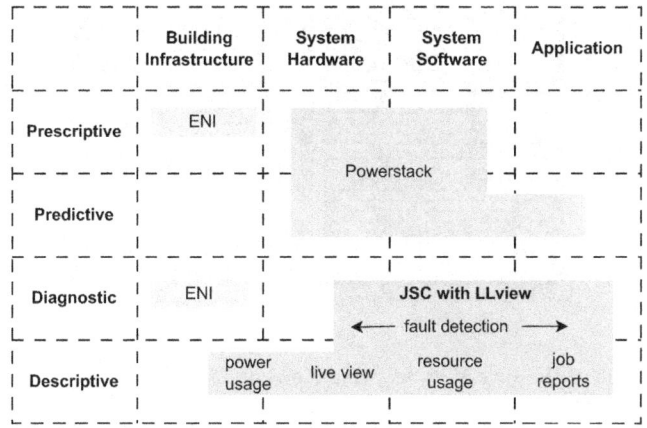

Fig. 2. Positioning of some ODA activities at JSC with LLview amongst the ODA infrastructure of ENI [4] and PowerStack [18] placed according to discussion in [13].

capability, providing quick feedback and enabling users to take prompt action when some issue is identified—avoiding wasting time and resources. In this paper we elaborate on several use cases and methods that leverage monitored information to support the investigation of user-level issues. By sharing these experiences and practices, we aim to help other HPC centres adopt and refine similar workflows to strengthen their own user support.

LLview began as a system-level reporting framework and later evolved to provide detailed job reports. The development of LLview began in 2004, initially aimed at reporting on systems managed by the IBM LoadLeveler workload manager (hence named LLview). Over time, it was generalised to support the reporting of systems with other workload managers, such as Slurm, PBS, Torque, etc. [9] [17]. LLview has been used at JSC to report on production grade supercomputers such as JUMP, JUGENE, JUROPA and IBM Blue Gene (JUGENE and JUQUEEN) in the past [7]. It is currently used to report on large scale systems JURECA [11], JUWELS (Cluster and Booster having in total more than 3500 compute nodes with over 3700 GPUs) [1], and other smaller clusters. LLview will also be used to report on JUPITER, the upcoming exascale system [10].

3 The Three Views and Their Analytical Use Cases

In this section, we describe the three views of LLview that are predominantly used to support HPC users. We provide examples of how each view assists users, administrators, and support staff in identifying both hardware and software issues.

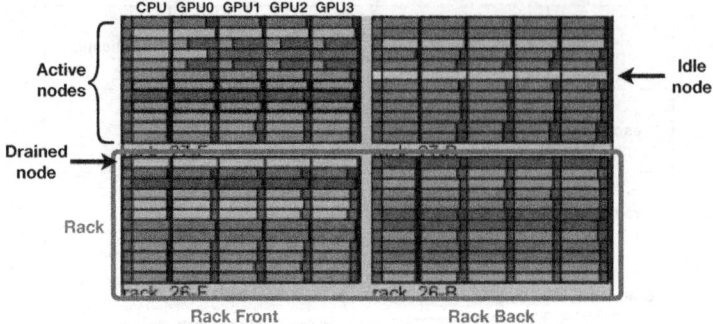

Fig. 3. A portion of the Live View showing 2 out of 36 racks of JUWELS Booster. The racks show the nodes, and the (colour-coded) jobs running on them.

3.1 Live View

In large-scale production systems with thousands of nodes, occasional node failures and performance variations in repeated job runs, often influenced by differences in system activity or job placement among the racks, are common. In these situations, identifying issues and taking prompt action is challenging due to the system's complexity and diverse workloads. The Live View aids in diagnosis by reporting a visualisation that aims to form a digital twin of the system, enhancing transparency and offering insights into system operations. Figure 3 shows the mapping between running jobs and the nodes on a portion of JUWELS Booster. Each rectangle represents a side (front or back) of the rack. Each side contains 12 nodes and each node have four NVIDIA A100 GPUs. In this visualisation, each node displays six status indicators: the first represents the node state (green indicates active nodes, yellow indicates idle nodes and red indicates nodes that are down), the second indicates CPU status (in use or idle), and the remaining four represent the utilisation levels of the four GPUs. Nodes belonging to the same job are highlighted in the same colour. Users can observe job placements across racks amongst other jobs in the system, and correlate their application's performance with a glimpse of the overall system activity. If they observe performance differences in repeated runs of the same job, they can reason out whether these variations are due to differences in job placement across racks. If a job fails due to unexpected node failures, Live View provides the first indication through its real-time visualisation.

3.2 Jobs Dashboard

With a large number of jobs running on the system, support staff or project leaders may need to quickly identify jobs that are not utilising system resources as expected. To this end, the Jobs Dashboard displays a list of jobs while allowing for hierarchical investigation. The first-level information includes a set of

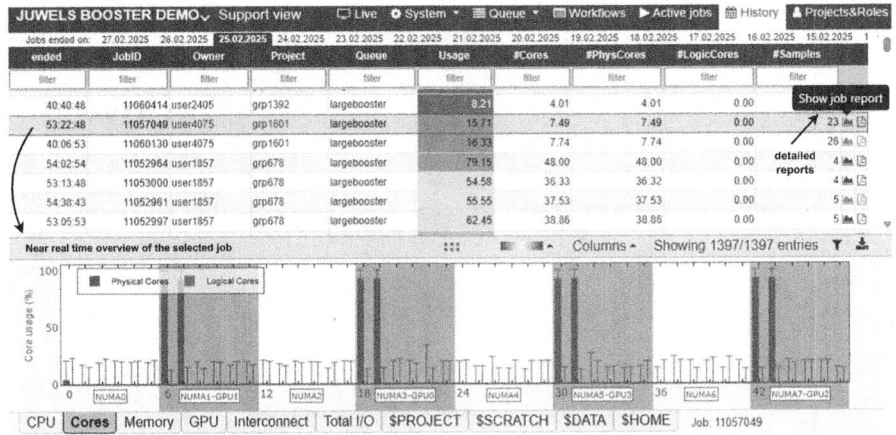

Fig. 4. A snapshot of the Jobs Dashboard showing a table representing one job per line, and each column containing one of its metrics. Some columns are colour-coded to indicate potential issues. Detailed job reports can be accessed in the rightmost columns. Selecting a line displays aggregated graphs on the bottom of the page.

summary statistics, with colour-coded indicators highlighting potentially underperforming jobs. For example, Fig. 4 shows a snapshot of jobs visible to a supporter, along with a configurable subset of statistics (additional stats can be toggled using the "Columns" button at the bottom right of the top panel). Average core usage across all nodes is colour-coded from red to green, with darker red indicating lower usage. Clicking on a job reveals second-level information, displayed as graphs in the bottom panel. One of the graphs displays per-core usage across all nodes using bar plots, offering detailed insights into load distribution among cores. In the example shown in Fig. 4, the job does not utilise all cores. If this usage pattern is unintended, it warrants further diagnosis. For the next level of information, such as viewing activity from each node, users can access comprehensive and interactive HTML reports (also available as PDF) containing more in-depth analysis and detailed insights.

3.3 Job Reports

Job reports are automatically generated and continuously updated in the background by LLview for all jobs running longer than a few minutes (depending on the number of jobs running on the system). These dynamic reports provide early, detailed insights that enable both users and support staff to promptly address emerging issues. In this section, we outline several common issues detected by our reporting infrastructure, illustrating each with a corresponding use case.

Memory Issues. Diagnosing memory issues can be challenging, especially when a user application crashes with a segmentation fault without providing additional

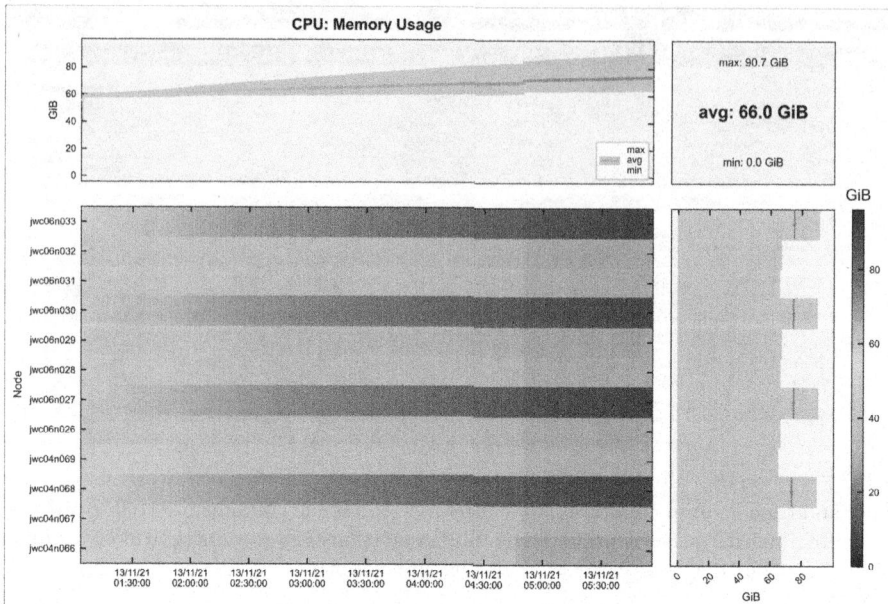

Fig. 5. Colorplot from a job report showing node memory usage over time (x-axis: time; y-axis: nodes). The top panel displays the average usage per timestamp with a shadowed min-max range; the bottom-right shows per-node averages with min-max regions; and the top-right summarises overall job statistics. In this case, some nodes exhibit a continuous memory increase until capacity is reached, leading to a job crash.

information. One recurring example evident in user reports is a steady increase in memory usage during simulations until the node's capacity is exhausted, ultimately resulting in a crash. Although this behaviour can occasionally be intentional—for instance, when an application incrementally accumulates data—it more frequently signals a memory leak, where unused memory is not properly released. Notably, even small increases in memory usage per minute can accumulate over extended periods, making it difficult to detect a memory leak by merely examining the current memory consumption of a job. This phenomenon is clearly demonstrated in the job reports as a monotonic increase in memory consumption across one or more nodes. Figure 5 reveals a memory leak affecting only specific nodes—even when overall consumption remains within acceptable limits—demonstrating the critical importance of granular node-level details for effective troubleshooting.

System Error Logs. In some scenarios, memory issues present themselves in a less gradual fashion: a simulation may suddenly request a large memory allocation that exceeds the available memory in a node. In such cases, the out-of-memory reaper terminates the job, leaving users without an immediate explanation since the detailed diagnostics reside only in the system logs, normally not

Job Finalization Report	Job State: FAILED	Return Code: 9	Signal Number: 0
System Error Report	# Msgs: 2 # Nodes: 1	(Out-of-memory)	
	This job has used approximately: 1 nodes × 48 cores × 0.186 hours = 8.93 core-h		

System Error Report

# Msgs: 2	# Nodes: 1

Error Messages:

```
2025-04-24T19:21:29+0200 jwb0163.juwels kernel: python invoked oom-killer:
gfp_mask=0x140dca(GFP_HIGHUSER_MOVABLE!__GFP_COMP!__GFP_ZERO), order=0, oom_score_adj=0
2025-04-24T19:21:29+0200 jwb0163.juwels kernel: Out of memory: Killed process 1556003 (python) total-
vm:902572524kB, anon-rss:496358356kB, file-rss:89856kB, shmem-rss:19200kB, UID:xxxxx pgtables:973944kB
oom_score_adj:0
```

Fig. 6. System errors are collected by LLview and displayed at the end of the job reports. The box on top is displayed in the beginning of the report, already describing common errors-as the 'Out-of-memory' indicator in the example above. The full system error message (bottom box) is displayed at the end of the reports.

available to the user. LLview mitigates this challenge by collecting such kind of error messages—deposited on the system side in a shared location—and incorporating them into the job report as seen in Fig. 6, thus enabling users to promptly identify the root cause of the crash.

An additional benefit of presenting system error logs to users is the enhanced capacity to diagnose issues - such as in network hardware failures. Under certain conditions, network adapters may experience transient link loss, which can provoke job failures. Given the inherent challenges in detecting such hardware malfunctions from a user's perspective, monitoring link-down events via system error logs is imperative. In the past, the absence of these logs in LLview reports compelled users to contact technical support, which subsequently (and often following extensive diagnostic procedures) involved system administrators to promptly ascertain whether a failure was attributable to the network issues.

This benefit is not limited to network problems; similar challenges arise when compute nodes crash due to sporadic, non-user-related faults. In these cases, explicit error messages in the system logs enable users to quickly recognise that the failure originates from the infrastructure rather than their own code, thereby reducing unnecessary diagnostic efforts and streamlining troubleshooting.

Inadequate Resource Usage. To extract the maximum capabilities of the HPC system, it is ideal for jobs to use all the available resources. Analysing job reports to assess resource utilisation can help users avoid unintentional waste and uncover opportunities for optimisation. Since these reports are generated and updated in near real time, potential issues can be identified and addressed promptly.

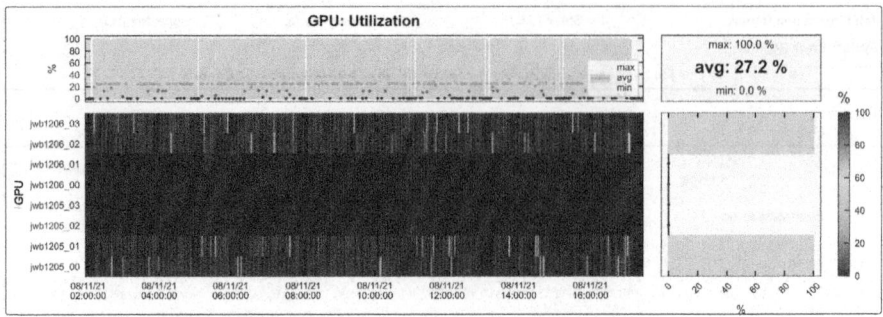

(a) Job allocated with 8 GPUs but using only 4 of them. The reports make it easier to recognise when jobs are not fully utilising the available resources.

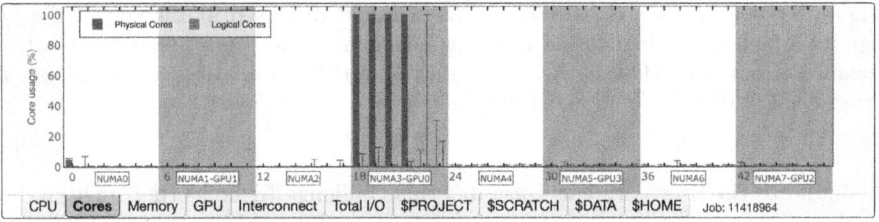

(b) Core usage of a GPU-focused job using four GPUs from four cores in a single NUMA domain that has direct access to one of the GPUs.

Fig. 7. Indications of inadequate GPU usage

For instance, some simulations reserve an entire node yet utilise only a fraction of the available cores or GPUs. This discrepancy is clearly illustrated in Fig. 7a, where the colorplot shows information for the 8 GPUs allocated for the job (in the y-axis), and four of them, depicted by the darker blue region, had zero utilisation as indicated by the averages per node shown on the lower-right plot. A subtler issue is depicted in the bar plot representing the core-usage of a job in Fig. 7b. The white and gray alternated areas mark the cores within different NUMA domains of a node, with each GPU being directly connected to the gray ones. In this example, all four GPUs are engaged by tasks confined to a single NUMA domain. Although such a configuration might be beneficial when shared memory access is preferred, it can adversely affect performance if intensive CPU–GPU communication is required. These scenarios often indicate misconfigurations; if undetected by the user, the support team can proactively intervene with recommendations for improvement.

Hardware Issues. LLview job reports help identify issues not only in user applications but also on the system side. Hardware problems can lead to restrictions and slowdowns that extend job runtimes. For example, Fig. 8 shows jobs affected by a GPU with high temperature (yellow in the bottom graph). In this case, GPU throttling was triggered (indicated in the top graph by the green

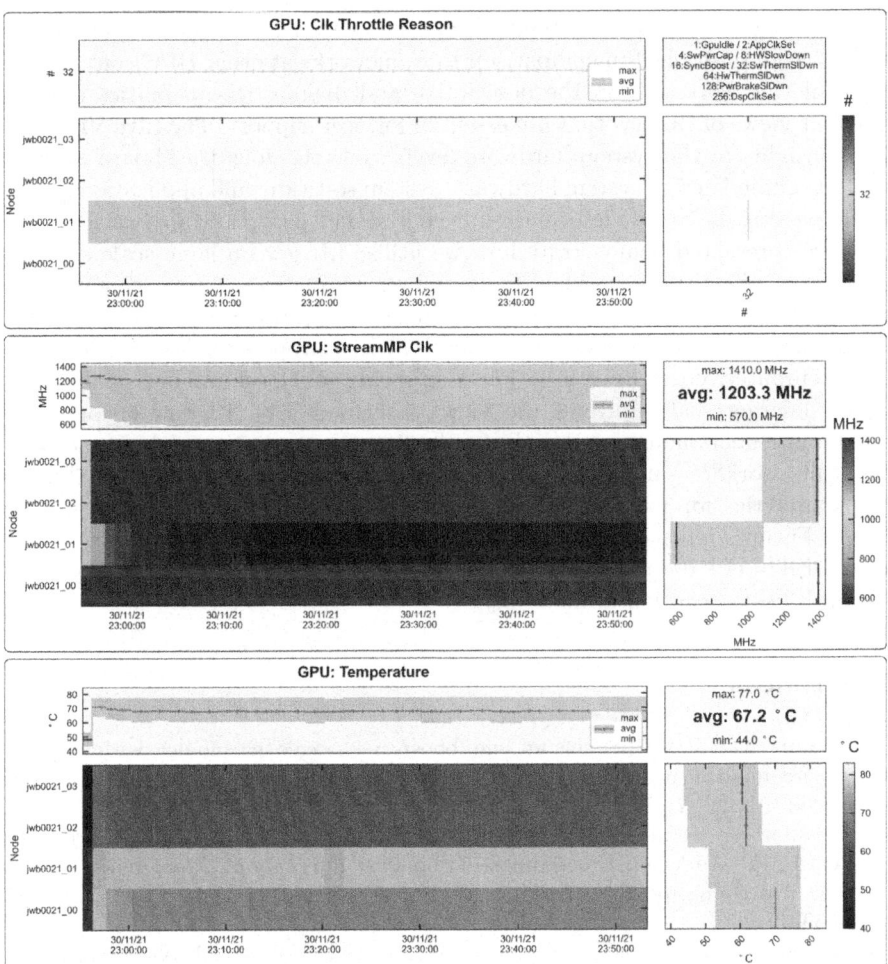

Fig. 8. Colorplots showing different metrics per node per timestamp of a job identified to be throttled down: Clock Throttle Reason (top) with green color indicating "Software Thermal Slow Down" value), Stream Multiprocessor Clock frequencies (middle) is highly decreased (dark blue) due to high temperatures (dark yellow) on a single GPU (bottom). (Color figure online)

color), reducing the GPU Streaming Multiprocessor clock frequency (darker blue in the middle graph). Even a single throttled GPU in a large calculation can cause significant delays, as other GPUs must wait for it to complete its computation.

4 Conclusions

In this paper, we presented an overview of LLview, a reporting infrastructure that aggregates data from multiple sources, applies additional analysis, and delivers it through a role-based web interface. The ODA activities done with LLview at JSC were positioned in comparison to frameworks at other HPC centres. The focus of this work was on the descriptive and diagnostic capabilities of three different views of LLview that are essential for user support: The Live View provides insights at the system hardware level, while the Jobs Dashboard and Job Reports extend across system hardware, system software, and applications, effectively passing diagnostic information from system logs to user applications. The use cases presented demonstrate how we utilise LLview on large scale systems, showing its effectiveness in identifying and resolving issues—from memory leaks to network-related failures—thereby significantly improving system oversight.

LLview is set to be deployed on JUPITER, Europe's forthcoming exascale supercomputer, ensuring robust job monitoring and performance analytics at an even larger scale. Beyond the views discussed here, LLview encompasses additional functionalities—including infrastructure reporting, job queue management, workflow analysis, and core usage pattern inspection—that further helps analytics for more support use cases, but are outside the scope of this paper. Future enhancements include the integration of long-term metrics analysis, REST-API data access, and comprehensive project reports to facilitate in-depth post-execution evaluations.

References

1. Alvarez, D.: JUWELS cluster and booster: exascale pathfinder with modular supercomputing architecture at juelich supercomputing centre. J. Large-Scale Res. Facilit. JLSRF **7**, A183 (2021). https://doi.org/10.17815/jlsrf-7-183
2. Bartolini, A., et al.: Paving the way toward energy-aware and automated datacentre. In: Workshop Proceedings of the 48th International Conference on Parallel Processing, pp. 1–8. ACM, Kyoto (2019). https://doi.org/10.1145/3339186.3339215
3. Bautista, E., Romanus, M., Davis, T., Whitney, C., Kubaska, T.: Collecting, monitoring, and analyzing facility and systems data at the national energy research scientific computing center. In: Workshop Proceedings of the 48th International Conference on Parallel Processing, pp. 1–9. ACM, Kyoto (2019). https://doi.org/10.1145/3339186.3339213
4. Bortot, L., Nardelli, W., Seto, P.: Data centers are a software development challenge. In: 48th Annual International Conference on Parallel Processing, pp. 1–5 (2019). https://www.hpcs.cs.tsukuba.ac.jp/icpp2019/data/posters/Poster4-abst.pdf
5. Bourassa, N., et al.: Operational data analytics: optimizing the national energy research scientific computing center cooling systems. In: Workshop Proceedings of the 48th International Conference on Parallel Processing, pp. 1–7. ACM, Kyoto (2019). https://doi.org/10.1145/3339186.3339210
6. Dietrich, R., Winkler, F., Knupfer, A., Nagel, W.: PIKA: center-wide and job-aware cluster monitoring. In: 2020 IEEE International Conference on Cluster Computing (CLUSTER), pp. 424–432. IEEE, Kobe (2020). https://doi.org/10.1109/CLUSTER49012.2020.00061

7. Norbert, E., Thomas, L.: Shaping the petaflop-era in Europe—supercomputing made in Jülich. In: Advances in Parallel Computing. IOS Press (2011). https://doi.org/10.3233/978-1-60750-803-8-31
8. Eitzinger, J., Gruber, T., Afzal, A., Zeiser, T., Wellein, G.: ClusterCockpit—a web application for job-specific performance monitoring. In: 2019 IEEE International Conference on Cluster Computing (CLUSTER), pp. 1–7. IEEE, Albuquerque (2019). https://doi.org/10.1109/CLUSTER.2019.8891017
9. Frings, W., et al.: LLview: user-level monitoring in computational grids and e-Science infrastructures. Baden-Baden, Germany (2007). https://pure.mpg.de/pubman/faces/ViewItemFullPage.jsp?itemId=item_1786610
10. Herten, A., et al.: Application-driven exascale: the JUPITER benchmark suite. In: SC24: International Conference for High Performance Computing, Networking, Storage and Analysis, pp. 1–45. IEEE, Atlanta (2024). https://doi.org/10.1109/SC41406.2024.00038
11. Krause, D., Thörnig, P.: JURECA: modular supercomputer at Jülich Supercomputing Centre. J. Large-Scale Res. Facilit. JLSRF **4**, A132 (2018). https://doi.org/10.17815/jlsrf-4-121-1
12. Müller, Y., Souza Mendes Guimarães, F., Karbach, C., Frings, W.: LLview (2024). https://doi.org/10.5281/ZENODO.12706843
13. Netti, A., Shin, W., Ott, M., Wilde, T., Bates, N.: A conceptual framework for HPC operational data analytics. In: 2021 IEEE International Conference on Cluster Computing (CLUSTER), pp. 596–603. IEEE, Portland (2021). https://doi.org/10.1109/Cluster48925.2021.00086
14. Palmer, J.T., et al.: Open XDMoD: a tool for the comprehensive management of high-performance computing resources. Comput. Sci. Eng. **17**(4), 52–62 (2015). https://doi.org/10.1109/MCSE.2015.68
15. Souza Mendes Guimarães, F., Lührs, S., Frings, W.: JURI (2024). https://doi.org/10.5281/ZENODO.12706831
16. Sîrbu, A., Babaoglu, O.: Towards operator-less data centers through data-driven, predictive, proactive autonomics. Clust. Comput. **19**(2), 865–878 (2016). https://doi.org/10.1007/s10586-016-0564-y
17. Watson, G.R., Frings, W., Knobloch, C., Karbach, C., Rossi, A.L.: Scalable control and monitoring of supercomputer applications using an integrated tool framework. In: 2011 40th International Conference on Parallel Processing Workshops, pp. 457–466. IEEE, Taipei City (2011). https://doi.org/10.1109/ICPPW.2011.53
18. Wu, X., et al.: Toward an end-to-end auto-tuning framework in HPC PowerStack. In: 2020 IEEE International Conference on Cluster Computing (CLUSTER), pp. 473–483. IEEE, Kobe (2020). https://doi.org/10.1109/CLUSTER49012.2020.00068

What Time Taught Us: Monitoring a Computing Technology Testbed Across Multiple Years

Eva Siegmann[1]($\boxtimes$), David Carlson[1], Nikolay A. Simakov[2], Anthony Curtis[1], Alan Calder[1], and Robert J. Harrison[1]

[1] Institute for Advanced Computational Science, Stony Brook University, Stony Brook, USA
eva.siegmann@stonybrook.edu
[2] Center for Computational Research, SUNY University at Buffalo, Buffalo, NY 14203, USA

Abstract. Testbeds for computing technologies play a crucial role in evaluating novel architectures and optimizing the user experience is critical to enabling meaningful and efficient use and testing of the platform. In this paper, we share our experience with Ookami, a computing technology testbed that has been operational for over four years, serving more than 500 users. Due to the novel nature of its technology and architecture, typical usage patterns differ significantly from those observed in conventional high-performance computing (HPC) systems. To monitor system performance and user interactions, we implemented a tracking approach that helps us assess project progress, identify beneficial and non-beneficial decisions, and continuously refine both system usage and user experience. Based on our findings, we provide recommendations for other testbed centers on key metrics to monitor and how to leverage collected data for system and user optimization. Additionally, we highlight aspects that in hindsight, would have been helpful, offering insights for future testbed development. This work serves as a practical guide for institutions managing similar testbeds, helping them make informed decisions on data collection, analysis, and operational improvements.

Keywords: HPC · Testbed · Monitoring · Usage Metrics · User Engagement · Scientific Impact

1 Introduction

1.1 The Ookami Testbed

The observed system, Ookami, is a cluster with 176 Fujitsu A64FX processors, one NVIDIA Grace Superchip, an Intel Skylake CPU, an AMD Milan node, and two Marvell ThunderX2 login nodes [1]. The focus of the system is the Fujitsu A64FX processor, which at the time of deployment (2020) had also been used in the at that time fastest machine worldwide [2], Fugaku, located at the RIKEN supercomputing center in Japan [3]. The Ookami testbed, located at Stony Brook University USA, gives researchers worldwide access to these CPUs. Ookami was the first open deployment of this technology outside Japan.

The Fujitsu A64FX processor is based on the ARM instruction set, it supports SVE (scalable vector extension), and promises high performance paired with energy efficiency. By focusing on crucial architectural details, the 48 core, 512-bit SIMD-vector processor with ultrahigh-bandwidth memory promises to retain familiar and successful programming models while achieving very high performance for a wide range of applications.

1.2 XDMoD

For monitoring the performance, overall utilization, job statistics, and other quality of service metrics on Ookami, we utilized XDMoD, an open-source tool designed to support the management of high-performance computing systems [4,5]. Its portal offers a comprehensive set of analysis and visualization tools, enabling users to efficiently explore a wide range of job accounting metrics over any specified timeframe. To enhance its functionality, two additional tools have been integrated, providing quality-of-service metrics and job-level performance insights. Together, these components form a unified system that facilitates comprehensive HPC resource management. By leveraging Open XDMoD, HPC administrators can monitor system efficiency, track application performance, and analyze resource consumption—key factors in optimizing overall system performance.

2 Monitoring

In addition to automated monitoring through XDMoD, we manually tracked relevant metrics, such as the number of executed events, to capture additional workload characteristics. Furthermore, we implemented supplementary monitoring mechanisms, including an automated Google Scholar search, to assess the impact of computational workloads on scientific output. This combined approach ensured a more comprehensive understanding of resource usage and its broader influence on research productivity.

In the following sections, we present various metrics collected during the monitoring process, explain their significance, and discuss their limitations, including aspects that were not tracked but, in hindsight, would have provided valuable insights into resource utilization and impact.

2.1 Utilization

Tracking overall utilization and active user engagement is crucial for assessing the effectiveness of an HPC testbed. Unlike production systems, where maximizing resource usage is a primary objective, a testbed serves as an experimental environment where users explore and familiarize themselves with new technologies. Therefore, monitoring not only the total computational workload but also the number of active users provides insights into adoption and accessibility. Additionally, evaluating how efficiently users leverage the available resources such as job success rates, queue wait times, and resource allocation efficiency—helps identify potential barriers to usability. By focusing on both utilization patterns and user experience, we can better understand how the testbed supports learning and experimentation, ultimately guiding improvements in usability and accessibility.

Ookami became openly available to researchers worldwide at the beginning of 2021. There was a continuous open call for allocations, and researchers could easily apply for time on the cluster. Before 2021, the system was open to a group of friendly users, allowing the project team to refine and optimize the testbed before a broader rollout. This early access phase was instrumental in identifying necessary software installations, such as libraries and compilers, and ensuring the system met user needs. Additionally, it provided an opportunity to develop user documentation, streamline the workflow for reviewing allocation requests, and establish procedures for setting up new projects. This preparatory phase helped create a more structured and accessible environment for a wider audience c.f. [6–8].

Figure 1 shows how the cumulative number of users and the cumulative number of projects evolved over time. After being broadly open to researchers, Ookami served 166 projects and 503 users. The allocation requests came in steadily, with an initial bump at the beginning of 2021. Since this is when Ookami became available, this bump is reasonable and shows the initial interest in testing a new technology. The same holds for the number of users. The projects using Ookami are supported by 92 external grants from national agencies and other institutions, 50 from the National Science Foundation (NSF), 18 from the Department of Energy (DOE), 6 from the National Institutes of Health (NIH), and the others from smaller agencies.

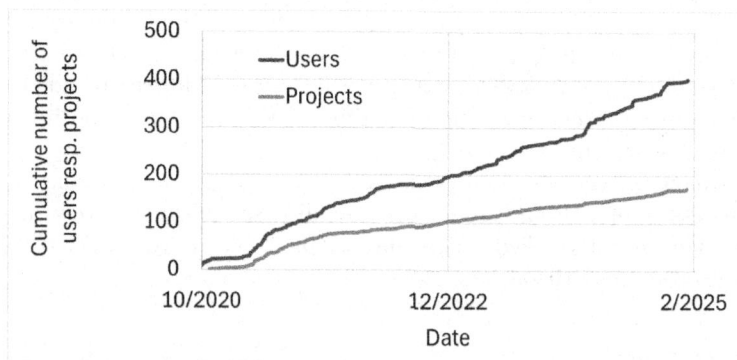

Fig. 1. Cumulative number of projects and users using Ookami.

While a significant number of users have accounts on the system, not all of them remain consistently active. Usage patterns vary depending on research demands, project timelines, and familiarity with the HPC environment and the goals of the users. In some cases, users performed a study or made comparisons, but did not follow these with production runs. Some users may log in only occasionally for specific tasks, while others engage more frequently. Therefore, analyzing the number of active users over time provides a more accurate picture of the testbed's adoption and accessibility (see Fig. 2). Tracking active user trends helps assess engagement levels, identify potential barriers to sustained usage, and inform strategies for improving support and outreach efforts. The number of active users fluctuates between 20 to 60 without significant increases or decreases over time.

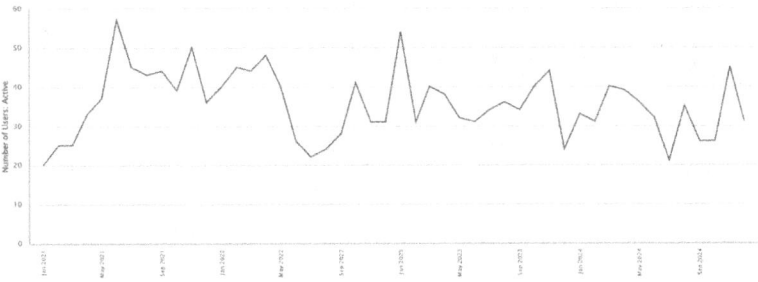

Fig. 2. Number of active Ookami users.

Analyzing overall cluster utilization (see Fig. 3), measured by the number of active nodes, provides valuable insights into resource demand and scheduling efficiency. The plot shows the average monthly utilization (blue) for the whole project duration, and the daily utilization for the last months (orange). The daily utilization was added to investigate the utilization in more detail. The curve shows that there are several days where the cluster is fully or nearly fully utilized, broken up by days with lower utilization. To allow for better visibility the detailed data is added just for the last months. Given the nature of the testbed, achieving 100% utilization is neither expected nor a primary goal. Unlike production HPC systems, where maximizing usage is critical, the testbed must accommodate users experimenting with different workloads, which often requires reserving nodes to satisfy jobs with higher node requests. As a result, utilization fluctuates based on workload characteristics and scheduling constraints. Understanding these patterns helps optimize resource availability while ensuring users have the flexibility needed for exploration and learning. The utilization shows a continuous increase over the project years with a significant under-utilization at the end of 2022. A detailed examination of the data suggests that even though the cluster was actively used before and after, the Christmas holidays appeared to have a significant effect on the utilization. During this period the cluster was mainly used by two big research groups, both of whom decreased their workloads over the holidays. Given that Ookami is a relatively small cluster (176 nodes), the drop out of single projects can have a big effect on utilization.

The overall usage of Ookami enjoyed a steady increase throughout the Ookami lifetime as measured by total core hours (Fig. 4.A). Interestingly, while the total core hours increase over time, the number of jobs stays relatively flat. The increase in the total core hours is caused by an increase in job sizes (core count) and longer wall times (Fig. 4.B). It can be an indication that users moved from shorter test jobs to longer, more useful, and possibly production-level jobs. There were over 39 different applications executed on Ookami (Fig. 5). The top five applications by CPU hours used are ROMS (ocean modeling), OpenFoam (computational fluid dynamics), R (statistical analysis), cp2k (molecular dynamics), and siesta (computational chemistry). Overall, a diverse set of applications has been successfully run on the system.

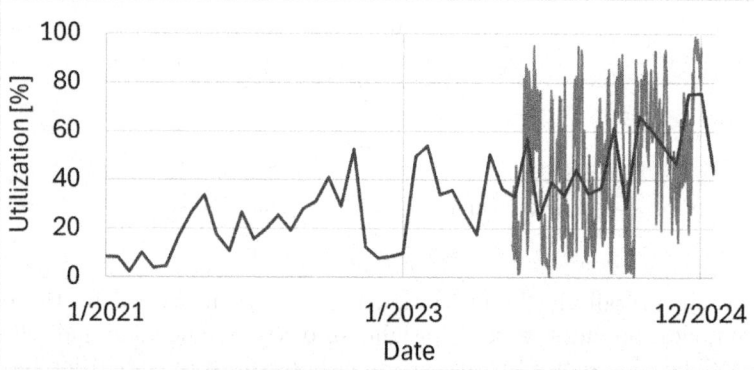

Fig. 3. Overall cluster utilization over time. The blue line shows the averaged monthly utilization and the orange one the daily utilization. (Color figure online)

2.2 User Support

To support users in effectively utilizing Ookami, the project team organized various events, including webinars focused on specific tools and best practices [9]. These sessions aimed to enhance user proficiency, address common challenges, and foster a collaborative learning environment. The number of such events was tracked over time to assess engagement efforts and adapt our outreach strategies based on user needs (see Fig. 6).

We observed that as more users became familiar with the testbed, the demand shifted from general introductory sessions to more specialized topics. This trend highlighted the growing expertise within the user base and the importance of adapting training efforts accordingly. In addition, the data helped identify gaps where further support was needed, guiding the development of future workshops and resources to better assist users in effectively using the system.

Our experience with workshops and webinars was overwhelmingly positive and we were particularly pleased with the evolution to more specialized

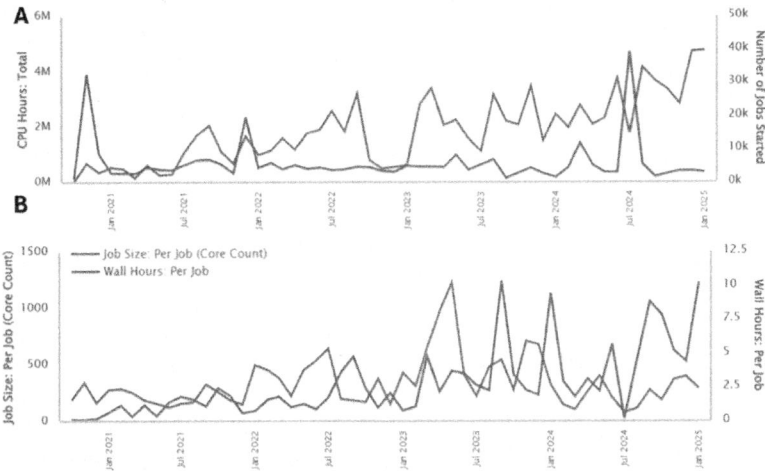

Fig. 4. A. Monthly cluster utilization over time. **B.** Average job characteristics over time, job size (core count), and walltime (hours) are shown. The dark blue line shows the trend from 2020 to the end of 2023.

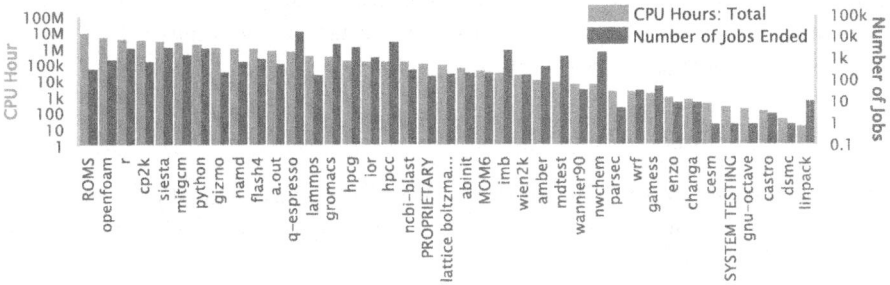

Fig. 5. Applications used on Ookami

topics. These were a critical part of our educational efforts, details of which can be found in [9].

The Ookami team also offers other support via a ticketing system, a Slack channel, and regular virtual office hours. New users are invited to complete a survey approximately one to two months after receiving their account. This survey is designed to gather feedback on their initial experience, challenges encountered, and overall satisfaction with the system. By analyzing responses, the team can identify areas for improvement, refine user support, and tailor training sessions and documentation to better meet user needs. This feedback-driven approach helps enhance the accessibility and usability of the testbed, ensuring that it effectively supports a diverse research community.

To assess user experience with the system, we conducted a survey targeting users who had interacted with the platform for a period of 1–2 months. The survey provided an opportunity for users to share their feedback and evaluate their

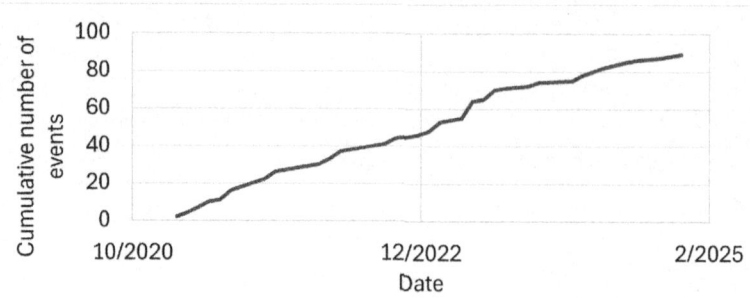

Fig. 6. Cumulative number of support events.

overall experience. Notably, 90% of respondents rated their experience as either "very good" or "good," indicating a high level of satisfaction. Participants were also asked about the compilers they had used, with the option to select multiple responses. The GCC compiler emerged as the most commonly used, with 78.1% of users reporting its use. This was followed by the Arm compiler (42.6%), Fujitsu (40.6%), and Cray (21.9%). The prominence of GCC is likely due to users' priorr familiarity with it from other systems, suggesting that familiarity and ease of transition play a significant role in user preference.

2.3 Publications

The number of publications (see Fig. 7) generated using a cluster is one of the most important metrics for evaluating its impact on research. This metric directly reflects the usefulness of the resource in enabling scientific advancements. To gain a more detailed understanding, we distinguished between publications from the project team—such as those describing the system, benchmarking results, and methodological improvements—and publications by external users conducting research on various scientific topics. Tracking both categories allowed us to assess not only the testbed's technical contributions but also its broader adoption and influence across different research domains. One can see that the number of publications by the Ookami team has remained nearly constant over the years, whereas the number of user publications is increasing. This highlights the fact that the system that started as a pure technology testbed, interesting for a few very technically savvy users doing testing and exploration, is getting more and more used by research groups using the computational power for their science projects.

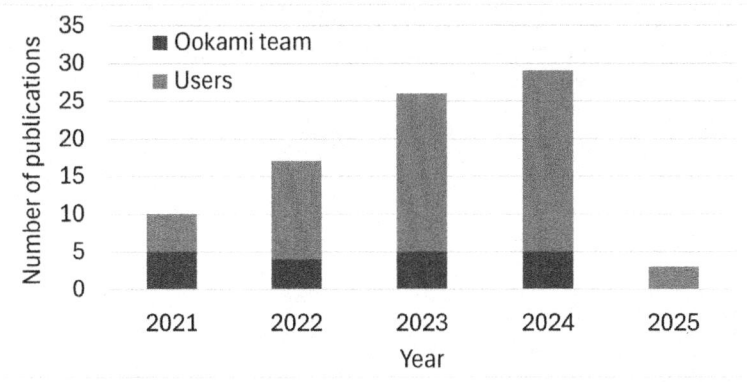

Fig. 7. Number of publications using Ookami per year. Publications from the Ookami team are blue and publications by Ookami users are orange. (Color figure online)

2.4 Energy

Energy monitoring is crucial for the HPC resource operation. The average drawn power for all compute nodes over time is shown in Fig. 8. It is relatively flat with a mean of 19.5 kW and a max of 22.4 kW. Such flatness is due to a small difference in ARM Fujitsu A64FX power draw under idle and load is practically the same and averages 114 W. The obvious spikes of low power occurred when a significant fraction of the nodes were down for maintenance or system upgrades.

Monitoring the energy consumption allowed us to assess the energy efficiency of the platform. In our previous work [10–13], we extensively studied ARM systems and their x86 counterparts in terms of computational and energy efficiency. We found that although the ARM Fujitsu A64FX is not particularly performant

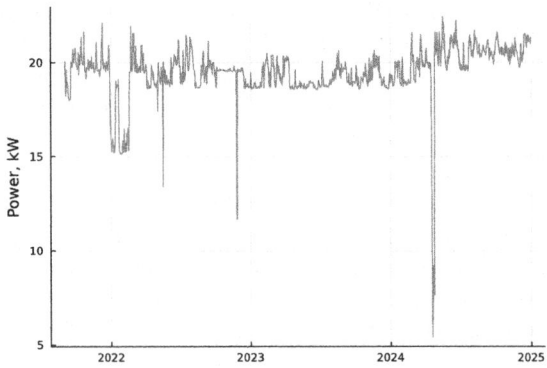

Fig. 8. Daily average total compute nodes electric power over time. The power includes only the electricity drawn by the compute nodes.

in most real-world applications, modern ARM CPUs offer a wide range of high-performing solutions in terms of both energy efficiency and computational power (See Fig. 9 for Gromacs example).

System	Cores	Simulation Speed, ns/day	Simulation Speed per Core, ns/day/core	Power, W	Energy Efficiency, ns/kWh
CPU Only Calculation					
ARM Fujitsu A64FX, SVE 512bit (SBU-Ookami, Fujitsu)	48	22.8 ± 0.3	0.48	105 ± 5	9.1 ± 0.4
ARM Cavium ThunderX2 (SBU-Ookami)	64	28.8 ± 4.2	0.45		
ARM Amazon Graviton 2, Neoverse N1 (AWS)	48	37.8 ± 0.1	0.79		
ARM Amazon Graviton 3, Neoverse V1, SVE 256bit (AWS)	64	71.4 ± 1.0	1.12		
ARM Ampere Altra, Neoverse N1 (Azure)	64	56.5 ± 0.6	0.88		
ARM Ampere One A192-32X, Neoverse N1 (Ampere)	192	172.1 ± 2.3	0.90	512 ± 5	14.0 ± 0.1
ARM NVIDIA Grace, Neoverse V2, SVE 128bit (SBU)	144	235.2 ± 0.4	1.63	709 ± 41	18.9 ± 0.8
x86 AMD EPYC 7742 Zen2(Rome), AVX2 (PSC Bridges-2)	128	109.6 ± 4.8	0.86		
x86 AMD EPYC 7763 Zen3(Milan), AVX2 (Purdue Anvil)	128	169.9 ± 4.4	1.33		
x86 Intel Xeon Plat. 8160, Skylake-X, AVX512 (TACC-Stampede 2)	48	70.4 ± 0.8	1.47		
x86 Intel Xeon Plat. 8380, Ice Lake, AVX512 (TACC-Stampede 2)	80	133.3 ± 6.0	1.67		
x86 Intel Xeon Gold 6130, Skylake-X, AVX512 (UBHPC)	32	39.3 ± 0.9	1.23	367 ± 35	4.5 ± 0.5
x86 Intel Xeon Gold 6330, Ice Lake, AVX512 (UBHPC)	56	103.0 ± 2.0	1.84	619 ± 17	6.9 ± 0.2
x86 Intel Xeon Max 9468, Sapphire Rapids, AVX512 (SBU)	96	193.08 ± 2.3	2.01	820 ± 7	9.8 ± 0.1
CPU-GPU Calculations					
x86 Intel Xeon Gold 6130, NVIDIA V100x2 (UBHPC)	32	145.1 ± 2.8		435 ± 7	13.9 ± 0.3
x86 Intel Xeon Gold 6330, NVIDIA A100x2 (UBHPC)	56	236.5 ± 10.8		707 ± 9	13.9 ± 0.8
AMD Ryzen 9 7950X (16 Cores Used)/NVIDIA RTX 4090	16	284.82			
NVIDIA Grace Hopper Superchip ES	72	429			

Fig. 9. Benchmarking Gromacs (82k atoms membrane protein system) across range of ARM and x86. This is a relatively small system, and the hardware performance ranking can change on larger systems (see, for example, [13]). The energy measurements were not available on all systems. CPU core normalized simulation speed was omitted for CPU-GPU systems because a large portion of calculations were done on GPU.

2.5 Continuous Performance Monitoring

HPC resources are complex systems, and their performance monitoring is crucial for successful operation. Without proper monitoring, many performance-degrading events may go unnoticed, and relying on users to report such issues is not an ideal approach. The continuous performance monitoring module of XDMoD [14] enables proactive identification of performance degradation by regularly executing synthetic and real application-based benchmarks and analyzing their performance. A particularly exciting aspect of applying continuous performance monitoring to Ookami is the ability to observe how application performance improves over time as the technology gains wider adoption in the computational community. Figure 10 illustrates the performance improvement of the GROMACS application [15,16] over time. For more details on continuous performance monitoring on Ookami, see our dedicated publication [17].

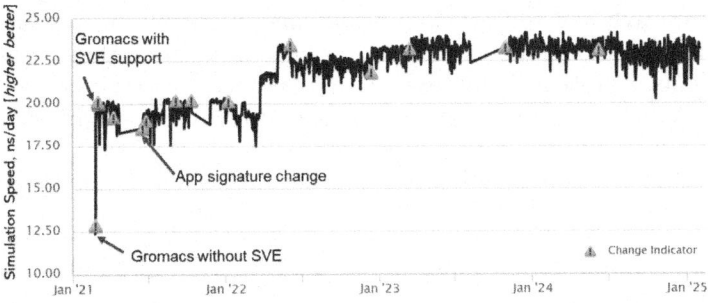

Fig. 10. Single node performance of Gromacs over time. Change indicators show the change for the application signature change, which is calculated as a hash-sum on the binary executable and the used dynamic shared libraries.

3 Lessons Learned

Over the past years, the team has gained significant insights into tracking and gathering meaningful metrics to assess the impact of the HPC testbed. In hindsight, certain metrics would have provided deeper insights and will be incorporated into future projects. These include explicitly linking user participation in office hours and webinars to job efficiency and job volume, allowing the project team to assess the tangible impact of training efforts. Additionally, improving the tracking of degrees granted as a result of using computational resources will help measure the long-term educational benefits of the system. These enhancements will enable a more comprehensive evaluation of the testbed's effectiveness and its contribution to research and education.

In hindsight, also systematically logging and categorizing compiler errors would have provided valuable insights into potential compiler bugs and recurring issues that users frequently encounter. Unfortunately, this data was not collected in previous years, but it stands as a key lesson learned for future system monitoring and user support strategies.

4 Outlook

As the Ookami testbed continues to evolve, future efforts will focus on refining monitoring strategies, improving user engagement, and expanding the scope of tracked metrics to better assess the system's impact. Key areas of development include integrating more detailed efficiency metrics, linking training participation to job performance, and improving the tracking of research outcomes, such as degrees granted. Additionally, we aim to enhance automation in data collection and analysis, reducing manual efforts while increasing the accuracy of insights. By continuously adapting the approach based on user feedback and lessons learned, the project will ensure that the testbed remains a valuable resource for both research and education, fostering innovation and broader adoption of HPC technologies. Moving forward, the team will integrate the lessons learned into the daily operations of future HPC systems, ensuring that monitoring, user support, and impact assessment are more structured and data-driven.

Acknowledgements. The authors would like to thank Stony Brook Research Computing and Cyberinfrastructure, and the Institute for Advanced Computational Science at Stony Brook University for access to the innovative high-performance Ookami computing system, which was made possible by a $5M National Science Foundation grant (#1927880).

References

1. Stony Brook University, "Ookami" (2020). https://www.stonybrook.edu/ookami/
2. Top500.org (2020). https://www.top500.org/
3. RIKEN Center for Computational Science, "Fugaku" (2021). https://www.r-ccs.riken.jp/en/fugaku/
4. University at Buffalo Center for Computational Research (2021). https://ookami.ccr.xdmod.org/index.php/
5. Palmer, J.T., et al.: Open xdmod: a tool for the comprehensive management of high-performance computing resources. Comput. Sci. Eng. **17**(4), 52–62 (2015)
6. Burford, A., et al.: "Ookami: deployment and initial experiences. In: Practice and Experience in Advanced Research Computing, PEARC 2021. NY, USA), Association for Computing Machinery, New York (2021)
7. Feldman, C., Michalowicz, B., Siegmann, E., Curtis, T., Calder, A., Harrison, R.: Experiences with porting the flash code to ookami, an hpe apollo 80 a64fx platform. In: International Conference on High Performance Computing in Asia-Pacific Region Workshops, HPCAsia 2022 Workshop, pp. 72–77. Association for Computing Machinery, New York (2022)
8. Calder, A.C.: Ookami: an a64fx computing resource. J. Phys: Conf. Ser. **2742**, 012019 (2024)
9. Siegmann, E., Calder, A., Feldman, C., Harrison, R.J.: Educating hpc users in the use of advanced computing technology. In: 2021 IEEE/ACM Ninth Workshop on Education for High Performance Computing (EduHPC), pp. 16–23 (2021)
10. Simakov, N.A., et al.: Are we ready for broader adoption of arm in the hpc community: performance and energy efficiency analysis of benchmarks and applications executed on high-end arm systems. In: Proceedings of the HPC Asia 2023 Workshops, HPC Asia '23 Workshops, pp. 78–86. Association for Computing Machinery, New York (2023)
11. Siegmann, E., et al.: First impressions of the sapphire rapids processor with hbm for scientific workloads. SN Comput. Sci. **5**, 623 (2024)
12. Simakov, N.A., Jones, M.D., Furlani, T.R., Siegmann, E., Harrison, R.J.: First impressions of the NVIDIA grace CPU superchip and NVIDIA grace hopper superchip for scientific workloads. In: HPCAsia 2024 Workshops, p. 36–44. Association for Computing Machinery, New York (2024)
13. Carlson, D., et al.: The ampereone a192-32x in perspective: benchmarking a new standard. In: Proceedings of the 2025 International Conference on High Performance Computing in Asia-Pacific Region Workshops, HPC Asia 2025 Workshops, pp. 23–35. Association for Computing Machinery, New York (2025)

14. Simakov, N.A., et al.: Application kernels: Hpc resources performance monitoring and variance analysis. Concurrency Comput. Pract. Experience **27**(17), 5238–5260 (2015)
15. Kutzner, C., Páll, S., Fechner, M., Esztermann, A., de Groot, B.L., Grubmüller, H.: Best bang for your buck: GPU nodes for gromacs biomolecular simulations. J. Comput. Chem. **36**(26), 1990–2008 (2015)
16. Páll, S., et al.: Heterogeneous parallelization and acceleration of molecular dynamics simulations in gromacs. J. Chem. Phys. **153**(13), 134110 (2020)
17. Simakov, N.A., et al.: Benchmarking and continuous performance monitoring of ookami, an arm fujitsu a64fx testbed cluster. In: SC24-W: Workshops of the International Conference for High Performance Computing, pp. 588–594. Networking, Storage and Analysis (2024)

9th International Workshop on In Situ Visualization (WOIV'25)

WOIV 2025 Preface

Objectives/Topics

The ever-increasing scale of today's HPC simulations with their inherent I/O bottleneck makes in situ an essential approach for data analysis. Nowadays, the rate of data generation significantly exceeds the available bandwidth of storage capabilities. Consequently, analysis and visualization have to be coupled in situ to a live simulation to facilitate comprehensive investigation. In doing so, data abstracts are generated that capture much more information than is otherwise possible.

The International Workshop on In Situ Visualization provides a venue for speakers to share practical expertise and experience with in situ visualization approaches. We host contributed talks and papers on methods and workflows that have been applied in this field. Papers detail whether and how the application drove abstractions or other kinds of data reductions and how these interacted with the expressiveness and flexibility of the visualization for exploratory analysis.

Of particular interest to WOIV and its attendees are recent developments for in situ libraries and software. As in the previous years, for this 9th edition of the workshop, we also strongly encouraged submissions on approaches that either did not work at all or did not live up to their expectations. We therefore expected to get first-hand reports on lessons learned and pitfalls to be avoided.

Our goal is to appeal to a wide-ranging audience of computational scientists, visualization scientists, and simulation developers, who closely collaborate in order to develop, deploy, and maintain in situ visualization approaches on HPC infrastructures. We hope to provide practical take-away techniques and insights that serve as inspiration for attendees to implement or refine in their own HPC environments and to avoid pitfalls.

Workshop Organization

François Mazen	Kitware Europe, France
James Kress	KAUST, Saudi Arabia
Tom Vierjahn	Westphalian University of Applied Sciences, Germany
Marcel Krüger	RWTH Aachen University, Germany
Jean Favre	Swiss National Supercomputer Center, Switzerland

Enabling Modular In-Situ Workflows Through *CatalystMaestro* and *CatalystComposer*

Marcel Krüger[✉][iD], Torsten W. Kuhlen[iD], and Tim Gerrits[iD]

Visual Computing Institute, RWTH Aachen University, Aachen, Germany
krueger@vis.rwth-aachen.de

Abstract. In-situ paradigms have become a key component for modern research endeavors confronted with large amounts of data. By incorporating in-situ approaches, hardware can be utilized more efficiently due to reduced requirements for I/O-overhead and storage while providing near real-time insights into the simulation for domain scientists. However, most in-situ tools are designed as large monolithic blocks that are challenging to maintain, adapt, or reuse. We believe that modularity is a key contributor to reducing maintenance, code duplication, and increasing flexibility, which are important properties of the in-situ software ecosystem. This paper presents and demonstrates CatalystMaestro (https://github.com/VRGroupRWTH/CatalystMaestro) and CatalystComposer (https://github.com/VRGroupRWTH/CatalystComposer), a Catalyst2 implementation and accompanying graphical editor that allow building complex in-situ workflows by composing modular in-situ implementations.

Keywords: In-situ · In-Transit · Workflows · Catalyst2

1 Introduction

As exascale computing becomes a reality in today's compute landscape, in-situ and in-transit visualization and analysis have become essential components of contemporary and future research. While traditionally, the primary motivation for using in-situ methods was to overcome I/O bottlenecks, nowadays, early feedback and interactivity play equally important roles in enhancing research workflows. Even for small experiments that finish within minutes, domain scientists can benefit from gaining insights into their simulations as early as possible. Despite the clear benefits of in-situ workflows, the adoption of these concepts remains relatively low. Current research has focused on establishing common standards, such as APIs like Catalyst2, and improving accessibility; however, typical in-situ workflows are still relatively inert and rigid. One reason for this is that three primary demographics are typically involved: Domain developers, (in-situ) tools developers, and end-users. Domain developers produce code and infrastructure as data sources, e.g., simulations. Tool developers contribute to code that uses and transforms the produced data, e.g., through analysis or visualization. And finally, end-users, typically domain experts, utilize these workflows in their research, e.g., by testing model assumptions. All three groups play an equally vital role in increasing adoption rates due to the significant effects of interaction among them. Domain developers will only invest resources on implementing necessary changes if sufficient potential users benefit from the effort. At the same time, end-users often depend on the domain developers' willingness and the availability of accessible tools. In turn, tool developers rely on domain developers to adopt their tools and end-users' feedback to refine them. One aspect that can hinder adoption, development progress, and versatility is that existing solutions are often monolithic, which makes them hard to adapt and reuse. All functionality is provided by one implementation that either fulfills the needed criteria or not. Due to their complexity, changing or reusing these implementations for different needs can be a laborious task. We believe a more modular approach can significantly improve the developer and user experience by allowing flexible use, reuse and adaptation during development and usage.

In this paper, we present *CatalystMaestro* and *CatalystComposer*, a Catalyst2 implementation and accompanying graphical editor that allows the creation and use of flexible, modular in-situ workflows through composition. CatalystMaestro aims to improve the experience of all three demographics by providing a framework that enables building complex workflows by combining multiple Catalyst2-compatible implementations through a graph-like structure. We discuss our design considerations and demonstrate its usefulness through several example workflows.

2 Background and Related Work

The in-situ environment comprises a multitude of coupling and in-situ codes ranging from bespoke solutions [11,14,21] to various libraries that are mostly agnostic to the task. Libraries such as Catalyst1[1] [3], SENSEI [5] and VisIt LibSim [20] make use of the Visualization Toolkit (VTK) [17] format to describe data that is processed in-situ. While Catalyst1 and VisIt Libsim are built around a tightly-coupled approach, SENSEI can be used as a tightly-coupled or loosely-coupled system. Even though VTK is a popular data format for visualization, using it implies that VTK becomes a dependency, i.e., simulation developers must familiarize themselves with the library and provide their data as VTK data objects. To alleviate this, Ascent [12] and Catalyst2 [4] use Conduit [9] - Conduit Mesh Blueprints to be precise - to describe data instead. It is designed to provide data transport in HPC environments while focusing on a straightforward API that allows describing complex data. As copying and/or marshaling data is an expensive process, Conduit is built to support passing data via pointers to external memory while allowing the augmentation of the data with additional allocated memory. The support of deep and shallow copies and the

---

[1] To improve reading flow, we refer to ParaView Catalyst pre v5.8 as *Catalyst1*.

efficient design make Conduit a prime data format for in-situ systems. Additionally, Catalyst2 limits its footprint within the simulation code by using only 5 API calls and providing a stable ABI. Thus, it can be understood as a common interface that allows loading implementations rather than a concrete visualization or analysis library. Visualization and analysis compatibilities are provided through other libraries that implement the Catalyst2 API, such as ParaView Catalyst (post v5.9) [1], Ascent Catalyst [12], Adios Catalyst [15,16] as well as InsitUE [10]. Due to its stable ABI, Catalyst2 implementations can be changed before starting the simulation by providing the path and name to the library via Conduit parameters or environment variables. However, only one implementation can be loaded and used per simulation run. Therefore, while being static, implementations typically provide means to instruct different visualizations and analysis tasks, e.g., through other files that describe the operations. However, this means that workflows are limited to features within the respective implementation, restricting the flexibility of systems and interoperability of tools.

3 From Monolith to Modular In-situ Workflows

The concept of modular software and workflows is an established and successful paradigm. While found in several domains [2,6,13], two prominent examples can be found in the UNIX philosophy and web development. A key component of the UNIX philosophy is to *"do one thing and do it well"*, which is evident in typical workflows in UNIX-based systems. Users frequently *pipe* output from one program to another, using single programs as intermediate steps. The true power lies in combining these limited-functionality programs to achieve complex tasks beyond their individual capabilities. Similarly, web development has shifted towards microservice architectures, moving away from large monolithic applications. There is an observable trend to break down functionality into smaller, self-contained services integrated into larger architectures to achieve more complex functionality. The modular nature of these systems can be seen as the key component to their success, offering numerous advantages. Components only define input and output and can thus act as standalone applications with smaller independent codebases, more explicit responsibilities, better test coverage, and easier reusability. It supports easier versioning and replacement of functionality, leading to increased robustness in larger systems. Similar assumptions can also apply to in-situ workflows. Pugmire et al. [19] argue that the monolithic nature of current in-situ systems is restrictive and identify this as one of four major challenges that need to be solved to achieve pervasive use of in-situ applications. To illustrate this potential advantage, consider a developer who publishes a novel and highly-improved algorithm for iso-surface extraction. In the context of existing large monolithic codebases that currently implement iso-surface extraction, updating and testing could require substantial effort: The need for an update leads to a change in version for all other unaffected library components as well, and all library vendors need to implement the new algorithm individually. In contrast, a modular approach allows iso-surface generation to be implemented and tested as a standalone module. Developers can focus on implementing and releasing the improved algorithm while users can easily swap out the iso-surface component in their workflow without affecting other parts.

In the following, we present *CatalystMaestro* - a first approach that brings a modular and federated design approach into in-situ workflows.

3.1 CatalystMaestro

CatalystMaestro is a Catalyst2 implementation that acts as middleware between simulation and various Catalyst2 implementations, orchestrating data flow without providing business logic itself. For simplicity, we refer to any other external Catalyst2 implementations hereafter as *modules*. To provide an easy-to-use and easy-to-integrate tool, we developed CatalystMaestro based on the following requirements:

1. Function as a drop-in replacement for existing Catalyst2 implementations
2. Modules must be oblivious to being part of a CatalystMaestro workflow
3. Minimize overhead to ensure performance efficiency

The first requirement ensures that CatalystMaestro does not introduce additional dependencies or requires changes in simulation code that is already capable of using Catalyst2, allowing developers and users to view it as just another Catalyst2 implementation that can be used without requiring additional work. The second requirement guarantees that modules are not dependent on being part of the CatalystMaestro workflow but can be used as standalone Catalyst2 implementations. Thus, existing and future models require no modifications to function within or outside CatalystMaestro. Finally, minimizing performance overhead is crucial, as performance is a key factor in in-situ systems. Negative impact on performance must not outweigh any benefits gained.

The core idea behind CatalystMaestro is to enable users to define data flow between different modules, providing them with means to construct complex systems from comparably simple modules. To understand its capabilities, we briefly revisit the Catalyst2 API architecture and discuss how it is leveraged in our approach. The Catalyst2 API consists of five function calls: *initialize, execute, result, finalize*, and *about*, called at different points within a simulation run. Each call receives a Conduit data object as its only parameter, which is used as either input or output, i.e., the function uses data described by Conduit or changes the Conduit object to include new data resulting from the implementation. The functions *initialize* and *finalize* are called at the start and end of simulations to handle setup and teardown tasks, typically called only once, and receive configuration information via Conduit. *Execute* and *result* are typically called in tandem after each timestep. *Execute* receives the simulation data of the corresponding timestep via Conduit and executes visualization or analysis functionality on it. At the same time, *result* is expected to fill the passed Conduit object with data that results from the execute step. The caller, i.e., a simulation, can then use this information again for further processing or steering. Lastly, the *about* function can be used to query information about the implementation and can be called from anywhere.

To keep CatalystMaestro lightweight, most functionality is provided by separate modules. However, not all functionality can be provided by external modules because they are designed to work self-contained. Especially non-linear flows, e.g., branching, would not be possible without making a module aware that it is part of a CatalystMaestro workflow and introducing loading of other modules. Consequently, we implemented core logic for the workflow as part of CatalystMaestro itself. We call these functions *nodes* as they are the building blocks of the graph-like workflow.

Execute Module. The *Execute Module* node is the most fundamental node and calls other modules within the workflow. It includes three variables: *Module Name* (the specific Catalyst2 implementation), *Variable Name* (to differentiate instances), *Input* (specifying which Conduit node serves as input) and *Function* (indicating which method to execute). As implementations can have a state, it is important that a user can decide to call a specific instance of a plugin. The variable name distinguishes between different instances of the same plugin class, allowing the same instance to be referenced at different points in the workflow. The node saves the function that should be invoked on the module, e.g., *initialize, execute, result,* or *finalize*. The input specifies what Conduit node is used as input to the method call. By default, it uses the node passed from the simulation but also supports inputs from the result method of other modules or *Conduit Literal* nodes. Specifying and using the input of other modules is essential to building modular workflows as it allows building sequences of processing steps.

Branch. This node models if/else branching in workflows to control the execution at runtime depending on the evaluated value. It is specified via four parameters: *Evaluation Expression, Input Value, True Case Successor Node,* and *False Case Successor Node*. Successor nodes can be any other node, including further branch nodes, allowing us to model "if else" relationships by chaining branch nodes. The evaluation expression can take expressions in the form "conduit_node_path OP value" or "conduit_node_path % num OP value" where OP can be one of $==, <, >, <=, >=, !=$ and % presents the modulo operator. Num can be int or double and value can be an int, double or string. CatalystMaestro supports combining multiple expressions via logical and (&&) as well as logical or (||) and defining precedence via parentheses. Like the Execute Module node, the input is configurable to evaluate values on different inputs.

Filter. The Filter node retains specific fields from a Conduit node before passing them on to other nodes or modules, i.e., only the specified fields remain in the output Conduit node. The filter node creates a new Conduit node, which references the original data, thus, data that is filtered out is not modified or deleted. It is configured via two parameters: *Input Name*, and a list containing the fields to retain.

Merge. The Merge node combines an arbitrary amount of inputs into one Conduit output. It is configured by one variable that describes a list of inputs to be merged. As the Catalyst2 API only accepts one Conduit node as input, this node helps to combine multiple Conduit nodes into one for use by other nodes.

Conduit Literal. This node creates new Conduit nodes within workflows to make configuration or additional information available to the pipeline without needing to pass it via simulation. It has two parameters: a JSON or YAML string that describes the content of the Conduit node, and a variable name parameter to enable reuse in the graph.

Sequence. The Sequence node specifies an ordered execution sequence of designated nodes via a single parameter: a list of nodes that should be executed in sequence.

Additionally, all nodes have an additional parameter called nodeID, which must be unique, used to identify the node in the graph. Node relationships are modeled as directed edges between Node A and Node B, where Node B is executed after Node A has finished. To start the workflow in CatalystMaestro, four "Event Nodes" act as the source nodes in the workflow graph: *On Initialize*, *On Execute*, *On Result* and *On Finalize*. The implementation calls these Event Nodes whenever the simulation calls the respective function.

Complete workflows can be described using text-based configuration files in TOML or JSON format containing entries for each node with their corresponding parameters and a list of graph edges. Edges are represented by tuples [Predecessor, Successor] where Predecessor is a string of the format "nodeID.OutputEvent". Output events are defined for each node type; nodes with only one successor only have the output event "Out". Branch nodes on the other hand have the output events "True" and "False" while the sequence node enumerates their outputs starting with zero. The Successor is defined by string in the form "nodeID.FunctionToExecute", where FunctionToExecute is "In" for all nodes that only have one input (Branch, Filter, Merge, Sequence) or the name of the Catalyst2 function that should be called on the module when using the Execute Module node. Assuming that node 1 is an "On Execute" Event Node while node 2 is a Execute Module node. The example tuple [`1.Out,2.Execute`] describes that after node 1 is evaluated, node 2 will call the *execute* function on the module. A small but complete configuration can look like this:

```
execute_edges = [
[1.Out,2.Execute],
[2.Out,3.Execute]]

[[nodes]]
NodeID = 1
Type = 'OnExecute'
```

```
[[nodes]]
NodeID = 2
PluginName = 'paraview'
VariableName = 'ParaviewModule1'

[[nodes]]
NodeID = 3
PluginName = 'printer'
VariableName = 'PrinterModule1'
Input = 'ParaviewModule1'
```

When the simulation calls Catalyst's *initialize* function, the config file is parsed to build the graph structure. Event Nodes are inserted into one of four priority queues corresponding to the event type *initialize, execute, result*, and *finalize*. Once the graph is built, all other calls to the Catalyst2 interface by the simulation will instruct CatalystMaestroto remove the first item in the priority queue and evaluate the whole path in the workflow graph. Once the last node in the path is reached, i.e., a node with no successor, the next event node will be removed from the priority queue until it is empty, leading to the eventual return of the simulation's Catalyst call. During graph construction, our implementation identifies required inputs for each node. If some nodes depend on outputs from other nodes within the graph structure, our system ensures that the results are buffered so that consuming nodes receive the appropriate Conduit node containing the correct saved results.

3.2 CatalystComposer

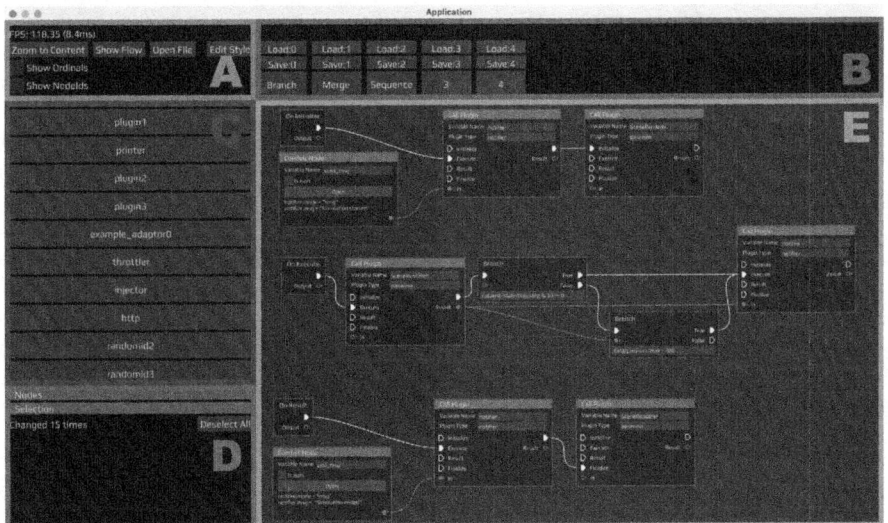

Fig. 1. CatalystComposer user interface. Area A: Files/Settings, Area B: Toolbar, Area C: Module Picker, Area D: Node List, Area E: Graph Canvas showing the graph of workflow 3 in Sect. 4.3.

As described in the previous section, we chose a human-readable configuration format to set up CatalystMaestro workflows. This is a deliberate choice to make configuration as accessible as possible, particularly for simple workflows. For more involved workflows, however, TOML descriptions can quickly become confusing. One possible solution is to allow configuration via visual graph editors. Graph editors are successfully applied in various commercial products and other scientific workflow solutions [7,18]. To leverage this concept with CatalystMaestro, we developed CatalystComposer, a GUI tool that allows users to create CatalystMaestro workflows using a visual graph editor. Figure 1 shows the interface of CatalystComposer which consists of five areas: The largest section, area E, hosts the graph representation of the workflow. Users can freely place nodes on the canvas and create connections by dragging from one node's pin to another. Creating new nodes can be done using either hotkeys, a right-click context menu, or the drag-and-drop from the buttons in areas B and C. Area B is a toolbar containing shortcuts for all node types described earlier. For instance, users can drag and drop the corresponding button into the graph area to add a branch node. Area C contains shortcuts for creating "Execute Module" nodes for different module names, enabling quickly adding various Execute Module nodes. Finally, area A contains buttons to control and configure the editor, while area D displays a list of nodes in the graph with functionality for selecting nodes from the list and zooming in on them. The editor is designed to directly load and write configuration files compatible with CatalystMaestro. This feature allows users to read workflows created outside of CatalystComposer and manually change the TOML config files without using the GUI.

4 Results

To demonstrate our tool, we decided to implement five small proof-of-concept Catalyst2 implementations that we use alongside ParaView Catalyst to build three example workflows. The five modules are:

Debugger. The *Debugger* provides an embedded HTTP server to control the execution of workflows via REST API. It allows setting breakpoints on time steps, step-by-step execution, continuing after breaks, and terminating the run. Breaking behavior can also be controlled through the Conduit node passed to the module, allowing for breaking on conditions other than time.

Web Injector. The *Web Injector* module injects parameters and other information into the workflow through an embedded HTTP server. The module provides an HTTP REST API that supports creating, modifying, and deleting Conduit fields, making it a versatile tool when combined with other modules.

Throttler. The *Throttler* module is also intended for debugging purposes. It delays the progression of time steps given a user-defined maximum throughput. This allows testing workflow at different (simulation) speeds and enables interactive workflows even in small test configurations that would otherwise run too fast to follow.

Conduit Printer. The *Conduit Printer* module can be configured with a list of Conduit paths and an accompanying verbosity level. It utilizes Conduit's built-in printing functionalities to print Conduit nodes more granularly than printing the full Conduit node. Additionally, it supports saving the output to file.

Process Caller. The *Process Caller* module executes any other binary as a subprocess. Conduit input configures the binary's path, and the arguments passed to the binary. Allowing to include functionality from external executables into workflows running within CatalystMaestro.

The workflows' feasibility was tested on the CLAIX-23 cluster at RWTH Aachen University using SLURM in a three-node MPI setup with 96 cores and 256GB RAM per node. We used SPH-EXA [8] as a representative simulation.

4.1 Workflow 1

The first workflow is based on our experience supporting domain developers who implement in-situ support for their application. The goal is to utilize the modular architecture to provide various levels of debugging logic embedded into the in-situ workflow, enabling developers to switch between different debugging levels. It utilizes the Branch, Filter and Execute Module nodes allowing users to transition gradually from simple debug output to a production-ready in-situ workflow. The debug level is set via an HTTP Injector module at the start. During early development stages, using the highest debug level, developers can choose an easy step-by-step and verbose path through the workflow by using the Throttler, Debugger and Printer modules to print the data passed from the simulation. After verifying that the simulation outputs the correct data, developers can switch to a lower debug level, which maintains throttling, and debugging, while printing only the output of ParaView Catalyst. The final debug level only incorporates the Branch node and Debugger module to break if a specific field does not yield an expected value. The domain developer can use process debuggers and other tools to inspect the current state of the execution for further analysis. By using CatalystMaestro workflows, domain developers can easily switch debugging levels or disable debugging on the system during runtime via the HTTP injector. This means debugging capabilities can be added to various workflows independently of the ParaView Pipeline. Furthermore, it allows domain developers to experiment with different implementations such as Catalyst Ascent or InsitUE without replicating the debugging workflow in all implementations. As CatalystMaestro is designed to incur minimal overhead, the workflow can default to leave debugging disabled and retaining the option to enable debugging on runtime when needed.

4.2 Workflow 2

The second workflow is a simple yet efficient workflow for in-situ tool developers to verify equivalence and thus correctness between two implementations without requiring modification for testing purposes. It consists of Execute Module nodes, Merge node, Branch node, two modules that are evaluated, and the Conduit Printer module. The workflow executes two module implementations that may either be different versions of the same implementation or entirely distinct implementations. Results from both modules are combined using a Merge node and fed into a Catalyst implementation that compares the results. If there is a mismatch between them, the Conduit Printer module saves the results' output and the data passed from the simulation to the disk for further analysis. The key advantage of using workflow orchestration tools such as CatalystMaestro is that implementations remain unaware of the test cases while still allowing to run tests in-situ; data is only written to disk upon failure. The same concept could also be applied through a module that loads verified data snapshot to compare against. As the comparison logic is part of the CatalystMaestro workflow itself, individual modules do not need built-in testing functionality themselves, which is especially useful when comparing different implementations.

4.3 Workflow 3

The last example workflow presents an end-user perspective by providing users with an easy and accessible way to track their simulation and visualizations while running batch jobs scheduled on computing resources. The workflow allows real-time updates about simulation parameters and progress status through messages in a chat client (Mattermost) while delivering rendered images at specified intervals and certain conditions. The workflow utilizes the Conduit Literal node, Execute Module, and Branch node alongside a ParaView Catalyst module for rendering and Process Caller module to call Python scripts to send messages and images via Mattermost - a popular collaboration platform that supports communication between users in channels on different servers. The Python script sends messages and files via arguments defining the mode and channel ID, followed by text or a path to an image that should be sent.

At the start of the simulation, the user is informed about the initiation while the ParaView Catalyst is initialized simultaneously. In each execution step, the ParaView node renders particles and their pressure into an image. Utilizing the Branch nodes, this image is sent via Mattermost every 10th timestep or whenever maximum pressure falls below a value of 200. After the simulation, another message informs the user about its completion and the *finalize* function of the ParaView Catalyst module is called. Figure 2 shows the result while Fig. 1 shows the graph in area E.

5 Performance Evaluation

As performance is a key characteristics of in-situ solutions, a low performance overhead was one of the key requirements we stipulated in Sect. 3.1. To assess the impact of our design, we instrumented the CatalystMaestro code with timing calls to measure the introduced overhead. Two main phases that must be considered regarding this overhead: at the beginning of the execution, modules need to be loaded, and the workflow graph must be generated. To evaluate potential scaling effects, we conducted test simulations using five test workflow graphs consisting of 10, 20, 30, 40 and 50 nodes, respectively. We found that parsing configuration files and generating the workflow graph representation incurs a

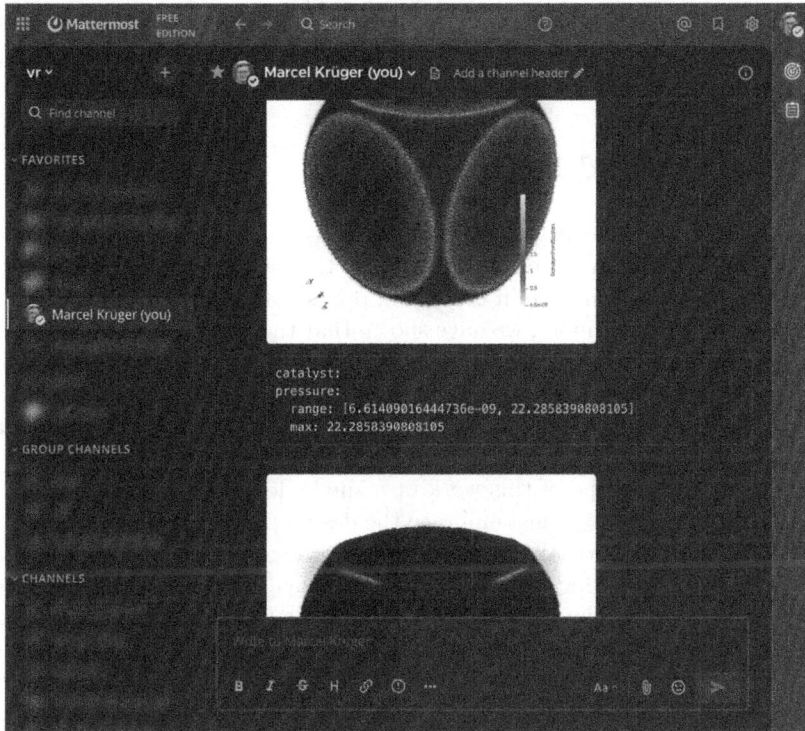

Fig. 2. SPH-EXA renderings are sent via Mattermost on every 10th timestep accompanied by information of the pressure field.

one-time cost that scales linearly at an average of 35 µs per node. This outcome aligns with our expectation since the workflow graph is represented by four priority queues and a set of linked-list-like data structures. While one-time costs incurred at the beginning of the simulation are less critical, it is more important to measure the overhead associated with each execute call. Using the same five workflow graphs as before, we profiled the time spent in CatalystMaestro's execute function, i.e., the elapsed time between invoking the simulation's execute call and returning the control back to it. In our test workflow, we utilized catalyst implementations that simply returned an OK status; thus, while calls into these modules were made, no computation time was consumed. This setup allowed us to isolate and measure the overhead created by calling modules and evaluating the workflow graph. Our measurements indicated that overhead per invocation scales linearly at approximately 625 ns per node. This low overhead aligns with our expectations because external modules (i.e., other Catalyst2 implementations) are loaded as shared libraries and stored in a hash map at execution start-up; consequently, calling these modules essentially amounts to making function calls. Additionally, CatalystMaestro passes data through Conduit nodes either as pointers or utilizes move semantics, respectively, avoiding additional costs for data movement. In comparison to computational costs associated with simulation timesteps and analysis/visualization algorithms, we conclude that the introduced overhead is negligible.

6 Discussion and Limitations

The approach presented in the previous sections gives a glimpse into the solution's flexibility. The presented test cases show that even a few modules, designed with the modularity principle in mind, can provide a lot of possibilities for complex workflows. Furthermore, we have shown that the approach introduces negligible overhead. The functionality for the rendering, however, was utilized through ParaView Catalyst, which is arguably a monolithic implementation. To fully utilize a modular design, it would be necessary to break functionality into modules. Even providing a collection of modules that covers only the most popular use cases is beyond the scope of this work or a single developer. To fully utilize the approach, the community must embrace the design pattern and contribute modules as a collective effort. We believe that following such an approach can also benefit existing monolithic implementations such as ParaView Catalyst, Ascent, etc. One advantage of the presented architecture is that a gradual shift is possible as monolithic implementations can still be used while pulling more and more functionality into small modules. New implementations, especially, can leverage the approach to minimize work. Adios Catalyst [16] and InsitUE [10] have a similar approach to their hybrid architecture by utilizing ParaView Catalyst for on-node processing and sending the results off-node for further processing. CatalystMaestro allows that both implementations are only tasked with data-transfer by treating the output of other modules as generic Conduit nodes that need to be transferred. Reducing the amount of code that is functionally equivalent between the two implementations, and opening up the method to other implementations for the on-node processing besides ParaView Catalyst without any changes. In the specific case of Adios Catalyst and InstUE, it must be noted that the on-node processing is optional, which means that it could already be utilized with CatalystMaestro to create hybrid pipelines easily.

Another aspect is that it can be challenging to decide what functionality should be part of CatalystMaestro's implementation or should be realized by external modules. The debugger, for example, could also be part of CatalystMaestro itself and not as a standalone module. Embedding it into CatalystMaestro would allow deeper access to the workflow and internal states but would increase maintenance and dependencies. Lastly, other useful nodes such as loops, switches, reading environment variables, etc. are still missing but can be easily added. Overall, the feature set of CatalystMaestro has to grow with demands and use-cases and the presented solution presents only a first step towards a modular in-situ ecosystem.

7 Conclusion and Future Work

Modular software development has been an established practice in other domains for quite some time. However, the advantages of such approaches, such as de-duplicating code, better versioning, replacing parts of the architecture, etc., can also be helpful for in-situ software. In this paper, we presented CatalystMaestro. This first prototypical implementation tackles modular in-situ by utilizing Catalyst2 and providing an implementation that allows the formation of complex workflows out of other Catalyst2 implementations. CatalystMaestro allows defining complex in-situ workflows through describing them as non-linear non-cyclic graphs. It provides all the functionality needed to use Catalyst2 implementations as building blocks to build workflows that are useful for end-users and can also help domain developers and in-situ tool developers. Alongside CatalystMaestro we presented CatalystComposer, a graphical user interface that allows users to build workflows in a visual editor and export the workflow for use with CatalystMaestro. While the presented method is not limited to Catalyst2, we believe that Catalyst2 is very suitable for this kind of approach due to its design. Furthermore, we believe the presented implementation can be the starting point to foster a community shift towards modular design patterns in the in-situ ecosystem. In the future, we will focus on three main aspects: first, we will seek feedback from the community to evaluate if crucial features are missing. Second, we plan to evaluate more workflows, especially ones utilizing hybrid processing. Lastly, we aim to publish evaluated example workflows as "compositions" that allow new users to start using CatalystMaestro easily.

Acknowledgments. The authors gratefully acknowledge the German Federal Ministry of Education and Research (BMBF) and the NRW state government for supporting this work/project as part of the NHR funding.

References

1. Ahrens, J., Geveci, B., Law, C.: Visualization Handbook, chap. ParaView: An End-User Tool for Large Data Visualization. Elsevier Inc., Burlington, MA, USA (2005)
2. Atkinson, M., Gesing, S., Montagnat, J., Taylor, I.: Scientific workflows: Past, present and future (2017)
3. Ayachit, U., et al.: Paraview catalyst: enabling in situ data analysis and visualization. In: ISAV2015, Association for Computing Machinery, New York (2015)
4. Ayachit, U., et al.: Catalyst revised: rethinking the ParaView in situ analysis and visualization API. In: Jagode, H., Anzt, H., Ltaief, H., Luszczek, P. (eds.) ISC High Performance 2021. LNCS, vol. 12761, pp. 484–494. Springer, Cham (2021). https://doi.org/10.1007/978-3-030-90539-2_33
5. Ayachit, U., et al.: The sensei generic in situ interface. In: 2016 Second Workshop on In Situ Infrastructures for Enabling Extreme-Scale Analysis and Visualization (ISAV) (2016)

6. Colonnelli, I., Cantalupo, B., Merelli, I., Aldinucci, M.: Streamflow: cross-breeding cloud with HPC. IEEE Trans. Emerg. Top. Comput. **9**(4) (2020)
7. Grüning, B.A., et al.: Jupyter and galaxy: easing entry barriers into complex data analyses for biomedical researchers. PLoS Comput. Biol. **13**(5), e1005425 (2017)
8. Guerrera, D., et al.: SPH-EXA: enhancing the scalability of SPH codes via an exascale-ready SPH mini-app (2019)
9. Harrison, C., Larsen, M., Ryujin, B.S., Kunen, A., Capps, A., Privitera, J.: Conduit: a successful strategy for describing and sharing data in situ. In: 2022 IEEE/ACM International Workshop on In Situ Infrastructures for Enabling Extreme-Scale Analysis and Visualization (ISAV). IEEE (2022)
10. Krüger, M., Milke, J.F., Kuhlen, T.W., Gerrits, T.: Insitue - enabling hybrid in-situ visualizations through unreal engine and catalyst. In: High Performance Computing. ISC High Performance 2024 International Workshops. Springer, Cham (2025)
11. Krüger, M., et al.: Insite: a pipeline enabling in-transit visualization and analysis for neuronal network simulations. In: High Performance Computing. ISC High Performance 2022 International Workshops. Springer, Cham (2022)
12. Larsen, M., Brugger, E., Childs, H., Harrison, C.: Ascent: a flyweight in situ library for exascale simulations. In: In Situ Visualization For Computational Science. Mathematics and Visualization Book Series from Springer, Cham, Switzerland (2022)
13. Liu, J., Pacitti, E., Valduriez, P., Mattoso, M.: A survey of data-intensive scientific workflow management. J. Grid Comput. **13**, 457–493 (2015)
14. Malakar, P., Natarajan, V., Vadhiyar, S.S.: Inst: an integrated steering framework for critical weather applications. Procedia Comput. Sci. **4** (2011)
15. Mazen, F., Givord, L., Gueunet, C.: Catalyst-adios2: in transit analysis for numerical simulations using catalyst 2 API. In: International Conference on High Performance Computing. Springer, Cham (2023)
16. Mazen, F., Gombert, L., Givord, L., Gueunet, C.: In situ in transit hybrid analysis with catalyst-adios2. In: High Performance Computing. ISC High Performance 2024 International Workshops. Springer, Cham (2025)
17. Moreland, K., et al.: VTK-m: accelerating the visualization toolkit for massively threaded architectures. IEEE Comput. Graph. Appl. **36**(3) (2016)
18. Oinn, T., et al.: Taverna: a tool for the composition and enactment of bioinformatics workflows. Bioinformatics **20**(17), 3045–3054 (2004)
19. Pugmire, D., Huang, J., Moreland, K., Klasky, S.: The need for pervasive in situ analysis and visualization (p-isav). In: High Performance Computing. ISC High Performance 2022 International Workshops: Hamburg, Germany, 2022, Revised Selected Papers. Springer, Cham (2023)
20. Whitlock, B., Favre, J.M., Meredith, J.S.: Parallel in situ coupling of simulation with a fully featured visualization system. In: Eurographics Symposium on Parallel Graphics and Visualization. The Eurographics Association (2011)
21. Ziegeler, S., Atkins, C., Bauer, A., Pettey, L.: In situ analysis as a parallel i/o problem. In: Proceedings of the First Workshop on In Situ Infrastructures for Enabling Extreme-Scale Analysis and Visualization (2015)

Updating Inshimtu with Catalyst2 and Integrating an HPC MiniApp: Lessons Learned

James Kress[1]([✉]) and Thomas Theußl[1,2]

[1] King Abdullah University of Science and Technology (KAUST),
Thuwal, Saudi Arabia
james.kress@kaust.edu.sa
[2] Consivi KG, Deutschlandsberg, Austria
thomas.theussl@consivi.com

Abstract. The growing disparity between system processing power and I/O and storage capabilities has underscored the importance of in situ visualization and analysis. However, adoption of these technologies remains limited due to hesitancy around new coding techniques, perceived workflow complexity, and concerns over resource costs. To address this and better educate users, we previously introduced Inshimtu, an in situ "shim" library designed to facilitate experimentation with in situ techniques and serve as a pedagogical tool, allowing users to experience in situ workflows before committing to full-scale integration. Building on this work, we have updated Inshimtu to utilize the Catalyst2 standard. We have also developed a version of the Gray-Scott reaction-diffusion MiniApp—a two-variable application using a memory-bound 7-point stencil kernel—to demonstrate in situ workflows at scale. This paper details the process of converting Inshimtu from Legacy ParaView Catalyst to Catalyst2, discusses the complexities and lessons learned, describes the integration of Inshimtu with the Gray-Scott MiniApp for scalability testing, and demonstrates the combined functionality within a scientific workflow on the Shaheen III supercomputer.

Inshimtu is available for download at:
https://github.com/kaust-vislab/Inshimtu-basic
Our version of the Gray-Scott MiniApp is available for download at:
https://gitlab.kitware.com/jameskress/KAUST_Visualization_Vignettes.

1 Introduction

Supercomputer users are increasingly facing challenges with data processing. Simulation data generation rates are outpacing disk write speeds, and disk quota limitations complicate data storage. As a result, simulation teams often reduce data writing frequency or save only a subset of variables to disk to accelerate simulations and minimize disk usage. Consequently, vital simulation phenomena can be missed, leading to less reliable and potentially incomplete data analysis.

In situ visualization and analysis provide a potential solution. The visualization community has developed powerful in situ tools that reduce a simulation's reliance on disk storage while enabling more frequent temporal analysis. However, significant challenges impede the widespread integration of these in situ technologies, due to concerns about integration time, code maintenance, additional computational costs, data integrity, resilience, and a lack of understanding regarding the capabilities and suitability of in situ for specific use cases [11,14].

To address these challenges, we previously introduced Inshimtu [15], an in situ shim that serves as a pedagogical tool and allows simulation codes to explore and evaluate in situ visualization without requiring code modifications. The initial version of Inshimtu was based on Legacy ParaView Catalyst.

With the shift towards Catalyst2, a more modern and flexible API, upgrading Inshimtu was necessary. Our goal was to simplify the user experience by adopting Catalyst2 and its more versatile Python scripting capabilities. To further enhance Inshimtu's educational utility, we developed and integrated the Gray-Scott reaction-diffusion MiniApp [25] for demonstration purposes. This MiniApp enables the demonstration of live in situ workflows using Inshimtu, without the need for full-scale simulations, making it an ideal environment for teaching and learning, allowing users to quickly observe, execute, and modify both simulation output and visualization. The Gray-Scott MiniApp has been tested with large datasets on up to 11,264 cores across 1,024 nodes of the Shaheen III supercomputer.

The combination of a readily available MiniApp for teaching and the ability to process users' simulation output from disk makes Inshimtu and Gray-Scott ideal tools for promoting in situ techniques within the simulation community. It is important to note that, like its predecessor, this version of Inshimtu is intended as a teaching aid and a first step toward full-scale in situ integration, not as a replacement for established, fully-featured in situ tools.

This paper details the lessons learned during the upgrade of Inshimtu from Legacy ParaView Catalyst to Catalyst2, its integration with the Gray-Scott MiniApp, and a demonstration on Shaheen III. Section 3 describes the upgrade process and key insights. Section 4 presents the Gray-Scott MiniApp implementation and a workflow example showcasing live visualization with Inshimtu. Finally, Sect. 5 summarizes the work and outlines potential future directions.

2 Related Work

In situ visualization has emerged as a crucial technique to address the growing disparity between simulation data generation rates and Input/Output and storage capabilities [1]. It generally falls into two main paradigms: in-line [7] and in-transit [24] in situ. In-line in situ involves performing visualization and analysis within the simulation code itself, while in-transit in situ moves data to separate processes for analysis. The way data is handled and visualization pipelines are constructed differs significantly between these paradigms [13], often leading simulations to choose one over the other [18]. To facilitate these diverse in situ approaches, a variety of tools and frameworks have been developed, which we will now explore.

2.1 Overview of Key In Situ Visualization Tools

Several tools and frameworks have been developed to facilitate in situ visualization and analysis:

- **Ascent** [19]: An HPC-ready in situ visualization and analysis infrastructure focusing on both MPI and node-level parallelism.
- **ADIOS2** [10]: A data management system for HPC that supports both in-line and in-transit visualization. It provides access to simulation memory through either direct memory access or data staging [9].
- **Catalyst2** [4]: An API specification for in situ data analysis and visualization, designed for direct integration into simulation codes. Visualization tasks are performed by a separate consumer-side implementation (e.g., ParaView, Cinema, or custom Python scripts).
- **ParaView Catalyst** [12]: The reference implementation of the Catalyst2 API, introduced in ParaView 5.9, providing access to the extensive ParaView visualization ecosystem.
- **AdiosCatalyst** [22]: An implementation of the Catalyst2 API that uses ADIOS2 for data transport. It supports hybrid in-line and in-transit workflows [23], addressing scalability limitations in certain visualization algorithms.
- **Legacy ParaView Catalyst** [5]: An earlier version of Catalyst, enabling in situ visualization via embedded ParaView pipelines. It lacks the modularity and extensibility of Catalyst2.
- **LibSim** [31]: An in situ interface for VisIt, enabling users to leverage the full VisIt ecosystem from within simulation codes.
- **SENSEI** [3]: A generic in situ interface supporting multiple backends including ADIOS2, Ascent, Legacy ParaView Catalyst, and emerging Catalyst2 support. It abstracts in situ implementations, allowing code portability across different visualization engines.
- **Kombyne** [20]: A commercial in situ and in-transit co-processing framework aimed at addressing data movement and storage challenges in large-scale simulations. It supports multiple data transport protocols (e.g., MPI, ADIOS2, ZeroMQ) and endpoints (e.g., ParaView, VisIt, direct rendering).

While these tools offer substantial capabilities, their adoption is not without challenges, which we briefly discuss next.

2.2 Addressing Adoption Challenges and Successes

Adopting in situ tools can lead to efficient and performant workflows [8] that save time [16,21,32] and cost [6,17,28] compared to post-hoc visualization. Despite these potential benefits, there can also be less successful implementations [2] due to improper tool selection, wrong in situ approach, non-optimal tool tuning, and even poor work distribution [30], often leading to wasted time and computational resources. This, combined with a lack of awareness and training, contributes to the continued reliance on post-hoc methods [26]. As simulation needs grow and in situ solutions mature (e.g., visualization as a service [27] and Fides [29]), adoption resistance should decrease. Against this backdrop of existing tools and adoption considerations, Inshimtu has been developed with a specific purpose and target audience in mind.

2.3 Connecting Inshimtu to the Existing Landscape

While numerous full-featured in situ visualization tools exist, a significant barrier to entry remains for users seeking to learn and experiment with these techniques without extensive development effort. Inshimtu addresses this gap by providing an educational tool that mimics in situ visualization. It operates solely off of files, passing them to the Catalyst2 in situ API, effectively serving as a stepping stone for users rather than a replacement for full-featured tools.

Inshimtu was developed to reduce the effort required to learn about and test in situ concepts. Previously, users would have to develop their own in situ readers or integrate in situ into their simulation code to see the benefits using their own data. With Inshimtu, however, no development is required, allowing users to experiment with in situ techniques using their own data without modifying their simulation codes.

Inshimtu's upgrade to Catalyst2 significantly simplifies the learning process. By using the most current Catalyst2 API and recent versions of ParaView, it showcases the streamlined Catalyst2 API when explaining to users how to create their own integrations. Furthermore, newer versions of ParaView support a simplified Python script format that is more maintainable and accessible for users, reducing the learning curve. In essence, Inshimtu provides a low-barrier, hands-on environment for users to explore and understand in situ visualization techniques.

3 Updating Inshimtu to Catalyst2 and Lessons Learned

3.1 Introduction to Inshimtu and Motivation for Upgrade

Inshimtu is an in situ "shim" library designed as a pedagogical tool to allow simulation codes to experiment with in situ visualization without significant modifications. Originally implemented using Legacy ParaView Catalyst, Inshimtu needed to be upgraded to the more modern Catalyst2 standard. This upgrade was necessary to leverage the improved API, enhanced Python scripting capabilities, and ongoing development of Catalyst2.

Code: Subsections below reference files and methods in the Inshimtu repository: github.com/kaust-vislab/Inshimtu-basic[1].

---

[1] This paper uses Inshimtu-basic git commit: *657d8db*.

3.2 Legacy ParaView Catalyst and Catalyst2 Overview

Legacy ParaView Catalyst was an earlier system for enabling in situ visualization, where visualization capabilities were achieved by embedding ParaView pipelines directly within the simulation code. Unlike the more modular Catalyst2, Legacy ParaView Catalyst had a more monolithic structure which could complicate integration and updates. Data was typically passed to the embedded ParaView pipelines using a specific `datadescription` API for input binding. The execution of in situ tasks was often managed through a function like `DoCoProcessing()`, with pipeline setup occurring within functions such as `CreateCoProcessor()` and `_CreatePipeline()`. The Python scripts generated for Legacy ParaView Catalyst were notably different from standard ParaView Python scripts and those used in Catalyst2 (an example is shown in Listing 1.2 within Fig. 1). These scripts often involved a more complex, nested structure, summarized in Table 1, which made them less reusable and more challenging to create and maintain. Furthermore, its approach lacked the flexibility of using tools like Conduit for data description and transfer.

Catalyst2 is an API specification for in situ data analysis and visualization. A key aspect of its design is its modernized approach to Python scripting for defining in situ pipelines. Catalyst2 enables the use of straightforward, flat Python scripts where the visualization pipeline is typically defined at the top level and executed directly (an example is shown in Listing 1.1 within Fig. 1). This structure, along with features like automatic input binding via `PVTrivialProducer`

Table 1. Comparison of Legacy and Catalyst2 Python scripting in ParaView.

Feature	Legacy ParaView Catalyst	ParaView Catalyst2
Script structure	Function-based; pipeline created in a helper function	Flat script; pipeline defined at top level
Execution entry	Runtime calls `DoCoProcessing()`	Script runs in `__main__` with `SaveExtracts...()`
Pipeline setup	Inside `CreateCoProcessor()` and `_CreatePipeline()`	Declared directly in global scope
Input binding	Manual via `datadescription` API	Automatic via `PVTrivialProducer` by name
Extractor use	Created with `CreateExtractor()`, triggered manually	Same, but can use `Options()` for config
Reusability	Low; deeply nested and tightly coupled	High; modular and easy to reuse or test
Extensibility	Requires modifying embedded functions	Add pipelines and extractors directly
Version support	ParaView ≤ 5.8 (deprecated in newer versions)	ParaView ≥ 5.9

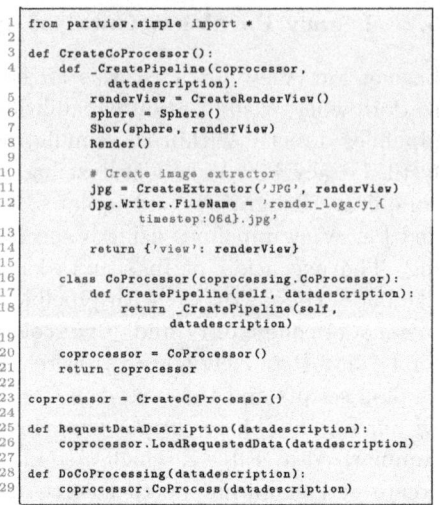

```
1  from paraview.simple import *
2  import paraview
3  paraview.compatibility.major = 5
4  paraview.compatibility.minor = 13
5
6  # View and layout
7  renderView = CreateView('RenderView')
8  layout = CreateLayout()
9  layout.AssignView(0, renderView)
10
11 # Pipeline
12 sphere = Sphere()
13 Show(sphere, renderView)
14 Render()
15
16 # Extractor
17 jpg = CreateExtractor('JPG', renderView,
                         registrationName='JPG1')
18 jpg.Writer.FileName = 'render_catalyst2_{timestep
                        :06d}.jpg'
19
20 # Catalyst options
21 from paraview import catalyst
22 options = catalyst.Options()
23 options.GlobalTrigger = 'Time Step'
24
25 if __name__ == '__main__':
26     from paraview.simple import
            SaveExtractsUsingCatalystOptions
27     SaveExtractsUsingCatalystOptions(options)
```

Listing (1.1) ParaView Version 5.9+ Catalyst2 Python Script.

```
1  from paraview.simple import *
2
3  def CreateCoProcessor():
4      def _CreatePipeline(coprocessor,
                            datadescription):
5          renderView = CreateRenderView()
6          sphere = Sphere()
7          Show(sphere, renderView)
8          Render()
9
10         # Create image extractor
11         jpg = CreateExtractor('JPG', renderView)
12         jpg.Writer.FileName = 'render_legacy_{
                                  timestep:06d}.jpg'
13
14         return {'view': renderView}
15
16     class CoProcessor(coprocessing.CoProcessor):
17         def CreatePipeline(self, datadescription):
18             return _CreatePipeline(self,
                                       datadescription)
19
20     coprocessor = CoProcessor()
21     return coprocessor
22
23 coprocessor = CreateCoProcessor()
24
25 def RequestDataDescription(datadescription):
26     coprocessor.LoadRequestedData(datadescription)
27
28 def DoCoProcessing(datadescription):
29     coprocessor.CoProcess(datadescription)
```

Listing (1.2) Legacy ParaView Catalyst Script.

Fig. 1. Side-by-side comparison of ParaView Version $\geq$ 5.9 Catalyst2 and Legacy ParaView Catalyst Python scripts.

by name and easier extensibility, contributes to higher reusability and a more maintainable scripting experience, as detailed in Table 1.

This streamlined scripting approach offers helpful improvements over Legacy ParaView Catalyst, which often involved more complex, function-based script structures with pipeline definitions nested within helper functions. Beyond scripting, Catalyst2 also employs a different data handling mechanism, notably through the use of Conduit, a software tool for describing hierarchical scientific data. Conduit facilitates efficient data passing between the simulation and the visualization pipeline within ParaView. To integrate with a simulation, a Catalyst2 adaptor implements a well-defined interface, requiring four methods (`catalyst_initialize`, `catalyst_execute`, `catalyst_finalize`, `catalyst_results`) and one optional method (`catalyst_about`).

Furthermore, Catalyst2 accommodates the use of *stub* implementations. A stub implementation provides the minimal Catalyst API interface for a simulation code, allowing calls to functions like `catalyst_initialize` and `catalyst_execute` without engaging a full visualization engine or performing actual data processing. This approach is valuable for verifying API integration, testing simulation logic in isolation by bypassing in situ components, facilitating incremental development before full visualization pipelines are ready, or for running in environments with limited visualization resources. Essentially, a stub acts as a lightweight or no-operation stand-in for the full Catalyst machinery, streamlining development and testing.

3.3 Conversion Process

To update Inshimtu to Catalyst2, we created a new adaptor adhering to the Catalyst2 standard. Previously, our code was instrumented with Legacy ParaView Catalyst, see source/processing/adaptor.cxx within the Inshimtu source. This transition was complicated by its significantly different structure, which involved a more monolithic design centered around a single co-processing entry point and a complex setup mechanism. This legacy structure was not inherently modular and relied on several custom helper classes within Inshimtu (primarily Adaptor and its associated methods that were tightly coupled with the ParaView Legacy Catalyst API specifics. These helper classes managed data handling, pipeline construction, and communication in a way that was not directly compatible with Catalyst2's more streamlined, five-method interface.

The primary challenge was retrofitting this new, clearly defined API structure onto our existing Inshimtu infrastructure, that was originally built to support the older, more integrated Legacy ParaView Catalyst model. For instance, tasks that were previously handled by our bespoke helper functions now needed to be mapped and refactored to fit within the distinct lifecycle phases defined by the Catalyst2 methods. This involved not just implementing the new API calls, but carefully disentangling the logic within our original Adaptor::coprocess method and other helper routines to align with Catalyst2's expectations for initialization, per-timestep execution, and finalization.

Given that a significant portion of Inshimtu's existing functionality depended on this established structure, a complete rewrite of the Adaptor logic was deemed impractical within the project's scope. Instead, we focused on carefully tailoring the new Catalyst2 implementation (now in source/processing/adaptorV2.cxx) to interface with the existing helper classes where possible, while refactoring them as needed to support the new data flow and control mechanisms mandated by Catalyst2, particularly concerning how data is described and passed using Conduit. This pragmatic approach, while enabling the upgrade, inherently introduced complexities that would likely be absent in a fresh Catalyst2 integration.

3.4 Data Conversion Details

A significant aspect of updating Inshimtu to Catalyst2 involved managing the data flow from our existing VTK-based data structures to the Conduit data model adopted by Catalyst2. Catalyst2 utilizes Conduit (conduit_cpp::Node) to describe and pass hierarchical scientific data to the processing pipeline (e.g., ParaView). Within Inshimtu, simulation data is primarily handled as vtkDataObject instances. Therefore, a crucial step in the conversion process was to correctly populate Conduit nodes with the information from these `vtkDataObjects`.

VTK itself provides mechanisms to facilitate this interface. When a `vtkDataObject` is passed to a Catalyst2 pipeline (like ParaView Catalyst), internal VTK and ParaView Catalyst components handle the wrapping or conversion of this VTK data structure into a Conduit node representation that Catalyst2 can understand. This process is designed to be efficient, leveraging Conduit's zero-copy capabilities where possible by allowing Conduit nodes to directly reference the memory arrays within the `vtkDataObject`.

However, this interaction, particularly the zero-copy aspect, introduced a subtle challenge in our updated Inshimtu implementation. Our initial approach involved taking data prepared similarly to how it was for the legacy `Adaptor::coprocess` method, where a `vtkDataObject` (managed by Inshimtu's Adaptor logic) was then used to populate a `conduit_cpp::Node` for Catalyst2 to consume via `catalyst_execute`. We discovered that in certain cases, the `vtkDataObject` instance was being destructed (or its data arrays deallocated) after the Conduit node was populated but before the Catalyst2 visualization pipeline had fully processed the data. This premature deallocation led to the Conduit node referencing freed and potentially overwritten memory, manifesting as corrupted data or incorrect values in the resulting visualizations.

To resolve this data integrity issue, which stemmed from the lifecycle mismatch between our Inshimtu-managed `vtkDataObject` and its usage by Catalyst2 via Conduit, we employed an instance of our `Descriptor` helper class (defined in `source/processing/adaptorV2.h`) to manage the lifecycle of the `vtkDataObject` within our updated Adaptor. This `Descriptor` instance ensured its `descriptor_data` member retained the data object for the required duration. This experience highlighted the importance of carefully managing data object lifecycles when interfacing VTK data structures with Conduit in a Catalyst2 environment.

3.5 Lessons Learned

The process of upgrading Inshimtu from Legacy ParaView Catalyst to Catalyst2, while ultimately successful, provided several key insights that may be beneficial to others undertaking similar transitions or new in situ integrations:

1. **Retrofitting New APIs into Existing Architectures is Inherently Complex:** Our primary challenge, as detailed in the *Conversion Process* section (Sect. 3.3), was integrating the distinct five-method Catalyst2 API into Inshimtu's established infrastructure, that was designed around the more monolithic Legacy ParaView Catalyst. While a complete overhaul was impractical for our project, adapting the existing codebase to the new API's lifecycle and data handling paradigms extended development time. This experience underscores that migrating an existing, tightly-coupled system to a new

standard like Catalyst2 can be substantially more involved than a fresh implementation, where the architecture can be designed around the new API from the outset.

2. **Careful Management of Data Lifecycles is Crucial:** The adoption of Conduit in Catalyst2, with its support for zero-copy data sharing, introduced subtleties regarding data object lifecycles. As discussed in *Data Conversion Details* (Sect. 3.4), we encountered data corruption issues stemming from `vtkDataObject` instances being deallocated prematurely before Catalyst2's Conduit-based pipeline had finished processing them. Resolving this required explicit measures to ensure data persistence. This highlights that while new data models offer performance benefits, they necessitate a thorough understanding and careful management of memory and object lifecycles, especially when interfacing with existing data management schemes within VTK or other libraries.

3. **API Stability and Maintenance Burden Remain Key Concerns for In Situ Adoption:** This upgrade experience reinforces the broader challenge that evolving standards and API changes pose for the maintainers and users of in situ tools. Each significant update to core in situ libraries, such as the transition from Legacy ParaView Catalyst to Catalyst2, can necessitate considerable rework in user implementations, contributing to the ongoing maintenance burden that can deter wider adoption. While breaking changes are sometimes unavoidable for progress, the pursuit of long-term API stability and clear migration paths is vital for retaining and growing the in situ user community. Catalyst2's more streamlined and modular API, with its well-defined interface, is a positive step in this direction, aiming to simplify future integrations and maintenance efforts.

4 Implementing Gray-Scott and Example HPC Workflow

This section provides an overview of our implementation of the Gray-Scott MiniApp and its integration with Inshimtu. Subsection 4.1 details the integration, while Subsect. 4.2 discusses the workflow on the Shaheen III supercomputer and the lessons learned from this specific application.

Code: Subsections below use both Inshimtu and Gray-Scott:
github.com/kaust-vislab/Inshimtu-basic[2],
gitlab.kitware.com/jameskress/KAUST_Visualization_Vignettes[3].

4.1 Integrating Inshimtu with the Gray-Scott MiniApp

We developed our own version of the Gray-Scott MiniApp with the explicit goal of having an easy-to-use and scalable data generator that we could use for testing, demonstrating, and teaching in situ workflows to users. The code and details

---

[2] This paper uses Inshimtu-basic git commit: *657d8db*.
[3] This paper uses KAUST_Visualization_Vignettes commit: *64e068fa*.

are available on GitLab shown above in Sect. 4. Gray-Scott is a 3D 7-point stencil program that simulates the Gray-Scott reaction-diffusion model. It is scalable across nodes with MPI and we have currently enabled three different visualization options within the program: 1) PVTI writer, 2) Catalyst2 integration with file writer, and 3) Catalyst2 in situ capabilities. Further development of the MiniApp and a detailed report of its capabilities and performance is planned for a future paper.

For this work we focused on testing the *PVTI* writing capabilities of Gray-Scott, as Inshimtu mimics in situ by reading files from disk, leaving the other configurations as future work. Testing included multiple node configurations, up to 1,024 nodes, with the largest configuration being 11,264 cores on 1,024 nodes. We found that the PVTI writer takes a significant amount of time to write data when writing from 11,264 different processes, much slower than a single simulation step. While slow, it did work, and demonstrates the scalability and capabilities of the MiniApp.

Build instructions are available on GitLab and have been validated on Linux. Inshimtu has a PVTI reader, so we directly used the output from Gray-Scott to feed as input into Inshimtu. Once ingested by Inshimtu, Catalyst2 Visualization scripts were executed.

4.2 Gray-Scott and Inshimtu Workflow

We ran the workflow on Shaheen III's CPU partition, on 192-core AMD Genoa nodes. Gray-Scott ran on 256 processes, 16 nodes, with a grid resolution of 1024^3, producing data sets that were 12 GB per step. Inshimtu ran on 4 processes, 4 nodes, with 370 GB of RAM per node. Inshimtu and Gray-Scott were launched simultaneously (using the script `sites/shaheen/gray-scott-configs/run.sbat`): Inshimtu watching the output directory of Gray-Scott, waiting for new files. We used the following Catalyst2 script from the Inshimtu repository: `sites/shaheen/gray-scott-configs/gray-scott-1024-png-clip.py`. This script uses standard ParaView techniques, and serves to demonstrate the full pipeline from data ingestion in Inshimtu, to execution using a ParaView Catalyst2 script. The visualization operations are simple: First, the volume is clipped in half, with one half being rendered as a surface. Second, the other half is rotated 90°, a contour is applied, and the contour is rendered. This representation was chosen to clearly display the evolution of the Gray-Scott simulation.

Figure 2 shows images from four different simulation steps, 1,000, 4,000, 7,000, and 10,000, illustrating the evolution of the reaction-diffusion equation. From these runs we have two primary insights: First, file-based in situ, as expected, introduces significant inefficiencies. Not only were the writes of the data slow, but the reading of the data was also slow. This underscores the advantages of memory-based in situ, which offers much faster data access. Second, our Catalyst2 pipelines were memory intensive (primarily due to the generation of unstructured grid geometry for surfaces and contours from the volumetric data). We originally ran larger simulations at 2048^3 and 4096^3, but these required us to

(a) Step 1,000, showing the U variable.

(b) Step 4,000, showing the U variable.

(c) Step 7,000, showing the U variable.

(d) Step 10,000, showing the U variable.

Fig. 2. Four images from the Gray-Scott and Inshimtu workflow run on Shaheen III, visualizing 1024^3 grid of data. These visualizations show the data clipped in half, with the right half being rotated and a contour being applied, showing the progression of the chemical reaction. (Color figure online)

resample the data to much smaller dimensions (using the Resample to Image filter) before clipping and creating unstructured grids. This had the implication that fine-grained features could have been lost in the down-sampling. To avoid this, we used the 1024^3 simulation.

This workflow showcases the ability to link Gray-Scott and Inshimtu together to create an in situ demonstration tool. We demonstrated that Gray-Scott is highly scalable, but suffers slowdown when writing many files to disk. We then showed Inshimtu's ability to read data from Gray-Scott as it was being produced, and process it with Catalyst2.

5 Conclusions and Future Work

Despite the availability of powerful in situ visualization libraries and frameworks, their widespread adoption remains limited. This is often due to challenges such as lack of awareness, complexity in integration, and concerns about resource costs. This paper addressed these challenges by enhancing Inshimtu, an educational tool designed to teach users about in situ using their own data with no coding required. Originally based on Legacy ParaView Catalyst, Inshimtu has been successfully updated to the Catalyst2 standard, leveraging its modern and flexible API.

We detailed the complexities encountered during this upgrade process, providing lessons learned for other researchers transitioning to Catalyst2. Furthermore, we developed and integrated the Gray-Scott MiniApp, a scalable reaction-diffusion model, to demonstrate in situ workflows at scale, including testing on 11,264 cores of the Shaheen III supercomputer. This integration allowed us to showcase live visualization and analysis, emphasizing Inshimtu's utility as a pedagogical tool.

Future work will focus on adding additional file reading options, optimizing parallel performance, and finishing development of a stream capable reader in Inshimtu in order to bypass the disk, which is a current limitation of Inshimtu. Additionally, we plan to conduct user testing with interested simulation scientists here at KAUST and globally, to further promote in situ adoption and educate users about the benefits and capabilities of in situ visualization and analysis.

Acknowledgments. We thank Kitware for their support in developing the Gray-Scott MiniApp and for their guidance in converting Inshimtu from Legacy ParaView Catalyst to Catalyst2. This work was supported by King Abdullah University of Science and Technology (KAUST) and made use of resources provided by the Visualization and Supercomputing Laboratories at KAUST.

References

1. Adhinarayanan, V., Feng, W-C., Rogers, D., Ahrens, J., Pakin, S.: Characterizing and modeling power and energy for extreme-scale in-situ visualization. In: IEEE Parallel and Distributed Processing Symposium (IPDPS), pp. 978–987 (2017)
2. Atzori, M., et al.: In situ visualization of large-scale turbulence simulations in nek5000 with paraview catalyst. J. Supercomput. **78**(3), 3605–3620 (2022)
3. Ayachit, U., et al.: The SENSEI generic in situ interface. In: Workshop on In Situ Infrastructures for Enabling Extreme-Scale Analysis and Visualization (ISAV), pp. 40–44 (2016)
4. Ayachit, U., et al.: Catalyst revised: rethinking the ParaView in situ analysis and visualization API. In: Jagode, H., Anzt, H., Ltaief, H., Luszczek, P. (eds.) ISC High Performance 2021. LNCS, vol. 12761, pp. 484–494. Springer, Cham (2021). https://doi.org/10.1007/978-3-030-90539-2_33
5. Ayachit, U., et al.: ParaView catalyst: enabling in situ data analysis and visualization. In: Workshop on In Situ Infrastructures for Enabling Extreme-Scale Analysis and Visualization (ISAV), pp. 25–29 (2015)
6. Ayachit, U., et al.: Performance analysis, design considerations, and applications of extreme-scale In Situ infrastructures. In: ACM/IEEE Conference for High Performance Computing, Networking, Storage and Analysis (SC16) (2016)
7. Bauer, A.C., et al.: In Situ methods, infrastructures, and applications on high performance computing platforms, a state-of-the-art (STAR) report. In: Computer Graphics Forum, Proceedings of Eurovis 2016, vol. 35, no. 3 (2016)
8. Childs, H., et al.: Visualization at extreme scale concurrency. In: High Performance Visualization: Enabling Extreme-Scale Scientific Insight. CRC Press, Boca Raton (2012)

9. Gainaru, A., et al.: Understanding the impact of data staging for coupled scientific workflows. IEEE Trans. Parallel Distrib. Syst. **33**(12), 4134–4147 (2022)
10. Godoy, W.F., et al.: Adios 2: the adaptable input output system. a framework for high-performance data management. SoftwareX, **12**, 100561 (2020)
11. Kim, M.: In situ analysis and visualization of fusion simulations: lessons learned. In: Yokota, R., Weiland, M., Shalf, J., Alam, S. (eds.) ISC High Performance 2018. LNCS, vol. 11203, pp. 230–242. Springer, Cham (2018). https://doi.org/10.1007/978-3-030-02465-9_16
12. Kitware, Inc. Paraview catalyst documentation (2025). https://docs.paraview.org/en/latest/Catalyst/index.html. Accessed 21 Apr 2025
13. Kress, J., Churchill, R.M., Klasky, S., Kim, M., Childs, H., Pugmire, D.: Preparing for in situ processing on upcoming leading-edge supercomputers. Supercomput. Front. Innov. **3**(4), 49–65 (2016)
14. Kress, J., et al.: Loosely coupled in situ visualization: a perspective on why it's here to stay. In: Workshop on In Situ Infrastructures for Enabling Extreme-Scale Analysis and Visualization (ISAV), pp. 1–6 (2015)
15. Kress, J., Holst, G., Dasari, H., Afzal, S., Hoteit, I., Theußl, T.: Inshimtu – A Lightweight In Situ Visualization "Shim", pp. 257–268 (2023)
16. Kress, J., et al.: Comparing time-to-solution for in situ visualization paradigms at scale. In: 2020 IEEE 10th Symposium on Large Data Analysis and Visualization (LDAV), pp. 22–26. IEEE (2020)
17. Kress, J., et al.: Opportunities for cost savings with in-transit visualization. In: Sadayappan, P., Chamberlain, B.L., Juckeland, G., Ltaief, H. (eds.) ISC High Performance 2020. LNCS, vol. 12151, pp. 146–165. Springer, Cham (2020). https://doi.org/10.1007/978-3-030-50743-5_8
18. Kress, J., Pugmire, D., Klasky, S., Childs, H.: Visualization and analysis requirements for in situ processing for a large-scale fusion simulation code. In: Proceedings of the 2nd Workshop on In Situ Infrastructures for Enabling Extreme-scale Analysis and Visualization, pp. 45–50. IEEE Press (2016)
19. Larsen, M., et al.: The ALPINE in situ infrastructure: ascending from the ashes of strawman. In: Workshop on In Situ Infrastructures on Enabling Extreme-Scale Analysis and Visualization (ISAV), pp. 42–46 (2017)
20. Legensky, S.M., et al.: Industrial and biomedical CFD workflows enhanced via coprocessing for knowledge capture and computational steering. In: Eleventh International Conference on Computational Fluid Dynamics (ICCFD11) (2022)
21. Mateevitsi, V.A., et al.: Scaling computational fluid dynamics: in situ visualization of nekrs using sensei. In: Proceedings of the SC'23 Workshops of the International Conference on High Performance Computing, Network, Storage, and Analysis, pp. 862–867 (2023)
22. Mazen, F., Givord, L., Gueunet, C.: Catalyst-adios2: in transit analysis for numerical simulations using catalyst 2 api. In: Bienz, A., Weiland, M., Baboulin, M., Kruse, C., (eds.) High Performance Computing, pp. 269–276. Springer, Cham (2023)
23. Mazen, F., Gombert, L., Givord, L., Gueunet, C.: In situ in transit hybrid analysis with catalyst-adios2. In: International Conference on High Performance Computing, pp. 482–489. Springer, Cham (2025)
24. Moreland, K., et al.: Examples of in transit visualization. In: Proceedings of the 2nd International Workshop on Petascale Data Analytics: Challenges and Opportunities, pp. 1–6. ACM (2011)
25. Pearson, J.E.: Complex patterns in a simple system. Science **261**(5118), 189–192 (1993)

26. Pugmire, D., Huang, J., Moreland, K., Klasky, S.: The need for pervasive in situ analysis and visualization (P-ISAV), pp. 306–316 (2023)
27. Pugmire, D., et al.: Visualization as a service for scientific data. In: Nichols, J., Verastegui, B., Maccabe, A.B., Hernandez, O., Parete-Koon, S., Ahearn, T. (eds.) SMC 2020. CCIS, vol. 1315, pp. 157–174. Springer, Cham (2020). https://doi.org/10.1007/978-3-030-63393-6_11
28. Pugmire, D., et al.: Visualization and analysis for near-real-time decision making in distributed workflows. In: Parallel and Distributed Processing Symposium Workshops, 2016 IEEE International, pp. 1007–1013. IEEE (2016)
29. Pugmire, D., et al.: Fides: a general purpose data model library for streaming data. In: Jagode, H., Anzt, H., Ltaief, H., Luszczek, P. (eds.) ISC High Performance 2021. LNCS, vol. 12761, pp. 495–507. Springer, Cham (2021). https://doi.org/10.1007/978-3-030-90539-2_34
30. Rau, T., Gralka, P., Fernandes, O., Reina, G., Frey, S., Ertl, T.: The impact of work distribution on in situ visualization: a case study. In: Proceedings of the Workshop on In Situ Infrastructures for Enabling Extreme-Scale Analysis and Visualization, pp. 17–22 (2019)
31. Whitlock, B., Favre, J., Meredith, J.: Parallel in situ coupling of simulation with a fully featured visualization system. In: In Proceedings of the 11th Eurographics Conference on Parallel Graphics and Visualization, pp. 101–109 (2011)
32. Wu, Q., Insley, J.A., Mateevitsi, V.A., Rizzi, S., Papka, M.E., Ma, K.L.: Distributed neural representation for reactive in situ visualization. IEEE Trans. Vis. Comput. Graph. (2024)

Issues and Challenges of Deploying in-Situ Visualization for SPH Codes

Jean M. Favre[✉] and Jean-Guillaume Piccinali

Swiss National Supercomputing Center, Via Trevano 131, 6900 Lugano, Switzerland
{jean.favre,jgp}@cscs.ch
https://www.cscs.ch

Abstract. In this work, we present our test and development strategies to instrument two SPH codes with in situ visualization and analysis. We discuss the multiple requirements of such applications, and the lessons learned while interfacing the simulation codes with three in situ libraries (VTK-m, ParaView Catalyst and Ascent). We discuss the compromises made to adopt solutions scaling beyond the 55-billion particle simulation sets and comment on memory consumption and performance for these tightly coupled solutions.

Keywords: SPH · in-situ Visualization

1 Introduction

Exascale computing is now a reality due to massive scaling of computing cores available in the top HPC environments [1]. As of November 2024, three supercomputing systems are listed above the exa-scale limit. Yet, as noted already by many authors, the increase in disk bandwidth in the last decade has not at all followed the trend seen by the increase of raw compute power. Thus, our ability to save numerical results to storage is greatly diminished, often at much reduced spatial and temporal resolution to avoid throttling numerical simulations. Given these hard facts, the field of in situ scientific visualization has been very active, proposing multiple scenarios and libraries to couple the execution of simulation codes with analysis and visualization methods. A comprehensive taxonomy of this landscape is offered in [2]. In this work, we focus on a subclass of solutions that provide a tight coupling of the visualization code in the same compute and memory space as the simulation. The interplay of simulation and visualization is achieved on-the-node, favoring whenever possible a direct access to data via shallow copies. With simulation and in situ visualization sharing the same physical compute resources, execution is split time-wise, alternating simulation steps and visualization and analysis with the current timestep.

1.1 Custom-Made Visualization Code or API-Driven Data Access

Following the terminology in [2], we chose to test three different but related libraries.

VTK-M: Providing a Bespoke Interface. VTK-m supports the fine-grained concurrency commonly found in modern devices (CPU and GPU) [3]. It provides data analysis and feature extraction algorithms suitable for the most common cases of in situ visualization. With a custom interface to the simulation codes, we can access the data in the most efficient manner and at discrete-time samples, giving us the opportunity to test several visualization algorithms. However, the programming effort is non-trivial and cannot easily be reused across multiple applications. VTK-m is also limited to on-the-node parallelism, focusing on accelerated computing on GPU or multithreaded hardware.

VTK-m provides a lightweight rendering package. Its authors have deliberately not attempted to provide more than a basic renderer. It is a good fit for an in situ visualization scenario. Users wanting a fully featured rendering system are invited to use for example VTK, which is already integrated with VTK-m and has sophisticated rendering layers (e.g. with OptiX, Ospray, or ANARI).

Ascent or ParaView Catalyst: Sharing Data In Situ via a Data API. Providing an abstraction to describe simulation data in memory offers a lot more portability and flexibility. For this purpose, Ascent [4] and Catalyst [5] use the Conduit Mesh Blueprint as a set of hierarchical conventions to describe the simulation data [6]. Conduit is used for data coupling between packages in-core, serialization, and I/O tasks. Sharing or passing data between simulation codes and in situ libraries can be done with a very light-weight data API which can respect zero-copy data access in most cases. Matching the MPI-based parallelism which ParaView Catalyst provides natively, Ascent also provides hybrid parallelism via its VTK-h layer. One can consider that support for parallel visualization for host-resident data is quite complete, including image generation.

DummySPH, a Mini-App to Enable Flexible Testing. To test these different strategies and validate the output generated for multiple configuration setups, we created a mini-app which the readers can download and install for their own testing [7]. We also use DummySPH to generate in situ visualization tutorial exercises. It can generate in-memory particle datasets with different CMake and run-time flags, with the following varying characteristics:

- **in situ library:** None, VTK-m, ParaView Catalyst, Ascent
- **execution model:** serial vs. MPI-based parallelism
- **numerical precision:** float32 vs. float64
- **data layout:** AOS (interleaved data) vs. SOA (compact data arrays)
- **data location:** Host vs. Device-resident data

The particle datasets generated are then either passed to VTK-m via shared memory pointers or to Ascent or ParaView Catalyst via Conduit nodes.

2 Background

2.1 Smoothed Particle Hydrodynamics Codes

Smoothed Particle Hydrodynamics (SPH) codes are a family of simulation codes based on a mesh-less set of particles. Based on a purely Lagrangian technique, SPH particles are free to move with fluids or deforming solid structures. It has been successfully used for several decades to simulate free-surface flows, solid mechanics, multi-phase, fluid-structure interaction and astrophysics. For a non exhaustive list of SPH codes, see for example [8].

Independent of the physical models coded in the different applications, one fundamental difference between all SPH implementations is the method of storing the physical quantities of each particle in memory. Two approaches are found. The first method is to store each physical data item in separate data arrays, providing contiguous memory access per independent physical quantity, leading to the definition of a *structure-of-arrays* (SOA) data layout. Conversely, one might prefer to keep all physical quantities pertaining to an individual particle close together, in a so-called *array-of-structures* (AOS) layout. Table 1 gives a pseudo-code example of the two strategies. One can immediately see that each strategy has a huge impact on the performance and memory costs associated with read-/write operations to disk, or within the memory hierarchy (CPU and/or GPU) of a simulation.

Table 1. Typical SOA, and AOS data structures and allocation methods holding the particles' characteristics

structure-of-arrays (SOA) data	array-of-structs (AOS) data
	struct tipsySph {
std::vector<float> mass;	float mass;
std::vector<float> posx, posy, posz;	float positions[3];
std::vector<float> velx, vely, velz;	float velocities[3];
std::vector<float> density;	float density;
std::vector<float> temperature;	float temperature;
std::vector<float> phi;	float phi;
	}
	std::vector<tipsySph> scalarsAOS;

Interfacing an SPH code with an in situ library has the same challenge of providing I/O services. Sharing memory pointers to provide zero-copy access to data between the simulation codes and the in situ libraries is crucial to offer an optimized solution, in particular with simulation scenarios in a parallel, distributed and GPU-based environment. To address the needs of two SPH production codes running in our compute infrastructure [9], we tested multiple deployment strategies for in situ visualization services. Our first SPH application, called PKDGRAV3 [10], uses an AOS memory layout; our second application, called SPH-EXA [11], uses the SOA strategy. In our study, we found out that the different in situ visualization and analysis services are not always optimal.

2.2 Testing and Deployment Methods

Using DummySPH as a mini-app for rapid prototyping has been much more cost-conscious to let us test the support offered by the different libraries. DummySPH uses a compile-time configurable data layout which mimics our two SPH applications. In fact, in addition to creating some trivial time-varying data, it can also initialize its arrays with data dumps created by PKDGRAV3 (using the Tipsy file format), or SPH-EXA (using the H5part format).

Since the field is in constant evolution, we chose to work with the most recent development versions of the software (VTK-m v2.3, Catalyst from the ParaView master (tag dec34694), and Ascent's develop branch (tag 8d139a4).

Going through the effort of implementing the VTK-m support, or tracing the execution path of the Ascent support for particle data has also shown that a list of indices for connectivity should be explicitly provided, even though defining the Conduit node data with mesh[``topologies/mesh/type''] = ``points'' should make the list implicit. In fact, Ascent's VTK-h Data Adapter method PointsImplicitBlueprintToVTKmDataSet() cannot do better at the moment than calling the GetExplicitCoordinateSystem<float64>() method. There is no free lunch! This latter observation has also revealed an implementation detail of great interest when counting the memory consumption of in-situ operation. In the presence of a Conduit node representing coordinates as interleaved arrays, Ascent's VTK-h Data adaptor skips over the fact, and reconstructs an array of compact coordinates with a call to a make_ArrayHandleSOA(). This is in contrast to our custom VTK-m interface, which is able to pass coordinates in a true zero-copy fashion via a make_ArrayHandleCompositeVector() call. Using the VTK-m API directly offers the benefit of providing the most efficient solution thanks to an interface that is crafted to match the data layout and characteristics, but it comes as a high programming cost. It speaks well for trying to favor a higher level interface as provided with Ascent or ParaView Catalyst. VTK-m's rendering layer provides mappers for glyphs, point, surface and volumes. The MapperPoint class does a great job for pseudo-colored particle datasets, and works both for AOS and SOA data layouts (see Fig. 1).

3 Visualization Methods of Interest

Data Reduction by Geometric Clip or Scalar Thresholding. An absolute *must-have* in any visualization toolkits, is the need to extract sub-regions of space (e.g. orthonormal slices), or threshold-based selection. Figure 1 below shows two clipping regions centered around the $Y = 0$ and $Z = 0$ axis, and iso-volumes of density between a given min and max values.

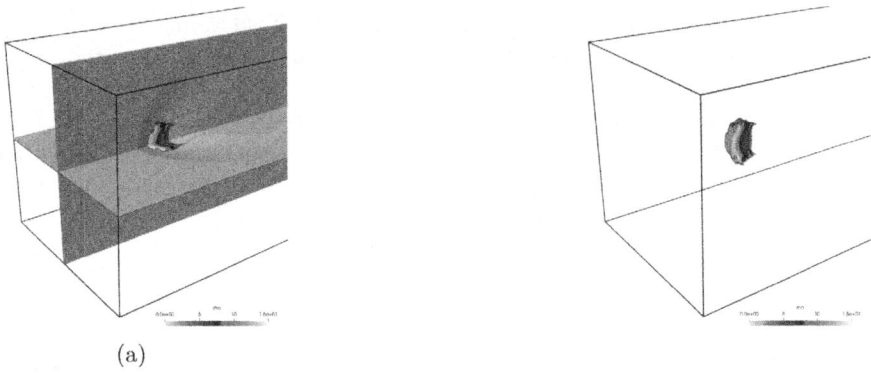

Fig. 1. Clipping planes (left) and scalar-thresholded particles (right)

Histogram-Based Sub-Sampling. While there exist different ways of subsampling a set of particles, the most common offset-based subsampling, while trivial to implement, does not give very good results with 3D datasets where feature of interests can be lost, or hidden by non interesting data. Of particular interest in our toolbox, we wish to use data-driven adaptive sampling (see Fig. 2). In a recent publication, the authors present an algorithm that preserves rare field values and outliers [12]. It has been implemented in VTK-m and in Ascent.

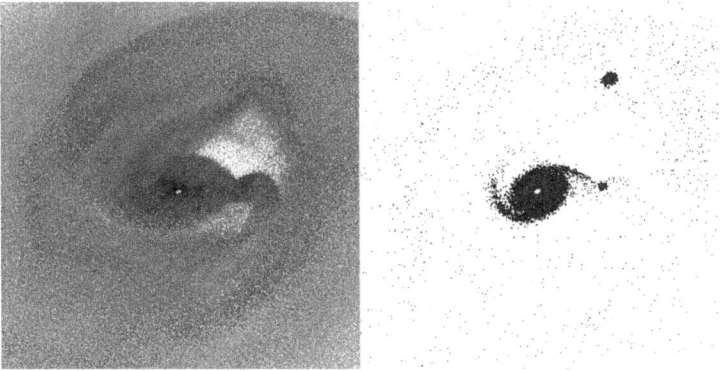

Fig. 2. Illustration of Histogram-based sampling. Original dataset (left), and sampled data at 5% (right)

3.1 Data Binning

Popularized with the VisIt interactive application [13], Data Binning/Derived Data Field capability is a method akin to a multi-dimensional histogram. Data binning can operate on either spatial coordinates or field values, and the data aggregation into bins uses a set of reduction functions (sum, average, min, max, variance, etc.) depending on the type of analysis desired (see Fig. 3a).

A common approach in many scientific fields is to compute Probability Density Function (PDF) of one variable against another one. These data aggregation and analysis methods provide 2D plotting functionalities of paramount importance for publication in scientific journals. (see Fig. 3b)

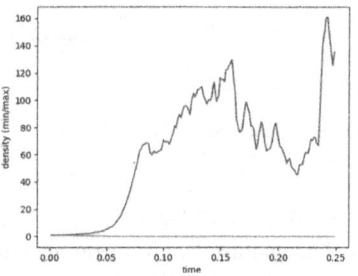 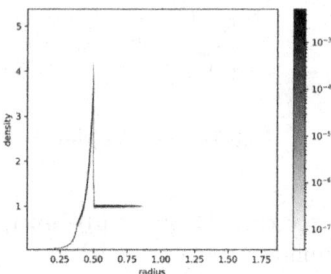

Fig. 3. Minimum and maximum of Density over time (left) and PDF (Density vs. Radius) (right)

4 Support for PKDGRAV3 (AOS Data Layout)

VTK-M: Our implementation of data clipping is straighforward, using VTK-m's `entity_extraction::ThresholdPoints`. Similarly, our tests of VTK-m's `density_estimate::Histogram` on serial runs of DummySPH initialized with PKDGRAV3 output has been very positive. On a recent laptop (Intel CPU 20 OpenMP threads), we can process datasets in the range of 100 million particles, doing extraction at a 10% ratio in under 2 s of wall time. Scaling up to beyond 300 million particles, we observe crashes (by the libgomp.so library) although we are not limited by CPU memory. While implementations of standard data-reductions techniques are available, we did not find a direct implementation of PDFs in VTK-m, as a predefined operator.

ParaView Catalyst: Validating a ParaView Catalyst support for PKD-GRAV3, we exposed some implementation limitations. In fact, while execution does not complain with error messages, we find that the outputs generated are not usable. Grid coordinates and scalar field values are out-of-order. Uncertain about the checks performed by the *conduit_blueprint_verify()* method and to debug potential problems in our implementation, we used Catalyst's ability to serialize Conduit nodes with its light-weight *stub* implementation which lets us inspect the data dumped to disk (see the Debugging and Catalyst Replay section of [5]). We then went the extra mile to convert the Catalyst JSON outputs to

Conduit Blueprint HDF5 files, which are fully supported by VisIt [13]. The following Python code does the required conversion.

```
import numpy as np
import conduit.relay as relay
mesh = conduit.Node()
relay.io.load(mesh, "execute_invc4_params.conduit_bin.1.0")
data = mesh["catalyst/channels/grid"]
relay.io.blueprint.write_mesh(data, "blueprint","hdf5")
```
Listing 1.1. Conduit Blueprint example

This gives us the guarantee that the Conduit nodes we pass to the ParaView Catalyst implementation contain valid data. We conclude that the interpretation of the Conduit nodes content for AOS data is not properly handled by ParaView Catalyst. This has also been reported by other users [15]. We intend to work with the ParaView Catalyst development team to document and address this issue, which constitutes a blocker at this time. Note that we also developed a ParaView Python plugin to read Conduit Blueprint HDF5 files. This is still a prototype, but can be shared with readers upon request. Finally, we also note that we were unable to find an implementation of PDFs in ParaView.

Ascent: Switching our testing to Ascent, we again verify the validity of the Conduit nodes created with the following YAML extract code.

```
action: add_extracts
  extracts:
    e1:
      params:
        path: "/dev/shm/foobar"
        protocol: "blueprint/mesh/hdf5"
        fields:
          - vx
          - vy
          - vz
          - rho
      type: relay
```
Listing 1.2. Yaml extract example

While the execution of the histogram-based adaptive sampling algorithm works well in our custom VTK-m interface, we do not succeed to make it work with Ascent. Ascent reports errors related to not finding appropriate cast for array in CastAndCall VTK-m operations.

Confirming that the Conduit meta-data passed to Ascent are correct, we successfully executed other Ascent actions (e.g., "clip", "threshold"), producing valid data, which unfortunately cannot be rendered on the fly with Ascent. This issue has also been reported by other users [16]. We are thus constrained to write data to disk, for a classic post-mortem rendering.

We met another challenge with the PKDGRAV3 simulation data where binning does not work, complaining that a DataType float64 is expected, while our data is float32. Switching back to our mini-app simulator DummySPH, we are indeed able to compute PDFs with 8-byte floating point interleaved data. We summarize in Table 2 our tests with the AOS data layout.

Table 2. Level of support for different in situ services with AOS data layout

PKDGRAV3 (AOS data)	VTK-m	Ascent	ParaView Catalyst
in situ rendering	Yes, but parallel image compositing is not provided.	Failing, although saving the data as Conduit Blueprint HDF5 works, validating our Conduit meta-data.	Using the same Conduit meta-data, there are un-explained offsets making the visualization un-usable.
Geometric clipping, thresholding by scalar	Yes	Yes	n.a (see comment above)
composing vector with individual array components	Yes	Action "composite_vector" failing.	n.a (see comment above)
Data binning	did not try	Failing with float32 data types, OK with float64	n.a (see comment above)
Histogram-based sampling	Yes	Failing	n.a (see comment above)

5 Support for SPH-EXA (SOA Data Layout)

Switching to the more common SOA data layout, we found that support was generally better. Our three in-situ visualization back-ends (VTK-m, Ascent and ParaView Catalyst) are able to handle most of our requirements. The use of ParaView Catalyst is a lot more robust, and offers also the interactive ParaView client as an easy path to prototype visualization pipelines, since it is able to write out the Python code to be reused at run-time. Here again we summarize our findings in Table 3.

Yet, our highest priority is to support GPU-based simulations. ParaView Catalyst is currently missing production-ready support for it. Data access with device-resident data is still at a proof-of-concept status [14]. A couple of Merge Request were proposed in Jan. 2024 but are still open. They deal with the management of external memory pointers by the vtkConduitSource data adaptor and

Issues and Challenges of Deploying in-Situ Visualization for SPH Codes   103

Table 3. Level of support for different in situ services with SOA data layout

SPH-EXA (SOA data)	VTK-m	Ascent	ParaView Catalyst
in situ rendering	Yes, but parallel image compositing is not provided.	Yes, supporting also parallel Image Compositing.	Yes, supporting also parallel Image Compositing.
Geometric clipping, thresholding by scalar	Yes	Yes	Yes. Few VTK-m filters are available, at the cost of a VTK to VTK-m dataset conversion.
composing vector with individual array components	Yes	Yes.	Yes, at the price of a severe warning: vtkSOA-DataArrayTemplate "This is very expensive for non-array-of-structs subclasses"
Data binning	did not try	Failing with float32 data types, OK with float64	not available
Histogram-based sampling	Yes	Yes	not available

a refining of the vtkCellArray implementation. Since we give priority to running GPU-based codes on our ALPS infrastructure, we prioritized our deployment efforts for in situ visualization with Ascent. After the initial check for functionality ran with our CPU-based version of the SPH-EXA code, we conclude our testing with results obtained with the GPU code.

6 Benchmarks

6.1 Production Runs with SPH-EXA

Our scale production test is an astrophysical problem that has been extensively studied in recent years [17]. The wind-cloud collision scenario involves several pieces of physics such as strong shocks and mixing due to the KelvinâĂŞHelmholtz instability, in a two-phase medium with a large density contrast. In this test, a spherical cloud of cold gas, initially at rest, is swept by a low-density stream of gas (the wind) moving supersonically. We have conducted an analysis of execution time and memory consumption by Ascent on CSCS Alps GPU system [9].

Figure 4 reports the execution times (in seconds) for the wind-cloud test with three configurations: running SPH-EXA-cuda for 10 steps without writing any HDF5 or PNG file (used as reference time), running the same simulation for 10 steps and saving the Temperature field $(-s10 - w5 - fx, y, z, temp)$ in HDF5 output files every 5 steps (2 output files per simulation), and running the same simulation for 10 steps and creating ortho-normal slices of the Temperature field as PNG files using the Ascent library every 5 steps (2 output files per simulation).

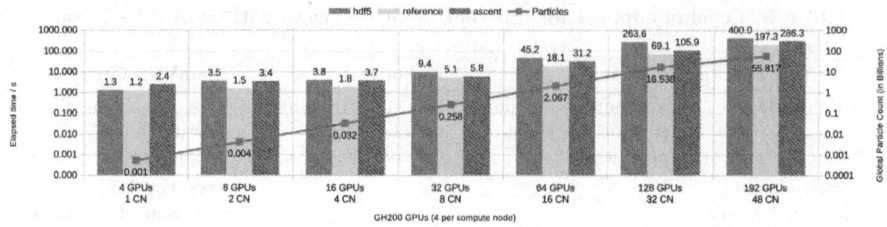

Fig. 4. Elapsed time of the Wind-Cloud test with HDF5 I/O and Ascent in situ

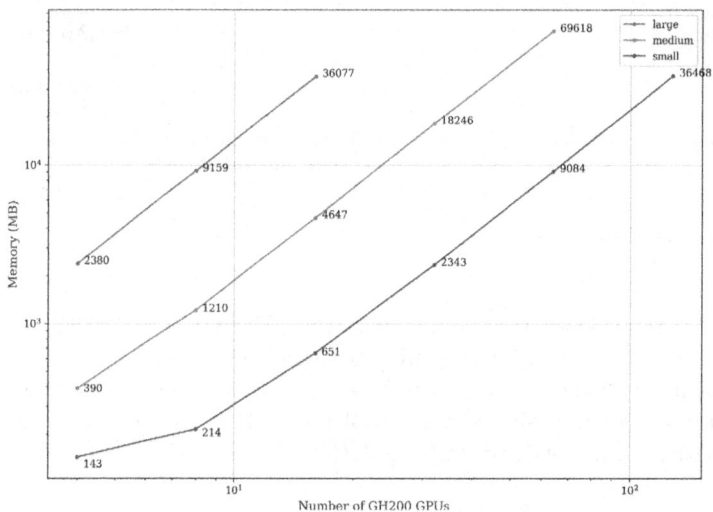

Fig. 5. Impact of Ascent on Managed GH200 GPU Memory Usage (weak scaling)

The tests were conducted across 1, 2, 4, 8, 16, 32 and 48 compute nodes (each equipped with 4 GH200 GPUs) with an increasing number of global particles starting with 0.5 million global particles on 1 compute node and reaching a total number of 55.8 billion global particles on 48 compute nodes. The overhead associated with using Ascent for image generation is negligible, especially when dealing with a large number of particles. For instance, it takes only 286.3 s on 192 GPUs to generate 2 PNG files, while it takes 400 s to generate the HDF5 output file. An illustration of the output generated with Ascent is shown in Fig. 1 and the Ascent yaml file used for the simulation is listed in Listing 1.3.

We report in Fig. 5 the additional memory used (in MB per GPU) for the same wind-cloud Temperature field clipping test, using three simulation sizes: small (same as above), medium (8 times more global particles than the small size) and large (8 times more global particles than the medium size) tested across 1, 2, 4, 8, 16 and 32 compute nodes (each equipped with 4 GH200 GPUs per node). As memory usage increases with the number of global particles and compute nodes, Ascent is able to scale up to 16.5 billion particles, requiring as much as 69 GB of managed extra memory per GPU, approaching the memory limit of the GPU device.

Figure 6 reports the evolution of memory usage (in GB) of a single GPU while Ascent creates slices of the Temperature field as PNG files every 5 steps. Ascent leverages the NVIDIA Hopper GPU unified memory model to transparently access both CPU-resident and GPU-resident memory. As the usage of managed memory increases to accommodate visualization tasks, the memory is released once these tasks are completed. This seems to be an efficient memory management approach as it enables the simulation code to leverage the full capacity of the available device memory, ensuring optimal resource utilization for both computation and visualization.

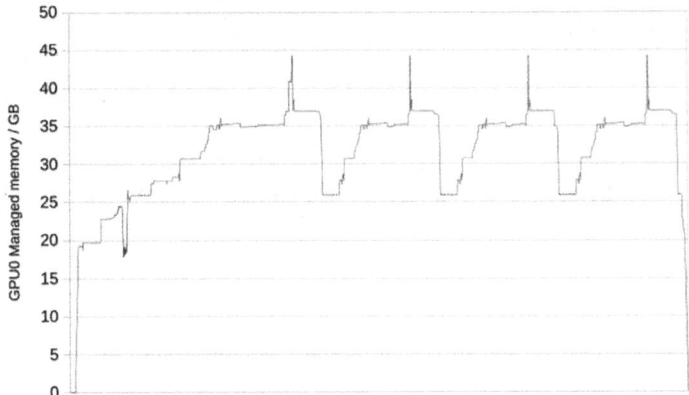

Fig. 6. Impact of Ascent on Managed and Device GH200 GPU Memory Usage

6.2 Future Deployment Strategy

At this moment in time, Ascent offers the simplest path to run in situ visualization at scale with GPU-enabled codes. To encourage its use during production runs, we need to provide scientists with more pre-baked YAML scripts describing the Ascent visualization pipelines for common operations, and to validate the support for GPU-resident data. In fact, we have found that unit testing in Ascent for the cuda backend is the strict minimum. We plan to provide more unit tests for the DummySPH mini-app to cover and summarize the different tests we have validated. The VTK-m library, discontinued in its current form, is being replaced by Viskores (https://github.com/Viskores/viskores) and is actively being pushed into VTK (Commit b7f5567c). We will thus migrate to it as soon as it is stable.

Disclosure of Interests. The authors have no competing interests to declare that are relevant to the content of this article.

7 Appendix

7.1 Ortho-Normal Slices of Particles with Ascent

```
action: "add_pipelines"
pipelines:
  pl_threshold_clip_z:                    pl_threshold_clip_y:
    f1:                                     f1:
      type: "threshold"                       type: "threshold"
      params:                                 params:
        field: "z"                              field: "y"
        min_value: 0.12425                      min_value: 0.12425
        max_value: 0.12575                      max_value: 0.12575

action: "add_scenes"
scenes:
  s1:
    plots:
      p0:                                     p1:
        type: "pseudocolor"                     type: "pseudocolor"
        pipeline: "pl_threshold_clip_z"         pipeline: "pl_threshold_clip_y"
        field: "Temperature"                    field: "Temperature"
        min_value: 4.5e-9                       min_value: 4.5e-9
        max_value: 2.9e-7                       max_value: 2.9e-7
        color_table:                            color_table:
          name: "viridis"                         name: "viridis"
        points:                                   annotation: "false"
          radius: 0.001                         points:
                                                  radius: 0.001
    renders:
      r1:
        image_prefix: "datasets/Temperature.%05d"
```

Listing 1.3. Wind-cloud test clipping with Ascent

References

1. The TOP500 most powerful commercially available computer systems. https://www.top500.org
2. Childs, H., et al.: A terminology for in situ visualization and analysis systems. Int. J. High Perform. Comput. Appl. **34**(6), 676–691 (2020). https://doi.org/10.1177/1094342020935991
3. Moreland, K., et al.: VTK-m: accelerating the visualization toolkit for massively threaded architectures. IEEE Comput. Graphics Appl. **36**(3), 48–58 (2016). https://doi.org/10.1109/MCG.2016.48
4. Larsen, M., Brugger, E., Childs, H., Harrison, C.: Ascent: a flyweight in situ library for exascale simulations. In: In Situ Visualization For Computational Science. Mathematics and Visualization book series from Springer, Cham (2022)
5. Catalyst documentation. https://catalyst-in-situ.readthedocs.io/en/latest/index.html
6. Conduit Mesh Blueprint. https://tinyurl.com/bd85mjmj
7. "DummySPH". https://github.com/jfavre/DummySPH
8. SPH Codes. https://www.spheric-sph.org/sph-projects-and-codes
9. ALPS, a Research Infrastructure for science with extreme-scale data and computing needs. https://www.cscs.ch/computers/alps
10. Potter D., Stadel J., Teyssier R.: PKDGRAV3: beyond trillion particle cosmological simulations for the next era of galaxy surveys. https://doi.org/10.48550/arXiv.1609.08621
11. Cavelan, A., Cabezon, R., Grabarczyk, M., Ciorba F.: A smoothed particle hydrodynamics mini-app for exascale. In: PASC 2020: Proceedings of the Platform for Advanced Scientific Computing Conference, pp. 1–11. https://doi.org/10.1145/3394277.3401855

12. Biswas A., Dutta S., Pulido J., Ahrens, J.: In situ data-driven adaptive sampling for large-scale simulation data summarization. In: ISAV 2018, Proceedings of the Workshop on In Situ Infrastructures for Enabling Extreme-Scale Analysis and Visualization, pp. 13–18 (2018). https://doi.org/10.1145/3281464.328146
13. Childs, H., et al.: VisIt: an end-user tool for visualizing and analyzing very large data. In: High Performance Visualization–Enabling Extreme-Scale Scientific Insight, pp. 357-372 (2012). https://doi.org/10.1201/b12985
14. Catalyst2: GPU resident workflows. https://www.kitware.com/catalyst2-gpu-resident-workflows/
15. Catalyst issue #19. https://gitlab.kitware.com/paraview/catalyst/-/issues/19
16. Ascent issue #1468. https://github.com/Alpine-DAV/ascent/issues/1468
17. García-Senz D., Cabezón R., Jose A. Escartín J.A.: Conservative, density-based smoothed particle hydrodynamics with improved partition of the unity and better estimation of gradients, in Astronomy & Astrophysics. https://doi.org/10.1051/0004-6361/202141877

5th International Workshop on Computational Aspects of Deep Learning (CADL)

CADL 2025 Preface

Objectives/Topics

The 5th Workshop on Computational Aspects of Deep Learning (CADL) at ISC 2025 addresses critical challenges at the intersection of Deep Learning and High-Performance Computing. As AI continues to revolutionize various fields, the demand for computational resources has skyrocketed, particularly with the advent of transformer-based models. This shift has transformed AI into a computational science where massive models are trained on large-scale infrastructures, accelerating scientific discovery and improving results in numerous applications. CADL aims to bring together AI and HPC experts to discuss challenges, exchange ideas, and identify solutions that advance the field in a computationally efficient and energy-saving manner. The workshop focuses on exploring innovative solutions for cost-effective AI, democratizing access to state-of-the-art AI research and development, and fostering effective convergence of AI and HPC.

Key topics include:

- Applied AI in resource-constrained environments
- Novel architectures for data-intensive scenarios
- Energy-efficient training frameworks and algorithms
- Distributed and efficient reinforcement learning
- Large-scale pre-training techniques for real-world applications
- HPC and massively parallel architectures for AI
- Model compression techniques
- Hardware accelerators
- Efficient integration of vision and language models

Workshop Organization

Giuseppe Fiameni	NVIDIA, Italy
Iuri Frosio	NVIDIA, Italy
Lorenzo Baraldi	University of Modena and Reggio Emilia, Italy
Marcel Krüger	CINECA, Italy
Dario Garcia-Gasulla	Barcelona Supercomputing Center, Spain

Direct Feedback Alignment for Recurrent Neural Networks

Sara Folchini[1], Andrea Cossu[2(✉)], Andrea Ceni[2], Vincenzo Lomonaco[2], Davide Bacciu[2], and Claudio Gallicchio[2]

[1] International School of Advanced Studies (SISSA), Trieste, Italy
[2] University of Pisa, Pisa, Italy
andrea.cossu@unipi.it

Abstract. Time series and sequential data are widespread in many real-world environments. However, implementing physical and adaptive dynamical systems remains a challenge. Direct Feedback Alignment (DFA) is a learning algorithm for neural networks that overcomes some of the limits of backpropagation and can be implemented in neuromorphic hardware (e.g., photonic accelerators). Until now, DFA has been investigated mainly for feedforward architectures. We adapt DFA for both "vanilla" and gated recurrent networks. Unlike backpropagation, the update rule of our DFA can be applied in parallel across time steps, thus removing the sequential propagation of errors. We benchmark DFA on 4 datasets for sequence classification tasks. Although backpropagation still achieves a better predictive accuracy, our DFA shows promising results, especially for environments and physical systems where backpropagation is unavailable.

Keywords: Biologically plausible algorithms · Recurrent Neural Networks · Time Series Classification

1 Introduction

Backpropagation [24] is the long-standing algorithm for credit assignment in artificial neural networks. Its efficient implementation in digital computers has supported the surge of machine and deep learning techniques as one of the key advancements in the field of artificial intelligence [14]. However, with a few exceptions [27], the adoption of backpropagation-based learning systems is still mainly limited to digital computers and simulations. It is well known that backpropagation cannot be easily implemented and deployed in physical systems [16,19]. For example, due to issues like the weight transport where the synaptic weights of the backward circuit need to be constantly synchronized with the synaptic weights of the forward circuit [1,15].

Physical deployment of backpropagation is even more challenging in Recurrent Neural Networks (RNNs) [7], where credit assignment must be performed across time. The most used algorithm to date is BackPropagation Through Time (BPTT) [26], which extends backpropagation to recurrent architectures.

Over time, several backpropagation-free algorithms have been proposed (see Sect. 2 for a non-exhaustive overview), some of them with the explicit objective of being compatible with the implementation in physical systems or on unconventional hardware (e.g., neuromorphic, optical).

We focus on Direct Feedback Alignment (DFA) [21], a backpropagation-free algorithm for credit assignment that removes the weight transport issue and also allows parallel computation of the weight update. DFA has already been implemented in nonconventional hardware, especially photonic [8]. The photonic co-processor introduced in [13] scales DFA to trillion-parameter random projections.

We briefly review DFA for feedforward networks in Sect. 3. We propose an extension of DFA tailored to recurrent neural networks. Our approach is able to compute the update of the recurrent parameters in parallel over all the time steps of the input sequence, thus removing one of the major drawbacks of BPTT. In fact, BPTT sends the error signal computed at the end of the input sequence *back in time* to compute the network parameters update. Instead, the update computed by our version of DFA is local at each time step, as it does not rely on the update computed for other time steps. Due to the weight sharing present in RNNs, the local update is eventually aggregated at the end of the input sequence to compute the final update. The aggregation operation includes information from all the time steps, thus enabling learning of temporal dependencies.

We develop DFA for both a "Vanilla" RNN and a Gated Recurrent Unit (GRU) network [2,3]. We benchmark both architectures against BPTT on four time-series classification datasets and we find that DFA can achieve non-trivial performances in all of the tested datasets but cannot always attain a performance comparable to BPTT. In general, DFA shows strength in datasets with more than 2 classes and in datasets with a limited number of training samples, although BPTT still surpasses its performance. We show that the GRU architecture trained with DFA is able to learn longer temporal correlations than a "Vanilla" RNN.

2 Related Works

Although backpropagation is the most popular learning algorithm [24], several alternatives exist: from target propagation [18] to signal propagation [11] to ad-hoc algorithms for adaptive dynamical systems like equilibrium propagation [12,25].

We start by considering the Feedback Alignment algorithm (FA), proposed in [15] as a biologically plausible gradient-free learning rule for deep learning. The key idea of FA is to project the errors from the last layer of a deep feedforward architecture to the first layer via random projections between consecutive layers. This simple algorithm has shown competitive performance on the MNIST classification task against the commonly used backpropagation algorithm.

Pushing the FA idea to the extreme, [21] proposed DFA, where the error is randomly projected back to each layer with a direct shortcut connection.

Practical applications of DFA to RNNs have been explored in [20]. The authors performed physical deep learning with an optoelectronic recurrent neural network. However, in their pioneering work, they do not explore the DFA algorithm in the context of fully trainable RNNs, since they only provide a proof-of-concept using a reservoir computing model with untrained reservoir connections [17]. In this paper, we investigate the potential of DFA on fully-trainable RNNs.

[9] investigated a DFA-inspired algorithm for RNNs. However, their version of DFA is restricted and cannot be applied to any recurrent or gated architecture, like our approach. First, they implement an upper triangular modular structure. Second, they use random projections as powers of the same matrix, which effectively resembles an FA algorithm applied to RNNs rather than a DFA algorithm for RNNs. Overall, our approach stems directly from DFA and closely follows its assumptions without requiring any customization, thus remaining more general and targeting any recurrent model.

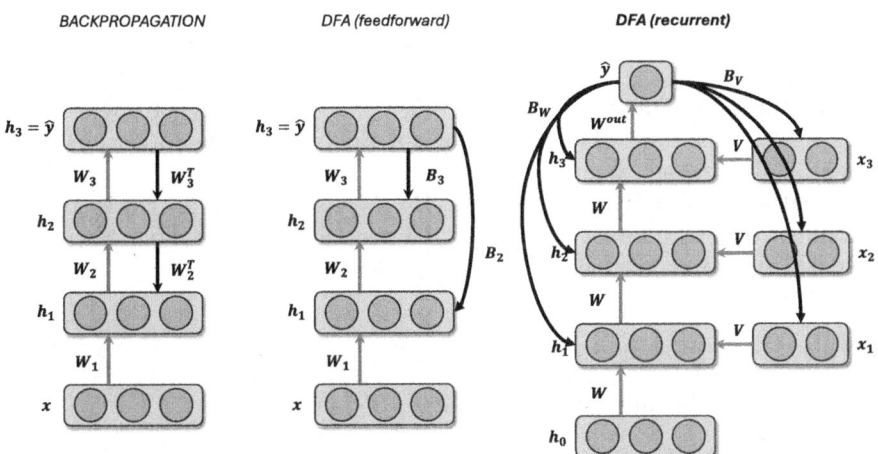

Fig. 1. We propose DFA applied to recurrent networks (right). The error is projected through random matrices B_W and B_V. We also show backpropagation (left) and DFA (middle) applied to feedforward networks. Grey arrows denote the forward phase, black arrows denote the update phase. Note that in the RNN, the matrices W and V are shared across time steps (layers), while in feedforward networks each layer has a different matrix. Also, the RNN receives a different input x_t at each time step (here, the input sequence has 3 time steps), while the feedforward network only receives one input x.

3 DFA for Feedforward Networks

We first introduce DFA for feedforward neural networks (Fig. 1, middle), to prepare the notation and set the stage for its extension to recurrent neural networks. Consider a fully-connected, feedforward neural network with an arbitrary number of L layers (including input and output layers), input size I, hidden size H and output size O. Each layer l computes its preactivation a_l through a linear projection.

$$a_l = W_l u_l + b_l, \tag{1}$$

where $W_l \in \mathbb{R}^{H \times I}, \mathbb{R}^{H \times H}, \mathbb{R}^{O \times H}$ is the weight matrix for the input, hidden and output layers, respectively. Similarly, $b_l \in \mathbb{R}^H$, $l < L$ is the bias vector for the input and hidden layer and $b_L \in \mathbb{R}^O$ is the bias vector for the output layer. The input u_l corresponds to the data sample x for the input layer ($u_1 \in \mathbb{R}^I$) and to the output of the previous layer for all other layers ($u_l \in \mathbb{R}^H, l > 1$). The preactivation at each layer is passed through an element-wise nonlinear function σ (e.g., hyperbolic tangent) to generate the layer's activation h_l. The output of the network $\hat{y}$ is read out from the last layer.

$$h_l = \sigma(a_l) \tag{2}$$
$$\hat{y} = h_L \tag{3}$$

For each input example x, the loss function $J(\hat{y}, y)$ (e.g., cross-entropy or mean-squared error) measures the error between the output and the target prediction y associated with the example x.

Updating the last layer's parameters W_L, b_L via gradient descent is straightforward as there is a direct dependency between $\hat{y}$ and the loss function J. For the cross-entropy or the mean-squared error loss.

$$e = \frac{\partial J}{\partial a_L} = \hat{y} - y \tag{4}$$

Therefore, e can be directly used to update W_L and b_L.

$$W_L \leftarrow W_L - \eta e h_{L-1}^T \tag{5}$$
$$b_L \leftarrow b_L - \eta e, \tag{6}$$

where η is the learning rate. The update of the last layer's parameters is the same for both backpropagation and DFA.

For the hidden layers, backpropagation computes the update by propagating the error signal e sequentially to lower layers (Fig. 1, left). For any hidden layer, we have

$$W_l \leftarrow W_l - \eta(\ (W_{l+1}^T \delta a_{l+1} \odot \sigma'(a_l))\ u_l^T), \tag{7}$$

where $\odot$ denotes element-wise multiplication and δa_{l+1} is the error signal coming from *the layer above*. This last term requires the error to be computed sequentially one layer at a time. This dependency prevents updating all layers in parallel.

DFA removes this limitation by projecting the error e *directly* to all layers, through a random matrix $B \in \mathbb{R}^{H \times O}$. B can also be different for each layer. Crucially, the matrix B is kept fixed and only governs the weights update. It does not take any part in the forward phase.

DFA updates each hidden layer via

$$W_l \leftarrow W_l - \eta(\ (Be \odot \sigma'(a_l))\ u_l^T), \qquad (8)$$
$$b_l \leftarrow b_l - \eta(\ Be \odot \sigma'(a_l)\ ). \qquad (9)$$

These updates can be applied to each layer independently, thus enabling embarrassingly parallel computation for all layers.

DFA also removes the weight alignment issue, as the update circuit uses random connections instead of connections that always need to be synchronized with the forward circuit, like in backpropagation.

4 DFA for Recurrent Networks

We develop a version of DFA that is compatible with RNNs for sequential data processing (Fig. 1, right). We closely follow the DFA approach devised for feedforward networks and we extend it to the recurrent case. Each example x is a sequence of T input vectors:

$$x = (x_1, \ldots, x_T), \qquad (10)$$

where $x_i \in \mathbb{R}^I$. We consider the sequence classification task where each sequence x is associated with a target class y. The RNN keeps an internal hidden state $h \in \mathbb{R}^H$ which is updated at each time step. We first focus on the "Vanilla" RNN [7], whose state update of reads:

$$h_{t+1} = \sigma(Wh_t + Vx_{t+1} + b), \qquad (11)$$

where $V \in \mathbb{R}^{H \times I}$ is the input-to-hidden matrix and we call a_t (pre-activations at time t) the terms inside σ. In RNNs, the same layer is applied to all time steps (weight sharing). The output $\hat{y}$ of the RNN is computed from the hidden state:

$$\hat{y} = \sigma(W^{\text{out}} h_t + b^{\text{out}}), \qquad (12)$$

where $W^{\text{out}} \in \mathbb{R}^{O \times H}$ and $b^{\text{out}} \in \mathbb{R}^O$. The nonlinear function σ can be different from the one used in the hidden layers. For sequence classification tasks the output is computed at the end of the input sequence from h_L.

Due to the weight sharing, the forward pass of an RNN can be interpreted as the unrolling of the state update function over time. At each time step, the matrix W and V (and the bias as well) are used to compute the next hidden state, much like the matrix W_l is used to compute the layer's output in a feedforward network. The backpropagation algorithm applied to RNNs, called backpropagation through time (BPTT) updates the hidden-to-hidden weight W via

$$\nabla_W J(\hat{y}, y) = \frac{\partial J}{\partial \hat{y}} \sum_{t=1}^{T} \frac{\partial \hat{y}}{\partial h_t} \frac{\partial h_t}{\partial W} \tag{13}$$

The term $\frac{\partial \hat{y}}{\partial h_t}$ hides a dependency between hidden states $\prod_{j=1}^{t-1} \frac{\partial h_{j+1}}{\partial h_j}$ which is due to the sequential propagation of the error over the time steps.

Our DFA-based algorithm for RNN removes this propagation and updates W by computing the term $\frac{\partial J}{\partial \hat{y}} \sum_{t=1}^{T} \frac{\partial h_t}{\partial W}$. The error signal e is projected via a random matrix B, randomly initialized and kept fixed.

The equations for the update of W and V via DFA read:

$$W \leftarrow W - \eta \sum_{t=1}^{T} (\, Be \odot \sigma'(a_t) \,) \, h_{t-1}^T, \tag{14}$$

$$V \leftarrow V - \eta \sum_{t=1}^{T} (\, Be \odot \sigma'(a_t) \,) \, x_t^T \tag{15}$$

The bias is updated by omitting the outer product.

DFA for Gated Recurrent Networks. In addition to the development of DFA for "Vanilla" RNNs (Eq. 11), we also developed a version of DFA for gated recurrent networks, focusing in particular on the GRU network [2,3]. The state update (forward pass) for a GRU reads:

$$z_{t+1} = \text{sig}(W_z h_t + V_z x_{t+1} + b_z),$$
$$r_{t+1} = \text{sig}(W_r h_t + V_r x_{t+1} + b_r),$$
$$c_{t+1} = \tanh(W_c(h_t \odot r_{t+1}) + V_c x_{t+1} + b_c),$$
$$h_{t+1} = (1 - z_{t+1}) \odot c_{t+1} + z_{t+1} \odot h_t,$$

where *tanh* and *sig* are the hyperbolic tangent and sigmoid functions, respectively. Our DFA update for all parameters of the GRU is provided in Appendix A. The output $\hat{y}$ of the network is computed from the hidden state h_t as previously discussed.

5 Experiments

We implemented all our experiments in PyTorch [23]. Although DFA does not compute a true gradient, we filled the "grad" attribute of each weight tensor with the DFA update. This enabled us to use any PyTorch optimizer to apply the update. We used the Adam optimizer for all experiments.

We assessed the performance of DFA against BPTT on the aforementioned "Vanilla" RNN and GRU. We report the average test accuracy and standard

Table 1. Summary of datasets statistics and average test accuracy and standard deviation over 5 repetitions for all datasets and models.

	Strawberry	LIBRAS	ECG200	Row-MNIST
Input size	1	2	1	28
Number of classes	2	15	2	10
Sequence length	235	90	96	28
Dataset size	983	360	200	70000
DFA GRU	79.73 ± 1.23	67.50 ± 3.68	80.6 ± 2.25	72.49 ± 1.1
BPTT GRU	92.05 ± 2.54	80.83 ± 9.19	82.10 ± 1.14	99.23 ± 0.03
DFA RNN	67.84 ± 2.66	47.92 ± 3.3	78.2 ± 1.47	87.48 ± 0.74
BPTT RNN	79.08 ± 4.18	54.30 ± 18.32	83.30 ± 2.1	96.69 ± 0.24

deviation computed over 5 runs[1]. Table 1 reports a summary of the time series datasets statistics. We considered 4 different datasets:

1. *Libras*[2] [6] contains 15 classes associated with a different hand movement type. The hand movement is represented as a bi-dimensional curve performed by the hand in a given period of time;
2. *Row-MNIST* [5]: each image of the MNIST dataset is presented to the recurrent model one row at a time;
3. *ECG200* [22]: where each time series traces the electrical activity of a subject recorded during one heartbeat. The task is a binary classification prediction between a normal heartbeat and one highlighting a Myocardial Infarction;
4. *Strawberry* [10] consists in classifying food spectrographs, a task with applications in food safety and quality assurance. The classes are strawberry (authentic samples) and non-strawberry (adulterated strawberries and other fruits).

The datasets are divided into train, validation and test sets according to the proportions 60%-20%-20%. The hyperparameters have been selected based on a model selection with a grid search (see Appendix B for the details).

Table 1 reports the test accuracy achieved by all methods, alongside the specifics of the datasets. Overall, BPTT still outperforms DFA across most datasets. Specifically, BPTT outperforms DFA with GRU architectures except for the ECG200 dataset, in which both learning algorithms achieve a comparable performance.

With "Vanilla"RNN architectures, BPTT outperforms DFA except for the ECG200 and the Libras datasets, where the average test accuracy of DFA (Fig. 2 top-left panel, orange line) is higher than BPTT's one (red line) after the first 150 epochs. Moreover, in this dataset, DFA has the same learning slope of BPTT either with vanilla RNNs (for the first 150 epochs) or for GRUs (for the first 50 Epochs).

---

[1] We will publicly release the code upon paper acceptance.
[2] LIBRAS is the acronym of the Portuguese name"Lingua BRAsileira de Sinais", is the official Brazilian sign language.

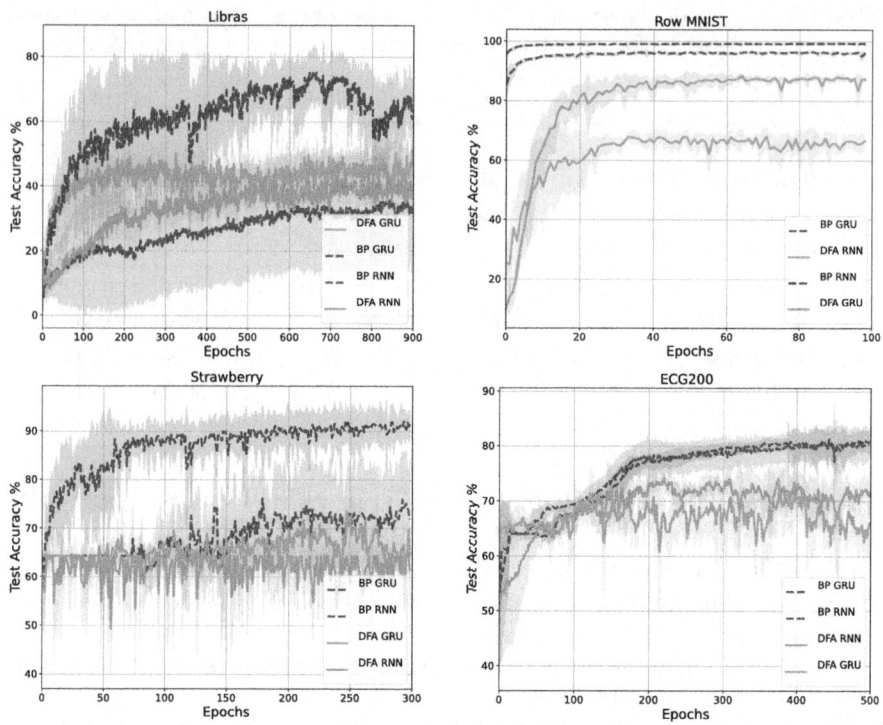

Fig. 2. Results on the Libras, Row-MNIST, Strawberry and ECG-200 datasets with a "Vanilla" RNN architecture (orange and red) and with a GRU (blue and cyan). The models are trained with DFA (lighter colors, full line) and BPTT (darker colors, dashed line). Error shades denote one standard deviation computed over 5 repetitions with different seeds. (Color figure online)

DFA seems to struggle with unbalanced datasets, like ECG200 and Strawberry. In the ECG dataset, which is the one with the smallest amount of data, the test accuracy of RNN with DFA is above the random performance of 12%. In the Strawberry dataset, the same model with DFA shows an accuracy which is above the random performance of only 5%. In the case of balanced datasets, RNNs trained with DFA are generally successful at learning temporal correlations.

Overall, while BPTT generally resulted in higher test accuracy, DFA demonstrated comparable performance particularly for ECG200 in both GRU and RNN models. This suggests that although DFA is less accurate overall, it may be a viable alternative in scenarios where strong parallelization combined with a physical implementation is a possibility.

6 Conclusion and Future Work

We proposed a learning algorithm for recurrent neural networks based on DFA [21]. Our DFA enables parallel updates across the time steps, thus removing the sequential update constraint of BPTT. The parallel update phase is particularly interesting for physical implementations of adaptive dynamical systems, as the signal needs not be propagated sequentially back in time. On digital computers, the parallel update allows speed-up when implemented on customized CUDA kernels or with low-level programming interfaces. Unfortunately, in native Python, the speed-up cannot be observed due to the GIL and the large overhead of process spawning. Starting from our publicly available code, future works can refine the implementation, perhaps by integrating the parallel DFA update within the C++ PyTorch API.

There are still other aspects that require further consideration. For example, the choice of the random feedback matrix is crucial, as it affects the trajectory of the parameters during training. Moreover, different matrix structures are amenable to different implementations in neuromorphic or unconventional hardware. [4] implemented DFA for feedforward architectures on neuromorphic hardware with a sparse feedback matrix, at minimal or no performance loss.

Our algorithm can also be easily extended to deal with time series forecasting tasks, where the prediction step is taken after each time step, instead of only at the end of the input sequence. Further benchmarking of our DFA in these settings is required to understand its effectiveness.

Acknowledgments. This work was supported by the EU-EIC project EMERGE (Grant number 101070918).

Disclosure of Interests. The authors have no competing interests to declare that are relevant to the content of this article.

A Appendix DFA for Gated Recurrent Unit Network

We provide the update rule of DFA for all the parameters of the GRU.

$$W_z \leftarrow W_z - \eta \sum_{t=1}^{T}(Be \odot h_{t-1} - Be \odot c_t) \odot (r_t \odot (1 - r_t))h_{t-1}^T,$$

$$V_z \leftarrow V_z - \eta \sum_{t=1}^{T}(Be \odot h_{t-1} - Be \odot c_t) \odot (r_t \odot (1 - r_t))x_t^T,$$

$$W_r \leftarrow W_r - \eta \sum_{t=1}^{T}(W_r(Be \odot (1 - z_t)) * (1 - c_t \odot c_t)h_{t-1}) \odot (r_t \odot (1 - r_t))h_{t-1}^T,$$

$$V_r \leftarrow V_r - \eta \sum_{t=1}^{T}(W_r(Be \odot (1 - z_t)) * (1 - c_t \odot c_t)h_{t-1}) \odot (r_t \odot (1 - r_t))x_t^T,$$

$$W_c \leftarrow W_c - \eta \sum_{t=1}^{T}(W_r(Be \odot (1-z_t)))*(1-c_t \odot c_t)(r_t \odot h_{t-1})^T,$$

$$V_c \leftarrow V_c - \eta \sum_{t=1}^{T}(W_r(Be \odot (1-z_t)))*(1-c_t \odot c_t)x_t^T.$$

As in the "Vanilla" RNN, all the bias vectors are updated by omitting the outer product in the corresponding W or V update. The matrix B can also be a different random matrix for each parameter.

B Appendix Hyperparameter Search

Hyperparameters are selected based on the best performances on a validation set among these possible values: hsize$\in$ [50,512], lr$\in$ [0.0005, 0.001,0.005,0.01], bs$\in$ [10,100,256], clip=2. The values selected by the model selection are:

1. Libras: Learning rate = 0.0005 (except for BPTT GRU: learning rate= 0.01), Hidden size = 512, Batch size = 10, Epochs= 900.
2. Strawberry: Learning rate = 0.0005 (except for BPTT GRU: learning rate= 0.005), Hidden size = 50 (except for RNN DFA: hidden size= 512), Batch size = 10 (except for RNN DFA: bs=100 and for RNN BPTT: bs= 256), Epochs= 300.
3. ECG200: [Learning rate = 0.0005 (Except for DFA GRU, lr=0.01), Hidden size = 50, Batch size = 256, Epochs = 500.
4. ROW-MNIST: [Learning rate=0.0005 (Except for RNN DFA and GRU DFA, lr=0.005), Hidden size = 512 (Except for RNN BPTT, hs= 50), Batch size = 100 (Except for RNN BPTT, bs = 10)].

In Fig. 2 we show the learning curves of the test accuracy for the datasets ECG200 and Strawberry. The fact that the lines start at a different level is because the train, test, and validation sets are divided randomly so the test set can be particularly imbalanced. In these cases, the learning lines of DFA are not visibly growing. We believe that the restricted range of the hyperparameters prevented us to find solutions of DFA that work at best for these datasets.

References

1. Akrout, M., Wilson, C., Humphreys, P., Lillicrap, T., Tweed, D.B.: Deep learning without weight transport. In: Wallach, H., Larochelle, H., Beygelzimer, A., dAlché-Buc, F., Fox, E., Garnett, R. (eds.) Advances in Neural Information Processing Systems, vol. 32, pp. 976–984. Curran Associates, Inc. (2019)
2. Cho, K., van Merriënboer, B., Bahdanau, D., Bengio, Y.: On the properties of neural machine translation: encoder–decoder approaches. In: Proceedings of SSST-8, Eighth Workshop on Syntax, Semantics and Structure in Statistical Translation, pp. 103–111. Association for Computational Linguistics, Doha, Qatar (2014). https://doi.org/10.3115/v1/W14-4012

3. Chung, J., Gulcehre, C., Cho, K., Bengio, Y.: Empirical Evaluation of Gated Recurrent Neural Networks on Sequence Modeling (2014)
4. Crafton, B., Parihar, A., Gebhardt, E., Raychowdhury, A.: Direct feedback alignment with sparse connections for local learning. Front. Neurosci. **13** (2019). https://doi.org/10.3389/fnins.2019.00525
5. Deng, L.: The MNIST database of handwritten digit images for machine learning research. IEEE Signal Process. Mag. **29**(6), 141–142 (2012)
6. Dias Daniel, P.S., Helton, B.: Libras Movement. UCI Machine Learning Repository (2009). https://doi.org/10.24432/C5GC82
7. Elman, J.L.: Finding structure in time. Cogn. Sci. **14**(2), 179–211 (1990). https://doi.org/10.1207/s15516709cog1402_1
8. Filipovich, M.J., et al.: Silicon photonic architecture for training deep neural networks with direct feedback alignment. Optica **9**(12), 1323–1332 (2022). https://doi.org/10.1364/OPTICA.475493
9. Han, D., Park, G., Ryu, J., Yoo, H.: Extension of Direct Feedback Alignment to Convolutional and Recurrent Neural Network for Bio-plausible Deep Learning (2020). https://doi.org/10.48550/arXiv.2006.12830
10. K. Kemsley, A.B.: Strawberry. https://timeseriesclassification.com/description.php?Dataset=Strawberry
11. Kohan, A., Rietman, E.A., Siegelmann, H.T.: Signal Propagation: A Framework for Learning and Inference in a Forward Pass (2022). https://doi.org/10.48550/arXiv.2204.01723
12. Laborieux, A., Ernoult, M., Scellier, B., Bengio, Y., Grollier, J., Querlioz, D.: Scaling equilibrium propagation to deep ConvNets by drastically reducing its gradient estimator bias. Front. Neurosci. **15** (2021)
13. Launay, J., et al.: Hardware Beyond Backpropagation: A Photonic Co-Processor for Direct Feedback Alignment (2020). https://doi.org/10.48550/arXiv.2012.06373
14. LeCun, Y., Bengio, Y., Hinton, G.: Deep learning. Nature **521**(7553), 436–444 (2015). https://doi.org/10.1038/nature14539
15. Lillicrap, T.P., Cownden, D., Tweed, D.B., Akerman, C.J.: Random synaptic feedback weights support error backpropagation for deep learning. Nat. Commun. **7**(1), 1–10 (2016). https://doi.org/10.1038/ncomms13276
16. Lillicrap, T.P., Santoro, A., Marris, L., Akerman, C.J., Hinton, G.: Backpropagation and the brain. Nat. Rev. Neurosci. 1–12 (2020). https://doi.org/10.1038/s41583-020-0277-3
17. Lukoševičius, M., Jaeger, H.: Reservoir computing approaches to recurrent neural network training. Comput. Sci. Rev. **3**(3), 127–149 (2009). https://doi.org/10.1016/j.cosrev.2009.03.005
18. Manchev, N., Spratling, M.: Target propagation in recurrent neural networks. J. Mach. Learn. Res. **21**(1), 7:250–7:282 (2020)
19. Momeni, A., Rahmani, B., Malléjac, M., del Hougne, P., Fleury, R.: Backpropagation-free training of deep physical neural networks. Science **382**(6676), 1297–1303 (2023). https://doi.org/10.1126/science.adi8474
20. Nakajima, M., Inoue, K., Tanaka, K., Kuniyoshi, Y., Hashimoto, T., Nakajima, K.: Physical deep learning with biologically inspired training method: gradient-free approach for physical hardware. Nat. Commun. **13**(1), 7847 (2022). https://doi.org/10.1038/s41467-022-35216-2
21. Nøkland, A.: Direct feedback alignment provides learning in deep neural networks. In: Lee, D.D., Sugiyama, M., Luxburg, U.V., Guyon, I., Garnett, R. (eds.) Advances in Neural Information Processing Systems, vol. 29, pp. 1037–1045. Curran Associates, Inc. (2016)

22. Olszewski, R.T., Maxion, R., Siewiorek, D.: Generalized feature extraction for structural pattern recognition in time-series data. Ph.D. thesis, USA (2001)
23. Paszke, A., et al.: PyTorch: an imperative style, high-performance deep learning library. In: Advances in Neural Information Processing Systems, vol. 32. Curran Associates, Inc. (2019)
24. Rumelhart, D.E., Hinton, G.E., Williams, R.J.: Learning representations by back-propagating errors. Nature **323**(6088), 533–536 (1986). https://doi.org/10.1038/323533a0
25. Scellier, B., Bengio, Y.: Equilibrium propagation: bridging the gap between energy-based models and backpropagation. Front. Comput. Neurosci. **11** (2017)
26. Werbos, P.: Backpropagation through time: what it does and how to do it. Proc. IEEE **78**(10), 1550–1560 (1990). https://doi.org/10.1109/5.58337
27. Wright, L.G., et al.: Deep physical neural networks trained with backpropagation. Nature **601**(7894), 549–555 (2022). https://doi.org/10.1038/s41586-021-04223-6

Assessing Tenstorrent's RISC-V MatMul Acceleration Capabilities

Hiari Pizzini Cavagna[1(✉)], Daniele Cesarini[2], and Andrea Bartolini[1]

[1] University of Bologna, 40136 Bologna, BO, Italy
{hiari.pizzinicavagna,a.bartolini}@unibo.it
[2] Cineca, 40033 Casalecchio di Reno, BO, Italy
d.cesarini@cineca.it

Abstract. The increasing demand for generative AI as Large Language Models (LLMs) services has driven the need for specialized hardware architectures that optimize computational efficiency and energy consumption. This paper evaluates the performance of the Tenstorrent Grayskull e75 RISC-V accelerator for basic linear algebra kernels at reduced numerical precision, a fundamental operation in LLM computations. We present a detailed characterization of Grayskull's execution model, grid size, matrix dimensions, data formats, and numerical precision impact on computational efficiency. Furthermore, we compare Grayskull's performance against state-of-the-art architectures with tensor acceleration, including Intel Sapphire Rapids processors and two NVIDIA GPUs (V100 and A100). Whilst NVIDIA GPUs dominate raw performance, Grayskull demonstrates a competitive trade-off between power consumption and computational throughput, reaching a peak of 1.55 TFLOPs/Watt with BF16.

Keywords: RISC-V · Tenstorrent Grayskull · Matrix Multiplication · Hardware Acceleration · Energy Efficiency

1 Introduction

Large Language Models, based on Transformer architecture [8], achieve state-of-the-art (SoA) results in various NLP tasks. Their ability to generalize a multitude of tasks is related with their size, allowing them to achieve excellent results even for tasks for which they have not been directly trained. Alongside with the growing demand for LLMs services, there has been an increasing need for architectures that allow for efficient use in terms of both performance and energy consumption. With billions—or even hundreds of billions—of parameters, models like GPT-4 demand substantial memory and computational resources, making efficient deployment a significant challenge.

From a computational perspective, a significant part of the workload in Transformer, and Deep Neural Network in general, consists of matrix-matrix multiplication (MatMul) operations. Thus, the efficiency of these operations that depends on the underlying hardware architecture and the specific data movement strategies employed, can greatly influence the overall performance.

In the literature, various architectures are used for LLMs execution, ranging from general-purpose devices such as CPUs and GPUs to more specialized accelerators as FPGA-based devices. Whilst GPUs currently dominate the market, emerging architectures are being explored to further enhance computational performance and reduce energy consumption. Some examples of new solutions are given by Sambanova [5], Groq [1], Cerebras [3] and Tenstorrent [7]. In particular, Tenstorrent is producing RISC-V based accelerators designed specifically to accelerate AI workloads. They product lineup covers a broad spectrum of needs, ranging from lightweight workloads to large-scale, compute-intensive applications. Their architecture is inspired by the idea of looking at AI models as graphs, developing an architecture that capitalizes on this structure by organizing the components of the graph into a grid of processors. This arrangement allows data to flow easily among various operations, maximizing the overlap between computation and communication, leading to a promising solution that warrants further exploration.

In this manuscript, we propose: (i) A characterization of the Tenstorrent Grayskull e75 accelerator in performing MatMul kernel under different configurations, both in terms of performance and power consumption, discussing the execution model and showing the obtained results. (ii) With respect of the execution model our characterization shows that there is a significant performance difference between the first execution of a computational kernel and subsequent executions. Our evaluation shows that in the first run the execution time is dominated by the matrix tiling and the matrix multiplication kernels compilation, accounting for the 31% and 66% of the total time, respectively. In contrast, subsequent runs are primarily dominated by data transfer times (62%). (iii) Considering only the kernel execution time, we characterized how processor grid size, matrix dimensions, data format and numerical fidelity impact the computational efficiency. Our results highlight substantial differences in achievable performance based on different configurations. (iv) A comparison with other SoA architectures, namely a Intel Sapphire Processor, a NVIDIA V100 GPU and a NVIDIA A100 GPU, showing the remarkable efficiency of Tenstorrent accelerator.

2 Background

Tenstorrent develops a family of accelerators, based upon the same architecture. Among them, the Grayskull e75 is the smallest card in the lineup. Its architecture consists of a grid of 96 Tensix cores, each designed to separate communication components from computational ones, enhancing efficiency. Fabricated using 12nm process, the card features eight LPDDR4 memory channels (DRAM) positioned at the top and at the bottom of the processors grid, providing a total capacity of 8 GB and a bandwidth of 102.4 GB/sec. Operating at 1 GHz, it delivers a peak performance of 55 TFLOPs for floating-point 16. Whilst the Grayskull e75 has reduced peak performance, these are scaled up in the Wormhole family where bigger grid of Tensix Cores are interconnected at board and system level.

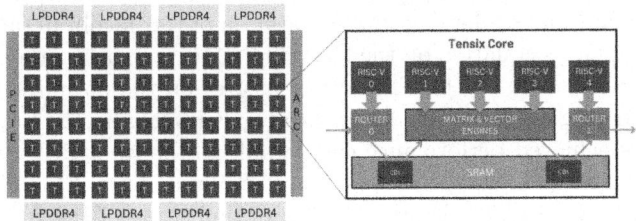

Fig. 1. A schema of the Grayskull's grid architecture and of the Tensix Core.

In details, each Tensix Core consists of five programmable *"baby"* RISC-V cores, one local SRAM memory of 1 MB (also referred as L1 memory), a SIMD Matrix & Vector engine and the Network on Chip (NoC) routers, as shown in Fig. 1. The first and the last cores (RISC-V 0 and RISC-V 4) execute Data Movement kernels, managing the asynchronous reads and writes across the other cores' SRAMs, the external DRAM banks and the local SRAM. The remaining three cores are interfacing with the Matrix & Vector engine, executing the Compute kernels. More specifically, the three Compute cores serve distinct roles: the first one unpacks the data, the second performs the computational kernels and the third handles data packing. The cores within the Tensix Core communicate using Circular Buffers (CB) in the SRAM, as shown in the figure, storing data from external memories and intermediate results.

Tenstorrent's Grayskull supports a broad range of Data Formats. Along with standard floating point formats, it supports Brain Floating Point (BF) and Block Floating Point (BFP). BFP allows the storage of blocks of 16 elements, by grouping them within a block under a shared common exponent, reducing memory footprint and improving performance. The BFP format is supported for 4, 8 and 16-bit configurations.

Additionally, it supports four levels of Math Fidelity, which determine the computing precision by specifying the number of bits which are used for the computing operation. These levels ranges from the lower fidelity, Low Fidelity, which consumes only the most significant bits (MSB) of the mantissas of both operands, to the highest, High Fidelity 4, which consumes all the bits of both operands. The two intermediate levels, High Fidelity 2 and 3, respectively consume the MSB of the first input and the LSB of the second one, and vice-versa. Higher fidelity levels require more bits for computation, leading to an increased number of cycles per operation, resulting in lower FLOPs.

3 Related Works

Whilst several works have focused on characterizing the performance of SoA CPU and GPU architectures, only a few have analyzed the efficiency of Tenstorrent architecture and compared it with current SoA technologies for tensor algebra acceleration.

In [2], the authors explore an implementation of the Jacobi iterative method for solving Laplace's equation on the Grayskull e150, comparing the results with an Intel Xeon Platinum CPU. Their work focuses on the optimization, exploring and comparing optimal data access strategies leveraging the low-level C++ kernels. They achieved performance comparable to the Intel CPU, whilst using around five times less energy, despite the CPU running in FP32 whereas the Grayskull in BF16. In [6] it is presented an optimization of the Attention layer using a fused kernel, achieving a significant speedup by leveraging the SRAM cores' memory. Additionally, Tenstorrent published a report[1] in its documentation, showcasing the absolute performance of the MatMul kernel on their device Wormhole.

Despite these initial characterizations, there is a lack of a comparative analysis of simple dense tensor algebra kernel with SoA architectures featuring tensorial acceleration. In this manuscript, we provide an analysis of the MatMul kernel running on the Tenstorrent Grayskull accelerator, benchmarking its performance and comparing its efficiency against other SoA devices in terms of both performance and energy efficiency.

4 Methodology

In this section, we describe the Tenstorrent software stack and the software abstraction of the Tensix Cores, showing some code examples.

4.1 TTNN

The TTNN Python library is a Tenstorrent's open-source library, built upon the TT-Metal software stack. It provides an API similar to PyTorch, implementing many PyTorch operations in a functional style. Under the hood, TTNN leverages C++ kernels to execute operations whilst exposing a user-friendly API. The execution model of TTNN consists of five steps:

1. Initialization of the program:
   - Buffers are allocated in the L1 (SRAM) memory of each core to facilitate data synchronization.
   - The program is compiled, generating the RISC-V binary code.
   - The compiled program and runtime configurations (e.g., memory addresses) are loaded into L1 memory.
2. Creation of the DRAM buffers for data storage.
3. Loading of the data from the host to the device's DRAM.
4. Program execution.
5. The results are stored back to the DRAM.

---

[1] Available in Tenstorrent's GitHub repository.

4.2 Software Abstraction

Compared to PyTorch, TTNN requires users to manage Tenstorrent's memory and computation configuration. To do so, it provides control over how the data is stored across the underlying hardware, allowing users to specify the destination memory (DRAM or L1) and the tensor memory layout.

Tensor Layout. Tensors are stored in the memory space as 2D objects by flattening the outer dimensions. For example, a tensor with dimension $[1 \times 2 \times 4 \times 8]$ is stored as $[8 \times 8]$. At the lowest level, a memory block containing part of the tensor is called a page. There are two possible ways to map a tensor to its pages. In Row-Major layout, each row is assigned to a separate page, storing the tensor row by row from top to bottom. Alternatively, the tensor can be tiled, meaning it is stored in fixed-size blocks, the default Tenstorrent tile size is 32×32. To be used for a MatMul, the tensors must be in Tile layout.

Memory Layout. The tensor's pages can be stored in memory using two mechanisms: Interleaved or Sharded. In the Interleaved configuration, the tensor is divided into multiple pages, which are then distributed across different memory banks in a round-robin fashion. This is the default memory storage used for both the DRAM and L1 memory. Conversely, the Sharded memory configuration divides the tensor into shards and distributes them across the L1 cores' memories according to a specified mapping. This approach allows users to define a specific data distribution across the processing grid, ensuring that each core has local access to the data in its L1 memory. It is possible to define the sharding strategy (in height, width or per blocks) and orientation, which determine the order with the shards are placed on the grid.

Code Example. In Listing 1.1 is an example of how to allocate a matrix onto the device, setting its layout, the storage strategy and the format. Using this method, it is also possible to use more advanced memory strategies, as the sharded layout, showed in Listing 1.2, which could be passed to the `from_torch()` method to be applied to the input.

```
import torch
import ttnn
device = ttnn.open_device(device_id=0)
in0 = torch.randn((512,512))
in0_t = ttnn.from_torch(
    in0,
    device=device,
    tile=ttnn.Tile((32,32)),
    layout=ttnn.TILE_LAYOUT,
    memory_config=ttnn.DRAM_MEMORY_CONFIG,
    dtype=ttnn.bfloat16 )
```
Listing 1.1. Input offloading

```
memory_config=ttnn.create_sharded_memory_config(
    (1, 1, 512, 512),
    core_grid=ttnn.CoreGrid(y=8, x=8),
    strategy=ttnn.ShardStrategy.BLOCK,
    orientation=ttnn.ShardOrientation.ROW_MAJOR,)
```
Listing 1.2. Memory configuration definition

In Listing 1.3 is the example of a simple MatMul kernel execution, with the Math Fidelity configuration. It is possible to execute more advanced kernels by passing to the argument `program_config` a kernel configuration.

```
output= ttnn.matmul(
    in0_t,
    in1_t,
    dtype=ttnn.bfloat16,
    memory_config=ttnn.DRAM_MEMORY_CONFIG,
    compute_kernel_config=ttnn.GrayskullComputeKernelConfig(
        math_fidelity=ttnn.MathFidelity.HiFi4),
    #program_config=...)
```

Listing 1.3. MatMul kernel execution

5 Experimental Results

In this section, we present the characterization results for the efficiency, energy consumption and performance of the Tenstorrent Grayskull when executing the matrix-multiplication kernel. We compared these results against SoA "general-purpose" computing systems optimized for matrix multiplication and tensor linear algebra, including two NVIDIA GPUs and an Intel Xeon Platinum 8480+ processor from the Sapphire Rapids server lineup. The tests have been conducted on the Grayskull e75, which has a peak performance of 55 TFLOPs (BF16). The Grayskull e75 is Tenstorrent's most affordable accelerator, designed for edge computing. In Tenstorrent's lineup, other accelerators are specifically designed for large-scale computing, such as the Wormhole card, which offers a peak performance of 131 TFLOPs (BF16) and can be clustered to build high-performance computing clusters.

5.1 Experimental Setup

The Grayskull e75 is connected via PCIe 4.0 x16 to an Intel Core i7 Coffee Lake host running Ubuntu 20.04.

To characterize the Tenstorrent accelerator, various tests have been conducted to explore the matrix multiplication execution under different conditions. We performed the following characterizations:

– **Offload and execution**: Analysis of the Tenstorrent execution model, consisting of the comparison between the first execution, which requires the computational kernels to be compiled, against the subsequent executions.
– **Performance of the MatMul kernel**: Evaluation of the performance under different configurations, including different Data Formats, Math Fidelity and grid cores selection.
– **Optimized MatMul kernel**: Assessment of the performance improvement of an optimized MatMul implementation, leveraging the cores L1 memory and a more sophisticated kernel.
– **Energy efficiency**: Measurement and comparison of power consumption relative to performance.

The power consumption is measured using pynvml Python module for GPUs, and TT-SMI for Grayskull, a Tenstorrent telemetry tool. Both tools report instantaneous power usage, which has been averaged over the duration of the computation.

5.2 Offload and Execution Model

The first execution of a kernel on the Tenstorrent Grayskull requires program compilation, which demands a substantial amount of time in comparison to the execution itself. Figure 2 reports the execution time of the first run and the subsequent ones. From the first run, it is possible to notice that the compilation times leads to significant overhead, which happens during the first execution of the kernels: indeed we can notice that the execution time is dominated by the *tiling* and the MatMul kernel *run*.

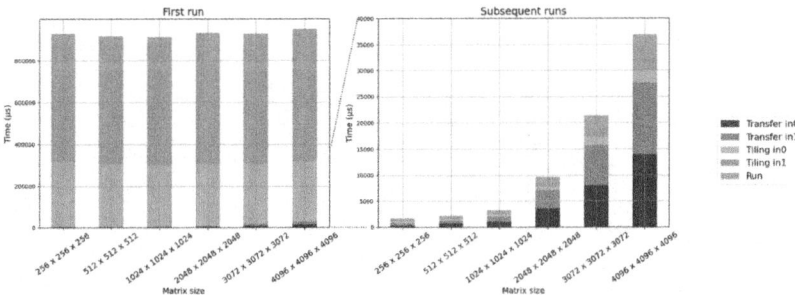

Fig. 2. First run and subsequent runs timings, for different matrix dimensions. The bars show the timings of the required steps: Transfer to the device of both the inputs, Tiling from Row Major to Tile layout, and the MatMul run.

After the first execution, the program does not need to be re-compiled, leading to a significant speedup in subsequent runs for both the *tiling* and the *MatMul operation* run. With respect to the tiling in the first-run plot, the tiling of the first input (in0) is three orders of magnitude greater than the tiling of the second matrix (in1), as the tiling of the second matrix will reuse the already compiled tiling program for the first one. By calculating the compilation time as the difference between the execution times of the first and subsequent executions, we obtain that the tiling kernel requires 296 ms to compile, regardless of the matrix dimensions. Whilst, the tiling execution time ranges from 351 µs for the 256×256 matrix to 2256 µs for a 4096×4096 matrix. On the other hand, the MatMul kernel requires 620 ms for compilation, with executing times ranging from 328 µs to 4783 µs for the same matrix sizes.

In subsequent runs, data transfer timings from the host to the device become the primary overhead, accounting, on average, for 62% of the timings. However, as the compilation, this overhead is only incurred when the matrices are located in the host. Once loaded onto the device, the operation can be executed without any transfer cost. Therefore, in the next experiments, we will consider only the execution time of the MatMul kernel, assuming data stationarity.

5.3 Performance of the MatMul Kernel

Table 1. The different configurations tested.

Configuration Name	Data Type	Math Fidelity
FP32 M4	floating point 32	High Fidelity 4
BF16 M4	brain floating point 16	High Fidelity 4
BF16 M2	brain floating point 16	High Fidelity 2
BFP8 M2	Block Float 8	High Fidelity 2
BFP8 M0	Block Float 8	Low Fidelity
BFP4 M0	Block Float 4	Low Fidelity

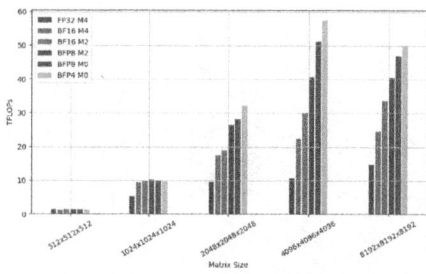

(a) TFLOPs obtained using different configurations, reported in Table 1

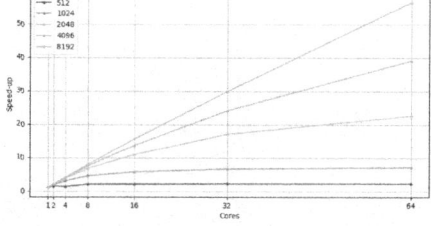

(b) The MatMul speedup with respect to the single core using different set of cores, using the configuration BF16 M4.

Fig. 3. Performance using different configurations and grid size.

We tested and compared a set of configurations reported in Table 1, combining different Data Type and Math Fidelity. In Fig. 3a, we compare the MatMul TFLOPs across different configurations. As expected, performance decreases with longer Data Format and higher Math Fidelity. This is particularly evident for larger matrices dimensions, where performance ranges from 14.72 TFLOPs using floating point 32 with the highest math fidelity to 49.78 TFLOPs using Block Floating Point 4 with Low Fidelity. Considering the theoretical peak of 55 TFLOPs using BF16, the current results remain far from optimal efficiency. In the following section, we will explore optimizations of the MatMul kernel leveraging the internal L1 SRAM and the vendor-optimized MatMul kernel.

Figure 3b shows the speedup of the MatMul kernel for different sets of cores, ranging from 1 core to 64 cores, corresponding respectively to the grid core selection $(0,0)$ and $(8,8)$.

As shown in the figure, smaller matrix sizes saturate the performance with few cores, whilst with larger matrix is possible to appreciate an almost linear speedup using a larger set of cores, reaching a speedup of 56x using 64 cores.

5.4 Optimized MatMul Kernel

In addition to the default MatMul configurations, Tenstorrent's software stack allows for further performance optimization by leveraging advanced kernels that utilize sharded memory configurations, distributing the matrix across multiple cores' local SRAM. In the previous experiments, both the input matrices were allocated in DRAM using the interleaved memory storage strategy. However, performances can be further improved by sharding one of the input matrices and distributing the shards onto the L1 memory of the computing cores. A kernel that takes advantage of this storing strategy and intermediate data reuse is the `MatmulMultiCoreReuseMultiCast` kernel, which achieves the highest performance.

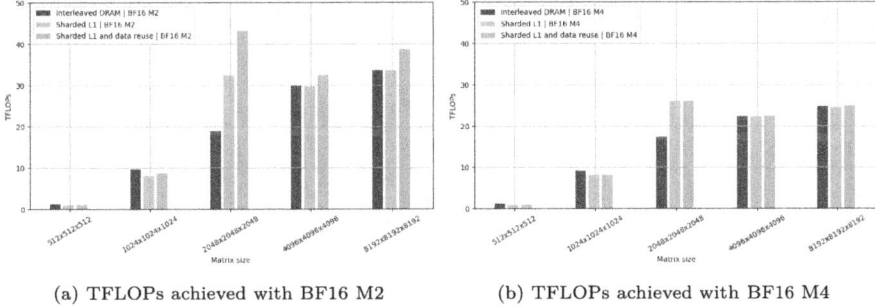

(a) TFLOPs achieved with BF16 M2   (b) TFLOPs achieved with BF16 M4

Fig. 4. Comparison of TFLOPs achieved using the default kernel configuration, a sharded memory configuration and the optimized kernel with BF16 with High Fidelity 2 and 4.

In Fig. 4a, is shown a comparison of the default MatMul kernel (with both inputs stored in the DRAM using the interleaved configuration, shown in blue), against configurations with one input sharded in L1 memory (yellow) and the sharded memory combined with the optimized kernel. For smaller matrix sizes, both the optimized kernel and the L1 memory configuration exhibit similar or slightly lower performance due to the sharded memory overhead. The advantages of the memory configuration are particularly evident for the BF16 M2 configuration and the 2048 × 2048 MatMul, as this is the largest matrix dimension of the matrices set which can be stored in the L1 cores' memory. From the Figure, we can see that for larger matrices sizes that exceed L1 memory capacity, the shared memory optimization is no more effective, but there is still a marginal improvement in performance for the optimized kernel.

From Fig. 4b, we can see that using the BF16 M4 configuration, the sharded memory optimization provides a similar performance improvement as observed in the M2 configuration. However, the optimized kernel does not appear particularly effective in this case.

Being the most performing one, we will use the optimized kernels for the following comparisons.

Performance Comparison. The obtained performance results have been compared against the PyTorch MatMul kernel execution on three SoA architectures: two GPUs, the NVIDIA A100 SXM4 40GB (w. peak BF16 throughput of 312 TFLOPs) and the NVIDIA V100S PCIe 32GB (w. peak FP16 throughput of 32 TFLOPs), and the Intel Sapphire Rapids server processor (w. peak BF16 throughput of 229 TFLOPs)[2]. The comparison is shown in Fig. 5a. The Sapphire Rapids Intel processor is equipped with the Intel Advanced Matrix Extensions (AMX) to optimize MatMul execution in BF16 and INT8 formats, which are leveraged by the PyTorch's MatMul kernel. The NVIDIA GPUs obtain remarkable performance thanks to the introduction of Tensor Cores, which accelerate the MatMul computation using BF16 and FP16 formats.

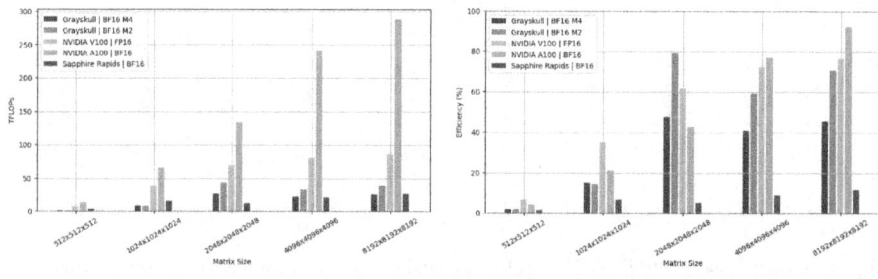

(a) TFLOPS achieved in the MatMul execution.   (b) Efficiency calculated against peak TFLOPs.

Fig. 5. A comparison of the performance between the devices.

As shown in the figure, the two NVIDIA GPUs dominate the performances for each matrix dimension, followed by the Grayskull accelerator and the Sapphire Rapids processor. As discussed earlier, the comparison serves as a reference to other So solutions, given that these devices are designed for different market segments. Nevertheless, Grayskull outperforms the Intel Sapphire Rapids processor in terms of raw performance.

In Fig. 5b, the efficiency is presented as the percentage of achieved TFLOPs relative to the theoretical peak TFLOPs. For smaller matrices, compute efficiency is limited but improves as matrix size increases. As shown, the Grayskull's efficiency is comparable to that of other devices, reaching a peak of 79.36% with 2048×2048 matrices, the largest matrix size in the test set that fits within the L1 core's memory and can benefit from sharded memory optimization.

---

[2] Calculated considering AMX's 1024 FLOPS/Cycle, 112 cores and 2.0 GHz frequency.

5.5 Energy Efficiency

Energy efficiency is a critical factor for today's systems' sustainability, scalability and operation costs. Memory accesses and arithmetic operations are the most relevant terms for power and energy consumption. While energy consumed for arithmetic operations can be lowered by advance technology nodes and reduced precision numerical formats, the memory access energy consumed strongly depends on the memory technology used and distance between the memory device and the compute unit [4]. The Tenstorrent Grayskull architecture, with its grid of Tensix Cores, stores data near the processing elements to achieve higher energy efficiency and reduce memory access time.

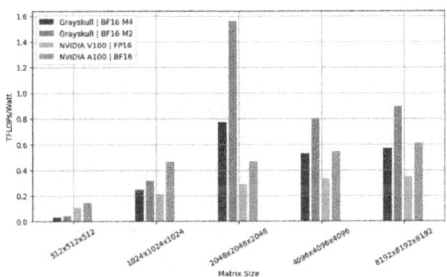

Fig. 6. Comparison of achieved TFLOPs per Watt.

Figure 6 shows the TFLOPs per Watt achieved by the examined devices. In line with the previous considerations, the Grayskull achieves the highest efficiency, reaching a peak of 1.56 TFLOPs/Watt (BF16, M2). As previously discussed, this peak efficiency is obtained with the largest matrix size among the ones tested, which fits the grid L1 memory. It is worth noting that beyond this specific scenario, Grayskull's TFLOPs/Watt ratio remains lower than that of NVIDIA A100 when using the highest Mathematical Fidelity but surpasses it when operating at reduced precision.

6 Conclusions

In this manuscript, we evaluated the performance and efficiency of the Tenstorrent Grayskull e75 RISC-V accelerator in executing matrix-matrix multiplication (MatMul), a fundamental operation in deep learning. Our analysis characterized its execution model, revealing significant differences between initial and subsequent runs due to compilation and data movement overheads. We examined the impact of processor grid size, matrix dimensions, data formats and numerical fidelity on computational performance. The results demonstrate that Grayskull achieves competitive performance in terms of TFLOPs per Watt relative to SoA architectures, such as two NVIDIA GPUs (A100 and V100) and an Intel Sapphire Rapids processor. Whilst GPUs deliver higher raw throughput, Grayskull provides a promising alternative with a strong balance between performance and energy efficiency.

Overall, this study highlights the potential of RISC-V-based accelerators in accelerating AI workloads and contributes to the ongoing discussion on efficient AI hardware design.

Acknowledgments. This activity has been supported by the HE EU Graph-Massivizer (g.a. 101093202), DECICE (g.a. 101092582), and DARE (g.a. 101143421) projects, as well as the Italian Research Center on High Performance Computing, Big Data, and Quantum Computing.

References

1. Abts, D., et al.: A software-defined tensor streaming multiprocessor for large-scale machine learning. In: Proceedings of the 49th Annual International Symposium on Computer Architecture, ISCA 2022, pp. 567–580. Association for Computing Machinery, New York (2022). https://doi.org/10.1145/3470496.3527405
2. Brown, N., Barton, R.: Accelerating stencils on the tenstorrent grayskull RISC-V accelerator (2024). https://arxiv.org/abs/2409.18835
3. Dey, N., et al.: Cerebras-GPT: open compute-optimal language models trained on the cerebras wafer-scale cluster (2023). https://arxiv.org/abs/2304.03208
4. Mutlu, O., Ghose, S., Gómez-Luna, J., Ausavarungnirun, R., Sadrosadati, M., Oliveira, G.F.: A modern primer on processing in memory (2025). https://arxiv.org/abs/2012.03112
5. Prabhakar, R., et al.: Sambanova sn40l: scaling the AI memory wall with dataflow and composition of experts. In: 2024 57th IEEE/ACM International Symposium on Microarchitecture (MICRO), pp. 1353–1366. IEEE (2024). https://doi.org/10.1109/micro61859.2024.00100
6. Thüning, M.: Attention in sram on tenstorrent grayskull (2024). https://arxiv.org/abs/2407.13885
7. Vasiljevic, J., et al.: Compute substrate for software 2.0. IEEE Micro **41**(2), 50–55 (2021). https://doi.org/10.1109/MM.2021.3061912
8. Vaswani, A., et al.: Attention is all you need (2023)

Automatically Parallelizing Batch Inference on Deep Neural Networks Using Fiats and Fortran 2023 "Do Concurrent"

Damian Rouson[1](✉), Zhe Bai[1], Dan Bonachea[1], Kareem Ergawy[2], Ethan Gutmann[3], Michael Klemm[2], Katherine Rasmussen[1], Brad Richardson[1], Sameer Shende[4], David Torres[5], and Yunhao Zhang[1]

[1] Lawrence Berkeley National Laboratory, Berkeley, CA 94720, USA
rouson@lbl.gov
[2] Advanced Micro Devices GmbH, 85622 Aschheim, Germany
[3] National Center for Atmospheric Research, Boulder, CO 80305, USA
[4] University of Oregon, Eugene, OR 97403, USA
[5] Northern New Mexico College, Española, NM 87532, USA

Abstract. This paper introduces novel programming strategies that leverage features of the Fortran 2023 standard of the International Standards Organization (ISO) to automatically parallelize computations on deep neural networks. The paper focuses on the interplay of object-oriented, parallel, and functional programming paradigms in the Fiats deep learning library. We demonstrate how several infrequently-used language features play a role in enabling efficient, parallel execution. Specifically, the ability to explicitly declare that a procedure is pure facilitates inference in the context of the language's loop-parallelism construct `do concurrent`. Also, explicitly prohibiting the overriding of a parent type's type-bound procedures eliminates the need for dynamic dispatch in performance-critical code. Finally, this paper uses batch inference calculations on a neural network surrogate for atmospheric aerosol dynamics to demonstrate that LLVM Flang compiler's automatic parallelization of `do concurrent` achieves roughly the same performance and scalability as achieved by OpenMP compiler directives. We also demonstrate that double-precision inference costs 37–72% longer runtime than default-real precision with most values in the range 57–60%.

Keywords: Atmospheric Sciences · Deep learning · Fortran

1 Introduction

1.1 Background and Motivation

Fortran programs occupy a significant fraction of the cycles on high-performance computing (HPC) platforms [1]. In recent years, the developers of many such applications have evaluated or adopted deep neural networks as surrogate models. At least two categories of solutions have emerged to satisfy the inference and training needs of Fortran applications: (1) application programming interfaces (APIs) that expose functionality provided by software packages written primarily in C++ and (2) packages with most or all of the deep learning algorithms written in Fortran. TorchFort [14] and FTorch [8], for example, offer Fortran APIs for the LibTorch C++ library that also serves as the back end for the PyTorch Python deep learning library, whereas Fortran-t-f-lib [7] provides a Fortran API for the Tensorflow machine-learning library's C interface. By contrast, neural-fortran [4,13], Athena [20] and Fiats [9] implement inference and training in native Fortran. This paper introduces Fiats, describes its approach to expressing deep learning algorithms, and presents initial results of parallel performance experiments for inference on the Perlmutter supercomputer at the National Energy Research Scientific Computing Center (NERSC).

Several considerations motivate exploring ways to express deep learning algorithms in Fortran. One motivation relates to generality. The aforementioned APIs with C++ back-ends rely on Fortran interoperability features with C, which provides standard-conforming and thus portable ways to call C from Fortran and vice versa. Doing so, however, requires that each procedure argument be of an interoperable type and kind.[1] By contrast, native Fortran deep learning libraries can support any type/kind combination supported by the chosen Fortran compiler.

Additional motivations for native Fortran libraries include interface size and complexity. In order to allow users to directly manipulate tensor data, the FTorch interface provides 30 procedures that convert C pointers to Fortran pointers for each combination of the fix supported ranks and five supported type/kind combinations. Another 30 functions do the reverse conversion. A native Fortran solution would obviate the need for these 60 procedures, thereby reducing the size of the interface. The resulting simplification of the interface also has robustness implications by avoiding the possibility that the metadata could mistakenly become inconsistent with the corresponding data.

A third motivation that distinguishes Fiats from the APIs for C++ libraries and from one of the Fortran native libraries relates to the choice of parallel programming models. Starting with the standard informally known as Fortran 2008, Fortran has provided explicit support for single-program, dultiple-data (SPMD) parallelism involving the execution of multiple images (instances) of a program, with a control model analogous to the execution of multiple ranks in the widely used Message Passing Interface (MPI). Dating back more than a decade, several groups have demonstrated that Fortran's SPMD features can produce executable programs that run in shared or distributed memory on as many as over 100,000 cores, exhibiting a performance and parallel efficiency comparable to or faster than MPI [5,16,18]. No explicit reference to parallelism appears in the

---

[1] Most Fortran data types are parameterized by "kind," a parameter that determines properties of the type. In the case of numeric types, for example, the kind value determines the range of representable values.

FTorch, Fortran-TF-Lib, or Athena interfaces, whereas the TorchFort interface uses MPI and only neural-fortran uses Fortran's SPMD features.

Also since Fortran 2008, the `do concurrent` construct exposes loop-level parallelism, which is of special relevance in deep learning because it can support parallel execution on graphics processing units (GPUs) in addition to central processing units (CPUs). Over the past five years, studies have demonstrated that automatically parallelized `do concurrent` constructs perform comparably to a variety of alternatives, including the OpenMP® API, the OpenACC® API, and the CUDA® model, in benchmarks and mini-apps [6,11] and with mixed results in full applications [3,19]. For a library targeting inclusion in user applications, a critical language constraint requires that any procedure invoked in a `do concurrent` iteration must be `pure`, an attribute inspired by the functional programming paradigm. A pure function produces the same result given the same arguments without side effects, including no mutation of the actual arguments. Functional purity plays a very important role when performing large batches of inferences, such as when a multiphysics simulation code performs inference at every time step on every grid point on a three-dimensional (3D) grid comprised of billions of grid points. An application can automatically parallelize across such a batch by invoking a deep learning inference procedure inside `do concurrent` only if the inference procedure is `pure`.

Among the competing library alternatives, only neural-fortran offers a `pure` forward pass (inference algorithm). However the library does so with various versions of a Fortran `subroutine`, which allows for mutating arguments declared with `intent(inout)` and which happens in the neural-fortran forward pass. The Fortran 2023 standard states that "Pure subroutines are included to allow subroutine calls from pure procedures in a safe way, [...]" suggesting the intention that `pure` subroutines serve supporting roles and thus implying that `pure` functions are primary. A `pure` function's arguments must have the `intent(in)` attribute, which eases the compiler analysis that underlies automatic parallelization. This subtlety motivates the Fiats choice of offering inference via `pure` functions, which differs from every alternative of which we are aware. Section 2 discusses two patterns that lead to `pure` functions producing immutable state, which aligns with functional programming practice.

1.2 Objectives

Developed by the Computer Languages and Systems Software (CLaSS) Group at Lawrence Berkeley National Laboratory and collaborators [10], Fiats provides a platform for exploring novel uses of advanced programming language features in deep learning. As such, CLaSS aims to push the envelope of what is possible with Fortran. For this reason, CLaSS also contributes to advancing compilers by isolating and reporting compiler bugs, and by developing a parallel runtime library for supporting SPMD features in Fortran compilers: Caffeine [17]. For the LLVM Flang compiler, CLaSS also writes unit tests, fixes front-end bugs, and collaborates on the implementation of parallel language features in the compiler. The principal objective of this paper is to describe the initial results of the collaboration between the Flang developers at Advanced Micro Devices, Inc. (AMD) and CLaSS on the automatic parallelization of `do concurrent`.

Section 2 describes the programming patterns and advanced language features supporting this work. Section 3 compares the parallel performance of batch inference with `do concurrent` versus OpenMP directives in the context of an important application: an atmospheric aerosol dynamics surrogate model. Section 3 also provides reproducibility information. Finally, Sect. 4 concludes and describes plans for future work.

2 Methodology

2.1 Use Cases

The first use case driving the examples in this paper stems from ongoing work in CLaSS on training a neural-network surrogate model for cloud microphysics in the Intermediate Complexity Atmospheric Research Model (ICAR) developed at the National Center for Atmospheric Research (NCAR). If successful, ICAR will perform inference at each time step at each vertex of a 3D Cartesian grid covering a region of the Earth's atmosphere. The results will predict cloud formation and precipitation. The ICAR use case inspires the three-level loop nesting and 3D arrays of `inputs` and `outputs` objects of type `tensor_t`[2] employed in the remainder of this paper. ICAR also inspires the example batch sizes of $latitudes \times levels \times longitudes = 263 \times 15 \times 317 = 1,250,565$ inferences, representing a common grid size for ICAR production runs. In order to be useful, the surrogate must reproduce the physics-based model's results in a shorter execution time and with acceptable accuracy. For this application, inference is the time-critical performance bottleneck; it's assumed network training was performed offline based on the physics equations, which don't change from one run to the next.

Because the training and evaluation of a neural-network surrogate for cloud microphysics in ICAR remains ongoing, this paper employs a previously trained network from a second, similar use case: predicting atmospheric aerosol dynamics for the Department of Energy (DOE) national laboratory community's Energy Exascale Earth System Model (E3SM). The aerosol model was trained in PyTorch [15]. Figure 7 shows a favorable comparison of the surrogate predictions with those of a physics-based E3SM aerosol model [2] on the accumulation-mode concentration.

2.2 Programming Paradigms and Patterns

Figure 1 shows a code snippet from the `concurrent-inferences.f90` program in the Fiats `example` subdirectory. This code invokes a pure `infer` function on a `neural_network` object. This code exhibits a common pattern with directives-based parallelization: nested, serial `do` loops annotated by comments (denoted by a leading exclamation mark: `!`) containing compiler directives (denoted by a

---

[2] Fiats employs a convention of appending "_t" to the names of derived types.

```
!$omp parallel do default(none) &
!$omp    shared(neural_network,inputs,outputs) collapse(3)
do j=1,lon
  do k=1,lev
    do i=1,lat
      outputs(i,k,j) = neural_network%infer(inputs(i,k,j))
    end do
  end do
end do
```

Fig. 1. OpenMP parallel do pattern.

```
do concurrent(i=1:lat, k=1:lev, j=1:lon)
  outputs(i,k,j) = neural_network%infer(inputs(i,k,j))
end do
```

Fig. 2. The do concurrent pattern.

```
!$omp workshare
outputs = neural_network%infer(inputs)
!$omp end workshare
```

Fig. 3. OpenMP workshare pattern with elemental inference.

subsequent $omp) telling the compiler to collapse the loops into one loop and to execute the loop iterations in parallel.

Figure 2 shows that do concurrent supports a pattern in which the iterations are syntactically and semantically collapsed with no implied ordering.[3]

Figure 3 depicts the simplest parallel programming pattern that Fiats supports: an array statement exploiting the fact that the Fiats infer function is declared elemental. Since Fortran 95, applying the elemental attribute to a procedure facilitates writing the procedure with scalar dummy arguments but passing an array as the actual argument, which in the most general case, might even be a non-contiguous slice of a multidimensional array with non-unit strides or vector subscripts. The compiler generates code that executes an elemental procedure on every element of the actual argument and produces an array result. Fortran's elemental procedures are pure unless declared otherwise and there is no implied ordering of the operations on each element of the 3D input array. Considering that outputs, neural_network, and inputs are objects, Line 2

---

[3] Fortran 2018 and 2023 added locality specifiers analogous to the default(none) and shared OpenMP clauses. Support for locality specifiers is under development in LLVM Flang, which is the only compiler that the current release of Fiats supports. Previous releases supported additional compilers that we expect to support again in upcoming releases of those compilers.

in Fig. 3 combines functional, object-oriented, parallel, and array programming, demonstrating the elegance and compactness achievable in modern Fortran.

Unfortunately, most compilers do not yet parallelize array statements even when bracketed by an OpenMP **workshare** directive as shown in Fig. 3. In Sect. 3, we therefore use the **elemental** execution time as the baseline serial execution time to normalize the OpenMP **parallel do** and the **do concurrent** execution times when discussing parallel performance and scalability.

Supporting inference with functions rather than subroutines aligns with the functional programming paradigm's emphasis on immutability. For example, instead of the usual declare-then-define pattern in Fortran, an invocation of **infer** could be placed within an **associate** statement or could be an actual argument in another procedure invocation. Both of the latter approaches would make the result immutable within the scope wherein the function result is accessible.

2.3 Preventing Dynamic Dispatch

By default, a program statement that invokes a type-bound procedure, such as **infer**, on an object, such as **neural_network**, implicitly involves polymorphism: the compiler has to generate code for checking the object's dynamic type to decide the actual procedure to invoke, allowing for the possibility that the object could be of a child type that overrides the procedure definition of the base type. To illustrate, consider the Unified Modeling Language (UML) class diagram of Fig. 4, where the child type **trainable_network_t** aggregates a private instance of type **workspace_t** for purposes of providing a dynamically allocated yet persistent scratchpad to the parent, which is of type **neural_network_t**. The motivation for defining the child type is that training requires a dynamically allocated but persistent scratchpad that is unnecessary if the neural network is used solely for inference. For this reason, the child type stores a workspace that it passes to the parent type's **learn** procedure inside the child's **train** procedure. This design pattern hides the workspace from user code and obviates the need to store a workspace in every **neural_network_t** object even if the object might be used only for inference, e.g., the pre-trained atmospheric aerosol surrogate described in Sect. 2.2.

Dynamic dispatch of procedure invocation imposes two important costs. First, it embeds additional memory references and indirection in performance-critical code. Second, support for dynamic dispatch on GPUs is prohibitively difficult. Neither the LLVM Fortran nor the LLVM C++ compiler currently support dynamic dispatch on GPUs. Fortunately, a seldom-used object-oriented programming (OOP) feature in Fortran facilitates removing the need for dynamic dispatch by applying the **non_overridable** attribute to a type-bound procedure. For this reason, all performance-critical type-bound procedures in Fiats are declared **non_overridable** and we have verified that the generated intermediate representation does not use dynamic dispatch for invoking procedures with this attribute. A search of each of the alternative libraries mentioned in Sect. 1.1 turns up no uses of **non_overridable**, making this pattern unique to Fiats as

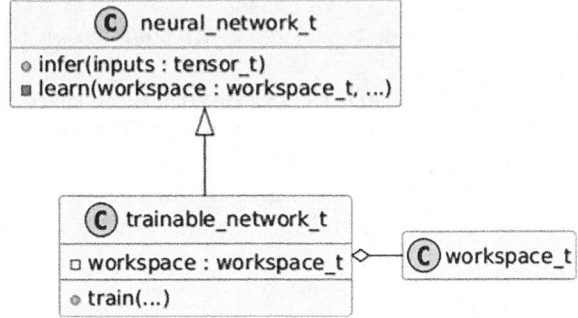

Fig. 4. Unified Modeling Language (UML) class diagram.

of this writing. In addition to any potential performance benefits on CPUs, this feature paves the way for automatically offloading performance-critical work to GPUs once we have access to compiler versions that can compile Fiats and that offer automatic offloading.

2.4 Parameterized Derived Types

Although many deep learning applications rely on low- or mixed-precision arithmetic, some scientific applications necessitate higher precision. We currently use Fortran's default `real` type for the ICAR cloud microphysics surrogate, whereas the E3SM atmospheric aerosol surrogate requires Fortran's `double precision`. In Fortran 2023, the `kind` type parameters that specify a numeric type's precision must be compile-time constants. In the case of user-defined derived types such as `neural_network_t`, this necessitates either compiling a separate version of a package for each supported combination of precisions or defining a different derived type for each combination. At compile time, one could arrange for the definition of a constant that is used wherever desired to determine the `kind` parameter of a type's components (data). Fiats instead defines parameterized derived types (PDTs) that support specifying an object's type parameters – and hence the precision of the object's components – in the object's declaration. Thus, one type definition supports multiple precisions without recompiling.[4]

Searches of the alternative APIs and libraries mentioned in Sect. 1.1 finds no uses of PDTs. In the APIs for C++ libraries, most types contain an opaque pointer that serves as a handle for data stored by the C++ library, which sets the precision. In neural-fortran, the precision is hardwired globally to default `real`. In Athena, derived-type components have `kind` parameters without the

---

[4] Although PDTs eliminate the need to either recompile or define multiple versions of a derived type, one still must write separate procedures for each kind value one intends to support. The next language revision, informally known as Fortran 2028, will include a generic programming facility that will alleviate this burden by empowering programmers to write templates that include type requirements to support writing type-safe generic algorithms.

type itself being parameterized, thus forcing a recompilation for each desired combination of precisions.

After debuting in Fortran 2003, PDTs proved notoriously difficult for compilers to support. Fiats 0.15.0, the first version with PDTs, broke our support for three of four previously supported compilers and generated tens of compiler bug reports. Based on resulting fixes in compilers and in Fiats, we anticipate resuming support for the other three compilers after upcoming compiler releases.

3 Discussion of Results

3.1 Batch Inference with an Aerosol Surrogate

Because this paper centers around novel programming paradigms and patterns, a discussion of raw performance could veer far afield by requiring a deeper consideration of various implementation choices. An example might be examining the choice to make derived type components private versus violating abstractions by granting direct access outside the encompassing scope of the derived type definition. Another example might involve choosing to encapsulate each tensor inside its own object versus aggregating all of the tensors into in one object, evoking a classic debate around whether to define a structure of arrays or an array of structures. Which choices achieve the highest performance can vary with application and hardware and thus fall outside the scope of this paper.

Instead, we focus on relative performance, seeking to answer the question, "For a fixed set of programming paradigms and patterns, does automatic parallelization achieve performance comparable to OpenMP directives?" Fig. 5 answers this question in the affirmative. Averaging across five trials, we find nearly linear speedup for the OpenMP inference code in Fig. 1 and the automatically parallelized `do concurrent`-based inference of Fig. 2. Both are normalized to the average performance of the effectively serial `elemental` inference shown in Fig. 3.

Figure 6 shows the performance for double-precision inference normalized by the corresponding performance for the Fortran default real kind (single-precision) inference for 1–128 cores. As in Fig. 5, the results are averaged over five trials on a dedicated Perlmutter CPU node [12]. The results indicate that using double-precision costs anywhere from a low of 37% slower on 32 cores to a maximum of 72% slower on 128 cores with five of the eight normalized values falling in the range of 57–60% slower.

3.2 Reproducibility

Table 1 describes the neural network employed to produce the results in this study. For purposes of reproducing the figures, a network matching the tabulated description can be instantiated with any weights and biases outside of problematic ranges that would cause floating-point exceptions. For verification of the network calculations, defining pass-through layers in which outputs are identical

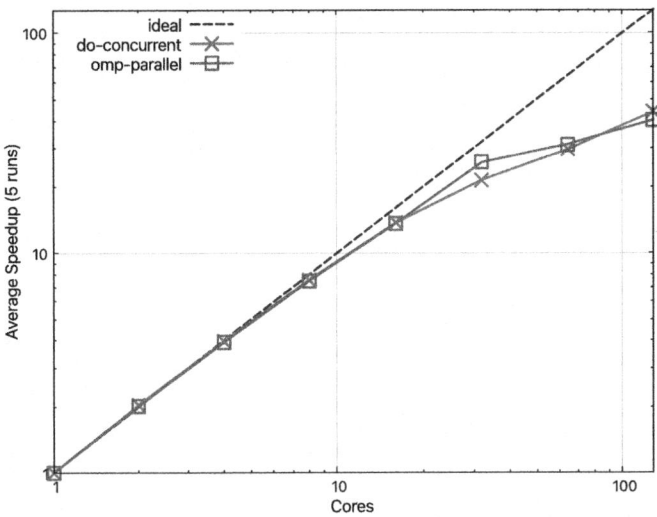

Fig. 5. Strong scaling with default-real (single-precision) of batch inference with the E3SM aerosol surrogate running on a dedicated node of the Perlmutter supercomputer

to inputs can be especially useful. Such layers have weights and biases corresponding to identity matrices and null vectors, respectively. The Fiats `example` subdirectory contains several examples of constructing such networks.

```
salloc --nodes 1 --qos interactive --time 02:00:00 \
       --constraint cpu --account <project-id>
```

Table 1. Neural Network Description

Network Architecture	Fully connected, feed-forward
Number of inputs	80
Nodes per hidden layer	256, 384, 256
Number of outputs	31
Activation function	GELU

For the results in Fig. 5, we requested an interactive, dedicated node on the CPU partition of the Perlmutter supercomputer, using the command:

The node has 2×64-core AMD EPYC^{TM} 7663 processors. Because the automatic parallelization patches had not yet been merged into LLVM, we built the compiler from source using the `build-rocm.sh` script from the handy-dandy repository. The LLVM Flang commit is on Berkeley Lab's flang-testing-project fork at `git tag paw-atm24-fiats` and was pulled from AMD's ROCm fork.

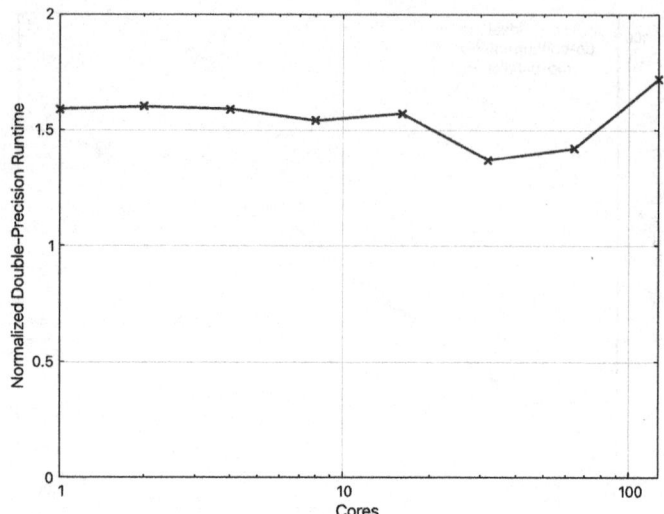

Fig. 6. Double-precision runtime normalized by single-precision time (5-run average).

With the present working directory set to the Fiats root directory and with the aerosol model in the same directory with the JavaScript object notation (JSON) format that Fiat defines, we ran commands of the following form:

```
OMP_NUM_THREADS=128 fpm run --example concurrent-inferences \
    --runner "srun --cpu_bind=cores -c 128 -n 1" \
    -- --network model.json
```

4 Conclusions and Future Work

We have described object-oriented, functional, and array programming paradigms and patterns supporting the automatic parallelization of inference calculations on deep neural networks using Fiats in Fortran 2023. We demonstrated that automatic parallelization performs comparably with OpenMP directives for an atmospheric aerosol application running on a dedicated CPU node of the Perlmutter supercomputer.

Future work will include applying similar strategies to the Fiats training algorithms, exploring automatically offloading inference and training to GPUs, and using Fortran's SPMD features for distributed-memory inference and training.

Acronyms

3D three-dimensional
AMD Advanced Micro Devices, Inc.
API application programming interface

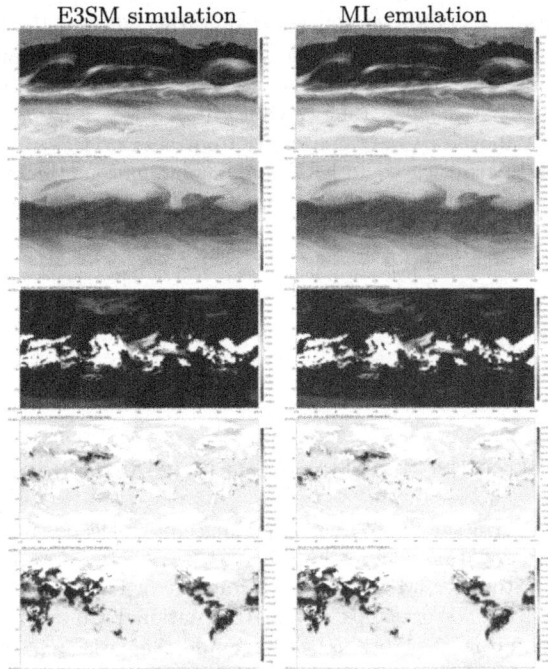

Fig. 7. Comparison of a first-principles simulation with E3SM (left) vs. machine learning (ML) emulation of the E3SM ODE solver (right): the tendency (delta due to the ODE solver) across atmospheric layers across altitudes (high to low) aerosol physics distribution at 00:30:00 UTC 01/24/2010 taking the input at 00:00:00 UTC of 01/24/2010.

CLaSS Computer Languages and Systems Software
CPU central processing unit
DOE United States Department of Energy
E3SM Energy Exascale Earth System Model
GPU graphics processing unit
HPC high-performance computing
ICAR Intermediate Complexity Atmospheric Research Model
ISO International Standards Organization
JSON JavaScript object notation
MPI Message Passing Interface
NCAR National Center for Atmospheric Research
NERSC National Energy Research Scientific Computing Center
OOP object-oriented programming
PDT parameterized derived type
SPMD single-program, dultiple-data
UML Unified Modeling Language

Acknowledgments. This research was supported by the U.S. Department of Energy, Office of Science, Office of Advanced Scientific Computing Research and by the Exascale Computing Project (17-SC-20-SC), a collaborative effort of the U.S. Department of Energy Office of Science and the National Nuclear Security Administration. This research used resources of the National Energy Research Scientific Computing Center (NERSC), a U.S. Department of Energy Office of Science User Facility at Lawrence Berkeley National Laboratory, operated under Contract No. DE-AC02-05CH11231.

AMD, the AMD Arrow logo, and EPYC, and combinations thereof are trademarks of Advanced Micro Devices, Inc. Other product names used in this publication are for identification purposes only and may be trademarks of their respective companies.

Disclosure of Interests. The authors have no competing interests to declare that are relevant to the content of this article.

References

1. Austin, B., et al.: NERSC-10 Workload Analysis (2020). https://doi.org/10.25344/S4N30W
2. Bai, Z., Wan, H., Hassan, T., Zhang, K., Almgren, A.: Deep learning based aerosol microphysics surrogate model for E3SM. AGU24 (2024)
3. Caplan, R.M., Stulajter, M.M., et al.: Portability of Fortran's 'do concurrent' on GPUs. In: SC24-W: Workshops of the International Conference for High Performance Computing, Networking, Storage and Analysis, pp. 1904–1913 (2024). https://doi.org/10.1109/SCW63240.2024.00240
4. Curcic, M.: A parallel Fortran framework for neural networks and deep learning. In: ACM SIGPLAN Fortran Forum, vol. 38, no. 1, pp. 4–21. ACM, New York (2019). https://doi.org/10.1145/3323057.3323059
5. Garain, S., Balsara, D.S., Reid, J.: Comparing Coarray Fortran (CAF) with MPI for several structured mesh PDE applications. J. Comput. Phys. **297**, 237–253 (2015). https://doi.org/10.1016/j.jcp.2015.05.020
6. Hammond, J.R., Deakin, T., Cownie, J., McIntosh-Smith, S.: Benchmarking Fortran do concurrent on CPUs and GPUs using BabelStream. In: 2022 IEEE/ACM International Workshop on Performance Modeling, Benchmarking and Simulation of High Performance Computer Systems (PMBS), pp. 82–99. IEEE (2022). https://doi.org/10.1109/PMBS56514.2022.00013
7. Institute of Computing for Climate Science at the University of Cambridge: Fortran-TF-Lib. https://github.com/Cambridge-ICCS/fortran-tf-lib
8. Institute of Computing for Climate Science at the University of Cambridge: FTorch. https://github.com/Cambridge-ICCS/FTorch
9. Lawrence Berkeley National Laboratory: Fiats: Functional inference and training for surrogates. https://go.lbl.gov/fiats
10. Lawrence Berkeley National Laboratory (LBNL), Computer Languages and Systems Software (CLaSS) Group: Fortran at LBNL. https://fortran.lbl.gov/
11. Maqbool, S., Lee, B.J.: High performance additive manufacturing phase field simulation: Fortran do concurrent vs OpenMP. Comput. Mater. Sci. **252**, 113788 (2025). https://doi.org/10.1016/j.commatsci.2025.113788
12. National Energy Research Scientific Computing (NERSC): Perlmutter Architecture. https://docs.nersc.gov/systems/perlmutter/architecture/
13. neural-fortran. https://github.com/modern-fortran/neural-fortran
14. Nvidia Corporation: TorchFort. https://github.com/NVIDIA/TorchFort

15. Paszke, A., Gross, S., et al.: Pytorch: an imperative style, high-performance deep learning library. In: Advances in Neural Information Processing Systems, vol. 32 (2019). https://doi.org/10.48550/arxiv.1912.01703
16. Preissl, R., Wichmann, N., Long, B., Shalf, J., Ethier, S., Koniges, A.: Multi-threaded global address space communication techniques for gyrokinetic fusion applications on ultra-scale platforms. In: Proceedings of 2011 International Conference for High Performance Computing, Networking, Storage and Analysis, pp. 1–11 (2011). https://doi.org/10.1145/2063384.2063404
17. Rouson, D., Bonachea, D.: Caffeine: Coarray Fortran framework of efficient interfaces to network environments. In: 2022 IEEE/ACM Eighth Workshop on the LLVM Compiler Infrastructure in HPC (LLVM-HPC), pp. 34–42. IEEE (2022). https://doi.org/10.25344/S4459B
18. Rouson, D., Gutmann, E.D., Fanfarillo, A., Friesen, B.: Performance portability of an intermediate-complexity atmospheric research model in coarray Fortran. In: Proceedings of the Second Annual PGAS Applications Workshop, pp. 1–4 (2017). https://doi.org/10.1145/3144779.3169104
19. Stulajter, M.M., Caplan, R.M., Linker, J.A.: Can Fortran's 'do concurrent' replace directives for accelerated computing? In: International Workshop on Accelerator Programming Using Directives, pp. 3–21. Springer, Cham (2021). https://doi.org/10.1007/978-3-030-97759-7_1
20. Taylor, N.T.: Athena: a Fortran package for neural networks. J. Open Source Softw. **9**(99), 6492 (2024). https://doi.org/10.21105/joss.06492

Optimizing Edge AI Models on HPC Systems with the Edge in the Loop

Marcel Aach[1]([✉]) [iD], Cyril Blanc[2] [iD], Andreas Lintermann[1] [iD], and Kurt De Grave[2] [iD]

[1] Jülich Supercomputing Centre, Jülich, Germany
{m.aach,a.lintermann}@fz-juelich.de
[2] ProductionS Core Lab, Flanders Make, Lommel/Leuven, Belgium
{cyril.blanc,kurt.degrave}@flandersmake.be

Abstract. Artificial Intelligence (AI) and Machine Learning (ML) models deployed on edge devices, e.g., for quality control in Additive Manufacturing (AM), are frequently small in size. Such models usually have to deliver highly accurate results within a short time frame. Methods that are commonly employed in literature start out with larger trained models and try to reduce their memory and latency footprint by structural pruning, knowledge distillation, or quantization. It is, however, also possible to leverage hardware-aware Neural Architecture Search (NAS), an approach that seeks to systematically explore the architecture space to find optimized configurations. In this study, a hardware-aware NAS workflow is introduced that couples an edge device located in Belgium with a powerful High-Performance Computing (HPC) system in Germany, to train possible architecture candidates as fast as possible while performing real-time latency measurements on the target hardware. The approach is verified on a use case in the AM domain, based on the open RAISE-LPBF dataset, achieving ≈ 8.8 times faster inference speed while simultaneously enhancing model quality by a factor of ≈ 1.35, compared to a human-designed baseline.

Keywords: Hyperparameter Optimization · Edge Computing · High-Performance Computing · Deep Learning · Computer Vision

1 Introduction

Deploying Machine Learning (ML) models on edge devices presents unique challenges, as these systems must deliver high accuracy while operating under strict memory and latency constraints. Edge Artificial Intelligence (AI) is widely used in applications requiring real-time decision-making. This includes industrial automation and process monitoring, where traditionally post-training optimization approaches like pruning and quantization are applied.

An alternative is hardware-aware Neural Architecture Search (NAS), which systematically explores model architectures to find a best-suited configuration for a given hardware platform. This study introduces a NAS workflow that pairs an edge device located in Belgium with a High-Performance Computing (HPC) system in Germany. This setup accelerates model training while simultaneously optimizing inference speed on the target hardware, ensuring a practical, improved, and efficient deployment. The corresponding code of the HPC2Edge workflow is available open-source on GitHub[1].

The approach is validated with a Laser Powder Bed Fusion (LPBF) application, an industrial Additive Manufacturing (AM) process that fabricates metal parts. Real-time anomaly detection is essential for preventing defects and reducing waste. The method uses a 20 kHz high-speed camera and a Neural Network (NN)-based ideo regression model to predict laser parameters. Deviations of the predicted laser parameters from ground-truth laser parameters indicate process anomalies [4]. For training and evaluation of the method, the RAISE-LPBF-Laser dataset (v1.1)[2], consisting of high-speed camera frames paired with various laser parameters, is used. Optimizing inference speed without sacrificing accuracy is key. Deploying the NAS-optimized model presented in this study on an edge device ensures seamless vision integration on any LPBF machine, while improving efficiency and reliability.

The paper is structured as follows: Sect. 2 summarizes the related work on hardware-aware NAS, Sect. 3 describes the developed workflow in detail, and Sect. 4 presents the empirical results. Finally, Sect. 5 provides a summary and a conclusion.

2 Related Work on Hardware-Aware NAS

To leverage high-performing ML and AI models in a practical setting on resource-limited edge devices, two approaches exist. On the one hand, an already optimized model is compressed to fit on the hardware, e.g., by quantization or structural pruning. On the other hand, hardware-aware NAS seeks to find the optimal building blocks for a model and then constructs its architecture from scratch. While in regular NAS the objective is to find the best performing NN architectures in terms of accuracy, hardware-aware NAS is inherently multi-objective as not only the accuracy of a model but also factors such as the model size and inference speed are of high relevance. Several methods for performing hardware-aware NAS for different types of edge devices have already been introduced in the literature and are summarized in the following, based on a general overview of the field in [2]. Facebook-Berkeley-Nets (FBNets) [16], a family of convolutional architectures for use on mobile devices, were discovered using a differential NAS approach and outperformed human crafted architectures (such as MobileNets [7]) at the time in terms of speed and accuracy. FNAS [8] leverages hardware-aware NAS for creating NN architectures that meet the specifications of Field Programmable

---

[1] HPC2Edge GitHub: https://github.com/Flanders-Make-vzw/HPC2edge.
[2] RAISE-LPBF-Laser dataset: https://www.makebench.eu.

Gate Arrays (FPGAs). It uses a multi-objective reinforcement learning NAS approach [17], where the latency of an architecture candidate is estimated and only verified after the NAS run on the target FPGA. In ProxylessNAS [5], the authors do measure latency on the target hardware, however only include measurements on one large Graphics Processing Unit (GPU), Central Processing Unit (CPU) and a mobile device. The Microcontroller Unit Network (MCUNet) in [11] focuses on microcontroller units, which feature even smaller memory than mobile phones. It also leverages a two stage process, where the NAS search space is first refined, such that all possible candidates fit the resource constraints of the edge device. Then, the NAS for the architecture with the best accuracy is launched. The memory footprint and the Floating Point Operation (FLOP) performance are calculated not on the edge device. From an optimization technique point of view, also Evolutionary Algorithms (EA) are a strong choice [6]. In EA, an initial population is sampled randomly. Subsequent generations are iteratively obtained from the previous one through selection (biased for fitness), mutations, and usually also crossover, i.e., sex. Measurement of fitness, which requires fully training the NNs candidates is here the expensive step.

A critical aspect of hardware-aware NAS is accurately measuring hardware costs. While the number of parameters and FLOPs required for the inference of an architecture candidate can be easily estimated, it has been shown that other quantities of interest, such as the inference time, cannot be reliably derived from these. This is, for instance, the case on different types of edge devices and especially relevant when GPUs are used [10]. For execution latency, real-world measurement has shown to be the most accurate technique. This may, however, increase the runtime of the NAS, as each network candidate needs to be transferred to the edge device, perform the measurement, and return the results. Therefore, many works rely on learning a surrogate model, use a look-up table or heuristics, to predict the latency on the target hardware. Even ML-based prediction models result in an error that is off by a factor of up to 3.8, compared to the actual latency [2]. Other important hardware cost measurements include energy consumption and memory footprint. While benchmarks exist that collect a large number of edge measurements on modern devices, they are often limited in scope. For Computer Vision (CV) workloads these are mainly focused on Convolutional Neural Networks (CNNs) [10], while the ones that focus on Transformer-based models tend to emphasize large language models [14].

3 Design and Implementation

This section introduces the database schema in Sect. 3.1, the AI model along with its architectural and optimizer-related hyperparameters in Sect. 3.2, and the setup of main HPC2Edge workflow in Sect. 3.3.

To enable a wide roll-out of monitoring of 3D printers, it is highly preferable to run the inference on embedded hardware near the printer rather than remotely and expensively on a power-hungry machine. Therefore, the community ultimately faces a multi-objective optimization problem: finding a model that is as accurate as possible and at the same time sufficiently fast and small for inferencing on embedded hardware.

Fig. 1. The edge device, an Nvidia Jetson AGX Orin (front), with a frame grabber PCIe card (green) for interfacing with high-speed cameras over fiber. (Color figure online)

The embedded system of choice is an NVIDIA Jetson AGX Orin^{TM} system, see Fig. 1. This system is fairly powerful and expensive ($\sim$2,000 EUR as of 03/2025) for an embedded device. The cost is, however, reasonable compared to the much more expensive metal printer and camera. The Jetson has an integrated 10 Gbps Ethernet Network Interface Card (NIC), a Peripheral Component Interconnect Express (PCIe) slot for hosting a frame grabber, and it can emulate smaller and cheaper devices of the same series. System and GPU memory are unified on the board. To demonstrate the flexibility of the approach, a limited ablation experiment is performed on a smaller and much more affordable (219 EUR as of 05/2025) Jetson Orin Nano Super Development Kit (actual, not emulated) with 8 GB unified RAM.

On the full AGX Orin, memory is not a constraining factor for storing the default NN architecture of the baseline model presented in this study. However, the speed of inference remains a constraint, as the system must be able to process the entire surface to catch all faults. The latency of this prediction should be low, i.e., feedback to the controller arrives within a few scanlines to avoid more damage and allow recovery of the fault. Ideally, this processing time should be not much longer than the time it takes to print a scanline.

The two objectives are therefore (i) inference speed and (ii) the Root Mean Square Error (RSME) of the predictions. The inference speed for a model architecture is influenced by many factors, such as the number of parameters. It can be roughly estimated/interpolated (see Sect. 2), but only an execution on the device itself can reveal the true inference performance. Therefore, the inference speed of all model variants considered in this study are directly measured on the embedded device.

A central relational database (in PostgreSQL) has been set up to allow bi-directional communication between the embedded device located in Belgium at Flanders Make and the HPC cluster located at the Jülich Supercomputing Centre, Forschungszentrum Jülich, in Germany. The schema is shown in Fig. 2. The optimizer consults the embedded device as soon as it conceives a new candidate NN architecture (hyperparameter setting), posting the architecture details to the database. The embedded device continuously polls the database for unmeasured architectures, compiles and optimizes the architecture with the NVIDIA TensorRT library[3], and (after warmup) runs a few inference steps to measure steady-state latency and throughput at several batch sizes. It subsequently reports its results back to the database.

The current setup lacks load balancing for multiple embedded devices of the same type, which is desirable for extremely large-scale optimizations, for efficient parallel operation also on the embedded side, as well as to achieve a degree of fault tolerance. At this point, further optimizations, such as the introduction of surrogate models, also become relevant.

3.1 Database Schema

The HPC2Edge database schema, shown in Fig. 2, consists of an essential part that supports basic communication between the HPC and edge systems (labeled 'HPC2Edge core' in the figure), and accessory tables to optionally store the full exploration of the optimizer. In terms of core schema, the edge device is GRANTed INSERT permission only into the edge_measurement table. The Hyperparameter Optimization (HPO) algorithm gets an account that can INSERT into the (neural) network_architecture and benchmark_result tables. All accounts can SELECT from all tables. The JSONB columns allow noSQL-equivalent freedom to evolve the system without changing the main schema, but can still be indexed and efficiently queried when needed.

The extended schema is designed to be compatible with OpenML[4] [15], which is an open platform for sharing datasets, algorithms, and experiments. OpenML has similarities to the more recent Hugging Face[5] platform, it is, however, more geared towards classical ML using tabular datasets. It offers Application Programming Interfaces (APIs) and supports experiment logging from several popular ML toolkits. The present work uses the publicly available code as of 08/2024[6]. Note that no full direct compatibility is achieved and OpenML has announced a full backend code rewrite, i.e., their future schema might be structured substantially different.

---

[3] NVIDIA TensorRT: https://developer.nvidia.com/tensorrt-getting-started.
[4] OpenML: https://openml.org.
[5] Hugging Face: https://huggingface.co.
[6] OpenML 08/2024: https://github.com/openml/OpenML/tree/develop/data/sql.

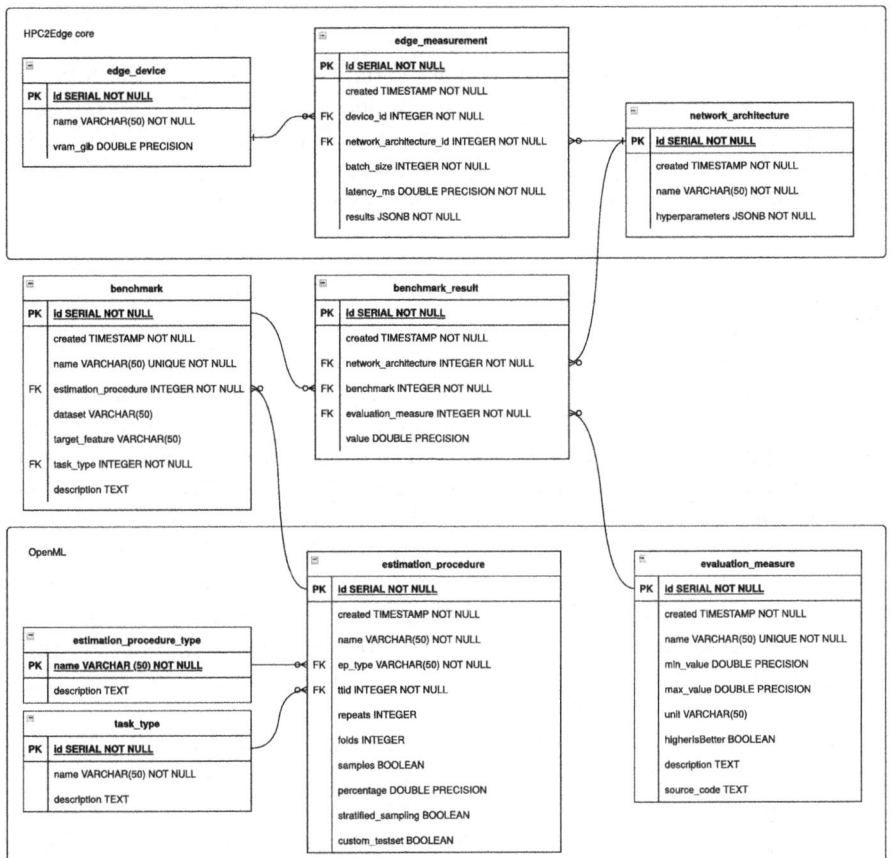

Fig. 2. Relational database schema for connecting the HPC-based HPO with an embedded device for inference measurements.

OpenML uses an extremely flexible, untyped schema. Here, some untyped, string-serialized fields were specialized to double precision, and the table `math_function` to `estimation_procedure`. Only reference records relevant for regression are stored, without loss of generality. The tables `benchmark` and `benchmark_result` correspond conceptually to tasks and runs in OpenML. It should be noted that the corresponding Data Definition Language (DDL) was not available publicly to ensure some level of compatibility. Future work may consider running a full OpenML server for experiment logging—or some other logging method like MLflow[7] or ClearML[8]—extended with only the HPC2Edge core schema.

---

[7] MLflow: https://mlflow.org/.
[8] ClearML: https://clear.ml/.

3.2 AI Model

The model used to predict the laser parameters and to produce the following results (see Sect. 4) is a Video Swin Transformer [12] with a modified fully connected end layer for power and speed regression. The data pre-processing is the same as described in [3]. The RAISE-LPBF-Laser dataset (v1.1) [3], consisting of high-speed camera frames paired with various laser parameters, is used. Training and validation focus on a single object (C027) with an 80-20 split, while object C028 is used for testing. The proposed NAS framework directly optimizes performance for edge deployment, balancing both speed and accuracy, while leveraging HPC for acceleration. This work provides an efficient solution for real-time AI-driven industrial applications.

The input to the model consists of a window of 16 consecutive frames that are randomly sampled from each scanline and then normalized and resized to a model input shape of (256, 256) pixels. The output of the model corresponds to the ground-truth values, consisting of a pair of setpoints for laser dot speed and power for each scanline, which are normalized by dividing by their nominal values of $900 mm/s$ and $215W$, respectively. The choice of using a Video Swin model for prediction is motivated by the fact that it is the best performing attention-based model from [12] and that its architecture can be easily modified. Specifically, the model's hyperparameters are well-designed to minimize conflicts and interdependencies, reducing the likelihood of parameterization issues during the optimization run.

The hyperparameters of the model that are optimized during the NAS run are listed in Tab. 1. The search space includes various Transformer-specific architectural parameters, i.e., the video patch size, which controls the temporal and spatial granularity of the input, the embedded dimensions influencing the dimensions of the tokens, the depths of each model stage, the number of attention heads, the window size of the self attention, and the ratio of feed-forward Multi-layer Perceptron (MLP) layers between attention blocks. The classical optimizer-related parameters are the base learning rate of the Adam optimizer [9] and the scheduler-specific step-size and learning rate decay factor. The search space is chosen to be high-dimensional to allow for an extensive exploration of model size and model quality.

3.3 Workflow Setup

The setup of the HPC2Edge workflow is shown in Fig. 3. The training of the different models is performed on the Extreme-Scale Booster partition of the DEEP-EST HPC machine [13] at the Jülich Supercomputing Centre, Forschungszentrum Jülich, in Germany. It features a total of 75 nodes, each one equipped with one NVIDIA V100 GPU and an Intel Xeon 4215 CPU with 8 cores and a base frequency of 2.5 GHz. To achieve results in a reasonable amount of time, the training of the different NNs is performed in data-parallel fashion with the PyTorch-DDP library[9]. Orchestration of the HPO runs is handled by the Ray

---

[9] PyTorch-DDP: https://pytorch.org/docs/stable/notes/ddp.html.

Table 1. Hyperparameter search space, consisting of architectural and optimizer-related hyperparameters of the Video Swin Transformer model.

Name	Description	Default	Sampling Range
Patch size	Video patch size for transformer tokenization	[2, 4, 4]	[2, 4] each
Embedded dimensions	Number of linear projection output channels	96	[24, 48]
Depths	Depths of each Video Swin Transformer stage	[2, 2, 6, 2]	[1, 2, 4] each
Heads number	Number of attention heads of each stage	[3, 6, 12, 24]	[3, 6, 12, 24] each
MLP ratio	Ratio of MLP hidden dim. to embedding dim.	4	[1, 2, 3, 4]
Learning rate	Controls how much to adjust model weights during training	$1e^{-4}$	$\log[1e-5, 1]$
Learning rate step size	Interval of learning rate adjustment	10	[10, 20, 40]
Learning rate γ	Learning rate decay factor	0.5	(0.1, 0.9)

Tune framework[10]. The optimization process leverages the Nevergrad library[11], a gradient-free optimization tool. Nevergrad performs evolutionary optimization in settings where the computation of gradients is hard or impossible. It is, therefore, a suitable solution for black box optimization problems such as HPO and NAS. It features a variety of optimization methods, that can be selected based on the search space and available computing budget. For the present work, the (1 + 1) EA was chosen. The algorithm starts with an initial parent population and then creates one offspring for each parent via mutation. It subsequently evaluates the fitness of both the parent and the offspring. In case the offspring achieves a better fitness value than the parent, it replaces the parent in the subsequent generation. For the present experiments, the population size is fixed at 8, while the total number of evaluations is varied from 16 to 64.

The edge device periodically queries the database for new, unevaluated entries that match its configuration, i.e., for supported edge device types. Upon finding a relevant entry, it loads the model parameters and performs ten inference runs to compute an average timing. This process is repeated for each configured batch size (1, 2, 4, and 8 in this case). The measured inference times, along with other measurements not exploited in this method, e.g., memory usage, CPU usage, or GPU usage, are entered in the database to be leveraged by the optimizer. Once a hyperparameter candidate is chosen, four GPUs are allocated to its training, balancing the allocation of GPUs to the data-parallel training loop and the overall HPO run [1]. With a population size of 8, this results in 32 GPUs

---
[10] Ray Tune: https://www.ray.io/.
[11] Nevergrad: https://facebookresearch.github.io/nevergrad/.

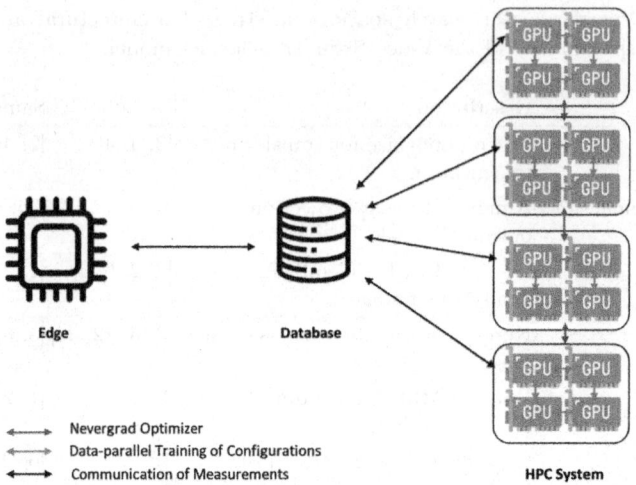

Fig. 3. Orchestration of the Hardware-aware NAS search, with communication between the HPC system, located at the Jülich Supercomputing Centre, Forschungszentrum Jülich, in Germany, and the edge device, located at Flanders Make in Belgium.

being used at the same time. Before launching the training, the head GPU submits the architectural details to the database for latency measurement on the edge device. After training for two epochs, the head node reads back this runtime measurement and combines it with the achieved validation loss. Submitting the architecture to the edge device before training the model and inquiring about the runtime measurement only after the model is trained hides the latency of communication between the HPC system and edge device.

$$score_{val} = loss_{val} \cdot 1000 + time_{inference} \qquad (1)$$

A weighted validation score value, based on validation loss and inference time in milliseconds (see Eq. 1) is then reported back to the optimizer and minimized. The best performing model is chosen according to the lowest score achieved. This model is then evaluated on the unseen test dataset, where also a test score is computed in a similar way.

Table 2. Results at different scales (averaged over five seeds).

Num. Samples	Val. Score	Val. Loss	Inference Time	Test Score	Test Loss
0 (baseline)	412.81	0.0807	332.11 ms	457.51	0.1254
16	146.02	0.0937	52.30 ms	156.66	0.1044
32	140.26	0.0959	44.34 ms	140.53	0.0962
64	129.99	0.0923	37.72 ms	130.58	0.0929

4 Empirical Results

The empirical results of running the hybrid workflow are shown in Tab. 2. It compares the default hyperparameter configuration, which was chosen by an expert (baseline) based on experience and several experiments, against running hardware-aware NAS with an increasing number of samples $n = \{16, 32, 64\}$. The training times of a single configuration range between 1–3 h, while the whole HPO run on the HPC system took between 8–19 h, stretching the maximum allowed job time of 20 h on the HPC system. The evaluation metrics include the validation loss l_v, the inferences time t and the test loss l_t of the best configuration, which is chosen according to the lowest validation score metric s_v, see Eq. (1). The most significant reduction in comparison to the baseline can be observed for the inference time metric. Using just 16 samples decreases the inference time by a factor of ≈ 6.35 from 332 ms to 52 ms. Increasing the number of samples to 64 even leads to a reduction factor of ≈ 8.8 in comparison to the baseline, which highlights the potential of the hybrid HPC2Edge workflow.

In terms of model quality, the validation loss metric shows varying performance across different sample sizes. At 16 samples, the validation loss increases to 0.0937, while at 64 samples it still remains higher at 0.0923, compared to the baseline. In contrast, the 64 samples NAS run results in the best model, decreasing the test loss by a factor of ≈ 1.35 compared to the baseline model. It is hypothesized that the fluctuations in the validation loss metric are due to the weighting of both metrics into a single one, see Eq. (1), and thus a larger focus is on the inference time. However, as shown by the decreasing test loss, the model still seems to be able to achieve a higher solution quality than the baseline. Both metrics, the model quality on the test set and the inference time in general decrease for the model on the edge as the number of samples (and thus the compute resources spent on the NAS loop) is increased. In Fig. 4, the pareto curves of the different configurations are depicted, showing the optimal trade-off points between validation loss and inference time. As can be seen, in all cases the pareto curves do move to the left bottom of the plots, indicating better models.

To assess the importance of the architectural and optimizer-related parameters on the model performance, the top 10% models found during the 5 NAS runs with 64 samples are examined through their median hyperparameter values. The results show that a small learning rate of $\approx 4.7 \cdot 10^{-4}$, combined with

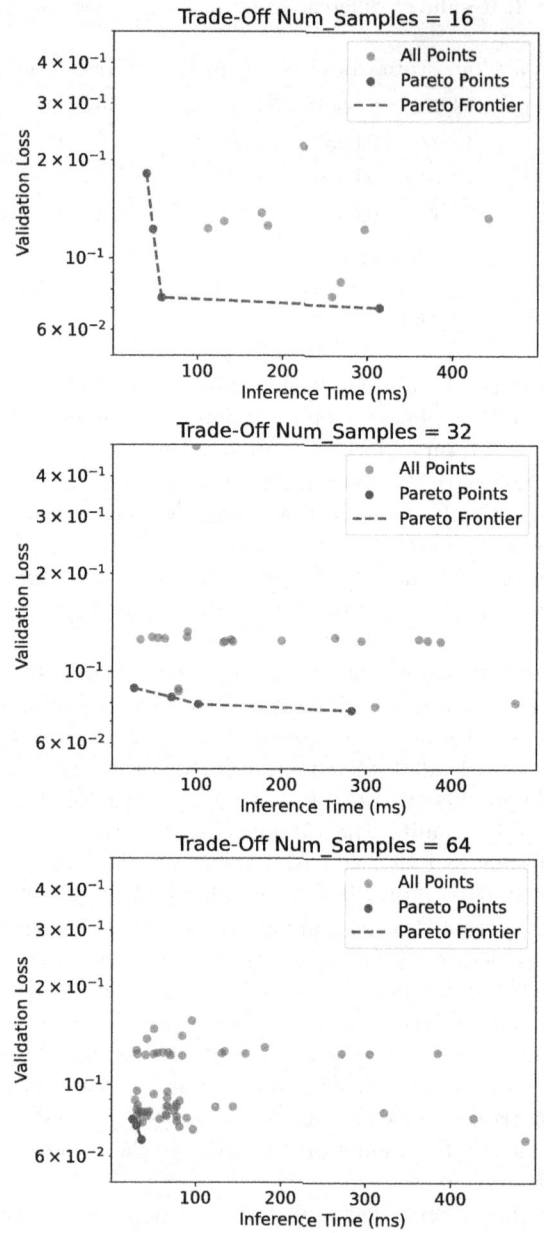

Fig. 4. Results at different scales, showing the median best run.

a large decay factor of ≈0.75 and a moderate adjustment interval of 20 steps results in the lowest validation score values. From an input data perspective, a median patch size of [4, 4, 4] suggests larger patches to be more favorable. From an architectural point of view, a median depth of $[1, 1, 2, 1]$, a median attention head number of $[3, 6, 3, 12]$, and a median embedding dimension of 24 suggests smaller models to be favorable. This is expected as these parameters usually also result in shorter inference times, which is one of the two objectives of the multi-objective optimizer.

4.1 Comparison of Edge Devices

To assess the impact of the capabilities of the edge device, apart from the full AGX Orin, also a Jetson Orin Nano Super Development Kit, a much smaller device, was used in an additional experiment. As can be seen from the results in Fig. 5 the main difference to the AGX Orin device are the inference time values. When evaluating 16 samples, the AGX Orin was able to achieve an average inference time as low as 52.30 ms, while the best configuration found by Orin Nano Super device on average requires 109.61 ms of inference time. This difference of ≈ 2.1 is expected, as the Orin Nano Super device is smaller and less powerful, therefore inference in general would take longer. Compared to the baseline configuration, which required an inference time of 947.46 ms on the Orin Nano Super, this still represents a significant improvement by a factor of ≈ 8.64. At an average test loss of 0.1052, the presented workflow is also in this case able to improve upon the baseline model (see Table 2) in terms of test set performance.

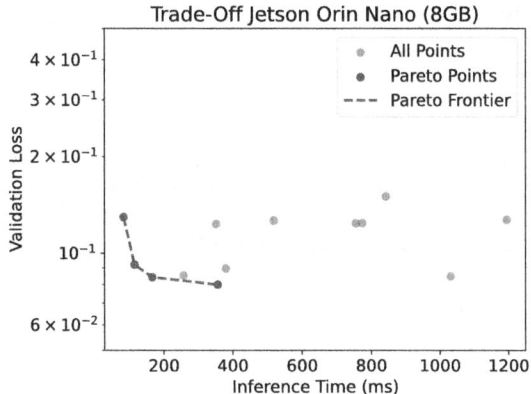

Fig. 5. Results on Jetson Orin Nano Super Development Kit.

5 Summary and Conclusion

In this work, a hybrid, cross-border, hardware-aware NAS workflow that runs in parallel on an HPC system and an edge device was presented. The workflow leverages the powerful GPUs of the HPC system to train different model configurations with data-parallel training while performing the inference time measurement of the models on the actual target device, resulting in an accurate measurement. To hide communication latency, each candidate model architecture is sent to the inference device before training on the HPC system. The empirical results clearly highlight how large savings in terms of inference time and model quality (in terms of final test loss) can be achieved on two representative edge devices, a more capable AGX Orin and a more constrained Orin Nano Super device. As a key finding, this research demonstrates empirically that increasing the computational resources of the HPO loop can lead to a smaller computational resource usage during the inference on the edge device. In the future, such workflows could therefore be used to find architectures with even higher speed (compared to expert baselines) or fitting on even smaller edge devices, which is an important feature not only in AM but in any field where fast ML models are deployed on small devices.

Acknowledgments. The CoE RAISE project has received funding from the European Union's Horizon 2020 Research and Innovation Framework Programme H2020-INFRAEDI-2019-1 under grant agreement no. 951733. This research was also partially supported by Flanders Make, the strategic research centre for the manufacturing industry, and specifically by its RELAI project. Resources for the database were provided by the VSC (Flemish Supercomputer Center), funded by the Research Foundation - Flanders (FWO) and the Flemish Government.

Disclosure of Interests. The authors have no competing interests to declare that are relevant to the content of this article.

References

1. Aach, M., Inanc, E., Sarma, R., Riedel, M., Lintermann, A.: Optimal resource allocation for early stopping-based neural architecture search methods. In: Faust, A., Garnett, R., White, C., Hutter, F., Gardner, J.R. (eds.) Proceedings of the Second International Conference on Automated Machine Learning. Proceedings of Machine Learning Research, vol. 224, pp. 12/1–17. PMLR (2023). https://proceedings.mlr.press/v224/aach23a.html
2. Benmeziane, H., Maghraoui, K.E., Ouarnoughi, H., Niar, S., Wistuba, M., Wang, N.: A comprehensive survey on hardware-aware neural architecture search (2021). https://arxiv.org/abs/2101.09336
3. Blanc, C., Ahar, A., De Grave, K.: Reference dataset and benchmark for reconstructing laser parameters from on-axis video in powder bed fusion of bulk stainless steel. Addit. Manuf. Lett. **7**, 100161 (2023)
4. Booth, B.G., Heylen, R., Nourazar, M., Verhees, D., Philips, W., Bey-Temsamani, A.: Encoding stability into laser powder bed fusion monitoring using temporal features and pore density modelling. Sensors **22**(10) (2022). https://doi.org/10.3390/s22103740
5. Cai, H., Zhu, L., Han, S.: ProxylessNAS: direct neural architecture search on target task and hardware. In: International Conference on Learning Representations (2019). https://openreview.net/forum?id=HylVB3AqYm

6. Eiben, A.E., Smith, J.E.: Introduction to Evolutionary Computing. Springer, Cham (2003)
7. Howard, A.G., et al.: MobileNets: efficient convolutional neural networks for mobile vision applications (2017). https://arxiv.org/abs/1704.04861
8. Jiang, W., et al.: Accuracy vs. efficiency: achieving both through FPGA-implementation aware neural architecture search. In: Proceedings of the 56th Annual Design Automation Conference 2019, DAC 2019. Association for Computing Machinery, New York (2019). https://doi.org/10.1145/3316781.3317757
9. Kingma, D.P., Ba, J.: Adam: a method for stochastic optimization. In: International Conference on Learning Representations (2015). http://arxiv.org/abs/1412.6980
10. Li, C., et al.: HW-NAS-bench: Hardware-aware neural architecture search benchmark. In: International Conference on Learning Representations (2021). https://openreview.net/forum?id=_0kaDkv3dVf
11. Lin, J., Chen, W.M., Lin, Y., Cohn, J., Gan, C., Han, S.: MCUNet: tiny deep learning on IoT devices. In: Proceedings of the 34th International Conference on Neural Information Processing Systems, NeurIPS 2020. Curran Associates Inc., Red Hook (2020)
12. Liu, Z., et al.: Video swin transformer. In: Proceedings of the IEEE/CVF Conference on Computer Vision and Pattern Recognition (CVPR), pp. 3202–3211 (2022)
13. Suarez, E., Kreuzer, A., Eicker, N., Lippert, T.: The DEEP-EST project, Schriften des Forschungszentrums Jülich IAS Series, vol. 48, pp. 9–25. Forschungszentrum Jülich GmbH Zentralbibliothek, Jülich (2021). https://juser.fz-juelich.de/record/905812
14. Sukthanker, R.S., et al.: HW-GPT-bench: hardware-aware architecture benchmark for language models. In: The Thirty-eight Conference on Neural Information Processing Systems Datasets and Benchmarks Track (2024). https://openreview.net/forum?id=urJyyMKs7E
15. Vanschoren, J., van Rijn, J.N., Bischl, B., Torgo, L.: OpenML: networked science in machine learning. SIGKDD Explor. **15**(2), 49–60 (2013). https://doi.org/10.1145/2641190.2641198
16. Wu, B., et al.: FBNet: hardware-aware efficient convnet design via differentiable neural architecture search. In: 2019 IEEE/CVF Conference on Computer Vision and Pattern Recognition (CVPR), pp. 10726–10734. IEEE Computer Society, Los Alamitos (2019). https://doi.org/10.1109/CVPR.2019.01099
17. Zoph, B., Le, Q.: Neural architecture search with reinforcement learning. In: International Conference on Learning Representations (2017). https://openreview.net/forum?id=r1Ue8Hcxg

Evaluation of Distributed Asynchronous Checkpointing in High-Performance Computing

Riccardo Scheda[✉][iD], Domitilla Brandoni[iD], Laura Cavalli[iD], and Laura Morselli[iD]

CINECA, SuperComputing Applications and Innovation (SCAI) Department,
Bologna, Italy
{n.scheda,n.brandoni,n.cavalli,n.morselli}@cineca.it

Abstract. During the training of large models, traditional checkpointing introduces significant overhead, as it requires pausing training while model states are copied from GPU memory to storage. At the same time, frequent checkpoint is needed to ensure an efficient use of resources.

Efficient checkpointing is crucial for large-scale training of Artificial Intelligence (AI) models, especially on high-performance computing (HPC) systems. In this work, we evaluate distributed asynchronous checkpointing (DACP) applied on various LLM models on the Leonardo supercomputer, hosted by CINECA. By integrating asynchronous checkpointing, we enable overlapping data transfer operations with training iterations, significantly reducing training time.

Our experiments span multiple LLM configurations, leveraging PyTorch DACP to optimize checkpointing frequency and minimize graphics processing unit (GPU) idle time. We evaluate this approach at scales of up to 256 GPUs using different model sizes. Results demonstrate a substantial reduction in checkpoint overhead, achieving up to a 6x improvement compared to synchronous methods. Our evaluations highlight the benefits of asynchronous checkpointing for large-scale training and provide insights into its practical deployment on HPC infrastructures.

Keywords: Asynchronous checkpointing · Training · HPC · LLMs

1 LLM Training

Training Large Language Models is a challenging task in terms of computational cost and time. Indeed, currently LLMs consist of billions and even trillions of parameters [8]. Due to the massive size of these model architectures, the learning process is significantly time-consuming. An average fine-tuning of a 70-billion-parameters model can take several hours to complete [4], and often require weeks to be trained from scratch [7]. However, several strategies and innovations have been developed to optimize the learning process, such as:

- Parameter reallocation and parallelization: techniques like ReaLHF optimize Reinforcement Learning from Human Feedback (RLHF) by dynamically redistributing parameters and adapting parallelization strategies, achieving significant speedups in training times [14];
- Compute-optimal training: research suggests that for compute-optimal training, both model size and the number of training tokens should be scaled equally. This approach has been shown to outperform larger models while using less computing for fine-tuning and inference [11];
- Distributed training strategies: efficient distributed training techniques, such as tensor and pipeline parallelism, have been developed to optimize the use of supercomputers, achieving high throughput and scaling efficiencies [6].

However, despite these advancements, the training process remains a time-intensive task due to the complexity and scale of modern models.

As a consequence, during training faults or sudden interruptions due to GPU failures can occur, as well as network disconnections between nodes, requiring the process to be restarted. These interruptions can cause the loss of the model weights trained since then, and thus a waste of costly compute resources. Moreover, despite failures, the training of a LLM can take an undesirable trajectory that leads to slow or no convergence, which can be avoided restarting the learning process [5]. To overcome these issues, developers adopted checkpointing.

Checkpointing consists in saving models' trained weights at intermediate stages of the learning process, enhancing fault tolerance of large model training [18]. To recover from a failure, the training process must stop and restart from the last saved checkpoint, instead of restarting from scratch.

However, adopting checkpointing can vastly increase training time, especially for very large models, where in some cases, saving the model can take over 2 h for a single checkpoint [15].

In a multi-node training setting, checkpointing becomes distributed (DCP), with each GPU and node saving their sharded part of the model. While using DCP avoids the need to aggregate tensors, the checkpointing overhead remains substantial compared to the training step. During checkpointing, the trainer must wait for the process to complete, effectively wasting costly GPU resources.

2 Asynchronous Checkpointing

Checkpointing faces two major bottlenecks: copying tensors from GPU to CPU memory (referred to as âĂIJStagingâĂİ) and transferring tensors from CPU memory to persistent storage (see Fig. 1). Figure 1 depicts three different tasks (training, staging and model saving) along the time axis (x-axis), requiring the process to pause training and switch to perform staging and then the model saving (or persistent step). For modern models, staging overhead typically lasts a few seconds, while the persistence step can take anywhere from tens to hundreds of seconds, depending on the storage system. To overcome this problem, PyTorch recently proposed a new type of distributed checkpointing, called asynchronous distributed checkpointing [2].

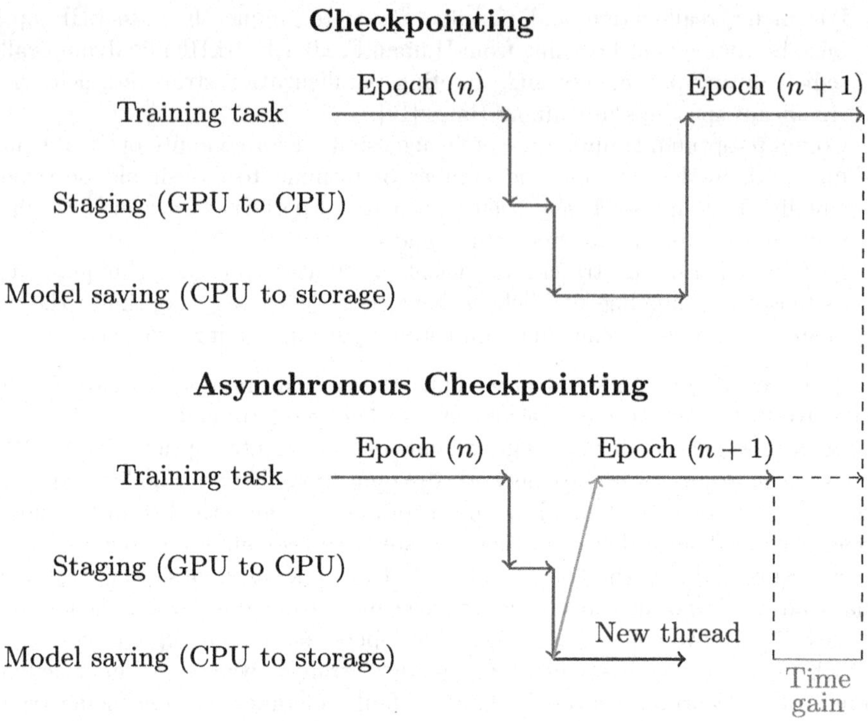

Checkpointing

Asynchronous Checkpointing

Fig. 1. Synchronous vs Asynchronous checkpointing. The diagram shows how the workflow is down during the training epochs. After staging, asynchronous checkpoint divide the workflow into two different processes, one for the training of the model on the GPU (orange), and the other one to save the model from the CPU to the storage (blue). Image readapted from [1] (Color figure online).

Indeed, the fundamental principle behind asynchronous checkpointing is turning the model saving step concurrently with the training step on a separate thread, as it doesn't involve GPUs. With asynchronous checkpointing, the process begins with the main training pausing to copy tensors from GPU to CPU memory (Fig. 1). After this, the main training thread resumes the training task, while the model saving is delegated to another thread: non-blocking CPU threads process the tensors arrived from the GPU, completing the full checkpointing and serialization process to disk for persistent storage. In this way, we have a modularization of the checkpointing process into two parts rather than one monolithic process.

Recently, a new type of asynchronous checkpoitning has been proposed [13]. This work introduces a technique (called Lazy Asynchronous Checkpointing, (LAC)) to improve checkpointing efficiency during the training of LLMs. Authors propose an asynchronous multi-level checkpointing approach that minimizes I/O overheads by overlapping data transfers with training operations.

In this work, we investigated the performances of PyTorch asynchronous checkpointing in different settings. Lazy asynchronous checkpointing in HPC will be investigated in future works.

3 Experimental Evaluation

3.1 Hardware Setup

We ran the experiments on Leonardo HPC system (Table 1). Leonardo is the pre-exascale Tier-0 EuroHPC Joint Undertaking supercomputer hosted by CINECA and located in the Bologna Technopole, in Italy [3]. It is based on two new specifically-designed compute blades, which are available through two distinct SLURM partitions on the cluster:

- **3456 nodes**: X2135 GPU blade based on NVIDIA Ampere A100-64 accelerators - LEONARDO Booster partition
- **1536 nodes**: X2140 CPU-only blade based on Intel Sapphire Rapids processors - LEONARDO Data Centric General Purpose (DCGP) partition

The overall system architecture also uses NVIDIA Mellanox InfiniBand High Data Rate (HDR) connectivity, with smart in-network computing acceleration engines that enable extremely low latency and high data throughput to provide the highest AI and HPC application performance and scalability. The system also includes a Capacity Tier and a Fast Tier storage, based on DDN Exascaler (Table 1).

3.2 Software Setup

To evaluate the performance of asynchronous checkpointing, we performed it on many trainings with different models and different sizes: LLama-2 [19],Llama-3.1 [7] and Mamba [9] (see Table 2), which correspond to the average sizes of the checkpoint files. In Table 2 are shown average checkpoint times for each model using standard checkpointing in PyTorch. Asynchronous checkpointing was perfomed using PyTorch [12]. To enable distributed training, we used Hugging Face Accelerate: A flexible API designed to simplify multi-GPU and multi-node training [10]. The main strategy used for distributed training was Fully Sharded Data Parallel (FSDP), a memory-efficient method that shards model parameters across GPUs, reducing memory overhead [20].

3.3 Methodology

In the first part, to make a comparison between checkpoint timing on different storage types, we performed a training for each model three times, with 200 iterations, saving a checkpoint after each iteration. The experiments were conducted across multiple configurations using 2,4,8 and 16 nodes, going from 8 GPUs up to 64 GPUs (4 GPUs per node).

Table 1. Hardware specifications of the Leonardo Booster partition.

Model	Atos Bull Sequana X2135 "Da Vinci" Blade
Racks	116
Compute Nodes	3456
Processors	Single socket 32 cores Intel Ice Lake CPU 1 × Intel Xeon Platinum 8358, 2.60GHz, TDP 250W
Accelerators	4 × NVIDIA Ampere GPUs/node, 64GB HBM2e NVLink 3.0 (200GB/s)
Cores	32 cores/node
RAM	512GB (8 × 64GB) DDR4 3200 MHz
Peak Performance	About 309 Pflop/s
Internal Network	DragonFly+ 200 Gbps (NVIDIA Mellanox Infiniband HDR) 2 × dual port HDR100 per node
Storage (raw capacity)	137.6 PB based on DDN ES7990X and Hard Drive Disks (Capacity Tier) 5.7 PB based on DDN ES400NVX2 and Solid State Drives (Fast Tier)

Table 2. Number of parameters, memory size of different Llama models and average checkpoint time of models using torch.save() function, not distributed. The size is computed assuming full precision (FP32).

Model	# of parameters (billions)	Checkpoint Size (GB)	Standard Checkpoint time (s)
Mamba	2.8	11	25
Llama2	7	28	49
Llama3.1	8	32	54
Llama2	13	52	92
Llama3.1	70	280	131

We used the fine-tuning dataset "Rotten Tomatoes" [16], which consists of movie reviews with labeled sentiments.

In the second part, we focused on a pre-training of different models, to see the difference in asynchronous checkpoint timing for different models on different number of nodes. The experiments were conducted across multiple configurations using 2,4,8,16,32 and 64 nodes, going from 8 GPUs up to 256 GPUs (4 GPUs per node). In this case the dataset utilized was the open-source "FineWeb" [17], a 15-trillion token dataset derived from 96 Common Crawl snapshots.

4 Results

Figure 2, shows the checkpoint saving times on Hard Drive Disks (HDDs) changing with respect to model size and number of resources. Clearly, for both of Llama-2 and Llama-3.1 models, as the model gets bigger, the saving time increases. Moreover, for each model, original checkpoint time decraseses as the number of nodes increases. This is due to FSDP, which shards the model equally on each GPU, so as the number of GPUs increases, the checkpoint size decreases for each GPU, reducing saving time. For Asynchronous checkpointing instead, we can see that it significantly reduces saving time on disk with respect to original distributed checkpointing; however, there is no such a clear correlation between saving time and number of nodes involved. However, it is not evident whether the absence of a clear correlation between saving time and the number of nodes involved aligns with expected behavior.

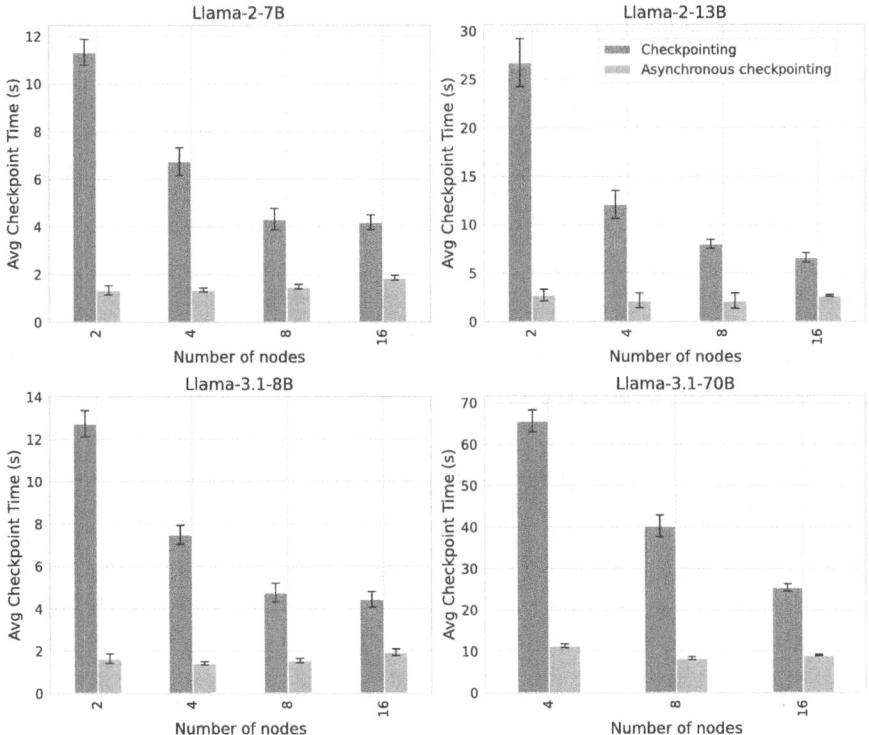

Fig. 2. Comparison between average time in checkpointing and asynchronous checkpointing, on Hard Drive Disks (Capacity Tier), for different models. Blue bars: original distributed checkpointing; orange bars: asynchronous distributed checkpointing. Error lines: standard deviation. (Color figure online)

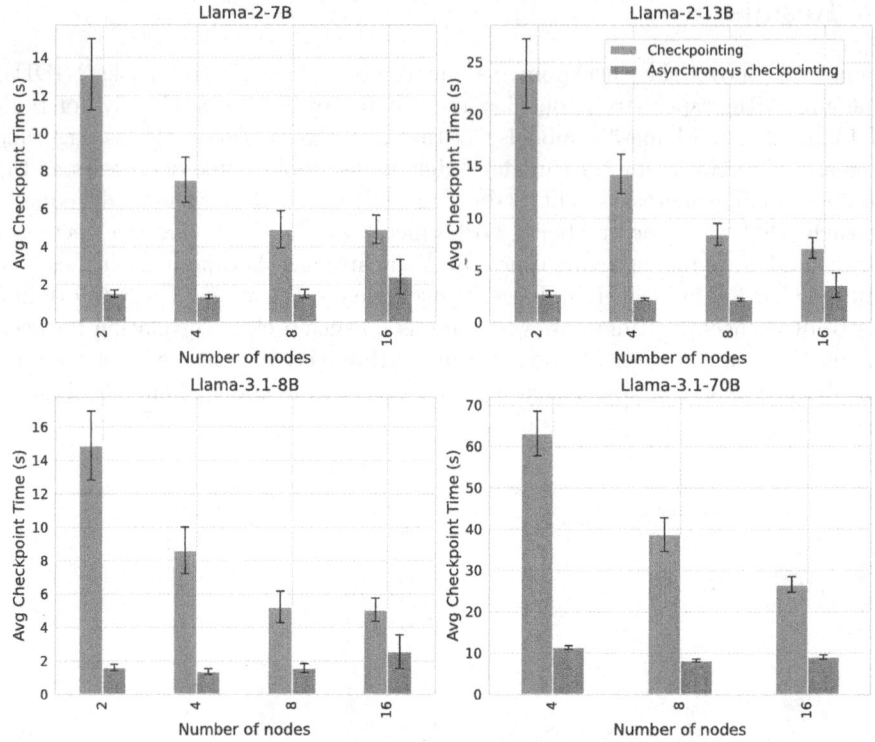

Fig. 3. Comparison between average time in checkpointing and asynchronous checkpointing time, on Solid State Drives (SSD), for different models. green bars: original distributed checkpointing; red bars: asynchronous distributed checkpointing. Error lines: standard deviation. (Color figure online)

For Solide State Drives (SSD), in Fig. 3, we can see different checkpoint saving times, changing models and number of nodes per training. Similarly to the previous case, for each model, original checkpoint time decraseses as the number of nodes increases. For asynchronous checkpointing instead, we can see that it significantly reduces saving time on disk with respect to original distributed checkpointing; however, as in the previous case, there is no such correlation between saving time and number of nodes involved.

Both Fig. 2 and Fig. 3, show that saving models using standard checkpointing on different storage types is almost equal for all the models and number of nodes. This can be due by the size of the files: since for the first three models (Llama-2 7B, Llama-2 13B, Llama-3.1 8B) the file sizes are light-weight, there is no such real difference between HDD ans SSD storage. While for the 70B-model, we can see a slightly improvement in saving time on the SSD.

Moreover, both Fig. 2 and Fig. 3 show that saving checkpoints in the SSDs takes the same time on average.

Figure 4 shows average asynchronous checkpointing times of different models during a pre-training, varying the number of nodes for each model up to 64 (256 GPUs). We can see that for each model, the time slightly increases as the number of nodes increases. This is likely due primarily to communication overhead between the nodes. Additionally, models of similar size (e.g. Llama-2 7B and Llama-3.1 8B) exhibit comparable average checkpointing times, whereas LLaMA 2 13B takes nearly twice as long to checkpoint compared to the smaller models. We can see that Mamba pre-training with 32 nodes has wide standard deviation, this can be due by the fact that in this case we had only one repetition of the experiments.

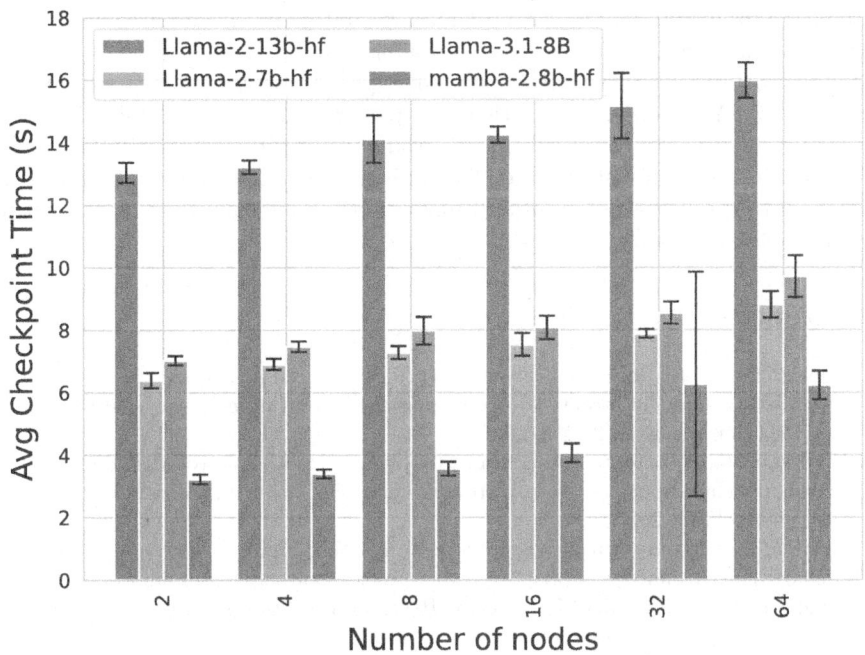

Fig. 4. Comparison of average asynchronous checkpointing time for pre-training with FineWeb dataset, on different models. Error lines: standard deviation.

5 Conclusion and Next Steps

In this study, we evaluated the impact of distributed asynchronous checkpointing on large-scale language model fine tuning and pre-training in a HPC environment. We compared asynchronous checkpointing for fine-tuning between HDD and SSD storage for different models. Our experiments on the Leonardo system demonstrated that, in some cases, DACP can significantly reduce checkpointing overhead compared to traditional distributed methods, achieving up to a 6x times improvement in checkpointing efficiency (Fig. 2). By overlapping data transfer operations with training iterations, DACP minimizes GPU idle time and enhances overall training throughput. We have seen that for LLMs with model sizes up to 70B parameters, there is no such difference on using asynchronous checkpointing using HDD or SSD storage. For pre-training, we evaluated asynchronous checkpointing for different model architectures, scaling up to 64 nodes (256 GPUs). We have seen that increasing the number of nodes the average checkpoint time has no major variations, likely due primarily to communication overhead between the nodes.

However, our results confirm that integrating asynchronous checkpointing into distributed training pipelines potentially enables better resource utilization, reducing computational waste and improving scalability for future LLM workloads. As future work, we will test different types of asynchronous checkpointing, such as [13]. Additionally, to further test performance and scalability of asynchronous checkpointing, we will focus on analyzing the convergence properties of the models to ensure stable and efficient learning. These steps will allow us to better understand the potential and limitations of asynchronous checkpointing in HPC infrastructures.

References

1. Optimizing checkpointing efficiency with pytorch dcp. https://discuss.pytorch.org/t/distributed-w-torchtitan-optimizing-checkpointing-efficiency-with-pytorch-dcp/211250, Accessed 24 Feb 2025
2. Reducing model checkpointing times by over 10x with pytorch distributed asynchronous checkpointing. https://pytorch.org/blog/reducing-checkpointing-times, Accessed 24 Feb 2025
3. Cineca, supercomputing centre, supercomputing applications and innovation department, leonardo: a pan-european pre-exascale supercomputer for hpc and ai applications. Journal of Large-Scale Research Facilities **8**, A186 (2024). https://doi.org/10.17815/jlsrf-8-186
4. Chen, M., et al.: Efficientqat: efficient quantization-aware training for large language models. ArXiv abs/2407.11062 (2024).https://doi.org/10.48550/arXiv.2407.11062
5. Chowdhery, A., et al.: Palm: scaling language modeling with pathways (2022). https://arxiv.org/abs/2204.02311
6. Dash, S., et al.: Optimizing distributed training on frontier for large language models, pp. 1–11 (2023). https://doi.org/10.48550/arXiv.2312.12705
7. Dubey, A., et al.: The llama 3 herd of models. arXiv preprint arXiv:2407.21783 (2024)
8. Fedus, W., Zoph, B., Shazeer, N.: Switch transformers: Scaling to trillion parameter models with simple and efficient sparsity (2022). https://arxiv.org/abs/2101.03961
9. Gu, A., Dao, T.: Mamba: linear-time sequence modeling with selective state spaces. arXiv preprint arXiv:2312.00752 (2023)
10. Gugger, S., et al.: Accelerate: training and inference at scale made simple, efficient and adaptable. https://github.com/huggingface/accelerate (2022)

11. Hoffmann, J., et al.: Training compute-optimal large language models. ArXiv abs/2203.15556 (2022). https://doi.org/10.48550/arXiv.2203.15556
12. Liang, W., et al.: Torchtitan: one-stop pytorch native solution for production ready LLM pre-training (2024). https://arxiv.org/abs/2410.06511
13. Maurya, A., Underwood, R., Rafique, M.M., Cappello, F., Nicolae, B.: Datastates-LLM: Lazy asynchronous checkpointing for large language models. In: Proceedings of the 33rd International Symposium on High-Performance Parallel and Distributed Computing, pp. 227–239. HPDC '24, ACM (2024). https://doi.org/10.1145/3625549.3658685
14. Mei, Z., Fu, W., Li, K., Wang, G., Zhang, H., Wu, Y.: Realhf: optimized RLHF training for large language models through parameter reallocation. ArXiv (2024). https://doi.org/10.48550/arXiv.2406.14088
15. Mohan, J., Phanishayee, A., Chidambaram, V.: {CheckFreq}: Frequent,{Fine-Grained}{DNN} checkpointing. In: 19th USENIX Conference on File and Storage Technologies (FAST 21), pp. 203–216 (2021)
16. Pang, B., Lee, L.: Seeing stars: exploiting class relationships for sentiment categorization with respect to rating scales. In: Proceedings of the ACL (2005)
17. Penedo, G., et al.: The fineweb datasets: decanting the web for the finest text data at scale. Adv. Neural. Inf. Process. Syst. **37**, 30811–30849 (2024)
18. Rojas, E., Kahira, A.N., Meneses, E., Gomez, L.B., Badia, R.M.: A study of checkpointing in large scale training of deep neural networks (2021). https://arxiv.org/abs/2012.00825
19. Touvron, H., et al.: Llama 2: open foundation and fine-tuned chat models (2023). https://arxiv.org/abs/2307.09288
20. Zhao, Y., et al.: Pytorch fsdp: experiences on scaling fully sharded data parallel (2023). https://arxiv.org/abs/2304.11277

Energy Efficiency with Sustainable Performance: Techniques, Tools, and Best Practices (EESP)

EESP 2025 Preface

Objectives/Topics

This workshop fosters an exchange of innovative strategies, tools, resources, and industry best practices to enhance energy efficiency in computing environments. As the challenges of rising energy costs, ambitious sustainability goals, and global environmental concerns continue to grow, optimizing energy use has become a crucial priority for managing computing infrastructure.

The EESP workshop focuses on advancing sustainable computing in alignment with Sustainable Development Goals, encouraging collaboration between the HPC and AI communities to foster a positive relationship between HPC, AI, and environmental health. It provides guidance to system operators and facility managers on reducing Power Usage Effectiveness (PUE) and sourcing green energy, while supporting users in making energy-conscious decisions through thoughtful experiment design. By providing visibility into energy consumption and CO_2 emissions, users can make informed choices. Although tenders today often prioritize TOP500 rankings or hardware counts, the EESP workshop emphasizes that sustained (application) performance, rather than peak performance, is crucial for future success.

EESP explores how to optimize computing environments by effectively balancing performance, power consumption, and sustainability trade-offs. The workshop provides participants with a comprehensive guidebook, including strategies designed for exascale, Tier-1, and Tier-2 supercomputing centers. By learning and exchanging about how to adopt greener, cost-effective, and energy-efficient practices, attendees and readers gain a competitive advantage in driving sustainability across their systems.

While there are only a few exascale systems (Tier-0 level), the majority of supercomputing centers globally operate at the Tier-2 level. These centers, including those in Germany, often face challenges such as high power costs and limited resources for frequent hardware upgrades. In the coming years, energy efficiency may become a critical bottleneck for their operations. Tier-0/1 and Tier-2 centers differ significantly in terms of funding, with Tier-0/1 centers typically having better opportunities to invest in energy-efficient technologies. This workshop creates a platform for dialogue between these centers, exploring how the energy-savings mechanisms used in Tier-0/1 systems can be adapted for Tier-2 centers, particularly those with limited budgets for major hardware investments. Such a dialogue is crucial for advancing global energy efficiency and aligning with broader sustainability goals. The workshop focuses on solutions that are not only financially viable but also technically sound for diverse computing environments, including data centers, cloud infrastructure, and HPC clusters.

Workshop Organization

Ayesha Afzal (General Chair) — Erlangen National High Performance Computing Center (NHR@FAU), Germany

Natalie Bates (Program Chair) — Energy Efficient HPC Working Group (EE HPC WG), USA

Siddhartha Jana (Program Chair) — Intel, USA

Sarah Neuwirth (Program Chair) — Johannes Gutenberg University Mainz, Germany

Radita Liem (Proceedings Chair) — RWTH Aachen University, Germany

Characterizing GPU Energy Usage in Exascale-Ready Portable Science Applications

William F. Godoy[1(✉)], Oscar Hernandez[1], Paul R. C. Kent[1], Maria Patrou[1], Kazi Asifuzzaman[1], Narasinga Rao Miniskar[1], Pedro Valero-Lara[1], Jeffrey S. Vetter[1], Matthew D. Sinclair[2], Jason Lowe-Power[3], and Bobby R. Bruce[3]

[1] Oak Ridge National Laboratory, Oak Ridge, TN, USA
{godoywf,oscar,kentpr,patroum,asifuzzamank,miniskarnr,valerolarap,vetter}@ornl.gov
[2] University of Wisconsin-Madison, Madison, WI, USA
sinclair@cs.wisc.edu
[3] University of California, Davis, Davis, CA, USA
{jlowepower,bbruce}@ucdavis.edu

Abstract. We characterize the GPU energy usage of two widely adopted exascale-ready applications representing two classes of particle and mesh solvers: (i) QMCPACK, a quantum Monte Carlo package, and (ii) AMReX-Castro, an adaptive mesh astrophysical code. We analyze power, temperature, utilization, and energy traces from double-/single (mixed)-precision benchmarks on NVIDIA's A100 and H100 and AMD's MI250X GPUs using queries in NVML and rocm_smi_lib, respectively. We explore application-specific metrics to provide insights on energy vs. performance trade-offs. Our results suggest that mixed-precision energy savings range between 6–25% on QMCPACK and 45% on AMReX-Castro. Also, we found gaps in the AMD tooling used on Frontier GPUs that need to be understood, while query resolutions on NVML have little variability between 1 ms-1 s. Overall, application level knowledge is crucial to define energy-cost/science-benefit opportunities for the codesign of future supercomputer architectures in the post-Moore era.

Keywords: Energy efficiency · HPC Applications · GPU Power

1 Introduction

As energy consumption and costs have grown exponentially in the post-Moore exascale era, high-performance computing (HPC) faces new challenges [23]. Interest in the energy-cost/science-benefit trade-offs is again gaining traction[1] as HPC systems become more heterogeneous [32]. Since HPC traditionally focused on optimizing time-to-solution, it is crucial to understand applications characteristics to design future energy-efficient hardware. Here, we provide insights

---
[1] https://www.orau.gov/2024EECWorkshop.

on the GPU energy characteristics of two applications developed under the US Department of Energy's (DOE's) Exascale Computing Project (ECP, 2016–2023) [16] that are widely used at HPC production facilities across the world: (i) QMCPACK [14,15,19], a quantum Monte Carlo (QMC) package, and (ii) the mesh-based AMReX-Castro's [1] compressible astrophysics code. We capture power, utilization, temperature, and calculate energy traces on NVIDIA's A100 and H100 GPUs and AMD's MI250X GPU. To capture these measurements, we designed an open-source `HWEnergyTracer.jl`[2] tool that runs side-by-side with an application and captures queries from NVIDIA's Management Library (NVML), and AMD's ROCm System Management Interface Library (`rocm_smi_lib`).

The paper is organized as follows: Sect. 2 provides information for QMCPACK, AMReX-Castro and selected benchmarks. Section 3 describes our methodology and the targeted GPU systems. Section 4 presents our results and analysis of the applications' energy characteristics. Related work in HPC is shown in Sect. 5. Finally, Sect. 6 provides our conclusions and future directions. To the best of our knowledge, our contributions on quantifying science-per-energy has not previously been an integral part of the applications' development process.

2 Background

QMCPACK and the NiO benchmark: QMCPACK is an open-source, many-body, ab-initio QMC framework solving the Schrödinger equation for atoms, molecules, 2D nanomaterials, and solids. QMC methods lead to far greater accuracy, but at a much greater computational cost. Key recent QMCPACK improvements made during the ECP included (i) a redesigned diffusion Monte Carlo (DMC) solver [19] – the focus on this study – using OpenMP offload capabilities on GPUs, and (ii) software engineering improvements for CPU/GPUs [9]. We use the nickel oxide (NiO) supercell benchmark[3] which is characterized by the total number of electrons, for which its required memory grows quadratically, while its computation increases at a cubic rate.

AMReX-Castro and the Sedov case: AMReX [36] is a widely used adaptive mesh refinement framework that powers several HPC applications running at scale. AMReX decomposes a problem into levels of adaptive resolution and rectangular patches. During the ECP, AMReX's solver capabilities were advanced for new CPU/GPU architectures, while energy-efficiency is in the product roadmap [22]. We use the Castro astrophysical radiation-magneto-hydrodynamics code that builds on AMReX to run the 2D Sedov spherical blast wave standard problem on a rectangular AMR mesh. Its computational costs are typically driven by the time evolution of the total number of AMR cells [8].

---

[2] https://github.com/JuliaORNL/HWEnergyTracer.jl.
[3] https://www.olcf.ornl.gov/wp-content/uploads/OLCF-6_QMCPACK_description-1.pdf.

3 Methodology

We use the Julia language [3] to call queries listed in Table 1 in NVIDIA's NVML by using the CUDA.jl package [2], and AMD's rocm_smi_lib C API using Julia's foreign function interface. The result is the HWEnergyTracer.jl tool that runs 15 s before the start and 10 s after the end of the application run to guarantee a steady static power state. Power values are integrated over time to obtain energy traces, and to minimize observed false positives (over-/under-shoots). We use three different GPU systems, 2 NVIDIA and 1 AMD, as described in Table 2. No power capping was applied in this work.

Table 1. Queries used for NVIDIA's NVML and AMD's rocm_smi_lib

Metric	Relevant Query	Description
NVIDIA	**nvmlDeviceGet***	
Power (W)	PowerUsage	Power usage of the GPU and its associated circuitry (e.g., memory) averaged over a 1 s interval [34]
Utilization (%)	UtilizationRates	Percent of time over the past sample period, between 1 and $\frac{1}{6}$ s, during which kernels were executing
Temperature (°C)	Temperature	Current temperature readings for the device
AMD	**rsmi_dev_***	
Power (W)	power_ave_get	device energy counter average for a short time (1 ms)
Utilization (%)	busy_percent_get	Percentage of time busy processing
Temperature (°C)	temp_metric_get	Retrieved from the temperature sensor for the device

Table 2. System hardware and software used in this study

System	Milan0	Hudson	Frontier
Hardware			
GPU-per-node	2 NVIDIA A100	2 NVIDIA H100	8 GCD AMD MI250X
Memory(GB)/Bandwidth(GB/s)	HBM2E 80/1,940	HBM3 94/1,940	HBM2E 64/3,276
Thermal Design Power (W)	300	400	500
Software			
GPU Tool Chain	NVHPC 24.9	NVHPC 24.9	ROCm 6.2
QMCPACK	v3.17.1	v3.17.1	v3.17.1
Compiler	Clang 19.1	Clang 19.1	AMDClang 6.2
Programming Model	OpenMP-offload	OpenMP-offload	OpenMP-offload
AMReX-Castro	v24.12	v24.12	v24.12
Compiler	GCC 13.2	GCC 13.2	GCC 12.3
Programming Model	CUDA 12.4	CUDA 12.4	HIP 6.2

4 Results

Results are presented for the application energy characteristics traces. We discuss: (i) regions of interests based on power consumption, (ii) measurement resolutions from 1 ms to 1 s to capture difference of the averages values given by the vendor tools, (iii) impact of double/single precision, and (iv) exploring application-specific energy-efficiency metrics (e.g. science/Joule).

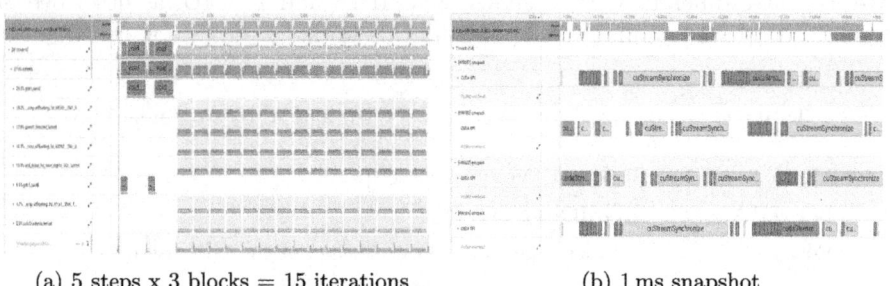

(a) 5 steps x 3 blocks = 15 iterations (b) 1 ms snapshot

Fig. 1. QMCPACK NiO Benchmark DMC GPU traces on an NVIDIA H100.

4.1 QMCPACK NiO Benchmark Results

We run the NiO benchmark for a representative supercell of 512 atoms and 6,144 electrons. Figure 1 shows the DMC code profile showing the asynchronous nature of kernel launching for each MC "walker" to maximize GPU usage (blue top row) [19]. The number of walkers is maximized to fit on GPU memory [6].

Figures 2 and 3 show the power, temperature, utilization and energy traces for the maximum number of walkers on the NVIDIA H100 and A100, and AMD MI250X GPUs, respectively, for different query time resolutions. In all cases, we use double-precision configurations. The query time resolution used in subsequent runs is highlighted as the larger figure. Also, the four run stages are captured by the traces for spline data initialization (showing low GPU activity), Variational Monte Carlo (VMC), matrix inversions, and DMC.

On the H100 and A100, the DMC power and utilization patterns match the kernel behavior shown in Fig. 1 a. As for the MI250X, the DMC stage power shows similar characteristics for minimum values, but peaks are not signaled as those in NVIDIA GPUs. This might be explained by the different query methodologies used by NVIDIA NVML, which has a wider time average frame of 1 s. The MI250X utilization shows fast variations between 100 and 0% highlighting the need for more robust energy tooling for further investigation. Energy consumption varies nearly linearly for all cases allowing for simple modeling of this benchmark. On the H100, the overall integrated energy usage ($\approx$112–115 kJ) shows little sensitivity, $\approx$2.6% up to 1 s, to the different resolutions. Importantly, the 1 ms resolution yields false positive results, as shown in the spikes in Fig. 2 a,

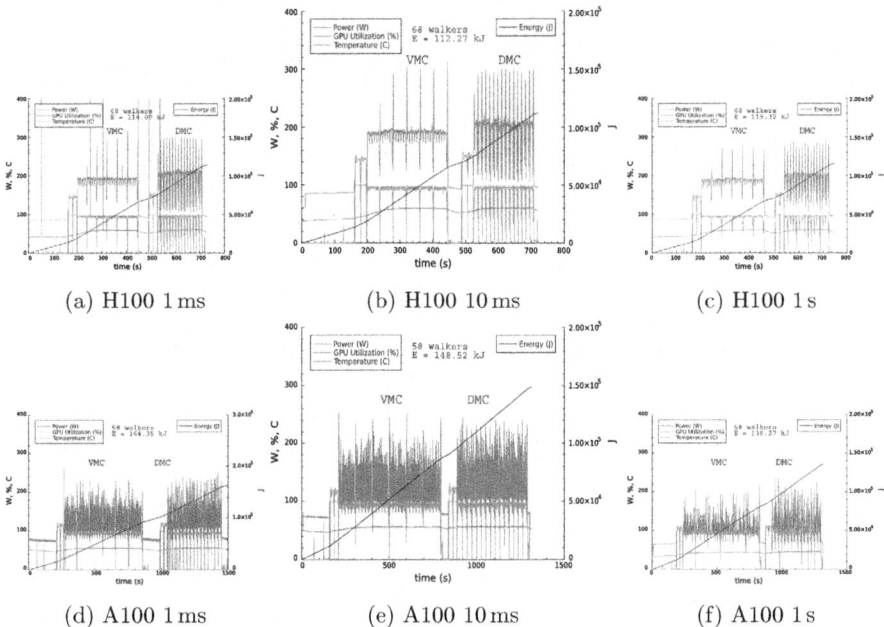

Fig. 2. Energy characteristics of the QMCPACK NiO benchmark on NVIDIA H100 and A100 for different query time resolutions.

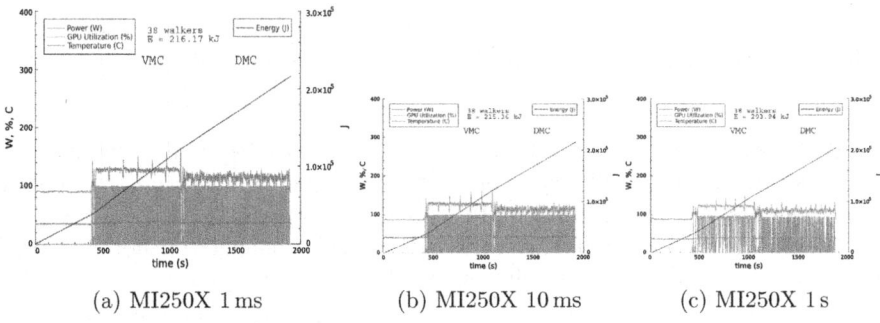

Fig. 3. Energy characteristics of the QMCPACK NiO benchmark on an AMD MI250X for different query time resolutions.

which are a repeatable pattern in our experiments. Additionally, the 1 s resolution is not enough to capture variations reinforcing the need for experimenting with finer resolutions. On the A100, the power traces have more variability than for the H100. It is unclear if this is due to changes in the methodology for measuring power in more recent NVIDIA GPUs or if it is an actual hardware characteristic. Importantly, querying at 1 ms introduces overhead in the time-to-solution on the A100, we ensured this is a repeatable pattern. Overall, both the A100 and H100 runs have similar energy characteristics, although as expected

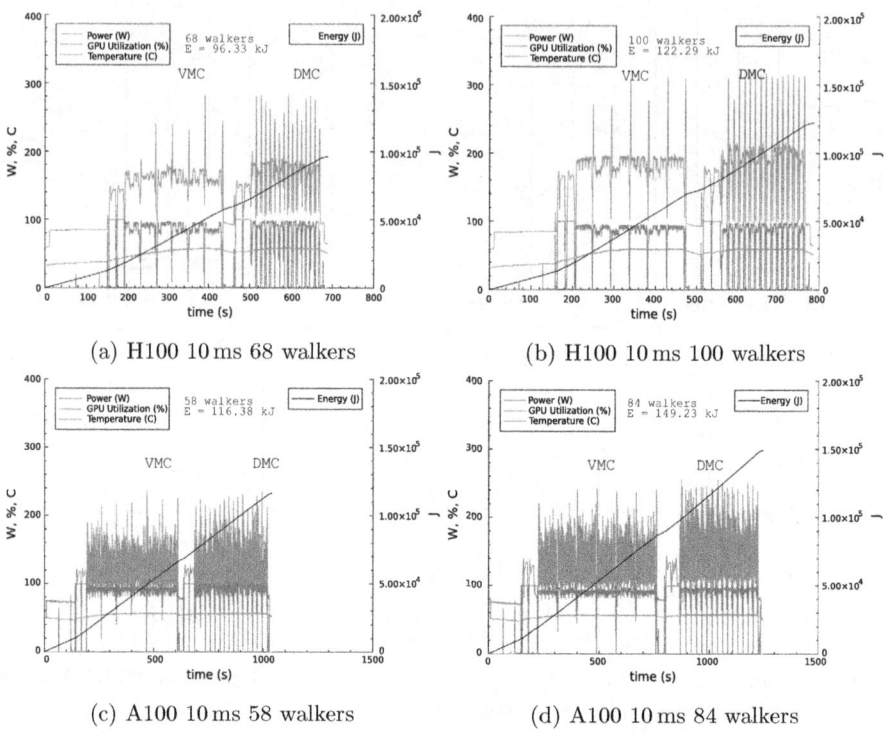

Fig. 4. Mixed-precision traces on NVIDIA H100 and A100 for (a) max double-precision walkers (68 and 58) and (b) max mixed-precision walkers (100 and 84).

the H100 is more performance and energy efficient. As for AMD, energy characteristics are slightly different. As for the cause, either the time-to-solution (and therefore the energy consumption) is higher than it is on the A100 (and the H100). Two things stand out: (i) ≤10 ms measurements do not introduce noticeable overhead, but 1 s resolutions might not be sufficient to capture variability for this workload. (ii) The DMC average power is lower for the AMD MI250X than for the NVIDIA GPUs at the expense of longer time-to-solution for a smaller number of walkers. In all cases, temperature values remain nearly constant, thereby indicating that thermal solutions for cooling the devices run efficiently for these benchmarks.

Mixed Precision Runs: QMCPACK uses a mixed-precision (single/double) option that reduces memory consumption at the expense of less accurate results. This is applied in two ways: (i) a shorter time-to-solution for the same number of walkers, or (ii) more walkers to fill the GPU's memory and increase utilization. These two options are illustrated in Figs. 4 and 5 for the NVIDIA H100 and A100, and AMD MI250X GPUs, respectively.

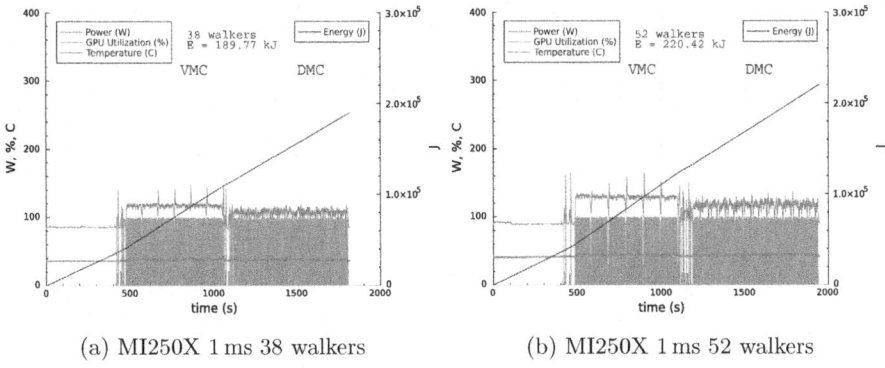

Fig. 5. AMD MI250X mixed-precision traces for (a) max double-precision walkers (38) and (b) max mixed-precision walkers (52).

For these cases, (a) and (c) contain the same number of walkers as the maximum double-precision runs, and (b) contains the maximum number of walkers for a mixed-precision run. In all cases, mixed-precision runs result in energy savings, thanks to faster times-to-solution than the double-precision runs. This is more evident on the runs with NVIDIA's H100 and A100 GPUs than with AMD's MI250X GPU. Because some components keep double-precision representations, the savings are not expected to be close to 50%. QMCPACK's mixed-precision has not been thoroughly studied for the latest GPUs. For example, this work identified different default behaviors (e.g., DMC mixed precision was running extra calculations) that has been corrected in QMCPACK. Thus showing the importance of monitoring energy characteristics during development. A simple power and utilization trace can showcase hardware usage correlations with expected algorithm behavior.

Energy Metric. The DMC performance metric (throughput) is measured as the computational cost of advancing walkers at each step and block [6]. We adapt this metric for energy efficiency (science/energy) by changing the denominator from time-to-solution to energy consumption in:

$$\text{Throughput}_{\text{Energy}} = \frac{\text{walkers} \times \text{blocks} \times \text{steps}}{\text{DMC energy}}, \quad (1)$$

where DMC energy is the energy needed by the DMC region.

Metric results are presented in Table 3 along with the average GPU power and utilization. Using the maximum number of walkers for mixed precision on H100 leads to the greatest science/energy ratio, and running in double precision draws higher energy rates. Energy savings from mixed-precision for the same number of walkers are on the order or 6%–25%. We also added cases to compare H100 versus A100, and A100 versus MI250X runs for the same number of walkers. Energy improvements between A100 and H100 cases are roughly 1.5×, whereas

Table 3. Energy metrics for QMCPACK's DMC on the NiO a512 benchmark for multiple GPU configurations

Configuration	Walkers *Max	Throughput Energy (1/kJ)	Power (W)	GPU (%)
NVIDIA				
H100-mixed	*100	38.69	190.02	72.54
H100-mixed	*68	33.20	172.60	74.60
H100-double	*68	27.26	191.87	83.92
H100-mixed	84	37.56	182.31	74.69
H100-mixed	58	32.42	174.24	75.93
H100-double	58	26.28	181.89	78.58
A100-mixed	*84	25.25	136.10	85.76
A100-mixed	*58	20.86	121.59	85.08
A100-double	*58	17.31	124.97	88.03
A100-mixed	52	21.41	122.22	83.84
A100-mixed	38	16.13	109.01	86.92
A100-double	38	15.58	119.11	86.69
AMD				
MI250X-mixed	*52	9.12	115.97	39.33
MI250X-mixed	*38	7.57	106.36	40.12
MI250X-double	*38	6.19	112.61	39.27

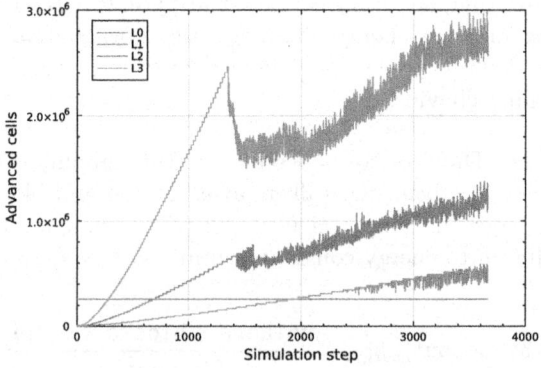

Fig. 6. AMReX-Castro Sedov problem advanced cells per AMR mesh level as a function of simulation step.

A100 runs are 2× more efficient than MI250X runs. Results for AMD's MI250X suggest that improvements are needed on either the software or vendor tool stack to achieve results comparable to NVIDIA's A100.

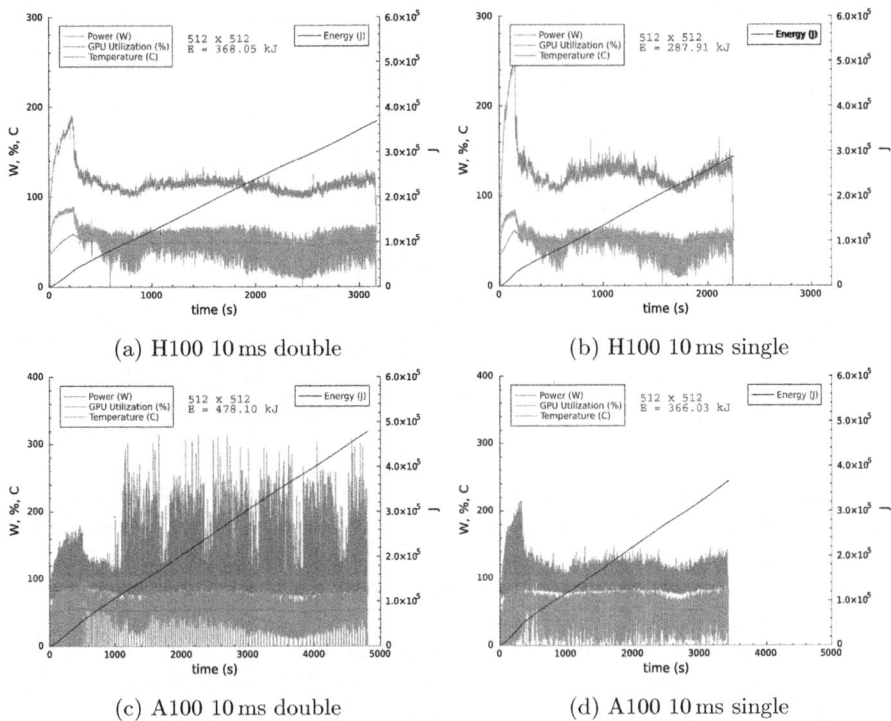

Fig. 7. AMReX-Castro Sedov energy characteristics on NVIDIA H100 and A100 for a 512×512 base mesh with CFL = 0.25 using (a) double and (b) single precision.

4.2 AMReX-Castro Sedov

We ran the 2D Sedov case to capture an AMR simulation's influence on energy characteristics. Compute activity comes from advancing a variable evolution (governed by PDEs) on cells placed at different mesh levels. Figure 6 shows the evolution of four mesh levels (L0–L3) in a coarser-to-finer order as a function of simulation steps. As seen, the finer mesh (L3) dominates the computation, and all of them except the base mesh (L0) evolve similarly. We expect that energy consumption would be dominated by this evolution and the use of double- or single-precision representations.

Double/single-precision In all cases, we use the previously set query resolution for NVIDIA (10 ms) and AMD (1 ms) GPUs, and fixed the Courant-Friedrichs-Lewy (CFL) condition to a value of 0.25. Figure 7 shows the traces on NVIDIA H100 and A100 runs when using the largest possible base 512×512 mesh and double- and single-precision representations. As expected, power and utilization show a strong correlation with the finer mesh evolution in Fig. 6. Power variability is high for the rapid evolution of the mesh levels (1,200–1,400 simulation steps), reaching an absolute peak and stabilizing until the end of the

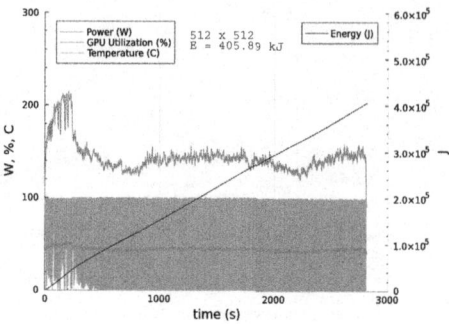

Fig. 8. AMReX-Castro Sedov energy characteristics on an AMD MI250X for a 512 × 512 base mesh using double precision, 1 ms resolution, and CFL = 0.25.

run. The use of single precision (Figs. 7 b and 7 d) represents a faster code execution ($\approx 2200/3200 = 68\%$) when compared with double precision (Figs. 7 a and 7 c) but a larger fraction in terms of energy ($\approx 287/368 = 78\%$). In fact, the initial peak power is higher than for double precision. Nevertheless, the H100 runs demonstrate the improvements in energy consumption over the previous A100 by using only 60% and 78% as much energy for the double- and single-precision cases, respectively. For AMD, the MI250X is more energy and time efficient than the A100 for the Sedov case when using double precision (Fig. 8). Power characteristics are very similar to those observed on NVIDIA's H100.

We did not observe differences between double- and single-precision runs on the MI250X, so the latter is not provided. Energy-efficiency metrics still need to be studied for this application as the influence of more complex performance and energy drivers (e.g., non-linear evolution in the AMR mesh sizes and CFL number) is highly problem- and hardware-dependent.

5 Related Work

Energy efficiency in HPC has garnered significant attention in recent years at all levels (including applications, facilities, and tools). Muriedas, et al. and Yang, et al. measured HPC application's energy consumption on Intel and NVIDIA GPUs [11,35]. Schieffer et al. characterized energy on AMD matrix cores using rocm_smi_lib [25]. Other work has designed a variety of tools for predicting GPU power consumption. This includes AccelWattch [12], machine learning models to predict power consumption [17,26,33], and flexible simulator interfaces [31]. However, most of these approaches focus on modeling and simulation tools, unlike our work. Simsek et al. [29,30] studied the energy efficiency of the SPH-EXA astrophysics application on CPUs and GPUs as well as the impact of dynamic frequency scaling using the open-source Power Measurement Toolkit [5]. Govind et al. [10] investigated the power characteristics of scientific and machine learning applications on the Perlmutter supercomputer. Zhao et al. studied power traces of the popular Vienna Ab initio Simulation Package on

NVIDIA A100 GPUs including power capping techniques [37]. Foster et al. [7] studied the energy efficiency of machine learning benchmarks. Mantovani et al. studied the performance and energy consumption of HPC workloads on Arm ThunderX2 CPU cores [20]. Mittal and Vetter presented a survey of methods for improving GPU energy efficiency [21]. Bridges et al. provided an overview of techniques for obtaining GPU power consumption data [4]. At the facility level, Karimi et al. presented a system-wide HPC monitoring framework on the Summit supercomputer [13]. Shin et al. introduced a comprehensive strategy for the sustainability of future HPC systems [27]. Silva et al. presented a comprehensive survey on the energy of state-of-the-art supercomputers [28]. Rrapaj et al. quantified the long-term energy consumption in systems of the National Energy Research Scientific Computing Center [24].

6 Discussion, Conclusions and Future Work

We quantified and analyzed the energy consumption characteristics of two science applications that are widely used in HPC systems—QMCPACK and AMReX-Castro—on recent NVIDIA A100 and H100, and AMD MI250X GPUs. Kernel characteristics were mapped to the power, temperature, utilization, and energy traces for different configurations, including reduced floating-point precision. Application-specific metrics were discussed compare the science-per-energy. Some key observations:

- **Observation 1:** small variability for the power, utilization, temperature traces and integrated energy calculations were observed for vendor APIs, NVML and rocm_smi_lib, in our application measurements.
- **Observation 2:** reduced floating-point precision resulted in more energy-efficient runs, while not at an ideal 50% rate these were on the order of 6%–25% on QMCPACK (on NVIDIA and AMD) and 45% for AMReX-Castro (on NVIDIA only).
- **Observation 3:** Energy-efficiency improvements (on the order of 1.5×) were shown for NVIDIA's H100 over their A100. Room for improvement exists for AMD's GPU tools and applications as the ecosystem matures.
- **Observation 4:** the proposed science-per-energy metric for QMCPACK allows for comparison across GPU vendors and generations. It factors in computational time aspects into the total energy required. A AMReX-Castro science-per-energy metric requires factoring-in the AMR variability in the number of cells advanced at every level.

Next steps include expanding to more HPC-relevant scientific workloads, understanding energy at the different GPU component levels, and integrating modeling for design space exploration (e.g., GEM5 [18]). As HPC facilities energy costs increase, we conclude that this type of analysis at the application level is crucial in the co-design of future supercomputing architectures.

Acknowledgements. This manuscript has been authored by UT-Battelle, LLC, under contract DE-AC05-00OR22725 with the US Department of Energy (DOE). The US government retains and the publisher, by accepting the article for publication, acknowledges that the US government retains a nonexclusive, paid-up, irrevocable, worldwide license to publish or reproduce the published form of this manuscript, or allow others to do so, for US government purposes. DOE will provide public access to these results of federally sponsored research in accordance with the DOE Public Access Plan (https://www.energy.gov/doe-public-access-plan). This material is based on work supported by the DOE's Office of Science, Office of Advanced Scientific Computing Research through EXPRESS: 2023 Exploratory Research for Extreme Scale Science. PRCK was supported by the DOE's Office of Science, Basic Energy Sciences, Materials Sciences and Engineering Division as part of the Computational Materials Sciences Program and the Center for Predictive Simulation of Functional Materials. This research used resources of the Oak Ridge Leadership Computing Facility and the Experimental Computing Laboratory at the Oak Ridge National Laboratory, which is supported by the DOE's Office of Science under Contract No. DE-AC05-00OR22725. WG would like to acknowledge Brandon Tran from the University of Wisconsin for the valuable discussion on NVML.

References

1. Almgren, A., et al.: Castro: a massively parallel compressible astrophysics simulation code. JOSS **5**(54) (2020). https://doi.org/10.21105/joss.02513
2. Besard, T., et al.: Effective extensible programming: unleashing julia on GPUs. IEEE TPDS **30**(4) (2019). https://doi.org/10.1109/TPDS.2018.2872064
3. Bezanson, J., et al.: Julia: a fresh approach to numerical computing. SIAM Rev. **59**(1), 65–98 (2017). https://doi.org/10.1137/141000671
4. Bridges, R.A., Imam, N., Mintz, T.M.: Understanding GPU power: a survey of profiling, modeling, and simulation methods. ACM Comput. Surv. **49**(3) (2016)
5. Corda, S., et al.: Pmt: power measurement toolkit. In: IEEE/ACM HUST Workshop (2022). https://doi.org/10.1109/HUST56722.2022.00011
6. Elwasif, W., et al.: Application experiences on a GPU-accelerated arm-based HPC testbed. In: Proceedings of the HPC Asia 2023 Workshops. p. 35–49. HPCAsia '23 Workshops, Association for Computing Machinery, New York (2023). https://doi.org/10.1145/3581576.3581621
7. Foster, B., et al.: Evaluating energy efficiency of GPUs using ML benchmarks. In: IPDPSW (2023). https://doi.org/10.1109/IPDPSW59300.2023.00019
8. Godoy, W.F., et al.: Modeling pre-exascale AMR Parallel I/O workloads via proxy applications. In: IPDPSW (2022). https://doi.org/10.1109/IPDPSW55747.2022.00153
9. Godoy, W.F., et al.: Software stewardship and advancement of a high-performance computing scientific application: QMCPACK. FGCS **163**, 107502 (2025)
10. Govind, A., et al.: Comparing power signatures of HPC workloads: machine learning vs simulation. In: SC-W (2023). https://doi.org/10.1145/3624062.3624274
11. Gutiérrez Hermosillo Muriedas, J.P., et al.: Perun: benchmarking energy consumption of high-performance computing applications. In: Euro-Par (2023). https://doi.org/10.1007/978-3-031-39698-4_2
12. Kandiah, V., et al.: AccelWattch: a power modeling framework for modern GPUs. In: MICRO (October 2021)

13. Karimi, A.M., et al.: Power profile monitoring and tracking evolution of system-wide HPC workloads. In: ICDCS (2024). https://doi.org/10.1109/ICDCS60910.2024.00018
14. Kent, P.R.C., et al.: QMCPACK: advances in the development, efficiency, and application of auxiliary field and real-space variational and diffusion quantum Monte Carlo. J. Chem. Phys. **152**(17) (2020). https://doi.org/10.1063/5.0004860
15. Kim, J., et al.: QMCPACK: an open source ab initio quantum Monte Carlo package for the electronic structure of atoms, molecules and solids. J. Phys. Cond Matter **30**(19), 195901 (2018)
16. Kothe, D., et al.: Exascale computing in the united states. CiSE **21**(1) (2019)
17. Lee, W., et al.: PowerTrain: a learning-based calibration of McPAT power models. In: ISLPED, pp. 189–194 (2015)
18. Lowe-Power, J., et al.: The gem5 simulator: V20.0 (2020). https://arxiv.org/abs/2007.03152
19. Luo, Y., Doak, P., Kent, P.: A high-performance design for hierarchical parallelism in the QMCPACK Monte Carlo code. In: SC-W HiPar (2022). https://doi.org/10.1109/HiPar56574.2022.00008
20. Mantovani, F., et al.: Performance and energy consumption of HPC workloads on a cluster based on Arm ThunderX2 CPU. FGCS **112** (2020)
21. Mittal, S., Vetter, J.S.: A survey of methods for analyzing and improving GPU energy efficiency. ACM Comput. Surv. **47**(2) (2014)
22. Myers, A., et al.: AMReX and pyAMReX: looking beyond the exascale computing project. IJHPCA **38**(6) (2024). https://doi.org/10.1177/10943420241271017
23. Reed, D., Gannon, D., Dongarra, J.: Reinventing high performance computing: challenges and opportunities (2022). https://arxiv.org/abs/2203.02544
24. Rrapaj, E., et al.: Power consumption trends in supercomputers: a study of NERSC's Cori and perlmutter machines. In: ISC (2024). https://doi.org/10.23919/ISC.2024.10528943
25. Schieffer, G., et al.: On the rise of AMD matrix cores: performance, power efficiency, and programmability. In: ISPASS (2024). https://doi.org/10.1109/ISPASS61541.2024.00022
26. Shim, J.S., et al.: DeepPM: transformer-based power and performance prediction for energy-aware software. In: DATE, pp. 1491–1496 (2022)
27. Shin, W., et al.: Towards sustainable post-exascale leadership computing. In: SC-W (2024). https://doi.org/10.1109/SCW63240.2024.00225
28. Silva, C., et al.: A review on the decarbonization of high-performance computing centers. Renew. Sustain. Energy Rev. **189**, 114019 (2024)
29. Simsek, O.S., et al.: Accurate measurement of application-level energy consumption for energy-aware large-scale simulations. In: SC-W (2023). https://doi.org/10.1145/3624062.3624272
30. Simsek, O.S., et al.: Increasing energy efficiency of astrophysics simulations through GPU frequency scaling. In: SC-W (2024). https://doi.org/10.1109/SCW63240.2024.00229
31. Smith, A., et al.: Designing generalizable power models for open-source architecture simulators. In: OSCAR (2024)
32. Vetter, J.S., et al.: Productive computational science in the era of extreme heterogeneity. Tech. rep., USDOE Office of Science (SC), Washington, D.C. (United States) (2018). https://doi.org/10.2172/1473756
33. Wu, G., et al.: GPGPU performance and power estimation using machine learning. In: HPCA, pp. 564–576 (2015). https://doi.org/10.1109/HPCA.2015.7056063

34. Yang, Z., et al.: Accurate and convenient energy measurements for GPUs: a detailed study of NVIDIA GPU's built-in power sensor. In: SC24 (2024). https://doi.org/10.1109/SC41406.2024.00028
35. Yang, Z., et al.: Accurate and convenient energy measurements for GPUs: a detailed study of NVIDIA GPU's built-in power sensor. In: SC (2024). https://doi.org/10.1109/SC41406.2024.00028
36. Zhang, W., et al.: AMReX: a framework for block-structured adaptive mesh refinement. JOSS **4**(37) (2019). https://doi.org/10.21105/joss.01370
37. Zhao, Z., et al.: Understanding VASP Power Profiles on NVIDIA A100 GPUs. In: SC-W (2024). https://doi.org/10.1109/SCW63240.2024.00189

What A Waste

Shaina Smith(✉), Jordan M. Abt, and Ryan E. Grant

Queen's University, Kingston, ON, Canada
{22sas7,jordan.abt,ryan.grant}@queensu.ca

Abstract. The immense demand for high performance computational resources has led to large increases in the energy consumption of data centers. Higher energy use tends to correlate with more waste heat being produced. This waste heat is often discarded, but it is a valuable resource that many data centers are starting to reuse for many different applications. In this paper we propose the Heat Reuse Factor (HRF) metric to quantify a data center's heat reuse approach. We then propose and define the Green Supercomputing Ratio (GSR) metric to determine the efficiency of a facility based on the HRF value and the amount of CO_2 emissions that are offset in accordance with green energy practices. Several examples of how to use the proposed metrics for varying heat reuse opportunities are covered using values for a Theoretical and a Practical data center. The resulting HRF and GSR values are provided to illustrate how HRF and GSR can be used to design more efficient data centers in the future.

Keywords: High Performance Computing · Data Center · Heat Reuse · Heat Recapture · Green Computing · Sustainability

1 Introduction

The increasing expansion and progression of technology in the past few decades has developed a growing need to store information and run applications such as Artificial Intelligence. This need has been filled by an increase in the number of data centers built around the world.

A data center (DC) is a large building that houses computational resources such as central processing units (CPUs) and graphical processing units (GPUs), in addition to cooling equipment, and mechanical and electrical components. DCs have become the cornerstone for conducting computational-based research in addition to being a necessity for several industries [1]. Due to the persistent immense demand for computational resources, DC operations require massive amounts of electricity to keep servers and cooling systems continuously working optimally. The United States Department of Energy reported that the energy used by DCs is 10–50 times more than an office building [2]. The International Energy Agency reported 1–1.3% of the global electricity use in 2022 was by DCs worldwide [3].

Most of the electricity supplied to a server is converted into heat, making cooling systems a necessity [4]. As DCs grow and the amount of electricity supplied to them increases, research on recapturing and reusing this dissipated waste heat has gained recognition. Reusing waste heat would improve energy consumption and greenhouse gas emissions produced by DCs [5]. Heat reuse is an important aspect to consider for the future of DCs because it uses a resource that is currently being wasted to reduce the costs of various applications.

The Power Usage Effectiveness (PUE) metric quantifies a DC's energy efficiency by providing a value based on the ratio between the total power consumption of the facility and the total IT power consumption. However, with the push towards sustainable and green computing, more DCs are moving toward reusing the generated heat from their servers for applications that would otherwise require power from the power grid. Using waste heat for useful purposes is important for efficiency and cost-effectiveness, and can help offset the environmental impact of DCs, but provides a complex problem: there is currently no way to quantify and compare the heat reuse approaches of DCs.

This has led to efforts using the PUE metric for heat recapture. Ljungqvist et al. conducted a study on free cooling methods using waste heat and used the PUE metric to demonstrate how heat reuse reduces energy consumption [6]. Haywood et al. proposed using recaptured heat to power an absorption-based cooling system for a DC [7]. Although the authors also found their proposed cooling system would decrease a DC's PUE to less than 1, using the PUE metric in this context is misleading since it captures facility power usage but does not reflect heat reuse. The Green Grid proposed the Energy Reuse Effectiveness (ERE) metric in 2010 [8]. The metric uses a defined Energy Reuse Factor (ERF) to form a relationship between the PUE and the ERE. The ERE metric measures and quantifies the energy that is being reused for other purposes divided by the total energy brought into a DC.

Since heat generation is a byproduct of the computation, the PUE and ERE metrics only capture the facility's electricity consumption. It does not capture how much of the total generated heat is being used in comparison to how much has been lost or wasted. These are both important factors to consider when examining the efficiency of a heat reuse approach. Due to the increase in energy required to cool servers in warmer climates, the PUE in colder climates will be lower and will seem to indicate an efficient facility, even if that is untrue from a heat reuse and green computing perspective. Furthermore, some heat reuse approaches use generated heat more effectively in comparison to others. The lack of an industry-wide quantifiable metric makes it challenging to understand how and why some approaches for DC heat reuse are objectively better.

This paper makes the following contributions:

1. Proposes the Heat Reuse Factor (HRF) metric;
2. Proposes the Green Supercomputing Ratio (GSR) metric;
3. Explores current heat reuse options and future possibilities;
4. Provides heat reuse examples of how to calculate the HRF and GSR.

2 Background

2.1 Energy Consumption and Heat Reuse

In 2022, approximately 460 TWh were consumed by DCs around the world [9], the majority of which was converted to heat. For some DCs, 40% of the consumed energy is required to cool the DC to prevent system damage, and the heat is released into the environment [10]. An alternative to releasing this waste heat is to capture and reuse the heat for other purposes. This reduces the carbon footprint of the DC and decreases costs (and emissions) for the application that substitutes waste heat for traditional heating methods. Zimmermann et al. introduced an equation for the economic value of heat, where it varies with the temperature and heat reuse application [11]. In this paper, we focus on determining how much heat can be reused and how much CO_2 can be offset in doing so. There are many difficulties in using this waste heat. DCs produce low-temperature waste heat, cooling methods can make heat difficult to capture, waste heat is challenging to transport, and cost can be a deterrent. An option to increase the quality of the heat is to use a heat pump, however, it does require electricity to operate. There are applications for waste heat that overcome these issues as well, some of which will be discussed in this paper.

2.2 Data Center Cooling

A common cooling practice for DCs is to place servers such that there are cold and hot aisles, with cold air passing through the servers. Fluid-air heat exchangers cool the servers with air and then cool the resulting hot air with liquid. Servers can be fitted with pipes that pass cool fluids across the equipment, allowing the equipment to stay dry. Direct liquid cooling (DLC) is a DC cooling option involving chiller-cooled water flowing over cold plates next to the heat source. Hot-water cooling is also an option for cooling DCs that produces high quality waste heat [12]. A newer model is liquid-immersion cooling, where the servers are placed inside dielectric fluids, allowing for better heat exchange as the surfaces of the equipment come in direct contact with the fluids. Each cooling option has different benefits in terms of ease of setup and efficiency, with some being better for heat reuse, as the waste heat is more concentrated or transportable.

In-house cooling systems in DCs can also be powered by waste heat. This option for heat reuse can decrease the amount of electricity needed from the power grid. A study by Haywood et al. explores using water as a heat transfer liquid; the heat from a CPU could be collected in a phase-change thermal storage unit to power an absorption chiller [7].

2.3 Heat Reuse Examples

Once recaptured, there are many potential uses in addition to power generation for the waste heat from servers, including district heating, greenhouse heating, and desalination.

District Heating. District heating distributes heat through pipes to homes and businesses to heat space and water. Significant infrastructure is needed to transport heat from the source to the buildings that use it; it is a heat distribution network. Fuel and heat sources include renewable heat such as geothermal wells and solar collectors, excess heat from combined heat and power plants, and industrial processes [13]. Yuan et al. reviewed waste heat recovery and uses in DCs, including a heating supply for residential and building heating, and heating nearby facilities such as greenhouses and swimming halls [14]. Due to heat having low relocation abilities, the location of the DC must be near a district heating-based area and requires access to its infrastructure.

Greenhouse Heating. Waste heat can also be reused to heat greenhouses. Some locations need heated greenhouses throughout the growing season to grow produce, as the climate does not allow it. Using DC waste heat can offset high heating costs, as seen in a study by Ljungvist et al. [15]. This option is useful for locations with poor climates for growing produce. In some locations, the time of year dictates whether the greenhouses need additional heating. For climates with diverse seasons, heating greenhouses may not be a practical use for waste heat as there will be warm periods where the heat will be wasted unless another use is found.

Desalination. There is a shortage of clean drinking water in many parts of the world. This pairs well with DC waste heat, as saltwater can be desalinated using heat to generate drinking water, and many places with clean water shortages have saltwater nearby. Water is required year-round, so more waste heat can be reused in this application, as seen in a study by Sondur et al. [16]. This application is limited to regions with large bodies of saltwater, where the DC can be supplied with saltwater to provide the surrounding area with drinking water.

3   Heat Reuse Factor and Green Supercomputing Ratio

We propose a Heat Reuse Factor (HRF) equation (Eq. (1)) for facilities to quantify the ratio of generated heat that is used for another purpose. The numerator is the total heat in British thermal units (BTU) that the facility reuses. This number will likely differ from the denominator (the amount of heat generated by IT equipment in BTU) due to loss. Loss is the heat wasted as a result of transmission or storage of the heat medium. For example, the loss will be small if the heat is not transported and can be controlled with insulated piping over longer distances. A result of 0 indicates no heat is being reused by the facility. A value of 1 indicates that all of the heat the facility is generating is being reused; however, this value is unlikely due to loss.

$$HRF = \frac{Heat\ Reused\ (BTU)}{Total\ Heat\ Generated\ (BTU)}, \quad 0 \leq HRF \leq 1 \quad (1)$$

The HRF equation only accounts for the heat reused in a DC and does not accurately assess how impactful a facility's practices are. To better understand how climate-friendly a facility is, we propose a CO_2 Offset equation to calculate the amount of CO_2 that would otherwise be emitted but has been offset by a facility's practices. The CO_2 Offset is capped at 1 and can be defined by Eq. (2) Both the numerator and the denominator must have the same unit of measurement. CO_2 *Saved* denotes all emissions that were prevented through heat reuse. CO_2 *Generated Energy Cost* is the emissions that would have occurred for all actions; this includes the energy used to power and cool the DC, and the energy that would have been used instead of the waste heat. Note that powering a DC with greener energy sources would generate fewer CO_2 emissions.

$$CO_2\ Offset = \frac{CO_2\ Saved}{CO_2\ Generated\ Energy\ Cost}\ ,\ \ 0 \leq CO_2\ Offset \leq 1 \qquad (2)$$

The Heat Reuse Factor and CO_2 Offset equations can be used to determine the Green Supercomputing Ratio (GSR) which provides a value that represents how green/efficient a facility's practices are (shown in Eq. (3)). A facility can need multiple HRF, CO_2 Offset, and GSR calculations throughout the year to get a range of values if the heat used fluctuates over time. The equation uses both the amount of heat reused and the CO_2 emissions that were prevented to provide a better picture of how efficient a facility is. A value of 1 is ideal but unrealistic due to heat losses, while a value of 0 would indicate the facility's practices are inefficient. GSR is designed to favor centers that reuse their heat for useful endeavors, ideally replacing existing uses that were otherwise serviced by traditional (CO_2 emitting) energy sources.

$$GSR = HRF \times CO_2\ Offset\ ,\ \ 0 \leq GSR \leq 1 \qquad (3)$$

4 HRF and GSR Calculation Granularity

There are many ways that the HRF, CO_2 Offset, and GSR values can be calculated. In this section we introduce three tiers of granularity for the calculations: theoretical, practical, and fine grained.

4.1 Tier 1: Theoretical

To understand how recapturing and reusing the generated heat from servers could save money and/or electricity, we will consider a theoretical DC based on publicly available average values for cost and electricity. An average full-scale DC is 100,000 ft^2 and uses about 37.99 TWh/year [17]. This is for compute floor space only and based on having CPU servers; as we are focusing on GPU servers (and therefore fewer servers are present as we only want to conserve compute power not number of devices), we halve the energy use. We choose a PUE of 1.1 (an efficient DC), that uses 91% of its energy for IT systems, 5.4% for cooling,

Table 1. Summary of theoretical DC information used for Tier 1 and Tier 2 analyses.

	Tier 1	Tier 2	Tier 2 Half Load
DC Size (ft^2)	100,000	100,000	100,000
Number of Racks	6,250	5,989	5,989
Electricity Cost (USD/kWh)	0.0733	0.0733	0.0733
DC Electricity (TWh/year)	19	4.28	2.33
Server Electricity Amount (TWh)	17.29	3.90	1.95
Cooling Electricity Amount (TWh)	1.03	0.23	0.23
Other Electricity Amount (TWh)	0.68	0.15	0.15
Type of Cooling System	Liquid	Liquid	Liquid
Server Electricity Cost (USD/year)	1.27 billion	285.7 million	171.1 million
Type of Power Plant[a]	coal	coal	coal
CO_2 Produced/million BTU (lb)	205.7	205.7	205.7

[a] Carbon emissions could be significantly reduced by using a greener power source than coal.

and 3.6% for power distribution units (PDUs), step down transformers, and other equipment. Electrical distribution systems can account for 10–12% of the energy consumption [18], but we choose distribution systems with platinum-level efficiency, consuming 3% of energy and an efficient step down transformer, with 1% of energy lost [19].

Our DC's electricity will cost 0.0733 USD per kWh [20]. This will be a liquid-cooled DC, based on most DCs moving towards liquid cooling. This means that electricity for only the servers in our large-scale commercial DC will cost approximately $1.27 billion a year. However, using the heat generated from the servers in a DC, this exorbitant number could be reduced for the DC and the industries around it. We also make the assumption that the waste heat from our DC is of a high enough quality that a heat pump to increase the temperature is unnecessary.

This theoretical DC will be powered by a bituminous coal-fired power plant, producing 205.7 lb of CO_2 per million British thermal units (BTU) [21]. The entire DC requires 64.8 trillion BTU, leading to 13.3 billion lb of CO_2 over a year.

4.2 Tier 2: Practical

A Tier 1 analysis is possible for all DCs, but it is the least accurate of approaches because it uses approximations of the required values. While this can be helpful for a DC in the planning stages, it will likely differ from the actual value. A Tier 2 analysis is more fine-grained; it uses measured values from a DC leading to more accurate HRF and GSR values. Here, we describe another theoretical DC with precise values.

A typical DC will have a CPU to GPU ratio of 1:4 or 1:8. We choose a ratio of 1 CPU to 8 GPUs for this theoretical DC. Racks in a DC house servers and switches and are typically 42U in height. Six U are used for the switch, and with 4U servers, we can fit nine servers in a single rack (72 GPUs per rack). Standard racks are 24 in. wide and 42 in. deep [22], requiring a front clearance of 47.2 in., a back clearance of 39.4 in., and 3.9 in. between racks [23]. Racks must also be 17.7 in. from the walls. With a DC area of 100,000 ft^2 and leaving 1,000 ft^2 of space between the racks and the walls, this allows approximately 6,250 racks. We assume that all electrical and facility equipment is not located on the compute floor, and we do not account for storage nodes in the DC to simplify presentation.

We base the power values on state-of-the-art hardware, such as NVIDIA's Blackwell GPU with a maximum Thermal Design Power (TDP) of 1000 W [24] and NVIDIA's Grace CPU C1 with a TDP of 250 W [25]. We neglect the power draw of the racks' switches as it is low compared to the server power requirements. Therefore, each rack can draw 74.25 kW of power. However, in our experience, the servers will only draw approximately half the power when running a typical load. We choose a PUE of 1.1 (based on maximum IT equipment power draw) to demonstrate that a highly efficient DC may not be very green. See Table 1 for the energy consumption values of the theoretical DC. The *Tier 2* column gives values for a full load, while the *Tier 2 Half Load* column gives the practical values that will be used in calculations later on. Note that all values should be measured for each DC, on a case-by-case basis; we are choosing these measurements for illustration purposes. This theoretical DC is also liquid-cooled, based on current cooling norms. Similarly to the Tier 1 DC, we assume this DC does not require the use of a heat pump to increase the quality of its waste heat. It is powered by a bituminous coal-fired power plant as well, so the DC at half load will require 7.97 trillion BTU over one year. This is equivalent to 1.64 billion lb of CO_2.

4.3 Tier 3: Fine-Grained

To increase the accuracy of the metrics, DCs may choose to do a more in-depth analysis than that of Tier 2. A Tier 3 analysis involves accounting for all power consumption within a DC, including power conversion losses in PDUs, and switches within racks that were not accounted for in the Tier 2 analysis. On the waste heat application side, it includes looking at precise heat loss values (in transport) and the carbon emissions of transporting things such as salt water, fresh water, or materials. It also accounts for the varying calculation loads over time. Due to the precise values needed, which cannot easily be created for a theoretical DC, we do not demonstrate a Tier 3 analysis in this paper.

4.4 Heat Reuse Calculation Example

Here, we demonstrate how to calculate the metrics with a Tier 1 analysis using the waste heat from our theoretical DC to heat surrounding buildings. If the proper infrastructure exists, using the heat from DC servers to heat buildings nearby would reduce heating costs because it would no longer require using 100% electrical or steam power. An analogy for this is heating water in a kettle. The water boils faster and requires less energy when the water in the kettle is already hot compared to when it is cold. We assume that it is a hot water system rather than a steam distribution system, as the DC can heat the water with waste heat to sufficient temperatures for hot water heating.

District Heating with a Tier 1 Analysis. The electricity used by the IT components in the theoretical DC is negligible, so we assume that all power is converted to heat. We convert the energy used by the servers in a year from kWh to BTU, since BTU is a common unit used in discussions about heating/cooling. An average building of 15,000 ft^2 needs approximately 675,000–825,000 BTU each hour to maintain a comfortable temperature [26]. With a heat loss of 10% due to transport, we use the remaining heat to calculate how many buildings can be heated: 7,340–8,971.

$$HRF = \frac{7,340 \ buildings * 825000 \ BTU/building * 24 \ hrs * 365.25 \ days}{58980375363000 \ BTU} = 0.9$$

Using our proposed Heat Reuse Factor, we divide the heat reused in BTU by the total heat generated in BTU to obtain a value of 0.9. However, if fewer buildings are heated, the leftover heat will be wasted, making the HRF much lower.

$$CO_{2,district} = 7340 \ buildings * \frac{825000 \ BTU}{building} * 24 \ hrs * 365.25 \ days * \frac{117 \ lb}{1000000 \ BTU}$$

$$CO_2 \ Offset = \frac{CO_{2,district}}{58980375363000 \ BTU * \frac{205.7 \ lb}{1000000 \ BTU} + CO_{2,district}} = 0.318$$

Using DC waste heat would offset the CO_2 emissions that would have been produced by heating the building with natural gas. According to the American Geosciences Institute, Natural Gas emits 117.0 lb of CO_2 per million BTU [21]. Using our CO_2 Offset equation (the emissions saved divided by emissions generated by the DC and district heating), we find that the CO_2 Offset is 0.318.

$$GSR = 0.9 * 0.318 = 0.286$$

Multiplying the HRF by the CO_2 Offset results in a GSR value of 0.286.

5 Waste Heat Reuse Examples

The HRF and GSR metrics can show a DC's efficiency when using waste heat for various purposes. We demonstrate Tier 2 analyses for the use of waste heat for district heating, agriculture, and desalination using our Practical DC values.

5.1 HRF and GSR District Heating Example

The calculations for a Tier 2 district heating analysis are similar to those shown in Sect. 4.4, but the values are precise. The DC's location impacts the heat lost in transport and when heating is required, as climate can cause HRF, CO_2 Offset, and GSR values to fluctuate throughout the year. We place our theoretical DC in Ottawa, Ontario, Canada, where some days would require constant heating, while others need none. Again, we base the CO_2 Offset on the buildings being originally heated by natural gas.

Table 2. The average number of days per month above $20\,^\circ\text{C}$ ($68\,^\circ\text{F}$) in Ottawa, Ontario [27], the billion BTU needed and produced, and resulting HRF, CO_2 Offset, and GSR values.

Month	Days 20 °C+	Billion BTU Need	Billion BTU Prod.	HRF	CO_2 Offset	GSR
Jan	0	508.01	564.45	0.900	0.299	0.269
Feb	0	462.94	514.38	0.900	0.299	0.269
Mar	0	508.01	564.45	0.900	0.299	0.269
Apr	3	442.46	546.25	0.810	0.278	0.225
May	13	294.97	564.45	0.523	0.199	0.104
Jun	24	98.32	546.25	0.180	0.079	0.014
Jul	30	16.39	564.45	0.029	0.014	0.000
Aug	28	49.16	564.45	0.087	0.040	0.003
Sep	16	229.42	546.25	0.420	0.166	0.070
Oct	3	458.85	564.45	0.813	0.279	0.226
Nov	0	491.62	546.25	0.900	0.299	0.269
Dec	0	508.01	564.45	0.900	0.299	0.269

The same calculations are done for the Tier 2 analysis as for Tier 1, except that they are completed by month. We determine the hourly heat produced by IT equipment, account for heat lost during transport (10%), and use a 15,000 square foot building, requiring approximately 750,000 BTU, to determine that approximately 910 buildings could be heated by the DC. We determine the amount of heat wasted using the number of days per month that will not require heating multiplied by the usable daily heat produced. Table 2 shows the approximate monthly heating requirements and the resulting performance values. During winter months, the DC has higher HRF and GSR values, but if heat is only reused for district heating, it is wasted during warmer months, leading to poor HRF and GSR values close to 0.

5.2 HRF and GSR Agriculture Example

Another option for waste heat reuse is using heating to improve yields in agriculture and avoid importing some produce to locations with poor growing conditions. Heating greenhouses is done to extend the growing season, so we place our Tier 2 theoretical DC in Juneau, Alaska for this case. The size of the greenhouse depends on multiple factors including the desired amount of food produced and the climate; colder climates require smaller greenhouses to maintain proper growing conditions. Based on the size of larger commercial greenhouses, the greenhouses we will heat with the theoretical DC will be 10,000 ft^2 [28]. To heat a greenhouse, 77 BTU/ft^2 is required [29]. This means that each 10,000 ft^2 greenhouse requires 770,000 BTU each hour. With a transport loss of 10%, we have a usable 682.8 million BTU produced each hour. We can heat 985 greenhouses with that heat; however, in 2022 it was estimated that there were over 8,750 greenhouses in the United States of America (USA) [30]. We provide an analysis for heating 600 greenhouses with waste heat based on Pennsylvania having the largest number of greenhouses in the USA at 593 [30].

According to the Environmental Defense Fund, the average truck carrying 2,000 lb of goods from 1,000 miles away would emit 3.24 metric tons of CO_2 [31], which is equal to 7142.98 lb of CO_2. Greenhouses produce approximately 2.5 lb of produce per square foot per year, so 600 greenhouses would produce 15,000,000 lb/year [32]. Growing this food locally is equivalent to replacing 7,500 trucks (and 53,572,350 lb of CO_2). Table 3 presents the monthly HRF, CO_2 Offset, and GSR values. There is a lot of wasted heat so the HRF and GSR values are poor. The remaining waste heat would need to be used for other purposes to improve the values.

Table 3. The average number of days per month above 16 °C (61 °F) in Juneau, Alaska, the billion BTU needed and produced, and resulting HRF, CO_2 Offset, and GSR values [33].

Month	Days 16 °C+	Billion BTU Need	Billion BTU Prod.	HRF	CO_2 Offset	GSR
Jan	0	343.73	564.45	0.61	0.032	0.019
Feb	0	313.24	514.38	0.61	0.032	0.019
Mar	0	343.73	564.45	0.61	0.032	0.019
Apr	2	310.46	546.25	0.57	0.032	0.018
May	12	210.67	564.45	0.37	0.032	0.012
Jun	18	133.06	546.25	0.24	0.032	0.008
Jul	22	99.79	564.45	0.18	0.032	0.006
Aug	19	133.06	564.45	0.24	0.032	0.007
Sep	7	255.02	546.25	0.47	0.032	0.015
Oct	0	343.73	564.45	0.61	0.032	0.019
Nov	0	332.64	546.25	0.61	0.032	0.019
Dec	0	343.73	564.45	0.61	0.032	0.019

5.3 HRF and GSR Desalination Example

Our final example of heat reuse is using it for desalination: turning saltwater into freshwater. Each kilogram of freshwater requires 1500 kJ/kg (1421.726 BTU) for desalination [34]. The heat wasted by DCs can contribute a lot of energy to the desalination process. Using two-phase liquid immersion cooling, such as in [35], the seawater is heated by the dielectric liquid's vapour, so we assume no heat is lost there. Assuming the desalination unit is part of the DC, the heat lost in transport is minimal (so we assume 1%). The hourly BTU production of the DC is 758.7 million, so 528,293.1 kg of water can be produced each hour (accounting for heat loss). We station the theoretical DC next to the Pacific Ocean in Los Angeles, California where there is a freshwater shortage, making desalination a good option. The average person in Los Angeles (LA) used 225.23 kg/day of water, from January 1 to May 31, 2023 [36]. In 2023, the population of LA was estimated to be 3,820,914, which means approximately 860,584,460.2 kg of water/day is needed [37]. The DC could supply approximately 1.5% of the population with fresh water from January to May using waste heat. We assume in the summer months more water would be consumed, which would change the percentage of population that could be supplied with water using waste heat from the DC. However, the amount of desalinated water produced would not be impacted. This results in an HRF of 0.99.

LA currently gets its water from groundwater (aqueducts) and purchases water from the Metropolitan Water District of Southern California [38]. As the population grows, this will not be practical. Desalination is a solution and a DC would offset some of the emissions created by building infrastructure to power a desalination plant. If desalination were done in the future in LA, instead of building a hydroelectric plant a DC's waste heat could be used. Hydro produces 24 g of CO_2-eq/kWh, so the DC waste heat would replace 102,096,443.3 lb of CO_2 each year, leading to a CO_2 Offset of 0.059 [39]. This results in a GSR of 0.058. Freshwater is required year-round, so the HRF and GSR values do not fluctuate over time. It is a good option for minimal heat loss, and all usable heat can go towards desalination.

6 Conclusion

We have proposed two metrics, the Heat Reuse Factor (HRF) and the Green Supercomputing Ratio (GSR), to encapsulate the efficiency and environmental impact of a DC. Many DCs have improved their cooling efficiency to achieve low PUE values, but continue to waste the heat produced rather than offset their environmental impact and potentially increase their revenue. Using these proposed metrics, DCs can determine which heat reuse options may be best suited to their location and size. We demonstrate with our theoretical DCs that district heating is best, followed by desalination, then greenhouse heating. Using a green power source would also greatly improve the HRF and GSR values.

We have shown an example of a very large commercial DC, but it is impractical to use all the generated heat because of the sheer amount. Future DCs should think about heat reuse options in the planning stages to improve their HRF and GSR values. Investigating the impact of using the waste heat for multiple applications and determining the best locations/climates for each approach is left for future work. Future work also involves examining the impact of heat reuse on cost. DCs may choose to sell their heat to offset electricity costs, which we will explore in future work.

References

1. Haleem, A., Javaid, M., Asim Qadri, M., Pratap Singh, R., Suman, R.: Artificial intelligence (AI) applications for marketing: a literature-based study. Int. J. Intell. Netw. **3**, 119–132 (2022). https://doi.org/10.1016/j.ijin.2022.08.005
2. Office of Energy Efficiency & Renewable Energy: Data Centers and Servers. https://www.energy.gov/eere/buildings/data-centers-and-servers. Accessed 04 June 2024
3. Rozite, V., Bertoli, E., Reidenbach, B.: Data centres & data transmission networks. https://www.iea.org/energy-system/buildings/data-centres-and-data-transmission-networks. Accessed 04 June 2024
4. Ebrahimi, K., Jones, G.F., Fleischer, A.S.: A review of data center cooling technology, operating conditions and the corresponding low-grade waste heat recovery opportunities. Renew. Sustain. Energy Rev. **31**, 622–638 (2014). https://doi.org/10.1016/j.rser.2013.12.007
5. Khalid, R., Wemhoff, A.P., Khuc, M., Nayar, A.J., Schon, S.: Data center waste heat reuse: an investment analysis. ASME J. Eng. Sustain. Build. Cities **6**, 021002 (2025). https://doi.org/10.1115/1.4067444
6. Ljungqvist, H.M., Risberg, M., Toffolo, A., Vesterlund, M.: A realistic view on heat reuse from direct free air-cooled data centres. Energy Convers. Manage.: X **20**, 100473 (2023). https://doi.org/10.1016/j.ecmx.2023.100473
7. Haywood, A., Sherbeck, J., Phelan, P., Varsamopoulos, G., Gupta, S.K.S.: Thermodynamic feasibility of harvesting data center waste heat to drive an absorption chiller. Energy Convers. Manage. **58**, 26–34 (2012). https://doi.org/10.1016/j.enconman.2011.12.017
8. Patterson, M., Tschudi, B., Vangeet, O., Cooley, J., Azevedo, D.: ERE: a metric for measuring the benefit of reuse energy from a data center. Green Grid (2010)
9. Government of Canada, C.E.R.: market snapshot: energy demand from data centers is steadily increasing, and AI development is a significant factor. https://tinyurl.com/5d95x6xa. Accessed 04 Feb 2024
10. Çam, E., Hungerford, Z., Schoch, N., Pinto Miranda, F., Yáñez de León, C.D.: Electricity 2024 - analysis and forecast to 2026. IEA 1–79 (2024)
11. Zimmermann, S., Meijer, I., Tiwari, M.K., Paredes, S., Michel, B., Poulikakos, D.: Aquasar: a hot water cooled data center with direct energy reuse. Energy. **43**, 237–245 (2012). https://doi.org/10.1016/j.energy.2012.04.037
12. Meyer, N., Ries, M., Solbrig, S., Wettig, T.: iDataCool: HPC with hot-water cooling and energy reuse (2013). http://arxiv.org/abs/1309.4887, https://doi.org/10.1007/978-3-642-38750-0_29
13. Werner, S.: International review of district heating and cooling. Energy **137**, 617–631 (2017). https://doi.org/10.1016/j.energy.2017.04.045
14. Yuan, X., Liang, Y., Hu, X., Xu, Y., Chen, Y., Kosonen, R.: Waste heat recoveries in data centers: a review. Renew. Sustain. Energy Rev. **188**, 113777 (2023). https://doi.org/10.1016/j.rser.2023.113777

15. Ljungqvist, H.M., Mattsson, L., Risberg, M., Vesterlund, M.: Data center heated greenhouses, a matter for enhanced food self-sufficiency in sub-arctic regions. Energy **215**, 119169 (2021). https://doi.org/10.1016/j.energy.2020.119169
16. Sondur, S., Gross, K., Li, M.: Data center cooling system integrated with low-temperature desalination and intelligent energy-aware control. In: 2018 Ninth International Green and Sustainable Computing Conf. (IGSC), pp. 1–6. IEEE, Pittsburgh (2018). https://doi.org/10.1109/IGCC.2018.8752108
17. DGTL Infra: Cities and regions with the highest concentration of data centers (2023). https://irei.com/publications/article/cities-regions-highest-concentration-data-centers/
18. Evaluating UPS system efficiency. https://www.csemag.com/articles/evaluating-ups-system-efficiency/. Accessed 15 Apr 2025
19. Step Down Transformer Diagram, Working, Applications, FAQs. https://www.electronicsforu.com/technology-trends/learn-electronics/step-down-transformer-working. Accessed 15 Apr 2025
20. Rareshide, M.: Power in the Data Center and its Cost Across the U.S. https://info.siteselectiongroup.com/blog/power-in-the-data-center-and-its-costs-across-the-united-states. Accessed 07 Feb 2025
21. Keane, C.: How much carbon dioxide is produced when different fuels are burned?. https://profession.americangeosciences.org/society/intersections/faq/how-much-carbon-dioxide-produced-when-different-fuels-are-burned/. Accessed 12 Feb 2025
22. Server Rack Sizes & Dimensions: Depth, Width, & Height. https://blog.enconnex.com/exploring-server-rack-sizes-and-dimensions-depth-width-height. Accessed 26 Feb 2025
23. Rack dimensions and service clearance requirements. https://www.ibm.com/docs/en/xiv-storage-system?topic=requirements-rack-dimensions-service-clearance. Accessed 26 Feb 2025
24. NVIDIA: NVIDIA Blackwell. https://nvdam.widen.net/s/wwnsxrhm2w/blackwell-datasheet-3384703. Accessed 25 Feb 2025
25. NVIDIA: NVIDIA Grace CPU Superchip Datasheet. https://resources.nvidia.com/en-us-grace-cpu/data-center-datasheet. Accessed 25 Feb 2025
26. Simning, B.: How Many BTU Per Square Foot to Heat or Cool Your Home. https://valleycomfortheatingandair.com/how-many-btu-per-square-foot-to-heat-or-cool-your-home/. Accessed 12 Feb 2025
27. Current Results: Ottawa ON Average Temperatures by Month. https://www.currentresults.com/Weather/Canada/Ontario/Places/ottawa-temperatures-by-month-average.php. Accessed 17 Feb 2025
28. Grodan: Commercial greenhouse growing. https://www.grodan.com/global/knowledge/root-zone-management/irrigation-and-nutrients/commercial-greenhouse-growing/. Accessed 17 Feb 2025
29. EnviroCept: Heating Greenhouses - Greenhouse Heaters and Requirements. https://www.envirocept.com/gh_guide/heating_greenhouses.html. Accessed 17 Feb 2025
30. Business Wire: North America Commercial Greenhouse Market Report 2022: Rising Populations and Growing Demand for Food Are Creating Greater Opportunities for Alternative Farming Methods. https://tinyurl.com/45cdybv4. Accessed 17 Feb 2025
31. Mathers, J.: Green Freight math: how to calculate emissions for a truck move. https://business.edf.org/insights/green-freight-math-how-to-calculate-emissions-for-a-truck-move/. Accessed 12 Feb 2025

32. BTL Liners-Geomembrane Systems: How much food can a greenhouse grow?. https://www.btlliners.com/how-much-food-can-a-greenhouse-grow. Accessed 17 Feb 2025
33. Current Results: Juneau AK Average Temperatures by Month. https://www.currentresults.com/Weather/Alaska/Places/juneau-temperatures-by-month-average.php. Accessed 24 Feb 2025
34. Gude, V.G., Nirmalakhandan, N., Deng, S., Maganti, A.: Feasibility study of a new two-stage low temperature desalination process. Energy Convers. Manage. **56**, 192–198 (2012). https://doi.org/10.1016/j.enconman.2011.11.026
35. Kanbur, B.B., Wu, C., Duan, F.: Multi-criteria thermoeconomic and thermodynamic assessments of the desalination-integrated two-phase liquid-immersion data center cooling system. Int. J. Energy Res. **44**, 10453–10470 (2020). https://doi.org/10.1002/er.5677
36. Chkarboul, C.: Residential water use in Los Angeles declines after winter rains. https://xtown.la/2023/09/05/residential-water-use-in-los-angeles-declines-11-after-winter-rains/. Accessed 17 Feb 2025
37. United States' Census Bureau: QuickFacts: Los Angeles city, California. https://www.census.gov/quickfacts/fact/table/losangelescitycalifornia/PST045223. Accessed 17 Feb 2025
38. Los Angeles Department of Water & Power: Sources of Supply. https://www.ladwp.com/who-we-are/water-system/sources-supply. Accessed 21 Feb 2025
39. International Hydropower Association: Hydropower's carbon footprint. https://www.hydropower.org/factsheets/greenhouse-gas-emissions. Accessed 25 Feb 2025

Pinpointing Idle-Power Regressions in Linux

Hannes Tröpgen[1]($^\boxtimes$), Till Smejkal[2], Thomas Ilsche[1],
Robert Schöne[1], and Horst Schirmeier[2]

[1] ZIH, CIDS, TU Dresden, 01062 Dresden, Germany
{hannes.troepgen,thomas.ilsche,robert.schoene}@tu-dresden.de
[2] Chair of Operating Systems, Faculty of CS, TU Dresden, 01062 Dresden, Germany
{till.smejkal,horst.schirmeier}@tu-dresden.de

Abstract. Energy-efficient idling of computers has a substantial influence on their lifetime energy consumption, total cost of ownership, and environmental impact. Mechanisms to reduce power consumption during idle rely on complex operating-system support, an area that is prone to regressions. Idle-power regressions are challenging to identify, even when actively looking for them: In-band measurements can easily perturb the monitored idle states. Additionally, as the idle power strongly depends on frequency and duration of interrupts, statistically sound comparisons require long observation periods.

In this paper, we present a measurement-based approach to pinpoint regressions in the Linux kernel that degrade the energy efficiency of idle systems. For that, we design an out-of-band measurement infrastructure that avoids the probe effect. Our approach based on bisection can isolate the culprit of regressions across a large number of code changes. We discuss the critical role of classification and present approaches to strengthen its reliability. Finally, we demonstrate our approach on a newly discovered power regression, as well as a known reference case by reliably finding the responsible code change.

1 Introduction

The energy demand of our daily used computers is growing every year. In 2016, data centers alone consumed about 286 TWh and are estimated to surpass 321 TWh in 2030 worldwide [28]. However, with growing environmental concerns and increasing energy costs, the importance of energy-aware computer systems increases. This also includes finding and correcting system behavior that leads to increased energy consumption. Modern programming tools already integrate means to analyze the energy consumption of specific software [12,18]. However, finding energy regressions – i.e., changes that lead to higher energy consumption – in a large code base in general is still an open problem.

While most of the energy is consumed when the systems are actively used, a considerable amount of energy is also accounted to idling phases. Although data center providers for example try to minimize their system's idle times, overprovisioning [19] and misconfigurations still lead to underused resources [7]. Also,

© The Author(s), under exclusive license to Springer Nature Switzerland AG 2026
S. Neuwirth et al. (Eds.): ISC High Performance 2025 Workshops, LNCS 16091, pp. 205–218, 2026.
https://doi.org/10.1007/978-3-032-07612-0_16

personal devices such as mobile phones, tablets or laptops are idling more than being actively used. Thus, the improvement of idle-energy consumption impacts the total energy consumption.

Monitoring applications in general or the power consumption of systems under stress in particular is a heavily studied field [2,13,14,27,29,33]. However, monitoring an *idling* system is a less studied scenario that comes with a unique set of challenges – one of them being that if monitoring tools run directly on the system under test, they influence its state. Thus, any in-band monitoring solution could perturb idle behavior, in turn hiding specific power-consumption problems. Furthermore, external influences such as interrupts or physical properties of the power supply make monitoring idle power complicated and difficult to reproduce.

If the monitoring finds an *idle-power regression* – either by targeted search, or by chance – the challenge remains to pinpoint the regression-causing code modification. A well-established approach to correlate behavioral changes with individual code modifications is *bisection* [15]. Although bisection was already applied to identify the reason for performance degradations [30] or functional changes [41], this paper is – to the best of our knowledge – the first to apply bisection to power consumption directly.

This paper presents a bisection approach that uses out-of-band power measurements to localize the root cause of idle-power regressions in the Linux kernel. In summary, we make the following contributions: We analyze difficulties in taking accurate idle-power consumption measurements (Sect. 2) and introduce our infrastructure enabling them (Sect. 3). We implement bisection with this infrastructure, show challenges to its success, and propose mitigations (Sect. 4). Finally, we demonstrate our approach in two scenarios (Sect. 5).

2 Related Work

Defect management (or *bug hunting*) in any form is a long-standing problem for all types of software and takes up most of the development time of modern software-development cycles. For example, 80% of a typical Linux-kernel release cycle is dedicated to fixing regression bugs [11].

Naive approaches for correlating regressions and individual code modifications become nearly impossible in big projects. In 2004, Johnson et al. [26] described a first approach for the GCC project to identify bugs that introduce regressions in its source code, and thereby follow the *bisection debugging* method described by Gross et al. in 1997 [15]. They apply a binary search on the individual source-code versions of the code base that follow every committed change. By classifying the source-code versions into either *old* (unaffected, also: *good*) or *new* (affected, also: *bad*), they find the culprit commit in $log_2 n$ steps, with n being the total number of changes between an *a priori* known-*old* and a known-*new* version. This culprit commit is referred to as the *first new commit*. Bisection is nowadays automated in most popular version-control systems [6,31,37].

Bisection is optimal with regard to the number of search steps [34], and many different approaches exist to even further improve its performance for example by parallelizing the search [4] or reducing the cost of the individual classification steps [32]. We adapt bisection for use with power measurements.

To initially identify a regression, excessive testing is necessary. In the Linux community as well as for other software systems, a wide variety of automatic regression testing frameworks exists [8,35,43,44]. One of the most popular ones in the Linux community is the *Linux Kernel Performance* [25] project. Here, fully automated tests are performed regularly for submitted patches. They can detect performance regressions and attempt to bisect them autonomously. However, these frameworks are mostly focused on runtime performance or functional regressions. Our work tackles regressions in power or energy consumption.

In order to identify regressions in power or energy consumption of a system, reliable power or energy measurements are necessary. In general, different approaches exist to gather power or energy measurements of systems at various temporal and spatial granularities. Nowadays popular are in-band on-chip measurement methods like the *Running Average Power Limit* (RAPL) registers available on Intel [24, Vol. 3B, 16.10] and AMD [3, Vol. 2, 17.5] systems. With RAPL, it is possible to read the energy consumptions of the CPU and some of its components with a typical update rate of 1 kSa/s [24, Vol. 3B, 16.10.3].[1] Due to their wide availability, energy measurements based on RAPL registers are frequently used in the literature [10,20,36]. However, in-band measurements are prone to the probe effect: The measurement or its tooling themselves may cause activity, thus disrupting the idle behavior to be monitored. In particular, recording time series requires one wake-up per recorded sample to read RAPL. Even when only collecting aggregated energy measurements, overflow detection and handling still necessitates recurring wake-ups every couple of minutes [24, Vol. 3B, 16.10.3]. Further, the energy consumption of components other than the CPU is more significant in idle, but not universally supported by RAPL.

Contrary, out-of-band measurements run exclusively on external equipment, avoiding the probe effect entirely. Such approaches may leverage values reported by *power supply/distribution units* (PSUs/PDUs) [16] or insert specialized sensors in the power cords of the individual system components [5,21]. This additional infrastructure can offer high-accuracy measurements at any scope physically accessible without influencing the *System Under Test* (SUT), rendering them best-suited for observations of idle. Our approach uses such out-of-band readouts of physical full-system power measurements; the full setup is detailed in Subsects. 3.1 and 5.1.

3 Bisecting Power Regressions

Although bisection can be applied manually to any list of code changes, a fully automated approach finds results faster and more reliably. However, automatic

---

[1] We use the unit Sa to refer to *sample*.

bisection necessitates (1) an automated reliable classification of commits into *new* and *old*, and (2) a persistent control process.

In this section, we introduce the necessary infrastructure and adaptations to the bisection process in order to pinpoint the root cause of a power regression in the Linux kernel.

3.1 Infrastructure

As outlined in Sect. 2, accurate idle-power measurements – as a basis to detect regressions in this area – require external instruments that enable out-of-band readouts. Our proposed infrastructure consists of three components:

System Under Test (SUT) is the observed system on which different versions of the Linux kernel are compiled and tested. It receives commands from the Control System and is monitored by the Measurement Infrastructure.

Measurement Infrastructure monitors and stores the power consumption of the SUT and reports the results to the Control System.

Control System coordinates and logs the experiments and measurements. This includes sending commands to the SUT (via SSH) and retrieving and analyzing the data from the Measurement Infrastructure.

Our out-of-band Measurement Infrastructure physically instruments the SUT and avoids any power-measurement perturbations. The measurements are reported by a high-precision power meter, which we combine with MetricQ [22] to collect and store its data. All subsequent requests, for example from the Control System in order to retrieve the measurement results, are directly handled by MetricQ and the attached database. The results can then be obtained post-mortem.

3.2 Bisection

To pinpoint the change from *old* to *new* behavior in the source code, the bisection demands the classification of a different commit in every step. This includes configuration, build, install, reboot, measurement and analysis of this kernel. We automate all these steps using the aforementioned infrastructure. Figure 1 outlines the general bisection process used by our approach. The entire procedure is controlled by an invocation of `git bisect run`. Since this command requires a persistent environment, this part of the bisection process is executed on the Control System, while the individual bisection steps are executed on the SUT.

3.3 Classification

To automate the classification during the bisection, we collect *reference measurements* of each behavior *old* and *new* before the actual bisection starts. To classify a commit, we build it, measure the resulting kernel, and compute its similarity to the reference measurements using a *distance function*. For simplicity, in this paper we calculate the arithmetic mean of all power samples for a

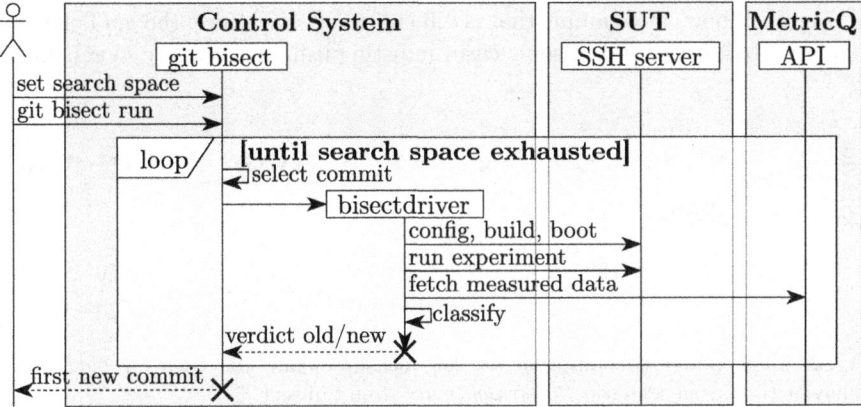

Fig. 1. Sequence of steps for the fully automated bisection process in order to track down power regressions.

kernel, and use the difference between means as the distance. This approach allows more flexibility than having a predefined classification rule set. We only have to ensure that all measurements are done on the same SUT under the same conditions to ensure comparability.

4 Robust Power Classification

The bisection process outlined in the previous section is a scalable algorithm to find the *first new commit*. However, this process is comparatively error-prone: If only a single commit – i.e., a single power-measurement time series – during the bisection is misclassified, the bisection focuses on an incorrectly reduced smaller search space, and the resulting *first new commit* is not correct. In this section, we discuss approaches that help to mitigate the resulting uncertainty.

4.1 The Distance Function

In order to find the first new commit with a 99% chance, the classification of each of the ~ 14 individual steps of a typical bisection between two Linux kernel versions[2] needs to be more than 99.9% accurate. Such a high accuracy is unrealistic: A classification is the result of the combined behavior of (1) *a distance function* applied to measurements of (2) *specific commits*, and (3) the *environment* it is running in, which includes both hardware variances and background noise. Even though a distance function can be optimized for a specific combination of these parameters, there is no general distance function that achieves the near-perfect classification accuracy required for high bisection success rates.

---

[2] Using the arithmetic mean of the commit counts between two Linux releases from Linux 3.0 to 6.12 yields the approximation of $\lceil \log_2 14468.73 \rceil = 14$ steps.

Figure 2 shows an example that is difficult to classify. Here, the *old* behavior is highly probabilistic, and in some cases indistinguishable from the *new* behavior.

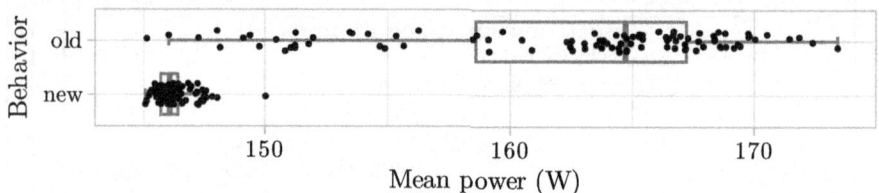

Fig. 2. Mean power consumption for 200 measurements, 100 each for *old* and *new* behavior (based on scenario *Powernightmare* from Subsect. 5.3).

4.2 Measurement Repetition

As shown in Fig. 2, single measurements can be too unreliable to classify the commit in a bisection step. To circumvent this problem, we propose to rely on multiple measurements in every part of the process to factor out outliers. This strategy relies on the independence of the measurements. Hence, the machine should be rebooted between measurements.

The number of repetitions required to achieve a reliable classification depends on the flakiness of the behavior in question. Thus, implausible bisection results might be a result of this flakiness and require more repetitions in order to become more stable.

4.3 Distance Ratio

The classification during a bisection does not specify its confidence. To assess this confidence, we propose to use the *distance ratio* defined as

$$distance\ ratio = 2\frac{\min\{d_{new}, d_{old}\}}{d_{new} + d_{old}},$$

where d_{new} and d_{old} are the distances to the *new* and *old* reference case, respectively. If $d_{new} = d_{old}$, i.e., the measurement is equally similar to the *new* and *old* reference case, this term approaches 1. If either $d_{new} \gg d_{old}$ or $d_{new} \ll d_{old}$, i.e., the measurement is much more similar to either the *new* or *old* reference case than the other, this term approaches 0. The distance ratio can be used as an indicator of uncertainty: The closer the distance ratio is to 0, the clearer the association with one of the reference cases is.

4.4 Verification Measurements

The bisection process as described earlier will (unless a catastrophic failure occurs) always report a commit that it deems to introduce the power regression. Even when assuming that no misclassification occurred during the whole process, it is still not clear at this point whether the identified commit is actually the isolated cause of the power regression. In order to verify that this commit is indeed necessary and sufficient to cause the power regression, our bisection process finishes with a verification step. This final step consists of two separate analyses.

To validate that the found commit is sufficient to trigger the regression, it is added to the kernel version with the *old* behavior. Therefore we apply (`git cherry-pick`) the identified commit on top of the *old* kernel. The resulting kernel is analyzed exactly like a bisection step and must classify as *new*. To validate that the found commit is necessary, we remove the commit from the kernel version with the *new* behavior. This time we remove (`git revert`) the identified commit from the *new* kernel. The resulting kernel is again analyzed as a bisection step and must classify as *old*.

If the isolated cherry-picking or reverting of individual commits fails or yields a non-buildable or non-booting kernel, manual intervention is required: (1) The source code can be manually adjusted to fix any errors. (2) Multiple commits can be cherry-picked or reverted together. (3) Finally, it can also be viable to skip the non-working test completely and begin a manual investigation.

In general, the verification measurements underline whether the entire bisection process search was successful. Though, even if some tests fail, the information gain might help to guide a more intensive and deeper debugging. However, if the search fails entirely – i.e. both verification measurements fail – no conclusions can be drawn towards possible causes.

5 Experiments

This section demonstrates our approach using two scenarios: First, a regression we found in our lab, which motivated us to explore the capabilities of bisection for power regressions. To the best of our knowledge, this regression (henceforth called *motivating example*) has not been described previously. Secondly, we reverse-engineer the fix for the so-called *Powernightmares* as a reference case for a change in power consumption behavior previously described in literature [23]. For both, we follow the procedure outlined in Sects. 3 and 4 consisting of (1) reference measurements, (2) bisection, and (3) verification measurements. Additionally, we demonstrate how a failed bisection can be investigated.

5.1 Setup

The *System Under Test* (SUT) is an *R282-Z90* system by GIGABYTE, equipped with two *AMD EPYC 7502 32-Core Processors*. The fans of the SUT are locked

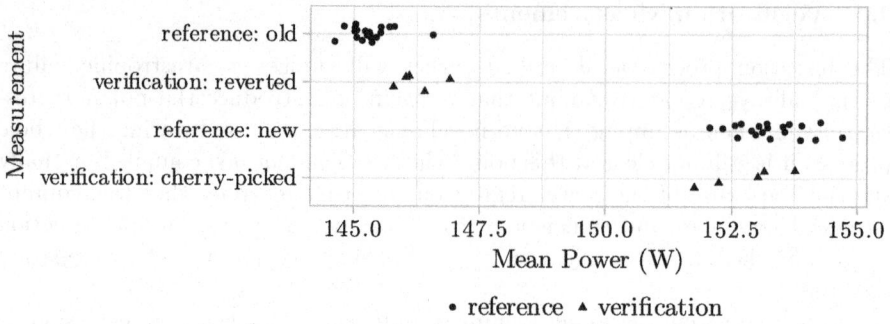

Fig. 3. Mean power consumption of reference and verification measurements for scenario *motivating example* for *first new commit* `cea79e7e2f24`.

at 80% of their maximum speed in order to avoid changes in power intake. The Measurement Infrastructure – split into a power meter and MetricQ [22] (see Subsect. 3.1) – instruments the FSP1200-20ERM power supply unit (80+ Platinum [9]) at its *alternating current* (AC) input. Thus, it can monitor the SUT's total power consumption accurately. The power meter is a ZES ZIMMER LMG95, which internally collects 100 kSa/s [42, 13.4.1, p. 230], exposed at 20 Sa/s. The installed Linux distribution is Ubuntu 18.04. The kernels built by the infrastructure always use the *default* configuration.

5.2 Motivating Example

After a routine update of the operating system on the SUT, we reviewed the out-of-band measurements from the LMG95 power meter. There, we noticed a minor, but persistent increase in power consumption – even though the SUT idled most of the time. Testing revealed that booting with the new Linux kernel caused this effect: Running Linux 4.15, the SUT drew a mean power of 144.9 W, which increased by 7.4% to 155.6 W under Linux 5.10. Using our approach, we tracked this change in power consumption to a source-code commit.

Based on the monitored behavior, the bisection starts with Linux 4.15 as *old* and Linux 5.10 as *new*. The experiment consists of booting the system, waiting for the system to be reachable again (via SSH) plus an additional 60 s to let the system settle, and then measuring the power consumed during the following idle period for 5 min. The reference measurements consist of 20 such measurements for each reference case. The bisection uses 5 measurements per step, and after 17 steps pinpoints commit `cea79e7e2f24` as the first commit with the increased power consumption. Figure 3 shows the verification step (see Subsect. 4.4). It verifies that commit `cea79e7e2f24` is the isolated cause for the regression.

The culprit commit removes the flag `TIMER_DEFERRABLE` from a timer setup. If the timer is marked as *deferrable*, the function call can be postponed. If the timeout occurs while the processors sleep in a power-saving state, a non-deferrable timer will cause a system wake-up, incurring considerable overhead in the power consumed. Conversely, if the timer is deferrable, the callback can be handled during a later wake-up. As a non-deferrable timer causes more wake-ups from power-saving states and thus more power consumption, the found *first new commit* can plausibly increase the power consumption. In this particular case, the interval for the timer is based on a value provided to the kernel through ACPI [1]. Hence, the impact of the *first new commit* on the power consumption may differ between systems.

5.3 Powernightmares

As a second scenario to test our approach, we tried to retroactively identify the (known) fix for Powernightmares in the Linux kernel. A Powernightmare is a phenomenon described by Ilsche et al. [23], where a sub-optimal power-saving state (also called *C-state*) is selected. C-states allow a processor to suspend operation and drastically cut its power consumption. A *deeper* C-state has a lower power consumption, but also a greater exit latency compared to a *shallower* C-state. For a long idle time, a deep C-state is desired, since more energy can be saved. During a Powernightmare, Linux remains in a shallow C-state, thereby consuming more energy than necessary – for up to 10 s, according to the original authors [23, 3.4].

Powernightmares were fixed with the release of Linux 4.17. Accordingly, we use Linux 4.16 (*old*) to 4.17 (*new*) as the search space. In practice, the occurrence of a Powernightmare is highly probabilistic. To make the tests more reliable, we employ an artificial user-space trigger described by the original authors [23, Listing 1]. An affected kernel (*old*) will have a distinctly higher power consumption when compared to an unaffected (*new*) kernel. Note that this would be swapped when examining a regression instead of a fix. However, this does not make a difference when applying our approach. The reference measurements are 20 measurements per behavior with the trigger running, each measured for 5 min. Each bisection step consists of 5 such measurements.

The found *first new commit* 554c8aa8ecad is part of a patch series with 7 commits [40]. Cherry-picking or reverting it individually for the verification measurements results in merge conflicts. Through manual investigation we identified sets of commits which allow cherry-picking and reverting. This list of commits can be found in the artifact accompanying this paper [38]. Their verification measurements are shown in Fig. 4. Together with the mailing-list thread for the patch series of the *first new commit* [40] mentioning the original Powernightmares publication [23], we are confident that the identified commit indeed is part of the commit series that fixes the Powernightmare regression: The bisection succeeded.

To demonstrate how faulty bisections can be handled, we launched an identical bisection, but used only 1 (instead of 5) repetitions per step. Here, the bisection identified e13e75b86ef2 as *first new commit*. Of the measures discussed in Sect. 4, verification measurements are not feasible, as this is a merge commit and can not be viewed in an isolated manner. Consulting the distance ratio introduced in Subsect. 4.3, Step 5 of the bisection in Table 1 stands out:

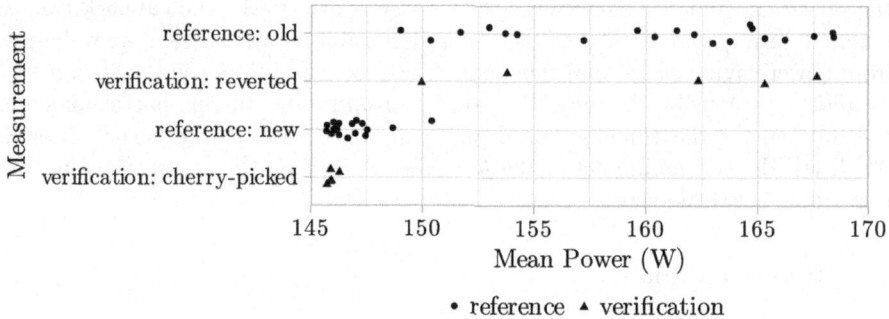

Fig. 4. Mean power consumption of reference and verification measurements for scenario *Powernightmare*.

For this scenario, we expect a low distance ratio for the *new* behavior. (For *old*, power, and thereby the distance ratio fluctuates more, cf. Figs. 2 and 4.) However, in Step 5 it is much greater than in the other *new* Steps 3 & 4, hinting towards a misclassification causing the bisection to fail. This is confirmed by the successful bisection above, where Step 5 is classified as *old* instead of *new*.

Table 1. First steps of a failed and successful Powernightmare bisection.

		Failed Bisection		Successful Bisection	
Step	Kernel (commit hash)	Verdict	Distance Ratio	Verdict	Distance Ratio
1	97b1255cb27c	old	0.56	old	0.46
2	5e630afdcb82	old	0.71	old	0.49
3	d19efb729f10	new	0.07	new	0.02
4	16e205cf42da	new	0.07	new	0.04
5	67698287031b	new	0.56	old	0.40

6 Conclusion and Future Work

As a step towards reducing the power consumption of idle systems, this work showed an approach to pinpoint the root cause of idle-power regressions in the Linux kernel. We outlined the challenges to accurately measuring idle-power consumption and designed an infrastructure around them. Using this infrastructure, we implemented an automated bisection-based approach to trace idle-power regressions to specific commits. In contrast to well-understood established bisection usages (e.g., [25,26]), our classification relies directly on power measurements. For such power measurements, we showed that similarity scoring is a practically viable and flexible approach to classification into *old* and *new*.

To ensure the robustness of the whole search process, we proposed measures to reduce and assess the remaining uncertainty.

With our approach we identified the root cause for two cases of power regressions in Linux. The first case was observed in our lab and showed an idle power increase of 7.4% after a system update. Our technique successfully pinpointed the cause of this regression to one specific commit. This commit removed the flag TIMER_DEFERRABLE from a timer, which we verified as the cause of the observed regression during the update. The second case reproduces an issue described in the literature [23]. Again, our approach successfully determined a particular commit that changed the specific behavior, in this case mitigated this issue.

Ultimately, our work shows that driving an automated bisection directly through power measurements is a promising approach to pinpoint power regressions, showing potential to effectively improve the energy efficiency of computer systems.

Future Work. So far our work is limited to only a single SUT. Expanding the testing infrastructure to support multiple SUTs could both speed up the search process through parallelization and produce more general results. It could also enable testing of multiple configurations or even perform searches in the large configuration space itself. Further, it could assess how consistent the impact of a specific regression is.

Another perspective to improve our work could be alternative algorithms to bisection. The literature describes comparable approaches that can handle misclassifications at individual steps [17,39]. Until now, a practical application of such algorithms for power regressions remains unclear and has to be investigated. Such a method, however, would simplify the classification and can hence reduce the overall analysis time. In general, a robust and universally applicable classification system of software systems into *old/new* for a given scenario remains an open challenge. Although our approach can successfully find the root cause of a power regression, a more general characterization framework for behavioral changes with regards to power consumption could supersede the search for scenario-optimal distance functions. Moreover, one could consider reducing the measurement infrastructure to a single machine. Dropping the focus on idle-power consumption would render in-band power measurements a feasible solution. Accordingly, a much simpler infrastructure without the need for a sophisticated out-of-band measurement setup could lead to a broader applicability of our approach.

Acknowledgments. This work is supported in part by the German National High Performance Computing (NHR@TUD), funded in equal parts by the state of Saxony and the Federal Ministry of Education and Research. Additionally, this work is supported by the Federal Ministry of Education and Research via the MCSE research project (16ME0663K). It is also financed on the basis of the budget passed by the Saxon State Parliament in Germany. We would like to thank Mario Bielert and the anonymous reviewers for their valuable input.

Data Availability. We provide the raw data of our experiments as well as the scripts of our infrastructure online [38].

References

1. ACPI Specification Working Group (ASWG), Tianocore Community Members, et al.: Advanced Configuration and Power Interface (ACPI) Specification. UEFI Forum, Inc., 3855 SW 153rd Drive, Beaverton, Oregon 97003 USA, release 6.5 edition, August 2022
2. Adhianto, L., Banerjee, S., Fagan, M.W., et al.: HPCToolkit: tools for performance analysis of optimized parallel programs (2009). https://doi.org/10.1002/cpe.1553
3. AMD64 Technology: AMD64 Architecture Programmer's Manual. In: Advanced Micro Devices, 4.08 edn, April 2024. Publication No. 40332, https://www.amd.com/content/dam/amd/en/documents/processor-tech-docs/programmer-references/40332.pdf
4. Bakhshalipour, M., Sarbazi-Azad, H.: Parallelizing bisection root-finding: a case for accelerating serial algorithms in multicore substrates (2018). https://doi.org/10.48550/arXiv.1805.07269
5. Bedard, D., Lim, M.Y., Fowler, R., Porterfield, A.: PowerMon: fine-grained and integrated power monitoring for commodity computer systems (2010). https://doi.org/10.1109/SECON.2010.5453824
6. BitMover, Inc. BitKeeper SCM (2016). https://www.bitkeeper.org/
7. Chapel, J.: The cloud is booming—but so is cloud waste, March 2020. https://devops.com/the-cloud-is-booming-but-so-is-cloud-waste/. Accessed 23 July 2023
8. Chen, H., Mao, Y., Wang, X., et al.: Linux kernel vulnerabilities: state-of-the-art defenses and open problems (2011). https://doi.org/10.1145/2103799.2103805
9. CLEAResult. What is 80 plus certified?, September 2022. https://www.clearesult.com/80plus/program-details
10. Colmant, M., Kurpicz, M., Felber, P., et al.: Process-level power estimation in VM-based systems. https://doi.org/10.1145/2741948.2741971
11. Couder, C.: Fighting regressions with git bisect. https://mirrors.edge.kernel.org/pub/software/scm/git/docs/git-bisect-lk2009.html
12. Georgiou, S., Rizou, S., Spinellis, D.: Software development lifecycle for energy efficiency: techniques and tools (2019). https://doi.org/10.1145/3337773
13. Gregg, B.: The flame graph (2016). https://doi.org/10.1145/2909476
14. Gregg, B., Mauro, J.: DTrace: Dynamic Tracing in Oracle Solaris, Mac OS X, and FreeBSD. Prentice Hall Professional (2011). ISBN 0132091518
15. Groß, T.R.: Bisection debugging (1997)
16. Hackenberg, D., Ilsche, T., Schuchart, J., et al.: HDEEM: high definition energy efficiency monitoring (2014). https://doi.org/10.1109/E2SC.2014.13
17. Henderson, T.A.D., Dorward, B., Nickell, E., et al.: Flake aware culprit finding (2023). https://doi.org/10.1109/ICST57152.2023.00041
18. Hönig, T., Janker, H., Eibel, C., et al.: Proactive energy-aware programming with PEEK (2014). https://www.usenix.org/system/files/conference/trios14/trios14-paper-hoenig.pdf
19. Hsu, C.-H., Deng, Q., Mars, J., Tang, L.: SmoothOperator: reducing power fragmentation and improving power utilization in large-scale datacenters (2018). https://doi.org/10.1145/3173162.3173190

20. Hähnel, M., Döbel, B., Völp, M., Härtig, H.: Measuring energy consumption for short code paths using RAPL. https://doi.org/10.1145/2425248.2425252
21. Ilsche, T., Hackenberg, D., Graul, S., et al.: Power measurements for compute nodes: improving sampling rates, granularity and accuracy (2015). https://doi.org/10.1109/IGCC.2015.7393710
22. Ilsche, T., Hackenberg, D., Schöne, R., et al.: MetricQ: a scalable infrastructure for processing high-resolution time series data (2019). https://doi.org/10.1109/DAAC49578.2019.00007
23. Ilsche, T., Hähnel, M., Schöne, R., et al.: Powernightmares: the challenge of efficiently using sleep states on multi-core systems (2018). https://doi.org/10.1007/978-3-319-75178-8_50
24. Intel Corporation: Intel® 64 and IA-32 Architectures Software Developer's Manual, March 2025. Order Number 325462. https://cdrdv2.intel.com/v1/dl/getContent/671200
25. Intel Corporation: Linux kernel performance, February 2025. https://www.intel.com/content/www/us/en/developer/topic-technology/open/linux-kernel-performance/overview.html
26. Johnson, J., Kenefick, J., Larson, P.: Hunting regressions in GCC and the Linux kernel (2004). http://mirror.linux.org.au/pub/linux.conf.au/2004/papers/41-janis-johnson-reghunt_kernel.pdf
27. Knüpfer, A, Rössel, C., Mey, D.A., et al.: Score-P: a joint performance measurement run-time infrastructure for Periscope, Scalasca, TAU, and Vampir (2012). https://doi.org/10.1007/978-3-642-31476-6_7
28. Koot, M., Wijnhoven, F.: Usage impact on data center electricity needs: a system dynamic forecasting model. https://doi.org/10.1016/j.apenergy.2021.116798
29. Linux Kernel Contributors. perf: Linux profiling with performance counters (2023). https://perf.wiki.kernel.org
30. Ocariza Jr., F.S.: On the effectiveness of bisection in performance regression localization (2022). https://doi.org/10.1007/s10664-022-10152-3
31. O'Sullivan, B.: Mercurial: The Definitive Guide. O'Reilly Media, Inc. (2009)
32. Saha, R., Gligoric, M.: Selective bisection debugging (2017). https://doi.org/10.1007/978-3-662-54494-5_4
33. Shende, S.S., Malony, A.D.: The Tau parallel performance system (2006). https://doi.org/10.1177/1094342006064482
34. Sikorski, K.: Bisection is optimal (1982). https://doi.org/10.1007/BF01459080
35. Silicon Graphics International, Open Source Development Labs, Bull, et al.: Linux test project. https://linux-test-project.github.io/
36. Smejkal, T., Hähnel, M., Ilsche, T., et al.: E-Team: practical energy accounting for multi-core systems. https://www.usenix.org/conference/atc17/technical-sessions/presentation/smejkal
37. Torvalds, L., Hamano, J.C., King, J.: et al.: Git, April 2023. https://git-scm.com/
38. Tröpgen, H., Smejkal, T., Ilsche, T., et al.: Artifacts to reproduce "Pinpointing Idle-Power Regressions in Linux", February 2025. https://doi.org/10.5281/zenodo.14938000
39. Wuffinga, E.: BBChop, August 2009. https://github.com/Ealdwulf/BBChop
40. Wysocki, R.J., et al.: [rft][patch v4 0/7] sched/cpuidle: Idle loop rework, March 2018. Thread on the Linux kernel mailing list
41. Zeller, A.: Yesterday, my program worked. Today, it does not. Why? (1999). https://doi.org/10.1145/318774.318946
42. ZES ZIMMER Electronic Systems GmbH, Tabaksmühlenweg 30, 61440 Oberursel. *1-Phasen-Präzisions-Leistungsmeßgerät LMG95 Benutzerhandbuch*, June 2007

43. Zhai, Y., Hao, Y., Zhang, H., et al.: UBITect: a precise and scalable method to detect use-before-initialization bugs in Linux kernel (2020). https://doi.org/10.1145/3368089.3409686
44. Zhai, Y., Hao, Y., Zhang, Z., et al.: Progressive scrutiny: incremental detection of UBI bugs in the Linux kernel (2022). https://doi.org/10.14722/ndss.2022.24380

DARE-ML: Democratized Accessible Resource Environment for Machine Learning in the SUPERCOM Platform

Matteo Mendula[1(✉)], Caterina Leonelli[2(✉)], Marco Miozzo[1], and Paolo Dini[1]

[1] Centre Tecnològic de Telecomunicacions de Catalunya, Catalunya, Spain
{mmendula,mmiozzo,pdini}@cttc.es
[2] University of Bologna, Bologna, Italy
caterina.leonelli2@studio.unibo.it

Abstract. The rise of Generative AI has renewed interest in Deep Learning across academia and industry, attracting smaller research groups and non-IT companies eager to leverage Machine Learning (ML). However, high infrastructure costs often make AI adoption impractical. Democratizing access to High-Performance Computing (HPC) is key to overcoming this barrier, enabling broader ML adoption while reducing e-waste by integrating existing resources.

DARE-ML (Democratized Accessible Resource Environment for Machine Learning) offers a framework to optimize resource allocation, lower energy use, and improve ML accessibility. By profiling models interactively in a heterogeneous, limited-GPU environment, DARE-ML collects key metadata—like training time and memory needs—before scheduling jobs. At its core, DARE-ML incorporates an efficient interactive profiling mechanism powered by ESN (Echo State Networks), enabling streamlined and resource-aware execution of deep learning tasks.

Experiments in real and simulated settings show DARE-ML improves ML job scheduling, reducing energy use up to 80-fold and cutting both average job completion time and waiting time per user by 15%.

Keywords: Energy Efficiency · HPC & AI · Power monitoring · Scheduling and resource management

1 Introduction

As Artificial Intelligence (AI) advances, the demand for High-Performance Computing (HPC) resources has surged, driven by the needs of Machine Learning (ML) and Deep Learning (DL) applications [1]. However, limited access to HPC infrastructure creates barriers for researchers and data scientists with constrained budgets, highlighting the need for solutions that democratize resource

---

M. Mendula and C. Leonelli—Equal contribution.

ⓒ The Author(s), under exclusive license to Springer Nature Switzerland AG 2026
S. Neuwirth et al. (Eds.): ISC High Performance 2025 Workshops, LNCS 16091, pp. 219–230, 2026.
https://doi.org/10.1007/978-3-032-07612-0_17

sharing. Additionally, the environmental impact of AI, including e-waste and CO_2 emissions which it is projected to reach 1.2–5.0 million tons by 2030 due to Generative AI [2], underscores the importance of reusing computational resources to promote sustainability and reduce the digital divide.

The DARE-ML framework (Democratized Accessible Resource Environment for Machine Learning) directly addresses this need by introducing an integrated framework that optimizes allocation and enhances accessibility of resources. Rather than requiring dedicated GPUs for each individual, DARE-ML offers a collaborative, shared environment where users can interactively profile their models. This environment tracks essential metadata—such as training time estimates and memory usage—allowing users to make informed decisions and manage computational demands effectively. By centralizing these capabilities, DARE-ML empowers users to profile and prepare models in a streamlined, resource-efficient setting, eliminating the bottlenecks and reducing the high costs associated with traditional HPC infrastructure when applied to ML training workloads. A key feature of DARE-ML is its intelligent training queue system, which dynamically adjusts resource allocation based on real-time workload demands and user-defined accuracy thresholds. Leveraging Kubernetes for orchestration, this system not only optimizes resource utilization but also significantly reduces energy consumption and training time. The project's framework includes interactive profiling tools, benchmark datasets, optimized job scheduling, and a robust monitoring interface—all of which contribute to a more sustainable and accessible ML/DL ecosystem.

Experimental results, conducted in a simulated environment using real monitoring data, demonstrate the capabilities of DARE-ML in ML job scheduling, achieving up to an 80-fold reduction in energy consumption and a 15% decrease in terms of average Job Completion Time (JCT) and waiting time per user.

2 Background and Problem Statement

In an era where increasingly complex and energy-intensive models set the benchmark for state-of-the-art predictive accuracy and performance in supervised learning, access to cutting-edge computational resources remains largely confined to organizations with substantial funding. While this exclusivity reflects the natural progression of a market driven by technological advancements, it poses significant challenges for researchers.

2.1 HPC and Reproducibility of Machine Learning

As highlighted by Varoquaux et al. [3], the prevailing "bigger-is-better" paradigm in AI exacerbates these challenges by driving a disproportionate focus on scaling models to ever-larger sizes, which not only strains resources but also narrows the scope of problems addressed by AI. This trend results in unsustainable economic and environmental costs, concentrating power and decision-making in the hands of a few well-resourced entities, while sidelining critical applications in fields that may not require such large-scale solutions. Consequently, the AI research landscape becomes less accessible, reinforcing inequalities and limiting the diversity of contributions from smaller academic and independent research groups.

A further challenge lies in the heterogeneous computing resources typical of many research environments. Unlike industrial setups, where older hardware is often retired or repurposed, research labs frequently operate with a mixture of outdated and newer components. This often includes older GPU models that, though functional for smaller models, lag behind newer GPUs in memory capacity and FLOPs. While many development frameworks support parallelization across multiple GPUs, efficiently allocating models across GPUs of varying capacities remains complex [4], especially when significant differences in GPU memory size are present [5]. This heterogeneity complicates model deployment and optimization, necessitating advanced resource management strategies to fully leverage mixed-hardware environments.

2.2 ML Job Scheduling

Recent research explores ML job scheduling optimizations, often using queuing mechanisms to improve job completion time (JCT), fairness, and accuracy. Optimus [6] minimizes JCT by evaluating training quality, while Slaq [7] dynamically reallocates jobs to enhance accuracy. These schedulers rely on preemption, which, despite its overhead, is essential for reducing JCT. However, fairness-focused schedulers [9] prioritize fairness over efficiency [10].

PCS [11] discusses job completion predictability and preemption's impact, though this is beyond our scope. In DARE-ML, we assume ML workloads are time-consuming and propose splitting long-running jobs based on accuracy thresholds, providing intermediate results for user decisions. This aligns with Auto-ML [12]. Wang et al. [13] propose removing tasks upon reaching accuracy goals under system overload; we extend this by applying accuracy-threshold preemption at the application level to manage limited GPU resources. DL2 [14] uses a neural network for real-time scheduling, optimizing JCT via reinforcement learning. Recent work also explores energy-aware scheduling, such as Rattihalli et al. [23], which integrates GPUs, CPUs, and specialized hardware.

While many studies address ML job estimation, they often overlook the full model lifecycle, including data preprocessing [15], hyperparameter tuning [16], and model validation [17].

2.3 Training Loss Estimation and Echo State Networks (ESNs)

Efforts to predict training quality trends, like loss and accuracy, often assume Machine Learning (ML) workflows converge predictably [11]. However, this assumption falters during dataset exploration, where data-driven dynamics and hyperparameter sensitivity dominate. Unlike these methods, our approach uses current loss and accuracy to trigger preemption, avoiding reliance on forecasting. Time series forecasting models, while useful, add computational overhead—e.g.,

GPU usage—that can detract from primary training tasks, often making them impractical.

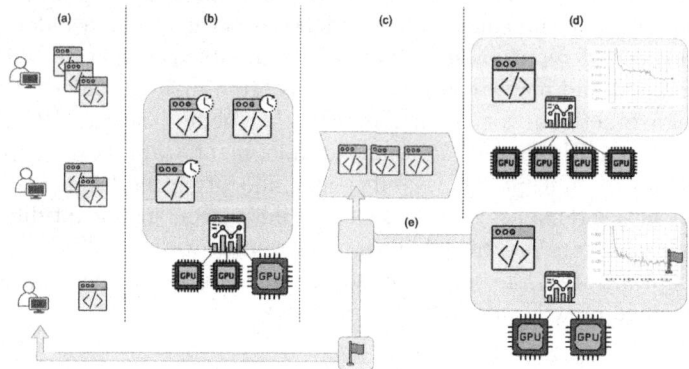

Fig. 1. DARE-ML framework architecture.

Echo State Networks (ESNs), a type of recurrent neural network (RNN), address traditional RNN limitations like training complexity [18]. With a fixed, random reservoir layer mapping inputs to a high-dimensional space, only the output layer is trained, simplifying the process. ESNs excel in tasks like time series forecasting [19], speech recognition [21], and system modeling [20], offering low-cost dynamic modeling [22]. In DARE-ML, ESNs efficiently estimate loss trends across epochs with minimal overhead, aiding model profiling.

3 DARE-ML Framework Architecture

To the purpose of providing an innovative framework for democratic sharing of HPC resources, here we detail the main components of our system:

- **Interactive Profiling Environment**: Provides researchers with a user interface to profile ML models using limited resources. Users can assess key metadata—training time, memory needs, and accuracy—enabling iterative refinements before full-scale training.
- **Job Scheduler**: Manages task queues using a First-In-First-Out (FIFO) strategy, optimizing resource usage, and minimizing wait times by dynamically adjusting to workload demands.
- **Resource Allocation Module**: Assigns GPUs based on profiling data, ensuring efficient execution. It monitors active jobs and adjusts allocations in real time as workload conditions change.
- **Training Management System**: Oversees ML training, halting jobs upon reaching target loss or accuracy. It saves model checkpoints, allowing researchers to resume training without losing progress.

Figure 1 illustrates the DARE-ML framework, where users train ML models with shared and heterogeneous cluster resources (a). Workloads are profiled within set time limits (b), then scheduled using policies like FIFO or Shortest Job First (c). Jobs receive GPUs based on profiling results and pause when a target loss is reached (d). The model checkpoint is then returned for further training or modification.

3.1 DARE-ML Profiling and Scheduling

Initially, each user access the session-based session with limited HPC resources to explore the target training dataset. In this phase the goal is to be able to produce a metadata description file which contains the memory and accuracy requirements for each job, while each GPU has its own memory budget.

Then the scheduling algorithm sets jobs in a queue for processing and iterates through each job to find an appropriate GPU. For each job, it checks each available GPU to determine if it meets the job's memory needs and is free for allocation. If a suitable GPU is available, the algorithm assigns the GPU to the job and initiates the training process. Once training is completed, the job's performance is evaluated against its target accuracy. If the target accuracy is reached, the model checkpoint is returned to the user, concluding that job's cycle. In contrast, if the target accuracy is not achieved, the job goes back to the queue for additional training. After each job completes or pauses, the allocated GPU is freed for use by other jobs. In order to limit infinite training loops, when the target accuracy is not reachable, a maximum number of retrain iterations is set at profiling time based on the task, the number of parameters of the model and the size of the dataset. If no compatible GPU is available for a job or if it requires additional training, the job is requeued to await the next available resource.

4 Experimental Testbed Description and Model Profiling

Real experiments are conducted on the SUPERCOM computing platform[1] which consists of four different host nodes with a heterogeneous set of seven GPUs. Those nodes are part of a Kubernetes cluster which hosts Jupyter Hub as interactive computing profiling environment and Kepler[2] as energy monitoring tool. Corresponding computing resources for currently existing nodes are listed in Table 1.

Our primary goal is to manage multiple training sessions with limited on-premises resources. To accomplish this, we focus on a specific type of high-demand task designed to push the SUPERCOM platform to its limits. We selected three distinct Large Language Models (LLMs), each with progressively increasing trainable parameters and memory requirements. Three different models are selected, each representing an incremental level of complexity in terms of trainable parameters and virtual memory requirements:

---

[1] https://supercom.cttc.es/.
[2] https://sustainable-computing.io/.

- **lucadiliello/bart-small**, 70.5M, 11GB;
- **google/flan-t5-small** with 77M, 11GB;
- **google/flan-t5-base** with 248M, 24GB.

We finetuned those models on DialogSum [24], a well-known dialog summarization dataset using LoRA+ [25]. Cross-entropy was chosen as the optimal loss function for all models tested. The learning rate is set to 2×10^{-4}, and the LoRA dropout rate to 0.1 across all models. Batch size is configured at 4 for the two smaller models and reduced to 2 for the most memory-intensive model. The additional virtual memory requirements of the flan-t5-base model present a practical challenge for complex job scheduling across a heterogeneous set of resources. In fact, this model only fits within three of the seven available GPUs, highlighting the difficulties of efficiently managing training workloads with varied hardware capabilities.

4.1 Loss Monitoring and Model Profiling

Predicting training loss dynamically is generally infeasible due to the inherent unpredictability of model convergence, contrary to the assumptions of many approaches that assume predictable convergence patterns [10]. Furthermore, any sophisticated prediction approach typically incurs considerable computational overhead, as it requires additional GPU resources to optimize usage, potentially

Table 1. SUPERCOM Platform Specifications for Each Computing Node of the Cluster

Node Tier	Component	Specification
Bronze	CPU	2x Xeon CascadeLake 6230 2.1 GHz, 40 cores
	GPU	4x NVIDIA RTX 2080 TI, 11 GB GDDR6
	RAM	192 GB
	HD	2 TB SSD
Silver	CPU	32x Intel(R) Xeon(R) Silver 4314, 2.40 GHz
	GPU	GeForce RTX 3090, 24 GB
	RAM	125 GB
	HD	8 TB SSD + 1 TB NVME
Silver	CPU	Xeon IceLake Silver 4314, 2.4 GHz, 16 cores
	GPU	NVIDIA RTX 3090 BLOWER, 24 GB GDDR6X
	RAM	128 GB
	HD	8 TB SSD
Gold	CPU	2x Xeon IceLake Platinum 8358, 32 cores, 2.6 GHz
	GPU	NVIDIA RTX 3090 BLOWER, 24 GB GDDR6X
	RAM	1024 GB
	HD	2 TB SSD, 3.84 TB NVME

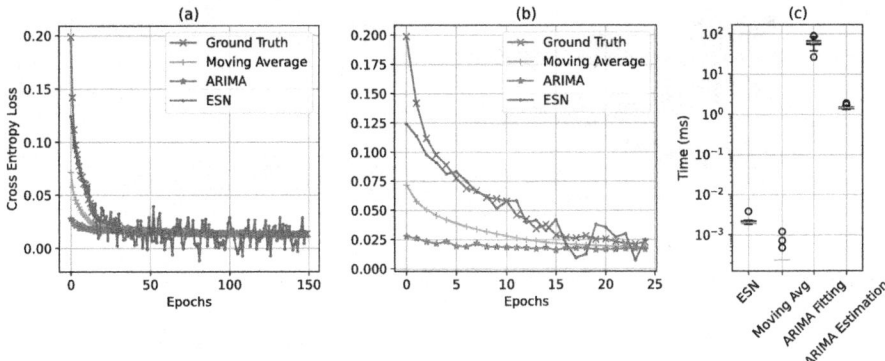

Fig. 2. Cross-entropy loss estimation for the BART-small model across all epochs (a), within the first 25 epochs (b), and the impact in terms of fitting time of each estimator (c).

leading to inefficiencies and reducing overall training performance. For these reasons, such prediction methods often prove impractical in real-world scenarios due to their high resource costs and limited reliability.

Our Interactive Profiling Environment addresses these challenges by allowing users to monitor training progress in real time using an ESN as future loss estimator. Figure 2 reports cross-entropy loss estimations across epochs for a smaller model, BART-small, comparing predictions by ESN, Moving Average, and ARIMA. The ESN consistently tracks the evolution of cross-entropy loss, while Moving Average and ARIMA, which rely on 50-point windows for prediction, struggle to capture the series' underlying dynamics accurately. ESNs achieve a reasonable balance, requiring only about two orders of magnitude more computational power than the Moving Average method while being nearly 40 times faster at fitting than ARIMA.

4.2 Power and Energy Consumption

At monitoring phase, we track the total power consumption for each considered training job. At this stage, we also checked the power consumption of models profiled against the full model training.

In Fig. 3, we present the calculated energy consumption for the entire training period, comparing scenarios with and without DARE-ML profiling, while incorporating the energy cost of the profiling process itself. In order to calculate the energy from the power consumption at each time step, we have used the Simpson's rule for numerical approximation integration [26]. As we can see, the DARE-ML profiling cuts significantly the amount of energy needed per single train, sparing about 21.79x the energy in bart-small training, 53.37x in flan-t5-base up to 92.7x in flan-t5-small.

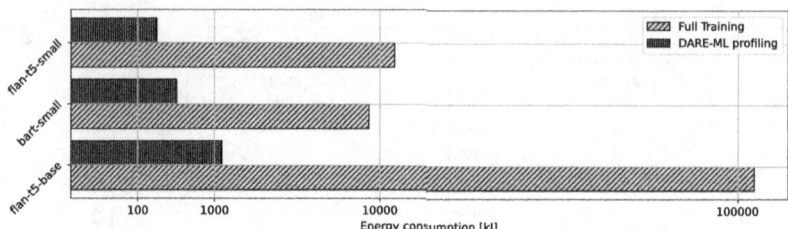

Fig. 3. Real total energy consumption per model with and without DARE-ML profiling.

5 DARE-ML Results

In this section, we simulate a scenario in which multiple users submit ML training jobs simultaneously. At simulation time, GPU sizes reflect the configurations of SUPERCOM according with specified memory budgets. Each user is a Python thread submitting a random number of ML training jobs at intervals sampled from a predefined pause range, with scaled-down memory and training times for faster simulation. Across the following set of experiments, we compare DARE-DL with (I) a baseline FIFO without logic and (II) a time-limited version where users have maximum session durations.

For reproducibility purposes, we also provide the code for our simulations[3].

5.1 Average Job Completion Time and Average Waiting Time

In Fig. 4, we illustrate three key metrics: the total waiting time across all jobs, the average waiting time per user, and the average job completion time $AvgJCT$. DARE-ML outperforms the alternatives by achieving the lowest total waiting time, average waiting time, and average job completion time. To clarify, the waiting time of a job is defined as the interval between its arrival time—when a user submits a job request—and its start time, when the scheduler assigns it to a GPU. These metrics underscore the efficiency of DARE-ML in reducing both waiting times and overall job completion times, making it a more responsive and efficient solution for managing ML workload.

5.2 Power Consumption Benchmark

In Fig. 5, we analyze GPU usage and energy consumption for 15 users under a fixed configuration.

The first subfigure, GPU Usage, shows balanced job distribution across GPUs, with memory-intensive tasks assigned to GPUs 1–3 (24 GB memory). Thanks to the introduction of the interactive enviroment, DARE-ML with Profiling (green bars), stops jobs once they meet the accuracy threshold, reducing

---

[3] https://gitlab.cttc.es/supercom/dare-ml-eesp-2025.

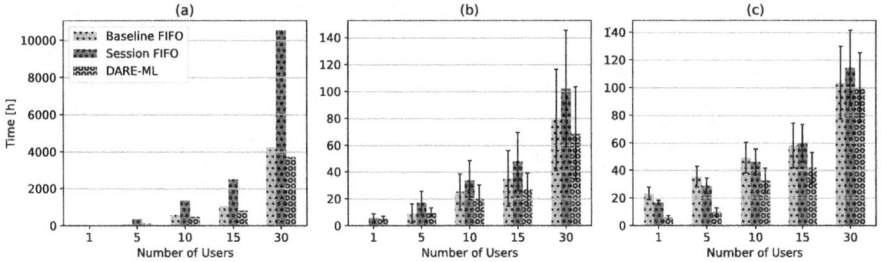

Fig. 4. Comparison of total waiting time, average waiting time per user, and average job completion time (AvgJCT) across scheduling strategies. *DARE-ML* scheduler achieves the lowest total waiting time (a), minimizes average waiting time per user (b), and yields the shortest Avg. JCT (c) across all user counts.

GPU usage to 10–15% of other scenarios. These values also account for the energy consumed during the profiling process.

The second subfigure, Total Energy Consumption, shows cumulative energy use across nodes. The worst-case scenario (DARE-ML, yellow bars) incurs higher energy costs due to preemption overhead, setting an upper bound on time and energy. In contrast, the best-case scenario (DARE-ML with Profiling) uses 83 times less energy by halting jobs at the accuracy threshold. Our solution balances these extremes, reducing GPU usage and energy consumption while maintaining user flexibility, offering a practical and efficient approach.

5.3 Job Scheduling Across Multiple GPUs

Next, we analyze job scheduling across GPUs. Figure 6 shows GPU task allocation under different configurations. Each row represents a GPU, with tasks color-coded by model type. GPUs 1–3 have 24 GB memory, while others have 11 GB. Red tasks require 24 GB and are scheduled only on the first three GPUs. We exclude DARE-ML with profiling as it simplifies the demonstration of reduced

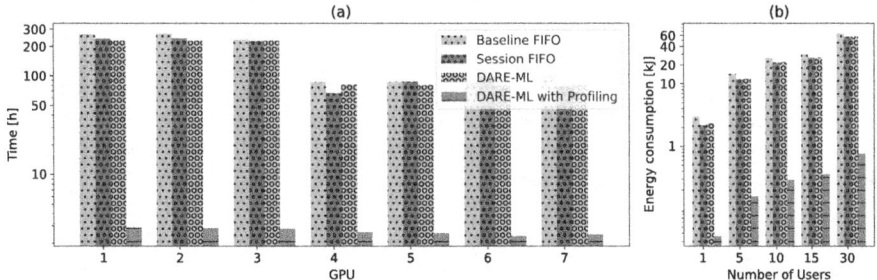

Fig. 5. GPU usage and energy consumption across scheduling scenarios for 15 users. The plot shows GPU usage (a) as a function of time and the total energy consumption (b) with different connected users.

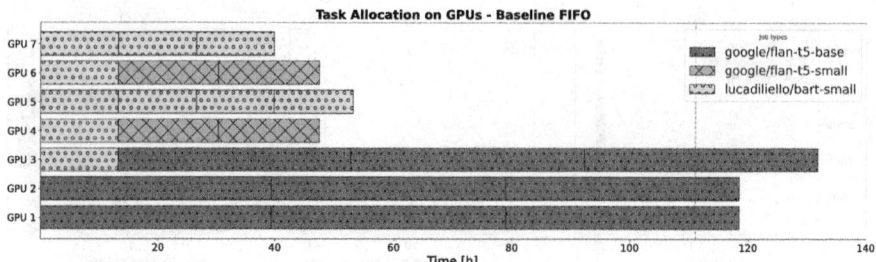

(a) Task allocation on GPUs using the Baseline FIFO policy. This configuration follows a strict first-in, first-out scheduling approach, leading to contiguous task blocks on each GPU since there is no preemption. The coarse task granularity results in less optimized GPU utilization.

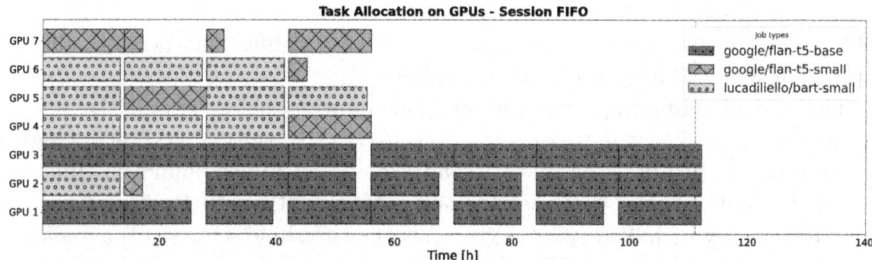

(b) Task allocation on GPUs using the Session FIFO policy. Here, tasks are scheduled in flexible sessions, leading to finer task granularity with more fragmented and interleaved task blocks.

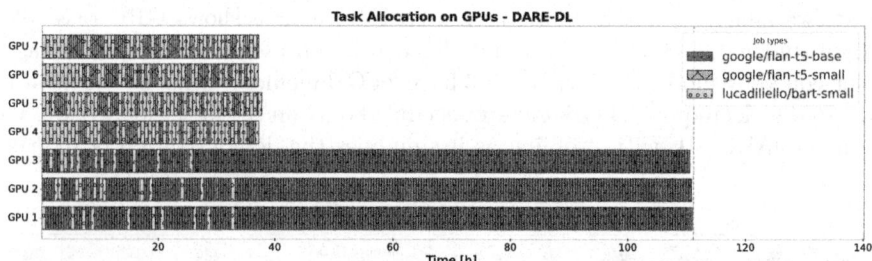

(c) Task allocation on GPUs using the DARE-ML policy. This policy maximizes GPU utilization by introducing the finest task granularity, packing tasks densely with minimal idle time. The highly fragmented allocation allows for efficient, continuous GPU usage across all available resources.

Fig. 6. Job Scheduling Allocation across GPUs against different preemption strategies.

training time. In Fig. 6 (a), tasks are scheduled sequentially (FIFO) without preemption. In Fig. 6 (b), we enhance FIFO with session-based preemption, suspending jobs after 14 h (matching Grid5000's reservation time). Although this reduces overall job time compared to Baseline FIFO, some idle periods persist.

Figure 6 provides the granularity of task allocation on GPUs. Granularity here refers to the detail and fragmentation level in task scheduling. In Fig. 6 (a) with Baseline FIFO, the level of grain is coarse, with longer, contiguous blocks of tasks. Figure 6 (b) with Session FIFO introduces finer grain, as tasks are more fragmented and interleaved, indicating a more flexible allocation within sessions, but noticeable idle gaps. Figure 6 (c) with DARE-ML has the highest grain level, with densely packed and highly fragmented tasks that minimize idle periods, suggesting an optimization strategy aimed at maximizing GPU utilization and handling tasks with greater granularity. DARE-ML completes all training jobs over 2 h faster than session-based FIFO with preemption and about 20 h faster than FIFO without preemption. The vertical line in the plots marks the shorter completion time.

6 Conclusion and Future Direction

In this article, we showed that DARE-ML's realistic ML job profiling cuts energy use and speeds up training in shared HPC environments. Our novel ESN-based loss estimator reduces resource use, lowering average JCT and wait times by 15% when retraining to overfitting, and up to 80x with loss-aware interruptions. In high-demand cases, energy consumption drops by up to 83x. Future work will integrate SUPERCOM's historical data to improve profiling accuracy and performance using task and data similarities. These advancements would strengthen DARE-ML's position as a valuable tool for sustainable AI, bridging the gap between high-performance computing and environmental responsibility.

References

1. Hacker, P., Engel, A., Mauer, M.: Regulating ChatGPT and other large generative AI models. In: ACM FAccT (2023)
2. Wang, P., Zhang, L.-Y., Tzachor, A.: E-waste challenges of generative artificial intelligence. Nature Comput, Sci (2024)
3. Varoquaux, G., Luccioni, A. S., Whittaker, M.: Hype, Sustainability, and the Price of the Bigger-is-Better Paradigm in AI. arXiv:2409.14160 (2024)
4. Zhang, J., Niu, G., Dai, Q., et al.: PipePar: enabling fast DNN pipeline parallel training in heterogeneous GPU clusters. Neurocomputing (2023)
5. Jia, X., Jiang, L., Wang, A., et al.: Whale: efficient giant model training over heterogeneous GPUs. In: USENIX ATC (2022)
6. Peng, Y., Bao, Y., Chen, Y., et al.: Optimus: an efficient dynamic resource scheduler for deep learning clusters. In: EuroSys (2018)
7. Zhang, H., Stafman, L., Or, A., et al.: SLAQ: quality-driven scheduling for distributed machine learning. In: SoCC (2017)
8. Mahajan, K., Balasubramanian, A., Singhvi, A., et al.: Themis: fair and efficient GPU cluster scheduling. In: NSDI (2020)

9. Chaudhary, S., Ramjee, R., Sivathanu, M., et al.: Balancing efficiency and fairness in heterogeneous GPU clusters for deep learning. In: EuroSys (2020)
10. Gu, J., Chowdhury, M., Shin, K.G., et al.: Tiresias: a GPU cluster manager for distributed deep learning. In: NSDI (2019)
11. Faisal, A., Martin, N., Bashir, H., et al.: When will my ML Job finish? Toward providing Completion Time Estimates through Predictability-Centric Scheduling, Usenix (2024)
12. Guyon, I., Sun-Hosoya, L., Boullé, M., et al.: Analysis of the AutoML challenge series 2015-2018. In: AutoML (2019)
13. Wang, H., Liu, Z., Shen, H.: Job scheduling for large-scale machine learning clusters. In: CoNEXT (2020)
14. Peng, Y., Bao, Y., Chen, Y., et al.: DL2: a deep learning-driven scheduler for deep learning clusters. CoRR (2019)
15. Oluwasakin, E., Torku, T., Tingting, S., et al.: Minimization of high computational cost in data preprocessing and modeling using MPI4Py. Mach. Learn, Appl (2023)
16. Wang, C., Liu, X., Awadallah, A.H.: Cost-effective hyperparameter optimization for large language model generation inference. In: AutoML (2023)
17. Ramezan, C. A., Warner, T. A., Maxwell, A. E.: Evaluation of sampling and cross-validation tuning strategies for regional-scale machine learning classification. Remote Sens. (2019)
18. Jaeger, H.: Echo state network. scholarpedia (2007)
19. Li, D., Han, M., Wang, J.: Chaotic time series prediction based on a novel robust echo state network. IEEE Trans. Neural Netw. Learn, Syst (2012)
20. Ullah, W., Hussain, T., Khan, Z. A., et al.: Intelligent dual stream CNN and echo state network for anomaly detection. Knowl.-Based Syst. (2022)
21. Pedrelli, L., Hinaut, X.: Hierarchical-task reservoir for online semantic analysis from continuous speech. IEEE Trans. Neural Netw. Learn, Syst (2021)
22. Yan, M., Huang, C., Bienstman, P., et al.: Emerging opportunities and challenges for the future of reservoir computing. Nature Commun. (2024)
23. Rattihalli, G., Hogade, N., Dhakal, A., et al.: Fine-grained heterogeneous execution framework with energy aware scheduling. In: IEEE CLOUD (2023)
24. Chen, Y., Liu, Y., Chen, L., et al.: DialogSum: a real-life scenario dialogue summarization dataset. In: ACL-IJCNLP Findings (2021)
25. Hayou, S., Ghosh, N., Yu, B.: LoRA+: efficient low rank adaptation of large models. arXiv:2402.12354 (2024)
26. Tallarida, R.J., Murray, R.B.: Area under a curve: trapezoidal and Simpson's rules. Manual Pharmacol, Calc (1987)

Power-Capping Metric Evaluation for Improving Energy Efficiency in HPC Applications

Maria Patrou[1]( ), Thomas Wang[2], Wael Elwasif[1], Markus Eisenbach[1], Ross Miller[1], William Godoy[1], and Oscar Hernandez[1]

[1] Oak Ridge National Laboratory, Oak Ridge, TN, USA
{patroum,elwasifwr,eisenbachm,rgmiller,godoywf,oscar}@ornl.gov
[2] Camas High School, Camas, WA, USA
twangapples@gmail.com

Abstract. With high-performance computing systems now running at exascale, optimizing power-scaling management and resource utilization has become more critical than ever. This paper explores runtime power-capping optimizations that leverage integrated CPU-GPU power management on architectures like the NVIDIA GH200 superchip. We evaluate energy-performance metrics that account for simultaneous CPU and GPU power-capping effects by using two complementary approaches: speedup-energy-delay and a Euclidean distance-based multi-objective optimization method. By targeting a mostly compute-bound exascale science application, the Locally Self-Consistent Multiple Scattering (LSMS), we explore challenging scenarios to identify potential opportunities for energy savings in exascale applications, and we recognize that even modest reductions in energy consumption can have significant overall impacts. Our results highlight how GPU task-specific dynamic power-cap adjustments combined with integrated CPU-GPU power steering can improve the energy utilization of certain GPU tasks, thereby laying the groundwork for future adaptive optimization strategies.

Keywords: Power Capping · Energy Efficiency · HPC · GH200 · Performance Metrics · Automatic Power Steering · Exascale Applications · LSMS

Notice: This manuscript has been authored by UT-Battelle LLC under contract DE-AC05-00OR22725 with the US Department of Energy (DOE). The US government retains and the publisher, by accepting the article for publication, acknowledges that the US government retains a nonexclusive, paid-up, irrevocable, worldwide license to publish or reproduce the published form of this manuscript, or allow others to do so, for US government purposes. DOE will provide public access to these results of federally sponsored research in accordance with the DOE Public Access Plan (https://www.energy.gov/doe-public-access-plan).

1 Introduction

GPUs have become crucial for exascale computing because of their high performance per watt compared with traditional CPUs, thus enabling significant improvements in application performance across diverse computational tasks. As a result, the high-performance computing (HPC) community has widely adopted GPUs and developed specialized programming models and numerical methods to maximize the benefits of GPU acceleration.

However, the slowdown of Moore's law has caused processors to lag behind the increasing compute and power demands of scientific application workloads. Thus, optimizing power and energy efficiency on HPC systems remains a critical and ongoing challenge. Although previous research has focused on optimizing application workloads and enabling facility-level improvements, more work is needed to fine-tune applications through dynamic tuning [17], mixed-precision methods, and computational batching to utilize accelerators more effectively [8]. Additionally, emerging hardware capabilities present new opportunities. Tightly integrated CPU-GPU superchips, such as the NVIDIA GH200, incorporate an automatic power-steering system that dynamically reallocates power between the CPU and GPU. This system can be used in conjunction with power capping to further improve energy efficiency. These new capabilities can now be exploited to improve the application's energy efficiency by applying finer-grained power capping based on the type of computations of the GPU tasks. Additionally, meaningful power-capping metrics play a critical role in guiding users to select appropriate optimization goals and tailor power-management strategies to individual application GPU tasks, thereby enabling users to define customized power-management settings for each application.

To this end, we took an initial step toward adaptive power-capping strategies by evaluating metrics to guide power-cap selection for a highly optimized exascale application. Even modest improvements in energy efficiency can yield substantial benefits at exascale, thus highlighting the relevance of this exploration. We used the NVIDIA GH200 Grace Hopper superchip and applied power-capping limits to control the chip's total (CPU-GPU) power consumption. We used automatic power steering to allow CPUs and GPUs to draw power within the set limits based on the application demands. For our study, we targeted key computational tasks, GPU kernels and GPU compute idle phases (where the CPU is executing work), of the Locally Self-Consistent Multiple Scattering (LSMS) exascale application (see Sect. 2.1) and identified the regions most impacted by the power-capping feature. We examined ways in which GPU task-specific power tuning can improve energy efficiency on compute- and memory-bound kernels within the self-consistent field (SCF) iterations. In our analysis, we evaluated and compared different decision-making metrics to identify suitable GH200 superchip power settings based on the execution characteristics of each GPU task. The speedup-energy-delay and Euclidean distance of normalized energy/runtime metrics provide complementary insights into power-capping effects and assist in finding optimized power settings for different GPU tasks executed during different application phases. We compared the results provided by each methodology and present their impacts on energy and runtime performance in ideal scenarios to identify the appropriate test cases for each one. Through our findings, we characterized scientific GPU tasks, identified methods for selecting appropriate power-cap settings, and contributed to power-capping tuning strategies that achieve greater energy efficiency.

2 Background

Research has shown that power capping improves energy efficiency, reduces hardware failures [19], and extends system lifespan. Haidar et al. [8] and Krzywaniak et al. [12] demonstrated how composite metrics, particularly energy-delay product (EDP), help manage GPU power limits and balance energy savings and performance. Abdulsalam et al. [1] introduced the Greenup, Powerup, and Speedup (GPS-UP) framework to categorize optimizations by their impact on execution time, power, and energy efficiency. Fine-grained power-capping strategies, such as the Global Extensible Open Power Manager [5], EE-HPC [18], and READEX [7], have proven more effective than static limits. Our approach is similar to fine-grained dynamic power optimizations but is driven by the exploration of effective optimization metrics.

Modern GPUs and CPUs independently regulate power via capping [11], but new-generation architectures, such as NVIDIA's GH200 superchip, regulate both CPU and GPU simultaneously. The GH200 incorporates power capping within its automatic power-steering system and dynamically reallocates power between the CPU and the GPU based on their usage. It initially allocates power to the CPU, thus transferring any unused capacity to the GPU, and enforces limits through Dynamic Voltage and Frequency Scaling (DVFS). When GPU power usage nears a power limit, the system reduces GPU clock speeds. This reduction affects compute-intensive workloads more significantly than memory-bound tasks. Other approaches for CPU-GPU power management with heuristic or machine learning methods have been explored by Saba et al. [16] and Azimi et al. [3], who dynamically allocate power between CPU and GPU. Our approach leverages the automatic power steering of the GH200 when setting a given power cap, thereby dynamically optimizing power allocation per application GPU task to improve both energy efficiency and performance.

2.1 Application

The LSMS exascale application [2,6] is a density functional theory code designed to compute the electronic properties of materials—particularly metals, alloys, and nanostructures. Instead of diagonalizing the Hamiltonian, LSMS utilizes the Korringa-Kohn-Rostoker method, which efficiently determines electronic interactions by computing Green's function. This approach allows LSMS to scale efficiently and support simulations beyond 100,000 atoms. The most computationally demanding tasks within LSMS involve dense-matrix operations, including matrix multiplications and block inversions, which contribute significantly to execution time. The code iteratively updates the electron density and potential through an SCF loop. Written in a combination of C++ and Fortran, LSMS achieves high scalability by leveraging the Message Passing Interface (MPI) for atom-level parallelization, OpenMP on CPUs for energy-level calculations, and CUDA/HIP to accelerate dense linear algebra operations on GPUs. This hybrid programming approach enables LSMS to maintain near-linear scaling on large-scale exascale supercomputing platforms [2].

3 Methodology

Our approach to optimize LSMS involves leveraging power capping to identify optimal maximum power settings that improve both energy efficiency and runtime performance. In this study, we systematically investigated the impact of varying power-capping levels on both fine-grained computational GPU tasks and overall application performance. We measured and analyzed execution time (seconds), energy consumption (joules), and power (watts) at the superchip level for the entire application, and we recorded the CPU- and GPU-specific power for each GPU task within the application run. These measurements were taken while applying incremental chip-level power constraints on the GH200 superchip, ranging from 200 W to the maximum power limit of 1,000 W (default). We executed the entire application at every superchip power limit and collected the data for every GPU task and idle period.

We collected the power data by using Score-P [10] in combination with a custom Performance Application Programming Interface (PAPI) component [9] designed to read power information from the GH200 monitoring infrastructure via the Linux */sys/class/hwmon* interface. Two Score-P plug-ins were employed: one used this PAPI component to monitor superchip and CPU power, whereas the other interfaced with the NVIDIA Management Library (NVML) to measure GPU power. Each plug-in ran on a dedicated thread per node and sampled power data every 5 ms. We calculated the total energy and runtime values in each run and aggregated the measurements together per GPU task. We performed three runs per power-cap setting and calculated the average values (total energy and runtime) per GPU task and power-cap setting. The runtime overhead per run for the power measurements was 1.3%. By evaluating these detailed power profiles and performance metrics across various power-cap settings, we calculated specific decision-making metrics to reveal the optimal power-limit configurations. This comprehensive analysis enables informed decision-making to maximize energy efficiency while minimizing application runtime performance degradation. Although the specific optimal power settings can vary across applications, the methodology and metrics can be adapted and used in every application/kernel of interest.

To evaluate our metrics and GPU task-specific power-capping strategies, we ran experiments by using the LSMS application (Sect. 2.1) on the Wombat testbed's NVIDIA GH200 nodes. Each node includes a 72-core Arm Neoverse-V2 CPU (3.52 GHz), 480 GB error-correction code (ECC) LPDDR5X memory, and a GH200 GPU with 96 GB ECC HBM3 memory. The software environment used Red Hat Enterprise Linux 9.4, NVIDIA driver 560.35.03, CUDA 12.6, an NVHPC 24.9 compiler suite, and GNU Compiler Collection 11.4.1. For our experimental runs, we configured LSMS to run with a single MPI rank, one OpenMP thread (OMP_NUM_THREADS=1), and one GPU per rank. These settings resemble those of an exascale MPI rank, thus ensuring precise, analyzable, and reproducible conditions. For the application input, we adjusted the *iron platinum* benchmark case[1] to achieve high GPU utilization.

Subsequent subsections detail the kernel selection process, the power-capping levels applied, and the analysis methods used to evaluate and identify the most energy-efficient configurations across different computational scenarios within LSMS.

3.1 Baseline Run of LSMS

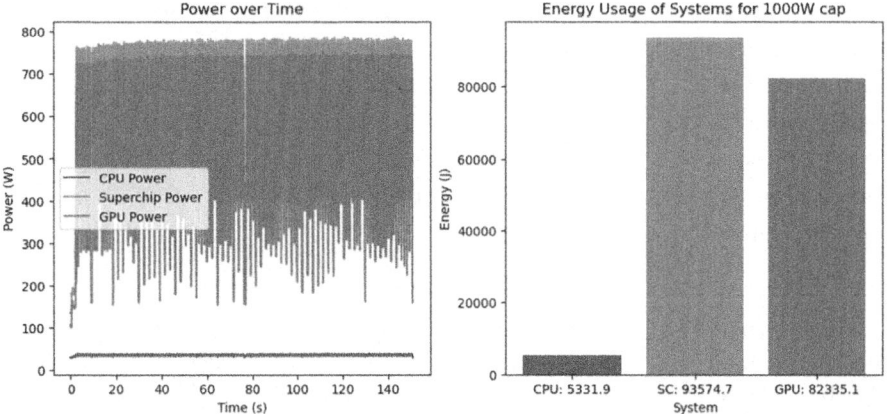

Fig. 1. Power and total energy consumed by LSMS on the GH200 superchip (SC), including CPU and GPU components, with the default maximum power setting of 1,000 W (no power capping).

We executed LSMS on the GH200 superchip by using the default power limit of 1,000 W (no power capping) as a baseline scenario. We measured kernel execution times along with power and total energy consumption for both CPU and GPU. The total runtime was 150.79 s, and the total energy consumption was 93,574.7 J. Figure 1 shows the power traces for the superchip, GPU, and CPU during the execution of LSMS and shows the cumulative energy usage for each component: 82,335.1 J for the GPU and 5,331.9 J for the CPU. The GPU predominantly drove both power consumption and total energy usage for this application. The trace distinctly captured two SCF iterations, and observable

---

[1] lmax=7; rLIZ=18; rsteps=89.5, 91.5, 93.2, 99.9; atom="Fe"; and Z=26.

power drops between iterations marked the transition of computations between the GPU and the CPU. Superchip power data was collected through `hwmon`. We subtracted CPU power from superchip power [4], thus yielding higher-resolution GPU power data points suitable for our fine-grained, GPU task-level analysis.

Because most power consumption occurs in the GPU, we focused on analyzing GPU kernels. Table 1 provides details of the GPU kernel execution with the default power setting, including total runtime, invocation counts, cumulative energy, and average power consumption. GPU tasks are listed in order of total energy consumption, thereby providing a clear prioritization for subsequent power-capping optimizations.

Table 1. Measurements at the default power setting (1,000 W, no power capping) per GPU kernel and GPU compute idle time.

Task	Total Time (s)	# Calls	Total Energy (J)	Avg. Power (W)
sm90_gemm_ts64x64x32	77.89	21,632	35,361.83	454.02
buildKKRMatrix	34.90	128	12,867.73	368.74
sm90_gemm_ts32x32x32	8.03	94,208	4,076.98	507.51
getrf_pivot(1)	4.07	16,384	2,694.54	662.05
getrf_pivot(2)	4.07	30,720	2,670.36	656.11
trsm_left_kernel	3.57	150,272	2,328.26	651.57
getrf_pivot(3)	1.82	8,192	1,146.70	630.06
gpu compute idle	8.83	601,345	2,425.49	274.80

The kernel `sm90_gemm_ts64x64x32` consumed the most energy overall (35,361.83 J). This amount far exceeded the second highest energy consumption (12,867.73 J), which came from the kernel `buildKKRMatrix`. However, invocation counts differed notably: `sm90_gemm_ts64x64x32` was invoked 21,632 times, whereas `buildKKRMatrix` was invoked only 128 times. This finding highlights the importance of analyzing each kernel's individual contribution to the execution characteristics to inform effective power-management strategies. We also profiled the GPU idle periods (`gpu compute idle`). These are phases in the application in which the CPU performs computations while the GPU remains idle. The phases occur mostly between SCF iterations. Identifying the GPU compute idle phases can inform design strategies for reducing GPU power with minimal impact on GPU runtime performance and steering the computational power to CPUs for efficient CPU runtime performance.

Below is a brief description of tasks that contribute significantly to both energy consumption and runtime:

- `sm90_gemm_ts64x64x32`: Compute-intensive cuBLAS zgemm operation; typically compute-bound
- `buildKKRMatrix`: Matrix construction primarily involving memory operations; memory-bound.

- `sm90_gemm_ts32x32x32`: Another compute-intensive cuBLAS zgemm kernel; compute-bound
- `getrf_pivot` kernels: Lower-upper factorization with pivoting; constrained by random memory accesses. We investigated three function invocations with different parameters.
- `trsm_left_kernel`: Triangular matrix solve (BLAS); typically memory-bound due to data access patterns
- `gpu compute idle`: Periods in which computations only occur on the CPU

These tasks represent distinct computational phases within LSMS: `buildKKRMatrix` constructs the multiple-scattering matrix, while the other kernels mainly solve dense linear equations. Identifying each kernel's characteristics is essential for fine-tuning GPU task-specific power caps to optimize energy efficiency and minimize the runtime performance impact.

3.2 Metrics

Traditional HPC optimizations prioritize execution time speedup. However, this performance alone does not guarantee energy efficiency because higher performance can come at the cost of increased power consumption. Achieving optimal energy efficiency requires exploring an optimization space that balances runtime and energy consumption. To evaluate this balance, we employed two complementary metrics: speedup-energy-delay [13] and Euclidean distance of normalized energy/runtime [15], each capturing different aspects of energy-performance trade-offs. We investigated the most appropriate power-cap settings in terms of energy efficiency and runtime performance for fine-grained computational regions (GPU tasks). These metrics help us to clearly quantify the impact of the underlying hardware power behavior as we scale the power-cap settings. Comparing the most energy-efficient solutions as defined by each metric helps us understand how a decision-making approach affects energy/runtime optimizations and determine the suitability of each metric.

Speedup-Energy-Delay Metric. To better evaluate the trade-offs between execution time and energy consumption, we employed a variation of the energy-delay product (EDP), known as the *speedup-energy-delay metric*. This metric provides a way to evaluate power optimizations by incorporating both performance improvements and energy efficiency into a single formula. This metric [13] is particularly useful for comparing different optimizations on HPC systems because it highlights the balance between reducing execution time and minimizing energy consumption. It is defined as follows:

$$SPEEDUP_{energy-delay} = \frac{\left[\frac{runtime_1}{runtime_n}\right]}{\left[\frac{energy_n}{energy_1}\right]} = \frac{[runtime_1 * energy_1]}{[runtime_n * energy_n]},$$

where

- $runtime_1$ and $energy_1$ refer to the baseline runtime and energy consumption, respectively, and
- $runtime_n$ and $energy_n$ represent the optimized runtime and energy consumption, respectively.

The purpose of this metric is to minimize the product of runtime and energy consumption for the optimized version of the code, as expressed by

$$\min [runtime_n * energy_n].$$

This formulation allows us to evaluate optimizations in a way that reflects both performance and energy trade-offs, thereby providing a useful basis for comparison with other metrics.

Euclidean Distance of Normalized Energy/Runtime Metric. This metric was previously used to identify the CPU frequency that offers the most efficient combination of energy consumption and runtime performance of web requests by applying the CPU DVFS technique [15]. It is based on the Global Criterion method for multi-objective optimization using Euclidean distance, which yields a Pareto-optimal solution, where no objective can be improved without compromising the other. [14]. We adapted the approach to evaluate GPU tasks at different power-cap settings while focusing on GPU accelerators.

First, we normalized the GPU energy $n_{energy_{ki}}$ for every GPU task k and power-cap setting i by using the feature scaling normalization method (min-max); see the formula below. We collected the total energy values for every GPU task at every available power-cap setting (200–1,000 W). Focusing on each GPU task, we found the minimum ($emin_k$) and maximum ($emax_k$) energy among these nine power-cap settings. The normalization process yielded values in the interval $(0, 1)$.

$$n_{energy_{ki}} = \frac{[e_{ki} - emin_k]}{[emax_k - emin_k]},$$

where

- $n_{energy_{ki}}$ refers to the normalized energy for a GPU task k at a specific power-cap setting i,
- e_{ki} refers to the energy measured for a specific GPU task k and power-cap setting i,
- $emin_k$ refers to the minimum energy measured for a specific GPU task k across all power-cap settings, and
- $emax_k$ refers to the maximum energy measured for a specific GPU task k across all power-cap settings.

Equivalently, we calculated the normalized runtime ($n_{runtime_{ki}} = \frac{[r_{ki} - rmin_k]}{[rmax_k - rmin_k]}$). Because energy and runtime are expressed at different scales, the normalization process ensures that we can include both metrics together in equal terms in subsequent calculations.

Second, we calculated the Euclidean distance of the normalized energy and normalized runtime for each GPU task k at every power-cap setting i:

$$distance_{ki} = \sqrt{n^2_{energy_{ki}} + n^2_{runtime_{ki}}}.$$

The purpose of this metric is to find the global minimum distance for each GPU task

$$min[distance_{ki}]$$

and indicate the power-cap setting that corresponds to it. It should indicate that with the selected power-cap setting, the scaled energy consumption cannot be decreased any further without increasing the scaled runtime performance [14], thereby revealing the optimal power-cap setting for efficiency.

4 Experimental Evaluation

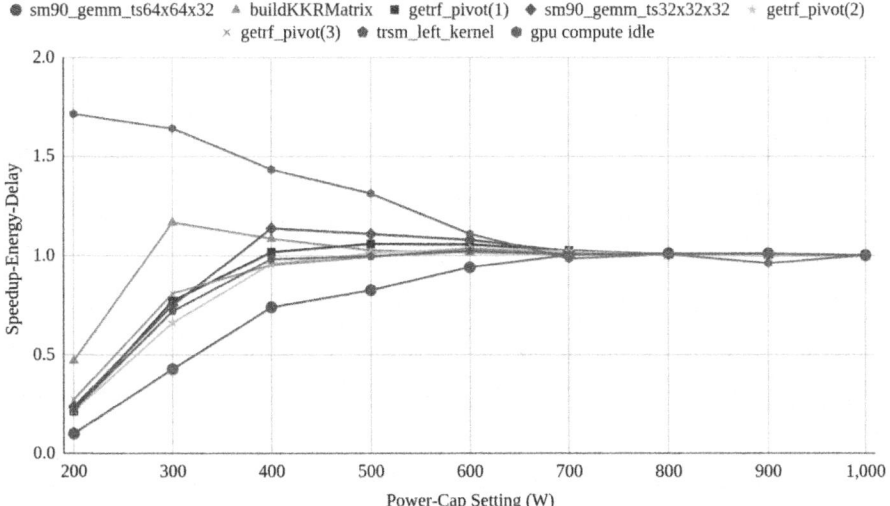

Fig. 2. Speedup-energy-delay per GPU task and power-cap setting. Higher is better.

Figure 2 shows the speedup-energy-delay metric across different power-cap settings for each previously described GPU task. The plot illustrates different behaviors depending on the type of GPU task and computational characteristics. For most GPU tasks, an initial significant increase in speedup-energy-delay is observed when increasing power-cap settings from the lowest level of 200 W, generally peaking between 300 W and 600 W with the exception of sm90_gemm_ts64x64x32, which is a compute-bound GPU task that reaches its peak at 900 W. After the peak, the metric generally slightly declines and stabilizes. This behavior indicates that further increases in the power cap do not yield any benefits. Kernels such as `trsm_left_kernel`, `getrf_pivot(1)`, `getrf_pivot(2)`, and `getrf_pivot(3)` show similar speedup-energy-delay trends and cluster around optimal power-cap settings of 600 W; `getrf_pivot(1)` reaches its optimal setting at 500 W. The `buildKKRMatrix` kernel, which is memory bound, reaches optimal speedup-energy-delay at a lower power cap of 300 W and stabilizes after 400 W.

The `gpu compute idle` phase closely follows the trend observed in the energy metric: it reaches its optimal speedup-energy-delay at the lowest power-cap setting (200 W) with a speedup value of 1.71, after which the values progressively decrease with increasing power settings. This graph highlights the importance of considering GPU task-specific characteristics when determining the best power-cap settings to achieve energy efficiency without substantial performance trade-offs.

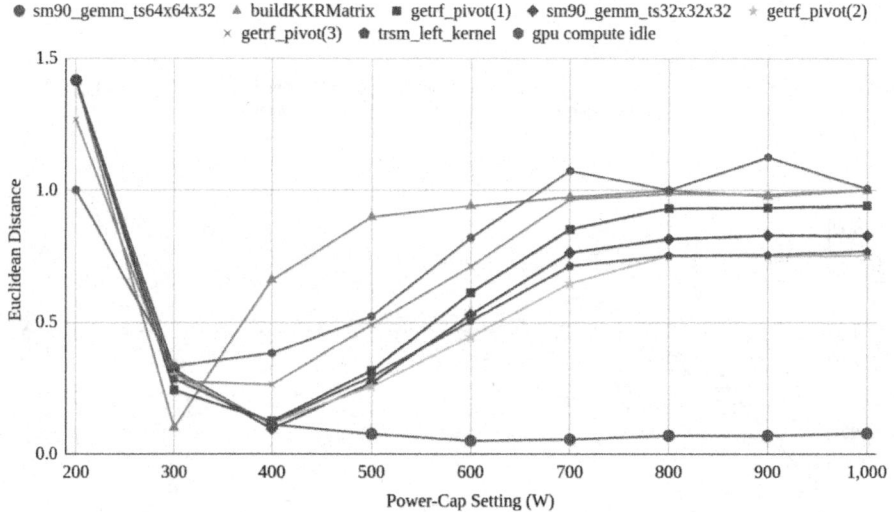

Fig. 3. Euclidean distance of normalized energy/runtime per GPU task and power-cap setting. Lower is better.

Figure 3 shows the Euclidean distance of GPU tasks for each power-cap setting. Most of the GPU tasks show the maximum distance at 200 W, so this is the least suitable setting according to the current metric. In some cases, the calculated distances exceed 1. This power setting increases execution time and produces the slowest runtimes; it also increases energy consumption and yields some of the highest energy usage. As we scale up the power cap, the GPU tasks' distances decrease and reach a minimum between 300 W and 600 W. Most of the GPU tasks reach their minimum distances at 400 W (five GPU tasks), and then their distances increase. At 700 W, their distances begin to stabilize. Thereafter, any power-cap setting does not substantially alter the distance values. The kernels trsm_left_kernel, getrf_pivot(1), getrf_pivot(2), and sm90_gemm_ts32x32x32 follow this pattern. Their trends form the tightest cluster among all GPU tasks. The pattern presents similarities with the CPU-driven requests described in previous work [14] and reveals a compute-intensive characteristic. The getrf_pivot(2) kernel follows a similar pattern. The buildKKRMatrix kernel demonstrates the minimum at 300 W, and the distance remains largely unchanged for power-cap increases after 600 W. In contrast, the distance for the sm90_gemm_ts64x64x32 kernel decreases at 600 W and then stabilizes at higher power-cap settings. Finally, the gpu compute idle phase reaches a minimum distance at 300 W, where it exhibits the second lowest energy consumption, and a maximum distance at 900 W, where the highest energy consumption is observed. The total energy consumption for this case increases as the power setting increases. Execution time is highest at the lowest power setting, and it fluctuates as the power increases. This fluctuation is similarly reflected in the distance metric. With the current measurements and metric, the memory-bound buildKKRMatrix and gpu compute idle phase exhibit the same optimal power setting.

Table 2. Runtime increase (%) and Energy reduction (%): default power compared with the most suitable power setting identified by speedup-energy-delay (SED) and Euclidean distance (ED) per GPU task.

GPU task	Power Cap (W)		Energy (%)		Runtime (%)	
	SED	ED	SED	ED	SED	ED
sm90_gemm_ts64x64x32	900	600	0.85	3.42	0.00	10.3
buildKKRMatrix	300	300	22.92	22.92	11.30	11.30
sm90_gemm_ts32x32x32	400	400	31.40	31.40	28.42	28.42
getrf_pivot(1)	500	400	20.61	28.50	19.16	37.67
getrf_pivot(2)	600	400	10.05	24.48	7.37	38.41
trsm_left_kernel	600	400	9.02	25.53	7.74	36.85
getrf_pivot(3)	600	400	9.10	24.15	6.59	38.46
gpu compute idle	200	300	46.58	39.69	9.25	1.17

For a comparison between the most suitable power-cap settings (as defined by each metric) and the system's default setting (1,000 W), Table 2 presents the percent change in energy and runtime for each GPU task. The energy change is calculated as $\frac{energy_i - energy_{1000}}{energy_{1000}} * 100$, in which the negative sign ($-$) is omitted, indicating energy reduction. The runtime change (or increase) is calculated as $\frac{runtime_i - runtime_{1000}}{runtime_{1000}} * 100$. In a few cases, both metrics define the same optimal power-cap setting. However, in most cases, they point to nearby settings that can affect energy savings and runtime performance quite differently.

Through a comparison of these two metrics, we identified significant opportunities for fine-grained energy optimization, especially notable in GPU tasks such as `buildKKRMatrix` and during GPU idle states. This optimization yields considerable energy savings with a small performance slowdown cost. GPU idle states are critical targets for power-capping optimization because they may occur frequently in HPC. Additionally, analyzing GPU task invocation frequency against energy consumption shows that even infrequently invoked GPU tasks can be good candidates for GPU task-specific power optimizations.

By aggregating the observed percentage values with speedup-energy-delay, we can achieve ~151% energy savings at the cost of a ~90% increase in execution time. Furthermore, with the Euclidean distance metric, we achieve ~200% energy reduction at the expense of a ~203% runtime increase. The speedup-energy-delay provides settings that can yield higher runtime performance and lower energy savings over the Euclidean distance metric. These numbers are simple aggregations of per-GPU task energy and runtime values and represent ideal scenarios with no overhead. However, they indicate the power-capping impact on individual GPU tasks and how the whole application can potentially be affected, presenting opportunities for energy reduction. Although LSMS is a compute-intensive application, our results show that kernel-level power-capping can yield greater energy savings than application-wide tuning. By adapting power caps to individual GPU kernels based on their characteristics, we can significantly reduce energy consumption and enhance overall application efficiency.

GPU task-level power-capping strategies can employ these metrics and provide energy savings that approximate the observed impact or performance-energy patterns by focusing on efficient power-capping tuning and transitions for the runtime. Further optimization could combine these two metrics with user-defined goals. Energy savings could be prioritized over runtime costs, thereby enabling users to filter results based on acceptable performance trade-offs at the GPU task level.

5 Conclusions

This work demonstrates the effectiveness of applying dynamic, GPU task-specific power-capping strategies that use the NVIDIA GH200 superchip's automatic power-steering system. We evaluated two complementary metrics—speedup-energy-delay and Euclidean distance–based normalization—to determine optimal power limits per computational GPU task in the LSMS application. Comparing the optimal power-capping settings suggested by each one, the Euclidean distance–based normalization considers both runtime and energy equal optimization objectives, while affected by the data distribution differently than the speedup-energy-delay. Our findings demonstrate significant energy savings achievable through fine-grained power management, thus emphasizing the balance between energy efficiency and performance. Future work will extend these methodologies, develop strategies for additional domains, and automate adaptive power-capping optimizations for easier integration into production HPC environments. These metrics can be seamlessly integrated into other GPU-accelerated

HPC applications through widely adopted tools such as Score-P and PAPI. This integration makes them immediately beneficial to the broader HPC community for experimentation.

Acknowledgments. This material is based on work supported by the US Department of Energy's Office of Science, Advanced Scientific Computing Research program through EXPRESS: 2023 Exploratory Research for Extreme-Scale Science. This research used resources of the Oak Ridge Leadership Computing Facility at Oak Ridge National Laboratory, which is supported by the Office of Science of the US Department of Energy under contract DE-AC05-00OR22725.

Disclosure of Interests. The authors have no competing interests to declare that are relevant to the content of this article.

References

1. Abdulsalam, S., Zong, Z., Gu, Q., Qiu, M.: Using the greenup, powerup, and speedup metrics to evaluate software energy efficiency. In: 20Haidar,15 Sixth International Green and Sustainable Computing Conference (IGSC), pp. 1–8 (2015). https://doi.org/10.1109/IGCC.2015.7393699
2. Atchley, S., Zimmer, C., et al.: Frontier: exploring exascale. In: Proceedings of the International Conference for High Performance Computing, Networking, Storage and Analysis. SC '23, Association for Computing Machinery, New York (2023). https://doi.org/10.1145/3581784.3607089
3. Azimi, R., Jing, C., Reda, S.: Powercoord: a coordinated power capping controller for multi-cpu/gpu servers. In: 2018 Ninth International Green and Sustainable Computing Conference (IGSC), pp. 1–9. IEEE (2018)
4. Corporation, N.: Nvidia grace performance tuning guide - power and thermals (2024). https://docs.nvidia.com/grace-perf-tuning-guide/power-thermals.html, Accessed 28 Feb 2025
5. Eastep, J., et al.: Global extensible open power manager: A vehicle for hpc community collaboration on co-designed energy management solutions. In: Kunkel, J.M., Yokota, R., Balaji, P., Keyes, D. (eds.) High Performance Computing, pp. 394–412. Springer International Publishing, Cham (2017)
6. Eisenbach, M., Larkin, J., Lutjens, J., Rennich, S., Rogers, J.H.: Gpu acceleration of the locally selfconsistent multiple scattering code for first principles calculation of the ground state and statistical physics of materials. Computer Physics Communications **211**, 2–7 (2017), high Performance Computing for Advanced Modeling and Simulation of Materials
7. Gerndt, M.: The readex project for dynamic energy efficiency tuning. In: Proceedings of the ACM Workshop on Software Engineering Methods for Parallel and High Performance Applications, pp. 11–12 (2016)
8. Haidar, A., Jagode, H., Vaccaro, P., YarKhan, A., Tomov, S., Dongarra, J.: Investigating power capping toward energy-efficient scientific applications. Concurr. Comput. Practice Experience **31**(6), e4485 (2019)
9. Hernandez, O., et al.: Preliminary study on fine-grained power and energy measurements on grace hopper gh200 with open-source performance tools. In: Proceedings of the 2025 International Conference on High Performance Computing in Asia-Pacific Region Workshops, pp. 11–22. HPC Asia '25 Workshops, Association

for Computing Machinery, New York (2025). https://doi.org/10.1145/3703001.3724383
10. Knüpfer, A., et al.: Score-p: A joint performance measurement run-time infrastructure for periscope, scalasca, tau, and vampir. In: Brunst, H., Müller, M.S., Nagel, W.E., Resch, M.M. (eds.) Tools for High Performance Computing 2011, pp. 79–91. Springer, Berlin Heidelberg, Berlin, Heidelberg (2012)
11. Krzywaniak, A., Czarnul, P.: Performance/energy aware optimization of parallel applications on GPUs under power capping. In: Wyrzykowski, R., Deelman, E., Dongarra, J., Karczewski, K. (eds.) Parallel Processing and Applied Mathematics. Springer International Publishing (2020)
12. Krzywaniak, A., Czarnul, P., Proficz, J.: GPU power capping for energy-performance trade-offs in training of deep CNNs. In: International Conference on Computational Science (ICCS), pp. 123–133. Springer (2022)
13. NVIDIA: Energy efficiency in high performance computing: Balancing speed and sustainability (2023). https://developer.nvidia.com/blog/energy-efficiency-in-high-performance-computing-balancing-speed-and-sustainability/, Accessed 23 Oct 2024
14. Patrou, M., Kent, K.B., Siu, J., Dawson, M.: Energy and runtime performance optimization of node.js web requests. In: 2021 IEEE International Conference on Cloud Engineering (IC2E), pp. 71–82 (2021). https://doi.org/10.1109/IC2E52221.2021.00021
15. Patrou, M., Kent, K.B., Siu, J., Dawson, M.: Optimizing energy efficiency of node.js applications with cpu dvfs awareness. In: 2022 IEEE 13th International Green and Sustainable Computing Conference (IGSC), pp. 1–8 (2022). https://doi.org/10.1109/IGSC55832.2022.9969367
16. Saba, I., Arima, E., Liu, D., Schulz, M.: Orchestrated co-scheduling, resource partitioning, and power capping on cpu-gpu heterogeneous systems via machine learning. In: Schulz, M., Trinitis, C., Papadopoulou, N., Pionteck, T. (eds.) Architecture of Computing Systems, pp. 51–67. Springer International Publishing, Cham (2022)
17. Sourouri, M., et al.: Towards fine-grained dynamic tuning of HPC applications on modern multi-core architectures. In: Proceedings of the International Conference for High Performance Computing, Networking, Storage and Analysis. SC '17, Association for Computing Machinery, New York (2017). https://doi.org/10.1145/3126908.3126945,
18. Terboven, C., et al.: Ee-HPC a framework for energy efficient HPC system management. In: SC24-W: Workshops of the International Conference for High Performance Computing, Networking, Storage and Analysis, pp. 1878–1882 (2024). https://doi.org/10.1109/SCW63240.2024.00236
19. Zhao, D., et al.: Sustainable supercomputing for AI: GPU power capping at HPC scale. In: Proceedings of the 2023 ACM Symposium on Cloud Computing, pp. 588–596 (2023)

Experience on Clock Rate Adjustment for Energy-Efficient GPU-Accelerated Real-World Codes

Giorgio Amati[1], Matteo Turisini[1], Andrea Monterubbiano[2], Mattia Paladino[3], Elisabetta Boella[3(✉)], Daniele Gregori[3], and Danilo Croce[4]

[1] CINECA, Rome, Italy
{g.amati,m.turisini}@cineca.it
[2] CINECA, Casalecchio di Reno, Italy
a.monterubbiano@cineca.it
[3] E4 Computer Engineering SpA, Scandiano, Italy
{mattia.paladino,elisabetta.boella,daniele.gregori}@e4company.com
[4] Università degli Studi di Roma Tor Vergata, Rome, Italy
croce@info.uniroma2.it

Abstract. Efficient energy utilization is crucial for High Performance Computing, especially for exascale supercomputers requiring tens of MW to operate. Increased energy awareness benefits both data center operators and code developers, focusing on balancing performance, energy, and power consumption. This work evaluates the impact of reducing GPU core clock frequency, running four production-grade codes on the latest NVIDIA Grace Hopper Superchip and comparing results with the previous Ampere A100 GPU. Findings indicate that a static clock speed adjustment can achieve over 10% energy savings with less than 5% degradation in time performance, offering valuable insights for the future sustainability of high-performance data centers.

1 Introduction

Nowadays the largest computing centers require $O(10)$ MW to meet the contemporary demands of Artificial Intelligence (AI) and High-Performance Computing (HPC) workloads, and the current technological trends indicate that this requirement will continue to grow with single processing units reaching a Thermal Design Power (TDP) of 1 kW or more. While this transformation is driving significant scientific advancements, its impact on energy consumption and sustainability can no longer be ignored.

A growing concern about efficient energy consumption in AI and HPC has led to the development of specialized tools for monitoring energy-related metrics alongside traditional HPC performance data [1,2]. These metrics include power consumption, as well as temperature and humidity measurements collected from sensors distributed throughout the facility, including the building itself. While all these instruments provide a complete view of energy utilization at facility level, other solutions focus on monitoring and optimizing individual HPC jobs to increase energy awareness of users and code developers [3,4].

In this work, we analyzed energy consumption and related metrics for four real-world GPU-based applications running on the latest NVIDIA *Grace Hopper* Superchip (GH200) and compared results with its predecessor, NVIDIA *Ampere* A100 GPU. In particular, we examined the impact of changing clock speed settings on four metrics: Time-To-Solution (TTS), Energy-To-Solution (ETS), average power absorption (AP), and average temperature (AT) of the device. We used the `nvidia-smi` command-line utility both to collect the relevant metrics and adjust GPU frequency settings. Thus, this work complements and expands upon similar recent studies [5–8].

The paper is organized as follows: experimental setups, metrics, codes, and data processing methodology are described in Sect. 2. Collected data are presented and analyzed in Sect. 3 and 4. Finally, Sect. 5 provides a summary of our findings and outlines directions for future research.

2 Methods

Two GPU models were tested by adjusting the clock rate (or clock speed) of their computing cores. The clock speed was set at the start of each job, monitored throughout execution, and reset to its default value upon completion[1].

Hardware Setups. Data collection was conducted using two air-cooled setups, both featuring NVIDIA GPUs running CUDA 12.5. The first platform is equipped with four A100-SXM4 GPUs, each with 80 GB of HBM2e memory. The second platform is a single GH200 node with 480 GB of HBM3 memory. The GH200 integrates both the GPU and an ARM-based CPU within the same chip package, with a total TDP of 1000 W. By default, GPUs remain idle when not in use and operate at their maximum clock rate under load with an internal protection mechanism to avoid thermal issues. Table 1 summarizes the characteristics of both platforms, including idle power consumption, TDP, and maximum clock speed.

Raw Data Collection and Metrics. Data were collected using the manufacturer's system management interface, `nvidia-smi`. This choice was preferred over the NVIDIA Management Library for its simplicity. Given a node, data acquisition scripts sample each GPU at a frequency of 1 Hz and record 1) the timestamp in millisecond, 2) the GPU board power consumption, with an estimated measurement error of five percent [9], 3) the temperature of GPU processor and HMB memory, measured in Celsius with a one-percent resolution, and 4) the clock speed of GPU processor and HBM. The time-series of all these variables were segmented into three distinct time windows to capture: 1) the idle state before the job starts; 2) the computational phase, representing the scalable and the most energy consuming part of the workload; 3) the thermal relaxation after job completion. Four metrics were derived for analysis:

- Time-To-Solution (TTS): duration of the simulation, in seconds.

---

[1] The clock rate adjustment operation requires administrative or *sudo* permissions.

Table 1. GPU specifications

GPU Model	A100	GH200
Max clock speed (MHz)	1410	1980
Max TDP, *GPU only*, (W)	500	700
Idle consumption (W)	60	65
Idle clock speed (MHz)	210	345
Total number of cores (#)	6912	16896
Memory size (GB)	80	480
Peak memory Bandwidth (TB/s)	2	4
Peak FP32 (TFLOP/s)	20	67
Peak TF32 (TFLOP/s)	156	494

- Energy-To-Solution (ETS): energy consumed by the board to complete the job, in kJoules.
- Average Temperature (AT): average temperature of the GPU cores, in Celsius.
- Average Power (AP): average power consumption of the GPU core components, in Watts.

These quantities were computed based solely on the numerical simulation, excluding the idle and relaxation phases. Average values were determined as time-averages over the scalable portion of the computation. Energy was calculated starting from raw data in two ways: as the discrete integral of the power over time and as the product of Time-To-Solution and average power absorption. Here, we used the second method. However, we verified that both methods yield the same result, as fluctuations during the computational phase were minimal.

Codes Under Test. Four codes from different application domains were used in this study: all codes were optimized for performance and have been proven to scale up to $O(1,000)$ GPUs. They are written in different programming languages and accelerated using various programming models, as outlined below. For this study, all codes were executed on a single GPU, with negligible time spent on initialization and finalization, ensuring that the vast majority of the execution time is spent in the main kernel. In detail:

BGK3D [10] is a Computational Fluid Dynamics (CFD) code that uses the Lattice Boltzmann Method. A three-dimensional lid-driven cavity flow on a $512 \times 512 \times 512$ grid at Reynolds number $Re = 256$ was modeled. BGK3D is a memory bandwidth-limited code, written in `Fortran90` and parallelized using `MPI+OpenACC`.

PipeFlow [11] is another CFD code, also bandwidth-limited. It directly solves the Navier-Stokes equations using finite differences. For this work, incompressible fluid flow in a circular pipe at $Re = 2.85 \times 10^5$ was simulated employing a staggered grid of $2305 \times 547 \times 298$ elements. The code is parallelized using `MPI` and accelerated for GPU with `CUDA Fortran` and `cuTENSOR`.

QISG [12] is a code for statistical mechanics studies on quantum complex systems composed of interacting spin glasses. The test case consists of a Monte Carlo simulation of a 2D ising quantum spin glass system using the Metropolis algorithm enhanced by the parallel tempering technique. It is written in C and explicitly parallelized for GPU with CUDA API. The code uses integer arithmetic and is bandwidth-limited.

BERT [13] is one of the first transformer-based models for natural language processing. It is written in Python and relies on TensorFlow, thus fully leveraging GPU power. For our tests, it was trained for 25 epochs using the bert-large-uncased variant (about 340 million parameters) with a batch size of 256. This extended training setup, exceeding typical usage, was designed to stress the single GPU and provide meaningful performance metrics under sustained computational loads. The training used a dataset of 5,500 labeled questions divided into six classes for a question classification task[2]. Tests on the GH200 platform were conducted in a containerized environment provided by NVIDIA, ensuring consistent and reproducible results. This code is compute-bound.

3 Results

This section is divided into four parts, each representing a step in the experimental procedure. First, for each GPU, the Memory Bandwidth (BW) and Floating Point (FP) arithmetic performance were measured as functions of clock speed. Second, the four codes were evaluated at the default clock speed to establish a baseline for performance comparison under standard configuration settings. In our setup, the default clock speed corresponds to the maximum clock speed of the GPU model used (see Table 1). Third, the codes were analyzed across different clock speeds. Lastly, the focus shifts to the GH200 device, where the relationship between temperature, power consumption, and clock speed was investigated in detail.

In this section, all quantities are considered normalized unless stated otherwise. Specifically, the clock speed is normalized by the maximum clock rate available for each device to facilitate comparison, while other quantities are normalized with respect to their values at the maximum clock speed. In contrast, all tables present absolute measured values.

Bandwidth and Floating Point Performance as Function of Clock Speed. The maximum achievable performance on A100 and GH200 was evaluated using an Open CL-based benchmark[3]. Data on BW and peak FP performance obtained by running the benchmark at different clock speeds are shown in Fig. 1. As expected, FP performance shows a linear monotonic dependence on clock speed for both GPUs. In contrast, memory BW exhibits a markedly different behavior, showing minimal sensitivity to clock speed reductions down to 0.6. The observed slight

---
[2] https://www.tensorflow.org/datasets/catalog/trec.
[3] https://github.com/ProjectPhysX/OpenCL-Benchmark.

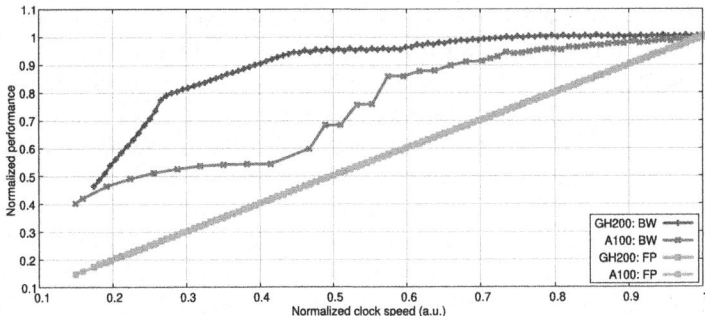

Fig. 1. Measured BW and FP performance vs clock speed for A100 (green and orange, respectively) and GH200 (purple and blue, respectively). (Color figure online)

decline in BW from a clock speed of 1 to 0.6 arises because the latter directly impacts GPU components such as the L2 cache, shared memory, texture cache, and registers, all of which collectively influence overall memory bandwidth [14]. Below a frequency of 0.6, the A100 experiences a substantial reduction in memory BW, while the GH200 maintains higher BW levels until the clock speed falls below 0.3. The underlying causes of these sudden drops are not fully understood and remain open questions. However, a detailed investigation lies beyond the scope of this work. Accordingly, we restrict our analysis to the core frequency range of [0.6–1.0]. Based on the results displayed in Fig. 1, we, therefore, expect that in this range the performance of a compute-bound application (like BERT) will be severely hindered, while bandwidth limited applications (like BGK3D, PipeFlow and QISG) will be less affected by reduced frequency values.

Comparison at Default Clock Speed. Table 2 presents the absolute values of Time-To-Solution, Energy-To-Solution, average power absorption, and average temperature measured by running the selected applications at the default (i.e., maximum) clock speed on both A100 and GH200 GPUs.

Table 2. Characterization at maximum clock speed for the four codes under test.

BGK3D	A100	GH200		QISG	A100	GH200
TTS (s)	424	254		TTS (s)	813	473
ETS (kJ)	155	155		ETS (kJ)	215	191
AP (W)	367	611		AP (W)	265	403
AT (°C)	56	62		AT (°C)	52	57
PipeFlow	A100	GH200		BERT	A100	GH200
TTS (s)	302	162		TTS (s)	567	66
ETS (kJ)	92	86		ETS (kJ)	184	38
AP (W)	304	530		AP (W)	327	530
AT (°C)	51	59		AT (°C)	57	53

A significant performance improvement is evident for GH200 with respect to A100 across all codes and variables considered. These results are broadly consistent with the hardware specifications listed in Table 1. In particular, GH200 shows a 2× Time-To-Solution improvement over A100 for all three bandwidth-limited codes (BGK3D, PipeFlow, and QISG), consistent with the 2× increase in peak memory bandwidth. This improvement is most likely due to the GH200 use of HBM3, a significant upgrade over the HBM2e used in the A100. In contrast, for the compute-bound BERT, the speedup on GH200 is more than 8×. This remarkable performance gain is likely attributable to several fundamental microarchitectural improvements, including support for WGMMa instructions, an increased number of streaming multiprocessors, higher clock speeds, improved L2 cache throughput, enhanced asynchronous execution, distributed shared memory, and support for dynamic programming instructions and asynchronous data transfers between thread blocks. Additionally, improvements in the low-level software stack and the increased efficiency of low-precision formats such as TF32 and FP16 may also contribute. However, identifying the exact cause would require deeper insight into the BERT code, which was treated largely as a black box in our experiments, and is left for future investigation.

Regarding Energy-To-Solution, memory-bound codes show similar values on both GPUs, with GH200 exhibiting slightly lower Energy-To-Solution. In contrast, for BERT, Energy-To-Solution is reduced by 3.6× on GH200, likely due to the improved performance of low-precision computations.

Finally, performance gains on GH200 come with only a modest increase in power consumption (less than 2× relative to the speedup) and minimal temperature changes, with some cases, such as AI training, even showing a slight decrease.

Measurements at Non-default Clock Speed. Results from clock scans are presented in Fig. 2, which displays normalized Energy-To-Solution and Time-To-Solution vs clock speed for the four applications. The energy exhibits a basin-shaped trend, indicating a minimum in energy consumption. This minimum occurs at approximately 80% of the clock speed for A100 and around 60% for GH200 across all applications. In absolute terms, the minimum is observed at a frequency of 1150 MHz for both devices. The maximum energy saving observed is about 30% compared to the default operating point, i.e. maximum speed. As expected, Time-To-Solution is a monotonic function of clock speed across all codes and devices considered in this study. In general, performance improves as clock frequency increases (i.e., the lower the Time-To-Solution, the better). The shortest execution time occurs at maximum clock speed, with a clear dependence on the specific combination of code and device. For the fluid dynamics codes (Fig. 2 top panels), the slope is relatively shallow, with a 10% increase in execution time between 70% and 80% of the clock speed. In contrast, for the other two codes (Fig. 2 bottom panels), the slope is steeper, and the same 10% increase in Time-To-Solution occurs at approximately 90% of the clock speed. The greater variability in the Time-To-Solution curve for AI training (Fig. 2 bottom right panel) may be attributed to hardware optimizations in

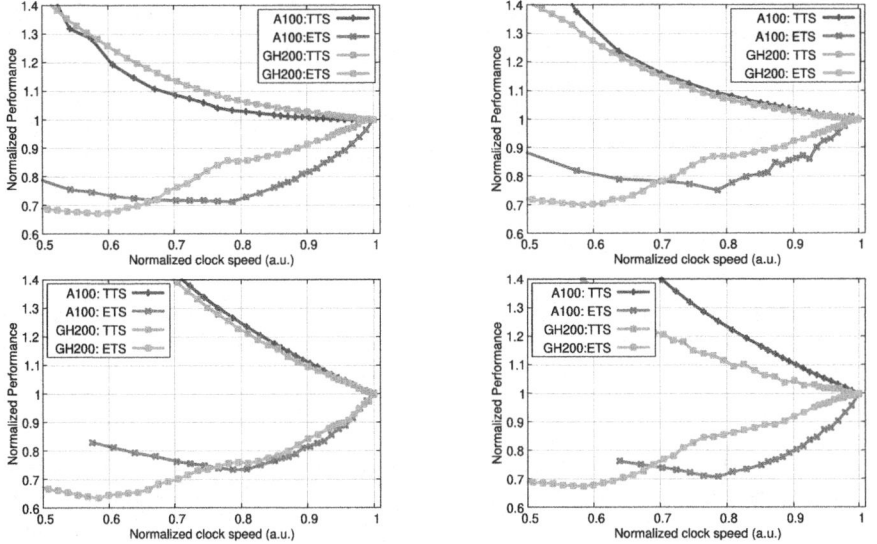

Fig. 2. Energy-To-Solution (green for A100 and orange for GH200) and Time-To-Solution (purple for A100 and blue for GH200) vs clock speed. Top left panel: BGK3D. Top right panel: PipeFlow. Bottom left panel: QISG. Bottom right panel: BERT. (Color figure online)

the GH200 device, which is specifically designed for AI workloads, as indicated by the previously observed 8× performance improvement.

In a production environment, a delay of up to 10% compared to the fastest execution time may be acceptable, and delays of 1% or less often considered negligible. Choosing the optimal clock speed for a given code requires balancing energy consumption and execution time. One option is to compute the energy-delay product (EDP), e.g. the product of Energy-To-Solution and Time-To-Solution, and select the clock speed that minimizes it. Alternatively, one can analyze the reduction in Energy-To-Solution relative to the increase in Time-To-Solution, an approach that we preferred in this work (see Fig. 4 for example). Additionally, through interpolation or an analytical model for each variable (time and energy separately), it is possible to estimate the clock speed needed to achieve a specific time delay and determine the corresponding energy consumption.

Power and Temperature on GH200. Here we analyze power and temperature loads of GH200, while executing the four applications. We limit the discussion to the most recent device because the focus is on infrastructural aspects. We consider only runs whose execution time does not exceed 20% of the fastest Time-To-Solution.

The average power consumption as a function of the normalized clock speed is shown in Fig. 3 (left panel). The reduction in power consumption scales almost

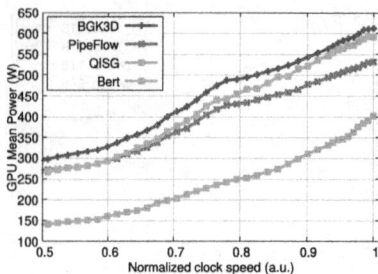 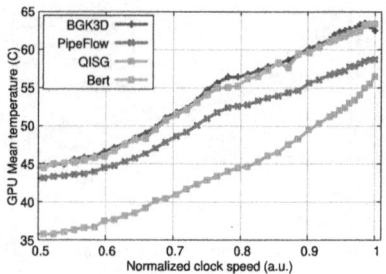

Fig. 3. Left panel: Average Power vs clock speed. Right panel: Average Temperature vs clock speed. Different colors correspond to different codes: purple for BGK3D, green for PipeFlow, blue for QISG, and orange for BERT. (Color figure online)

linearly with clock speed for all codes, with a noticeable change in slope around 0.8 of the maximum clock speed. At 0.8 clock speed, the two fluid dynamics codes, BGK3D and PipeFlow, consume an average of 100 W less than at maximum clock speed. For QISG and BERT, the reduction in average power is even greater, around 150 W. Given these values, if all users agree to accept a certain level of performance degradation during simulations, savings of the order of megawatts could be achieved, especially considering that a high-end data center can house $O(10^4)$ GPUs. Additionally, reducing peak power consumption would not only lower operating costs but also decrease total energy consumption, thus reducing the data center carbon footprint and operating temperature. This, in turn, could help mitigate hardware errors and failures, potentially lowering downtime and improving overall data center reliability. Furthermore, starting a simulation with thousands of GH200 could place significant stress on the electrical grid, requiring it to absorb megawatts of power in just a few seconds. Operating at a reduced frequency could help alleviate this strain. Furthermore, lowering the frequency would enable power oversubscription, which could help mitigating one of the most severe bottlenecks faced by modern data centers [15].

As shown in the right panel of Fig. 3, the thermal stress on the chips while running the four applications follows the same trend as power consumption, with temperature decreases being similar across all codes. At a normalized clock speed of 90%, the temperature drops between 4 and 7 °C, with QISG experiencing the largest variation in operating temperature. As noted earlier, this reduction in GPU temperature could help minimize failures in systems with $O(10^4)$ GPUs, offering significant benefits at the cost of only minor performance degradations.

GH200 Tuning Considerations. For practical use, establishing a numerical link between time degradation tolerance and energy savings is beneficial. The Energy-To-Solution variation as a function of Time-To-Solution variation on GH200 across different codes and clock speeds is displayed in Fig. 4. This visualization highlights that Energy-To-Solution varies more rapidly than Time-To-Solution, particularly in the region where time delay is between 0% and 5%. By

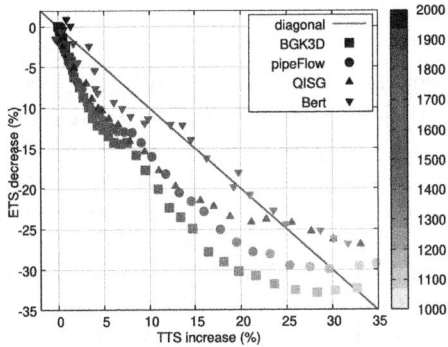

Fig. 4. GH200 Energy-To-Solution decrease vs Time-To-Solution increase. Colors indicates the clock speed in MHz. Different markers refer to the different codes under test. (Color figure online)

comparing this trend to the theoretical diagonal line, which represents a proportional relationship between energy, time, and clock speed, it is clear that most data points fall below the line, indicating net energy savings. The only exception is BERT, where deviations begin around a 10% TTS, gradually converging toward the diagonal. This suggests that beyond this threshold, further clock speed reductions yield minimal energy savings. A more comprehensive view is provided in Table 3, where the four metrics are presented for three time delay values: 2%, 5%, and 10%.

Table 3. GH200 metrics for different Time-To-Solution delay on the four tested codes.

BGK3D	default	+2%	+5%	+10%	QISG	default	+2%	+5%	+10%
f (MHz)	1980	1845	1635	1485	f (MHz)	1980	1935	1875	1785
TTS (s)	254	259	267	279	TTS (s)	473	482	496	518
ETS (kJ)	156	146	136	128	ETS (kJ)	191	181	171	161
AP (W)	611	563	508	459	AP (W)	403	376	345	311
AT (°C)	62	1	58	55	AT (°C)	56	54	52	49
PipeFlow	default	+2%	+5%	+10%	BERT	default	+2%	+5%	+10%
f (MHz)	1980	1845	1635	1485	f (MHz)	1980	1875	1725	1575
TTS (s)	325	331	344	359	TTS (s)	66	67	69	72
ETS (kJ)	174	163	151	145	ETS (kJ)	38	37	35	34
AP (W)	531	494	440	404	AP (W)	576	555	508	465
AT (°C)	59	57	53	51	AT (°C)	52	52	50	48

4 Discussion

Characterizing and understanding the energy and power behavior of typical HPC workloads is a crucial first step in reducing data center consumption and improving sustainability. The results presented in this paper show that both energy and time performance, for both HPC and AI workloads, are fundamentally influenced by hardware characteristics. As such, any quantitative modeling effort must be device-specific. Specifically, the data collected confirm that GH200 excels in AI training workloads, delivering exceptional time and energy performance compared to previous GPU models. However, for memory-bound scientific codes, the performance differences between the two GPU generations are less pronounced. It was also demonstrated that the relative energy savings exceed the relative time degradation when reducing the clock speed from the maximum to 90%. This observation thus challenges the assumption that optimizing energy efficiency by minimizing kernel execution time, following the so called race-to-idle approach, is always the best strategy [16].

An interesting finding is that in the same range of clock frequencies, a reduction in operating temperature is also observed, which could positively impact reliability and scalability. This is because thermal stress is a primary cause of throttling, leading to consequences such as unpredictable Time-To-Solution in single-GPU jobs or significant slowdowns in multi-GPU scenarios, where the performance of a single device can affect the overall latency of a many-GPU simulation.

While our study focused on *single-node single-GPU* runs, similar studies have shown that power consumption per node remains unchanged if the code maintains a parallel efficiency above 70% [5,6]. Therefore, we consider it reasonable to assume that our results could extend to multi-GPU executions.

The consistent pattern observed in production-grade codes suggests that similar opportunities for optimizing energy efficiency may exist across a broader range of applications. However, a key challenge is that the optimal balance between performance, energy, and power consumption cannot be achieved solely at the data center level, as it also depends on the objectives and design choices made by code developers.

5 Conclusion and Outlook

A comprehensive characterization of four production-grade codes was conducted as a function of the computing clock speed of the latest NVIDIA GPU models: A100 and GH200. The study evaluates time and energy-related metrics. Data were collected at user-level as multiple time-series, which were then processed to calculate energy consumption and derive key statistics for power and temperature. The clock speed was statically adjusted at the start of each execution and restored afterward, ensuring precise control over performance metrics. Test cases were selected from different application domains to analyze a variety of computational models and workloads, providing meaningful insights into the energy and power signatures of both HPC and AI applications. While this study focused on single-GPU runs, the findings provide valuable implications for future large-scale, energy-efficient computing. Based on the collected data, three main observations can be made. First, reducing the clock speed to 90% of its maximum value results in a slight degradation in time performance, accompanied by a more substantial energy saving across all codes and hardware combinations considered. Second, this clock speed reduction also leads to a decrease of few degrees Celsius in the GPU operating temperature, with the exact amount varying depending on the code and GPU model. Particularly in air-cooled environments, this reduction can positively affect system reliability and, consequently, enhance the scalability of workloads. Finally, transitioning from A100 to GH200 device brings significant improvements for the AI compute-bound test case, achieving a remarkable 8× reduction in execution time and more than 3× reduction in energy consumption. For the other memory-bound codes, significant improvements were observed mainly in execution time, with a performance boost of around 2×. However, in terms of Energy-To-Solution, the performance remained similar across the different GPU models.

A secondary outcome of this work is the development of a framework to allow monitoring GPU energy consumption, just at the cost of an additional process in user space. In contrast, adjusting the clock speed requires administrative privileges and a more complex integration with the infrastructure Resource and Job Management System (RJMS) to ensure user accessibility. Looking ahead, adopting a more systematic approach would be preferable to the current in-house solution. For this reason, an overview of widely adopted tools is essential. Regardless of the tool used, our investigation represents only a first step toward the systematic adoption of energy-related metrics in HPC and AI. For a more comprehensive understanding, further studies are needed. These should include testing GPUs from other manufacturers, such as AMD and Intel, extending energy profiling to platform and rack levels by incorporating CPU, memory, networking, and power distribution unit contributions, and focusing on multi-GPU and multi-node systems. Additionally, optimizing the clock scan protocol to reduce data acquisition time and expanding the set of monitored metrics to include GPU utilization would further enhance the analysis.

In terms of general considerations, allowing users to control clock speed has the potential to empower researchers and developers to make informed decisions about the energy consumption of their computations and ultimately reducing the sector carbon footprint [17]. Furthermore, integrating energy profiling as a standard practice could encourage users to adopt different strategies based on their priorities and needs, such as focusing on performance during development and testing phases while optimizing for efficiency in production. At the data center level, increased awareness of energy consumption could help optimize costs and reduce downtime. The current accounting model is based solely on CPU/GPU hours, but we believe that it should evolve to include energy consumption, enabling dynamic pricing based on actual power usage. At a finer granularity, a RJMS could operate in an energy-aware mode, helping to lower temperatures and, consequently, reducing the likelihood of component failures and the frequency of maintenance interventions, ultimately leading to less downtime. Finally, systematically evaluating energy usage can enhance the operational efficiency of existing data centers and contribute to the design of more advanced, energy-efficient computing infrastructures.

Acknowledgments. The authors gratefully acknowledge Prof. G. Falcucci (Università degli Studi di Roma Tor Vergata, Rome, Italy) for providing full access to the A100 system. Acknowledgments are also extended to Prof. S. Pirozzoli (Università degli Studi di Roma La Sapienza, Rome, Italy) and Dr. M. Bernaschi (Istituto per le Applicazioni del Calcolo, Consiglio Nazionale delle Ricerche, Rome, Italy) for their valuable support in customizing PipeFlow and QISG.

This work is partially supported by the Project ECS 0000024 Rome Technopole, - CUP B83C22002820006, NRP Mission 4 Component 2 Investment 1.5, Funded by the European Union - NextGenerationEU.

References

1. Beneventi, F., et al.: Continuous learning of HPC infrastructure models using big data analytics and in-memory processing tools. In: Design, Automation & Test in Europe Conference & Exhibition (DATE), pp. 1038–1043 (2017)
2. White, J.P., et al.: Monitoring and analysis of power consumption on HPC clusters using XDMoD. In: Practice and Experience in Advanced Research Computing 2020: Catch the Wave (PEARC 2020), pp. 112–119. ACM, New York (2020)
3. Corbalan, J., et al.: EAR: energy management framework for supercomputers. Barcelona Supercomputing Center (BSC) Working Paper (2019)
4. Vysocky, O., Beseda, M., Říha, L., Zapletal, J., Lysaght, M., Kannan, V.: MERIC and RADAR generator: tools for energy evaluation and runtime tuning of HPC applications. In: Kozubek, T., et al. (eds.) HPCSE 2017. LNCS, vol. 11087, pp. 144–159. Springer, Cham (2018). https://doi.org/10.1007/978-3-319-97136-0_11
5. Acun, F., et al.: Analysis of power consumption and GPU power capping for MILC. In: SC24-W: Workshops of the International Conference for High Performance Computing, Networking, Storage and Analysis, pp. 1856–1861 (2024)
6. Zhao, Z., et al.: Understanding VASP Power Profiles on NVIDIA A100 GPUs. In: Proceedings of the SC 2024 Workshops of the International Conference on High Performance Computing, Network, Storage, and Analysis, pp. 1496–1505. IEEE Press (2025)
7. Simsek, O.S., et al.: Increasing energy efficiency of astrophysics simulations through GPU frequency scaling. In: SC24-W: Workshops of the International Conference for High Performance Computing, Networking, Storage and Analysis, pp. 1826–1834 (2024)
8. Turisini, M., et al.: Energy efficiency: a lattice Boltzmann study. In: Proceedings of the 4th Workshop on Performance and Energy Efficiency in Concurrent and Distributed Systems, PECS 2024, Pisa, Italy, pp. 17–23. Association for Computing Machinery (2024)
9. Yang, Z., et al.: Accurate and convenient energy measurements for GPUs: a detailed study of NVIDIA GPU's built-in power sensor. In: SC24: International Conference for High Performance Computing, Networking, Storage and Analysis, pp. 1–17. IEEE (2024)

10. Falcucci, G., et al.: Extreme flow simulations reveal skeletal adaptations of deep-sea sponges. Nature **595**, 537–541 (2021)
11. Pirozzoli, S., et al.: One-point statistics for turbulent pipe flow up to $Re_\tau \approx 6000$. J. Fluid Mech. **926**, A28 (2021)
12. Bernaschi, M., et al.: The quantum transition of the two-dimensional ising spin glass. Nature **631**, 749–754 (2024)
13. Devlin, J., et al.: BERT: pre-training of deep bidirectional transformers for language understanding. In: Proceedings of 2019 Conference of the North American Chapter of the Association for Computational Linguistics: Human Language Technologies, pp. 4171–4186 (2019)
14. Wang, Q., Chu, X.: GPGPU performance estimation with core and memory frequency scaling. In: 2018 IEEE 24th International Conference on Parallel and Distributed Systems (ICPADS), pp. 417–424 (2018)
15. Patel, P., et al.: Characterizing power management opportunities for LLMs in the cloud. In: Proceedings of 29th ACM International Conference on Architectural Support for Programming Languages and Operating Systems, ASPLOS 2024,d La Jolla, CA, USA, pp. 207–222. Association for Computing Machinery (2024)
16. Schoonhoven, R., et al.: Going green: optimizing GPUs for energy efficiency through model-steered auto-tuning. In: 2022 IEEE/ACM International Workshop on Performance Modeling, Benchmarking and Simulation of High Performance Computer Systems (PMBS), pp. 48–59. IEEE Computer Society (2022)
17. Yang, X., et al.: Computational fluid dynamics: Its carbon footprint and role in carbon reduction. J. Renew. Sustain. Energy **16**, 055906 (2024)

Running Energy-Efficient HPL on APUs: Strategies and Best Practices

Jean-Yves Vet[1](✉)[iD] and Gabriel Hautreux[2][iD]

[1] Hewlett Packard Enterprise, Puteaux, France
vet@hpe.com
[2] CINES, Montpellier, France
https://www.cines.fr

Abstract. The increasing energy needs of supercomputers have highlighted the importance of energy efficiency for HPC and AI tasks. Accelerated Processing Units (APUs), which combine CPU and GPU in a package with shared memory, have the potential to enhance energy efficiency by reducing data movement. Nevertheless they bring management challenges. As opposed to conventional setups where CPUs, GPUs and memory have separate power allocations, APUs rely on a power limit that necessitates flexible distribution. Inefficient power allocation can lead to improper resource utilization and can hinder performance improvements while also raising concerns about energy usage. This research investigates methods for improving energy efficiency in APU systems with the High Performance Linpack Benchmark (HPL). We analyze the findings of the Adastra-2 partition of CINES, which ranked third on the SC24 Green500 list. This includes fixed resource utilization approaches, architectural challenges, and memory side effects. In addition, we offer recommendations on how to improve the efficiency of HPL runs, discuss power management strategies, and pinpoint areas where performance can be further enhanced. Our discoveries provide practical system guidelines for future APU-based HPC deployments.

Keywords: APU · HPL · Gren500 · Energy · Efficiency

1 Introduction

The energy consumption of supercomputers is increasing rapidly due to the growing need for high-performance computing (HPC) and AI training workloads. With increasing scale and complexity of computations comes a growing impact on the environment, especially as energy costs rise and sustainability becomes an issue. Today, energy efficiency is therefore a key factor in the design of HPC systems, affecting both the operational expenses of such systems and the carbon footprint of large-scale computing infrastructure. To meet these challenges, hardware architectures are being developed to increase computational performance while also improving energy efficiency. Over the past several years, there has been a notable shift to heterogeneous architectures that are tightly integrated with different types of compute resources. One such innovation is Accelerated Processing Unit (APU) that integrates CPU cores and GPU accelerators into one package, often featuring shared High Bandwidth Memory (HBM). This design offers several benefits that can enhance energy efficiency in some applications, including reducing data movement overhead [1,2] and improving memory bandwidth. However, it also raises new power management issues that need to be properly solved. Traditional HPC systems have clearly defined power budgets for CPUs, GPUs and memory; APUs however require that these components share a single fixed Thermal Design Power (TDP) budget. Incorrect power distribution may result in under-utilization of resources and unnecessary energy consumption, undermining the potential benefits of APUs.

Given these challenges, optimizing the behavior of the APUs is essential to improve energy efficiency in modern HPC systems. In this paper, we focus on the AMD Instinct MI300A APU [3,4] and derive insights from the Adastra supercomputer, which secured the third place on the SC24 Green500 list [5]. We discuss coarse-grained strategies for statically guiding resource utilization on APU based systems and point out some pathological behaviors that are specific to this architecture if not properly managed. In addition, we provide general information and best practices for system tuning to optimize both High Performance Linpack (HPL) runs for performance and energy efficiency.

HPL is a very high computational intensity benchmark that maximizes node power consumption by exploiting all components to their near limits. Tuning HPL for optimal performance is a practice commonly used at production sites to stress hardware components and verify stability after deployment. In addition, this benchmark is used proactively to monitor the health of the compute nodes [6]. This article does not dive into exploring HPL parameters or enhancing its implementation; instead, it concentrates on analyzing system parameters and refining optimization strategies. Overall, our findings contribute to a better understanding of energy-efficient computing with HPL and can be used as guidelines for future system deployments.

2 Related Work

Closed-source implementations of HPL have been designed to leverage heterogeneous architectures. For example, vendor-specific versions, such as HPE's implementation, are specifically designed for large-scale runs on exascale supercomputers, empowered by the HPE Cray Slingshot Interconnect [7]. Examples include Frontier [8] and El Capitan, the latter utilizing the same hardware as the one studied in this paper. rocHPL, AMD's open source implementation of the HPL benchmark, has been optimized and refined for previous generations of AMD Instinct GPUs, including the MI250X [9]. Several optimizations were introduced by Chalmers et al. to maximize performance when using high-throughput GPU accelerators and CPU resources. Key strategies include a multithreaded approach to panel factorization on CPUs, time sharing of CPU cores among processes, and techniques to hide MPI communication latency [10]. All of these techniques are also relevant to APUs and were enabled with the rocHPL version we used.

Beyond performance optimizations, multiple studies have focused on energy efficiency in HPC systems, particularly regarding CPU, GPU, and network configurations. Laros et al. demonstrated that static tuning of CPU frequency and network settings can produce significant energy savings [11]. Indrani et al. proposed a model capturing an application's frequency sensitivity, which served as the foundation for a dynamic, coordinated energy management scheme, improving the energy efficiency of AMD A-Series APUs [12]. Similarly, Simmendinger et al. introduced the PowerSched [13] framework, which dynamically optimizes the power consumption of HPC applications. Their results indicate that this approach may outperform static capping strategies both in terms of power savings and performance.

Additionally, hardware variability must be considered, as it can significantly impact performance, especially with GPUs. Vergara et al. observed up to a 5% variability between identical GPUs, highlighting the importance of hardware characterization in energy and performance studies [14].

3 System Description

This study was carried out during stabilization and adjustment of the extension of Adastra (alias Adastra-2), a GENCI [1] supercomputer hosted and operated by CINES in Montpellier. This extension brings 112 AMD Instinct MI300A APUs, integrated into a new HPE Cray EX4000 cabinet, with 14 HPE Cray EX255a accelerator blades exposing 28 nodes in total. Each node contains four APUs each connected to an HPE Slingshot 11 Network Interface Controller (NIC) running at 200 Gbps.

An AMD Instinct MI300A APU combines CPU and GPU chiplets, a 256 MB AMD Infinity Cache (memory-side cache), eight stacks of HBM3 memory, and various system-on-chip (SoC) components into a single processor package. It features a unified memory architecture with 128 GB of HBM3 memory that is coherently shared between the CPU and GPU chiplets. The CPU chiplets are based on AMD's Zen 4 architecture [15], while the GPU is built on the CDNA 3 architecture [16]. The GPU component consists of six accelerated Compute Dies (XCDs), each containing 38 compute units (CUs), and is presented to the system as a single GPU device. This configuration is used in our system to reduce the number of MPI tasks. Although referred to as a "GPU" for simplicity, this term is somewhat misleading, as the CDNA 3 architecture omits traditional graphics-oriented hardware such as pixel processing and ray tracing units. Nonetheless, we retain the term throughout this article for consistency and to align with common APU sub-component nomenclature. The CPU portion includes three Core

---

[1] GENCI (Grand Équipement National de Calcul Intensif) implements France's national strategy for supercomputing to support French and European open scientific research.

Chiplet Dies (CCDs), each with 8 cores, totaling 24 physical cores. Simultaneous multithreading (SMT) is enabled, resulting in 48 hardware threads per APU.

The system incorporates a fanless direct liquid cooling solution from HPE to dissipate 97% of the heat generated. An HPE Cray EX400 Coolant Distribution Unit (CDU) is used for heat exchange between the external loop and the inner loop of the system. The inner loop using glycol is cooled with an external closed loop that utilizes input water at 30^{circ}C. Employing warm water for cooling purposes helps to boost operational efficiency and efficiency while reducing expenses and supporting sustainability goals.

4 Methodology

In this section, we provide a comprehensive description of the software stack selected for the evaluation and the approach used for quantifying energy consumption, ensuring accuracy and reproducibility in our analysis.

4.1 Software Environment Selection

To establish an optimal software environment, we conducted a preliminary study to evaluate different configurations. Based on this analysis, we selected the *apu* branch of rocHPL 6.0 (commit a394f17) [17]. For compilation, we chose GCC 13.2, as it demonstrated compatibility and performance advantages. The following libraries were selected on the basis of their computational efficiency and performance stability:

- **BLIS 4.2** was used for CPU-based computations.
- **ROCm 6.2.0** provided the required GPU runtime and driver support.
- **rocBLAS 4.2.0** was chosen for its improved performance in matrix operations.
- **Cray MPICH 8.1.30** was selected for MPI operations enabling GPU-aware communications.
- **Slingshot Host Software (SHS) 11.0** providing libfabric 1.20.1 with Slingshot support.

Resource allocation and job management are handled via Slurm 23.02.6. The experiments were carried out on a system running Red Hat Enterprise Linux (RHEL) 9.4. and following AMD's recommended system optimizations [18]. These included enabling transparent huge pages, increasing allocatable memory by adjusting parameters of the *amdttm* kernel module, enabling compaction proactiveness, and disabling Non-Uniform Memory Access (NUMA) balancing.

4.2 Energy Measurement

To monitor power consumption at the node level, we use hardware telemetry, which provides real-time energy usage data. It is stored in node memory at /sys/cray/pm_counters/energy via the Cray Power Management (PM) counters [19]. This energy counter accumulator is updated approximately every 100 milliseconds. During execution, we track the progression of the energy counter every second. We also monitor the node's power draw every second to detect anomalies. To calculate the total energy consumption per node, we align the initial and final counter values with the start and end times of `HPL_pdgesv()` as indicated in the listing 1.1. This method provides an accurate measurement of energy consumption per node and per run. We calculate the GFLOPs/W per node, and then calculate the average across all nodes at the end of each run. The final Green500 level 1 submission also accounted for the contribution of network consumption.

```
T/V                    N        NB     P       Q              Time                    Gflops
WC10R2R4            995328      576    8       8             259.98                  2.529e+06
HPL_pdgesv()  start time  Wed Oct 23 22:15:25 2024
HPL_pdgesv()  end   time  Wed Oct 23 22:19:45 2024

||Ax-b||_oo/(eps*(||A||_oo*||x||_oo+||b||_oo)*N)=                 0.0001195 ...... PASSED
```

Listing 1.1. Output of the run ranked 3rd in the SC24 Green500 list.

5 Experiments

To optimize the energy efficiency of the system and maximize the HPL performance for Green500, we analyze the impact of various aspects. Some strategies are applicable to all types of architectures, while others are specifically relevant to APU-based systems.

We occasionally refer to raw performance, measured in GFLOPs, to illustrate how the hardware behaves when optimizing for minimal time to solution. In contrast, the Green500 list ranks systems based on performance per watt (GFLOPs/W). For a fixed-size problem with a known number of floating-point operations, this metric is proportional to the inverse of the total energy consumed. Since GFLOPs/W is numerically equivalent to GFLOP/J, it serves as a practical proxy for energy-to-solution.

5.1 Universal Optimization Strategies

Memory Free Capacity. The ability to use larger matrices and extend the duration of compute-intensive matrix multiplication (DGEMM) calls improves as the available memory on compute nodes increases. Compute nodes are configured to expose a single memory region per APU which functions as a NUMA node. Performance degrades when an APU accesses data from the HBM of another APU within the same compute node, due to NUMA effects. As a consequence, we ensure that memory accesses stay local to the NUMA node.

However, we observed that the system has over 1 GB less free memory on the first NUMA node, as shown in the Table 1. This behavior stems from standard Linux kernel practices: during early boot, the kernel is not yet aware of the full NUMA topology or optimal allocation policies and, therefore, defaults to allocating some memory from node 0. Moreover, the `crashkernel=` parameter reserves a contiguous region of physical memory, typically from NUMA node 0 for use by *kdump* mechanisms in the event of a kernel panic. Consequently, NUMA node 0 retains fixed reserved regions that are unavailable for general allocations, contributing to a persistent imbalance even when memory is otherwise uniformly distributed. This leads to a suboptimal situation, where increased memory reservation on a single NUMA node effectively reduces the usable memory across all NUMA nodes. This occurs because each MPI task is typically bound to a specific NUMA node and tends to allocate a similar amount of memory.

Table 1. Memory unbalances on NUMA node 0.

	NUMA node 0	NUMA node 1	NUMA node 2	NUMA node 3
size (MB)	127811	128719	128678	128706
free (MB)	125468	127104	127221	126564

In our configuration, the crashkernel reservation consumes approximately 400 MB. While this feature remains necessary to keep enabled for production environments, it can be safely disabled to perform HPL executions. We partially mitigated the imbalance by reducing the crashkernel parameter to 1M in the kernel command line. On top of that, approximately 500 MB more memory was reserved on the first NUMA node, causing an uneven distribution of free capacity across NUMA nodes. To improve memory distribution, we remounted some in-memory filesystems to avoid using the first NUMA node. This was done by remounting these filesystems with page interleaving skipping the first NUMA node. In addition, a drop cache must be forced for the changes to be effective as indicated in the listing 1.2. The first NUMA node received 1 GB additional usable memory through these changes, resulting in a total increase of 4 GB of usable memory per compute node.

```
$ mount | grep 'rootfs.rw'
tmpfs on /rootfs.rw type tmpfs (rw,[...],mpol=interleave:0-3)
$ mount -o remount,mpol=interleave:1-3 /rootfs.rw
$ mount | grep 'rootfs.rw'
tmpfs on /rootfs.rw type tmpfs (rw,[...],mpol=interleave:1-3)
$ echo 3 > /proc/sys/vm/drop_caches
```

Listing 1.2. Interleaving memory on last 3 NUMA nodes with a *tmpfs* mount point.

System Noise. Background noise could strongly impact performance and could cause large variability between runs. For example, a drop in power consumption was observed every 30 s, resulting in a drop in efficiency. When investigating the issue, we found that this problem was caused by the Slurm *acct_gather* plugins. No issues were observed in single-node runs, suggesting that the plugins may interfere with the internode communications among the MPI tasks. Figure 1 illustrates the variation in instantaneous power of a node while running a multi-node HPL. These plugins were turned off during the HPL runs. More detailed analysis will be needed to pinpoint the root cause of the problem and minimize its effects when the plugins are enabled in production.

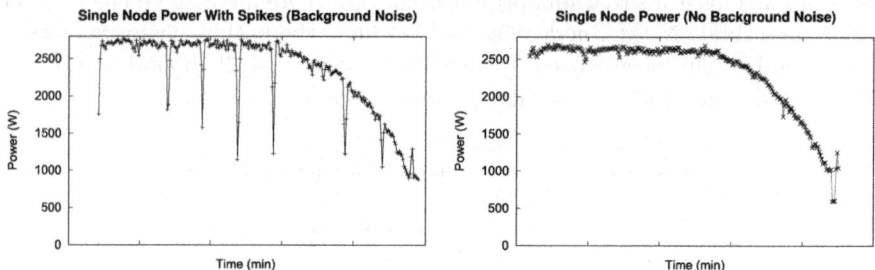

Fig. 1. Power measurements on one node while running a multi-node rocHPL. Slurm *acct_gather* plugin was generating background noise and interfering with HPL.

To enhance the reproducibility and stability of the results, the Address Space Layout Randomization (ASLR) was turned off (setarch x86_64 -R <app>) when running HPL. ASLR is an anti-exploitation feature that changes the memory locations to make it harder for attackers to know where to find potential vulnerabilities. It has been shown to introduce small overheads [20], but we noticed that it could also cause larger performance variations with other applications.

In addition, all interrupt requests (IRQs) were set to isolated hardware threads associated with cores that were not used by HPL. Critical IRQs such as *amdgpu* were also moved to keep NUMA affinities as shown in the listing 1.3.

```
# Isolating IRQs to dedicated cores
systemctl stop irqbalance
export IRQBALANCE_BANNED_CPUS=fefefffe,feffffe,fffefeff,fefefffe,feffffe,fffefeff
irqbalance
sleep 2
pkill irqbalance

# Manually moving amdgpu IRQs to isolated SMTs and keep NUMA affinities
GPU0_IRQ="0,00000000,00000000,00000001"
GPU1_IRQ="0000000,00000000,00000000,01000000"
GPU2_IRQ="00000,00000000,00000000,00010000,00000000"
GPU3_IRQ="000,00000000,00000000,00000100,00000000,00000000"
echo $GPU0_IRQ > /proc/irq/$(cat /sys/class/drm/card0/device/irq)/smp_affinity
echo $GPU1_IRQ > /proc/irq/$(cat /sys/class/drm/card8/device/irq)/smp_affinity
echo $GPU2_IRQ > /proc/irq/$(cat /sys/class/drm/card16/device/irq)/smp_affinity
echo $GPU3_IRQ > /proc/irq/$(cat /sys/class/drm/card24/device/irq)/smp_affinity
```

Listing 1.3. Moving IRQs to dedicated cores.

Node Selection. Because each chip is unique, it is not uncommon to see 5% variation in performance and efficiency with GPUs [14]. Figure 2 illustrates the performance distribution during a single node HPL run. There is exactly a 5% difference between the fastest and the slowest node. Of the 28 available nodes, we selected the 16 fastest based on single-node HPL performance, all of which achieve at least 170 TFLOPs. A small number of runs were performed to identify the optimal set of nodes for energy efficiency as well. The deployed strategy, which entailed monitoring the GFLOPs/W per node at the end of each run, helped us to identify the best performing nodes quickly. This simple method can be used again to exclude nodes in any HPL run aimed at energy efficiency or performance-oriented HPL runs based on pure TFLOPs.

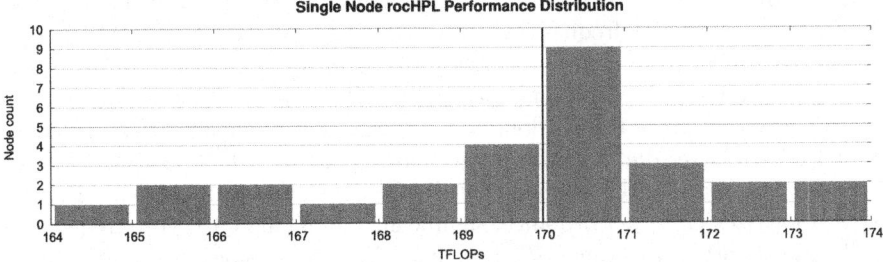

Fig. 2. Distribution of node performance among the 28 nodes (16 nodes are performing above 170 TFLOPs).

5.2 Memory Implications in APU Systems

The unified memory between CPUs and GPUs accelerates fragmentation, increasing allocation costs. This appears to be a drawback of the APU, causing severe performance degradation over time. AMD's system optimization guide recommends enabling proactive compaction and setting *compaction_proactiveness* to 20. However, this does not appear to resolve the issue in our system, probably because high memory utilization limits the effectiveness of the background compaction mechanism. Instead, running the memory compaction command on the node with root permissions and waiting a few minutes mitigates the fragmentation issue. This command can also be added to the workload manager's epilog script for automation. We observed an almost 5× slowdown when working with large matrices before and after compaction as shown in the Table 2.

Table 2. Single node HPL performance before and after memory compaction.

Matrix size (N)	Compaction (before the run)	HPL result (TFLOPs)
230400	no	167.6
243072	no	34.8
243072	yes	173.1

5.3 Power Management Strategies for APUs

We noticed a strong CPU-GPU dependency while running compute intensive workloads. For instance, we compared the performance of simultaneous CPU and

GPU stress tests in Fig. 3. The frequency of the 24 CPU cores is 3700 MHz (boost mode) when the system is idle, the GPU frequency is 94 MHz, while the APU consumes 80 W of power. First, a CPU stress test (*stress-ng* [21], matrix mode) on all 24 cores raises power to 215 W without altering the CPU frequency. At 21 s, launching a GPU stress test (*CoralGemm* [22] benchmark using rocBLAS DGEMM) drops CPU frequencies to about 2050 MHz, while the APU power reaches its 550 W power limit, indicating dynamic power allocation. This shows that the power envelope is dynamically shared between the two components. When the CPU stress test is done at 51 s, the power remains close to 550 W, the CPU cores are idle, and the frequencies return to 3700 MHz, with a small (100 MHz) increase in the frequency of the GPU. These results indicate that the APU prioritizes GPU performance, significantly reducing CPU core frequencies, while also slightly impacting GPU frequency. We now explore strategies to guide this arbitration and improve the efficiency of HPL execution.

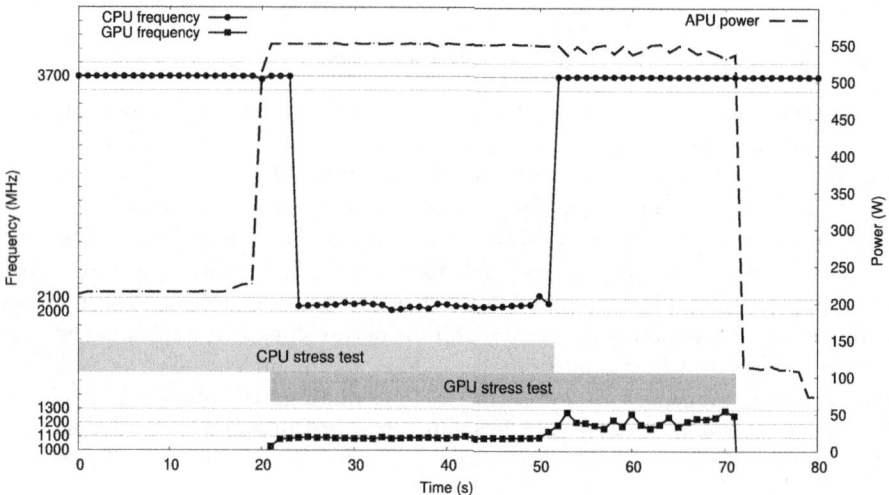

Fig. 3. CPU-GPU interdependency alters frequencies during intensive workloads, with one targeting the GPU and the other utilizing all 24 CPU cores of a single APU.

GPU Frequency Capping. Adjusting the frequency of the GPU was found to be an effective way of distributing power usage between the CPU and the GPU within the APU. Our analysis revealed a trade-off between performance and energy efficiency, and highlighted the importance of frequency tuning for optimal operation. Performance measurements indicated that the highest computational throughput was obtained at 1500 MHz, which makes it the most suitable for peak performance conditions. However, energy efficiency assessments showed that the optimal frequency range was between 1200 MHz and 1300 MHz, as shown in

Fig. 4. We chose 1275 MHz as it appeared to yield slightly better results in 16-node runs.

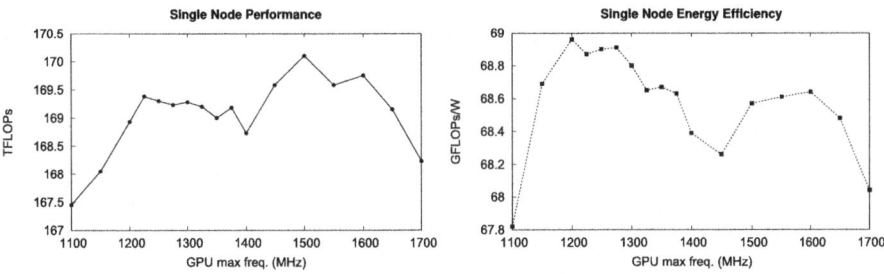

Fig. 4. rocHPL performance results and energy efficiency based on the maximum GPU frequency. Results were averaged over five runs. APU max power: 550 W, CPU maximum frequency: 37000 MHz, 24 OpenMP threads.

Quantity of CPU Cores. Each APU embeds 24 CPU cores. Using all 24 cores for HPL computations on CPUs with OpenMP leads to performance degradation likely due to resource contention, as at least one core is shared between HPL workloads and *amdgpu* IRQs. OpenMP places were used for thread affinities and, for a core count less than 24, the hardware threads used to bind the IRQs were avoided. Testing has been conducted and it has been found that setting the core count to 23 minimizes interference and improves performance. Further experiments revealed that HPL configured to run on 21 cores is the best for overall performance and energy efficiency as evidenced in Fig. 5, probably due to reduced CPU power consumption, allowing more power to be allocated to the GPU.

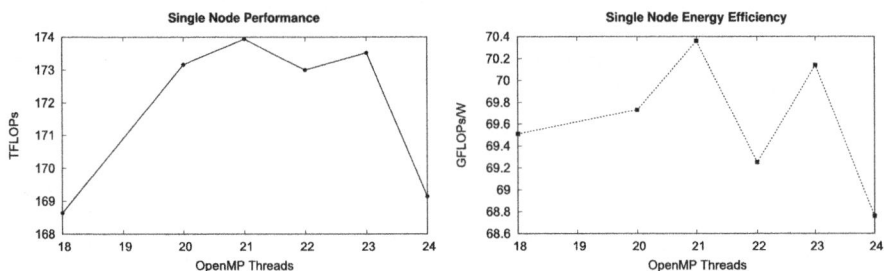

Fig. 5. rocHPL performance and energy efficiency vs. OpenMP threads, averaged over five runs. APU maximum power: 550 W, GPU maximum frequency: 1275 MHz, CPU maximum frequency: 3700 MHz, with balanced OpenMP placement across CCDs.

APU Power Capping. Capping each MI300A power consumption, while leading to a reduction in GFLOPs, can help improve energy efficiency. In some cases, limiting the APU power to 530 W and capping the GPU frequency at 1275 MHz has resulted in an efficiency gain of up to 1 GFLOPs/W.

5.4 Unfruitful Strategies

We investigated several alternative ways to improve performance and energy efficiency. However, none provided significant or sustainable enhancement in all test cases. The optimizations explored included:

- Changing the maximum memory frequency settings in the BIOS, both to increase and to decrease, to find the possible benefits and drawbacks of the changes made concerning bandwidth and power consumption.
- Switching the CPU mode in the BIOS from *Power* to *Performance* in an attempt to improve the stability of computational performance.
- Reducing the PCIe links from PCIe 5.0 to 4.0, 3.0 and 2.0 to determine the impact of the reduction in link speed on the performance and power consumption of the system.
- The use of other broadcast algorithms. Only one resulted in measurable improvement: *Ibcast* (=6) with HPL increased performance by approximately 1.5% on a single node. However, this optimization was not better than the default setting *1rg* (=0) when the number of nodes increased.

6 Discussion and Future Work

The effects of frequency and power capping on various workloads have already been studied on Adastra-1 using MI250X GPUs, demonstrating potential for reducing energy consumption or operational costs when needed, even temporarily [23]. These are the kinds of approaches we aim to democratize in production environments. However, with APUs, such strategies are more intricately tied to CPU behavior, introducing additional complexity. Despite these challenges, these techniques along with the ones mentioned earlier were successfully implemented, contributing to Adastra-2 achieving a remarkable rank of No. 3 on the November 2024 Green500 list. While this ranking is based solely on the HPL benchmark, it nonetheless illustrates how energy efficiency can be effectively optimized on this particular APU-based architecture for compute-intensive workloads.

To improve the energy efficiency score, we could have further refined the node selection. We created a tool to assess the power efficiency and performance of each APU by launching strided and batched matrix multiplication kernels on the GPUs. This tool pushes compute intensity further and also aids in detecting problems such as hardware failures or cooling issues like poor thermal paste application or a loose water block. We used this tool to evaluate the performance of all APUs and observed a variation of up to 15% in power efficiency between them. Although redistributing the most efficient APUs to selected nodes could have significantly improved overall efficiency, we chose not to implement this strategy in the current deployment.

Additionally, capping the CPU frequency at 2600 MHz occasionally improves energy efficiency. This implies that further performance enhancements could be achieved by fine-tuning CPU power consumption, particularly through guided frequency scaling during execution. GPU performance is most critical at the beginning of an HPL run, while computational demand gradually shifts toward the CPU as execution progresses. Optimizing power allocation in real time could improve overall energy efficiency, especially for small runs, where the fraction of total time spent on the CPU part is quite significant. As part of future work, we plan to examine the effectiveness of simple models and more dynamic approaches for adjusting frequencies and power capping. This investigation aims to determine whether an explicit programmatic approach to specifying compute unit priorities would be necessary for achieving optimal energy efficiency with APUs, as opposed to relying on a fully dynamic external mechanism.

7 Conclusion

In this article, we explored various techniques for optimizing HPL runs to enhance energy efficiency or raw performance on APUs. Some general strategies, such as cutting down background noise, increasing memory free capacity, and opting for the most efficient nodes, can be helpful for all kinds of hardware and may hold significance for upcoming setups. However, APUs need specific adjustments because of their integrated GPU, CPU and shared memory, causing new effects that have to be addressed. The most disruptive impact is the dynamic power distribution within the APU, as increasing the performance of one type of compute unit reduces the efficiency of the other as both share the same power envelope. Deciding which part to focus on is tricky since it is heavily dependent on the workload and can change dynamically during computing phases. Currently, runtime detection of the optimal balance remains difficult. That is the reason why we focused on static configurations in our research, including the number of CPU cores, GPU frequencies, and power capping. This approach enabled us to secure the third position in the Green500 ranking and surpass other systems using similar architecture.

References

1. Tandon, S., et al.: Porting HPC applications to AMD instinct MI300A using unified memory and OpenMP (2024)
2. Bertolli, C., et al.: Runtime handling of zero-copy for OpenMP programs on MI300A APUs. In: SC24-W (2024)
3. Smith, A., et al.: Realizing the AMD exascale heterogeneous processor vision. In: ISCA (2024)
4. Smith, A., et al.: AMD instinct MI300 series modular Chiplet package – HPC and AI accelerator. In: ISSCC (2024)

5. TOP500. Green500 List - Nov (2024). https://top500.org/lists/green500/2024/11/. Accessed 14 Feb 2025
6. Hagerty, N., et al.: Detecting defective hardware in exascale supercomputers. In: SC-W '23 (2023)
7. Roweth, D., et al.: HPE slingshot launched into network space. In: CUG (2022)
8. Atchley, S., et al.: Frontier: exploring exascale. In: SC '23 (2023)
9. AMD. *CDNA2 Architecture*, https://www.amd.com/content/dam/amd/en/documents/instinct-business-docs/white-papers/amd-cdna2-white-paper.pdf. Accessed 14 Feb 2025
10. Chalmers, N., et al.: Optimizing HPL for exascale accelerated architectures. In: SC '23 (2023)
11. Laros, J., et al.: Energy-based performance tuning for HPC systems. In: HPC Symposium (2012)
12. Paul, I., et al.: Coordinated energy management in heterogeneous processors. In: SC (2013)
13. Simmendinger, C., et al.: TPowerSched - managing power in overprovisioned systems. In: Cluster Workshops (2024)
14. Melesse Vergara, V., et al.: Matrix multiply performance on exascale-class HPE/cray systems. In: ORNL (2022)
15. AMD. *4th Gen AMD EPYC Processor Architecture*, https://www.amd.com/content/dam/amd/en/documents/products/epyc/4th-gen-epyc-processor-architecture-white-paper.pdf. Accessed 14 Feb 2025
16. AMD. *CDNA3 Architecture*, https://www.amd.com/content/dam/amd/en/documents/instinct-tech-docs/white-papers/amd-cdna-3-white-paper.pdf. Accessed 14 Feb 2025
17. GitHub. *rocHPL repository*, https://github.com/ROCm/rocHPL. Accessed 14 Feb 2025
18. AMD. *MI300A System Optimization*, https://rocm.docs.amd.com/en/docs-6.2.0/how-to/system-optimization/mi300a.html. Accessed 14 Feb 2025
19. Hart, A., et al.: User-level power monitoring on cray XC30 supercomputers. In: CUG (2014)
20. Detter, J., Mutschlechner, R.: Performance and Entropy of ASLR Implementations. Univ. Wisconsin-Madison, Tech. Rep. (2015)
21. Github. *stress-ng*, https://github.com/ColinIanKing/stress-ng. Accessed 14 Feb 2025
22. Github. *CoralGemm*, https://github.com/AMD-HPC/CoralGemm. Accessed 14 Feb 2025
23. Hautreux, G., Malaboeuf, E.: Reducing HPC energy footprint for large scale GPU accelerated workloads. In: SC-W '23 (2023)

Analysis of Application Power Characteristics Using Performance Counters on A64FX

Ryoma Ohara[1](✉), Keiji Yamamoto[2], and Toshihiro Hanawa[1]

[1] The University of Tokyo, Tokyo, Japan
ohara@cspp.cc.u-tokyo.ac.jp, hanawa@cc.u-tokyo.ac.jp
[2] R-CCS, RIKEN, Kobe, Japan
keiji.yamamoto@riken.jp

Abstract. In recent years, increasing power consumption and rising electricity costs associated with supercomputers have become critical concerns. The A64FX processor, developed for the Fugaku supercomputer, includes "Power Knob" capabilities that reduce power usage by adjusting specific hardware functions, such as clock frequency, the number of active floating-point units, and core states. This study investigates the correlation between these power knobs and application energy consumption using performance monitoring unit (PMU) counter values on the A64FX processor. By measuring the energy consumption of the eight microbenchmarks, we demonstrate that the optimal power knob configuration can reduce energy usage by up to 53.8%. Additionally, we collected all PMU event counter values and identified events that exhibited remarkable changes in response to power knob adjustments. Based on these observations and the characteristics of each application, we selected representative events most closely linked to application behavior. We then derived summary metrics to determine the optimal power knob settings. Using these metrics, we classified applications according to their power characteristics, demonstrating that optimal power knob configuration can be selected based on application-specific tendencies.

Keywords: Energy efficiency · A64FX processor · Performance counter

1 Introduction

In recent years, the increasing energy consumption of supercomputers has become a critical concern. Under these circumstances, it is essential to execute user jobs energy-efficiently. For example, the A64FX processor developed for the Fugaku supercomputer has 48 compute cores. A prototype of Fugaku achieved an energy efficiency of 16.8 GFLOPS/W and ranked first on the Green500 list in 2019 [2]. Additionally, to further reduce energy consumption, the A64FX has includes "Power knob" functions, which users can configure when executing jobs on the Fugaku system.

Table 1. Specifications of A64FX (Fugaku).

Item	Description
Architecture	Armv8.2-A SVE 512 bit
Number of compute cores	48 cores
CPU Frequency	2.0/2.2 GHz
Theoretical Performance	Double Precision (2.2 GHz): 3.3792 TFLOPS
Memory	HBM2 32 GiB, 1024 GB/s
Interconnect	Tofu Interconnect D (28 Gbps × 2 lanes × 10 ports)
I/O	PCIe Gen3 × 16
Technology	7 nm FinFET

In this study, we focus on reducing total energy consumption, not just instantaneous power, where total energy is defined as the product of average power and execution time. We analyze the energy consumption of applications based on the measurements obtained from the performance monitoring unit (PMU) counters embedded in the A64FX processors. By referring to the PMU counter values, users can identify the computational intensity and performance bottlenecks of their programs. We used these counter values to characterize application behavior.

The main contributions of this study are as follows: (1) We analyze how energy consumption and PMU counter values vary across different applications under various power knob settings. (2) We propose metrics that enable users to determine optimal power knob settings based on application characteristics and PMU counter values.

The remainder of this paper is organized as follows. Section 2 explains the power-saving mechanisms of the A64FX and related technologies. Section 3 presents measurements of microbenchmarks and analyzes the energy consumption under different power knob settings. Section 4 discusses the analysis of PMU counter values in these settings and explains how to estimate the optimal power knob configuration. Section 5 reviews related work, and Sect. 6 summarizes the results and discusses future directions.

2 Power-Aware Mechanisms of the A64FX

To enable energy-efficient computing on the Fugaku supercomputer using the A64FX processor, this section outlines the detailed architecture specifications, power-saving design settings, and power measurement functions.

2.1 Overview of Fugaku

The specifications of Fugaku, jointly developed by the RIKEN Center for Computational Science and Fujitsu, are shown in Table 1. Fugaku comprises 158,976

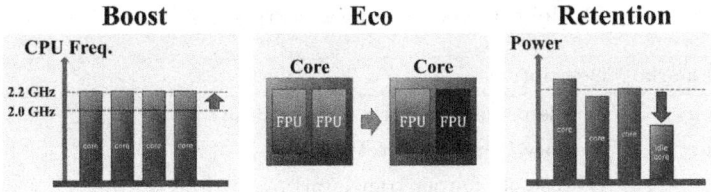

Fig. 1. "Power Knob" functions.

nodes with a single-chip processor—the Fujitsu A64FX [12]. The A64FX features 48 compute cores, internally organized into four core memory groups (CMGs), each comprising 12 cores, 8MB of L2 cache, and a memory controller. The internode network utilizes a six-dimensional mesh/torus topology called the Tofu Interconnect D (TofuD). The chip also integrates both network controllers and PCI Express functionality.

2.2 Power Knob

Fugaku incorporates a "Power Knob" mechanism designed to improve power efficiency by disabling unused circuits while maintaining application performance. By adjusting power knobs based on application requirements, efficient computation can be achieved. The three available power knob settings are described below and illustrated in the conceptual diagram in Fig. 1.

- **Boost**: This setting increases the A64FX clock frequency from the default 2.0–2.2 GHz. While this enhances performance, it also raises power consumption due to the increased power supply voltage.
- **Eco**: In this mode, A64FX restricts its two floating-point unit (FPU) pipelines to one during application execution. Since FPU is among the power-intensive components, so applying eco mode can lead to noticeable power savings.
- **Retention**: In this mode, unused cores enter a deeper low-power state to conserve energy. However, if a core is assigned to a process, it remains fully active, even if all cores are generally set to retention mode across the processor.

Typically, power knob settings are specified within the job script used to submit applications on Fugaku. Before execution, the system automatically adjusts the power knobs according to the job script's configuration. Futhermore, more granular control can be achieved at the application level using the Power API [6,8].

2.3 Power API

Fugaku provides a Power API for power measurement and control. It supports two types of measurements: measured power, which records actual power consumption with node-specific variations, and estimated power, which provides a

Table 2. Overview of benchmark applications.

Benchmark	Description
dgemm	double-precision matrix computation
stream	memory bandwidth test
fft	1D discrete fourier transform
ptrans	matrix transpose
IS	integer sort
EP	gaussian distribution computation (no intertask dependencies)
osu_mbw_mr	MPI Multi-pair bandwidth/message rate
osu_allreduce	MPI_Allreduce latency

Table 3. List of power knob settings.

Setting	Details
normal	Power knob: None
boost	CPU frequency: 2.2 GHz
eco	Only 1 FPU pipeline
retention	Retention mode
boost + eco	2.2 GHz, 1 FPU
boost + retention	2.2 GHz, retention mode
eco + retention	1 FPU, retention mode
boost + eco + retention	2.2 GHz, 1 FPU, retention mode

consistent estimate across nodes. Power values are updated every few milliseconds, and the average power is calculated based on differences over the measurement interval. Users can also use the Power API to adjust power knob settings via job scripts or direct function calls within their programs.

2.4 Performance Monitoring Unit

In this study, we use counter values obtained from the performance monitoring unit (PMU) to analyze the power characteristics of the target application. A PMU is a hardware component embedded within a computer's processor for real-time monitoring and measurement of performance-related data. It supports many events, such as the number of executed instructions and cache misses. Some events are configured by default. Tools like the perf command or PAPI (Performance API) in Linux environments can configure and monitor PMU events. The fapp command measures profiling data, allowing users to specify any PMU event for measurement. During this process, the source code section to be measured is enclosed with fapp function calls.

3 Evaluation of Microbenchmarks

In this section, we describe and evaluate the performance of microbenchmarks used to analyze PMU counters. We calculate the energy consumption and examine the energy-saving effects of adjusting the power knob settings. We then identify the optimal power knob settings during execution from an energy efficiency perspectives.

3.1 Power and Performance Impacts of the Power Knobs

In this study, we measured eight microbenchmarks to analyze PMU counter values. The microbenchmarks used are listed in Table 2. We selected dgemm, stream, fft, and ptrans from the HPC Challenge Benchmark [3]; IS and EP from the NAS Parallel Benchmarks [4]; and osu_mbw_mr and osu_allreduce from the OSU microbenchmarks [5], each with distinct characteristics.

Figure 2 presents the performance and power consumption graphs for eight types of microbenchmarks, categorized by the number of threads or processes and power knob settings. For non-MPI benchmarks, execution is performed on a single node, whereas MPI benchmarks (osu_mbw_mr, osu_allreduce) involve communication between two adjacent nodes. The horizontal axis represents the number of threads or processes. The left vertical axis indicates average power consumption, shown as a bar graph, while the right vertical axis displays execution time as a line graph. All combinations of power knobs settings are listed in Table 3. Each benchmark was configured to perform multiple iterations per run for every thread or process count. The number of iterations was adjusted such that, under the slowest configuration (4 threads or 96 processes), the total elapsed time was approximately 15 s or more.

Retention Mode. As shown in Fig. 2, the overall power consumption tends to be lower when the retention mode is enabled and the number of threads or processes is small. This suggests that when fewer cores are in use, more idle cores remain idle, and the retention mode further reduces power usage for these idle cores. Since retention mode only affects idle cores, it has minimal impact on the application performance.

Eco Mode. Eco mode provides some power savings, but its performance impact varies by application. In Figs. 2a and 2b, the performance degradation is substantial for dgemm and EP due to their heavy reliance on floating-point operations. In contrast, Figs. 2c, 2d, 2e, and 2f show minimal degradation because these applications are more memory-bound than CPU-bound, and the reduced FPU pipeline remains sufficient. Similarly, Figs. 2g and 2h show no performance degradation as communication-bound applications require little CPU computation. These results indicate that while eco mode offers limited energy-saving for dgemm and EP, it can achieve energy efficiency without considerable performance loss for memory- and communication-bound applications.

Boost Mode. Under boost mode, applications with intensive floating-point computations (Figs. 2a and 2b) experienced a noticeable reduction in execution

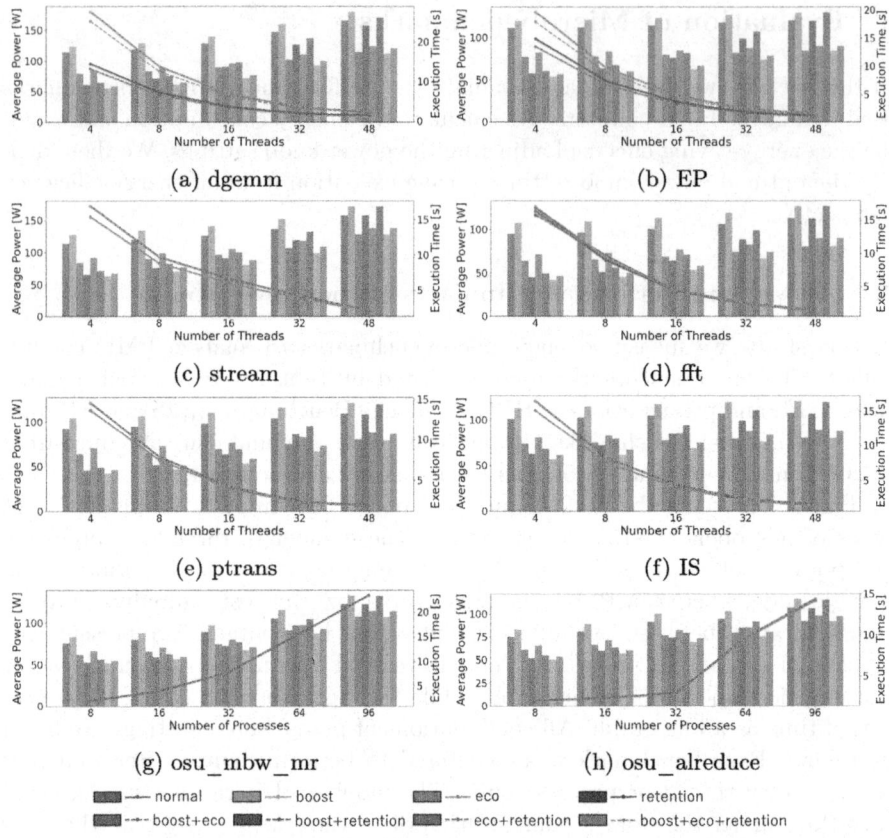

Fig. 2. Performance and power consumption of microbenchmarks.

time. Conversely, memory-bound applications (Figs. 2c-2f) exhibited minimal change, while communication-bound applications (Figs. 2g, 2h) remained unaffected. Therefore, for dgemm and EP, the reduced execution time in boost mode can outweigh the increased power consumption, potentially leading to lower overall energy usage.

3.2 Energy Consumption and Optimal Power Knobs

This section calculates the energy consumption from the power and execution time measurements and analyzes the energy-efficient power knob settings per application.

Figure 3 shows the energy consumption for each application at each thread or process count. The horizontal axis represents each power knob setting, and the vertical axis shows the normalized energy values. Each value is normalized to the "normal" value at the respective thread or process count, making the "normal" value equal to 1 for each thread or process count. The smaller the value, the more optimal the power knob setting is defined to be. It can be observed that the energy-saving effect of the retention-type power knobs becomes more pronounced with lower thread or process counts. Specifically, for fft in eco mode, there is up to a 53.8% energy saving at eight threads. For dgemm, the energy-saving effect of the boost mode is substantial. In CPU-bound applications where the boost mode substantially improves performance, selecting the boost-type power knobs can achieve energy savings. EP benefits from a boost but sees greater eco mode savings at higher threads, with boost+eco+retention yielding the most savings at 48 threads. For other applications, eco-type settings (e.g., eco+retention) are more effective, especially for memory- and communication-bound workloads where boost has little impact.

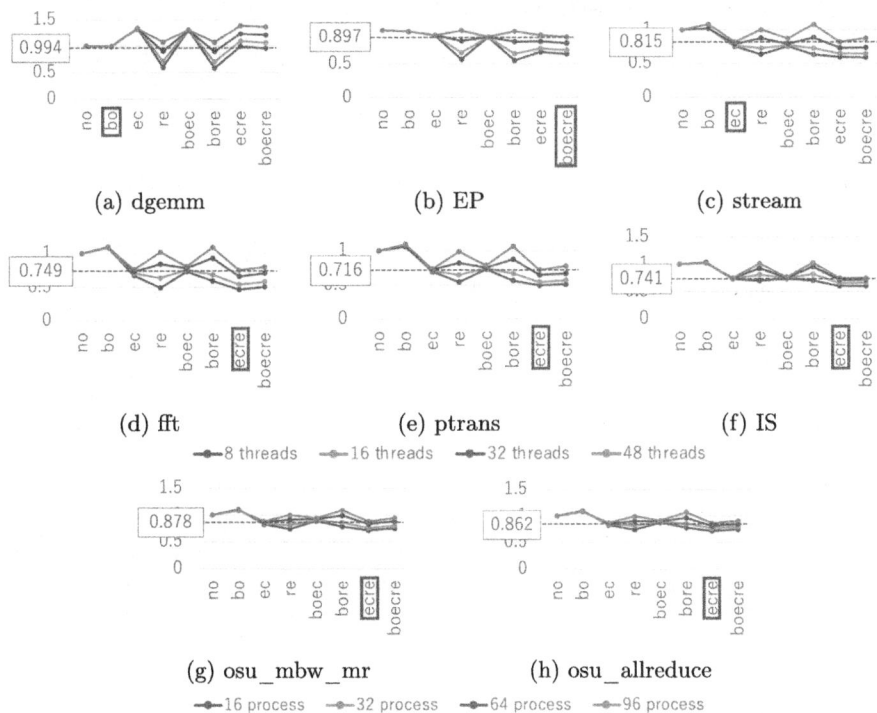

Fig. 3. Normalized energy per benchmark (8, 16, 32, 48 threads or 16, 32, 64, 96 processes). The power knob with the lowest energy consumption during the 48-thread or 96-process execution is highlighted, with the normalized energy value at that time shown in red. (Color figure online)

4 Analysis of the PMU Counter Values

We measured all 183 types of PMU events listed in the A64FX PMU Events [1]. For the eight types of microbenchmarks explained in Sect. 3, we measured all eight combinations of power knobs while changing the number of threads and processes, targeting a single node (non-MPI) and two adjacent nodes (MPI).

4.1 PMU Counter Values for Each Power Knob

We first measured all 183 types of PMU events for each power knob setting. Figure 4 shows the relative values of all PMU counter values, calculated as the ratio of "eco" values to "normal" values. These values indicate how much the counter values increased or decreased compared with the normal values. In Fig. 4, FPU pipelines decrease from two to one, substantially reducing the PMU counter values for floating-point-intensive tasks like dgemm and EP, while memory- and communication-bound applications (e.g., stream, fft, ptrans, IS, osu_mbw_mr, osu_allreduce) remain mostly unaffected.

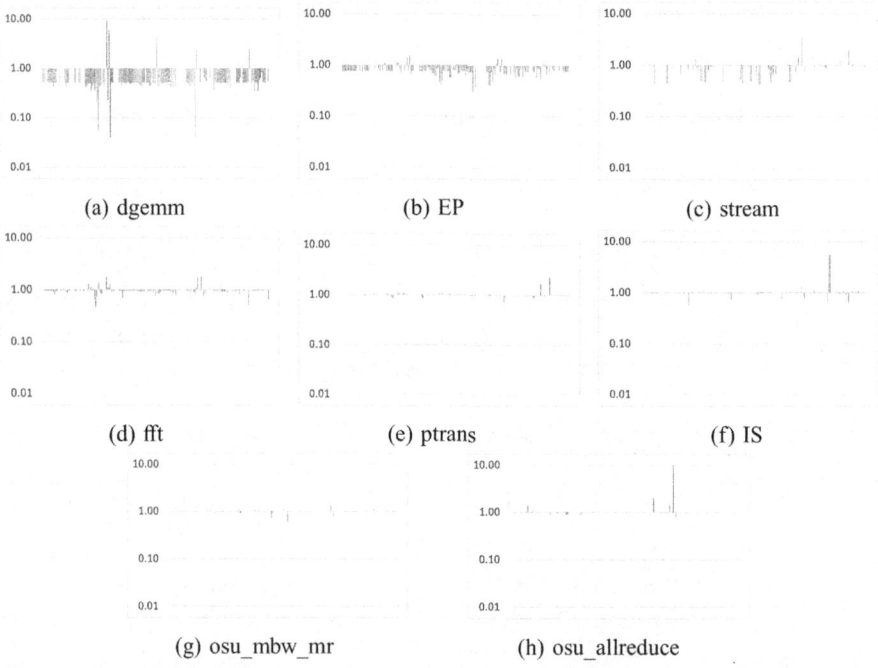

Fig. 4. Relative values of all PMU counters during the 48-thread or 96-process execution. The vertical axis shows the log-scale ratio of the counter values in eco mode compared to normal mode. The horizontal axis lists all 183 PMU event types. Each configuration was executed for approximately 15 s to collect the measurements.

From Fig. 4, it is evident that some of the 183 PMU counter values change substantially with power knob adjustments, while others do not. For estimating the optimal power knob based on the application power characteristics, PMU

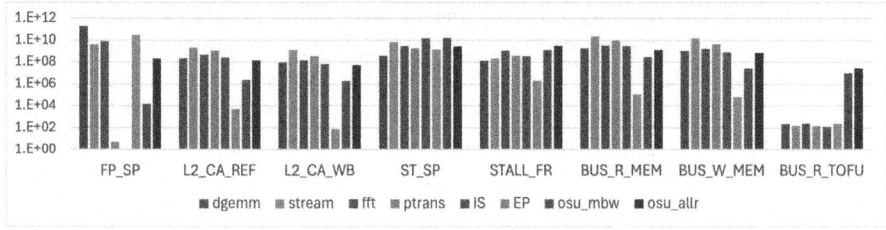

Fig. 5. Normalized counter values per second for representative Performance Monitoring Unit (PMU) events across benchmarks. The horizontal axis represents the abbreviated event names, while the vertical axis shows the counter values normalized by each application's execution time, plotted on a logarithmic scale.

Table 4. List of PMU events presented in this study.

Event Name	Abbrev.	Description
INST_SPEC	IN_SP	Every architecturally executed instruction.
FP_SPEC	FP_SP	Floating-point operation instructions.
L2D_CACHE_REFILL	L2_CA_REF	Operations that cause a refill of the L2 cache.
L2D_CACHE_WB	L2_CA_WB	Every write-back of data from the L2 cache.
STALL_FRONTEND	STALL_FR	Cycles in which no instruction was issued due to the absence of front-end operations.
BUS_READ_TOTAL_MEM	BUS_R_MEM	Read transactions from the local memory to the measured CMG.
BUS_WRITE_TOTAL_MEM	BUS_W_MEM	Write transactions to its local memory.
BUS_READ_TOTAL_TOFU	BUS_R_TOFU	Read transactions from the Tofu controller to the measured CMG.
BUS_WRITE_TOTAL_TOFU	BUS_W_TOFU	Write transactions to the Tofu controller.
FP_SCALE_OPS_SPEC	FP_SCA_SP	SVE scalable floating-point operations.
FP_FIXED_OPS_SPEC	FP_FIX_SP	Advanced SIMD and scalar floating-point arithmetic operations.
LD_SPEC	LD_SP	Architecturally executed load instructions.
ST_SPEC	ST_SP	Architecturally executed store instructions.
L2D_SWAP_DM	L2_SW_DM	Demand accesses that hit an L2 cache refill buffer allocated by prefetch.
L2D_CACHE_MIBMCH_PRF	L2_MI_PRF	Prefetch operations that hit an L2 cache refill buffer allocated by demand access.

events with notable changes are more informative. We summarize in Fig. 5 the key events from Fig. 4 that show substantial changes and closely align with the application's characteristics. The results are based on 48 threads on a single node (non-MPI) or 96 processes on two adjacent nodes (MPI)—additionally, Table 4 lists these PMU event names, their abbreviations, and descriptions. For FP_SP, PMU counter values are high for dgemm and EP, reflecting their CPU-bound characteristics. However, for L2_CA_REF, L2_CA_WB, BUS_R_MEM, and BUS_W_MEM, the counter values for stream, fft, and ptrans are relatively high, indicating their memory-bound characteristics due to L2 cache and memory access. Regarding IS, the counter values are not particularly high. Still, the value of ST_SP is notably large, which is attributed to the sorting application's heavy memory write instructions, highlighting its memory-bound nature. Futhermore, since the value of FP_SP is 0, the energy-saving effects from eco mode can be expected. The relatively low values for EP are due to its high data locality and efficient cache access. In osu_mbw_mr and osu_allreduce, the high values of BUS_R_TOFU indicate internode communication via Tofu. Additionally, the large values of STALL_FR suggest instruction issuance stalls due to synchronization waits and communication overhead between nodes. Moreover, the frequent data write operations result in high ST_SP values, emphasizing communication-bound characteristics.

4.2 Estimation of the Optimal Power Knob Setting

Based on the results from Sect. 4.1, the PMU events that are notably correlated with the application characteristics include the number of floating-point operations, L2 cache misses, and Tofu accesses. Additionally, Sect. 3.2 demonstrated that the most energy-efficient power knobs (optimal power knobs) can be classified according to the characteristics of the application. With these analysis results, it is possible to determine the energy-optimal power knob from the PMU counter values for each application. To estimate the optimal power knobs using only the PMU counter values, the calculation formulas shown in Equations (1) to (3) are used. The event names are indicated using abbreviations, and the event names used in the equations are listed in Table 4.

$$\text{Floating-point operation rate} = \frac{\text{FP\_SCALE} \times 512/128 + \text{FP\_FIXED}}{\text{INST\_SP} \times 2 \times 2 \times 8} \quad (1)$$

$$\text{L2 miss rate} = \frac{\text{L2\_CA\_REF} - \text{L2\_SW} - \text{L2\_PRF}}{\text{LD\_SP} + \text{ST\_SP}} \quad (2)$$

$$\text{Tofu access rate} = \frac{\text{BUS\_R\_TOFU} + \text{BUS\_W\_TOFU}}{\text{INST\_SP}} \quad (3)$$

The floating-point operation rate represents the number of actual floating-point operations executed per instruction. FP_SCA_SP counts the number of operations for the SVE instructions, while FP_FIX_SP counts the operations for the fixed-width vector and scalar instructions. On the A64FX, the SVE operation counts are measured in 128-bit units. To align them with the actual 512-bit SVE vector length, these counts must be scaled and normalized by multiplying by 512/128. The product $2 \times 2 \times 8$ (FMA unit count × FLOPs per unit × SIMD element count) represents the theoretical parallel operation count per instruction. The L2 cache miss rate indicates the proportion of L2 cache misses per load/store instruction. The numerator is computed by subtracting the prefetch and buffering effects from L2_CA_REF. The Tofu access rate represents the fraction of read/write transaction operations to the Tofu network.

Using the above formulas, the values for all eight combinations of power knobs during the execution of 8, 16, 32, and 48 threads, or 16, 32, 64, and 96 processes, are calculated and shown in Fig. 6. In the figure, applications that are

CPU-bound gather near the x-axis, those that are memory-bound gather along the y-axis, and those that are communication-bound gather along the z-axis. By combining this characteristic classification based on the metrics calculated from the PMU counters with the energy consumption graph in Fig. 3, the optimal power knob for each application can be determined as follows:

- **dgemm, EP** : High floating-point operation rate, CPU-bound; boost series is optimal.
- **stream, fft, ptrans, IS** : High L2 cache miss rate, memory-bound; eco series is optimal.
- **osu_mbw_mr, osu_allreduce** : High internode communication rate, communication-bound; eco series is optimal.

EP has a lower computational density than dgemm, as seen in the floating-point operation rate. The impact of reducing one FPU pipeline is small, and energy savings are achieved by combining boost and eco. Additionally, in all cases, Retention has minimal downsides and generally saves energy, making it best used with any power knob.

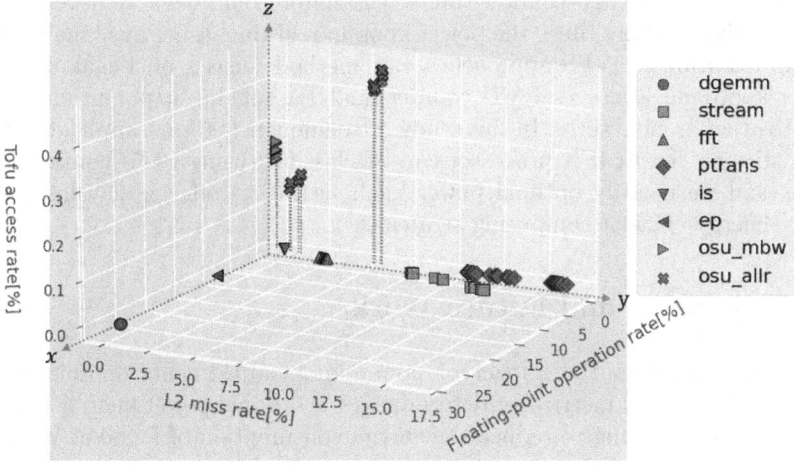

Fig. 6. Floating-point operation rate vs. L2 miss rate vs. Tofu access rate.

5 Related Work

In recent years, the rising energy consumption of supercomputers has become a significant concern, prompting the development of various energy-saving strategies. Papadimitriou et al. [10] sought to enhance the overall energy efficiency of servers by utilizing Dynamic Voltage and Frequency Scaling (DVFS) on

Micro's (now Ampere Computing) X-Gene 2 and X-Gene 3 processors. They developed a monitoring daemon that automatically adjusts DVFS settings and core allocations to optimize energy-efficient execution. Kusaba et al. [9] investigated node-level power efficiency variations in Fugaku and the University of Tokyo's Wisteria/BDEC-01 Odyssey, equipped with A64FX processors. By grouping nodes based on power efficiency and selectively shutting down less efficient nodes under specific constraints, they achieved greater power savings than conventional methods. Fan et al. [7] proposed a fine-grained energy-saving technique using machine learning. They statically extracted the computational characteristics of the applications at compile time and used this information to train a machine learning model. The approach demonstrated high prediction accuracy and validated energy-saving in a real GPU cluster environment. Several supercomputing centers have explored dynamic gear control for energy conservation. Simmendinger et al. [11] introduced PowerSched, a dynamic CPU power capping framework for the Hawk supercomputer at the High Performance Computing Center Stuttgart (HLRS). Compared to static capping, PowerSched substantially reduced performance degradation for CPU-bound applications and achieved even greater energy savings for memory-bound workloads.

Our study aims to improve the energy efficiency by adjusting Fugaku's power knob based on the PMU counter values. Ultimately, our goal is to develop a system that dynamically tunes the power knob in real time using machine learning. Unlike traditional DVFS approaches, our method focuses on Fugaku's unique power knob and leverages PMU counter analysis, making it potentially adaptable to other architectures. In this study, we demonstrated that application characteristics on the A64FX processor can be classified using PMU counter values alone, and we identify optimal power knob settings— offering key insights for future energy-efficient computing strategies.

6 Conclusion and Future Work

This study analyzes the impact of power knob adjustments on microbenchmarks and proposed metrics for determining the optimal power knob using PMU counter values, aiming to reduce the energy consumption of Fugaku. We examined how the performance and energy consumption of each application changed as the power knob was adjusted. We measured variations in the PMU counter values during these adjustments. Based on the results, we identified PMU counter values that are closely related to the application characteristics and power knob settings, and we calculated metrics for selecting the optimal power knobs.

For future work, we plan to measure a broader set of applications and explore methods to determine the optimal power knobs with greater accuracy. To achieve this, we intend to adopt machine learning approaches, building models that can flexibly set power knobs for a broader range of applications. Additionally, we aim to develop a system that dynamically controls the power knobs through machine learning by acquiring PMU counter values in real time. In this system, monitoring begins when the user's application starts, and PMU counter values are collected at regular intervals. Using time-series data and feature extraction from applications—such as detecting for-loops and specific function executions—the system will quickly estimate the optimal power knob and dynamically adjust it. Ultimately, we aim to extend this approach to heterogeneous environments that combine CPUs and GPUs beyond Fugaku.

References

1. A64FX PMU events. https://github.com/fujitsu/A64FX/blob/master/doc/A64FX_PMU_Events_v1.3.pdf. Accessed 19 Dec 2024
2. Green500 (2019). https://top500.org/lists/green500/2019/11/. Accessed 19 Dec 2024
3. HPC challenge benchmark. https://hpcchallenge.org/hpcc/. Accessed 19 Dec 2024
4. NAS Parallel Benchmarks. https://www.nas.nasa.gov/software/npb.html. Accessed 19 Dec 2024
5. OSU-Micro-benchmarks. https://github.com/forresti/osu-micro-benchmarks. Accessed 28 Feb 2025
6. Power API. https://pwrapi.github.io/. Accessed 22 Apr 2025
7. Fan, K., D'Antonio, M., Carpentieri, L., Cosenza, B., Ficarelli, F., Cesarini, D.: SYnergy: fine-grained Energy-Efficient Heterogeneous Computing for Scalable Energy Saving. In: Proceedings of the International Conference for High Performance Computing, Networking, Storage and Analysis pp. 1–13 (2023). https://doi.org/10.1145/3581784.3607055
8. Grant, R.E., Levenhagen, M., Olivier, S.L., DeBonis, D., Pedretti, K.T., Laros, J.H., III.: Standardizing power monitoring and control at EXASCALE. Computer **49**(10), 38–46 (2016). https://doi.org/10.1109/MC.2016.308
9. Kusaba, T., et al.: Power-efficiency variation on A64FX supercomputers and its application to system operation. In: 2024 IEEE International Conference on Cluster Computing Workshops (CLUSTER Workshops), pp. 55–65. IEEE (2024). https://doi.org/10.1109/CLUSTERWorkshops61563.2024.00018
10. Papadimitriou, G., Chatzidimitriou, A., Gizopoulos, D.: Adaptive voltage/frequency scaling and core allocation for balanced energy and performance on multicore CPUS. In: 2019 IEEE International Symposium on High Performance Computer Architecture (HPCA), pp. 133–146. IEEE (2019). https://doi.org/10.1109/HPCA.2019.00033
11. Simmendinger, C., Marquardt, M., Mäder, J., Schneider, R.: Powersched-managing power consumption in overprovisioned systems. In: 2024 IEEE International Conference on Cluster Computing Workshops (CLUSTER Workshops), pp. 1–8. IEEE (2024). https://doi.org/10.1109/CLUSTERWorkshops61563.2024.00012
12. Yoshida, T.: Fujitsu High Performance CPU for the Post-K Computer. In: Hot Chips, vol. 30, p. 22. IEEE Computer Society (2018)

Fifth Workshop on Compiler-Assisted Correctness Checking and Performance Optimization for HPC (C3PO'25)

C3PO 2025 Preface

Objectives/Topics

Practical compiler-enabled programming environments, applied analysis methodologies, and end-to-end toolchains can contribute significantly to performance portability in the exascale era. The practical and applied use of compilation techniques, methods, and technologies, including static analysis and transformation, are imperative to improve the performance, correctness, and scalability of high-performance applications, middleware, and reusable libraries.

This workshop brings together a diverse group of researchers with a shared interest in applying compilation and source-to-source translation methodologies, among others, to enhance explicit parallel programming such as MPI, OpenMP, PGAS, and hybrid models, but also heterogeneous programming on GPUs and FPGAs.

Since 2020, this workshop has sought innovative applications of such technologies singly and in combination to derive enhanced utility in parallel programs that are generalizable beyond a single case study or narrow application. Its original papers identify and solve challenges in the tradeoffs of scalability, performance, predictability, correctness, productivity, and portability on-node and at massive scale; strong-scaling, weak-scaling, and hybrid-scaling solutions assisted, augmented, and/or enabled by compiler technology are in scope. Topics of interest include but are not limited to: correctness checking of parallel programs, source-to-source translation of legacy MPI codes to improve performance-portability, instrumentation, and massively multipass FPGA compiler optimization strategies.

Workshop Organization

Julien Jaeger	CEA, France
Peter Pirkelbauer	Lawrence Livermore National Laboratory, USA
Anthony Skjellum	Tennessee Technological University, USA

CGPatch: Streamlining Static Call Graph Validation Using Selective Instrumentation

Sebastian Kreutzer[✉], Silas Martens, Peter Arzt, Tim Heldmann, and Christian Bischof

Scientific Computing, Technische Universität Darmstadt, Darmstadt, Germany
{sebastian.kreutzer,peter.arzt,tim.heldmann,
christian.bischof}@tu-darmstadt.de, silas.martens@stud.tu-darmstadt.de

Abstract. Static call graphs play a crucial role in program analysis, aiding in tasks such as security analysis, optimization, and performance profiling. However, dynamic language features, such as virtual functions and function pointers, may lead to missing edges in the call graph, which can affect the effectiveness of downstream analyses. Existing solutions rely on full program instrumentation to supplement static call graphs with dynamic information but incur significant runtime overhead, making them impractical for large-scale applications. In this work, we present CGPatch, a call graph validation and patching tool for C++ applications, combining link-time points-to analysis with selective instrumentation to efficiently resolve indirect function calls while minimizing runtime overhead. During execution, a runtime component captures missing edges, which are then used to augment the static call graph. Evaluation on three representative HPC applications demonstrates that CGPatch significantly reduces overhead compared to full program instrumentation while maintaining completeness, thus facilitating program analysis for large-scale applications.

Keywords: Call Graph Construction · Static Analysis · Clang/LLVM

1 Introduction

Static call graphs are fundamental to various program analysis tasks. In addition to their role in compilers for inter-procedural optimization [5], static call graphs are widely used in security analysis [18], debugging, and performance profiling tools [3,10]. For an accurate representation of a program's behavior, it is desirable that the static call graph represents a superset of all possible execution paths. However, the dynamic features of modern programming languages, such as virtual function calls and function pointers in C++, introduce challenges in achieving this goal. These features create function calls with targets that cannot always be resolved statically, leading to missing edges in the call graph. Such omissions can cause subgraphs to become disconnected, negatively impacting downstream analyses that rely on a complete and accurate representation of the program's structure.

While some of these inaccuracies can be mitigated through static analysis techniques, such as including all possible virtual function implementations, indirect calls via function pointers typically cannot be fully resolved statically. One approach to addressing this limitation is to supplement the static call graph with dynamic information gathered during program execution. MetaCG [11], a framework designed for constructing and managing static call graphs, provides a tool called CGValidate for this purpose. CGValidate takes a call path profile as input and compares the dynamically observed call graph with the static one to identify and insert missing edges. This approach, however, requires a fully instrumented version of the program to ensure consistency with the static call graph, which introduces significant run time overheads, often increasing execution time by orders of magnitude. As a result, this method becomes impractical for large-scale applications.

In this work, we present CGPatch, a hybrid call graph validation and patching tool for C/C++ applications, to address these limitations. CGPatch performs a link-time points-to analysis using the SVF framework [16] to try to resolve as many indirect calls as possible. This is combined with a selective instrumentation pass that specifically targets indirect function calls and emits lightweight runtime calls. During execution, a runtime library collects these calls and constructs a patch graph. This patch graph can be used to validate and, if necessary, augment the static call graph, thus improving its completeness for downstream analyses. While CGPatch is integrated into the MetaCG framework, it is designed to be compatible with other analysis tools, such as Phasar [14].

We make the following core contributions:

- Design and implementation of CGPatch, a call graph patching and validation tool for the Clang/LLVM compiler infrastructure that combines light-weight instrumentation with state-of-the-art static analysis.
- An in-depth evaluation of CGPatch on three representative HPC applications, focusing on completeness, as well as compile and run time overhead.

CGPatch is available as part of the MetaCG framework under the BSD 3-clause license at https://github.com/tudasc/MetaCG.

2 Background

This sections provides an introduction to static call graph construction and the MetaCG framework. In addition, it highlights relevant related work.

2.1 Call Graphs

A call graph is a directed graph that represents the calling relations between the functions of a program. They can be broadly divided into static and dynamic call graphs. Static call graphs are constructed by analyzing the source code or binary without running the program. A complete static call graph models every possible call relation, which may include calls that never occur in an actual run of the program [12]. At the same time, static analysis cannot fully resolve dynamic features which can lead to missing edges [1]. To reduce the number of missing edges, call graph construction algorithms may use over-approximation.

Dynamic call graphs, on the other hand, are generated at runtime. They can therefore fully resolve all visited call paths, but lack the generality of a static call graph. They are often used in profiling tools to represent program behavior.

2.2 Handling of Dynamic C++ Features

Some C++ features, such as dynamic dispatch (implemented via `virtual` function calls) and function pointers, cannot be fully resolved by static analysis.

Dynamic Dispatch: Dynamic dispatch can be handled by analyzing the set of possible call targets. There are two main algorithms. Class Hierarchy Analysis (CHA) [17] uses broad over-approximation. When encountering a virtual function call to a class `A`, CHA inserts edges to all overriding functions implemented in subclasses of `A`. This ensures that all possible call targets are represented. Rapid Type Analysis (RTA) [17] refines this approach, by only considering classes instantiated in the program.

Function pointers: C and C++ allow invoking arbitrary functions by address via function pointer calls. This feature is problematic for static analysis, as the exact call target is typically not statically decidable. In some cases, points-to analysis [13] can successfully identify call targets. This analysis tracks assignments to the called pointer to determine a set of possibly aliasing functions.

2.3 MetaCG

MetaCG [11] was developed as an extensible framework for generating and analyzing whole-program call graphs. It consist of the following components: **(1)** a file format for reusable annotated call graphs, **(2)** a library for loading, managing and analyzing call graphs in memory, and **(3)** CGCollector, a Clang-based tool for the construction and merging of call graphs. CGCollector uses CHA for resolving virtual calls and includes an experimental points-to analysis based on Zhang's FA analysis [13]. The workflow for generating a whole-program call graph is comprised of the following steps:

1. Collection of local call graphs for each translation-unit (TU).
2. Merging of individual local graphs into a unified whole-program call graph.
3. Completeness validation using `CGValidate` to compare, and if necessary, augment, the static call graph with a call path profile from a fully instrumented program run.

`CGPatch` aims to replace the current completeness validation method with a much more lightweight instrumentation-based approach.

2.4 Related Work

This section gives an overview of related work regarding the construction of static call graphs and the handling of dynamic features.

Lehr et al. [10] highlight the importance of complete call graphs in static analysis. They developed PIRA, an infrastructure aimed at automating the refinement of instrumentation configurations for performance analysis. Their tool relies on call graphs generated using MetaCG to iteratively refine the instrumentation configuration based on static and dynamic profiling data. The evaluation of this tool showed that missing edges due to function pointers could lead to the exclusion of performance-critical hotspots.

PhASAR [14] is a framework designed for performing inter-procedural static analysis on C/C++ programs at the LLVM-IR level. It supports static call graph construction, points-to analysis and data-flow analysis. However, it faces challenges in cases where function pointers are dynamically assigned or resolved through external libraries, thus leading to missing edges.

Antoniol, Calzolari and Tonella [1] examined how function pointers in C affect program comprehension, especially through its impact on the accuracy of call graphs. They implemented a flow-insensitive points-to analysis to solve this issue and tested it on 12 public domain programs and a large industrial system. Their findings reveal that on average, about 24% of functions in public domain programs were only reachable through function pointers. For the large industrial application they observed that 18% of functions were only reachable through function pointers.

Hubicka [5] developed the inter-procedural optimization framework for the GCC compiler, including an annotated call graph data structure. At later stages of compilation, this call graph is used to perform inlining. Indirect calls are not explicitly represented in the call graph. Functions that may be called by an indirect call are marked as externally visible and not inlined by the compiler.

Lhotak [12] presented a tool for comparing call graphs. This tool ranks edges by their likelihood of causing large differences in the call graph. When comparing a statically generated call graph with a dynamically generated one, they found missing edges due to dynamic calls. The tool can also be used to find superfluous edges reducing over-approximation of static call graphs.

Sui et al. [15] leveraged test suites with high coverage to approximate a dynamic ground truth call graph. This call graph was used to explore the limitations of static call graphs algorithms for four real-world Java applications. They highlight key issues like modeling dynamic language features, such as reflection.

Static and dynamic call graphs can be combined to produce more comprehensive call graphs. For example, the profiling tool Gprof [3] leverages the static call graph to augment edges not present in the dynamic call graph, as they may affect the overall structure.

In the context of Software Composition Analysis [18], both static and dynamic call graphs were employed to determine whether vulnerable library code is executed by an application. Foo et al. [2] developed a method of combining static and dynamic call graphs to improve accuracy. They evaluated their approach on four real-world Java projects and found that incorporating dynamic call graphs added on average 824% more vertices and 361% more edges, which resulted in more reachable vulnerable methods.

3 Design and Implementation

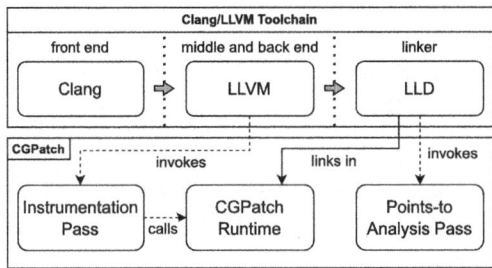

Fig. 1. Components of CGPatch and their interaction with the compiler toolchain.

This section describes the design and implementation of CGPatch. The proposed design is illustrated in Fig. 1 and consists of three primary components:

- A link-time whole-program analysis pass that attempts to statically resolve indirect calls.
- An LLVM pass that instruments function calls that cannot be statically resolved.
- A runtime library that collects information during execution and constructs a patch graph, representing potentially missing call edges.

To simplify integration, we provide a compiler wrapper that automatically sets the necessary flags, registers the analysis and instrumentation passes, and ensures correct linking of the runtime library. The workflow begins with each translation unit being processed by Clang, which generates LLVM IR. Our instrumentation pass is integrated into the optimization pipeline, where it detects and instruments indirect function calls. At link-time, an optional global points-to analysis is performed to attempt to statically resolve indirect calls. The CGPatch runtime library is then linked into the final executable, alongside the required LLVM and MetaCG dependencies. These dependencies are necessary for address symbolization and call graph construction, enabling the resolution of function addresses at runtime. Depending on the configuration, CGPatch requires compilation with either thin [6] or full link-time optimization (LTO).

3.1 Points-to Analysis

LLVM's built-in `basic-aa` pass does not support inter-procedural alias analysis and is, therefore, to limited for our purposes. Instead, our points-to analysis pass uses the `AndersenWaveDiff` analysis from the SVF framework [16]. For each indirect call, we determine the set of functions that may alias with the called pointer and insert corresponding edges into a static patch graph. This requires compilation with full LTO and can be costly to compute for large applications (see Fig. 4b).

3.2 Instrumentation Pass

The primary objective of the instrumentation pass is to detect and instrument function pointer calls in the LLVM IR. To track these calls, the pass inserts a runtime function call at relevant indirect call site in the IR. The pass operates in two phases:

Call detection and filtering: In this phase, the pass iterates over all call instructions in the translation unit (TU) and identifies indirect calls. These calls are then further analyzed to filter out virtual calls, as their targets can be resolved through static means. If enabled by the user, direct constructor and destructor calls are also considered, as they sometimes lead to missing edges when using source-based call graph construction [11].

Runtime call insertion: Once relevant indirect calls are identified, the pass inserts instrumentation calls to the runtime library. The inserted runtime function has the signature `__metacg_indirect_call(const char* caller, void* callee)`, where `caller` is the name of the caller function and `callee` the address of the call target. The function symbol corresponding to this address is not known at this point and must be resolved at runtime.

At the LLMV-IR level, calls to virtual functions look identical to calls via function pointers. Identifiying and filtering out virtual function calls is an important part of the pass, as it reduces the number of instrumented calls significantly. To distinguish these two types of indirect calls, we exploit the fact that virtual calls follow a specific pattern. This consists of loading the object address, loading its vtable pointer, computing the address of the vtable entry, loading the address of the underlying virtual function, and finally calling that function. By examining the def-use chain, we can identify the instruction that loads the vtable pointer. We can then query type metadata, emitted by Clang with `-fwhole-program-vtables`, to verify that the loaded address actually corresponds to a vtable. A drawback of this additional check is that Clang requires LTO (thin or full) to be active, to insert this metadata. It is, however, necessary in order to avoid falsely classifying regular indirect calls, mimicking the same pattern as virtual function calls.

3.3 Runtime Component

The CGPatch runtime library fulfills the task of collecting instrumented function calls and generating the patch graph. At the start of execution, the patch graph is empty. For every call to __metacg_indirect_call, the library first resolves the name of the function corresponding to the callee address. It then checks whether a call between the two functions has already been observed. If the edge is missing, the runtime ensures that both functions are present in the graph and then inserts the new call edge. At the end of execution, the graph is serialized and written to a file. To correlate dynamic addresses with the corresponding function name, we employ a symbol resolution mechanism from a previous project [8]. This method reads the memory map of the running process and extracts available symbols for each loaded object.

Handling MPI-parallel applications requires special consideration, since each rank executes an independent process. To maintain consistency, we first record separate patch graphs for each rank individually. We then intercept the call to MPI_Finalize using the MPI Profiling Interface (PMPI). At this point, we collect the local patch graphs and merge them into a single, unified graph in rank 0. This final graph is then written to a file.

3.4 Call Graph Construction and Patching Worfklow

Figure 2 visualizes the complete call graph construction and patching workflow. Starting with the source code, the static call graph is extracted by first creating TU-local call graphs, followed by the merge into one whole-program call graph. Using the CGPatch compiler wrapper, the application is compiled and instrumented. Optionally, points-to analysis is performed at link-time, resulting in a static patch graph that can be merged into the existing graph. Executing the instrumented binary yields a dynamic patch graph that can subsequently be used to validate or augment the static call graph.

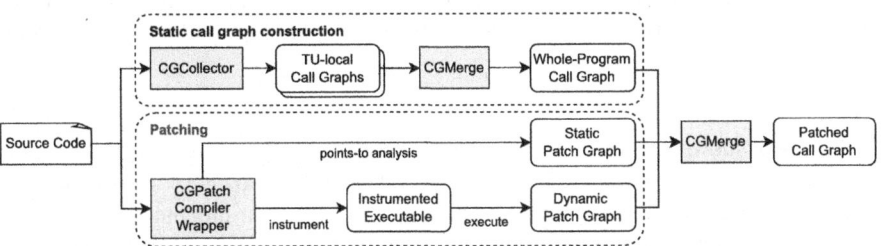

Fig. 2. Workflow for generating and patching call graphs with CGPatch. Shaded boxes represent tools and light boxes are artifacts. While our workflow relies on CGCollector for call graph construction, other tools can be integrated via a file format converter.

4 Evaluation

This section presents a detailed evaluation of CGPatch based on three representative applications: LULESH [7], a proxy application simulating hydrodynamic shock, AMG2013 [4], a parallel algebraic multigrid solver, and the much larger ISSM [9] code, used for ice sheet modeling and simulation. We compare CGPatch to the previously-used validation method from MetaCG, relying on full instrumentation. We consider the following core aspects:

1. **Completeness**: The extent to which our approach successfully identifies previously missing edges in the static call graph.
2. **Performance**: The amount of compile- and run time overhead incurred by CGPatch.

4.1 Setup and Methodology

Experiments were conducted on a single node of the Lichtenberg II cluster[1], comprised of 2 Intel Xeon Platinum 8470Q CPUs with a total of 104 cores and 512 GB main memory. All benchmarks were executed using 8 MPI processes.

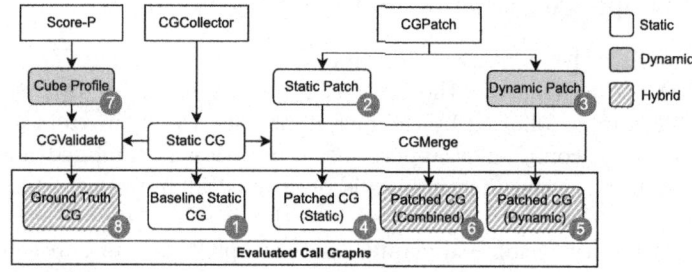

Fig. 3. Overview of the evaluation methodology. Different shading is used to differentiate between purely static call graphs (obtained through static analysis), purely dynamic call graphs (obtained through instrumented program execution) and hybrid call graphs (a combination thereof).

Figure 3 shows an overview of the evaluation methodology. CGCollector is used to obtain the static call graph (①). We use CGPatch to create a static patch (②), based on the point-to analysis, and a dynamic patch (③), using the selective instrumentation pass. In order to assess the completeness of our approach, we merge the patch graphs with the static call graph to obtain the patched call graphs (④ and ⑤). In addition, we create a *combined* variant (⑥) that uses both the static and dynamic patch. We validate the edges in the original static call graph and the three patched graphs with CGValidate. To this end, we

[1] https://www.hrz.tu-darmstadt.de/hlr/betrieb_hlr/hardware_hlr_1/hardware_und_konfiguration_hlr/index.en.jsp.

first create a fully instrumented binary and obtain a profile with Score-P (7). We then use CGValidate to detect and patch missing edges. The resulting call graph (8) serves as the ground truth for the completeness evaluation.

4.2 Completeness

Table 1. Completeness results for LULESH, AMG2013 and ISSM. Shown are the number of total edges (E), number of missing edges as detected by CGValidate (E_m), number of correctly reported missing edges ($\hat{E}_m$), number of functions reachable from main (F_r), and the relative increase in reachable functions compared to the static call graph (ΔF_r).

Application	Variant	E	E_m	$\hat{E}_m$	F_r	ΔF_r
LULESH	Static	5338	28	26	389	—
	Patched (static)	5338	28	26	389	0%
	Patched (dynamic)	5365	2	0	393	1%
	Patched (combined)	5365	2	0	393	1%
AMG2013	Static	3242	16	15	498	—
	Patched (static)	3244	15	14	498	0%
	Patched (dynamic)	3257	1	0	644	29%
	Patched (combined)	3258	1	0	644	29%
ISSM	Static	81674	122	3	3910	—
	Patched (static)	81813	121	2	7531	92%
	Patched (dynamic)	81679	119	0	7223	84%
	Patched (combined)	81817	119	0	7540	92%

Table 1 shows the results of the completeness evaluation. Some of the missing edges reported by CGValidate are false positives, and they are filtered out in the $\hat{E}_m$ column. A primary cause for these false positives are uninstrumented shared library dependencies. To illustrate this, consider a function A that invokes function B, with B defined in a shared library. If B calls a third function C, and C itself is instrumented (e.g., because it is defined in a header file), then the profiling tool will record an incorrect edge A→C. We consider third-party dependencies, which cannot be directly analyzed or compiled, to be out of scope of the analysis, and these defects can, thus, be safely ignored in this context. A secondary reason for false positives are destructor calls. On the source level, these calls are not always explicit and must be inferred by the call graph construction tool. We observe that in certain situations, calls to implicitly generated base class destructors are sometimes omitted by the compiler during code generation (i.e. before instrumentation is inserted). This can lead to slight inconsistencies between the static and the observed dynamic call graph, which we do not consider critical.

Excluding false positives, we observe between 3 and 26 true missing edges in the static call graph across the applications. Points-to analysis proved largely ineffective in resolving indirect calls for LULESH and AMG013. This can be explained by the fact that SVF is not able to track pointers stored in dynamically allocated heap memory. For ISSM, an important indirect call in the `FemModel::` `↪solve()` method can be resolved, adding 22 possible call targets and increasing the number of reachable functions by 92%.

With selective instrumentation, all missing calls are correctly identified and recorded across all applications. This has a pronounced effect on the number of reachable functions for AMG2013 and ISSM, increasing it by 29% and 84% respectively. Naturally, the best results can be gained by applying both the static and dynamic patch.

4.3 Performance

To assess run time overhead, we compare `CGPatch` with full pre-inlining instrumentation. All variants are compiled with full optimization (using the default optimization flags for each benchmark) and `-flto=thin` in order to eliminate effects due to different optimization. Figure 4a displays the increase in run time compared to the uninstrumented baseline. Full instrumentation significantly increases the run time for LULESH (68×) and ISSM (11×). The run time for AMG2013, a C code with fewer small functions, only increases by 15%. In contrast, the selective instrumentation with `CGPatch` incurs negligible overhead for the instrumentation itself, and approx. 3 s of constant overhead for initialization and IO.

Figure 4b compares the compile times of two `CGPatch` variants with the baseline build configuration. Compiling with thin LTO and selective instrumentation increases the compile time only moderately, with up to 12% for ISSM. The whole-program point-to analysis with full LTO, however, has a much bigger impact, increasing the ISSM compile time by a factor of 3.8×. For the smaller LULESH and AMG2013 applications, this effect is less pronounced.

4.4 Discussion

Results from the three evaluated applications demonstrate that `CGPatch` is an effective tool for patching static call graphs. It reaches the same level of completeness as a full instrumentation approach. The measured run time overheads, however, are orders of magnitude lower, thus significantly speeding up the validation and patching workflow. The small, near-constant overhead suggests that `CGPatch` could feasibly be enabled in production runs. `CGPatch`'s reliance on thin LTO, needed for accurate virtual call filtering, increased compile times only slightly. Whole-program points-to analysis with SVF yielded varying results and led to increased compile times. For very large applications, this static analysis approach may, therefore, be impractical. For ISSM, however, static patching was successful in creating a much more generalized call graph that covers execution paths for varying input configurations. Potential improvements could be made

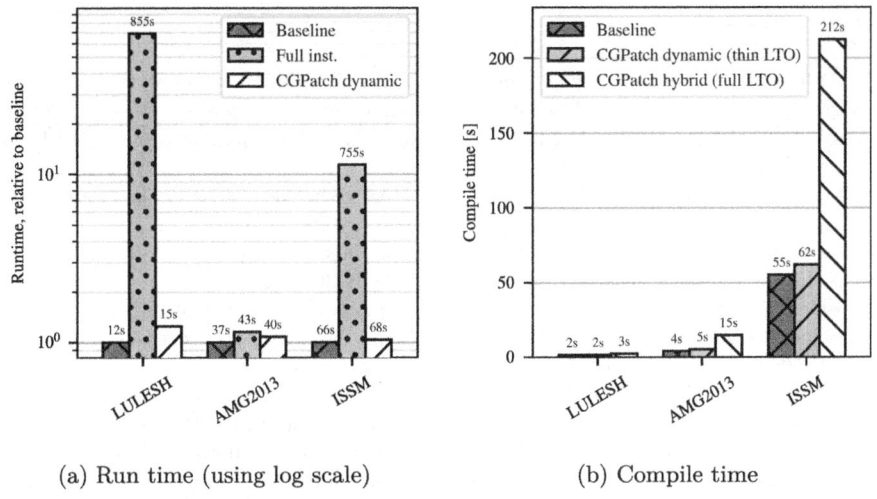

Fig. 4. Compile and run time results.

by applying an analysis that over-approximates w.r.t. memory operations on the heap, so as to track function pointers more effectively. For example, MetaCG's built-in source-based analysis is able to resolve all indirect calls in LULESH. However, it has issues with certain C++ language features and, as a consequence, does not work with complex codes, such as ISSM.

5 Conclusion

We present CGPatch, a tool to streamline static call graph validation and patching, using a combination of light-weight instrumentation and static analysis. A compiler pass identifies and instruments critical indirect functions, and a whole-program points-to analysis is used for further static resolution. We evaluated this approach on three applications, observing significantly reduced overheads compared to full instrumentation, while maintaining the same level of completeness. This greatly facilitates the call graph validation workflow for large-scale applications. Future work includes exploring alternative points-to analysis approaches to make static patching more effective and practical.

Acknowledgments. This work was in part supported by the Federal Ministry of Education and Research (BMBF) and the states of Hesse as part of the NHR program. The authors gratefully acknowledge the computing time provided to them on the high-performance computer Lichtenberg II.

Disclosure of Interests. The authors have no competing interests to declare that are relevant to the content of this article.

References

1. Antoniol, G., Calzolari, F., Tonella, P.: Impact of function pointers on the call graph. In: Proceedings of the Third European Conference on Software Maintenance and Reengineering (Cat. No. PR00090), pp. 51–59 (1999). https://doi.org/10.1109/CSMR.1999.756682
2. Foo, D., Yeo, J., Xiao, H., Sharma, A.: The dynamics of software composition analysis (2019). https://doi.org/10.48550/arXiv.1909.00973
3. Graham, S., Kessler, P.: Gprof: a call graph execution profiler. ACM SIGPLAN Notices **17** (1982). https://doi.org/10.1145/800230.806987
4. Henson, V.E., Yang, U.M.: BoomerAMG: a parallel algebraic multigrid solver and preconditioner. Appl. Numer. Math. **41**(1), 155–177 (2002). https://doi.org/10.1016/S0168-9274(01)00115-5
5. Hubicka, J.: The GCC call graph module: a framework for inter-procedural optimization. In: Proceedings of the GCC Developers' Summit 2004 (2004)
6. Johnson, T., Amini, M., David Li, X.: ThinLTO: scalable and incremental LTO. In: 2017 IEEE/ACM International Symposium on Code Generation and Optimization (CGO), pp. 111–121 (2017). https://doi.org/10.1109/CGO.2017.7863733
7. Karlin, I., Keasler, J., Neely, R.: Lulesh 2.0 updates and changes. Tech. Rep. LLNL-TR-641973 (2013). https://doi.org/10.2172/1090032
8. Kreutzer, S., Iwainsky, C., Lehr, J.P., Bischof, C.: Compiler-assisted instrumentation selection for large-scale C++ codes. In: Lecture Notes in Computer Science (including subseries Lecture Notes in Artificial Intelligence and Lecture Notes in Bioinformatics) **13387 LNCS**, pp. 5–19 (2022). https://doi.org/10.1007/978-3-031-23220-6_1
9. Larour, E., Seroussi, H., Morlighem, M., Rignot, E.: Continental scale, high order, high spatial resolution, ice sheet modeling using the ice sheet system model (ISSM). J. Geophys. Res. Earth Surf. **117**(F1) (2012). https://doi.org/10.1029/2011JF002140
10. Lehr, J.P., Hück, A., Bischof, C.: PIRA: performance instrumentation refinement automation. In: Proceedings of the 5th ACM SIGPLAN International Workshop on Artificial Intelligence and Empirical Methods for Software Engineering and Parallel Computing Systems, pp. 1–10. AI-SEPS 2018, Association for Computing Machinery, New York, NY, USA (2018). https://doi.org/10.1145/3281070.3281071
11. Lehr, J.P., Hück, A., Fischler, Y., Bischof, C.: MetaCG: annotated call-graphs to facilitate whole-program analysis. In: TAPAS 2020 - Proceedings of the 11th ACM SIGPLAN International Workshop on Tools for Automatic Program Analysis, Co-located with SPLASH 2020, pp. 3–9. Association for Computing Machinery, Inc, New York, NY, USA (2020). https://doi.org/10.1145/3427764.3428320
12. Lhoták, O.: Comparing call graphs. In: Proceedings of the 7th ACM SIGPLAN-SIGSOFT Workshop on Program Analysis for Software Tools and Engineering, pp. 37–42. PASTE '07, Association for Computing Machinery, New York, NY, USA (2007). https://doi.org/10.1145/1251535.1251542
13. Milanova, A.L., Rountev, A., Ryder, B.G.: Precise call graphs for C programs with function pointers. Aut. Softw. Eng. **11**, 7–26 (2004). https://doi.org/10.1023/B:AUSE.0000008666.56394.a1
14. Schubert, P.D., Hermann, B., Bodden, E.: PhASAR: an inter-procedural static analysis framework for C/C++. In: Lecture Notes in Computer Science (including subseries Lecture Notes in Artificial Intelligence and Lecture Notes in Bioinformatics) **11428 LNCS**, 393–410 (2019). https://doi.org/10.1007/978-3-030-17465-1_22/TABLES/1

15. Sui, L., Dietrich, J., Tahir, A., Fourtounis, G.: On the recall of static call graph construction in practice. In: Proceedings of the ACM/IEEE 42nd International Conference on Software Engineering, pp. 1049–1060. ICSE '20, Association for Computing Machinery, New York, NY, USA (2020). https://doi.org/10.1145/3377811.3380441
16. Sui, Y., Xue, J.: SVF: interprocedural static value-flow analysis in LLVM. In: Proceedings of the 25th International Conference on Compiler Construction, pp. 265–266. CC '16, Association for Computing Machinery, New York, NY, USA (2016). https://doi.org/10.1145/2892208.2892235
17. Tip, F., Palsberg, J.: Scalable propagation-based call graph construction algorithms. In: Proceedings of the 15th ACM SIGPLAN Conference on Object-Oriented Programming, Systems, Languages, and Applications, pp. 281–293. OOPSLA '00, Association for Computing Machinery, New York, NY, USA (2000). https://doi.org/10.1145/353171.353190
18. Zhao, L., et al.: Software composition analysis for vulnerability detection: an empirical study on java projects. In: Proceedings of the 31st ACM Joint European Software Engineering Conference and Symposium on the Foundations of Software Engineering. p. 960–972. ESEC/FSE 2023, Association for Computing Machinery, New York, NY, USA (2023). https://doi.org/10.1145/3611643.3616299

Speculative Recursion Unrolling

Tim Heldmann[✉][iD], Tim Ziegler[iD], Peter Arzt[iD], and Christian Bischof[iD]

Department for Computer Science, Institute for Scientific Computing, Technical University of Darmstadt, Hesse, Germany
tim.heldmann@tu-darmstadt.de

Abstract. In this paper, we propose a novel, annotation based approach to optimize recursive functions in C/C++ codes. It can be used to fully remove recursive structures, optimize the working pattern and gives the developer fine grain control over inlining behavior, leading to speedups of up to 40x. To achieve this we use Clang annotations and have developed an LLVM compiler pass that parses the developer given annotation and transforms the code accordingly. We demonstrate the effectiveness of this approach on 5 well known recursive algorithms. Our experiments show, that recursive functions that are not limited by memory bandwidth but computation intensity benefit the most from this optimization. Our code is available at https://github.com/tudasc/SpecRecUnroll.

Keywords: Recursion Optimization · Unrolling · LLVM

1 Introduction

When translating and optimizing code, a compiler needs to be conservative in its assumption about the codes behavior and most algorithms are designed to work for all possible inputs or cases. For most applications however additional information is known by the developer about the usage of these algorithms. If the compiler can get certain guarantees about the uses of an algorithm, be it due to domain knowledge of the developer or profiling of the application, it is possible to use these guarantees to generate significantly more performant code [1]. This especially relevant for recursive algorithms, which are especially hard to automatically analyze and optimize, because determining the exact behavior of any given call is dependent on the set of all possible program states that are reachable by any valid recursion. If a developer knows his depth-first search will only ever search through 10.000 nodes in a graph, the compiler could optimize the program with this knowledge. Here we present an approach, in which a programmer can annotate recursive function with guarantees about their recursion depth, expected recursion structure as well as the handling of the case where the assumption did not hold unexpectedly. The compiler will then optimize the program according to these guarantees, allowing it to fully remove the whole recursive tree if the given guarantee is strong enough, or generate code, which falls back to the original recursion pattern if the programmer specified a save assumption-violation behavior.

In this work we make the following contributions: (1) An annotation based optimization pass for recursive functions (2) An evaluation of its efficacy on some textbook recursive codes. (3) An analysis of the limitations and future possibilities of this approach. We will showcase our approach and explain our some of our implementation decisions in Sect. 2. The results of our approach will be evaluated in Sect. 3 and the limitations discussed in Sect. 4. We lastly give an overview of where this novel approach falls in the research field in Sect. 5.

2 Proposed Approach

2.1 Unrolling

The basic idea of unrolling a recursion is similar to inlining, in that the callee's function body is moved up towards the caller, with the exception, that in the case of recursive functions both functions are identical. Some recursive function like the faculty function (see Listing 1.1) only have point of recursion, where they will call one instance of themselves with a different set of arguments. This leads to a linear recursion structure (see Fig. 1). In these cases, we can simply inline an instantiation of the function body that has the new function parameters (see Listing 1.2. This leads to code that closely resembles what would be generated by loop unrolling.

```
int faculty(int n) {
    if(n<=0){return 1;}
    else{return n*fac(n-1);}
}
```

Listing 1.1. A textbook implementation of the faculty function.

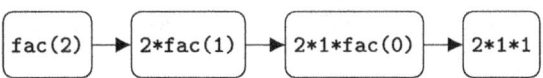

Fig. 1. The linear recursion chain of the faculty function, if instantiated with 2.

```
int facUnroll2(int n) {
    if(n<=0){ return 1;}
    else{
        if(n-1<=0){ return 1*n-1;}
        else{std::unreachable();}
    }
}
```

Listing 1.2. The same implementation but onrolled once. The developer gave the guarantee, that it is impossible to exceed a recursion depth of one.

Functions that do have a linear recursion structure like `faculty` are subject to the *TailCallElimination* optimization that is available in LLVM. This optimization can remove recursive calls and turn them into loops, if the recursive call is the last instruction of the function. This leads to a full elimination of functions like the faculty function, but also leads to a partial elimination in functions like Fibonacci (see Listing 1.3).

```
int fib(int n){
    // Base case
    if (n <= 1){return n;}
    // Recursive case
    return fib(n - 1) + fib(n - 2) ;
}
```

Listing 1.3. The green call to fib can be eliminated, as it is the last instruction before we return. The yellow call can not be eliminated. The function is therefore still recursive, with one less call path then before.

Functions that do not have their recursive call as their last instruction can not be optimized that way. Additionally functions that do not have a linear recursion structure, will still be recursive. Functions like Fibonacci have a tree like recursion structure (see Fig. 2). Quicksort's recursive structure follows that of a directed acyclic graph, while Depht First search's recursive structure is a general graph. These functions can still be subject to our recursion unrolling optimization, in which we iteratively inline every function call This might however lead to an exponential growth of the function body, if every function call spawns two or more new function calls.

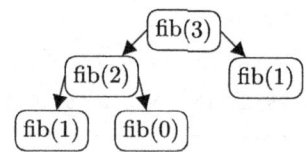

Fig. 2. A tree shaped recursive chain

For this there are two solutions. The first is to select which functions to inline and which to keep as a separate call. In the case of Quicksort for example, one can decide to only inline the recursive call to the top-level Quicksort function itself, and keep the partitioning and shuffling of elements as a separate call (see Listing 1.4. This approach can reduce the amount of instructions, but does not fully eliminate the exponential growth. For this we need to specify a tiered unrolling approach to suppress the exponential growth. We call this tiered approach *Chunking*.

```
void quicksort(int* vec, int low, int high) {
  if (low < high) {
    int pi = partition(vec, low, high) ;
    quicksort(vec, low, pi - 1) ;
    quicksort(vec, pi + 1, high) ;
  }
}
```

Listing 1.4. The green call to quicksort could be unrolled and inlined, but to keep instruction count lower, the yellow call to partition can be marked as excempt from inlining

2.2 Chunking

When unrolling a recursive function we can curb the exponential growth by generating the unrolled functions in chunks. Given a Mergesort that needs to sort 100,000 numbers, we would generate a tree with 17 layers. Assuming two instructions per level, one comparison and one swap, we would generate $2^{17} = 131072$ instructions. If we instead generate two chunks for this tree, we generate two functions with $2^{10} + 2^7 = 1024 + 128 = 1152$ instructions, which is much more manageable. This also allows us to handle cases where multiple different recursion depths are common. In the case of a recursive search algorithm, we might know that, if we do not find the correct element in the first 30 tries, we will probably need 100. If we did not find the correct element by then, we need to search through everything. One could then unroll this recursion with a chunk containing the first 30 unrolls, the common case, the first fallback case where one needed to search for 100 tries in total, and continue to search everything if this fails. This allows the compiler to generate more efficient code for the two common cases. This is akin to loop versioning. If no such behavior is either known of expected, it is still helpful to unroll the function into separate chunks to help with compile times and analysis complexity.

2.3 Annotation

To give the compiler the necessary information to do the transformations described above our approach uses the clang::annotate() mechanism, provided by Clang [2,3]. Placing these annotations in front of a declaration, like a function, Clang automatically connects the information provided in the annotation to the given function declaration. We then parse this annotation inside of LLVM [4] to transform the code accordingly. Our annotations folow the grammar shown in Listing 1.5. The basic form of a recursion unrolling annotation looks like this: [[clang::annotate(''SpecRecUnroll'', 5, ''↪SpecEndUnreachable'')]]. This will annotate the function with our custom SpecRecUnroll type annotation, that will unroll the recursion 5 times and will assume that a case where a greater unroll depth is needed, will never occur. In other words, we speculate the end to be unreachable (`SpecEndUnreachable`). Different options for the ending speculation are `SpecEndAbort`, in which case the compiler will generate code to abort the execution if the speculated assumption is invalidated, and `SpecEndContinue`, which falls back to the original implementation in case of violated assumptions. Unrolling the recursion then gives the compiler a better overview of the programs behavior and control flow, as the amount of code visible to the compiler inside a single function increase. The annotations can be extended to also hint the compiler towards expected recursion structure and to fine tune the unrolling behavior, with an annotation like: `[[clang::annotate(''SpecRecUnroll'', 30,70,1 ''SpecEndContinue'', ''parentInline'', ''markNoInline'', dfs)]]`. This annotation again is of type `SpecRecUnroll` but tells the compiler to generate chunks of sizes 30,70,1 and that we only want to unroll the part of the recursive chain that is opened by the function `dfs`, and keep other functions as calls. We then prohibit the compiler to do further inlining modifications on the functions generated by us with `markNoInline`.

```
annotation := 'clang :: annotate(" rec_unroll ",'( arg ',')* ')'
arg := functionRef | unrolldepth | '"' annotationLiteral
       '"'
annotationLiteral := 'SpecEndAbort' | 'SpecEndUnreachable'
       |
                     'SpecEndContinue' | 'this' |
                     'parentInline' | 'markNoInline'
unrolldepth := integer
functionRef := functionptr
```

Listing 1.5. This is the syntax of our pass in a BackusNaur form. Here integer can be any constant evaluatable integer and functionptr any valid constant evaluatable function reference in C++.

2.4 Assumption Violation Handling

This optimization uses annotations given by the programmer to achieve its improvements. Depending on how confident the user is in their assertion, they can decide what the program behavior should be, if the assertion is violated. This allows the compiler to do aggressive optimizations like the complete removal of all exception landing pads, as their reachability is now also subject to undefined behavior rules. If `SpecEndAbort` is chosen, the compiler needs to terminate the program, if the recursion depth is exhausted. This does allow for some of the aggressive optimizations discussed before, but optimizations passes like condition folding need to keep a default case with the abort statement. In both cases, the result is not valid if the recursion depth is achieved. If a programmer wants to achieve a valid result in the case of a violated assumption, the choice is `SpecEndContinue`, for which will keep on recursing. This can still give speed improvements for the more common cases while retaining correctness of the program. It is the safest choice and the default handling strategy if none is explicitly specified.

3 Evaluation

We evaluated our pass on five functions that are commonly implemented using recursion. We chose Fibonacci's function, Ackerman's function, a textbook Mergesort and Quicksort as well as a recursive Depth-First-Search. The relative runtime improvements are shown in Fig. 3, while the absolute runtimes are given in Table 1.

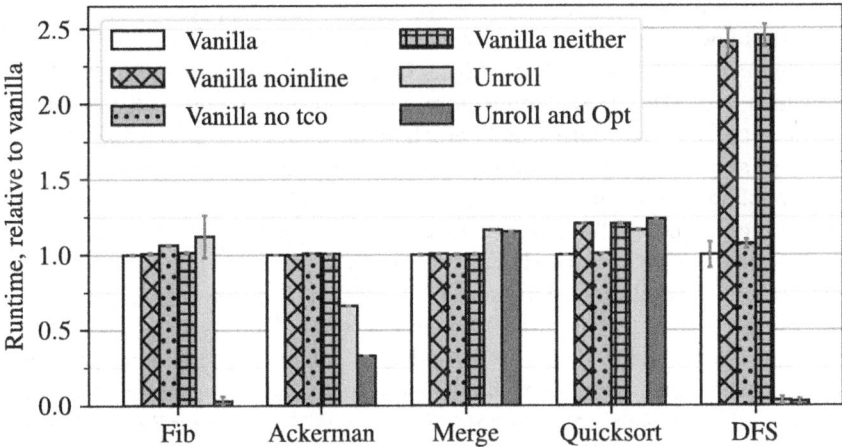

Fig. 3. The relative runtimes of the different compile variations. The white bar is the vanilla Clang -O3 pipeline. The hatched bars are variations of this vanilla pipeline, while the two filled gray bars are the results of the unrolling optimization. The error bars in red is the standard deviation. (Color figure online)

Fibonaccis function (Fib) was chosen as it shows the performance gains possible with complete recursion elimination for functions. Fib has two recursive calls, one of which can be subject to tail call elimination. As the other call needs to remain however, the overhead of calling a function still remains after the standard tail call elimination. When applying the unrolling optimization we need to consider that Fibs callstack grows in $O(2^n)$, which means we have to introduce chunks into the function. To reach the values given in Table 1, we gave the annotation: [[clang::annotate(''rec_unroll'', ↪ ''SpecEndUnreachable'', 10, 10,10,10, calcFib),gnu::pure]]. This generates four equally sized chunks. The unrolling optimization alone decreases the performance slightly, but running the O3 pipeline again will allow the compiler to generate a lookup table for each of the chunks, meaning this function has quasi-constant execution times.

Ackerman's function was chosen, as it is a common benchmark for recursive functions and their optimization. It shares the trait with Fib that it decreases one parameter until the parameter reaches zero. This means that we could technically eliminate the recursion fully as well. However, the recursion depth of the Ackerman function grows double exponentially. We therefore need to choose `SpecEndContinue` as our assertion for the compiler. We generate a chunk size of 3 with the annotation: `[[clang::annotate(''rec_unroll'',` `''SpecEndContinue'', 3, calcAck)]]`. As the Ackermann function itself does very little computation within each recursive call, unrolling alone decrease the runtime by about a third, as the compiler now does not need to create a separate function anymore. Running the unrolled function through a opt will improve the generated chunk again, reducing the runtime by another 50%. We see that chunking alone can be a good optimization in functions where compute overhead is low compared to the function call overhead.

Mergesorts shows behavior reaffirms this, as it is a non precomputable function, which is mostly limited to memory access speed. Mergesort has a fully predictable recursion structure which we thought would be exploitable. The time shown in Table 1 was for the annotation `[[clang::annotate(''rec_unroll'',` `''SpecEndUnreachable'', 17, mergeSort)]]`, generating a single large chunk, which we hoped to optimize. Our benchmarks however show, that Mergesort does not work well with this optimization.

Quicksort is similar to mergesort in its design, but does not show the same predictable recursion structure. We therefore could not give a guarantee for the maximum recursion depth and needed to resort to `''SpecEndContinue''`. We tried to generate larger chunks, similar to ackerman and continuing the recursion with `[[clang::annotate(''rec_unroll'', ''SpecEndContinue'',` `3, quickSort)]]`. We again saw however that Mergesort-like functions do not work well with this kind of optimization. Interestingly enough, trying to apply the unrolling optimization gives us performance that is similar to disabling inlining outright. It might be possible to get some additional performance if we specify the inlining behavior more strictly.

The recursive *Depth-First-Search* (DFS) however performs exceptionally well. It is linear in its recursive structure, meaning we can unroll to large depths without chunking. The unrolling alone is enough to

Table 1. Runtimes of the given function with the given compile pipeline, averaged over 5 runs.

Time in milliseconds	Vanilla	noinline	no tco	neither	Unrolled	Unrolled and Opt
Fib	2.424	2.442	2.577	2.456	2.718	0.074
Ackerman	1437.446	1437.720	1450.326	1445.602	951.321	471.802
Mergesort	15.223	15.306	15.235	15.262	17.707	17.533
Quicksort	15.562	18.768	15.674	18.759	18.098	19.235
DFS	0.813	1.957	0.870	1.991	0.028	0.024

give us a performance uplift of about 95%. Running the optimizer does improve this slightly to about 97%. The annotation was chosen as [[clang::annotate(``rec_unroll'', ``parentInline'', ``↪SpecEndUnreachable'', 100, &Graph::depthFirstFind)]].

All measurement runs for our evaluation have been conducted on the Lichtenberg cluster at TU Darmstadt on Intel® Xeon® Platinum 9242 CPUs with the different compile pipelines shown in Fig. 4.

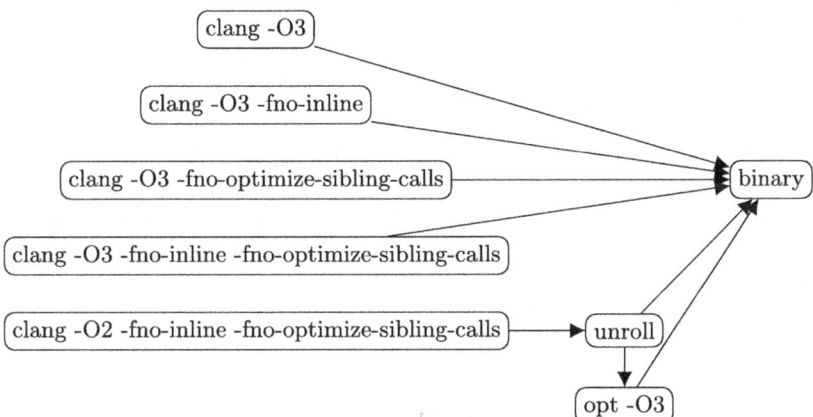

Fig. 4. The different compile pipelines, the unrolling optimizations needs some optimizations to happen before it runs but needs control over tail call elimination and inlining behavior. We therefore emit LLVM IR after it has gone through a O2 pipeline without those steps and then unroll it. We then run the unrolled code through the same O3 pipeline as all the other codes to get inlining and tail call elimination benefits where applicable.

4 Conclusion and Future Work

Our evaluation has shown our unrolling optimization to work well for cases in which the overhead of calling a function is high compared to the work done. The sorting algorithms did not benefit as much, as they are mostly limited by the memory speed. Quicksort proved especially difficult as it has no nicely predictable recursion scheme, and is double recursive. During our evaluation however, we have found three limitations of the current approach: (1) the need for the developer to give a good annotations, (2) the increase binary size, and (3) increase compile times.

We currently rely on the programmer to give us the necessary information on how to unroll, which pattern, and what to do in the case of a violated assumption the unrolling optimization can generate slower code in the case of a suboptimal annotation. Coming up with a suitable annotation is not only dependent on the developers knowledge of the functions behavior but sometimes also requires some trial and error. While some algorithms such as Depth-First-Search (DFS) benefit from as deep an unroll pattern as possible, this is not true for other functions like Mergesort. Generating a heuristic, which tries to choose the annotation parameters based on the observable recursion structure would be interesting, but leads back to the problem of recursive functions being hard to analyze from a compilers perspective.

Another limitation is the increased binary size after applying the unrolling optimizations. As we combine ideas from loop unrolling, which increases binary size, and inlining, which also can increase binary size, the resulting binaries after unrolling the recursion are larger as well. While this size increase can be observed very clearly in our lean benchmarking binaries, which consist mainly of the function to be benchmarked as well as some driver code, we argue that the binary size increase is less notable in real applications.

Compile times however are significantly longer. This is not due to the unrolling optimzation itself, which does not take to much time, but other passes that need to analyse and possible transform the large chunks generate by the unrolling transformation. We identified three passes which are significantly slower after unrolling: Instruction Combine, Inlining and Devirtualization ↪. Unrolling the recursion generates code with a many dependent arithmetic instructions, which need to be analyzed and checked for potential folding optimizations by the Instruction Combine pass. We can not reduce this, as we need this pass to optimize our generated code. The Inlining pass takes additional time, because incomplete unrolling generates many call sites, all of which have to be checked for potential inlining. In Listing 1.6 we see that unrolling without chunking squares the amount of call sites to be analyzed. The same is true for Devirtualization. It needs to analyze all call sites to find out if they call into a virtual function. We can either circumvent this by running later in the pipeline or, if possible, update their internal analysis state during our passes runtime.

```
int fib(int val) {
    if (val <= 1) return val;
    val1 = val - 1;
    if(val1 <= 1)fib_1 = val1;
    else fib_1 = fib(val1 - 1) + fib(val1 - 2);

    val2 = val - 2;
    if(val1 <= 1) : fib_2 = val2;
    else : fib_2 = fib(val2 - 1) + fib(val2 - 2);
    return fib_1 + fib_2;
}
```

Listing 1.6. Pseudocode for Fibonaccis function after being unrolled once with SpecEndContinue as the assumption violation behavior

5 State of the Art

While recursive algorithms can be very elegant with respect to how they are implemented, the execution overhead of a recursive function is typically higher compared to an equivalent iterative implementation of the same algorithm [5]. We want to give a quick overview of the existing optimization techniques for recursive functions, as well show to which extend the ideas of loop optimizations have been applied to recursive functions with out recursion unrolling approach.

Tail Call Elimination is one of the most helpful optimizations, transforming a recursive function into a loop, if the recursive calls result is the last instruction inside the function (or is the returned value). If this is the case the functions stack frame can be either be elided in interpreted languages or the whole recursive function turned into a loop. It completely removes the function creation overhead [6].

Hot-Cold-Splitting is the idea of splitting the control flow paths into a hot path, that is taken more often and a cold path, which is taken more rarely. Our unrolling optimization allows for a similar optimization with its chunking pattern. E.g. if a node is either found in 30 recursive steps or in 100 one can generate two chunks from the same DFS function.

Loop Versioning is similar to this, in that it generates two versions of the same loop, one with more agressive optimization assumptions than the other. These assumptions are then checked at runtime and the more aggressively optimized loop taken. Our approach takes inspiration in the assumption violation handling in that we allow the developer to fall back to a version of a function for which their annotation did not hold, at the price of some performance.

Flattening is an approach that is common when designing hardware. High-Level Synthesis (HLS) tools enable describing hardware in high-level languages like C, which support functions and recursion. While iterative algorithms can be translated into state machines, recursive algorithms must be flattened. Similar to our approach, these recursions are annotated with a depth, and flattened (inlined) until the specified depth is reached. The work by Stitt and Villarreal demonstrates that this method can eliminate recursion in some cases, enabling synthesis of previously impossible circuits, with hardware performance comparable to an iterative approach [7]. Our approach has similar effects and serves as a general-purpose optimization.

Rerolling recursive function has also been explored by [8]. They unroll the recursive function from the bottom, creating a larger and larger base case. After the specified size for the is reached for the base case, they reroll the basecase into a loop. This is possible because they now know the bounds.

References

1. Novillo, D.: SamplePGO - the power of profile guided optimizations without the usability burden. In: 2014 LLVM Compiler Infrastructure in HPC, pp. 22–28 (2014). https://doi.org/10.1109/LLVM-HPC.2014.8
2. Clang compiler user's manual (2025). https://clang.llvm.org/docs/UsersManual.html
3. Annotate LLVM Documentation (2025). https://clang.llvm.org/docs/AttributeReference.html#annotate
4. Lattner, C., Adve, V.: LLVM: a compilation framework for lifelong program analysis and transformation. In: Proceedings of the International Symposium on Code Generation and Optimization: Feedback-Directed and Runtime Optimization, CGO '04, pp. 75, USA (2004). IEEE Computer Society. ISBN 0769521029
5. Abelson, H., Sussman, G,J.: Structure and Interpretation of Computer Programs. MIT Press (2002). ISBN 9780262011532
6. Clinger, W.D.: Proper tail recursion and space efficiency. In: Proceedings of the ACM SIGPLAN 1998 Conference on Programming Language Design and Implementation, PLDI '98, pp. 174–185, New York, NY, USA (1998). Association for Computing Machinery. ISBN 0897919874. https://doi.org/10.1145/277650.277719
7. Stitt, G., Villarreal, J.: Recursion flattening. In: Proceedings of the 18th ACM Great Lakes Symposium on VLSI, GLSVLSI '08, pp. 131–134, New York, NY, USA (2008). Association for Computing Machinery. ISBN 9781595939999. https://doi.org/10.1145/1366110.1366143
8. Rugina, R., Rinard, M.: Recursion unrolling for divide and conquer programs. In: Samuel, P., (eds.), Languages and Compilers for Parallel Computing Ed. Berlin, Heidelberg: Springer Berlin Heidelberg, pp. 34–48 (2001). ISBN: 978-3-540-45574-5.

From C to Rust: Evaluating LLM Capabilities in Transpilation Through Compilation Errors

Andrea Valenzuela[✉], Marta Gonzalez-Mallo, Cristian Gutierrez, Dario Garcia-Gasulla, Gokcen Kestor, and Sara Royuela

Barcelona Supercomputing Center, Barcelona, Spain
andrea.valenzuela@bsc.es

Abstract. Migrating C code bases to Rust is increasingly attractive due to Rust's strong memory safety guarantees. However, code migration remains costly and time-consuming, motivating the use of Large Language Models (LLMs) to expedite the process while addressing limitations in traditional rule-based approaches. In this work, we evaluate the zero-shot performance of state-of-the-art open-source models on C-to-Safe-Rust transpilation, finding that general models achieve up to 50% in pass@1, with mid-sized coder models also performing competitively. Furthermore, we propose a hybrid approach where the C2Rust tool generates an initial unsafe Rust transpilation, which the LLM then refines into safe Rust. Results on this Unsafe-to-Safe-Rust transpilation task indicate general improvements across models, suggesting the usage of C2Rust as a preprocessing tool. Finally, we analyze common compilation errors, revealing LLM limitations in handling Rust-specific syntactic features such as null checks, C APIs, and iterators. Overall, this study characterizes the performance of LLMs for C-to-Rust transpilation and identifies their current limitations.

1 Introduction

Rust is a modern programming language that provides an innovative approach to traditional memory safety principles, particularly *ownership*, *borrowing*, and *lifetimes*, to enforce memory safety at compile time. This design enables Rust frameworks to prevent many code vulnerabilities before they manifest at program execution. Combining these safety guarantees and features like zero-cost abstractions positions Rust as a high-performance alternative to traditional low-level languages [2]. Rust is the only language besides C and Assembly integrated into the Linux kernel[1], underscoring its suitability for systems programming.

Despite Rust's increasing adoption in new projects, many legacy systems are written in low-level languages like C and C++. Although *transpilation*, i.e., converting source code to a different programming model while maintaining functionality and correctness, to Rust would enhance safety and maintainability, manual porting is prohibitively expensive and time-consuming.

---
[1] https://lwn.net/Articles/829858. Accessed: March 2025.

Different approaches have been proposed to automate C-to-Rust transpilation. The prominent *rule-based* tool is C2Rust[2] which analyzes the Abstract Syntax Tree (AST) of the C code to produce equivalent *unsafe* Rust code. Unsafe Rust does not fulfill Rust's memory safety requirements. Therefore, it can only bypass the compiler checks if explicitly marked with the unsafe keyword. This approach ensures semantic correctness by construction, i.e., I/O equivalence, but produces non-idiomatic and unsafe code that mirrors the original C code. Other rule-based approaches aim to rewrite the unsafe code produced by C2Rust into safer Rust constructs [4,5,8,14], mainly focusing on memory-related issues. However, these works disregard many other sources of unsafety, like calls to C standard libraries and the use of C-style unions and external variables.

Other transpilation methods involve Large Language Models (LLMs) [1], showing promising performance in transpilation tasks, thus facilitating the seamless migration and modernization of legacy software [6,7,13]. However, these works conclude the limitations of LLMs in ensuring functional equivalence and the need for techniques like meta-learning and feedback strategies. To cope with these limitations, hybrid approaches combining rule-based methods and program analysis have also been proposed to improve the LLMs' performance [9,11]. Even so, LLM-based transpilation presents a unique set of challenges, ranging from language paradigm differences, including memory models, type systems, and library mappings, to semantic preservation. Consequently, evaluating the effectiveness of various transpilation approaches and the available models is essential to understanding their limitations and potential for real-world adoption.

In this work, we evaluate the ability of state-of-the-art open-source LLMs to automatically translate C code into safe Rust (C-to-Safe-Rust) using *RustRepoTrans* [10], a benchmark specifically designed for repository-level C-to-Rust transpilation. Unlike competitive programming benchmarks [12], *RustRepoTrans* provides a more comprehensive evaluation by incorporating real-world software projects, ensuring that our assessment reflects practical challenges such as handling dependencies, complex control flows, and idiomatic Rust constraints. Beyond direct C-to-Safe-Rust transpilation, we introduce a hybrid approach that leverages the output of the C2Rust tool as an intermediate representation to assess the ability of LLMs to refine *unsafe* Rust into fully *safe* Rust (Unsafe-to-Safe-Rust). To better understand the limitations of these approaches, we conduct a detailed analysis of the compilation errors generated during transpilation. By categorizing and comparing these errors across both the C-to-Safe-Rust and Unsafe-to-Safe-Rust tasks, we identify common failure patterns. Through this comprehensive evaluation, we aim to understand the performance of state-of-the-art models across various C-to-Rust transpilation methods and provide insights for future improvements in automated transpilation techniques. Overall, this paper includes the following contributions:

– An evaluation of state-of-the-art LLMs in C-to-Safe-Rust transpilation.

---

[2] https://github.com/immunant/c2rust. Accessed: March 2025.

- A hybrid approach in which LLMs refine the unsafe Rust output of the C2Rust tool (Unsafe-to-Safe-Rust), shifting the focus from direct C transpilation to enhancing memory safety within the Rust ecosystem.
- An analysis of common compiler errors with the identification of patterns in C-to-Safe-Rust and Unsafe-to-Safe-Rust transpiled code.

1.1 Related Work

Rule-based transpilation prioritizes syntactic correctness over Rust's stringent memory safety guarantees, often failing to leverage idiomatic Rust abstractions such as ownership. The resulting Rust code is non-idiomatic and heavily relies on unsafe constructs. Several rule-based approaches aim to transform the unsafe code generated by C2Rust into safer equivalents. For example, *Zhang, H. et al.* incorporate Rust's ownership model to improve the safety of C2Rust-generated code [8]. *Emre, M. et al.* propose a method for analyzing the granularity of unsafe blocks produced by C2Rust and eliminating unnecessary uses of unsafe [5]. In a later work, they leverage compiler feedback to refactor a specific class of raw pointers into Rust references, improving both the safety and idiomatic quality of C2Rust output [4]. Finally, *Ling, M. et al.* focus on enhancing API safety by reducing the use of the unsafe keyword in function signatures [14]. However, none of these methods are capable of fully eliminating the unsafe constructs and non-idiomatic patterns generated by C2Rust.

LLM-based transpilation leverages model trained on code datasets to generate Rust code from C inputs. Unlike rule-based methods, LLMs are not bound by predefined transformation rules and can produce more idiomatic Rust code that aligns with best practices in memory safety and error handling. However, this approach lacks strong correctness guarantees, suffering from inconsistencies, especially when handling complex dependencies, API translations, or non-trivial C constructs.

Recent efforts aim to improve reliability through verification. For example, *Yang et al.* combine LLMs with formal verification to generate readable and functionally equivalent Rust code [13]. *Eniser et al.* propose using LLMs for direct C-to-Rust transpilation, validating correctness via differential fuzzing [6]. Finally, *Hong et al.* introduce a method that uses LLMs for accurate type migration during transpilation, addressing a common source of failure in LLMs [7].

Hybrid transpilation combines the strengths of rule-based methods and program analysis techniques with LLMs. *Shetty, M. et al.* propose dynamic analysis techniques to ensure semantic correctness and memory safety in the LLM-generated Rust code [11]. *Nitin, V. et al.* mirrors the rule-based approaches by converting the C code into unsafe Rust code using the C2Rust tool and using an LLM to convert the unsafe code into safer Rust [9]. These hybrid approaches balance correctness and idiomaticity, leveraging the systematic nature of program analysis and rule-based transpilation while incorporating LLMs' ability to generate more idiomatic Rust code.

2 Background

Rust is designed to provide memory safety and performance. Unlike traditional languages like C, it enforces memory safety guarantees at compile-time without a garbage collector. Despite its benefits, Rust's static analysis is conservative and only accepts programs that can be fully validated. This causes the rejection of code that might be correct when there is not enough information at compile-time, a common challenge in system-level applications involving low-level operations.

Rust provides a mechanism, namely *unsafe Rust*, to bypass strict guarantees: Code within the `unsafe` keyword can use memory unsafe operations, including dereferencing a raw pointer, calling an unsafe function, accessing a mutable static variable, implementing an unsafe trait, and accessing fields of a union. Listings 1.1 and 1.2 show an implementation that creates a variable and increments its value through its address using *safe* Rust and *unsafe* Rust, correspondingly. In the former case, a safe mutable reference is created and then dereferenced to perform the modification. In the latter case, a raw mutable pointer is used to access and modify the value directly. For compiling this unsafe operation, it needs to be embedded within an `unsafe` block as shown.

```
1  fn safe_modify() {
2      let mut value = 42;
3      // Safe mutable reference
4      let reference = &mut value;
5
6
7      // Safe modification
8      *reference += 1;
9      println!("Safe res: {}", value);
10
11 }
```

Listing 1.1. Safe Rust example.

```
1  fn unsafe_modify() {
2      let mut value = 42;
3      // Raw mutable pointer
4      let ptr = &mut value as *mut i32;
5
6      unsafe {
7          // Unsafe modification
8          *ptr += 1;
9          println!("Unsafe res: {}", *ptr);
10     }
11 }
```

Listing 1.2. Unsafe Rust example.

The Rust compiler detects a wide range of *compile-time errors* which help eliminate several memory safety issues before execution. These errors typically fall in three different categories: (1) *ownership and borrowing errors*, which prevent data races and ensure safe memory access, (2) *type mismatches*, which rely on the strong static type system of Rust, and (3) *lifetime errors*, which ensure that references are valid for the duration of their use and do not outlive the data they point to. Table 1 describes some of the errors emitted by the Rust compiler[3] and further analyzed in Sect. 4.

Although less frequent in safe Rust, *runtime errors* occur while the program runs in scenarios such as integer overflow (when not explicitly allowed) or panics due to assertions or out-of-bounds indexing. Rust's strong type system and compiler diagnostics make it a robust language, minimizing reliance on runtime checks while maximizing safety and performance.

---

[3] https://doc.rust-lang.org/error_codes/error-index.html. Accessed: March 2025.

Table 1. Examples of Rust error codes and the descriptions from the Rust manual.

Error Code	Description
E0038	A trait contains methods that are incompatible with dynamic dispatch.
E0061	An invalid number of arguments was passed when calling a function.
E0107	An incorrect number of generic arguments was provided.
E0252	Two items of the same name cannot be imported.
E0277	A type doesn't implement some expected trait.
E0308	Expected type did not match the received type.
E0425	An unresolved name was used.
E0432	An import was unresolved.
E0433	An undeclared crate, module, or type was used.
E0599	A method is used on a type which doesn't implement it.
E0609	Attempted to access a nonexistent field in a struct.
E0782	Trait objects must include the `dyn` keyword.

3 Evaluation Methodology

In this work, we focus on LLM-based and hybrid transpilation approaches to evaluate their ***syntactic correctness*** and ***functional equivalence***, ensuring that the resulting Rust code compiles successfully and preserves the expected behavior of the original C program. Syntactic correctness is assessed through successful compilation, while functional equivalence is checked with unit tests. While runtime performance and memory footprint are critical factors in practical software development, we defer their evaluation to future work.

In addition to correctness evaluations, we conduct a detailed compiler error analysis to categorize the types of errors introduced during the aforementioned transpilation processes. This analysis provides insight into the common failure patterns of each approach.

4 Evaluation

This section presents the results of the experiments conducted, including (1) the performance results of the state-of-the-art LLMs on `C-to-Safe-Rust` transpilation tasks in Sect. 4.2, (2) the results of changing the transpilation task from `C-to-Safe-Rust` to `Unsafe-to-Safe-Rust` in Sect. 4.3, and (3) the analysis of the most frequent errors occurring when LLMs address `C-to-Safe-Rust` and `Unsafe-to-Safe-Rust` transpilations in Sect. 4.4.

4.1 Evaluation Setup

To compare the performance across different LLMs, we implement the *RustRepoTrans* benchmark in the `BigCode Evaluation Harness`[4] framework, a widely adopted platform for the evaluation of coding tasks.

RustRepoTrans Benchmark: *RustRepoTrans* is a code transpilation benchmark that considers real C software projects which have been already migrated to Rust. For the benchmark construction, function pairs with equivalent functionality between the original C code and the Rust implementation are extracted, together with the function dependencies in the Rust code base. The target function signature is also supplied to the LLM, which is prompted to generate the complete target function. The correctness of the generated code is then verified by the compiler and the unit tests of the original Rust project, which report a 90% average test coverage.

The benchmark comprises 375 translation tasks, including projects initially written in C, C++, Java, and Python. We discard the non-C code bases from our analysis, resulting in 145 translation tasks. These functions belong to the *DeltaChat Core Library*[5], a messaging application with end-to-end encryption that relies on the IMAP/SMTP protocol, and to the cryptographic toolkit *Apache Milagro Crypto Library*[6]. Finally, we use the prompt provided by the *RustRepoTrans* benchmark and follow their hyperparameter definition, setting `temperature` to 0 to achieve greedy decoding.

Model Selection: We evaluate various open-source models, including popular ones such as Llama, Qwen and DeepSeek, considering the many categories and alternatives available. These alternatives include *general purpose models* trained mostly for natural language, *coder models* trained mostly with code, and also the LLMCompiler [3], a *domain-specific model* built upon CodeLlama (a Llama model trained for coding) and pre-trained to understand LLVM internal representation (LLVM-IR), several assembly languages, and optimization techniques. Finally, various sizes are included in the study to consider the role of scale, ranging from *small models* in the order of 7B parameters, to *medium models* under 70B parameters, and *big models* over 70B parameters. To cover all these categories, this work benchmarks 16 different LLMs.

Experiment Setup: We run the experiments on the *MareNostrum 5* supercomputer, using compute nodes with 4xH100 Nvidia GPUs. The number of nodes used goes from one node for smaller models to eight nodes for the larger ones. Results are reported using the `pass@k` metric, with k = 1, simulating the requirement of getting the right answer on the first try.

---

[4] https://github.com/bigcode-project/bigcode-evaluation-harness. Accessed: March 2025.
[5] https://rs.delta.chat/deltachat/. Accessed: March 2025.
[6] https://github.com/apache/incubator-milagro-crypto-rust. Accessed: March 2025.

4.2 Performance of C-to-Safe-Rust Transpilation

Let us now evaluate the `C-to-Safe-Rust` task using the selected state-of-the-art LLMs on the *RustRepoTrans* benchmark. Table 2 shows the model's performance according to the `pass@1` metric.

Table 2. Accuracy of different LLMs on *RustRepoTrans*, reported with `pass@k` when k = 1 (higher is better). Models are categorized according to their type: general models (top left), domain-specific models (bottom left, separated by the dashed line) and coder models (right). Models are sorted by performance within their respective categories. The general and coder models with the highest accuracy are highlighted in bold.

Model	pass@1	Model	pass@1
DeepSeek-R1-685B	**51.03**	**Qwen2.5-Coder-14B-Instr**	**35.86**
Llama-3.1-405B-Instr	38.62	DeepSeek-Coder-V2-236B-Instr	26.21
DeepSeek-R1-Distill-Qwen-32B	36.55	Qwen2.5-Coder-32B-Instr	25.52
Llama-3.3-70B-Instr	27.58	OpenCoder-8B-Instr	17.24
DeepSeek-R1-Distill-Qwen-14B	26.90	CodeGemma-7B-Instr	17.24
Qwen2.5-14B-Instr	18.62	StarChat2-v0.1-15B	13.10
Llama-3.1-8B-Instr	5.52	CodeLlama-7B-Instr	9.66
LLMCompiler-13B	18.62	DeepSeek-Coder-V2-16B-Instr	8.97

We do not observe a strong correlation between performance and model size from the results. Nevertheless, *DeepSeek-R1* considerably outperforms all other models under consideration, achieving 51.03% in `pass@k`—a +12.41% improvement over the second-best model, *Llama-3.1-405B-Instr*.

Qwen2.5-Coder-14B-Instr, among the coder models, and *DeepSeek-R1-Distill-Qwen-32B*, among the general models, also demonstrate competitive performance with 35.86% and 36.55% in `pass@k`, respectively, despite having significantly smaller model sizes than the top two models.

Surprisingly, the 32-billion-parameter variant of *Qwen2.5-Coder* shows a roughly 10% decrease in `pass@k` compared to its 14-billion-parameter counterpart. This suggests that while larger models may generalize better, they might sacrifice some domain-specific performance as a trade-off. Nevertheless, *Qwen2.5-Coder-32B-Instr* still shows competitive performance compared to larger models such as *Llama-3.3-70B-Instruct* and *DeepSeek-Coder-V2-236B-Instr*.

Finally, the distilled variants of *DeepSeek-R1* also achieve competitive performance relative to larger models, with *DeepSeek-R1-Distill-Qwen-32B* reporting a decrease of 14.48% in `pass@k` compared to *DeepSeek-R1*.

Regarding the domain-specific *LLMCompiler-13B*, we observe an approximately +9% increase in accuracy compared to its base model, *CodeLlama-7B-Instruct*, exposing promising results when using low-level languages like the

LLVM-IR that get rid of syntactic decorations and can let the model focus on the semantics.

Compared to the original *RustRepoTrans* study, we observe similar pass@k for the open-source models included in both studies, namely *Llama-3.1-8B-Instruct* and *DeepSeek-Coder-V2-16B-Instr*.

4.3 Performance of Unsafe-to-Safe-Rust Transpilation

The C-to-Safe-Rust task can be transformed, if previously using a rule-based tool like C2Rust, into a Unsafe-to-Safe-Rust task, where the input of the LLM is the unsafe Rust generated by such tool. This section explores how model performance changes under this new setting. To that end, we first transpile the *DeltaChat* code base present in *RustRepoTrans* with the C2Rust tool. Notably, we encountered ten E0061 compilation errors (see Table 1) due to multiple instances of two functions that take no arguments, but where one argument was supplied. After manually addressing these issues, we extract the unsafe functions to prompt the LLM with an Unsafe-to-Safe-Rust task.

During evaluation, the compiler explicitly forbids using any unsafe code through the #![forbid(unsafe_code)] compiler directive. We compare the

Table 3. Accuracy of different LLMs on *RustRepoTrans*, reported with pass@k (k = 1), for the C-to-Safe-Rust task (C-to-Safe column) and the proposed Unsafe-to-Safe-Rust task (Unsafe-to-Safe column) on the *DeltaChat* code base. Models are ordered by performance on the new Unsafe-to-Safe-Rust task. The general model and coder model with the highest performance increase are highlighted in bold.

Model Name	C-to-Safe	Unsafe-to-Safe	Diff
DeepSeek-R1	47.2	54.84	7.64
DeepSeek-R1-Distill-Qwen-32B	32.8	50.00	17.20
Qwen2.5-Coder-14B-Instr	33.6	48.39	14.79
Qwen2.5-Coder-32B-Instr	21.6	46.77	**25.17**
DeepSeek-Coder-V2-Instr	22.4	40.32	17.92
Llama-3.3-70B-Instr	20.0	39.52	19.52
OpenCoder-8B-Instr	14.4	36.29	21.89
Qwen2.5-14B-Instr	13.6	33.87	**20.27**
CodeGemma-7B-Instruct	17.6	31.45	13.85
LLMCompiler-13B	18.4	29.03	10.63
Llama-3.1-405B-Instr	31.2	25.81	−5.39
DeepSeek-Coder-V2-16B-Instr	4.0	24.19	20.19
Llama-3.1-8B-Instr	1.6	20.16	18.56
CodeLlama-7B-Instruct	8.8	17.74	8.74
DeepSeek-R1-Distill-Qwen-14B	20.8	12.9	−7.90
StarChat2-v0.1-15B	9.6	4.03	−5.57

model performance on the Unsafe-to-Safe-Rust task with that of regular C-to-Safe-Rust in Table 3.

Results show that a majority of models (13 out of 16) exhibit improved performance when translating from Unsafe-to-Safe-Rust, as compared to the standard C-to-Safe-Rust translation task. This finding suggests that, for most of the models, the Unsafe-to-Safe-Rust transformation may be more tractable, potentially due to the syntactic and semantic proximity between unsafe and safe Rust, which reduces the translation gap. Notably, code-specialized models like *Qwen2.5-Coder-32B-Instr* and *OpenCoder-8B-Instr* achieve substantial gains, with +25.17% and +21.89% respectively. On the other hand, some general-purpose models, such as *Llama-3.1-405B-Instr* and *DeepSeek-R1-Distill-Qwen-14B*, still show performance drops. These mixed outcomes indicate that while Unsafe-to-Safe-Rust transpilation is not universally easier, modern code-focused models can increasingly handle such transformations more effectively. Therefore, we observe the potential benefits of adding C2Rust as a preprocessing step on LLM-based approaches for specific models.

4.4 Compilation Error Analysis

After considering the proportion of cases in which code can be compiled without errors, we follow an open coding approach to process the error messages for each failing task and classify each error according to the error code. We run error deduplication based on the error message and line number within the same failing task. We then gather each model's 5 most frequent error codes, leading to the 12 errors previously shown in Table 1.

We analyze those errors on the C-to-Safe-Rust and Unsafe-to-Safe-Rust tasks and study their distribution. Results are reported using polar plots, showing the subset of the most frequent errors.

Figure 1 shows errors on the C-to-Safe-Rust task for the best performant models of our study. The plot shows how certain errors are recurrent and frequent across models when doing the C-to-Safe-Rust task (e.g., E0599, E0425 and E0061). Next paragraphs analyze in detail the sources of these errors.

E0599: A Method is Used on a Type Which Doesn't Implement It. The core cause of this error is missing trait implementations or method definitions when moving from C's free-function, pointer-driven style into Rust's trait-based system. One repeating source of this error points to a wrong translation of the C-style null checking. While in C, NULL is commonly checked directly (e.g., if (context == NULL)), Rust uses the None variant of the Option type to represent the absence of a value, or the built-in .is_none() method. Some transpilation instances use direct null checking as in the original C code. E0599 also includes instances of functions coming from job C management libraries (e.g., kill_job() or add_job()) or database transaction handling libraries (e.g., commit_transaction()) that are not native in Rust. To achieve equivalent functionality in Rust, the LLM should identify existing Rust crates (such as nix for process and signal management, or sqlx for database transactions) that provide

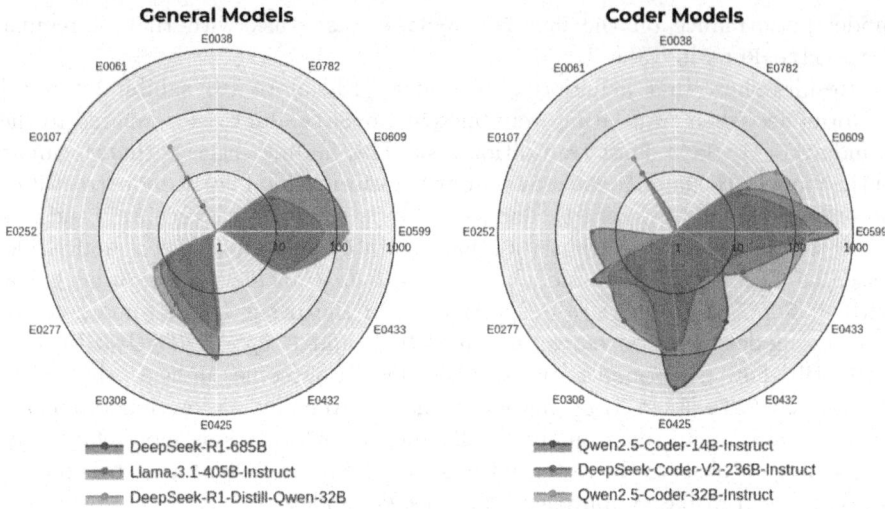

Fig. 1. Polar plot of the most frequent Rust compilation errors caused by the best-performing LLMs (log scale) in the `C-to-Safe-Rust` transpilation task. General models are on the left and coder models are on the right.

similar capabilities or explicitly implement the required functionalities. These findings show a lack of understanding of the Rust ecosystem or an assumption that the same method names from a C-style database API would apply directly. In a similar line, different instances of this error reveal the differences in iteration semantics between the two languages. In C, iterating over a container manually uses pointers and loops, whereas Rust requires types to implement the `Iterator` trait explicitly. We find instances where the LLM assumed an object was iterable without implementing the `Iterator` trait.

E0425: An Unresolved Name was Used. This error occurs when Rust code references identifiers that have not been declared in the current scope, often because they originated as C preprocessor macros or global symbols. In C, the preprocessor handles text substitution, conditional compilation, and code inclusion via `#define` macros, allowing descriptive names in place of literals. Nevertheless, Rust has no global preprocessor and every external name must be explicitly declared or brought into scope with `use`. We observe that this error arises from the LLM omitting these Rust declarations or imports.

Miscellaneous Errors. Among others, we observe a misunderstanding with the `self` keyword. While in C, `self` is not a language feature but a convention, in Rust it is a built-in keyword with specific behavior tied to Rust's ownership, mutability, and borrowing concepts. Failing to handle this correctly during transpilation leads to errors in method calls. Additionally, we encounter C functions and variables with names that conflict with Rust keywords. In those cases, the LLM should be able to identify those keywords and rename the original instance. Finally, another frequent issue arises from translating C macros into Rust functions. C macros are purely textual substitutions handled by the preprocessor, allowing them to be type-agnostic and accept various arguments. Rust functions, by contrast, are strongly typed, requiring explicit type annotations or generics. This difference means that naive translation of macros into Rust functions fails to compile without explicit type handling.

Error Complexity. We observe that the most frequent errors stem from a lack of understanding of the Rust ecosystem and foundational language features such as type lifting, keyword misuse, and incorrect API calls. Other reported errors include passing an invalid number of arguments to a function (E0061), referencing an undeclared crate, module, or type (E0433), and attempting to access a nonexistent field in a *struct* (E0609). Surprisingly, we did not observe errors directly related to Rust's ownership model, borrowing semantics, or lifetimes. To investigate this anomaly, we extracted error messages directly from the Rust compiler's borrow checker and explicitly checked for their presence, finding only isolated occurrences. We hypothesize that the complexity of repository-level benchmarks causes LLMs to struggle with surface-level coding errors rather than deeper language semantics.

Unsafe-to-Safe-Rust Errors. Figure 2 compares the error distribution of C-to-Safe-Rust and Unsafe-to-Safe-Rust tasks for the models reporting the highest increase in performance, namely *Qwen2.5-14B-Instr* from the general models and *Qwen2.5-Coder-32B-Instr* from the coder models. Overall, we observe a reduction on the number of errors for the Unsafe-to-Safe-Rust task. For example, we observe more errors regarding using undeclared crate, module or type (E0433) in the C-to-Safe-Rust task than in the Unsafe-to-Safe-Rust task. We hypothesize that the LLM might not be familiar with the Rust crates, modules or types that replace the C ones, leading to more E0433 errors.

Runtime and Functional Errors. In cases where compilation succeeded, we also observed instances of functional errors. During evaluation, we measured the proportion of transpilation tasks that both compiled and passed the unit tests. Table 4 presents the pass@k when considering only compilation in the evaluation, alongside the pass@k when both compilation and unit testing are considered during the evaluation. The last column shows the performance drop between compilation and unit testing. This analysis aims to determine whether the models face greater challenges in generating code that compiles or preserving the original code's intended functionality.

Overall, we observe a trend where the best-performing models in terms of compilation success also exhibit a notable decrease in pass@k when unit tests are considered, e.g. *DeepSeek-R1-685B* and *Llama-3.1-405B-Instr*. This suggests that while these models are adept at generating syntactically correct code that compiles, they struggle to maintain the intended functionality.

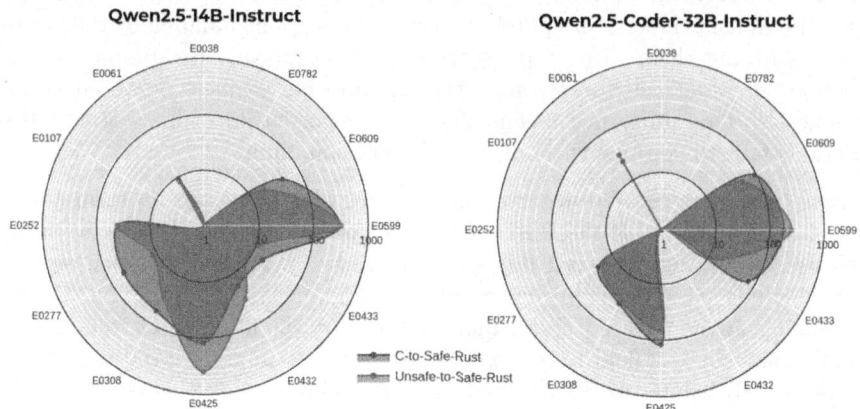

Fig. 2. Polar plot of the most frequent Rust compilation errors in the different transpilation tasks (log scale). In blue, `C-to-Safe-Rust`. In red, `Unsafe-to-Safe-Rust`. (Color figure online)

Table 4. Accuracy of the different LLMs, reported with `pass@k` (k = 1), when comparing evaluation based only on syntactic correctness (*Compilation* column) and evaluation based on syntactic correctness and functional equivalence (*Unit tests* column). The *Diff* column shows the performance drop between both approaches. Models are sorted as in Table 2 and the highest accuracy drop is highlighted in bold.

Model Name	Compilation	Unit tests	Diff
DeepSeek-R1-685B	51.03	60.00	-8.97
Llama-3.1-405B-Instr	38.62	48.97	**-10.35**
DeepSeek-R1-Distill-Qwen-32B	36.55	43.45	-6.90
Llama-3.3-70B-Instr	27.58	34.48	-6.90
DeepSeek-R1-Distill-Qwen-14B	26.90	28.97	-2.07
Qwen2.5-14B-Instr	18.62	20.69	-2.07
Llama-3.1-8B-Instr	5.52	6.21	-0.69
LLMCompiler-13B	18.62	20.00	-1.38
Qwen2.5-Coder-14B-Instr	35.86	39.31	-3.45
DeepSeek-Coder-V2-Instr	26.21	32.41	-6.20
Qwen2.5-Coder-32B-Instr	25.52	33.10	-7.58
OpenCoder-8B-Instr	17.24	17.93	-0.69
CodeGemma-7B-Instruct	17.24	19.31	-2.07
StarChat2-v0.1-15B	13.10	14.48	-1.38
CodeLlama-7B-Instruct	9.66	10.34	-0.68
DeepSeek-Coder-V2-16B-Instr	8.97	9.66	-0.69

5 Conclusions and Future Work

This study shows that state-of-the-art general models achieve up to 50% in pass@1 on the C-to-Safe-Rust transpilation task, with mid-sized coder models ranking among the top performers, reaching up to 35% in pass@1. In contrast, we find that most models improved their performance when targeting the Unsafe-to-Safe-Rust task, with pass@1 improvements of up to 25%. We observe that this task appears well within reach for many code-specialized models. These findings highlight the potential of LLMs in converting unsafe Rust to safe Rust, shifting the focus from the regular C-to-Rust transpilation to a more refined task. This also suggests the potential benefits of integrating the C2Rust tool as a preprocessing step for LLM-based approaches.

Furthermore, we identify that the most recurrent compilation errors made by LLMs during transpilation stem from a lack of understanding of the Rust ecosystem and its syntactic rules. These errors often include direct transpilation of C-style features such as null-checking, C API calls, and the misuse of Rust-specific keywords. We observe that models fail the transpilation task due to surface-level coding errors rather than deeper language semantics like ownership and advanced Rust features.

We also characterize the error distribution for the Unsafe-to-Safe-Rust task. We find that although the number of errors is reduced, the overall shape of the distribution remains consistent. Finally, we observe that models with higher pass@k scores struggle to maintain code functionality relative to the number of generated samples that successfully compile.

As future work, we plan to continue exploring the usage of the C2Rust tool as a preprocessing step to guide the LLM in the transpilation process, specifically focusing on the limitations of starting the transpilation task from unsafe Rust. Furthermore, regarding the error analysis, we plan to explore the impact of simplifying the translation tasks, e.g., by employing competitive programming benchmarks. Such a controlled environment could reveal whether LLM transpilation shifts away from shallow syntactic errors and progresses further along the compilation chain, potentially uncovering issues detectable by the borrow checker. This may allow us to characterize how effectively LLMs handle Rust's memory system features, offering deeper insights into their understanding of ownership, borrowing, and lifetimes.

Energy Consumption. The execution of the experiments presented in this work resulted in a total energy consumption of 927.1 MJ approximately, corresponding to an estimated 259.6 kg of CO_2 emissions.

Acknowledgments. This work was partially funded by the HiPART project, with reference PID2023-148117NA-I00, financed by MICIU/AEI /10.13039/501100011033 and FEDER, UE. Andrea Valenzuela, Critian Gutierrez and Gokcen Kestor fellowships within the "Generación D" initiative, Red.es, Ministerio para la Transformación Digital y de la Función Pública, for talent attraction (C005/24-ED CV1). Funded by the European Union NextGenerationEU funds, through PRTR.

References

1. Bhatia, S., Qiu, J., Hasabnis, N., Seshia, S., Cheung, A.: Verified code transpilation with LLMs. Adv. Neural. Inf. Process. Syst. **37**, 41394–41424 (2024)
2. Bugden, W., Alahmar, A.: Rust: the programming language for safety and performance. arXiv preprint arXiv:2206.05503 (2022)
3. Cummins, C., et al.: LLM compiler: foundation language models for compiler optimization. In: Proceedings of the 34th ACM SIGPLAN International Conference on Compiler Construction, pp. 141–153 (2025)
4. Emre, M., Boyland, P., Parekh, A., Schroeder, R., Dewey, K., Hardekopf, B.: Aliasing limits on translating C to safe Rust. Proc. ACM Program. Lang. **7**(OOPSLA1), 551–579 (2023)
5. Emre, M., Schroeder, R., Dewey, K., Hardekopf, B.: Translating C to safer Rust. Proc. ACM Program. Lang. **5**(OOPSLA), 1–29 (2021)
6. Eniser, H.F., et al.: Towards translating real-world code with LLMs: a study of translating to Rust. arXiv:2405.11514 (2024)
7. Hong, J., Ryu, S.: Type-migrating C-to-Rust translation using a large language model. Empir. Softw. Eng. **30**(1), 3 (2025)
8. Ling, M., Yu, Y., Wu, H., Wang, Y., Cordy, J.R., Hassan, A.E.: In Rust we trust: a transpiler from unsafe C to safer Rust. In: Proceedings of the ACM/IEEE 44th International Conference on Software Engineering: Companion Proceedings, pp. 354–355 (2022)
9. Nitin, V., Krishna, R., Valle, L.L.d., Ray, B.: C2SaferRust: transforming C projects into safer rust with neurosymbolic techniques. arXiv preprint arXiv:2501.14257 (2025)
10. Ou, G., Liu, M., Chen, Y., Peng, X., Zheng, Z.: Repository-level code translation benchmark targeting Rust. arXiv:2411.13990 (2024)
11. Shetty, M., Jain, N., Godbole, A., Seshia, S.A., Sen, K.: Syzygy: dual code-test C to (safe) rust translation using LLMs and dynamic analysis. arXiv:2412.14234 (2024)
12. Yan, W., Tian, Y., Li, Y., Chen, Q., Wang, W.: CodeTransOcean: a comprehensive multilingual benchmark for code translation. arXiv:2310.04951 (2023)
13. Yang, A.Z., Takashima, Y., Paulsen, B., Dodds, J., Kroening, D.: VERT: verified equivalent rust transpilation with large language models as few-shot learners. arXiv:2404.18852 (2024)
14. Zhang, H., David, C., Yu, Y., Wang, M.: Ownership guided C to Rust translation. In: International Conference on Computer Aided Verification, pp. 459–482. Springer (2023)

CompilerGPT: Leveraging Large Language Models for Analyzing and Acting on Compiler Optimization Reports

Peter Pirkelbauer[✉][iD] and Chunhua Liao[iD]

Lawrence Livermore National Laboratory, Livermore, CA 94550, USA
{pirkelbauer2,liao6}@llnl.gov

Abstract. Current compiler optimization reports often present complex, technical information that is difficult for programmers to interpret and act upon effectively. This paper assesses the capability of large language models (LLM) to understand compiler optimization reports and automatically rewrite the code accordingly.

To this end, the paper introduces CompilerGPT, a novel framework that automates the interaction between compilers, LLMs, and user defined test and evaluation harness. CompilerGPT's workflow runs several iterations and reports on the obtained results.

Experiments with two leading LLM models (GPT-4o and Claude Sonnet), optimization reports from two compilers (Clang and GCC), and five benchmark codes demonstrate the potential of this approach. Speedups of up to 6.5x were obtained, though not consistently in every test. This method holds promise for improving compiler usability and streamlining the software optimization process.

1 Introduction

Compilers translate source code into optimized machine code that can be executed by computers. The code generation and optimization passes are opaque to software engineers. Compilers such as Clang/LLVM and GCC can generate optimization reports to make the optimization process more transparent. However, compiler optimization reports are often hard to understand, requiring considerable expertise to interpret and act upon. This complexity hinders the effective utilization of compiler optimization capabilities, limiting their potential impact on software development.

Large language models (LLMs), such as GPT-4, Claude, and Gemini, with their capabilities in natural language understanding and code generation, offer

---

This manuscript has been authored by Lawrence Livermore National Security, LLC under Contract No. DE-AC52-07NA27344 with the US. Department of Energy. The United States Government retains, and the publisher, by accepting the article for publication, acknowledges that the United States Government retains a non-exclusive, paid-up, irrevocable, world-wide license to publish or reproduce the published form of this manuscript, or allow others to do so, for United States Government purposes.

© The Author(s), under exclusive license to Springer Nature Switzerland AG 2026
S. Neuwirth et al. (Eds.): ISC High Performance 2025 Workshops, LNCS 16091, pp. 325–338, 2026.
https://doi.org/10.1007/978-3-032-07612-0_25

Table 1. Challenges and Solutions when Designing CompilerGPT

Challenge	Solution
Complex Process	Chain-of-thought (CoT) style prompting
Hallucination	Iterative Compilation, Testing and Correction
Context Window Limit	Code snippet optimization
Verbose Reports	LLM prioritization of high-impact optimizations
Unwanted Outputs	Negative Prompting
Context Sensitive	Maintaining a conversation history

a promising avenue for bridging the semantic gap between compiler output and human understanding. Using a technique called self-supervised learning, LLMs are trained on massive datasets of text and code. This process allows them to learn complex patterns, relationships, and contextual information, enabling them to generate human-quality text and code and perform a variety of other code-related tasks, including code completion, bug detection, and code summarization.

Our *research hypothesis* is that LLMs, when appropriately integrated with a compiler and a robust evaluation framework, can significantly improve the efficiency and effectiveness of code optimization by accurately interpreting compiler optimization reports and generating effective code transformations.

To test our hypotheses, we design and implement CompilerGPT, a framework that leverages the power of LLMs for automated and enhanced performance tuning. Our approach tackles the issues of cryptic compiler output, the need for iterative refinement, and the inherent limitations of LLMs in handling complex codebases. CompilerGPT has been released as open-source on https://github.com/LLNL/CompilerGPT/.

The paper offers the following contributions:

1. An *iterative LLM-guided optimization framework* called CompilerGPT, and a detailed description of its design.
2. *Effective prompt engineering:* We present effective prompt engineering strategies, including chain-of-thought prompting and negative prompting, tailored to guide the LLM in performing specific optimization tasks.
3. An *empirical evaluation* using five benchmark programs applied to two different LLMs (GPT-4o and Claude Sonnet 3.7) and two different compilers (Clang and GCC).
4. *Addressing LLM challenges in code optimization:* We explicitly address and propose solutions to several common challenges like hallucination, context window limitations, and the management of rich context.

The remainder of the paper is organized as follows. Section 2 introduces background and motivation for this paper. Section 3 describes the design of the CompilerGPT framework. Section 4 presents our evaluation. Section 5 puts our work in context of the existing literature, and Sect. 6 concludes the paper with an outlook on future work.

2 Background

We define compiler optimization reports as diagnostic messages generated by a compiler (such as LLVM, GCC and Intel Compilers) to explain its internal optimization decisions to users. These reports may reveal which optimizations were successfully performed, which were missed, and why certain optimizations could not be applied. They offer valuable insights about optimization techniques employed by the compiler, assisting developers in diagnosing performance bottlenecks and tailoring their code to achieve optimal results. However, interpreting compiler optimization reports and understanding when optimizations are applied or not applied can be challenging, even for compiler experts.

We will use a matrix multiplication kernel as the running example. Figure 1 shows the code we would like to optimize and the interface of the SimpleMatrix class. SimpleMatrix's implementation stores matrices in row-major order. Note, matrix elements use type `long double` as opposed to the more common `double`. This requires the AI model to maintain the correct type in transformations.

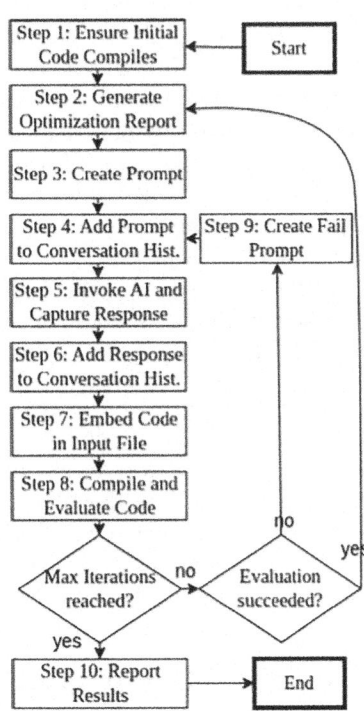

```
     // from header file
 2   struct SimpleMatrix {
         using value_type = long double; // element type
 4       SimpleMatrix(int rows, int cols); // constructor
         value_type operator()(int row, int col) const; // read
 6       value_type& operator()(int row, int col); // write
         int rows() const; // returns number of rows
 8       int columns() const; // returns number of columns
         ..
10   };

12   // matrix multiplication implementation
     SimpleMatrix
14   operator*(const SimpleMatrix& lhs,
               const SimpleMatrix& rhs) {
16       if (lhs.columns() != rhs.rows())
             throw runtime_error{"lhs.columns() != rhs.rows()"};
18
         SimpleMatrix res{lhs.rows(), rhs.columns()};
20       for (int i = 0; i < res.rows(); ++i) {
22           for (int j = 0; j < res.columns(); ++j) {
                 res(i,j) = 0;
24               for (int k = 0; k < lhs.columns(); ++k)
26                   res(i,j) += lhs(i, k) * rhs(k, j);
             }
28       }
         return res;
30   }
```

Fig. 1. Matrix multiplication in C++

Fig. 2. CompilerGPT Flow

```
simplematrix.cc:19:18: remark: failed to move load with loop-invariant address because the
loop may invalidate its value [-Rpass-missed=licm]
  19 |         res(i,j) += lhs(i, k) * rhs(k, j);
     |                 ^
simplematrix.cc:19:18: remark: failed to hoist load with loop-invariant address because load
is conditionally executed [-Rpass-missed=licm]
simplematrix.cc:19:18: remark: failed to move load with loop-invariant address because the
loop may invalidate its value [-Rpass-missed=licm]
simplematrix.cc:18:7: remark: loop not vectorized [-Rpass-missed=loop-vectorize]
  18 |       for (int k = 0; k < lhs.columns(); ++k)
     |       ^
simplematrix.cc:14:5: remark: 1 reloads 1.249999e+02 total reloads cost 4 folded reloads
8.124992e+02 total folded reloads cost 4 virtual registers copies 5.312495e+02 total copies
cost generated in loop [-Rpass-missed=regalloc]
  14 |     for (int j = 0; j < res.columns(); ++j)
     |     ^
```

Fig. 3. An excerpt of a Clang/LLVM optimization report for code in Fig. 1. The clang version is 18.1.8 and the compile arguments were -Rpass-missed=. -O3 -march=native -DNDEBUG=1 -c.

Figure 3 shows an example output that LLVM produces for the matrix multiplication kernel in Fig. 1. The excerpt is difficult to understand and act upon directly. Several factors contribute to this difficulty:

- The reports use highly technical terminology (*e.g.*, licm, loop-vectorize, regalloc) and often present information in an abbreviated, cryptic manner. These terms are not readily understandable without significant compiler expertise.
- Line numbers only indicate *where* the problem is detected, but not *why*. The report doesn't explicitly state what code transformations *should* be applied to address the underlying issues (*e.g.*, failed to move load...because the loop may invalidate its value). This leaves programmers to infer the necessary changes based on limited information.
- Optimization reports can be extremely verbose. The sheer volume of messages, many of which might be related and intertwined, makes it difficult to identify the most impactful issues.
- The structure and content of optimization reports differ between compilers (*e.g.*, GCC vs. Clang). Programmers need familiarity with each compiler's reporting style to interpret messages effectively, adding to the complexity.

On the other hand, large language models (LLMs) have recently emerged as powerful aids in software development, showing promise in tasks like code generation, debugging, and documentation. Notably, LLMs have demonstrated an ability to explain and even fix compiler errors in simpler programming contexts. This is why we are interested in leveraging LLMs to bridge the semantic gap between the raw compiler output and human-understandable action items.

3 Design of CompilerGPT

The goal of CompilerGPT is to make compiler optimization reports more accessible and actionable with minimal user intervention and delegate many of the tedious steps to the AI model. As shown in Table 1, there are several key challenges faced when designing CompilerGPT. We address these challenges in the following way: We break down the task into sub-tasks (*e.g.*, analyze reports, prioritize optimizations, apply optimizations).

Iterative compilation, testing and correction are used to address the hallucinations of LLMs. A robust evaluation harness provides detailed feedback on compilation and correctness. Negative prompting explicitly instructs the LLM to avoid certain code constructs (*e.g.*, "Do not add OpenMP"). A code snippet optimization strategy focuses the LLM on relevant code sections on larger codes. CompilerGPT extracts a user defined code range and trims the diagnostic output accordingly. The LLMs is tasked to identify and prioritize most beneficial transformations. Keeping a conversation history across iterations enables context-rich, informative prompts that guide the LLM through successive iterations.

3.1 Design and Key Components

CompilerGPT is a driver that ties together three loosely coupled components: (1) the compiler (*e.g.*, Clang) is used for compiling code and generating the optimization report; (2) the AI model (*e.g.*, GPT-4o) interprets the prompt and optimization report to rewrite the input code, and (3) a user provided evaluation harness tests for correctness and measures the runtime.

Figure 2 shows CompilerGPT's iterative workflow. Step 1 checks that the initial input code is compilable with the specified compiler. Step 2 uses the compiler to generate an optimization report, and Step 3 generates the first prompt. Step 4 starts the conversation history by adding the initial prompt. Step 5 invokes the AI model with the conversation history and captures its output. Step 6 appends the response to the conversation history, while Step 7 extracts the generated code from the response and replaces the original code in the input file with the generated code. Step 8 uses the compiler to test if the code compiles, and the evaluation harness to run correctness and performance tests. Unless this is the final iteration, CompilerGPT checks if the evaluation succeeded. If successful, CompilerGPT continues with Step 2 to generate an optimization report of the latest version of the code and a success prompt. If the evaluation failed, CompilerGPT generates a fail prompt asking the AI model to correct the problem using the captured output of the evaluation harness as problem context. After the final iteration, CompilerGPT generates a summary of the iterations and recorded correctness and performance evaluations.

Note, in every iteration the prompt and response are recorded and added to the conversation history. Each invocation of the AI model receives the full conversation history as input.

CompilerGPT runs an automatic and iterative optimization process. The tasks of the software engineer are the following: (1) configure CompilerGPT with prompts (Sect. 3.2); (2) define an evaluation harness that provides proper error messages so that the AI can address any issue in a following run; (3) define a code region in the input code that should be optimized; (4) interpret the obtained results.

Table 2. Matrix multiplication prompt of CompilerGPT

ID	Prompt
Context	You are an expert in C++ compiler optimizations and code performance tuning for modern Intel x86.
First Prompt	You are provided with the following code snippet: <<code>>. The execution time for 10 runs of the code is <<scoreint>> milliseconds. The compiler, <<compilerfamily>>, has generated the following optimization report: <<report>>. Your goal is to focus on high-impact optimizations that significantly reduce execution time. Follow these tasks carefully: **Task 1**: Report Analysis - Analyze the optimization report and extract a prioritized list of the top 3 issues that are most likely to have a significant impact on performance.- Focus on issues that are directly related to execution time bottlenecks or critical paths in the code. **Task 2**: Code Analysis - Based on the extracted prioritized list, select the single highest-impact issue. Identify the specific code segments that are directly related to this issue. Do not suggest changes to unrelated or low-impact parts of the code. **Task 3**: Code Improvement - Rewrite only the identified code segments from Task 2 to address the selected issue and enable better compiler optimizations. Ensure the rewritten code is functionally equivalent to the original code. Return the entire code in a single code block.
Success Prompt	The execution time for 10 runs of the latest code is <<scoreint>> milliseconds. ... *The full prompt continues like the first prompt and is omitted for brevity.*
Compile Error Prompt	This version did not compile. Here are the error messages: <<report>>. Try again.
Failing Test Prompt	This version failed the regression tests. Here are the error messages: <<report>>. Try again.

3.2 Prompts Used

As shown in Table 2, the prompts used in CompilerGPT are designed to guide the AI in analyzing and improving C++ code. Prompts are user configured and may contain variables, marked by <<>> filled in by CompilerGPT. The prompts shall ensure that the AI can systematically approach the optimization task while adhering to defined constraints.

The context establishes the role of the AI as a compiler expert focused on C++ code optimization for modern Intel x86 computers. It sets the objective to improve the existing code, which is crucial for aligning the AI's responses with the user's goals.

The *first prompt* instructs the AI to consider the provided input code and the optimization report generated by the compiler. Using a Chain-of-Thought style, it breaks down the optimization task into a series of smaller tasks, including optimization report analysis, code analysis to identify target code regions, and code transformations. This approach aims at focusing and constraining the AI model to address the issues mentioned in the optimization report.

When the AI-generated code does not compile or fails the regression tests, the *error prompts* are utilized. The prompts inform the AI of the failure and provide the specific error messages generated by the compiler or test harness.

The *success prompt* is used for follow-up prompts to further optimize the latest code. It is similar to the first prompt in style.

Overall, these prompts work together to create a structured framework for the AI, enabling it to perform iterative optimizations on C++ code while maintaining a focus on performance and correctness.

4 Evaluation and Experimental Results

We have evaluated CompilerGPT on five source codes, four of which use OpenMP. (1) Naive matrix multiplication, our running example, (2) a C++ version of prefix scan [1], (3) a C++ version of Smith-Waterman [3,12], (4) NAS-FT, (5) and a subset of NAS-BT from the NASA OpenMP benchmark suite [9].

Table 3. Summary of obtained speedups

Benchmark	AI Model	Clang			GCC		
		Max.	Avg.	Num.	Max.	Avg.	Num.
Matmul	GPT-4o	2.4	1.90	5	2.4	1.73	5
Matmul	Sonnet 3.7	3.1	2.10	5	2.4	1.77	5
Prefix	GPT-4o	1.0	1.00	0	1.0	1.00	0
Prefix	Sonnet 3.7	2.6	2.11	4	6.5	2.73	4
SW	GPT-4o	1.4	1.07	1	1.0	1.03	5
SW	Sonnet 3.7	1.4	1.38	5	1.0	1.02	4
NAS/BT	GPT-4o	1.0	1.00	0	1.0	1.01	1
NAS/BT	Sonnet 3.7	1.1	1.05	2	1.1	1.02	2
NAS/FT	GPT-4o	1.0	1.02	5	1.1	1.03	3
NAS/FT	Sonnet 3.7	1.1	1.03	5	1.1	1.07	5

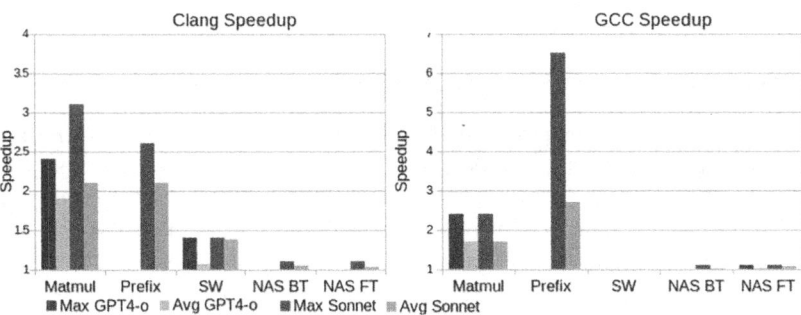

Fig. 4. Comparison of maximum and average speedups achieved by GPT-4o and Claude Sonnet 3.7 across different benchmarks using Clang and GCC compilers.

We tested CompilerGPT with these five benchmarks compiled with two different compilers (Clang 18.1.8 Red Hat and GCC 12.2.1 Red Hat) using -O3 -march=native -DNDEBUG=1 and tested two different AI models (GPT-4o by OpenAI and Claude Sonnet 3.7 by Anthropic). CompilerGPT ran each configuration five times for six iterations. Any correct code was run on an Intel

Xeon(R) Gold 6248R CPU at 3.00 GHz system (with 48 CPUs and 96 hardware threads) to produce a performance score (sum of ten runs). OpenMP tests used 24 threads.

Table 3 shows the obtained results. Columns Max and Avg show the maximum and average speedups obtained over their base line (*i.e.*, GCC is compared to a base line compiled with GCC and the Clang to a base line compiled with Clang). The column Num shows how many of the five CompilerGPT runs did produce any speedup. Figure 4 displays the obtained speedups in bar chart form.

This section summarizes notable results. Complete conversation histories of the best runs are available on https://github.com/LLNL/CompilerGPT/tree/c3po-preconf/evaluation

CompilerGPT's runtime and cost vary significantly across benchmarks and AI models. For example, the matrix-matrix multiplication kernel is the shortest benchmark with 25 lines or 500 characters. Its runs take roughly 4.3 min with GPT-o and 5 min with Sonnet. About 50 s (GPT4-o) and 65 s (Sonnet) are spent on AI alone. The cost is 0.01 USD (GPT4-o) and 0.13 USD (Sonnet). For NAS BT, the code section submitted for optimization contains 422 lines or 12695 characters. A run of CompilerGPT takes about 8.88 min (4.5 min AI alone) for GPT-4o and 22.5 min (9.2 min AI). The cost is 0.13 USD and 1.31 USD for GPT-4o and Sonnet respectively (measured on May 15, 2025).

The differences between Sonnet 3.7 and GPT-4o observed in our experiments may be partially attributed to their respective design goals and training philosophies—though both models are closed. Sonnet 3.7 consistently ranks higher on public leaderboards for programming and math tasks, likely reflecting its focus on structured reasoning and text-intensive problem-solving. In contrast, GPT-4o is a general-purpose, multimodal model optimized for a broad range of tasks.

4.1 Sequential Matrix-Matrix Multiply

The *evaluation harness* checks that (1) loop unrolling is correct by using matrix dimensions that are prime numbers, by (2) testing matrix values that require at least the original datatype. This ensures that the AI does not incorrectly optimize by using smaller datatypes, such as `double` instead of `long double`.

(3) We test whether wrong matrix sizes preserve the exception behavior, and (4) in general test the correctness of the computation. A failing test ideally uses a descriptive message that would guide the AI in the next iteration to fix the problem. For example, if a wrong datatype is used, the test emits the error message: "datatype too short; use SimpleMatrix::value_type".

Best Result: The best speedup (3.1x as shown in Fig. 5) was obtained by Sonnet optimizing code for Clang. The fifth run proceeded as follows: **Iteration 0**: Sonnet identified three high-impact optimizations: (1) Failed Vectorization of the inner loops, (2) Register use due to numerous spills and reloads, and (3) Loop-invariant loads not being hoisted. The resulting code reorders the innermost loops and uses a local variable to avoid repeated loads of the left-hand side

```
   // Use a tiled approach with 2x2 blocks to reduce register pressure
2  for (int i = 0; i < M; i += 2) {
     const int iLimit = (i + 1 < M) ? i + 2 : i + 1;
4    for (int j = 0; j < N; j += 2) {
6      const int jLimit = (j + 1 < N) ? j + 2 : j + 1;
8      // Initialize accumulators for this 2x2 block
       SimpleMatrix::value_type acc00=0, acc01=0, acc02=0, acc03=0;
10     for (int k = 0; k < K; ++k) {
12       const SimpleMatrix::value_type lhs_ik = (i < M) ? lhs(i, k) : 0;
         const SimpleMatrix::value_type lhs_i1k = (i+1 < M) ? lhs(i+1, k) : 0;
14       const SimpleMatrix::value_type rhs_kj = (j < N) ? rhs(k, j) : 0;
         const SimpleMatrix::value_type rhs_kj1 = (j+1 < N) ? rhs(k, j+1) : 0;
16       if (i < M && j < N) acc00 += lhs_ik * rhs_kj;
18       if (i < M && j+1 < N) acc01 += lhs_ik * rhs_kj1;
         if (i+1 < M && j < N) acc10 += lhs_i1k * rhs_kj;
20       if (i+1 < M && j+1 < N) acc11 += lhs_i1k * rhs_kj1;
       }
22     // Write accumulated results back to result matrix
       if (i < M && j < N) res(i, j) = acc00;
24     if (i < M && j+1 < N) res(i, j+1) = acc01;
       if (i+1 < M && j < N) res(i+1, j) = acc10;
26     if (i+1 < M && j+1 < N) res(i+1, j+1) = acc11;
     }
28 }
```

Fig. 5. Sonnet optimized code for Clang: Iteration 6 yielded the best result.

matrix value. **Iteration 1**: The code failed regression tests due to the datatype being too small. **Iteration 3**: After this was corrected in **Iteration 2**, Sonnet still identifies missed vectorization opportunities, register pressure, and memory access patterns. Sonnet introduces 4×4 blocking and loop unrolling but undoes the loop interchange. **Iteration 4**: Sonnet starts to identify load elimination failures, register spills, loop invariant code motion as high impact. **Iteration 6**: After having to correct the datatype size issue in **Iteration 5** again, Sonnet reduces the blocking to 2×2 to reduce register pressure further.

Other runs of CompilerGPT produced improved results in the range of 1.3x to 2.3x speedup in all configurations.

4.2 Parallel Prefix Sum

Prefix sum is an instance of prefix scan and computes the prefix sum for each element of a `vector<long double>`. The algorithm consists of two nested loops. The inner for loop is marked as OpenMP parallel, but the parallel region does not extend to the outer loop. In addition, the input code uses C++ vectors and inefficiently creates copies with each iteration of the outer loop.

Best Result: The best speedup was by Sonnet optimizing code for GCC. The first run proceeded as follows: **Iteration 0** identified issues: (1) vector creation and copying inefficiency; (2) insufficient loop vectorization; (3) OpenMP parallelization overhead due to frequent thread creation/destruction. This issue is not obvious from the original report as the related message is: "statement clobbers memory: __builtin_GOMP_parallel". Sonnet generated code that hoists the temporary vector outside the loop nests and marks the OpenMP loops as SIMD. The vector is initialized by adding a second parallel for loop. **Iteration 1** shows 3.3x speedup, but the optimization report still indicates (1) insufficient loop vectorization; (2) memory management inefficiencies; (3) OpenMP parallel overhead. The generated version switches from using vectors to raw memory managed by unique pointers, which gives a speedup of almost 2x over the previous version. In further iterations, Sonnet attempts to vectorize the inner loops but it does not improve performance.

Other runs with Sonnet produced improved results in the range of 1x to 2x speedup for both Clang and GCC. GPT-4o did not produce versions with significant speedup, though the analysis of the report found the same issues identified by Sonnet. Noteworthy, the Clang optimization report indicates that type of `long double` is unsupported by SIMD vectorizer. GPT-4o attempts to modify the function signature to use `vector<double>` but that failed in the tests.

4.3 Parallel Smith Waterman (SW)

SW is a wavefront algorithm that finds longest similar subsequences of two strings and is fundamental for protein folding. The initial code is OpenMP parallel and consists of five functions spanning 110 lines of code (LOC). The outermost function contains an OpenMP parallel section with two nested loops, where only the inner loop is parallel. The initial version uses a double-checked locking pattern to not always enter a critical section in the innermost loop to update `maxPos` (storing the best solution).

Best Result: The best improvement was obtained by Sonnet optimizing code for Clang. **Iteration 0** identified the following issues: (1) memory access patterns and cache misses; (2) critical section bottleneck. "The'#pragma omp critical' section for updating maxPos is likely causing thread contention and serialization, especially given the number of virtual register copies reported around this code."[1] (3) loop vectorization failures. Claude's generated code privatizes the local maximum variable and synchronizes them at the end, and it adds memory prefetch instructions to the inner loop. **Iteration 1** attributed missed optimizations to (1) loop vectorization failure; (2) memory access patterns; (3) excessive register spills. **Iteration 2** failed to compile and **Iteration 3** failed regression tests. **Iteration 4** made small improvements such as declaring local variables const, resulting in a measured speedup of 1.4x over the base. Further iterations did not produce better results.

Other Runs: Sonnet produced consistent results over the five runs. GPT-4o had only one run with comparable results. Other runs did not generate code optimizations for Clang. With GCC, the initial performance was already 1.4x faster than Clang. Neither Sonnet nor GPT-4o produced any substantial speedup.

---

[1] The optimization report does not mention the critical section explicitly, though register pressure and loads are mentioned.

4.4 NAS Parallel Benchmarks

We used OpenMP versions of BT and FT from the NAS benchmark suite. The initial code was mildly modified to co-locate all functions that we wanted to optimization. The kernel of FT kernel is 332 lines long (including comments and blank lines). BT's kernel is about 1800 LOC, which is too large to fit several iterations of the code and optimization report within the context window. Thus, we only optimized and timed the function compute_rhs spanning 420 LOC. To test the generated code, we rely on the tests provided by the benchmark suite.
BT: The *best run* of 1.1x speedup was Sonnet optimizing GCC code. **Iteration 0** suggested the following issues: (1) nested loops with poor data access patterns; (2) multiple deeply nested loops; (3) loop structure and loop invariant computation. Sonnet eliminates some common subexpressions and hoists them outside a loop, and it marks innermost loops with fixed bounds as SIMD. **Iteration 1**: Although the report remains similar, Sonnet reports a different root case as (3) loop directives and scheduling. The generated code restructures the computation of common terms and removes the SIMD annotations. **Iterations 2 and 3**: The report remains similar, and Sonnet suggests that (3) memory layout and cache efficiency should be improved. **Iteration 4** fixed that by unrolling an innermost loop with fixed size bounds. A similar speedup was obtained with Clang.

Other Runs: Other runs of Sonnet produced smaller speedups or degraded performance. GPT-4o did not return the complete code. CompilerGPT can currently not detect such issue and follow up with a meaningful prompt.

FT: The *best run* of 1.08x speedup was Sonnet optimizing GCC code. In **Iteration 0**, Sonnet identifies the following missed optimization opportunities: (1) complicated memory access patterns; (2) OpenMP barrier overhead; (3) Function call overhead, since inlining cannot be performed. Sonnet converts outer OpenMP loops to static schedule and marks inner loops as SIMD. Further iterations did not produce better speedup.

Other Runs: Other configurations also produced a small speedup in the range of 1.02–1.05x.

4.5 Discussion

While CompilerGPT is designed to automate many aspects of the optimization process, there remain several scenarios where human intervention is essential. First, large language models are prone to hallucination due to factors such as limited domain knowledge, prompt ambiguity, or the inherent stochasticity of generative models. Second, the limited context window size of current LLMs restricts their ability to access relevant information. This includes key optimization opportunities or constraints, which may fall outside the visible scope of the model. This is especially problematic for large or modular codebases. Third, optimization prioritization remains an open research challenge: accurately predicting the performance impact of a given transformation is notoriously difficult, particularly in the presence of complex hardware behavior and compiler heuristics. In such cases, domain expertise is often required to correctly interpret reports, validate AI-suggested changes, and steer the optimization process toward high-impact improvements.

LLMs can summarize optimization reports (Clang and GCC). While the summaries do not always identify the same key issues that need to be addressed, the listed issues are mostly consistent with optimization reports. At times, an LLM infers issues that are not mentioned in the optimization report, such as potential contention in concurrent code as observed in the Smith-Waterman tests. The actual code transformation produces mixed results. While LLMs may tackle optimizations that go beyond what a typical compiler would do (*e.g.*, rewrite synchronization in the SW code), larger codes seem to be pose more difficulties. However optimizing codes like the NAS benchmark is non-trivial and challenging even for experts.

Unlike traditional code translators, LLMs can operate on incomplete or erroneous codes. This is essential to keep the communication context concise, as it allows to trim irrelevant parts or parts that cannot be optimized (*e.g.*,, headers).

An AI model's code transformation may introduce subtle errors, such as reducing the precision of a matrix element. Thus, providing unit tests (or tool support) to uncover subtle errors in the generated code is fundamental to prevent code defects. Ideally, the tests can generate meaningful messages so that the LLM can fix issues in subsequent iterations. If the unit tests are not comprehensive, software engineers need to validate the optimized code.

We did not compare the results with CompilerGPT configurations that omit the optimization reports. The reason for this omission is that such alternative prompts would not constrain AI models in the same way. Such configurations may lead to algorithmic optimizations that we attempted to prohibit by using prompts that guide AI models to focus on optimization reports.

5 Related Work

Several tools have been developed to assist developers in analyzing and visualizing compiler optimization reports, making them more accessible and actionable.

Intel has released *oneAPI 2025.0*, which includes improved optimization reports for both their DPC++/C++ and Fortran compilers [2]. These reports offer more detailed information on optimizations performed or missed, with a focus on inlining, profile-guided optimization (PGO), loop optimization, vectorization, OpenMP, and code generation reports. *LLVM's opt-viewer.py* transforms serialized optimization remarks in YAML format into visual HTML representations. *FAROS* [7] utilizes LLVM's optimization remarks for generating and comparing reports of optimization remarks between serial and OpenMP compilation. FAROS enables researchers and developers to gain deeper insights into the compilation process of OpenMP programs.

LLMs have also been studied in the context of compilers. A study [5] presents a 7-billion-parameter transformer model trained from scratch to optimize LLVM assembly for code size. The Meta Large Language Model Compiler [6] is built on Code Llama and trained on 546 billion tokens of LLVM-IR and assembly code. It interprets compiler behavior and supports tasks like code size optimization and disassembly. Another study [15] revealed that LLMs, such as GPT-4, outperform Stack Overflow in explaining compiler errors. Similarly, studies [11,13] showed that students find GPT-4's explanations helpful for fixing compile-errors.

Large language models (LLMs) have been increasingly applied to a wide range of software engineering tasks, including code repair, refactoring, translation, code generation, and optimization [8,10]. Notable examples include GitHub Copilot [17], SWE-Agent [16], Devin [4], and OpenHands (formerly OpenDevin) [14]. While our work shares similarities with these in leveraging LLMs and iterative processes for automation, it focuses on the novel domain of directly interpreting and acting upon compiler optimization reports to guide code optimization.

6 Conclusion

CompilerGPT, a novel framework that leverages LLMs to significantly improve the productivity of code optimization, is an approach that addresses inherent difficulties in understanding and acting upon the often hard to understand compiler optimization reports. It guides an LLM to systematically refine code based on compiler feedback and correctness constraints. Experimental results demonstrated significant performance improvements on some benchmark codes (*i.e.*, 6.5x improvement for prefix sum), highlighting the potential of this approach. The prioritization lists that are part of the LLM response demonstrate the benefits of using LLMs to summarize and interpret complex compiler-generated reports, aiding software engineers in understanding the results.

The current work has several limitations that we aim to address in future work: (1) The evaluation process currently requires user-defined tests, such as unit tests. (2) Optimization of large-scale codebases depends on users selecting specific code regions for improvement. (3) The outputs generated by large language models exhibit significant variability across different runs.

To address these challenges, we propose several key strategies: leveraging profiling to identify performance-critical hotspots in large-scale codebases, utilizing automated unit test generators to significantly reduce the manual effort required for creating effective test harnesses, and employing advanced prompt engineering alongside fine-tuning of open-weight models to enhance the consistency and reliability of AI-generated outputs. These approaches refine our methodology and aim to further reduce human intervention in the optimization loop.

Acknowledgment. We thank the anonymous referees for their helpful suggestions for improvements. This work was performed under the auspices of the U.S. Department of Energy by Lawrence Livermore National Laboratory under Contract DE-AC52-07NA27344. LLNL-CONF-2001471.

References

1. A parallel implementation of a left-associative prefix sum using OpenMP. https://github.com/robfarr/openmp-prefix-sum. Accessed 15 May 2025
2. Faster with Compiler Optimization Reports — intel.com. https://www.intel.com/content/www/us/en/developer/articles/technical/compiler-optimization-report-news-2025.html. Accessed 15 May 2025
3. TheFighters/Smith-Waterman: Parallel implementation of Smith–Waterman using OpenMP. https://github.com/TheFighters/Smith-Waterman. Accessed 15 May 2025
4. cognition.ai. Cognition | Introducing Devin, the first AI software engineer — cognition.ai. https://www.cognition.ai/blog/introducing-devin. Accessed 15 May 2025
5. Cummins, C., et al.: Large language models for compiler optimization. *arXiv preprint* arXiv:2309.07062 (2023)
6. Cummins, C., et al.: Meta large language model compiler: foundation models of compiler optimization. *arXiv preprint* arXiv:2407.02524 (2024)
7. Georgakoudis, G., Doerfert, J., Laguna, I., Scogland, T.R.W.: FAROS: a framework to analyze openMP compilation through benchmarking and compiler optimization analysis. In: Milfeld, K., de Supinski, B.R., Koesterke, L., Klinkenberg, J. (eds.) IWOMP 2020. LNCS, vol. 12295, pp. 3–17. Springer, Cham (2020). https://doi.org/10.1007/978-3-030-58144-2_1
8. Hou, X., et al.: A systematic literature review. ACM Trans. Softw. Eng. Methodol. Large Lang. Models Softw. Eng. (2023)
9. Jin, H.-Q., Frumkin, M., Yan, J.: The openMP implementation of NAS parallel benchmarks and its performance (1999)
10. Nikolaidis, N., et al.: A comparison of the effectiveness of chatGPT and co-pilot for generating quality python code solutions. In: 2024 SANER-C, pp. 93–101. IEEE (2024)
11. Pankiewicz, M., Baker, R.S.: Navigating compiler errors with AI assistance-a study of GPT hints in an introductory programming course. In: Proceedings of the 2024 on Innovation and Technology in Computer Science Education V. 1, pp. 94–100 (2024)
12. Smith, T.F., Waterman, M.S., et al.: Identification of common molecular subsequences. J. Mol. Biol. **147**(1), 195–197 (1981)
13. Taylor, A., Vassar, A., Renzella, J., Pearce, H.: DCC–help: transforming the role of the compiler by generating context-aware error explanations with large language models. In: Proceedings of the 55th ACM Technical Symposium on Computer Science Education V. 1, pp. 1314–1320 (2024)
14. Wang, X., et al.: Openhands: an open platform for AI software developers as generalist agents. *arXiv preprint* arXiv:2407.16741 (2024)
15. Widjojo, P., Treude, C.: Addressing compiler errors: stack overflow or large language models? *arXiv preprint* arXiv:2307.10793 (2023)
16. Yang, J., et al.: SWE-agent: agent-computer interfaces enable automated software engineering. *arXiv preprint* arXiv:2405.15793 (2024)
17. Zhang, B., Liang, P., Zhou, X., Ahmad, A., Waseem, M.: Demystifying practices, challenges and expected features of using github copilot. *arXiv preprint* arXiv:2309.05687 (2023)

Improving Compiler Support for SIMD Offload Using Arm Streaming SVE

Mohamed Husain Noor Mohamed[1], Adarsh Patil[2(✉)], Latchesar Ionkov[1], and Eric Van Hensbergen[1]

[1] Arm, Austin, USA
[2] Arm, Cambridge, UK
adarsh.patil@arm.com

Abstract. The wider adoption of tightly coupled core-adjacent accelerators, such as Arm Scalable Matrix Extension (SME), hinges on lowering software programming complexity. In this paper, we focus on enabling the use of SME architecture in Streaming Scalable Vector Extension (SSVE) mode for workloads written in C/C++. While current compilers optimize loops for all types of SIMD instructions, these techniques primarily target vector units within the core and falter when applied to disaggregated, core-adjacent SIMD accelerators. Our goal is to enable the compiler to automatically generate code for such accelerators only *when profitable*.

To this end, we investigate a path towards performant, precise, and repeatable computation offloading through two compiler ecosystems. We revisit LLVM compiler passes, MLIR transforms and their associated cost models, and heuristics. We hope that these insights can provide directions for evolving compiler capabilities towards automatic code generation for this next-generation vector processing paradigm.

Keywords: Auto-vectorization · Arm SME · Arm Streaming SVE

1 Introduction

Modern CPUs feature specialized accelerators adjacent to the main core to offload fine-grained computational tasks. The SME architecture in Armv9 exemplifies this architecture, accelerating matmul and wide vector width computations, providing dual benefits of energy-efficient execution and reduced design complexity for specialization. The most versatile way of lowering programming complexity for such architectures is to use compiler ecosystems to automatically offload computations to these accelerators when profitable.

Streaming SVE (SSVE) Mode: Arm SME defines SSVE mode [4] which allows execution of a subset of SVE2 instructions with a flexible, implementation-dependent vector width. This Streaming SVE Vector Length (SVL) can be any power of two in the range of 128–2048 bits. SSVE mode can be enabled by programming the `PSTATE.SM` field. The focus of this paper is to enable the use of SSVE mode to perform vector operations, for workloads written in C/C++. Therefore, we generate SSVE vector pipes, i.e., SVE code running in streaming mode with wider vector width. We do not target Matmul with outer-product and accumulate (MOPA) or Matmul with multi-vector instructions or instructions that use the ZA register storage. Specifically, the target is instructions that are valid in PSTATE.SM=1 and PSTATE.ZA=0, commonly referred to as "streaming compatible instructions" (Fig. 1) [3].

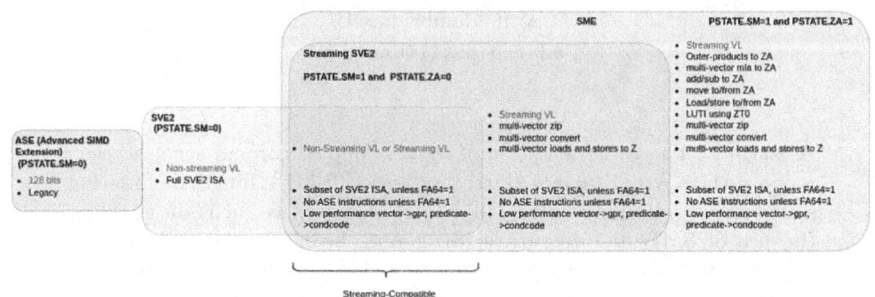

Fig. 1. A venn diagram of Arm vector ISA extensions. This study focuses on SVE2 streaming-compatible instructions to utilize the wider vectors of the SME hardware.

SSVE Architecture: A potential implementation of SME would support Streaming SVE mode with an SVL as a power of two in the range 128–2048 bits inclusive [12]. Each core supports fixed 128-bit vector length NEON SIMD and does not support SVE natively. Architecturally, these SME units act as part of each core i.e., instructions are sent to the SME unit when streaming mode is enabled on a core. This control data like addresses and offsets are sent over a dedicated control bus. Other data are accessed by the SME unit through loads and stores. The SME units have a private L1 cache and a high-bandwidth connection to a shared cache. Note that the closest common cache for both the core and the SME unit is the shared cache, i.e. whatever data is written to the memory by the core will be read by the SME unit from the cache and vice versa.

Compiler Auto-vec Limitations: Contemporary compilers possess the capability to identify and optimize loops to generate SIMD instructions that execute on vector units located within the core. In contrast, SSVE architectures have disaggregated SIMD units outside of the core. Consequently, the entire infrastructure for estimating profitability of vectorization is relatively simple and ill-suited for architectures implementing streaming SVE. We revisit the applicability of existing techniques for generating vectorization candidates, transforms, cost models, and heuristics to achieve automatic offload capability in a variety of compilers.

The heuristic of whether to generate SVE instructions vs fixed-width NEON instructions should include the microarchitectural features, e.g., cost of switching into/out of streaming mode, the associated costs of running in streaming mode, performance of fall back path. An incorrect decision can potentially make the performance worse than falling back to fixed-width vector/scalar mode.

Contributions:

(i) We demonstrate compiler limitations in auto-vectorizing for SSVE offload, using a variety of benchmarks on a SME supported processor (Sect. 2).
(ii) We propose the enhancements necessary for LLVM and MLIR-based compilers to facilitate the generation of SSVE code (Sect. 3).

2 Motivation

Compiler Limitations: Auto-vectorization is disabled in LLVM for streaming-enabled functions. Using the following experimental flag,

`-mllvm -enable-scalable-autovec-in-streaming-mode`

forces auto-vec which generates SVE code without a streaming-mode switch. Developers must then annotate the function with `__arm_streaming` to enable streaming mode. In addition, careful analysis and profiling are needed to ensure:

(a) *correctness* - the auto-vectorizer's *code-generator* may vectorize using SVE instructions that are not streaming compatible, e.g. scatter/gather, leading to `EXC_BAD_INSTR`

(b) *performance* - the auto-vectorizer does not have a *cost-model* to decide profitability of vectorization using SSVE leading to severely degraded performance, potentially worse than scalar execution.

Code-Gen Performance Analysis: We benchmark to assess compiler auto-vectorization capability and architecture performance (config in Table 1). We use the -mcpu flag to tune the cost model for the vector lengths of our processor architecture. Recall that the SME unit in the processor offers SIMD vector widths much wider than that of the NEON unit on the core. Consequently, we expect to see some improvements in performance for certain workloads even with such a rudimentary compilation [5].

Table 1. Experimental setup for SSVE benchmarking

Clang	clang version 19.1.4; Target: arm64
Platform Arch	Processor with support for 128-bit NEON and 512-bit SVL
SSVE	-O3 -fstrict-aliasing -mllvm -enable-scalable-autovec-in-streaming-mode
NEON	-O3 -fstrict-aliasing -fvectorize
Scalar	-O3 -fstrict-aliasing -fno-vectorize

≻ **TSCV_2 suite** [9]: (Iterations 100000, Sizes: LEN_1D 32000, LEN_2D 256). Among the 146 loops in the TSVC suite, we observe.

(i) *Performance:* Baselining to scalar execution, compiling to SSVE sees a geomean of 0.52x (upto 153x slowdown). Only 53% of the loops show improved performance with SSVE. Note that compiling to NEON shows a geomean speedup of 1.62x over scalar. *Baselining to NEON,* SSVE shows a geomean of 0.32x (upto 268x slowdown) with only 22 loops showing better performance with SSVE.

(ii) *SSVE auto-vectorization:* Almost 90% of the loops were auto-vectorized to NEON but only 35% were auto-vectorized to SSVE by the compiler. Specifically, we highlight five loops that were autovectorized to SSVE with significant slowdowns compared to NEON and Scalar (s115, s132, s2233, s1281, s443). Across this subset of loops, SSVE shows geomean of 0.14x over NEON and 0.37 over scalar. This clearly highlights the compiler's inadequate cost-model, given that it produced SSVE code even though it led to performance reductions compared to NEON and scalar.

➤ **Mandelbrot set** [7] (Input sizes: 180×135, 360×270, 720×540, 1440×1080)
For the C++ source, the compiler SSVE auto-vec failed due to an early exit loop condition. Instead, we used an implementation of the kernel with intrinsics. Across these input sizes, SSVE sees a geomean of 0.35x over NEON. Specifically, we observe that the slowdown decreases linearly with increasing input sizes, since the cost of offload is amortized relative to the execution latency.

➤ **SPEC 2017** [6] We observe a 1.9x slowdown over NEON for the notoriously difficult to optimize mcf benchmark (rate mode) in the SPEC 2017 suite.

Motivation Summary: Although 4x wider SSVE SIMD units offer potential performance gains, most benchmarks show significant slowdowns The issue largely stems from compilers' inability to generate optimal code. Relying on programmer expertise to diagnose issues or simply isolating acclerator interaction through expertly hand-written libraries limits the use of SME architecture.

3 Extensions for Auto-vectorization to SSVE

We offer a brief overview of the two approaches (LLVM and MLIR-based) to generate SSVE instructions, highlighting their constraints and limitations.

3.1 LLVM Approach

Enhancing the Loop Vectorizer (LV) Pass: LV widens instructions in loops to operate on multiple consecutive iterations. LV uses a Vectorization Factor (VF) to model the profitability of vectorization over scalar execution, representing the number of vector lanes in the architecture. For SVE auto-vec the cost model was enhanced to support unknown number of lanes. Since the vector length is unknown, the compiler needs to ensure that vectorization is beneficial for all vector sizes. To avoid having to check all potential vector lengths for profitability, LV assumes that speedup is constant or strictly increasing with vector size, i.e., code beneficial for vectorizing at $VF = 4$ is also advantageous at VF = 16. It therefore performs a single cost analysis for the smallest possible vector size.

➤ **Implementation details:** To support SVE in LV, *VectorType* was split into *FixedVectorType* and *ScalableVectorType*. The parameter *vscale* was introduced to support scalable vector types in LV [11]. A scalable vector type is specified of the form $< vscale \times N \times Ty >$ where '*N*' is the minimum number of elements of type '*Ty*' contained within the vector, and '*vscale*' indicates that the total element count is an integer multiple of '*N*'. *vscale* is an unknown at compile time and takes a value greater than 0 and in the range specified by *vscale_range(min[,max])*. For example, a vector containing an unknown integer multiple of four i32s is represented as $< vscale \times 4 \times i32 >$.

VF for profitability analysis is expressed as $< vscale \times N >$. Flag -mtune=<cpu> is used to tune for specific vscale based on the microarchitecture. For example -mtune=neoverse-v1 uses vscale=2. If the parameter is not specified, the code generated remains compatible with any *vscale* in the specified *vscale_range*.

➤ **Extending the cost-model:** The cost model analysis uses the codegen to approximate the cost of any IR instruction when lowered to machine instructions. The cost results are unit-less and the cost number represents the throughput of the machine assuming that all loads hit the cache, all branches are predicted, etc. Cost numbers can be added to compare two or more transformation alternatives.

The current cost model does not take into account that speedups might not scale perfectly linearly and increasing vector lengths using SSVE can have added performance impacts on speedups. The cost-model must account for the performance overheads of running in SSVE mode and the associated non-linear performance scaling for various vector lengths in *vscale_range(min[,max])*. In addition, since SSVE only supports a subset of SVE2 instructions, invalid SVE operations, such as scatter-gather, now need to be excluded from the cost-model calculations.

Note that simply changing the instruction costs in the compiler table will not work. The cost of an SVE2 instruction can be different in streaming vs non-streaming mode. Additionally, the cost overheads of SSVE instructions are not associated with individual instructions but are amortized over a basic block.

Enhancing Vectorization Plan (VPlan): A VPlan is a representation of a distinct way to vectorize a loop nest, called a vectorized candidate. This candidate is represented using a hierarchical CFG. VPlan supports estimating the cost and driving the generation of the output IR code. The Hierarchical CFG models the planned control-flow, whose nodes are basic blocks (VPBasicBlock).

The LoopVectorizationPlanner handles the vectorization of a loop or a loop nest. It constructs, optimizes, and discards one or more VPlans, each VPlan modeling a distinct way to vectorize the loop or the loop nest. Once the best VPlan is determined, including the best VF and UF, this VPlan drives the generation of the output IR. A VPBasicBlock holds a sequence of zero or more VPRecipes which model the cost and generation of the output IR instructions.

➤ **Extending the cost model:** VPlan cost modeling totals each instruction's cost in the loop body to estimate a plan's cost. It calls cost() on VPlans, which recurses into VPBasicBlocks and into VPRecipes. Most cost() methods for individual recipes currently call CostModel.getInstructionCost which uses the lookup of the tables for instruction costs. We propose adding costs to VPlans that employ streaming SSVE. The cost() method for an SSVE VPlan's cost() method should be instantiated with a static cost to account for streaming mode overheads before calculating instruction costs.

3.2 MLIR Approach

Enhancing Polygeist [10]: We describe extensions to Polygeist - a C/C++ compilation flow using MLIR [8]. Polygeist currently auto-vectorizes loops for fixed width vector NEON instructions only and cannot generate SVE.

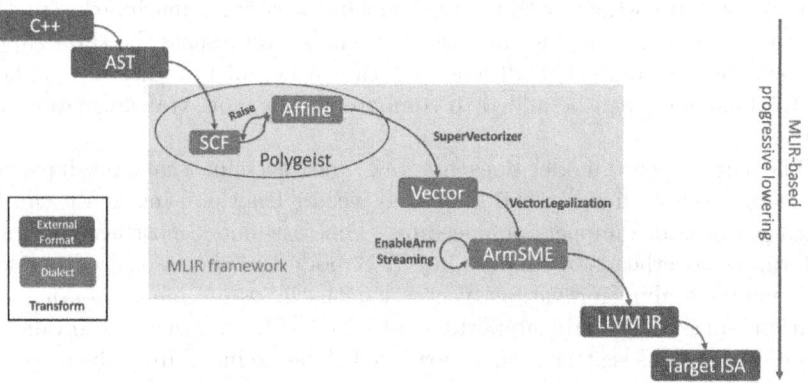

Fig. 2. The proposed extensions for lowering for generating SSVE. Within the MLIR framework (yellow box), only the red circle is currently present in Polygeist. (Color figure online)

➤ **Implementation details:** Figure 2 illustrates the proposed compilation pipeline, which extends Polygeist, to generate SSVE code. Polygeist currently generates and optimizes the code only at the Affine level. The proposed pipeline enhances existing transforms and dialects to generate SSVE as detailed below.

SuperVectorizer Transform: We propose to apply the SuperVectorizer transform to lower the optimized Affine dialect to the Vector dialect. A "super-vector is loosely defined as a vector type that is a multiple of a "good" vector size so the hardware can efficiently implement a set of high-level primitives. Loops and operations are emitted that operate on those super-vector shapes, which are later lowered to hardware-specific vector sizes. Currently, the SuperVectorization transform currently does not generate scalable vectors, and doing so requires also adding a cost-model heuristic in the transformation.

Vector Dialect: Vector dialect currently supports representing scalable vectors. As an example, a fixed-width vector represented as $vector < 4 \times 8 \times 128 \times f32 >$ lowers to $!llvm < [4 \times [8 \times < 128 \times float >]] >$ in LLVM IR.

A scalable vector representation represented as $vector < 4 \times 8 \times [128] \times f32 >$ lowers to $!llvm < [4 \times [8 \times < vscale \times 128 \times float >]] >$ in LLVM IR.

ArmSME and ArmSVE Dialect: The ArmSVE dialect currently does not flag streaming compatible SVE instructions. As SSVE is an ArmSME feature, we suggest extending the ArmSME dialect with SSVE operations, using the same sematics as in ArmSVE. ArmSME does provide an operation to query the streaming length `arm_sme.streaming_vl`. Extending the ArmSME dialect allows us to use its transforms to generate streaming SVE (see below).

VectorLegalization and EnableArmStreaming Transforms: These transforms are part of the ArmSME dialect. They currently have very limited support for the SSVE operations that are in scope for this study. The *VectorLegalization* transform legalizes vector operations for ArmSME, focusing on SME tiling. This transform needs extensions for SSVE operations. A similar legalization transform is performed when lowering vector operations in ArmSVE via LegalizeVectorStorage. *EnableArmStreaming* transform enables streaming mode by adding arm_streaming or arm_locally_streaming functions. The LLVM backend will emit 'smstart sm'/'smstop sm' [4] around calls to streaming functions.

3.3 Architectural Considerations for the SSVE Cost-Model

To calibrate the auto-vectorizers cost model for streaming-SVE, we outline the architectural consideration of the SME unit that affect the performance of the generated code.

Synchronizations: Synchronizations between core and the SME unit stall execution. Minimizing these will improve performance of the generated code.

- *GPR and FPR synchronization:* In streaming mode, the floating-point operations are dispatched to the SME unit which has a private L1 cache. When both that SME unit and the scalar core access the same cache lines on the stack, the memory-ordering hardware must stall on one side until the other retires its access. To reduce the probability of such events during streaming execution, the AArch64 back-end in LLVM can insert a tunable pad (specified by `-aarch64-stack-hazard-size` flag) between stack objects predominantly accessed through GPRs and those accessed through FPRs. The padding pushes FPR-only data to the middle of the frame and GPR-only data at the edges.
  This heuristic cannot isolate variable-length arrays, argument spill slots, or objects referenced by both register classes [1]. Micro-benchmarking on the

SME platform shows that the residual stall penalty is 17% for a single streaming loop, grows roughly linearly to 61% for 100 concatenated loops, and then mostly saturates.
- *Predicates synchronization:* The predicate registers are used to select the active lanes in the SME unit. Both the core and the SME unit can produce predicates. If the core uses the produced predicate from the SME, e.g. the load-store instructions in streaming mode, synchronization of predicates produced on the core adds tens of cycles of latency. In code generation, to avoid this synchronization replacing the predicates with the vectors registers and placing the predicates usage as far as possible will help improve the performance.

Memory Interactions: Memory interactions between the SME unit occur through the shared cache. Minimizing such interactions in the generated code will improve performance.
- *Load-Store Region Table (LSRT) Hazards:* The SME unit relies on the core's MMU for address translation for each load/store instruction. The core maintains the LSRT for the physical address and is synchronized to the SME unit using LSRT sync-up packets. Each time the SME unit requests a load or store, if the region is unallocated, a new LSRT region gets created and synchronized with the SME unit. The core is also responsible for verifying that the transfer is successful by checking translation faults, alignment faults, and watchpoints. The address translation in the LSRT is instantiated at 4 KB granularity.

  A core access is stalled until the completion of all the SME unit accesses to the same region are completed and visible by the coherency. Similarly, the access cannot be sent to the SME unit if it conflicts with a core access in the same region. The core uses the LSRT to detect these hazards between the core requests and the SME unit. Accesses within the same region are monitored by the LSRT table. Each LSRT entry implements counters to track these hazards at an aligned 1 KB granularity regions. LSRT hazards lead to performance slowdowns.

  To avoid these hazards, the compiler can generate spills and fills of both scalar/vector data accessing the same region. Secondly, the compiler can keep 1 KB aligned regions in the stack if it is accessed both by the core and the SME unit, and at least one executes write accesses.

  We observe that the QPSK modulation kernel in Arm RAL [2] compiled for SSVE causes shows 6× slowdown over NEON. Using the above technique to avoid the LSRT hazard improves the performance of the kernel.
- *Scaling behavior:* The performance gains of streaming SVE over regular NEON or scalar is dependent on the input length. For smaller input lengths, offloading to the SME unit incurs higher costs (warming up SME caches, memory access characteristics of the loop, chances of LSRT stalls due to the source and destination memory mapping to the same 1 KB LSRT region, etc.). We note that most loops tend to show a performance knee, a point after which SSVE is more performant than NEON, amortizing the costs of

offload to the SME unit Compiler cost-model decision-making heuristics can be conservative, defaulting to NEON, as the consequences of an inefficient offload can degrade performance.
- *Prefetcher:* The SME unit prefetcher is based on strided and nested access patterns and is less capable of tracking arbitrary access efficiently. Arbitrary access can pollute training and prevent useful prefetching. The compiler can revert to NEON if pointers or data-dependent addresses are used in the loop.
- *Gather loads and scatter stores:* These instructions are unavailable in streaming SVE. Regular strided accesses can be converted to regular load/store SSVE instructions using ZIP/UZIP instructions. However, random stride cause performance slowdowns, Therefore, the general guidance for compiler code generation is to execute loops with gather/scatter operations using NEON instructions.

4 Conclusions and Call to Action

Compiler auto-vectorizers need updating to support core-adjacent offload vector computation. It is crucial to factor in the architectural characteristics such as mode switch/synchronization costs and data access via accelerator caches to assess offload profitability. More generally, this paper motivates compiler researchers to enable a transition to this more efficient paradigm of compute offloading, especially as application stacks evolve to be architecture-agnostic.

References

1. LLVM 20: AArch64FrameLowering. https://github.com/llvm/llvm-project/blob/llvmorg-20.1.5/llvm/lib/Target/AArch64/AArch64FrameLowering.cpp. Stack hazards for GPR and FPR
2. Arm: Arm 5G RAN Acceleration Library (ArmRAL). https://learn.arm.com/learning-paths/servers-and-cloud-computing/ran/. RAL library for various vector processing technologies
3. ARM: The scalable matrix extension (SME), for ARMV9-A. https://developer.arm.com/documentation/ddi0616/latest/. Arm Architecture Reference Manual Supplement
4. Arm: Streaming SVE mode. https://developer.arm.com/documentation/109246/0100/SME-Overview/Streaming-SVE-mode
5. Arm: What is new in LLVM 20? https://community.arm.com/arm-community-blogs/b/tools-software-ides-blog/posts/whats-new-in-llvm-20. LLVM 20
6. Bucek, J., Lange, K.D., v. Kistowski, J.: SPEC CPU2017: next-generation compute benchmark. In: Companion of the 2018 ACM/SPEC International Conference on Performance Engineering, ICPE 2018, pp. 41–42. Association for Computing Machinery, New York (2018). https://doi.org/10.1145/3185768.3185771
7. Wellons, C.: Mandelbrot set in SSE, AVX, and NEON. https://github.com/skeeto/mandel-simd
8. Lattner, C., et al.: MLIR: a compiler infrastructure for the end of Moore's law (2020). https://arxiv.org/abs/2002.11054

9. Maleki, S., Gao, Y., Garzarán, M.J., Wong, T., Padua, D.A.: An evaluation of vectorizing compilers. In: 2011 International Conference on Parallel Architectures and Compilation Techniques, pp. 372–382 (2011). https://doi.org/10.1109/PACT.2011.68
10. Moses, W.S., Chelini, L., Zhao, R., Zinenko, O.: Polygeist: raising C to polyhedral MLIR. In: Proceedings of the ACM International Conference on Parallel Architectures and Compilation Techniques, PACT 2021. Association for Computing Machinery, New York (2021)
11. de Smalen, S.: Optimizing code for scalable vector architectures. https://llvm.org/devmtg/2021-11/slides/2021-OptimizingCodeForScalableVectorArchitectures.pdf
12. Wilkinson, F., McIntosh-Smith, S.: An initial evaluation of arm's scalable matrix extension. In: 2022 IEEE/ACM International Workshop on Performance Modeling, Benchmarking and Simulation of High Performance Computer Systems (PMBS) (2022). https://doi.org/10.1109/PMBS56514.2022.00018

Fifth Workshop on Interactive and Urgent HPC (WIUHPC)

WIUHPC 2025 Preface

Objectives/Topics

Interactivity enables the exploitation of HPC in new and revolutionary ways, delivering many new and exciting opportunities for our community. Interactive HPC involves users being in the loop during job execution where a human is monitoring a job, steering the experiment, or visualising results to make immediate decisions about the results to influence the current or subsequent interactive jobs. Likewise, urgent computing combines interactive computational modelling with the near-real-time detection of unfolding disasters to take real-time actions. Supporting interactive and urgent workloads on HPC requires expertise in a wide range of areas and the solving of numerous technical and organisational challenges, including organisational and system policies; effective scheduling; effective technologies and tools; data management; and user education and training.

This workshop brings together stakeholders, researchers and practitioners from across interactive and urgent computing with the wider HPC community. We share success stories, case studies and technologies to continue community building around leveraging interactive HPC as an important tool responding to disasters, societal issues, rapid prototyping and data analysis.

Workshop Organization

Albert Reuther	MIT Lincoln Laboratory Supercomputing Center, USA
Robert Henschel	Indiana University, USA
William Arndt	National Energy Research Scientific Computing Center, USA

Workshop Synopsis

WIUHPC at ISC 2025 included an introduction, keynote talk, three research paper talks and a panel session.

Dynamic Resource Management Framework for Elastic Computing

Arjun Parab[(✉)], Amir Raoofy, and Josef Weidendorfer

Leibniz Supercomputing Centre, Munich, Germany
{arjun.parab,amir.raoofy,josef.weidendorfer}@lrz.de

Abstract. The landscape of High Performance Computing (HPC) is rapidly evolving, resulting in significant increases in computational power. This advancement enables individuals to address tasks with larger workloads, where resources are allocated statically at the beginning. However, with static allocation, not all workloads can fully utilize the available compute power throughout the duration of the task. Furthermore, the ever-growing usage of HPC leads to more diverse workloads in terms of priority, ranging from time-critical to those that can be delayed. This creates a need for a scalable cluster management and job scheduling system (SCMJSS) capable of dynamically allocating resources, with the potential for co-scheduling [3] to best manage such diverse workloads. We introduce FlexiAlloc, a fast prototype version of scheduler with dynamic resource management framework aiming to address the aforementioned challenges and facilitate the study of scheduling strategies enabled by the malleability of HPC jobs. We also demonstrate the programming model, which is particularly well suited to capitalize on resource dynamicity. Our evaluation of dynamic job resource allocation and co-scheduling with FlexiAlloc shows an increase in throughput and ≈4x faster execution compared to static allocation. In addition, we showcase how it handles dynamic workloads by preempting lower priority job to prioritize urgent job taking ≈517 ms and the elasticity of a job across two clusters.

Keywords: Dynamic resource allocation · Co-scheduling · Elastic computing

1 Introduction

The Scalable cluster management and job scheduling system (SCMJSS) is critical in high-performance computing (HPC) environments, aiding the parallel execution of numerous jobs to enhance resource utilization efficiency. These jobs are submitted by a diverse group of users, promoting resource sharing. Meanwhile, the HPC landscape is rapidly changing, leading to more heterogeneity of hardware components that challenge the effectiveness of SCMJSS. Furthermore, the rapid expansion of new computing centers emphasizes the need for SCMJSS that can handle size and heterogeneity on a large scale effectively. On the other hand, existing SCMJSS allocate resources statically at the beginning of the job. However, not all users can fully utilize all the available compute power, which is provided by the static allocation, throughout the duration of the job. Consequently, there is a clear need from many applications for dynamic resource allocation to allow jobs to expand or contract their resource usage as necessary, facilitating job malleability. This creates a need for dynamic resource allocation features in SCMJSS which allows jobs to adjust their computing resource allocations as needed dynamically, addressing the issue of under utilization and improving throughput. Moreover, establishing a communication channel between jobs and SCMJSS is crucial for dynamic resource management and allocation. In addition, it should provide opportunities to handle allocation from multiple perspectives, such as performance-focused or energy-aware scheduling.

This paper presents FlexiAlloc, a fast prototype version of scheduler with dynamic resource management framework that serves as a research vehicle to study scheduling strategies enabled by malleability of HPC jobs. In addition, there is a need for a framework like this for the HPC community that enables fast and flexible prototyping by being written in Python. Furthermore, to evaluate strategies, we need to define a benchmark with concrete use cases, to be able to compare strategies identified by the HPC community. We provide FlexiAlloc and two example use cases to start this effort and to better understand the features required in SCMJSS that actively makes use of malleable jobs. With the experience gained through FlexiAlloc, we aim to develop a more stable version, potentially as a scheduling plugin in Flux. The paper contributes the following: we ...

- propose a fast prototyping version of a scheduler to facilitate studies around job malleability.
- identified promising use cases, including enabling interactivity and improving throughput, and demonstrated that FlexiAlloc is flexible with low overhead, enhancing evaluation results.
- showcase priority scheduling facilitating urgent computing and cross cluster elasticity of a job.

2 Related Work

This section delves into an overview of scheduler platforms in HPC or libraries relevant to dynamic resource allocation or co-scheduling.

2.1 SLURM

Simple Linux Utility for Resource Management (SLURM) [15], originally developed for large Linux clusters at Lawrence Livermore National Laboratory (LLNL), is a robust cluster management system capable of scaling to thousands of processors. It is designed to be flexible and fault-tolerant and can be ported to clusters of varying sizes and architectures with minimal effort. Several updates have been made by SchedMD to supporting job preemption, PMIx, and Gang Scheduling. Currently, SLURM offers static resource allocation at the start of an application. However, resizing between job steps is possible, but is usually disabled, as this requires restarts of MPI applications per step.

2.2 LSF

IBM Spectrum LSF [13] is a workload management system designed to enhance resource allocation and job scheduling. It facilitates dynamic hybrid cloud configurations, allowing organizations to seamlessly extend their on-premises clusters into public clouds and support preemptive scheduling. However, for dynamic resizing, LSF uses tasks as abstractions for units of work requiring system resources. This approach, while effective, may lead to resource inefficiency, increased complexity, and reduced fine-grained control.

2.3 Flux

Flux [1] is an open source hierarchical resource management and scheduling framework designed to prioritize flexibility and elasticity. It permits the nesting of Flux instances in a tiered manner, facilitating more precise resource allocation and accommodating a broader array of use cases, notably including co-scheduling. It is also capable of nesting instances within a batch resource allocation provided by other resource managers, such as SLURM. Currently, Flux provides detailed resource management with static resource allocation.

2.4 Dynamic Resource Management of MPI Jobs

The dynamic resource management of MPI jobs [7,8] relies on MPI Sessions [6,14] and PMIx [4], demonstrated by a prototype platform that utilizes an extended Open MPI, OpenPMIx, and PRRTE to flexibly allocate resources at the node level. Resources are depicted as modifiable sets through set operations, organized hierarchically. The overhead of dynamic resource management in the application is relatively low, with re-allocation taking between 71–180 ms when scaling across four nodes.

3 Scheduler-Guided Elastic Leader-Follower SPMD Model

We introduce the Scheduler-Guided Elastic Leader-Follower model, inspired by social media platforms, as depicted in Fig. 1. This model is defined using an executable file that follows a single program multiple data (SPMD).

The executable file specifies the job, the roles (leader/follower), and their functionality, with the experimental flexibility to switch roles for elastic scaling across a cluster or job migration. The executable file also includes role discovery,

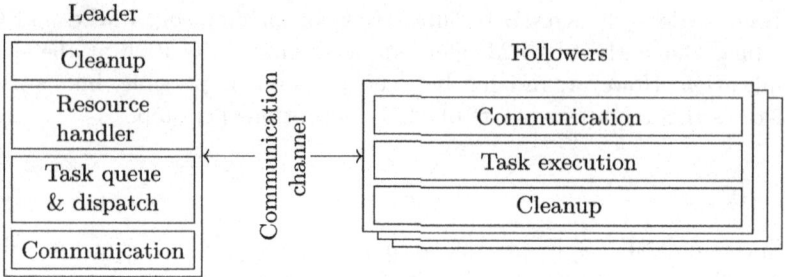

Fig. 1. Overview of the Leader-Follower programming model with their main components.

allowing dynamic assignment of Leader or Follower roles upon execution. Additionally, it features a resource handler that tracks Followers. A job refers to a computational operation that users wish to perform, which can be divided into smaller discrete units of work called tasks. These tasks are organized and managed in a task queue, similar to the task-based programming model. The Leader functions as the central manager, handling critical operations such as maintaining the communication channel and managing the task queue to distribute computational tasks to Followers. The Follower connects to the Leader via the communication channel and executes tasks assigned by the Leader. In our model, Followers receive the necessary computational resources from FlexiAlloc. Both Leader and Followers include cleanup functionality to ensure smooth teardown of communication and termination upon completion. When the task queue is completed, the Leader initiates a cleanup process and resource release. This model emphasizes elasticity, allowing the Leader to dynamically scale the number of Followers up or down. In addition, FlexiAlloc can guide this scaling process automatically, based on current workloads and objectives. This includes performance scaling, which aims to maximize resource allocation for improved throughput, and priority scaling, which first shrinks the low-priority job resources and then allocates the maximum available resources for high-priority job. Currently, application developers need to adhere to this model. However, with the stable version of FlexiAlloc, potentially as a scheduling plugin in Flux, this will not be necessary. Most of the features will be integrated or extended, and many of the components are similar.

4 FlexiAlloc: A Dynamic Resource Management Framework

FlexiAlloc is a fast prototype version of a scheduler with dynamic resource management framework. The primary motivation for developing a FlexiAlloc was to address dynamic resource allocation within SCMJSS to support job malleability.

Figure 2 presents the architectural framework of FlexiAlloc. The FlexiAlloc master is the primary instance of the FlexiAlloc, composed of several compo-

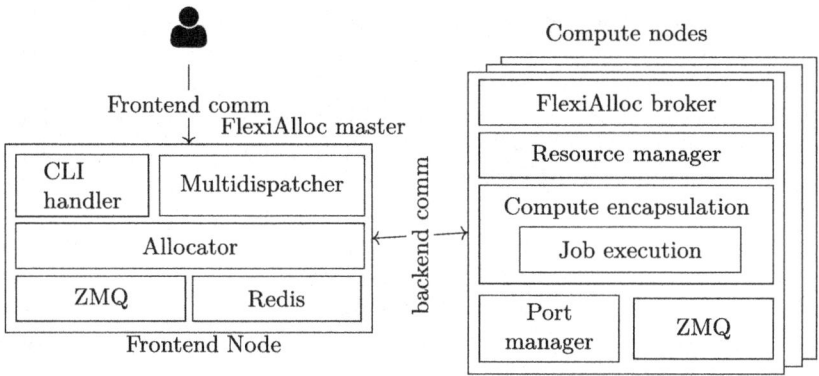

Fig. 2. Overview of the FlexiAlloc framework with encompassed components.

nents running on a frontend node. The CLI handler, which is the first contact point for users, oversees job submissions by checking mandatory details like initial CPU core, executable file, and priority. Following this, the Multidispatcher facilitates smooth job processing, ensuring that they follow priority through multiple job state queues like pending and running. These job state queues not only enable clear distinction based on their states but also aid in job migration from the 'running' queue to the 'pending' queue to make way for urgent/high-priority jobs. Redis [10] is an in-memory database known for its low latency and high throughput capabilities. It can scale using Redis Cluster, making it ideal for large HPC environments with multiple nodes. The Key Value Store (KVS) is a fundamental concept in Redis, where data are stored as a collection of keys and associated values. Therefore, Redis was chosen to serve as the KVS to store the job, resource, and other details of FlexiAlloc. ZeroMQ (ZMQ) [2] serves as an essential communication backbone, making it ideal for the development of distributed and scalable applications. It offers low-latency, high-throughput messaging, along with adaptable patterns and resilience to faults. Also, it is extensively utilized in HPC schedulers for inter process and internode communication. The FlexiAlloc broker denotes the system-level instance of FlexiAlloc, tasked with managing system resources via the resource manager and executing allocated jobs via compute encapsulation. The compute encapsulation acts as the core mechanism of FlexiAlloc, similar to a wrapper, capable of handling dynamic resource allocation, provided that the necessary resources are available. Each compute encapsulation is assigned a unique identifier, such as c1, c2, etc., within the FlexiAlloc broker. As depicted in Fig. 2, it accommodates several types of communication channels, including the frontend comm for user interaction, the backend comm to coordinate activities among FlexiAlloc components, and the compute comm to facilitate interactions between jobs and compute encapsulation. These communication channels utilize TCP sockets, with ports allocated by the port manager. It is presumed that jobs will be submitted using the CLI. Jobs are expected to be submitted with only the minimal required resources for execution, so that they can begin as soon as possible, while additional resources can be dynamically requested within the executable file. Figure 3 depicts the hierarchical structure of FlexiAlloc, including the FlexiAlloc master, brokers, and compute encapsulations. The dotted lines illustrate the capability to dynamically modify resource allocation, achieved through Control Groups (cgroups) [5] a feature of the Linux kernel that enables fine-grained resource (CPU, memory, I/O etc.) control for processes, making them ideal for dynamic resource allocation. FlexiAlloc presently offers dynamic allocation for CPU and memory resources. During the startup, FlexiAlloc establishes a top-level cgroup, termed `flexialloc` for each FlexiAlloc broker. The top-level cgroup consists of a parent-child hierarchy of cgroups. Here, a parent cgroup, e.g., `c1`, is linked with compute encapsulation `c1`, and the child cgroups, e.g., 1, 2, etc., are associated with executable file processes. Upon the startup of FlexiAlloc, the user can submit the job in which the FlexiAlloc master assigns the job to the available FlexiAlloc broker. When the FlexiAlloc broker discovers an incoming job, it verifies the compute encapsulation's availability. If available, it assigns the job; otherwise, it waits. Subsequently, the compute encapsulation prepares by allocating a port for compute comm and exports this, along with the compute encapsulation ID (e.g., c1/c2), as an environment variable. The executable file is then executed, and its related processes are binded to the core using child cgroups.

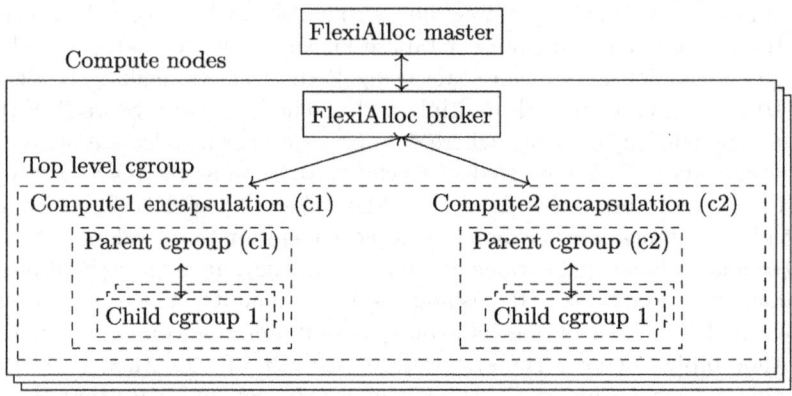

Fig. 3. Hierarchical structure of FlexiAlloc running on three compute nodes, including the master, broker, and compute encapsulations.

FlexiAlloc offers two resource allocation commands: `ADD` to allocate additional CPU cores and `DEL` to release allocated CPU cores. To manage resource allocation expansion, the job Leader requests cores by providing the compute encapsulation ID, and the type, e.g. `ADD 1`. The compute encapsulation then checks with the broker to confirm resource availability. If approved, the broker expands the core allocation for the parent cgroup linked to the compute encapsulation. This is followed by execution of the same executable file, spawning new child followers that integrate with the compute comm followed by binding to the core using a child group. The Follower greets the job Leader process once ready, which can assign tasks to these new followers. When it comes to shrinking, the job Leader can submit a request to free up resources by specifying the compute encapsulation ID, resources to release (e.g., DEL 2 if two cores are being freed), which is passed to the compute encapsulation. This subsequently updates the FlexiAlloc broker followed by termination of the Followers and core release. Additionally, the compute encapsulation tracks the process IDs of all processes under it, including the Leader and its Follower processes. If these processes do not terminate gracefully, they can be forcibly terminated. In the current allocation scheme, we have two resource abstractions for the CPU i.e. socket and cores. There are two methods for allocating CPU resources. The first is random allocation, where free cores are randomly assigned. The second is socket-based allocation, which involves mapping the compute encapsulation ID to a socket; it is assumed that the number of compute encapsulations started corresponds to the available sockets. Once compute encapsulations are initialized, core allocation is confined to those within the specific socket. It is also assumed that cores are sequentially numbered within sockets. In addition, mutexes are used in the allocation scheme to avoid race conditions and ensure unique core allocation when multiple compute encapsulations are involved. Also, resource allocation requests are processed in a FIFO fashion.

5 Evaluations

FlexiAlloc evaluations were carried out using the `ice, wolpy` systems that have an Intel Xeon 8360Y CPU(2 sockets each having 36 cores), mainly by estimating pi using the Monte Carlo method. Here, a random point (x, y) is generated within a square, centered at the origin. Followed by checking if this point lies within the inscribed unit circle by verifying if $x^2 + y^2 \leq 1$. This procedure is repeated for a large number of sample points. In addition, for some evaluations, our in-house benchmarking platform AutoBench [11] was used.

5.1 Dynamic Resource Allocation

In HPC environments, dynamic resource allocation provides flexibility for job resources beyond fixed system configurations. Additionally, this flexibility can facilitate resource reallocation during periods of idle nodes, leading to faster execution and improved throughput. Figure 4 illustrates the dynamic resource allocation of a job that estimates π (with 1,0000,000,000 samples) with FlexiAlloc, using performance scaling and socket-based allocation. Initially, two cores are utilized, one for the Leader and the other for the Follower. The total number of cores are increased progressively, for instance, with a 50% allocation, 17 Followers are added in round one, followed by eight in round two, and nine in round three where in reallocation occurs periodically at every six seconds. When free cores fall below 10, Followers are assigned directly to 100% to reduce the overhead associated with smaller allocations. As additional cores are allocated in subsequent phases, the execution time decreases. The speed is approximately 4x times faster with 100% core allocation compared to the single core execution time of 393 s. Furthermore, we present a detailed breakdown of the elapsed time into compute, resource allocation, and cleanup. This suggests that the overheads related to resource allocation and cleanup are minimal (max 1.3 s), allowing scalable applications to benefit from dynamic resource allocation.

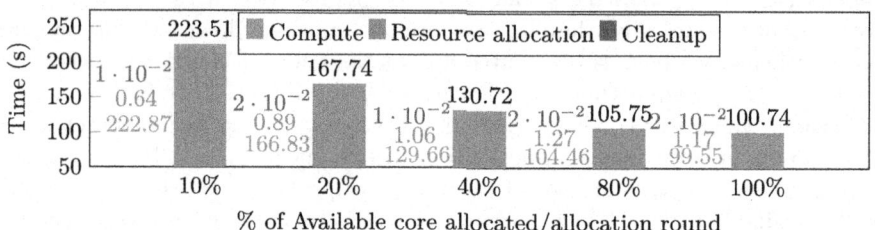

Fig. 4. Dynamic scaling CPU cores allocation for a job showing effective scaling with overheads.

5.2 Enhanced Job Throughput Through FlexiAlloc

The existing SCMJSS allocate resources statically at the beginning of the job. However, not all jobs can fully utilize all the available compute resources throughout the entire duration of the job, which affects the cluster's job throughput. FlexiAlloc facilitates co-scheduling by employing compute encapsulation, resulting in an increased throughput rate for jobs in a cluster. When paired with dynamic resource allocation, it can enhance throughput even further. To assess this, a scenario was tested in which jobs tasked with computing π using the Monte Carlo method (with 100,000,0000 samples), were statically allocated 15 cores (15 followers) within two compute encapsulations using performance scaling and socket-based allocation facilitating co-scheduling, resulting in double the speed out of the box. Furthermore, when the same jobs were assigned additional cores through dynamic allocation using performance scaling with 100% allocation of free cores, the number of followers eventually increased to 35. Figure 5 illustrates the execution times for SLURM, Flux, and FlexiAlloc across varied workloads detailing the elapsed time. For Flux, two child instances (each for one job) were created inside the parent Flux instance, which can be used to allocate the resources at the fine-grained level, allowing for effective co-scheduling. FlexiAlloc shows a speed-up of ≈1.9x over Flux and ≈4x over SLURM, highlighting the benefits of dynamic allocation. However, there is potential for further improvements, especially in relation to overheads from resource allocation and cleanup.

Dynamic Resource Management Framework for Elastic Computing 359

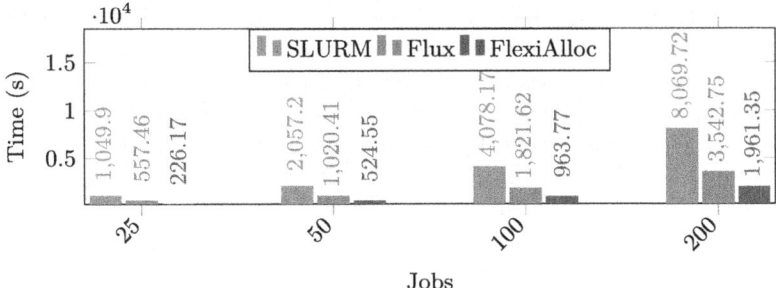

Fig. 5. Showcasing total execution time for different scheduler with varying workloads.

6 Showcase

This section emphasizes several key showcase capabilities of FlexiAlloc, primarily featuring priority scheduling with job preemption, facilitating urgent computing and job elasticity across a cluster.

6.1 Priority Scheduling with Job Preemption and Re-queuing Facilitating Urgent Computing

In HPC, users submit a diverse set of jobs, each having varied priority levels. Some are urgent and require immediate processing, while others can tolerate delays without major consequences. To address this, low-priority jobs can be preempted and placed back in the pending queue, freeing up resources for high-priority job arrivals. This method of priority scheduling enables urgent jobs with high priority to be processed swiftly, enhancing overall performance by adapting to workload changes and preventing starvation.

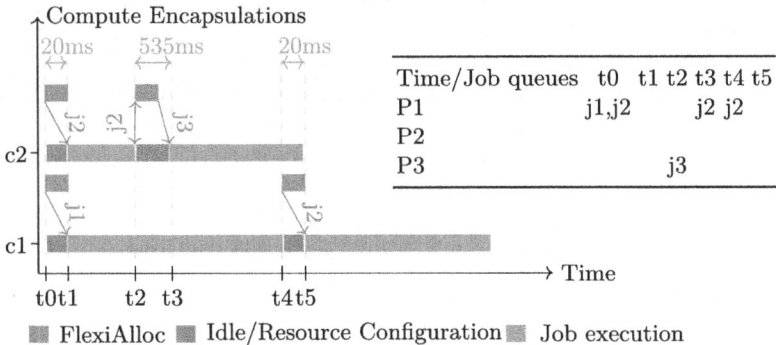

Fig. 6. Showcases the on demand job preemption and re-queuing of the low priority job on the arrival of the urgent high priority job.

Figure 6 illustrates the FlexiAlloc allocation using three different job priority queues (p1 being the lowest and p3 the highest) with two compute encapsulations (c1 and c2) using priority scaling and socket-based allocation. Here, jobs are estimating π (with 100,000,0000 samples). At timestamp 0 (t0), FlexiAlloc receives two jobs (j1, j2) in the queue P1 and assigns them to compute encapsulation at time step (t1). At timestep (t2), a high-priority urgent job (j3) is received, prompting a request to compute encapsulation (c2) to preempt and requeue the job (j2) to the P1 queue, allowing the job (j3) to be processed. At timestep (t3), c2 completes cleanup tasks (halting the previous job and reassigning resources) and starts job (j3). Also, due to priority scaling, the resources of job (j1) are reduced and granted to the job (j3), e.g. 50% CPU cores, leading to faster execution. Subsequently, c1 starts job (j2) after completing job (j1) in timestep (t5). The job (j2) was executed with two Follower processes, and the preemption and requeuing process took approximately 517 ms, an acceptable duration.

6.2 Elastic Computing Across the Cluster

As the complexity of job workflows increases, they often demand varying levels of computational resources throughout their execution cycle, and dynamic resource allocation across the cluster can significantly enhance such workflows, resulting in faster processing times. This underscores the necessity for job elasticity across the cluster. Figure 7 illustrates the extension of Follower beyond a single node by starting a new Follower on the `ice` node within the BEAST cluster, while the compute encapsulation is initially running on the isolated `wolpy` node. Once connected, the Leader begins delegating tasks to the newly initiated Follower. In particular, the Follower on the `ice` node was manually initiated using the IP and port number, as assigned by the compute encapsulation to manage the compute comm with the `woolpy` node. This setup assumes that the user has access to both machines and the required job details. After joining (Step 1), the new `Follower3` sends a switch request (Step 2) to the current `Leader`, aiming to assume the role of Leader, and subsequently forwarding the switch request to `Follower1` and `Follower2`. The request includes the `ice` IP and port number and culminates with closing the current connection, prompting them to connect to the new connection exposed by `Follower3` as followers, where the `Leader` relinquishes its role as Leader and joins as Follower. Subsequently, `Follower3` assumes the Leader role (Step 4). This paves the way to address job flexibility beyond a single node, allowing several Follower processes to be initiated as needed and facilitating the relocation of the job Leader and eventually enhancing job migration capabilities across the cluster.

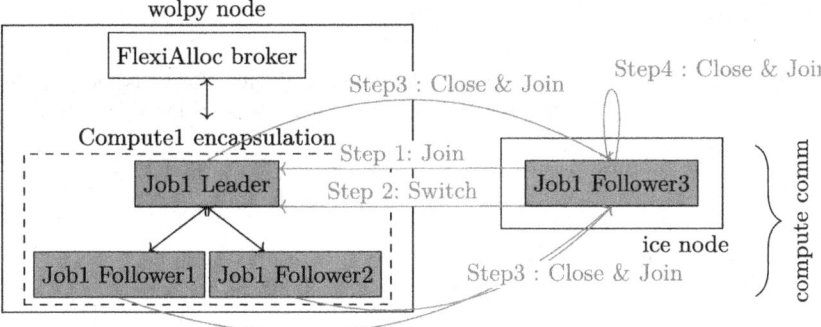

Fig. 7. Showcasing job elasticity by initiating a Follower process on the `ice` node and integrating it into the existing compute encapsulation (c1) on the `wolpy` node, and then promoting it to a leader.

7 Conclusion

In this paper, we introduce FlexiAlloc, a fast prototype version of scheduler with dynamic resource management framework. It allows for dynamic CPU core and memory allocation within a node for job processing. FlexiAlloc supports parallel job execution through compute encapsulation, advancing towards co-scheduling, and introduces the Leader-Follower programming model. We demonstrated how FlexiAlloc can dynamically allocate CPU cores, resulting in reduced execution times and improved cluster throughput. The integration of co-scheduling along with dynamic resource allocation through compute encapsulation can improve resource optimization. We showcased responsiveness to changing workloads by employing priority scheduling, allowing for the preemption and re-queuing of low-priority jobs to prioritize urgent job. We also examine cross-cluster job elasticity, planning for comprehensive integration, and detailed evaluations in the future. In the future, we aim to extend this to include GPU and accelerator allocations at the inter-node level. Additionally, we plan to address data distribution between tasks using the LAIK library [9]. Furthermore, there are plans to integrate this work into existing SCMJSS systems, such as Flux [12], through plugins.

Acknowledgments. This paper is partially funded by the CoMPS project, funding number 16ME0647 from the Federal Ministry of Education and Research (BMBF). This includes funding by the European Union - NextGenerationEU.

A Appendix: Artifact Availability/Artifact Evaluation

Artifacts: ⚭ — Code: ⚭ — Code licenses : MIT License

References

1. Ahn, D.H., et al.: Flux: overcoming scheduling challenges for exascale workflows. In: 2018 IEEE/ACM Workflows in Support of Large-Scale Science (WORKS), pp. 10–19 (2018)
2. The ZeroMQ authors: ZeroMQ. https://zeromq.org/. Accessed 28 Jan 2025
3. Carsten Trinitis, J.W.: Co-Scheduling of HPC Applications. Advances in Parallel Computing, vol. 28. IOS Press, Amsterdam (2017)
4. Castain, R.H., Hursey, J., Bouteiller, A., Solt, D.: PMIx: process management for exascale environments. Parallel Comput. **79**, 9–29 (2018)
5. The Kernel Development Community: Control group v2 - the linux kernel documentation. https://docs.kernel.org/admin-guide/cgroup-v2.html. Accessed 28 Jan 2025
6. Holmes, D., et al.: MPI sessions: leveraging runtime infrastructure to increase scalability of applications at exascale. In: Proceedings of the 23rd European MPI Users' Group Meeting, EuroMPI 2016, pp. 121–129. Association for Computing Machinery, New York (2016)
7. Huber, D., Schreiber, M., Schulz, M.: A case study on PMIX-usage for dynamic resource management. In: Bienz, A., Weiland, M., Baboulin, M., Kruse, C. (eds.) High Performance Computing, pp. 42–55. Springer, Cham (2023). https://doi.org/10.1007/978-3-031-40843-4_4
8. Huber, D., Streubel, M., Comprés, I., Schulz, M., Schreiber, M., Pritchard, H.: Towards dynamic resource management with MPI sessions and PMIX. In: Proceedings of the 29th European MPI Users' Group Meeting, EuroMPI/USA 2022, pp. 57–67. Association for Computing Machinery, New York (2022)
9. Weidendorfer, J., Yang, D., Trinitis, C.: LAIK: a library for fault tolerant distribution of global data for parallel applications. In: Konferenzband des PARS 2017 Workshops, p. 10. Gesellschaft der Informatik (2017)
10. Redis Ltd.: Docs. https://redis.io/docs/latest/. Accessed 28 Jan 2025
11. Parab, A., Raoofy, A.: AutoBench: a holistic platform for automated and reproducible benchmarking in HPC testbeds (2025). https://doi.org/10.5281/zenodo.14732455
12. Patki, T., et al.: Fluxion: a scalable graph-based resource model for HPC scheduling challenges. In: Proceedings of the SC 2023 Workshops of The International Conference on High Performance Computing, Network, Storage, and Analysis, SC-W 2023, pp. 2077–2088. Association for Computing Machinery, New York (2023)
13. Quintero, D., et al.: IBM Platform Computing Solutions for High Performance and Technical Computing Workloads. IBM Redbooks (2015)
14. Ureña, I.A.C., Riepen, M., Konow, M., Gerndt, M.: Invasive MPI on Intel's single-chip cloud computer. In: Herkersdorf, A., Römer, K., Brinkschulte, U. (eds.) ARCS 2012. LNCS, vol. 7179, pp. 74–85. Springer, Heidelberg (2012). https://doi.org/10.1007/978-3-642-28293-5_7
15. Yoo, A.B., Jette, M.A., Grondona, M.: SLURM: simple linux utility for resource management. In: Feitelson, D., Rudolph, L., Schwiegelshohn, U. (eds.) JSSPP 2003. LNCS, vol. 2862, pp. 44–60. Springer, Heidelberg (2003). https://doi.org/10.1007/10968987_3

Enabling Seamless Transitions from Experimental to Production HPC for Interactive Workflows

Brian D. Etz, David M. Rogers, Michael J. Brim, Ketan Maheshwari, Kellen Leland, Tyler J. Skluzacek, Jack Lange, Daniel Pelfrey, Jordan Webb, Patrick Widener, Ryan Adamson, Christopher Zimmer, Verónica G. Melesse Vergara, Mallikarjun Shankar, Sarp Oral, and Rafael Ferreira da Silva(✉)

Oak Ridge National Laboratory, Oak Ridge, TN 37831, USA
silvarf@ornl.gov

Abstract. The evolving landscape of scientific computing requires seamless transitions from experimental to production HPC environments for interactive workflows. This paper presents a structured transition pathway developed at OLCF that bridges the gap between development testbeds and production systems. We address both technological and policy challenges, introducing frameworks for data streaming architectures, secure service interfaces, and adaptive resource scheduling for time-sensitive workloads and improved HPC interactivity. Our approach transforms traditional batch-oriented HPC into a more dynamic ecosystem capable of supporting modern scientific workflows that require near real-time data analysis, experimental steering, and cross-facility integration.

Keywords: Interactive HPC Workflows · Time-Sensitive Computing · Cross-Facility Integration · High Performance Computing

1 Introduction

High performance computing (HPC) has traditionally operated in a batch-oriented paradigm, where jobs are submitted to queues, executed when resources

---

This manuscript has been authored in part by UT-Battelle, LLC, under contract DE-AC05-00OR22725 with the US Department of Energy (DOE). The US government retains and the publisher, by accepting the article for publication, acknowledges that the US government retains a nonexclusive, paid-up, irrevocable, worldwide license to publish or reproduce the published form of this manuscript, or allow others to do so, for US government purposes. DOE will provide public access to these results of federally sponsored research in accordance with the DOE Public Access Plan (http://energy.gov/downloads/doepublic-access-plan).

© The Author(s), under exclusive license to Springer Nature Switzerland AG 2026
S. Neuwirth et al. (Eds.): ISC High Performance 2025 Workshops, LNCS 16091, pp. 363–375, 2026.
https://doi.org/10.1007/978-3-032-07612-0_28

become available, and results are retrieved after completion [8]. However, modern scientific workflows increasingly demand interactive capabilities that allow researchers to steer computations in near real time, analyze data as it is generated, and make informed decisions during the execution of experiments [12,13]. This shift is driven by scientific machine learning (ML) models that guide exploration and by experimental facilities that produce data at unprecedented rates [2,9]. Therefore, as these workflows mature, alternative interactive computing strategies that complement traditional computing operations are required for seamless integration across facility boundaries.

Time-sensitive applications present particularly challenging requirements for HPC systems. These applications require time-critical/sensitive access to computing resources (i.e., real time or near real time), motivated by a need for timely decision making, experiment steering, virtual proximity, or loss of data fidelity [10,12]. Experiments such as the Linac Coherent Light Source (LCLS-II) require near real-time data analysis and instrument steering within strict time constraints [14]. This requires preemptive scheduling and advance reservations to align computational resources with experiment timelines. Similarly, data-intensive integration workflows for DIII-D tokamak fusion experiments [1] require robust data movement and flexible authentication across institutional boundaries. Current HPC technologies and policies, designed primarily for batch processing, are often ill-equipped to support these emerging patterns of scientific computing.

Testbeds offer an attractive approach to evaluate and address interactive HPC challenges, yet a significant barrier remains between testbed and production environments. While testbeds provide flexibility for innovative workflows, they lack the scale, reliability, and security required for production science. Conversely, production HPC systems are optimized for traditional batch workloads with policies that often impede interactive applications. This disconnect forces researchers to substantially modify workflows when transitioning to production from sandboxed testbed environments, slowing scientific progress and limiting the adoption of cutting-edge methodologies.

At the Oak Ridge Leadership Computing Facility (OLCF), we are establishing a transition pathway that bridges the gap between development testbeds and production HPC environments (Sect. 6). This pathway provides a rubric for researchers to easily and systematically adapt their interactive workflows through progressively enhanced computing environments, while at the same time providing useful information on how OLCF might need to adapt our production environments in the future. Our approach is motivated by close collaboration with users to enable their interactive workflows and combines the necessary policy adaptations for security, operations, and resource allocation with important technological innovations in data streaming, secure service interfaces, and flexible resource scheduling (Fig. 1). This paper examines these policy and technological requirements, using a practical case study to demonstrate effective strategies for seamless transitions from experimental to production environments.

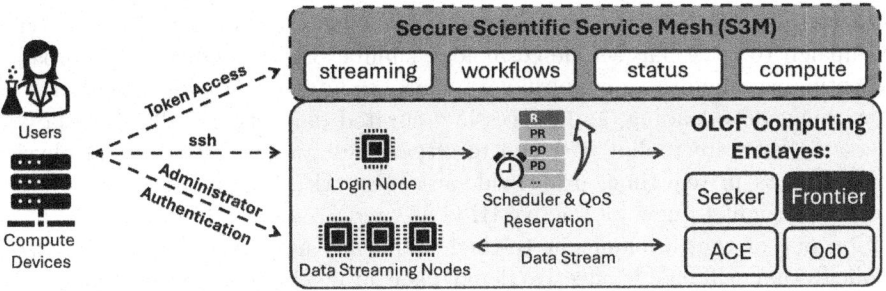

Fig. 1. OLCF's integrated approach to interactive computing. External users connect via secure authentication methods, accessing a suite of specialized services for status monitoring, computation, workflow management, and data streaming that collectively enable seamless interactivity across the computing environments.

2 Computing Landscape at OLCF

OLCF has a long history of delivering, operating, and conducting research on world-leading supercomputers. The most recent being Frontier, the world's first exascale system. Frontier exemplifies the evolution of leadership computing, pushing beyond traditional HPC architectures to achieve unprecedented performance [3]. As a leadership system, Frontier provides a platform for solving the most complex scientific and engineering challenges that demand exascale computing resources while still operating under the traditional batch-oriented HPC paradigm.

To accommodate the ever-changing landscape of scientific discovery utilizing HPC, OLCF has implemented programs for active development, such as the Advanced Computing Ecosystem (ACE) [11] and the Quantum Computing User Program (QCUP). These programs aid the OLCF by providing environments for testing new technologies, developing interactive workflows across facilities, and evaluating necessary changes to traditional HPC policies that limit the interactive use of HPC. The ACE testbed has enabled significant progress in technology development and evaluation, exploration of diverse computing workflows that exemplify the architectural patterns identified by the DOE's Integrated Research Infrastructure (IRI) program [10], and support for early-stage development of science pilots spanning the breadth of the DOE-SC program. Similarly, QCUP has provided a program for users to explore the integration of quantum computing with traditional HPC and to evaluate application, infrastructure, and policy constraints surrounding new paradigms in computing [4].

Transitioning interactive workflows from development to production within leadership computing environments requires a systematic approach tailored to the project scope that addresses evolving requirements across different computing enclaves. Three use cases will be discussed to showcase how different project scopes drive new HPC interactivity. LCLStream involves streaming data from SLAC's LCLS beamlines to compute nodes at OLCF to perform high-throughput analysis and AI modeling on experimental X-ray data. OpenCosmo is a long-term campaign to make large-scale cosmology simulations accessible to the broader scientific community to support data sharing and provide capabilities such as searching, downloading, and processing, curated datasets. Finally, Deleria is a versatile software toolkit designed to stream and analyze results from physics experiments in real-time, using wide-area networks. These three case studies provide insight to new interactive HPC use and are currently undergoing transition out of the development testbed, requiring supporting technologies and policies that will enable effective deployment in production environments.

3 End-to-End Interactive Workflow

Modern scientific computing demands both specialized infrastructure and efficient data exchange mechanisms. This section presents OLCF's computing environments for interactive workflow development and introduces a project that implements experimental data streaming for near real-time analysis.

3.1 Computing Landscape at OLCF

OLCF provides a spectrum of computing environments designed to facilitate transitions from experimental to production workflows. Frontier [3], the world's first exascale system, delivers unprecedented performance while operating within traditional batch-oriented HPC paradigms. Frontier serves as the ultimate destination for mature workflows that require leadership-class computing capabilities (i.e., jobs consuming 20% or more compute nodes at any given time).

To bridge the development-to-production gap, OLCF has established the Advanced Computing Ecosystem (ACE) [11] and Quantum Computing User Program (QCUP). These environments enable researchers to explore interactive workflows across facilities, test emerging technologies, and evaluate necessary policy adaptations before transitioning to production systems. ACE enables significant progress in technology development and supports diverse computing patterns identified by DOE's Integrated Research Infrastructure (IRI) program [10], while QCUP allows exploration of quantum computing integration with traditional HPC resources [4].

ACE has played a pivotal role in advancing interactive HPC capabilities by providing a flexible environment for experimentation with emerging technologies and collaboration with external users across experimental and computational facilities. The testbed supports diverse computational patterns, allowing researchers to prototype innovative workflows that require near real-time data analysis, experimental steering, and cross-facility integration. ACE's infrastructure accommodates the development of custom authentication mechanisms, data streaming architectures, and specialized resource scheduling required by interactive applications. This environment has proven particularly valuable for time-sensitive workloads like the LCLS-II experiments, where near real-time analysis of experimental data guides ongoing scientific discoveries. By creating a sandbox environment, ACE enables rapid iteration on complex multi-facility workflows before they must contend with the stricter policies of production systems.

3.2 Streaming Experimental Data for Near Real-Time Analysis

The LCLStream project exemplifies the challenges of transitioning interactive workflows to production environments, aiming to accelerate scientific discovery by processing beamline data from SLAC's LCLS facility on OLCF's HPC resources [15]. This workflow enables researchers to launch compute jobs during their scheduled beamtime or interactive analysis sessions, establishing high-bandwidth data paths between the data transfer nodes and allocated HPC resources.

Despite its conceptual simplicity, the LCLS implementation encountered three fundamental challenges that would later inform our holistic framework for interactive HPC:

1. High-performance data movement required innovations in network architecture. For LCLStream's high-speed data transfer needs, we implemented experimental network configurations that connected the Energy Sciences Network (ESNet) testbed and science DMZ networks to ACE compute nodes, with carefully managed firewall rules and SLURM integration to maintain security boundaries. Although successful in achieving full switching capacity throughput, these approaches proved too complex for production environments, prompting the development of the memory-to-memory data streaming framework described in Sect. 5.1 as a more scalable solution.
2. Authentication and access control emerged as a critical barrier. OLCF security models traditionally rely on human-verified SSH sessions rather than programmatic API access, creating a significant obstacle for automated workflows that require machine-to-machine communication across facility boundaries. To address this challenge, we implemented a container-based solution to deploy custom REST APIs that satisfy security requirements while enabling programmatic resource access. These APIs allow LCLS users to authenticate once through multifactor verification and delegate secure access tokens to their software, a pattern that directly informed the development of our Secure Scientific Service Mesh (S3M) framework detailed in Sect. 5.2.
3. Time-sensitive resource allocation required fundamental rethinking of scheduling models. In an environment optimized for large batch jobs, interactive workflows with strict timing requirements demanded innovative approaches to resource prioritization. Our solution implemented on ACE utilizes SLURM's preemptive scheduling capabilities, refined through a "Quality of Service (QoS) reservation" system that provides guaranteed availability without the resource inefficiency of traditional node reservations. This approach, detailed in Sect. 5.3, allows specific user groups to receive elevated priority during scheduled periods, ensuring that their workflows start immediately while minimizing system-wide impact.

The LCLStream experience directly shaped our comprehensive approach to interactive HPC workflows. Through this project, we discovered that successful cross-facility integration requires simultaneous evolution in three interconnected domains: security, operations, and resource allocation. On the security front, we had to reimagine authentication from a user-centric model to a service-oriented framework with delegated credentials and fine-grained access controls, preserving strong security boundaries while enabling automated data flows. Operationally, the project revealed a fundamental tension between the unpredictable timing of experimental facilities and the rigid maintenance schedules of production HPC systems, necessitating new service level agreements and incident response protocols specifically designed for time-sensitive workloads. Perhaps most significantly, LCLStream challenged traditional resource allocation metrics based solely on system utilization, highlighting the scientific value of immediate but short-duration access to computing resources aligned with experimental beamtime. These insights, together with similar requirements from other applications, formed the foundation of our policy considerations (Sect. 4) and drove the development of technologies that could systematically address these interrelated challenges while providing a clear pathway from experimental to production deployment.

As these solutions mature, they establish patterns to address similar requirements in other interactive HPC applications transitioning to production environments, and guide our structured transition pathway detailed in Sect. 6. The LCLStream project demonstrates how each stage of the transition from ACE to production systems requires careful consideration of both technological capabilities and policy frameworks to maintain workflow functionality while enhancing security and reliability.

4 Policy Considerations and Challenges

Enabling interactive HPC workflows requires fundamental policy adaptations beyond the technological solutions. Traditional HPC policies, designed primarily for batch processing, must evolve to accommodate the dynamic and time-sensitive nature of interactive workflows while ensuring system security and efficiency.

4.1 Security Policy Adaptations

Security policies are designed to ensure high assurance for the appropriateness of data access and correctness of workflow execution. Interactive workflows challenge traditional HPC security models by requiring external data streams to access supercomputing resources on demand. This represents a significant departure from conventional isolated computing environments, where access is mediated exclusively through SSH sessions. For projects like LCLStream, where experimental facilities need to initiate workflows and stream data to computing resources in real-time, security policies must be reimagined while ensuring every user and their actions are authenticated, authorized, and evaluated for appropriate use and intent for the corresponding computing environment.

We have developed a security framework that implements token-based authentication with time-limited credentials alongside API gateways on secure access nodes with fine-grained authorization controls. Application-aware traffic governance through S3M (Sect. 5.2) provides an additional layer of protection. This approach maintains robust security boundaries while enabling the necessary external connections for interactive science.

Our experience indicates that traditional network firewalls often become bottlenecks for interactive workloads. Instead, science DMZ architectures with dedicated network interfaces for interactive services provide better performance while maintaining security through isolated VLANs and strict access controls. Security protocols must evolve from a closed fortress model to a selectively permeable membrane that allows data and computations to flow as needed for science, but under tight scrutiny and control.

4.2 Operational Policy for Time-Sensitive Workloads

Interactive workflows require operational guarantees that conflict with traditional maintenance and resource allocation policies. To accommodate these needs, maintenance windows must be carefully scheduled, communicated, and tightly coupled with resource reservations, with provisions for critical interactive services to remain operational, when possible. Service Level Agreements (SLAs) for interactive services with defined uptime requirements provide clear expectations for both users and system administrators.

Specialized incident response protocols now prioritize restoration of time-sensitive services when issues arise. Change management procedures include an additional risk assessment for modifications that could affect interactive services, with increased testing requirements and fallback provisions. These operational adaptations recognize that interruptions to interactive workflows can have major scientific consequences, especially when coordinated with experimental facilities.

4.3 Resource Allocation and Scheduling Policies

Perhaps the most challenging policy shift involves fairly allocating resources between traditional batch jobs and interactive workflows with strict timing requirements. Our approach includes QoS-based preemptive scheduling tiers that enable time-critical applications to interrupt lower-priority workloads when necessary. Resource allocation and scheduling mechanisms guarantee availability without the inefficiency of traditional node reservations by elevating priority for specific user groups during scheduled periods.

Multi-tenancy policies now allow appropriate resource sharing while maintaining security and performance boundaries between users. In experimental environments, containerization technologies like Docker and OpenShift provide sufficient isolation, but production HPC systems require more robust mechanisms such as virtual machines and confidential computing enclaves to guarantee both security and performance isolation. These differences require policy frameworks that can be translated across enforcement mechanisms as workflows transition from testbed to production. We have implemented formalized justification processes for requesting prioritized access to balance system-wide resource utilization with the needs of time-sensitive applications, with well-defined authorization workflows for accessing shared resources.

The transition from experimental to production environments involves progressively stricter resource allocation policies. While testbeds such as ACE allow flexible, on-demand access, production systems require structured approval processes that balance the needs of interactive workflows against broader system utilization. Resource allocation committees must develop new evaluation criteria that account for the value of time sensitivity, rather than focusing exclusively on core hours or node utilization metrics that have traditionally governed HPC allocation decisions.

5 Technology Framework for Interactive HPC

After addressing policy considerations in Sect. 4, we now present the technological frameworks required to implement these policies effectively. Our framework balances innovation with security, reliability, and the scale required for production operations. This section describes three core components that collectively enable interactive workflows to successfully transition from testbeds to production environments (Fig. 1).

5.1 Memory-to-Memory Data Streaming Framework

Interactive HPC applications increasingly require near real-time data movement between experimental facilities and computational resources as outlined for LCLStream (Sect. 3.2). Our data streaming architecture [5] enables direct memory-to-memory transfers between producer and consumer endpoints, significantly reducing latency compared to traditional file-based transfers, while providing capabilities to connect compute jobs with experimental control applications. This architecture is accessed through an API embedded in S3M (Sect. 4.2) that provisions RabbitMQ or Redis messaging services on dedicated data streaming nodes (DSNs).

A defining feature is separation of the control and data planes to maintain security while maximizing performance. Control interfaces allow system administrators to implement authentication mechanisms and network access policies independently of high-throughput data paths. DSNs handle these data paths, operating either as application gateways with application-level context awareness (OSI layer 7) or as dedicated routers with selective traffic forwarding (OSI layer 4). The application gateway approach provides better security control but sacrifices some performance, while the router configuration offers higher throughput but relies on firewall rules rather than the application context.

DSNs connect to both external and internal HPC networks through high-speed interfaces, creating a controlled pathway between these environments. System administrators manage DSN configurations through templates, allowing application teams to specify limited parameters such as allowed external addresses, targeted internal nodes, and buffer settings. This maintains control and security while offering the necessary flexibility for diverse interactive workloads.

5.2 Cross-Facility Authentication and API Gateway

The Secure Scientific Service Mesh (S3M) [11] builds on existing scientific APIs (e.g. Superfacility [7] and FirecREST [6]) but distinguishes itself through a service mesh architecture that provides a unified framework for customizable services not possible in traditional API gateways such as, policy enforcement, dynamic routing, authentication, authorization, and traffic management between external services and internal HPC resources. A user's interaction with S3M is generally as follows: (1) access token generation through my OLCF web platform, (2) embed token in requests from client applications, and (3) S3M verifies the user and project permissions, authorizes, and executes the requested task.

This approach enables fine-grained access control to HPC resources through standardized APIs for low-latency data streaming and seamless workflow orchestration, allowing external workflows to interact with computation and storage resources without compromising security boundaries. S3M incorporates policy-as-code capabilities for defining secure access patterns, implements rate limiting to prevent resource exhaustion, and provides comprehensive logging for security auditing. The mesh architecture abstracts the underlying complexity of cross-facility authentication, allowing scientific workflows to focus on core functionality while security policies are consistently enforced at the infrastructure level.

5.3 Time-Sensitive Workload Prioritization System

Supporting time-sensitive interactive workflows requires fundamental changes in resource scheduling approaches. Our adaptive scheduling framework incorporates preemptive capabilities that allow high-priority interactive jobs to interrupt lower-priority batch workloads when necessary. This ensures resource availability for time-critical analysis while maintaining overall system utilization.

QoS implementations define service levels with associated resource guarantees, allowing administrators to assign appropriate priorities to different workflow types. SLURM's QoS features have been tailored to assign varying levels of priority and preemption capabilities to specific projects based on their time-sensitivity requirements. Users can select the appropriate QoS level when submitting jobs, with a project-based inheritance of these capabilities.

For workflows with more predictable schedules, we have implemented a refined "QoS reservation" system that provides guaranteed availability without the resource inefficiency of traditional node reservations. This approach requires coordination between users and system administrators to elevate specific user groups priority during scheduled periods, ensuring that their workflows start immediately while minimizing system-wide impact. Our validation test of the SLURM workflow manager scheme demonstrated that this approach effectively balances interactive and batch workloads across diverse user communities [11].

6 Experiment to Production Transition Architecture

We have devised a practical transition guide that researchers can follow to navigate the path from early prototyping to full-scale production deployment. By understanding the key considerations at each stage of this journey, developers can design their interactive workflows to minimize rework and maximize scientific productivity across the complete computing spectrum. This pathway can be conceptualized as a progression through distinct enclaves: open development environments, open production systems, and moderate security production platforms, each with specific requirements and capabilities.

Open development environments provide flexibility for rapid prototyping and experimentation, allowing researchers to establish workflow patterns and verify technical approaches. As workflows mature, they transition to open production systems, where operational stability becomes more critical, although authentication requirements remain relatively lightweight. The final stage involves deployment to moderate security production environments, where multi-factor authentication and stricter security policies are enforced to protect high-value computational resources. At OLCF, this pathway is implemented through a series of platforms: ACE provides the experimental testbed environment, Odo offers a production-like development system in the open enclave, Seeker serves as a production-development system in the moderate security enclave, and Frontier represents the ultimate production environment (Fig. 2).

This transition path provides a rubric to production; however, each use case is not built the same and may require different technology and policy considerations. Therefore, each step must be tailored to the specific scope of the project and requires careful consideration of authentication mechanisms, API access patterns, and resource allocation strategies to ensure that workflows remain functional while meeting increasing security requirements. This structured progression enables researchers to gradually evolve their workflows to adapt to the constraints of each environment without the need to re-engineer their workflows.

Table 1 summarizes the key technologies in our interactive HPC framework alongside their associated policy considerations. This holistic view highlights how each technological component requires specific policy adaptations across different computing environments. As workflows transition from development testbeds to production systems, these technologies and policies must evolve together, with increasing emphasis on security, reliability, and scalability. The framework provides a structured approach for researchers and system administrators to identify and address the specific requirements at each stage of the transition pathway, ensuring that interactive scientific workflows can successfully bridge the gap between experimental flexibility and production-level robustness.

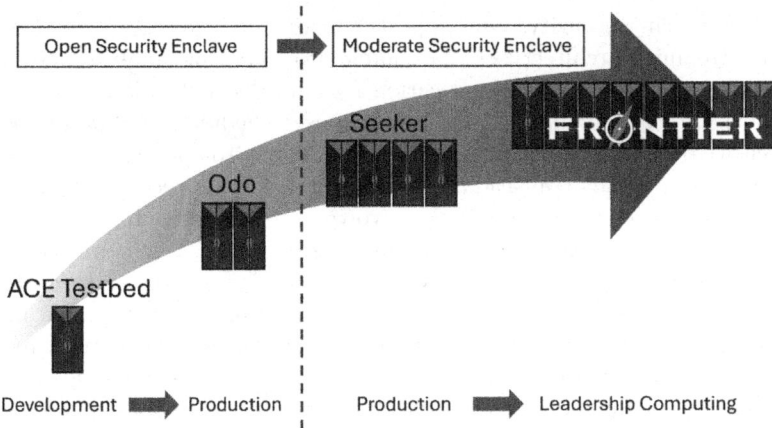

Fig. 2. OLCF transition path illustrating progression from the developmental testbed to production HPC to leadership computing, while spanning security enclaves.

Table 1. Interactive HPC Technologies and Associated Policy Considerations

Technology	Policy Considerations/Recommendations	Computing Environment
Memory-to-Memory Data Streaming Framework	- Token-based authentication with time-limited credentials - Separation of control and data planes - Science DMZ architectures with dedicated network interfaces - Templates for DSN configurations with limited user parameters	Development (ACE) → Production (Odo/Seeker)
Secure Scientific Service Mesh (S3M)	- Centralized authentication services - Fine-grained access control through standardized APIs - Policy-as-code capabilities for secure access patterns - Rate limiting to prevent resource exhaustion - Comprehensive logging for security auditing	Production (Odo/Seeker) → Leadership (Frontier)
Time-Sensitive Workload Prioritization	- QoS-based preemptive scheduling tiers - Resource reservation mechanisms without traditional inefficiency - Project-based inheritance of QoS capabilities - Formalized processes for requesting prioritized access	All Environments
Multi-tenancy Resource Sharing	- Containerization (Docker/OpenShift) for development - Virtual machines and confidential computing enclaves for production - Well-defined authorization for accessing shared resources	Development (ACE) → Production (Odo/Seeker)
Cross-Facility Integration	- Synchronized maintenance scheduling aligned with experimental facilities - Service level agreements with defined requirements - Specialized incident response for time-sensitive services - Change management procedures with risk assessment	Production (Odo/Seeker) → Leadership (Frontier)
Security Framework	- Application-aware traffic governance - Isolated VLANs with strict access controls - Evolution from closed fortress model to selectively permeable membrane - Increased testing requirements and fallback provisions	All Environments
Resource Allocation	- New evaluation criteria accounting for time sensitivity - Balance interactive workflows with broader system utilization - Structured approval processes for production systems - Flexible, on-demand access for development environments	All Environments

7 Conclusion

The transition from experimental to production HPC environments represents a critical challenge for interactive scientific workflows. Through our work at OLCF and in close collaboration with many users, we have demonstrated that a carefully structured pathway, combining technological innovations with policy adaptations, can successfully bridge this gap while preserving functionality and enhancing security. Our approach addresses three core requirements: (1) data streaming architectures that enable near real-time analysis across facility boundaries, (2) secure authentication frameworks that balance accessibility with robust protection, and (3) adaptive resource scheduling that accommodates time-sensitive workloads within traditional HPC environments.

The success of this transition framework depends on recognizing that each workflow has unique requirements that evolve as it progresses from development through production to leadership computing. By tailoring authentication mechanisms, API access patterns, and resource allocation strategies to each stage of this journey, researchers can maintain scientific productivity while meeting increasingly stringent security and reliability requirements. This structured progression transforms traditional batch-oriented HPC into a dynamic ecosystem capable of supporting modern scientific discovery processes that depend on interactive, time-sensitive computation.

As experimental facilities generate ever larger data volumes and scientific exploration becomes increasingly guided by machine learning models, the need for seamless integration between experimental workflows and production HPC will only grow. The transition pathway we have established provides a foundation for this integration, enabling researchers to harness the full potential of leadership computing resources for interactive scientific discovery.

Acknowledgments. This research used resources of the Oak Ridge Leadership Computing Facility at the Oak Ridge National Laboratory, supported by the Office of Science of the U.S. Department of Energy under Contract No. DE-AC05-00OR22725.

References

1. Bechtel Amara, T., et al.: Accelerating discoveries at DIII-D with the integrated research infrastructure. Front. Phys. **12** (2025). https://doi.org/10.3389/fphy.2024.1524041
2. Antypas, K.B., et al.: Enabling discovery data science through cross-facility workflows. In: 2021 IEEE International Conference on Big Data (Big Data), pp. 3671–3680 (2021). https://doi.org/10.1109/BigData52589.2021.9671421
3. Atchley, S., et al.: Frontier: exploring exascale. In: Proceedings of the International Conference for High Performance Computing, Networking, Storage and Analysis,. SC 2023 (2023). https://doi.org/10.1145/3581784.3607089
4. Beck, T., et al.: Integrating quantum computing resources into scientific hpc ecosystems. Futur. Gener. Comput. Syst. **161**, 11–25 (2024). https://doi.org/10.1016/j.future.2024.06.058
5. Brim, M.J., et al.: A High-level Design for Bidirectional Data Streaming to High-Performance Computing Systems from External Science Facilities. Tech. rep., Oak Ridge National Laboratory (ORNL), Oak Ridge, TN (United States) (Mar 2024). https://doi.org/10.2172/2338264
6. Cruz, F.A., et al.: Firecrest: a restful api to hpc systems. In: 2020 IEEE/ACM International Workshop on Interoperability of Supercomputing and Cloud Technologies (SuperCompCloud), pp. 21–26 (2020). https://doi.org/10.1109/SuperCompCloud51944.2020.00009

7. Enders, B., et al.: Cross-facility science with the Superfacility Project at LBNL. In: 2nd Annual Workshop on Large-Scale Experiment-in-the-Loop-Computing, pp. 1–7 (2020). https://doi.org/10.1109/XLOOP51963.2020.00006
8. Endo, T., et al.: Challenges in computing resource sharing towards next-gen interactive accelerated HPC. In: High Performance Computing. ISC High Performance 2024 International Workshops, pp. 231–242 (2025). https://doi.org/10.1007/978-3-031-73716-9_16
9. Jha, S., Pascuzzi, V.R., Turilli, M.: AI-coupled HPC workflows. arXiv preprint arXiv:2208.11745 (2022)
10. Miller, W.L., et al.: Integrated Research Infrastructure Architecture Blueprint Activity (Final Report 2023) (July 2023). https://doi.org/10.2172/1984466
11. Oral, S., et al.: Olcf's advanced computing ecosystem (ace): Fy24 efforts for the doe integrated research infrastructure (iri) program. Tech. rep., Oak Ridge National Laboratory (ORNL), Oak Ridge, TN (United States) (Nov 2024). https://doi.org/10.2172/2477506
12. Reuther, A., et al.: Interactive and urgent hpc: Challenges and opportunities (2024). https://arxiv.org/abs/2401.14550
13. da Silva, R.F., et al.: Frontiers in scientific workflows: pervasive integration with HPC. IEEE Comput. **57**(8) (2024). https://doi.org/10.1109/MC.2024.3401542
14. Thayer, J., et al.: Massive scale data analytics at LCLS-II. EPJ Web of Conf. **295** (2024). https://doi.org/10.1051/epjconf/202429513002
15. Wang, C., et al.: End-to-end deep learning pipeline for real-time bragg peak segmentation: from training to large-scale deployment. Front. High Perform. Comput. **3** (2025) https://doi.org/10.3389/fhpcp.2025.1536471

A Novel Approach to Dynamic Computing Using Slurm

Leonardo Sala[✉], Ivano Talamo, Borys Sharapov, Greta Assmann, and Alvise Dorigo

Paul Scherrer Institute, Forschungsstrasse 111, 5232 Villigen PSI, Switzerland
leonardo.sala@psi.ch

Abstract. During operations of the Swiss Light Source (SLS), it was customary for the high-volume scientific beamlines to have statically dedicated resources assigned to them. While providing a simple and predicting approach to resources assignation, this systematically led either to resource starvation during peak times, or waste of idle compute cycles. The push for better resources utilization during the operations of the upgraded facility (SLS2), and a more dynamical assignation of them, led to explore a novel approach to cluster management using a workload manager such as Slurm. By combining different Slurm and Systemd functionalities, we architected a way to move computing resources dynamically between clusters that may have different rules and requirements (e.g. accesses to different file systems), and we called it *flurm*, as in *flexible slurm*. The advantage over normal resources assignation such as reservations or dedicated partitions resides in the customization possibilities (storage mountpoints, running services) that this architecture allows. This feature is offered directly to the final users, that upon certain conditions can stear resources without the admins intervention. In this paper we describe the situation during SLS operations, the novel architecture that was designed and its implementation, its current status and way forward.

Keywords: Workload management · Dynamic computing

1 The Swiss Light Source and Its Compute Resources Usage

1.1 A Short Introduction to SLS

The Swiss Light Source (SLS) at the Paul Scherrer Institut is a synchrotron light source, which operated as third-generation synchrotron between June 2001 and October 2023. The upgrade project as fourth-generation light source (SLS2.0 project [1]) is currently ongoing, with user operations expected in 2026.

1.2 Compute Resources Utilization During SLS Operations

During the operations of the SLS, compute resources were bought by and assigned to the various experimental groups, and the central IT team would run and maintain them through their lifetimes. This approach enabled the scientists to have access to a predictable, always-on pool of resources, but it also showed limitations over the years:

1. Scientists had to wait for the lifecycle of their resources before being able to access new technologies, e.g. up-to-date compute architecture
2. Testing new technologies during experiments (e.g. GPUs) was impossible
3. It was not possible to temporarily increase resources during compute-intensive experiments
4. Compute nodes were mostly idle

These limitations hit different facility personnel with different impact: while the access to more dynamic and easily accessible resources is a priority for scientists, a better resource usage optimization and a reduction of idle cycles is a main concern for facility managers, in order to better optimise costs. Figure 1 clearly exemplifies the usage pattern during an operational year at SLS. Statically assigned resources are used with different loads among the experimental groups, and substantial differences can be seen even on a day-by-day case. In this usage sample, some groups might have profited from more resources (e.g. Group 5), while others were under-utilizing the assigned resources (e.g. Group 2): overall, the total used is reasonably flat around 30-40%, which suggests that a more efficient allocation should be possible.

Another effect of this approach was that compute nodes were treated as "pets", with unique names and hand-crafted configurations. This caused also various issues when the compute nodes had to be decommissioned and replaced. This tension became more evident when the Data Analysis cluster "Ra" came into operations in 2018, providing access to a more standard and homogeneous pool of resources.

2 A More Dynamical Approach to Resources Allocation

2.1 Requirements

Based on the usage and pattern analysis of compute nodes load, the Science IT team decided to proceed with a novel approach to the allocation of compute resources. The base requirements that defined the architecture were:

1. Enable scientists to have a baseline amount of compute resources, if needed
2. Enable scientists to request additional compute resources during an experiment
3. Support reproducible customization based on the scientist community, including storage mountpoints
4. Base the allocated compute resources from a common pool of compute nodes

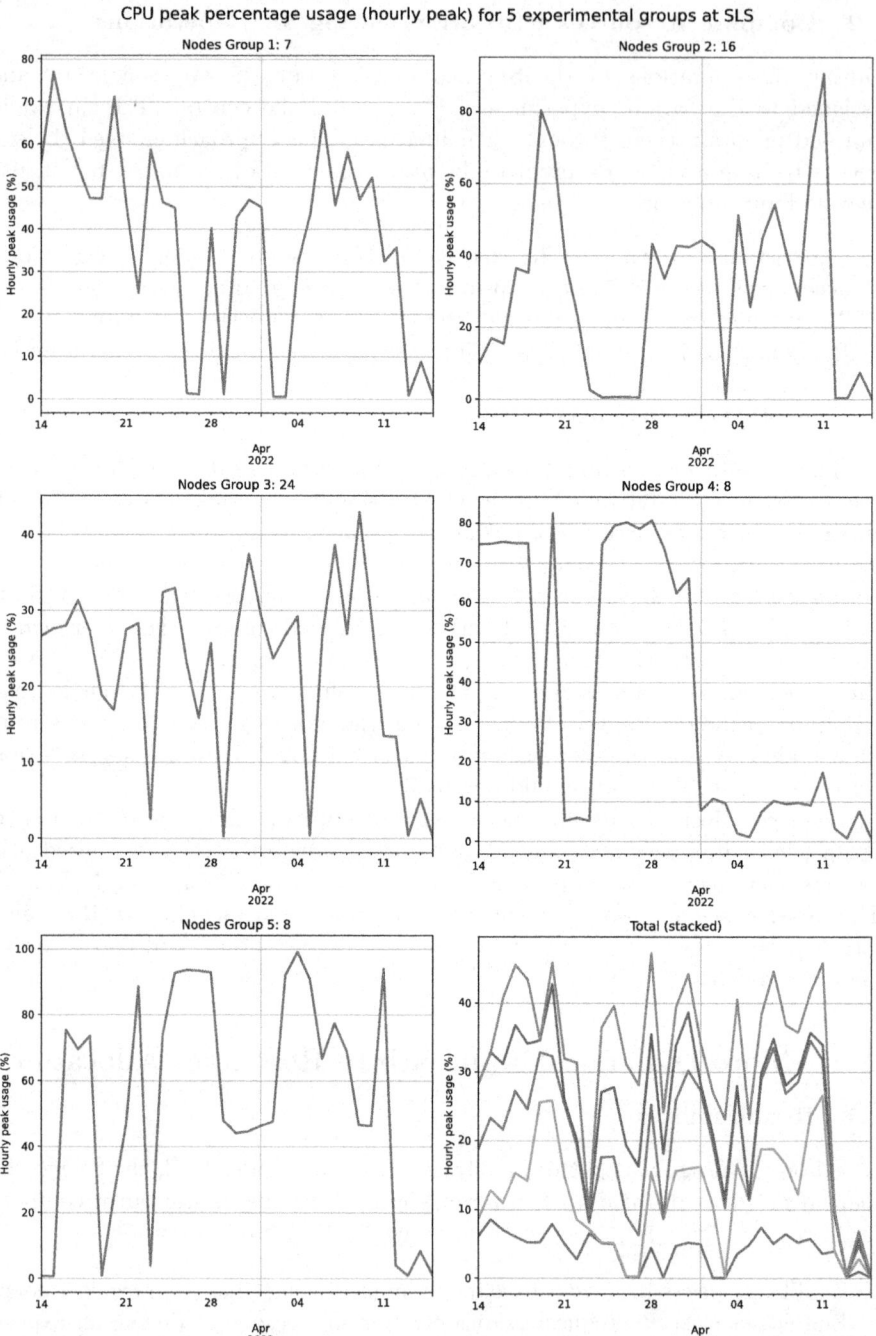

Fig. 1. CPU percentage usage between 2022-04-14 and 2022-05-16 for the 5 SLS experimental groups owning dedicated resources. The hourly peak has been computed summing the CPU user usage over all available cores, and normalizing it by the total cores number in the sample. The time range has been chosen as it was one with substantial load among the various groups.

5. Enable self-service, so that the whole process can be triggered by authorized scientists (within certain rules)

The common pool of compute nodes would be the one provided by the general data analysis cluster Ra, thus enabling the strategy of disentangling the lifecycle management from the single scientists communities.

2.2 Using Slurm for Dynamical Resources Allocation

Slurm [2] has been the workload management of choice since the beginning of the Ra cluster, and so the idea to manage resources using separate Slurm clusters came naturally. One major issue that we initially faced was that our Slurm instances had a static configuration file, describing all the nodes and relative partitions. As our linux hosts configurations are managed over Puppet and Hiera files, this was hindering the possibility of self-servicing for the users. We decided to profit from the "configless" mode of Slurm [2] to overcome this limitation, and to initially split our compute resources in two Slurm clusters: a *base* one, representing the common pool of compute resources (in our case, the Ra data analysis cluster), and a *dynamic* one, both managed in "configless" mode. Within the *base* cluster, some nodes are available to be moved across clusters. Slurm configuration parameters are passed to the SLURMD_OPTIONS variable in the /etc./default/slurmd configuration file, e.g.:

```
SLURMD_OPTIONS='-Z --conf Feature=myfeature \
   --conf-server slurm-controller.domain.com'
```

where slurm-controller.domain.com is the FQDN of the Slurm controller server, and myfeature is a comma-separated list of Slurm Features applied to the node (more on the usage of features later). A simplified view of the intended flow is represented in Fig. 2.

We then evaluated various possibilities as mechanism for the configuration change, including Puppet-driven changes and Ansible playbooks. In the end we decided to rely on Systemd targets, as it provided a very generic and easy to extend mechanism common to the majority of Linux distributions.

We then faced the issue of how to label resources for the move, and ensure that no jobs would land on them during the process. Slurm Reservations proved to be a very flexible tool in this respect, allowing us to cordon compute nodes and release them as soon as possible, and leaving to Slurm the job of selecting the proper nodes based on requirements and current usage. We used a predefined naming pattern for the reservations, to that they could be easily distinguished from normal reservations. Systemd timers running on the compute nodes would then check for these special reservations, and trigger the required operations.

2.3 Implementation

The overall implementation schema logic is reported in Fig. 3. The workflow consists of the following steps:

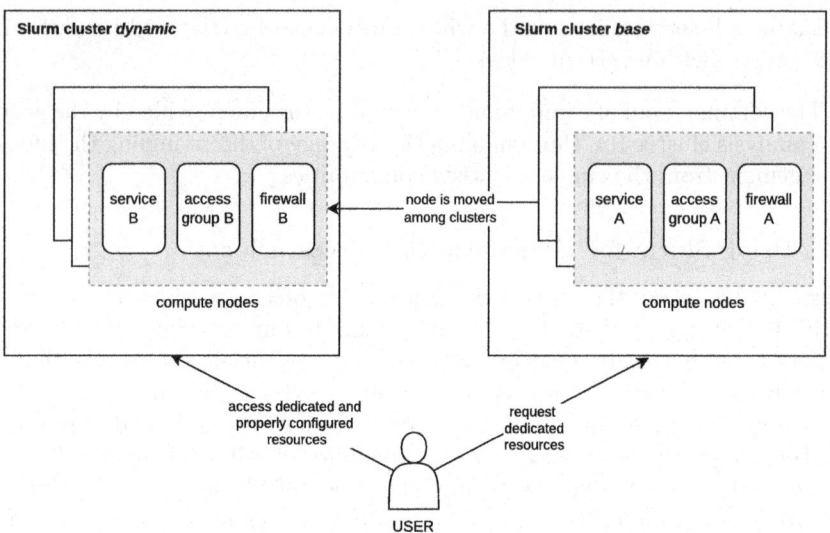

Fig. 2. Simplified view of dynamic resources allocation flow.

1. A request for resources (e.g. 2 compute nodes) is requested by group **GroupA**
2. A corresponding Slurm reservation is created per each requested node, e.g. flurm-<cluster>-<partition>-<ib>, where <cluster> is the destination Slurm cluster, <partition> is the name of the destination partition (normally dedicated to a specific user group) and <id> a unique id, in our case a combination of a timestamp and an incremental integer
3. The systemd timer running on the compute nodes (e.g. cn2) see that a reservation for the node has been requested. If valid, it changes the systemd target and reboot the node (when necessary)
4. After reboot, the new cn2 target start a series of dedicated services, including mount of the required storage areas, and start up of eventual dedicated user services (e.g. for automated data processing)

Multiple partitions are provided in the *dynamic* cluster: by default a shared one, and usually one per scientific group when required. Nodes are assigned to partitions based on Slurm Features, which are also assigned as Systemd target names. We also profit from the possibility to create dependencies among Systemd targets, that enables the re-usage of common components. For example, GroupA.target requires sls.target, and starts additional services, including starting the Slurm service with the correct Feature enabled. To ensure that the compute node has the correct configuration, we do rely on the LBNL Node Health Check (NHC) Slurm plugin [3]

When the compute node is booted up in the *dynamic* cluster, a further Reservation is created (at the moment, through a drop-in override of the service checking for reservations). This reservation is scheduled to be active when the compute node must be moved back to the *base* cluster. The same systemd

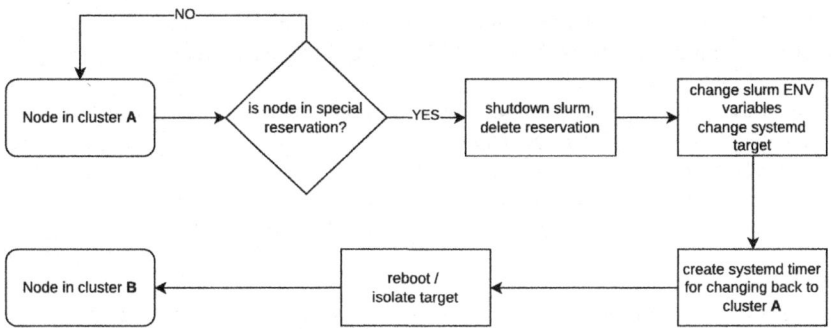

Fig. 3. Implementation schema logic for the migration of a compute node from *base* cluster to *dynamic* cluster.

timer that triggered the initial move will pick up also this reservation, and trigger the move back to the initial cluster. A node can be permanently moved to a cluster if the `sharedcompute-<group>-<n>` is created with an `duration=infinite` reservation: at the time of writing, Slurm treats this reservation as having one year duration, thus we had to implement some special checks in the code.

The node reboot is an optional step, as systemd targets allow for target switching through the `isolate` command. We found nevertherless that some services and processes may linger and keep some I/O operations alive, thus creating some instabilities in the node. While further debugging the various issues, we decided to reboot the node by default when switching targets, but maintaining support of the live-switching mode through `isolate`.

3 Results

During the second half of 2024 we were able to set up a proof of concept on our infrastructure, that showed us that the designed architecture was feasible in a production-like environment. We opted to distribute all the necessary code as RPM package, and build them automatically on our git service using a dedicated CI/CD pipeline. The resulting time for switching between clusters ranges between 10 and 30 min, mainly driven by the timers frequency, and boot time of the hardware itself (which is the main source of delay). In the following code example it can be seen a typical flow for a compute node, using some simple tools we developed.

```
# Node is in the base cluster
[root@ra2-c-007 ~]# flurm-status
Current cluster          ra
No pending moves
Next move check active. Next run: Tue 2025-05-27 21:10:00 CEST

# Creation of a reservation to trigger the move to dynamic cluster
```

```
[root@ra2-c-007 ~]# flurm-reserve_nodes -p mx -c sls -n 1 -d 1
Reservation sharedcompute_sls_mx_20250527210439_0 created

# Reservation is registered, will be applied at the next timer run
[root@ra2-c-007 ~]# flurm-status
Current cluster              ra
Moving to cluster=sls and partition=mx at 2025-05-27T21:04:39
Next move check active. Next run: Tue 2025-05-27 21:10:00 CEST


# Timer has been fired, and after reboot the node is in the dynamic
    cluster. A timer to trigger the move back to the base cluster is
    visible
[root@ra2-c-007 ~]# flurm-status
Current cluster              sls
Moving to cluster=ra and partition=ra at 2025-05-28T17:09:02
Next move check active. Next run: Tue 2025-05-27 21:10:00 CES
```

One known limitation of this architecture is that only full compute nodes can be assigned to an experiment, and not single resources like a GPU. We plan to lower the possible impact of it by statically assigning a minimal amount of resources to the *dynamic* cluster in a shared partition, thus minimizing the amount of idle cycles.

The current plan is to have the system in production in time for the SLS2 project commissioning time (end of 2025Q2). We also plan to add support for this workflow to our Resource Management API. The Resource Management API is a FastAPI-based RESTful API we developed, that allows user self-service assignation of IT resources, such us storage quotas and compute nodes reservations.

4 Comparison with Existing Solutions

Dynamic node allocation is a common pattern in cloud computing (public and on-premises), including Kubernetes-based [4] resources. While projects as OpenStack [5] effectively provide cloud-like scaling capabilities, they also require specialized personnel to operate. Due to the size of our team and compute resources, we decided to harness the existing knowledge in Slurm and Linux OS, to achieve the maximum result with the minimal development. Another factor it was taken into consideration was that our user communities were already accustomed to use Slurm as resource manager, and it was preferred to limit the knowledge toll on the scientific user communities.

During the review process of this paper, we became aware of the Flux Framework for resource management [6]. We will be closely watch its developments in the near future and evaluate it as soon as possible.

5 Conclusions

Peak and sparce resources usage is a common discussed topic in the Scientific IT community. We profited from our past experience during SLS operations, and the availability of a partially-predictable load (based on the experiments scheduling) to design a novel approach in dynamic resources assignation based on Slurm and Systemd. This approach allow us to manage a common pool of compute resources and dynamically allocate them to different Slurm compute clusters, with the possibility of user self-service and customizations. The current work (soon to be released on https://github.com/paulscherrerinstitute/flurm) will constitute the base architecture of the compute resources available for the upgraded SLS operations, allowing to balance efficient resources utilization and availability on resources on short demand. A further application that we are currently exploring is to use this mechanism to dynamically manage compute clusters for different user communities (so, not specifically bound to the SLS operations), by assigning resources from a common pool. One key aspects we found during development is that we can treat all Slurm clusters as equal (so, without any hierarchy as *base* and *dynamic*), opening the possibility to dynamically customize compute resources to different user communities based on a common configuration.

Acknowledgments. We would like to thank Marc Caubet for the invaluable help and support in better understanding Slurm, and all the Science IT department at PSI. This work was partially funded by the SLS2 Upgrade Project.

References

1. Streun, A., et al.: SLS-2 - the upgrade of the Swiss Light Source in. J. Synchrotron Rad. **25**, 631–641 (2018)
2. Jette, M.A., Wickberg, T.: Architecture of the slurm workload manager. In: Klusáček, D., Corbalán, J., Rodrigo, G.P. (eds.) Job Scheduling Strategies for Parallel Processing. JSSPP 2023. LNCSe, vol 14283. Springer, Cham (2023). https://doi.org/10.1007/978-3-031-43943-8_1
3. LBNL Node Health Check. https://github.com/mej/nhc, Accessed 14 Mar 2025
4. The Kubernetes website. https://kubernetes.io/, Accessed 14 Mar 2025
5. The Openstack project website. https://www.openstack.org/. Accessed 14 Mar 2025
6. The Flux Framework website. https://flux-framework.org/, Accessed 14 Mar 2025

Fifth Workshop on Communication, I/O, and Storage at Scale on Next-Generation Platforms – Scalable Infrastructures (ixpug-comm-io-storage)

IXPUG 2025 Preface

Objectives/Topics

Next-generation HPC platforms have increasing heterogeneity in their communications, I/O and storage subsystems. These subsystems include internal high-speed fabrics and SmartNICs for inter-node communication; storage systems integrated with programmable data processing units (DPUs) and infrastructure processing units (IPUs) to support software-defined networks; traditional storage infrastructures with parallel POSIX-based filesystems complemented with scalable object storage; and heterogeneous compute nodes configured with a diverse spectrum of CPUs and accelerators (e.g., GPU, FPGA, AI accelerators).

The IXPUG workshop pursues multiple objectives, including:

1. to develop and provide a holistic overview of next-generation platforms with an emphasis on communication, I/O, and storage at scale,
2. to showcase application-driven performance analysis with various HPC fabrics,
3. to present early experiences with emerging storage and I/O concepts such as object stores using next-generation HPC fabrics,
4. to share experience with performance tuning on heterogeneous platforms from multiple vendors, and
5. to share best practices for application programming with complex communication, I/O, and storage at scale.

Workshop Organization

David Martin	Argonne National Laboratory, USA
Amit Ruhela	Texas Advanced Computing Center, USA
Steffen Christgau	Zuse Institute Berlin, Germany
John Pennycook	Intel, UK
Glenn Brooke	Cornelis Networks, Inc., USA
Oscar Hernandez Mendoza	Oak Ridge National Laboratory, USA

Combining Malleability and Distributed Control Mechanisms to Reduce I/O Contention

Paula Sanchez-Checa(✉), Javier Garcia-Blas, Jesus Carretero, and David E. Singh

Computer Science Department, Universidad Carlos III de Madrid, Madrid, Spain
{paulasan,fjblas,jcarrete,dexposit}@inf.uc3m.es

Abstract. Some data-intensive applications perform periodic read and write operations, which can lead to slowdowns and contention when multiple applications are running simultaneously on a shared filesystem. In high-performance computing (HPC), malleability refers to the ability to dynamically adjust job resources at runtime to optimize performance, reduce execution times, and improve efficiency. This paper presents a decentralized probabilistic framework designed to reduce I/O contention in data-intensive malleable applications. A performance model is used to obtain the application maximum I/O performance, and an algorithm is used to detect when there is contention when running multiple applications. In such cases, malleability is applied to a subset of running applications to mitigate performance issues. We tested the model on a parallel, data-intensive, agent-based epidemiological simulator that performs periodic write operations. The results show that our model efficiently reduces contention, particularly during the most data-intensive critical stages of the execution, improving I/O throughput up to a 15%.

Keywords: I/O contention · malleability · performance modeling

1 Introduction

EpiGraph [14] is an agent-based simulator that models the spread of infectious diseases, such as influenza and SARS-CoV-2. Agent-based simulators consider the characteristics and behavior of each individual, and can effectively capture complex interaction patterns, enabling more precise predictions compared to other methods [8,12]. During the COVID-19 pandemic, EpiGraph was used to provide decision-making support to the Spanish and European Union Health Authorities [17,19]. EpiGraph is written in C and is parallelized using MPI. The simulator has been integrated with Flex-MPI [13], which provides malleable capabilities that allow to increase or decrease the number of processes at runtime. In this work, we analyze EpiGraph from both computational and I/O perspectives, identify I/O performance issues, and propose a methodology to

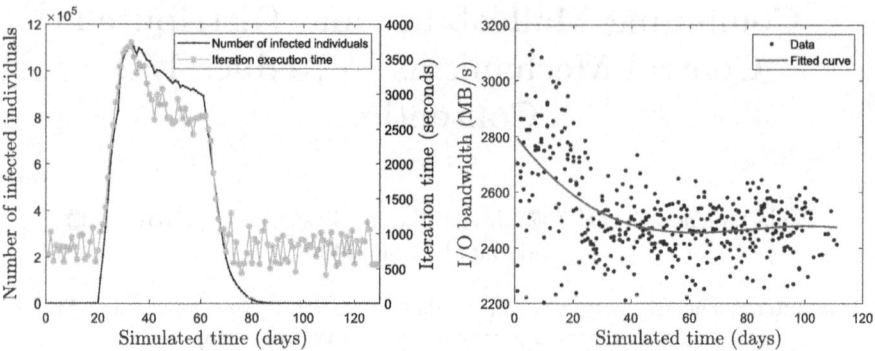

(a) Number of infected individuals and iteration execution times.

(b) I/O throughput per day. Combined results of five independent executions.

Fig. 1. EpiGraph performance analysis for a 144 process execution.

address them. In the remainder of this section, we describe the characteristics of EpiGraph and state the problem addressed in this work.

Figure 1a shows both the number of infected individuals and the iteration time for the scenario considered in this work, corresponding to the SARS-CoV-2 Omicron variant outbreak in Spain in November 2021, simulating 3.5 million individuals. Due to the higher transmission rate of this new variant, about two times higher than that of the Delta variant, it quickly spread throughout all cities and became the dominant strain in the country, creating a large infection wave. In Fig. 1a, we observe that the execution time of the iteration increases sharply with the infection wave (days 20–80). This is because the computational cost of the transmission algorithm, which models the disease propagation, is proportional to the number of infected individuals. Also note that the number of infections decreases (days 80–130) and the iteration execution time reaches a minimum value, which is related to other time-consuming operations that do not depend on the number of infections. These operations include updating the individual status, performing MPI communications, or I/O.

In order to allow a detailed analysis of the COVID-19 propagation, EpiGraph stores the simulation state every day, which includes individual characteristics and additional metadata (interaction patterns, vaccination status, etc.) related to each simulated individual. In this way, the application alternates CPU, communication, and I/O stages. Figure 1b shows the I/O throughput per day of five independent simulations, each one executed exclusively on BeeGFS, without interfering with other running applications. Note that there is significant variability in the I/O performance. Moreover, the I/O throughput tends to stabilize from day 20, and the performance values are independent of the number of infected individuals, reaching similar values around days 40 and 80. This is because the amount of output data of each I/O stage is the same during the whole simulation, as it is only dependent on the number of simulated individuals, which remains constant during the simulation period.

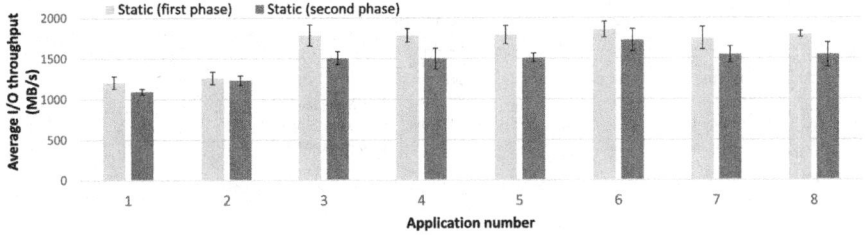

Fig. 2. EpiGraph average I/O throughput for the two simulation phases when eight applications are simultaneously executed (each one of them using 144 processes). The first phase ranges from days 0 to 80. The second phase ranges from days 80 to 130.

Figure 2 shows the average I/O throughput when eight simulations are executed simultaneously, each comprising 144 processes. In total, 905 GB of data are stored during the whole simulation by all running applications. In this figure, we consider two execution phases. The first phase ranges from day 0 to day 80 and corresponds to the main Omicron wave. The second phase ranges from day 80 to day 130 and corresponds to the remaining part of the simulation, when the incidence of COVID-19 is small. Each bar in the figure represents the average throughput value for all I/O operations within each phase. We can now identify two sources of I/O degradation. First, the I/O throughputs achieved are smaller than those achieved when the application is executed exclusively (Fig. 1b). This behavior is expected, given that in this scenario multiple EpiGraph instances are sharing access to the parallel filesystem. Second, there is an additional I/O performance degradation for the second simulation phase in comparison to the performance of the first phase. As Fig. 2 shows, this occurs for all running applications. The reason for this behavior is that the iteration time decreases in the second phase (see Fig. 1a), which increases the I/O operation frequency. This produces a contention situation when the eight applications are executing the second phase of the simulation. In contrast, in the first phase the I/O stages are more spaced in time, since the iterations take longer, reducing the pressure on the filesystem and the contention risk. Based on this behavior, we state the problem that we address in this paper.

Problem Statement: When multiple instances of EpiGraph are executed simultaneously, is it possible to detect I/O contention in runtime and reduce it using malleability?

This work presents the following contributions. First, we introduce EpiGraph as an interesting use case from both the CPU and I/O perspectives. Second, we introduce a novel technique based on malleability that reduces the I/O contention when multiple instances of EpiGraph are executed. It combines runtime application monitoring and a distributed decision-making framework. Third, we evaluate the solution on a real platform.

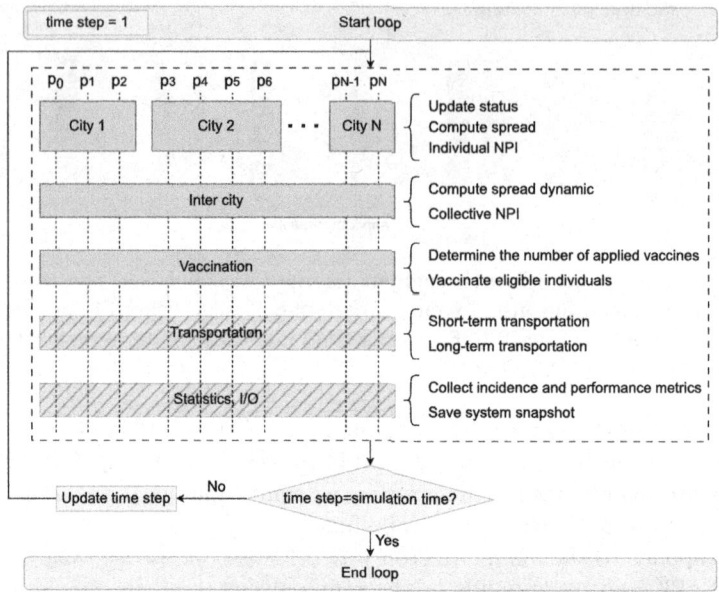

Fig. 3. EpiGraph simulation algorithm. Blue and green boxes represent the stages of the algorithm. Green dashed boxes represent stages in which there is communication. Yellow and orange boxes represent the loop of the algorithm. (Color figure online)

2 Background

2.1 EpiGraph

EpiGraph is an epidemiological simulator of infectious diseases, which consists of a social model, an epidemic model, and a transportation model. The social model reproduces social contacts related to the daily activities for each individual, such as going to work, school or family time. The epidemic model simulates the spread of the disease and its evolution in each infected individual. The epidemic model includes different states representing the stage of the infection in an individual, such as incubation, asymptomatic, and hospitalized. Finally, the transportation model represents the movements of individuals between different cities.

Figure 3 represents EpiGraph's simulation algorithm. This algorithm is executed every time step until the total simulation time is reached. Each iteration starts by performing city-level simulations. The cities are determined by the area in which the disease spread is simulated (one city, one or several provinces, or the whole country). For each city, the model updates the health status of each infected individual, and the social model simulates the spread of the infectious disease at individual-level. Then, the model simulates the possible non pharmaceutical interventions (NPI) taken by each individual (e.g., the use of face masks) in the city. At a global level, the model simulates the spread of the disease, as well as the possible collective NPIs (e.g., lockdowns). Next is the vaccination

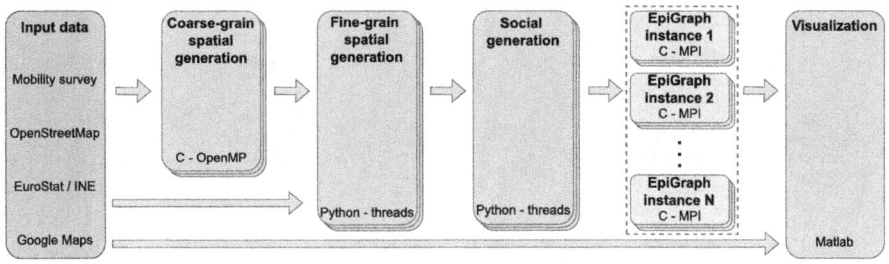

Fig. 4. Epidemiological simulation workflow for N applications. The leftmost box lists the data sources of the input data to the workflow. This work contributes to the red boxes surrounded by a dashed line. (Color figure online)

module, which is in charge of determining the number and type of vaccines that are applied. Moreover, the model takes into account vaccination policies and the availability of vaccines to determine which individuals are eligible for vaccination and with which type of vaccine. The transportation model takes into account short- and long-term transportation of individuals over medium and long distances (between cities) to travel, for work or study, or for leisure activities such as vacations. Finally, the statistics and I/O model is in charge of collecting incidence and performance metrics and storing a system snapshot in every iteration.

Figure 4 shows the epidemiological simulation workflow. The leftmost box in the diagram represents the data sources used to create the model. In the coarse-grain spatial generation stage, the simulator assigns the residence and work districts to each individual. In the fine-grained spatial generation stage, the model assigns a street number to give each individual a more specific residence and work address based on the district assigned during the coarse-grain spatial generation stage. The social generation stage uses spatial data to create a realistic social model with socio-economic indicators related to each individual [7]. Using this information, several EpiGraph instances are simultaneously executed. EpiGraph performs stochastic simulations, so it is necessary to run multiple simulations (around one hundred repetitions for each scenario) to perform a statistical analysis of the results. This means that, in practice, the problem introduced in this work (I/O interference related to multiple instance execution) appears frequently. The last stage corresponds to the visualization of the simulation results (e.g., evolution of the number of infections or number of hospitalizations).

2.2 Flex-MPI

The current version of EpiGraph is integrated with Flex-MPI, an extension of MPI that provides monitoring, load balancing, data redistribution, and malleable capabilities to parallel applications [13]. Using Flex-MPI, the application can dynamically expand or shrink the number of processes at runtime. Monitoring permits collecting performance metrics at runtime in a transparent way, without introducing changes in the source code. Computational metrics are captured via

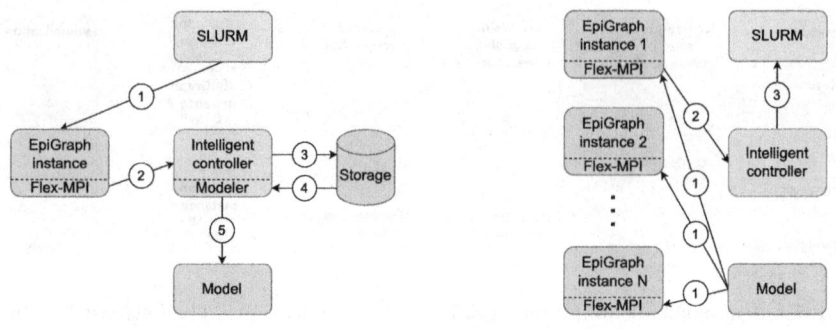

(a) Model generation. (b) Multiple instance execution.

Fig. 5. Overview of the decision-making framework.

hardware counters (using PAPI), and communication metrics via MPI profiling interface (PMPI). These performance metrics are used to detect load imbalance situations. When this happens, the application data (and consequently, the workload) are redistributed in order to mitigate it. Flex-MPI uses MPI standard messages to redistribute data from dense and sparse data structures. The current version of EpiGraph supports two malleability strategies, both enabled by FlexMPI. The first one relies on dynamic process creation and destruction combined with data redistribution. The second one uses a start-and-stop approach based on checkpointing. While both strategies have been implemented and tested, the results presented in this paper correspond to the second approach.

3 Methods

This work was carried out under the umbrella of the ADMIRE project [1], with the goal of reducing the I/O contention by means of holistic coordination, the use of computation and I/O malleability, and the design of novel scheduling I/O techniques. In this work, the aim is to mitigate the I/O contention when executing multiple applications that simultaneously share the same filesystem. To do so, in a first stage, we propose the creation of an offline model that represents the expected application I/O throughput that is achieved when EpiGraph is executed exclusively.

Figure 5a shows how this model is generated. First, in arrow 1, SLURM launches the job. During its execution, as shown by arrow 2, Flex-MPI monitors EpiGraph and collects I/O traces that are sent to the Intelligent Controller (IC). This controller provides a coordination layer for all the applications that are running and is able to detect when the EpiGraph instance is executed exclusively.

The traces are stored in REDIS (arrow 3) and then used to generate a performance model that combines the results of different executions (arrows 4 and 5). The proposed model consists of a polynomial fit of the average I/O throughput of independently executed simulations. Figure 1b shows the result of this model for the combination of five independent executions of EpiGraph.

When multiple instances are executed simultaneously, the application monitoring is performed in a distributed manner, without each application knowing the performance of the others. If I/O contention is detected, the idea is to reduce the performance of some of the running applications by shrinking the number of processes. The goal behind this idea is to change the application CPU time by using fewer processes, which also changes the I/O pattern of the application (temporal separation between I/O operations). We expect this strategy to reduce the degree of I/O interference.

Figure 5b shows the procedure used when multiple EpiGraph instances are run simultaneously. This situation is detected by the IC, which transfers the performance model to Flex-MPI's control logic of each running application (arrow 1) and activates the application's performance analytic component, which is part of Flex-MPI. Then, for each running application, the model's I/O performance is compared to the actual performance, which is collected by the Flex-MPI monitor using real-time monitoring metrics. If the average I/O throughput of the applications is below the threshold expected by the model, then there is a possible contention situation. We define *trigger point* as the iteration in which this threshold is reached. In this case, a certain percentage F of the applications (EpiGraph instance 1 in the example in Fig. 5b) reduce the number of processes. This is done by communicating to the IC (arrow 2) this decision [15]. Then, the IC requests a reduction of resources to SLURM (arrow 3) and, when fulfilled, the IC acknowledges it to the application. Finally, Flex-MPI shrinks the application.

The trigger point is calculated using the following procedure:

1. For every simulated day i, the average value of the last w real performance metrics (average real I/O throughput $\overline{TP}_i^{real}$) is calculated using Eq. 1. In our experiments, w was set to the value of 5.

$$\overline{TP}_i^{real} = \frac{\sum_{i-w}^{i} TP_i^{real}}{w} \quad (1)$$

2. Following a similar approach, the average of the last w modelled throughputs ($\overline{TP}_i^{model}$) is calculated using the performance model.
3. ΔTP_i is calculated as the difference between both values (Eq. 2).

$$\Delta TP_i = \overline{TP}_i^{model} - \overline{TP}_i^{real} \quad (2)$$

4. In our experiments, ΔTP_i values decrease at the beginning of the execution. We calculate the minimum ΔTP_i value, denoted as ΔTP_i^{min}. This value corresponds to the maximum I/O throughput achieved by the application.
5. Then, during the program execution, the distributed control algorithm compares the real and expected values. The trigger point corresponds to the first simulated day i where ΔTP_i is greater than 125% of the value of ΔTP_i^{min} during five consecutive days.

6. When the trigger point is reached, a random function ensures that only a fraction F of the applications reduce the number of processes, while the remaining ones continue to run with their original size.

Note that despite the main goal of the ADMIRE project being to develop a centralized control mechanism, in this work, we have followed a different approach, using decentralized decision-making, in which each application evaluates its own performance and decides to shrink independently. This new approach is more scalable and reduces the amount of resources used on the IC side.

EpiGraph performs I/O read operations only at the beginning of execution and all subsequent I/O accesses are write operations related to checkpointing. For this reason, we have only focused on write-related operations. Note that the methodology proposed in this paper can be extended to other applications that include phases with read operations. Since read and write I/O performance may differ, for these applications separate models and threshold parameters should be developed for each operation type.

4 Evaluation

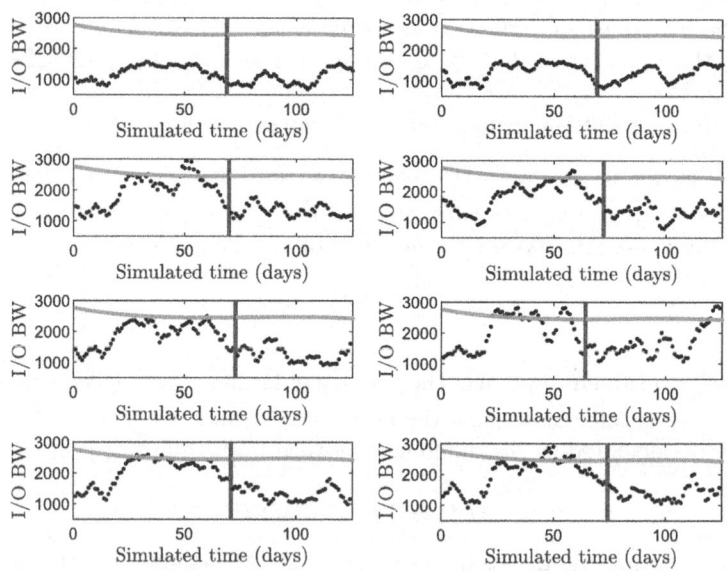

Fig. 6. EpiGraph I/O performance when eight instances are simultaneously executed. Each plot represents one application. The I/O throughput of each instance is represented in blue. The polynomial fit of the average I/O throughput when one single application is exclusively executed is shown in green. The trigger point is represented as a vertical red line. (Color figure online)

The evaluation has been carried out in the High-Performance Computing for Artificial Intelligence Center (HPC4AI Laboratory), co-located by the University of Turin and the Polytechnic University of Turin. This cluster is equipped with a 50 TB BeeGFS filesystem and SLURM workload manager. It consists of 68 Lenovo NeXtScale nx360 compute nodes, equipped with 2 18-core Intel Xeon E5-2697 CPUs, connected by Omni-Path 100 Gb/s.

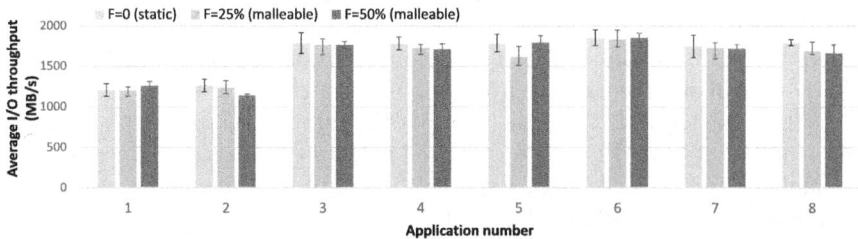

Fig. 7. EpiGraph I/O performance comparison for the first phase of the simulation.

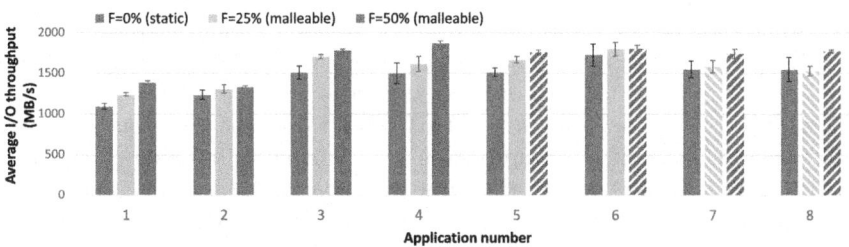

Fig. 8. EpiGraph I/O performance comparison for the second phase of the simulation. The malleable applications reduce the number of processes from 144 to 72 and are represented with dashed bars.

In our experiments, eight instances of EpiGraph (144 processes per application, 1,152 in total) were executed simultaneously in the workflow. Figure 6 shows in blue the I/O throughput achieved during each I/O stage for each running application. Note that, because of the I/O interference in the second phase, the average throughput for the first phase of the execution (from simulated days 0 to 80) is higher than for the second phase (from simulated days 80 to 130). Green is used in the figure to denote the fit of the average I/O throughput when a single application is executed exclusively, which corresponds to the one shown in Fig. 1b. The distributed control algorithm compares the real and expected values, detecting when there is a prolonged drop in performance. The trigger point (simulated day when this threshold is reached) is represented by a vertical red line. We can observe that the trigger points for all applications are around day

70. In our experiments, the fraction of applications that are reconfigured were $F = 0\%$ (all applications are static, i.e., non-malleable), $F = 25\%$ (approximately two are malleable), and $F = 50\%$ (approximately four are malleable).

Figures 7 and 8 show the performance comparison for each application phase and F values. Each experiment was repeated five times, and error bars are shown. Note that $F = 0\%$ corresponds to a static execution and is represented by the green bars, which are the same as those shown in Fig. 2.

Since trigger points are around day 70, application shrinkage will not occur until the end of the first phase (simulated day 80). That is, all experiments related to the first phase were run with similar configurations. For this reason, in Fig. 7 we can observe that the average I/O throughputs of the applications are barely the same for all F values. This is not the case for the second phase. In this phase, for $F = 25\%$ and $F = 50\%$, two and four applications dynamically reduce the number of processes to half, respectively. In Fig. 8 the malleable applications that reduce size are highlighted with dashed bars. In this figure, we can observe that the introduction of malleability increases I/O performance compared to the baseline scenario ($F = 0$). This increment is greater when more malleable applications are involved ($F = 50\%$). In general, for the second phase, the I/O throughputs improve 7% and 15%, for $F = 25\%$ and $F = 50\%$, respectively.

The cost of the malleable operation in EpiGraph (reducing from 144 to 72 processes) is around 11 s, which represents 2% of the overall execution time of the application. On rare occasions in our experiments, some applications reached the threshold point earlier (around day 50) or later (around day 100). In both cases, the effect was to bring forward or delay the reduction of the I/O congestion.

Finally, it is worth mentioning the trade-off between the performance of some applications, which can be compromised by reducing the number of resources, and the overall performance of the workflow. EpiGraph exhibits good scalability during the first execution phase. Given that this phase is the most time-consuming part of the application execution, EpiGraph application (as a whole) scales well until 216 processes. In our experiments, we observed that EpiGraph scalability was poor during the second phase; thus, a reduction in the number of processes does not lead to higher execution times during this phase. This is the reason that the use of malleability in the second execution phase does not introduce performance degradation.

5 Related Work

EpiGraph is an agent-based simulator of the spread of influenza and COVID-19. We can find other epidemiological simulators with similar characteristics. In [2], they simulate the effectiveness of defense strategies against COVID-19 in Germany and Poland. In [8], the authors presented a model developed to analyze the spread of COVID-19 in small populations or facilities. In addition, [16] and [12] developed models to study the effect of NPIs against COVID-19 in Switzerland and the UK, respectively.

In the context of HPC, malleability consists of dynamically adapting the computational and I/O resources of the applications at runtime, which can increase

I/O throughput and reduce execution times. The work carried out in [22] identifies different current challenges affecting malleability. One of them is the difficulty of dynamically managing hardware and software resources. In this sense, monitoring of the applications is key to be able to schedule and make redistribution decisions within a reasonable amount of time. Regarding application monitoring, the authors also identified some challenges, such as difficulties in managing the vast amounts of data captured during monitoring and the need to modify the source code of applications to extract performance information. In the context of our work, the IC and SLURM dynamically manage the application resources. Flex-MPI performs monitoring transparently at the application level. In addition, it is not necessary to deploy a complete system monitoring infrastructure. The models presented in this paper, although simple, also have a small processing overhead and are used by the applications in a distributed way.

When multiple applications are running at the same time, the goal of I/O scheduling techniques is to choose which applications should be prioritized and which ones should be delayed. There are different I/O scheduling approaches in this context. In [3,20] different scheduling techniques are proposed based on the periodicity of HPC applications. In [6], an optimization framework is proposed using multiple heuristics to address I/O contention when running multiple applications. In [21] a different approach is used to improve I/O throughput when multiple applications are executed. In this case, an I/O throughput capping is applied, at MPI level, to some running applications to reduce contention. There are some similarities between our proposed technique and the one presented in [21]. Both aim to reduce I/O contention, but our approach is focused on synchronous I/O and uses application malleability instead. In [18] application malleability is used to prevent I/O contention by shifting the time of I/O operations. The main difference with our approach is that it addresses specific I/O operations while the methodology presented in this paper is applied to multiple ones (the whole phase), not trying to avoid multiple I/O operations, but to reduce their impact on the filesystem.

A different approach to accelerate I/O operations and avoid bottleneck problems involves the use of ad hoc file systems. General purpose parallel file systems, such as Lustre [4] and BeeGFS [11], have a fixed number of I/O nodes and cannot be modified at runtime, which can lead to contention. In response to these limitations and the emergence of data-intensive HPC applications, ad hoc parallel file systems were developed [5]. Ad hoc file systems are temporary, and only run while the application is running. They act as intermediate file systems between the application and the backend file system, speeding up the I/O operations. We can find multiple ad hoc filesystems in the literature, such as Hercules [9], Expand Ad Hoc [10], and GekkoFS [23]. However, this approach adds the complexity of integrating the file system with the application.

6 Conclusion

This work presents a decentralized decision-making framework that leverages application malleability to reduce I/O contention when multiple instances of

EpiGraph are executed. In this approach, each application independently evaluates its performance and decides whether to shrink the number of processes if an I/O contention situation is detected. The proposed methodology improves the scalability of the central controller, by delegating part of the control logic to the applications, and reduces the resource consumption on the controller side. In addition, it does not require a centralized monitoring infrastructure, and the monitoring data processing, used to develop the application model, is lightweight. The results show that our model reduces contention and improves I/O throughput up to 15% during the most data-intensive phases of the simulation.

Despite these advantages, we have also identified some limitations. Firstly, the proposed solution assumes that the use of malleability can alleviate the I/O contention. However, it should be noted that this is not always the case. Other alternatives, such as the limitation of I/O throughput, could be considered instead. Secondly, it is important to note that the proposed solution is used when multiple instances of the same application are being executed, which is a realistic scenario. In future work, we plan to generalize the proposal to environments with different applications. Furthermore, the solution involves randomness, which is prone to generate multiple solutions. For instance, a value of $F = 50\%$ may apply malleability to 3 out of 8 applications, rather than 4. It is worth noting that, according to our results, there is a performance improvement even when a smaller number of applications change size. An alternative solution to overcome this problem is to centralize the control logic, which is a subject we plan to address in future research. For a more general use, application performance models should be used to support the decision-making process. In addition, although ad hoc file systems have not been used in this work because we wanted to provide a simple and easy to implement solution, they can help speed up the I/O operations of data-intensive applications. Therefore, while their integration with the application involves more complexity, it would be interesting to study their advantages in future work.

Acknowledgments. This publication has been partially funded by the project BCV-2024-2-0021 of Red Española de Supercomputación, and the I+D+i project PID2022-138050NB-I00 (New scalable I/O techniques for hybrid HPC and data intensive workloads - SCIOT), funded by MICIU/AEI/10.13039/501100011033/ "FEDER A way to do Europe".

Disclosure of Interests. The authors have no competing interests to declare that are relevant to the content of this article.

References

1. ADMIRE: Adaptative Multi-tier Intelligent data manager for Exascale – This project has received funding from the European Union's Horizon 2020 JTI-EuroHPC research and innovation programme, no 956748, https://admire-eurohpc.eu/

2. Adamik, B., et al.: Mitigation and herd immunity strategy for COVID-19 is likely to fail (May 2020)
3. Aupy, G., Gainaru, A., Fèvre, V.L.: I/O scheduling strategy for periodic applications. ACM Trans. Parallel Comput. **6**(2), 7:1–7:26 (2019)
4. Braam, P.J., Schwan, P.: Lustre: the intergalactic file system. In: Ottawa Linux Symposium, pp. 3429–3441 (2002)
5. Brinkmann, A., et al.: Ad hoc file systems for high-performance computing. J. Comput. Sci. Technol. **35**, 4–26 (2020)
6. Carretero, J., Jeannot, E., Pallez, G., Singh, D.E., Vidal, N.: Mapping and scheduling HPC applications for optimizing I/O. In: Proceedings of the 34th ACM International Conference on Supercomputing, ICS 2020, pp. 1–12. Association for Computing Machinery, New York(Jun 2020)
7. Cublier Martínez, A., Carretero, J., Singh, D.E.: Detailed parallel social modeling for the analysis of COVID-19 spread. J. Supercomput. **80**(9), 12408–12429 (2024)
8. Cuevas, E.: An agent-based model to evaluate the COVID-19 transmission risks in facilities. Comput. Biol. Med. **121**, 103827 (2020)
9. Garcia-Blas, J., Sanchez-Gallegos, G., Petre, C., Martinelli, A.R., Aldinucci, M., Carretero, J.: Hercules: scalable and network portable in-memory ad-hoc file system for data-centric and high-performance applications. In: Cano, J., Dikaiakos, M.D., Papadopoulos, G.A., Pericàs, M., Sakellariou, R. (eds.) Euro-Par 2023: Parallel Processing. Euro-Par 2023. LNCs, vol 14100. Springer, Cham. https://doi.org/10.1007/978-3-031-39698-4_46 (2023)
10. Garcia-Carballeira, F., Camarmas-Alonso, D., Caderon-Mateos, A., Carretero, J.: A new ad-hoc parallel file system for hpc environments based on the expand parallel file system. In: 2023 22nd International Symposium on Parallel and Distributed Computing (ISPDC), pp. 69–76 (2023)
11. Herold, F., Breuner, S., Heichler, J.: An introduction to beegfs. Tech. Rep, ThinkParQ, Kaiserslautern, Germany (2014)
12. Hinch, R., et al.: OpenABM-Covid19-An agent-based model for non-pharmaceutical interventions against COVID-19 including contact tracing. PLoS Comput. Biol. **17**(7), e1009146 (2021)
13. Martín, G., Marinescu, M.-C., Singh, D.E., Carretero, J.: FLEX-MPI: an MPI extension for supporting dynamic load balancing on heterogeneous non-dedicated systems. In: Wolf, F., Mohr, B., an Mey, D. (eds.) Euro-Par 2013. LNCS, vol. 8097, pp. 138–149. Springer, Heidelberg (2013). https://doi.org/10.1007/978-3-642-40047-6_16
14. Martín, G., Singh, D.E., Marinescu, M.C., Carretero, J.: Enhancing the performance of malleable MPI applications by using performance-aware dynamic reconfiguration. Parallel Comput. **46**, 60–77 (2015)
15. Muññoz, J.F., Cascajo García, A., Pérez, J.C.: Dynamic management of processes and communicators in malleable MPI applications. In: 2023 IEEE 29th International Conference on Parallel and Distributed Systems (ICPADS), pp. 848–855. IEEE, Ocean Flower Island, China (Dec 2023)
16. Shattock, A.J., et al.: Impact of vaccination and non-pharmaceutical interventions on SARS-CoV-2 dynamics in Switzerland. Epidemics **38**, 100535 (2022)
17. Sherratt, K., et al.: Predictive performance of multi-model ensemble forecasts of COVID-19 across European nations. eLife **12**, e81916 (2023)
18. Singh, D.E., Carretero, J.: Combining malleability and I/O control mechanisms to enhance the execution of multiple applications. J. Syst. Softw. **148**, 21–36 (2019)
19. Singh, D.E., et al.: Evaluation of vaccination strategies for the metropolitan area of Madrid via agent-based simulation. BMJ Open **12**(12), e065937 (2022)

20. Tarraf, A., Bandet, A., Boito, F., Pallez, G., Wolf, F.: Capturing Periodic I/O Using Frequency Techniques (2023)
21. Tarraf, A., Muñoz, J.F., Singh, D.E., Özden, T., Carretero, J., Wolf, F.: I/O behind the scenes: bandwidth requirements of HPC applications with asynchronous I/O. In: 2024 IEEE International Conference on Cluster Computing (CLUSTER), pp. 426–439. IEEE, Kobe, Japan (Sep 2024)
22. Tarraf, A., et al.: Malleability in modern HPC systems: current experiences, challenges, and future opportunities. IEEE Trans. Parallel Distrib. Syst. **35**(9), 1551–1564 (2024)
23. Vef, M., et al.: GekkoFS - a temporary distributed file system for HPC applications. In: 2018 IEEE International Conference on Cluster Computing, pp. 319–324 (2018)

DOCA UROM: A Vehicle for Offloading HPC and AI to DPUs

Ferrol Aderholdt, Zach Tiffany, Rohit Zambre[✉],
Manjunath Gorentla Venkata, Yuri Shatsman, Muhammad Abu Saleh,
and Gil Bloch

NVIDIA, Santa Clara, USA
{faderholdt,ztiffany,rzambre,manjunath,yshatsman,musaleh,gil}@nvidia.com

Abstract. Data processing units (DPUs) represent a significant advancement in networking technology. With their extensive capabilities, DPUs are well-positioned to accelerate AI and HPC workloads by offloading tasks that would otherwise rely on the host for additional resources. However, fully realizing the potential of DPUs is currently hindered by the lack of robust frameworks that facilitate the development of services on these devices. While DPU SDKs like NVIDIA's DOCA are rapidly evolving, they still fall short of providing seamless offloading to DPUs. To address this gap, we introduce DOCA Unified Resource and Offload Manager (UROM): a framework designed to enable seamless offloading of parallel computing tasks from the host to NVIDIA DPUs. This paper details the architecture of DOCA UROM, highlighting its key components and their functionalities, including resource discovery, host-DPU coordination, and task management on the DPU. We describe how developers can leverage DOCA UROM's flexible architecture to develop new DPU-based services. To demonstrate its versatility, we showcase three diverse DPU-based services developed using DOCA UROM: RDMOs, progress for non-blocking collectives, and utilizing DPU memory to enhance AI training. Our results illustrate the significant benefits these services offer, underscoring the potential of DOCA UROM in accelerating workloads.

Keywords: Data Processing Units · Smart NICs · Communication offloading · DOCA · BlueField · Super NIC

1 Introduction

The latest advancements in high-speed networks feature not just enhanced compute, but also improved memory, accelerators and storage through data processing units (DPUs). Prominent examples of DPUs include AMD Pensando platforms, NVIDIA BlueField networking platforms, and Intel Infrastructure Processing Units. These advancements have primarily been driven by cloud computing environments where DPUs excel at offloading key components of the cloud software stack.

F. Aderholdt, Z. Tiffany, R. Zambre, and M. Gorentla Venkata—Equal contribution.

© The Author(s), under exclusive license to Springer Nature Switzerland AG 2026
S. Neuwirth et al. (Eds.): ISC High Performance 2025 Workshops, LNCS 16091, pp. 401–415, 2026.
https://doi.org/10.1007/978-3-032-07612-0_31

DPUs hold strong potential to benefit HPC and AI workloads as well. The compute and memory resources on DPUs (detailed in Sect. 2) can both help address existing challenges, such as asynchronous progress for complex communication operations, and provide opportunities to design new communication semantics, such as RDMOs [16].

Different layers of the software stack present various opportunities for offloading with DPUs.

All offloading opportunities in HPC and AI, however, face the same critical hurdle: how to efficiently offload to the DPU? A DPU offloading study today requires developing an offloading infrastructure from scratch. Developing one is not trivial as it requires addressing several challenges: deployment of offload execution units (*e.g.*, processes) on the DPU, efficient communication of commands and data between execution units on the host and the DPU, and coordination between the groups of processes in the parallel program and the offload execution units. The complexity involved hinders the exploration of HPC offloading and increases the likelihood of standalone developments to be specifically tailored to the offload being experimented with, thereby restricting the framework's reusability by other offloads. The HPC and AI community is lacking a software framework that addresses the challenges involved in offloading to the DPU in a flexible and efficient manner.

In this paper, we present Unified Resource and Offload Manager (UROM) as a vehicle for exploring offloading ideas on NVIDIA's BlueField networking platform. UROM focuses primarily on *how* to efficiently offload to DPUs so that researchers can instead focus their efforts on *what* to offload. UROM addresses the challenges of offloading by providing well-defined abstractions for seamless offload development, management of offload execution units, process group management, and composability of multiple offloads within a single execution unit. With UROM, developers of a new offload define their offloading logic using the *UROM plugin* abstraction and launch instances of the plugin as *UROM workers* running on the DPU. The workers are launched via a *UROM service*, a daemon on the DPU that provides resource and offload management. UROM uses a client-server model for interaction between the host and the DPU, and it also provides *domains* as a group abstraction to address parallel process groups that are common in prevalent distributed programming models (*e.g.*, PyTorch ProcessGroup or MPI Communicator). We provide further details about UROM's component architecture and its design in Sect. 4.

The UROM project began as a research effort to explore the key components required in a DPU offloading framework. Today, UROM is deployed as part of the Data Center on a Chip Architecture (DOCA) SDK [3], which is the software programming framework for NVIDIA's BlueField networking platform. Even though we describe DOCA UROM in this paper, the architectural components of the framework would apply beyond NVIDIA DPUs. To that end, we make the following contributions.

1. We detail the architecture of DOCA UROM and its components (Sect. 4).

2. We describe how a researcher would use DOCA UROM to develop their offloads of interest (see Sect. 5).
3. We showcase the verstality of DOCA UROM using three diverse case studies—RDMOs, truly non-blocking collective progress, and supplemental memory—in Sect. 7. For each service, we show how DOCA UROM enables the development of the service, and we evaluate the effectiveness of the service.

2 Data Processing Unit Architecture

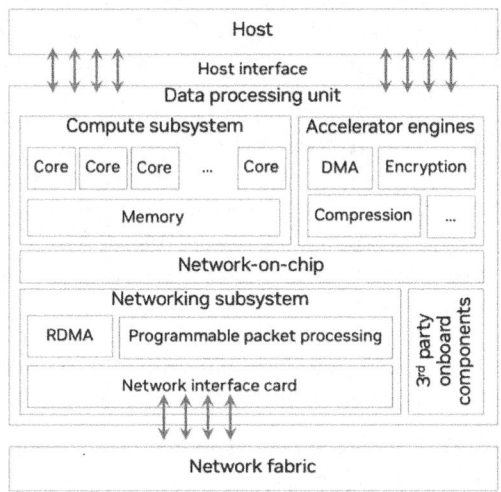

Fig. 1. General architecture of a data processing unit.

The DPU is a system-on-chip (SoC) that integrates 3 key components: (1) a high-performance networking subsystem, (2) a compute subsytem, and (3) a set of accelerator engines (see Fig. 1). These 3 components are consistent across different vendors. The SoC features a network-on-chip that tightly couples these components together. Today's DPUs connect to the host using a PCIe form factor. Additionally, the DPU incorporates its own PCIe root complex, allowing third-party components such as NVMe devices to connect directly to the DPU.

The networking subsystem comprises of an efficient interface that processes and transmits data over the network at high line rates (*e.g.*, ConnectX NICs). This subsytem also contains programmable silicon (*e.g.*, FPGA) that is capable of deploying custom network pipelines (typically via P4 [10]).

The compute subsystem consists of multiple high-performance general-purpose cores (typically Arm) that have access to memory via multiple levels of caches. These software-programmable cores run full OS instances and allow for flexible deployment of infrastructure services.

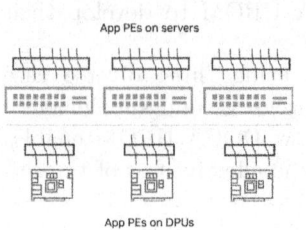 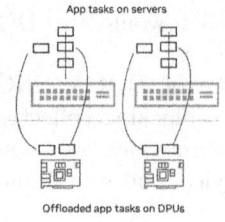 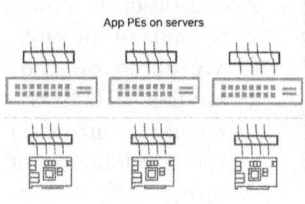

Fig. 2. Data parallelism.   **Fig. 3.** Task parallelism.   **Fig. 4.** Library offloads.

The accelerator engines are fixed-function units that provide fast implementations of common data processing routines. These units are programmable and examples include DMA, compression, and encryption of data.

3 DPU Offload Execution Models

To use the DPU's rich resources with existing programming models, we define three execution models: data parallelism, task parallelism and library offloads. These models fall into two categories—direct and indirect uses. The data and task parallelism execution models are direct uses of the DPU since the user is aware of the DPU's resources. In the library execution model, the user indirectly uses the DPU as the underlying framework transparently provides DPU-accelerated features. We elaborate on the execution models below.

Data Parallelism: DPU cores expand the compute parallelism available for applications using an SPMD programming model such as MPI or OpenSHMEM. The application's processing elements run on the DPU's cores (see Fig. 2).

Task Parallelism: DPU cores execute the application's tasks. The application on the host instructs the DPU to execute tasks when needed, and the DPU notifies the application upon completion of the offloaded task (see Fig. 3).

Library Offloads: DPU cores execute the functionalities of a library. The DPU-offload enabled library uses helper processing elements (red lines in Fig. 4) to execute functionality requested by the application's processing elements (purple lines in Fig. 4).

All three models rely on the same key functionalities: launching and termination of processes on the DPU, and communication between the host and the DPU. In this work, we focus on use cases that fall under the library-offloads execution model.

4 DOCA UROM Architecture Overview

DOCA UROM's primary goal is to enable flexible exploration of offloading to DPUs. We seek to provide flexibility to not just the end user but also to the

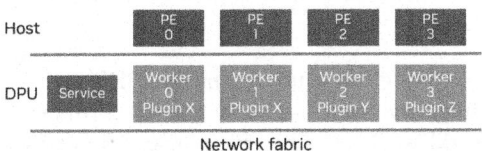

Fig. 5. A sample DOCA UROM deployment with a 1:1 mapping between host PEs and UROM workers.

developers of the framework. Hence, we design the architecture of DOCA UROM with three main objectives: flexible exploration of implementations, extensibility of features, and general applicability to a variety of users.

The framework should provide the end user with complete freedom to explore the designs of their offloading logic while abstracting away the complexities in orchestrating the deployment of the offload. The framework should cater to use cases that follow both a client-server execution (*e.g.*, key-value store) and a group-based execution (*e.g.*, an MPI application).

Figure 5 provides an overview of a typical deployment of DOCA UROM, where the processes of a distributed application on the host are its clients. Each DPU hosts a *UROM service* that manages a group of *UROM workers* responsible for executing the offloading logic (*UROM plugin*) requested by the client processes on the host. The typical usage of DOCA UROM can be summarized in four steps, which are executed by all processes in an application.

1. Host processes discover the UROM services.
2. UROM authenticates the client and provides details about the available offload services (plugins).
3. Host processes choose the appropriate plugin and launch UROM workers to run the offload functionality.
4. UROM workers execute the chosen plugin and send responses back to the application processes on the host.

To meet our flexibility objectives, we organize the DOCA UROM library with a modular component architecture that supports the exploration of various technologies and designs without sacrificing high performance [7]. UROM's component architecture is primarily based on three frameworks: *service*, *worker*, and *communication channel* which together constitute its functionalities. DOCA UROM's users interact only with the service and worker components, while the communication channel component is used internally by the library. The DOCA UROM library interoperates with DOCA *core* objects such as *devices*, *progress engines*, *contexts*, and *buffers*. The DOCA programming guide describes the different objects in detail [2]. In the following sections, we describe the different frameworks in DOCA UROM.

4.1 UROM Service

The UROM service is a daemon running on the DPU that is responsible for the discovery of offloading resources, secure control coordination with clients, and management of UROM workers. This daemon is assumed to be running on the DPU before the application connects to it.

The service daemon authenticates clients when they connect to it, after which clients can request particular types of offloads. When clients do so, the service spawns the UROM workers corresponding to the requested offload. Such requests can only be requested by client processes that have previously been authenticated by the daemon. After the UROM workers are ready to accept new connections, the service provides the clients with information about connecting to and disconnecting from the workers. The service destroys the UROM workers when authenticated clients request to do so.

4.2 UROM Plugin and Worker

Each type of supported UROM-based service corresponds to a distinct UROM plugin. Plugins define the core logic of the offloaded service. Developers would define new plugin types for their new offloads. A UROM worker is a unit of offload functionality (an OS process or thread) that executes one or more plugins. Developers can flexibly use the multiple cores on the DPU using process- or thread-level parallelism; both are valid UROM plugin designs. Each client process can spawn and map, via the UROM service, to one or many UROM workers. Each worker is uniquely identified within a single DPU by a *worker ID* or globally across multiple DPUs by a *domain ID* (see Sect. 4.4).

4.3 UROM Communication Channel

UROM's communication channel framework is the basis of all communication that occurs between UROM clients, services and workers. It uses an abstract push and pop interface for exchanging *commands* and *notifications* between the client processes and servers (UROM service and workers). UROM commands and notifications contain fields that are populated according to their type which are then packed and unpacked at the source and destination, respectively. UROM clients push commands to the services and workers, and they pop notifications. UROM service and workers, on the other hand, pop commands and push notifications to the clients.

The abstract interface for communication is designed to be versatile, supporting a wide range of components including UCX, gRPC, and DOCA Comm Channel. This flexibility facilitates the exploration of performance characteristics across both current and upcoming communication technologies, particularly in the context of host-DPU interfaces.

4.4 UROM Domains and Active Sets

Domains in UROM identify a group of UROM workers that have been spawned by client processes in a distributed application. Analogous to `MPI_COMM_WORLD`, there exists a `UROM_DOMAIN_WORLD` that comprises of the workers spawned by clients in the world group of processes. Each worker in the domain is uniquely identified with a *domain ID*. For example, in an MPI application where each process spawns one UROM worker, the domain ID of each worker would be equivalent to the MPI rank of the process that spawned it. Workers in a domain can communicate with each other.

Connections are established between the workers of a domain with the help of client processes. DOCA UROM's domain creation API takes in a pointer to an out-of-band allgather collective that runs on the clients. The DOCA UROM runtime uses this function to exchange the addresses of the spawned workers. The runtime then uses the UROM communication channel to pass worker addresses between the UROM worker and the client.

Notably, domain creation is expensive, but this overhead is incurred only once since applications can create new groups of workers using UROM active sets. Active sets are a group of workers that form a subset of the workers in `UROM_DOMAIN_WORLD`. Each active set is described by three pieces of information: `start_index`, `stride`, and `size` (like OpenSHMEM's active sets [6]).

Unlike domain creation, the creation of active sets does not incur significant overheads, as they are simply maps into the domain's connections.

5 Flexible DOCA UROM Plugin Development

To deploy new offloads with DOCA UROM, developers must create custom plugins by implementing two key components: a host component to manage commands from the host application, and a DPU component to executes the offloading logic on the DPU. These components provide developers with extensive flexibility to define and implement new operations tailored to specific workloads.

5.1 Host Plugin Component

The first step in creating a plugin is defining the commands (plugin APIs) that applications on the host will call to execute the functionalities offloaded by the plugin on the DPU. Command submission is asynchronous, so the plugin must also implement a (DOCA-UROM-defined) callback that executes whenever the command completes. Developers can choose to associate each command with (developer-defined) response data—for example, a command could initiate an operation on the offload and the response data could indicate the completion of the operation. So, depending on the command, the completion callback may execute only after receiving a notification from the worker on the DPU.

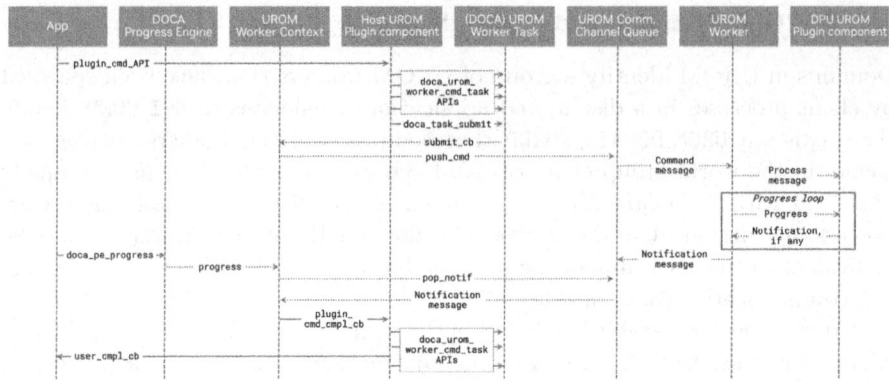

Fig. 6. Plugin command flow between the different components of DOCA UROM (solid arrows portray flows involving the DOCA UROM user: both plugin users and developers; dashed arrows portray flows between internal components).

The host component of the plugin utilizes DOCA UROM worker interfaces and data structures to manage user-invoked commands and their corresponding task objects. The plugin API can take several arguments, including the DOCA UROM worker, command attributes, and an optional pointer to a user (plugin-defined) callback. Plugins can use this callback to notify the user of task completion. Additionally, DOCA UROM provides a "user data" for each task, which is passed to the task's completion callback. Developers can use this data to store the task's context (*e.g.*, user's completion callback), enabling efficient tracking and management of task execution.

5.2 DPU Plugin Component

In the DPU component of the plugin, developers have complete flexibility in implementing the core logic of the offloads for different commands. To facilitate interaction with the DOCA UROM framework, we define 6 core interfaces that the plugin's DPU component must implement.

- **open** and **close**: initialization and destruction of the plugin's resources (*e.g.*, communication endpoint), respectively;
- **addr**: retrieving the address of the worker on which the plugin is running. Other processes can establish a connection to the worker using this address;
- **worker_cmd**: forwarding of incoming commands to the plugin to initiate offload execution;
- **progress**: entrypoint into the plugin to advance offload execution and retrieval of any available responses;
- **resp_pack**: packing of plugin response data into a buffer before pushing them to the host.

To deploy the DPU component of the plugin, the developer needs to compile the plugin as a shared library and place it in a location where the DOCA UROM service is configured to search for plugins.

5.3 End-to-End Flow

Figure 6 shows the end-to-end flow of a plugin command: from the application on the host to the DPU component of the plugin via the host plugin component and the various software components of both DOCA core objects and DOCA UROM. Once the application calls a plugin API, the host plugin component prepares the command and kicks off the execution of the task. The DOCA UROM worker context on the host pushes the command over the DOCA UROM communication channel to the worker on the DPU. The application polls for completion of the task via the DOCA progress engine which in turn checks for notifications from the communication channel in the worker context.

The DPU worker continuously loops over its progress engine which performs multiple tasks. These tasks include checking for commands from the host, monitoring notifications from any of the plugins it runs, and advancing offload execution using the progress interface. When the worker receives a command from the host, it forwards the command to the corresponding plugin via the worker_cmd interface. The plugin then begins executing the offload. Depending on the command, the plugin may enqueue a notification upon completion of the offload's execution. After serializing the notification using the resp_pack interface, the DPU worker pushes it to the host through the communication channel.

When the host DOCA UROM worker context pops a notification, it executes the plugin's completion callback for that task which in turn executes the application's completion callback.

6 Testbeds

We evaluate the DOCA UROM case studies described in Sect. 7 on systems and clusters containing the BlueField-3 (BF-3) networking platform. Each BF-3 contains multiple (up to 16) Arm A78 cores, a ConnectX-7 adapter that offers a networking throughput of 50 GB/s, and a memory capacity of up to 32 GB. We use two clusters: one at the HPC-AI Advisory Council [5] where each server hosts a single BF-3, and another DGX H100 cluster where each server hosts 8 BF-3s, each corresponding to a dedicated H100 GPU. Depending on the case study, we use the UCX, UCC, NCCL, and CUDA software frameworks.

7 DOCA UROM Case Studies

In this section we showcase the use of the DOCA UROM framework to develop efficient offloads for versatile use cases.

7.1 Remote Direct Memory Operations (RDMOs)

Much like Liu et al. [16], we define a Remote Direct Memory Operation (RDMO) as a new communication primitive that entails an RDMA communication coupled with a compute element at the destination. A DPU enables an efficient RDMO implementation since its cores can execute the compute element of an RDMO without needing involvement from any of the application's processing elements. We deploy RDMO servers on the BlueField networking platform via a DOCA UROM plugin.

Figure 7 outlines the different components—initiator, server, and target—of a DOCA UROM RDMO deployment and the connections involved. The application processes (DOCA UROM clients) on the host first create DOCA UROM workers on the DPU with RDMO capabilities. To bootstrap the required connections, the application processes use the RDMO plugin APIs to query the addresses of their local RDMO servers and exchange them with each other using an out-of-band (OOB) mechanism. When the target registers memory segments with the server, the UROM worker returns an ID which an initiator will use in its RDMO requests. The application processes exchange these memory region IDs with each other using an OOB mechanism. Once the bootstrapping phase is complete, the RDMO initiator communicates with the RDMO server using commands that we predefine in the RDMO plugin.

We showcase the efficiency of RDMOs using an RDMO *append* operation that atomically appends data into a queue in remote memory. The result of this operation is semantically equivalent to the result of two consecutive RDMA operations: a fetch-and-add atomic followed by a put to the fetched address (FADD+Put). Compared to FADD+Put, the RDMO operation incurs only one roundtrip (see Fig. 8).

Figure 9 compares the rate of append operations between two executions: an RDMA-based FADD+Put, and DOCA UROM RDMO's append operation. RDMO append operations achieve a much higher throughput, upto 10.57×, than FADD+Put does especially for smaller message sizes as the RDMO operation only incurs one roundtrip compared to FADD+Put.

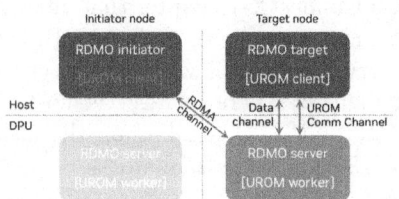

Fig. 7. RDMO service with DOCA UROM.

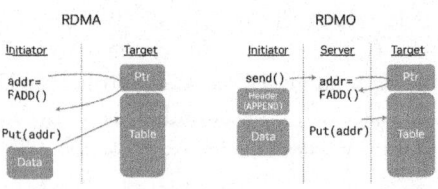

Fig. 8. Comparing RDMA-based and RDMO-based append operations.

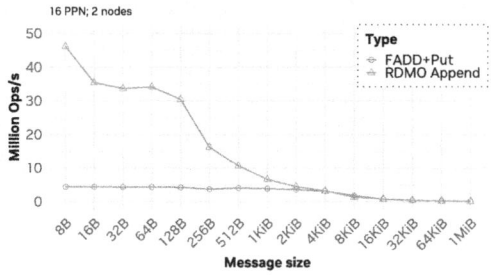

Fig. 9. Append rate with and without DOCA UROM.

7.2 True Non-blocking Collective Progress

The DPU's cores offer an opportunity to progress the schedule of a non-blocking collective in parallel to the application's overlapping computation without any involvement from the host's cores. Using a DOCA UROM plugin, we enable collective progress on the BlueField networking platform by offloading parts of the Unified Collective Communication (UCC) library. To utilize this offload, each process of a distributed application first creates a UROM worker that runs a DOCA UROM UCC plugin. The application processes then establish the UROM_DOMAIN_WORLD (see Sect. 4.4), connecting all UROM worker processes to one another. Finally, the application processes set up a data channel with their corresponding UROM worker using a cross GVMI memory key, allowing the UROM worker to issue network operations that access memory regions registered by the host [1,19]. The UCC library runtime executes these three steps, enabling existing uses of the UCC library to transparently leverage the DOCA UROM UCC service without any modifications. Figure 10 illustrates the various components and connections involved in an application utilizing the DOCA UROM UCC plugin.

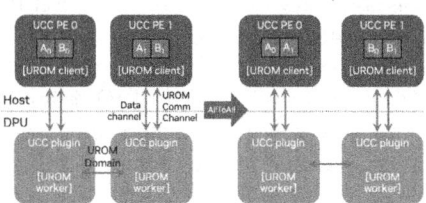

Fig. 10. UCC offload with DOCA UROM.

We showcase the benefits of offloading collective progress using OSU's non-blocking AllToAll MPI benchmark (osu_ialltoall). This benchmark runs an MPI_Ialltoall collective with overlapping computation. We run the benchmark with a UCC library that can toggle between offloading collective progress and

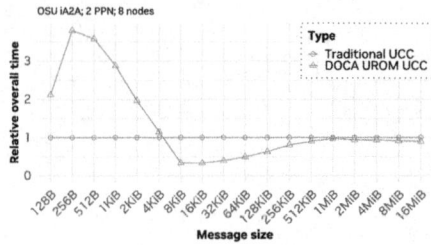 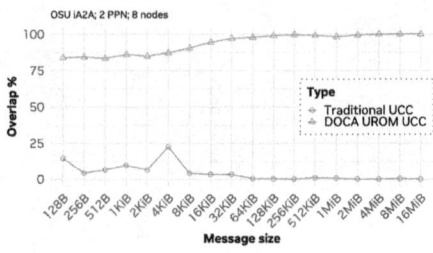

Fig. 11. Overall benchmark time with offloaded progress relative to that without offloading.

Fig. 12. Computation-communication overlap with and without offloaded collective progress.

not. Figure 11 presents the overall time taken by the benchmark with offloaded progress (DOCA UROM UCC) relative to that without offloaded progress (traditional UCC) for each message size. For small message sizes, offloaded progress hurts the execution time of the benchmark because of the overheads of offloading the collective to the DPU, which occupy a significant proportion of the overall collective execution time. For medium and large message sizes, however, the benchmark completes up to 3× faster with offloaded progress compared to without. This improvement is primary due to the overlap between computation and collective progress achieved by DOCA UROM UCC, which traditional UCC cannot match. Figure 12 demonstrates that DOCA UROM UCC achieves nearly 100% overlap between communication and computation for medium and large messages in the osu_ialltoall benchmark.

7.3 Memory Service for AI Model States

DPU SoCs feature an isolated memory subsystem, and they offer significant amounts of memory with DRAM and on-board NVMe. Collectively, the set of DPUs that constitute the distributed execution of a workload offer a memory pool that could serve as a second-tier memory location for applications like AI training that have large memory requirements.

Using a DOCA UROM plugin, we offload AI model states to the BlueField networking platform. We define a new DOCA UROM plugin—Object Manager—that provides object-level access to DPU-offered memory. Once the application creates a UROM worker with the Object Manager plugin, it can offload and prefetch objects using non-blocking put- and get-style commands defined in the plugin. Each command contains information identifying an object along with source (put) or destination (get) addresses on the host. These commands use data channel connections (see Fig. 13) that the application establishes with the worker during the bootstrapping phase. Using the data channel, the plugin orchestrates data movement between the host and the DPU-offered memory.

The BlueField-3 networking platform is rated for a max memory of 32 GB. Considering a DGX H100 cluster with a 1:1 GPU:DPU ratio, Fig. 14 shows that we can enable the training of a 500-billion-parameter model using as few as 512

GPUs by offloading model states to BF-3. Without offloading, we need more than 2048 GPUs to train the same model.

Using a mini-app that emulates the FWD pass in FSDP training, we observe that the communication and computational bandwidths with offloading are equivalent to those without offloading (see Figs. 15 and 16).

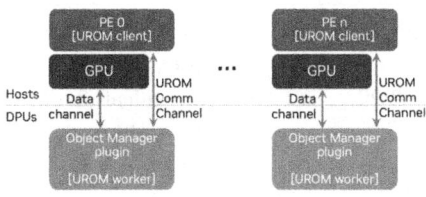

Fig. 13. Object Manager service with DOCA UROM.

8 Related Work

Various efforts on DPU accelerations for workloads have identified that offloading frameworks will play a critical role in simplifying the exploration and use of DPU-based services [8,14,15,18]. Prior offloading frameworks are either tied to a specific use case [12,17], or are not available for public use [20]. To best of our knowledge, UROM is the first of its kind to achieve both flexibility and efficiency.

The sPIN [11,13] framework enables programmable processing for each network packet. Like DOCA UROM plugins, users write sPIN handlers that run on execution units on the NIC. The sPIN framework is designed to execute relatively short custom handlers. With DOCA UROM workers, on the other hand, developers have the flexibility to run both lightweight and complex operations depending on the needs and goals of the offload. The Open Smart Network API (OpenSNAPI) project is another effort that shares the same goal of DOCA UROM: to abstract away the complexities involved in offloading from the user [9]. OpenSNAPI has explored the use of inline compiler directives [20]; DOCA UROM plugins require a higher amount of developer effort to deploy offloads, but their flexible design allows a seamless support for both communication and computational operations.

9 Concluding Remarks

Data Processing Units (DPUs) are part of the networking infrastructure, but they are more than just network endpoints. They are comprised of a rich set of resources including multiple server-grade cores, memory, and accelerator engines. HPC and AI applications seek to benefit from the capabilities of DPUs, but the

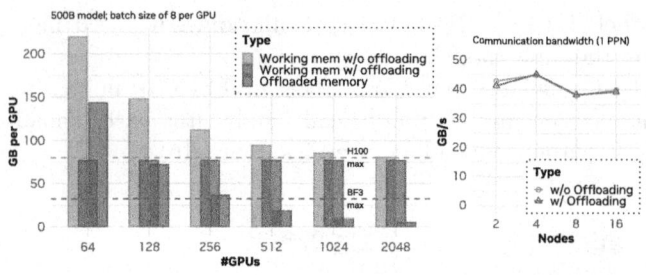
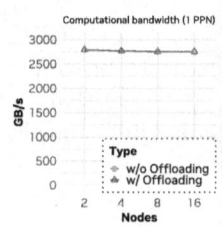

Fig. 14. Running larger models with offloading.

Fig. 15. Communication bandwidth.

Fig. 16. Computational bandwidth.

community lacks an efficient and flexible framework that enables a seamless exploration of DPU-based offloads. The DOCA UROM offloading framework that we detail in this paper provides a comprehensive solution to the existing challenges in DPU-based offloads. The core architectural designs of DOCA UROM are compatible with DPU offerings from various vendors. Originally developed as part of a research project, DOCA UROM is now accessible as a vital tool for researchers, enabling them to rapidly prototype DPU-based services on the BlueField networking platform for AI and HPC applications. It can be downloaded as part of the DOCA programming platform [4].

References

1. Cross-gvmi patches in the mlx5 driver. https://mails.dpdk.org/archives/dev/2022-December/257885.html
2. DOCA Core Programming Guide. https://docs.nvidia.com/doca/sdk/doca+core/index.html
3. DOCA documentation. https://docs.nvidia.com/doca/sdk/
4. DOCA downloads. https://developer.nvidia.com/doca-downloads
5. HPC-AI Advisory Council. https://www.hpcadvisorycouncil.com/
6. Aderholdt, F., Pophale, S., Gorentla Venkata, M., Imam, N.: OpenSHMEM sets and groups: an approach to worksharing and memory management. In: Pophale, S., Imam, N., Aderholdt, F., Gorentla Venkata, M. (eds.) OpenSHMEM 2018. LNCS, vol. 11283, pp. 3–21. Springer, Cham (2019). https://doi.org/10.1007/978-3-030-04918-8_1
7. Barrett, B., Squyres, J.M., Lumsdaine, A., Graham, R.L., Bosilca, G.: Analysis of the component architecture overhead in open MPI. In: Di Martino, B., Kranzlmüller, D., Dongarra, J. (eds.) EuroPVM/MPI 2005. LNCS, vol. 3666, pp. 175–182. Springer, Heidelberg (2005). https://doi.org/10.1007/11557265_25
8. Bayatpour, M., et al.: BluesMPI: efficient MPI non-blocking alltoall offloading designs on modern BlueField Smart NICs. In: Chamberlain, B.L., Varbanescu, AL., Ltaief, H., Luszczek, P. (eds.) High Performance Computing. ISC High Performance 2021. LNCS, vol. 12728. Springer, Cham (2021). https://doi.org/10.1007/978-3-030-78713-4_2

9. Beebe, M., Williams, B.K., Leidel, J., Chen, Y., Poole, S.W.: A path toward understanding the performance capabilities of smartnic devices [slides]. Tech. rep, Los Alamos National Laboratory (LANL), Los Alamos, NM (United States) (2022)
10. Bosshart, P., Daly, D., et al.: P4: programming protocol-independent packet processors. ACM SIGCOMM Comput. Comm. Rev. **44**(3), 87–95 (2014)
11. Di Girolamo, S., et al.: A risc-v in-network accelerator for flexible high-performance low-power packet processing. In: 2021 ACM/IEEE 48th Annual International Symposium on Computer Architecture (ISCA), pp. 958–971. IEEE (2021)
12. Graham, R., et al.: Optimizing application performance with bluefield: accelerating large-message blocking and nonblocking collective operations. In: ISC High Performance 2024 Research Paper Proceedings (39th International Conference), pp. 1–12. Prometeus GmbH (2024)
13. Hoefler, T., Di Girolamo, S., Taranov, K., Grant, R.E., Brightwell, R.: SPIN: high-performance streaming processing in the network. In: roceedings of the International Conference for High Performance Computing, Networking, Storage and Analysis, pp. 1–16 (2017)
14. Karamati, S., et al.: "smarter" nics for faster molecular dynamics: a case study. In: 2022 International Parallel and Distributed Processing Symposium (IPDPS), pp. 583–594. IEEE (2022)
15. Li, Y., et al.: Accelerating lossy and lossless compression on emerging bluefield dpu architectures. In: 2024 IEEE Intl. Parallel and Dist. Processing Symp. (IPDPS), pp. 373–385. IEEE (2024)
16. Liu, F., et al.: Beyond MPI: new communication interfaces for database systems and data-intensive applications. ACM SIGMOD Rec. **49**(4), 12–17 (2021)
17. Megan Grodowitz, Pavel Shamis, S.P.: Openshmem i/o extensions for fine-grained access to persistent memory storage. In: SMC 2020 (2020)
18. Sarkauskas, N., et al.: Large-message nonblocking mpi_iallgather and mpi ibcast offload via bluefield-2 dpu. In: 2021 IEEE 28th International Conference on High Performance Computing, Data, and Analytics (HiPC), pp. 388–393. IEEE (2021)
19. Suresh, K.K., et al.: A novel framework for efficient offloading of communication operations to bluefield smartnics. In: 2023 IEEE International Parallel and Distributed Processing Symposium, (IPDPS), pp. 123–133. IEEE (2023)
20. Usman, M., et al.: DPU offloading programming with the OpenMP API. In: Proc. of the SC 2023 Work. of the International Conference for High Performance Computing, Network, Storage, and Analysis. pp. 884–891 (2023)

Accelerating I/O in Scientific Workflows with the Impact of Apache Ignite's In-Memory File System

Vijayalakshmi Saravanan[1,2](✉), Sai Karthik Navuluru[2], Lakshman Tamil[2], and Khaled Ibrahim[3]

[1] Department of Electrical and Computer Engineering, University of Texas at Tyler, Tyler, TX, USA
[2] Department of Electrical and Computer Engineering, University of Texas at Dallas, Dallas, TX, USA
vsaravanan@uttyler.edu, {SaiKarthik.Navuluru,laxman}@utdallas.edu
[3] Lawrence Berkeley National Laboratory, Berkeley, CA, USA
KZIbrahim@lbl.gov

Abstract. Efficient storage and retrieval of large-scale scientific data remain critical challenges in HPC environments, especially as heterogeneous architecture and evolving system complexities continue to increase demands on application developers. This work-in-progress paper investigates the potential of in-memory computing file systems, specifically Ignite's Distributed File System (IDFS), for mitigating I/O bottlenecks in scientific workflows. We evaluate IDFS performance by single-node deployment at the NERSC Perlmutter supercomputer for latency in data access, throughput, and resource utilization. Our preliminary results prove the feasibility of using IDFS to improve I/O efficiency in large-scale scientific applications. This work adds to the current efforts in scalable data management and performance optimization, hence setting the base for future multi-node evaluations and integration with advanced parallel and distributed computing methodologies.

Keywords: In-memory computing · Distributed storage · HPC

1 Introduction

The continued increase in the use of advanced scientific computing has made handling and analysis of complex scientific data sets produced by high-performance computing simulations a reality. Some of these applications generate large amounts of data, leading to file I/O becoming a major consideration in HPC environments. Recent studies have shown that I/O operations can consume up to 70% of execution time in data-intensive scientific applications [9], creating a critical bottleneck that limits overall performance.

Traditionally, data management in HPC environments has included systems such as the Lustre system and the Hadoop Distributed File System (HDFS). Despite their solidity and expansibility, all these storage solutions inspire some concerns. Their major disadvantage is the use of physical storage devices with high I/O latency and limited throughput. While they are generally efficient and easy to scale, especially for larger data sets, scientific datasets continue to grow larger, and these systems begin to exhibit lower efficiency for real-time computations and large-scale simulations. In contrast, in-memory distributed file systems could provide an effective solution to the problem. Distributed File System named as Ignite Distributed File System (IDFS) integrated in Apache Ignite in-memory platform targets the I/O latency by storing files in the memory of nodes in the cluster. Because the IDFS has opted to embrace in-memory storage to achieve quicker storage and retrieval of data, the throughputs are bound to undergo a drastic hike even under rigorous scientific usage. While traditional systems such as Lustre, HDFS, and Ceph have been critical data management platforms to tackle large datasets in HPC, they have disk-based architectures that give rise to large I/O latency, low throughput, scalability, integration, and resource utilisation. Considering these limitations, it's crucial to explore alternative file systems that can better meet the needs of data-intensive scientific applications.

This research specifically addresses the following questions:

- How effectively can an in-memory file system like IDFS handle large-scale scientific datasets compared to traditional disk-based storage?
- What performance benefits can be realised for read/write operations in molecular dynamics simulations?
- How efficiently does IDFS utilise system resources during data-intensive operations?

The structure of this paper is as follows: Sect. 2 discusses the background and motivation; Sect. 3 presents the proposed methodology; Sect. 4 outlines the preliminary results; Sect. 5 presents the conclusions and future enhancements.

2 Related Work

Distributed file systems are crucial for managing the vast data generated by high-performance computing (HPC) workloads. Due to their scalability and performance, traditional systems like Lustre, Hadoop Distributed File System (HDFS), and Ceph are widely used in HPC environments. Lustre [4] excels in high-throughput scenarios, achieving tens of gigabytes per second in I/O bandwidth, making it ideal for large-scale simulations. However, its reliance on physical disk storage can lead to performance degradation during peak I/O demands. HDFS [1,7] prioritises fault tolerance through data replication but struggles with the low-latency demands of real-time scientific data processing [5]. Its disk-based nature and sequential write pattern make it less suitable for HPC workloads requiring frequent data writes and random access.

Ceph [8] is adaptive in supporting object, block, and file storage, but similar to Lustre and HDFS, its disk-based design cannot support I/O-intensive workloads in real-time systems cost-effectively. Apache Spark [2] uses in-memory computation for fast data processing and analysis but does not have a native distributed file system and must use external storage devices, which provide performance bottlenecks. Apache Ignite [3] overcomes these shortcomings through a complete in-memory computing platform with an in-built Ignite Distributed File System (IDFS). By storing frequently used data in memory across distributed nodes, Ignite lowers latency and removes most of the bottlenecks found in conventional disk-based systems. It provides ACID-compliant transactions and dynamic data rebalancing, making it even more applicable to HPC environments [8]. This in-memory architecture allows Ignite to support real-time data access and analysis with less latency, a possible solution for computationally intensive workloads in scientific computing that require rapid processing and data analysis. cite ignite-gpu.

Despite extensive research and development efforts invested in distributed file systems, there is a significant knowledge gap regarding the performance potential of in-memory file systems such as Apache Ignite's IDFS for high-performance computing applications. Although traditional disk-based systems are popular and attractive, they are fundamentally limited in their ability to support real-time data access and rapid simulations. The emergence of in-memory solutions offers an opportunity to overcome these limitations; however, their application within HPC environments for processing large-scale scientific data sets has not been thoroughly investigated.

In this paper, we aim to fill this research gap by evaluating the scalability of IDFS in managing huge NWChem simulation data compared to traditional distributed file systems. This evaluation will show the feasibility of using in-memory distributed file systems to improve future data handling for HPC applications.

3 Methodology

3.1 Experimental Setup and Configuration

We conducted our experiments on NERSC's Perlmutter [10], a GPU-boosted supercomputer at the Lawrence Berkeley National Laboratory (LBNL). Perlmutter consists of 1,536 GPU nodes, each equipped with an AMD EPYC 7763 (Milan) CPU and four NVIDIA A100 GPUs, each having 40 GB of memory. The GPUs are connected via NVLink for high-bandwidth communication and use an HPE Slingshot interconnect for a fast network backbone. The system features a fully-flash Lustre file system for efficient data access and storage.

We implemented Apache Ignite on a single Perlmutter node, leveraging its computing capabilities to run extensive NWChem molecular dynamics data. Apache Ignite was set up specifically with good amount of data storage capacity, PARTITIONED cache mode with backup snapshots, TRANSACTIONAL atomicity mode, and PRIMARYSYNC write synchronization mode. This setup ensured effective in-memory data processing and high-performance execution of our scientific workloads.

While Apache Ignite is intended for distributed processing over numerous nodes, here we aimed to test the performance of the Ignite Distributed File System (IDFS) processing large-scale datasets under the single-node condition. This will enable us to assess Ignite's read/write capability and query execution as much as processing and managing molecular dynamics simulation data. The Apache Ignite setup consisted of several main elements:

- In-Memory Caching: The data set was cached in memory to minimize disk I/O operations and decrease access times.
- Storage of Data: Ignite distributed in-memory file system (IDFS) was utilized to save the molecular data. Since the setup was a single node, multi-node replication was not necessary.
- ACID Transactions: All read and write operations were executed under ACID-compliant transactions to ensure data consistency and reliability.

3.2 Datasets

We utilized two datasets from the NWChem [11] molecular dynamics simulations:

Dataset Characteristics

- 1H9T Dataset:
  - 151 frames of molecular dynamics simulation
  - 8,993 atoms per frame
  - Each frame contains atomic coordinates (x, y, z positions) stored as double-precision floating-point values
  - Use case: Protein folding simulation of hemoglobin
- 1FME Dataset:
  - 26,283 frames of molecular dynamics simulation
  - 504 atoms per frame
  - Each frame contains atomic coordinates (x, y, z positions) stored as double-precision floating-point values
  - Use case: Molecular dynamics simulation of peptide folding

Frame Definition. In molecular dynamics simulations, a "frame" represents a snapshot of the atomic positions at a specific timestep. Each frame contains the 3D coordinates (x, y, z) of all atoms in the system at that moment. Consecutive frames show the evolution of the molecular system over time.

3.3 Operations Performed

To benchmark the performance of Apache Ignite with the 1H9T and 1FME datasets, we executed a series of read, write, and query operations to comprehensively assess Ignite's capabilities in managing large-scale molecular dynamics simulations. These operations targeted both sequential and random data access patterns, along with real-time data ingestion and complex query execution.

For read operations, we executed sequential reads from the entire dataset with access to the atomic coordinates (x, y, z positions) of all frames. This allowed us to analyze Ignite's performance on processing large volumes of data and data streams. We also executed random access reads, with particular atomic coordinates accessed from randomly chosen frames. This helped measure Ignite's latency and whether arbitrary data access was feasible without a loss of performance, particularly considering the complexity of molecular simulation data.

In the write operations, we simulated real-time data ingestion using concurrent writes of large-scale molecular data. The writes were batched, just like data flow normally encountered in molecular dynamics simulations, where there are streams of data that are constantly processed. Performance was normally gauged by how long it took to execute these writes, testing how well Ignite could store massive amounts of molecular data in memory with consistency and durability ensured by ACID-compliant transactions.

The query operations were aimed at retrieving atomic data and energy levels through the application of complex queries. Filters, for instance, were utilized to retrieve atoms with certain criteria, essentially simulating scientific queries that scientists can use during molecular studies. Aggregation operations were also performed to identify mean atomic displacements and energy levels per frame, providing insight into Ignite's query execution speed and overall computation overhead while executing complex data manipulation.

3.4 Disruption Simulation

To validate Ignite's recovery and resilience to interruptions, we took a systematic approach to replicate interruptions in I/O operations:

Methodology for Simulating Disruptions

- Duration of disruption: ranged from 100ms to 5000ms to mimic various system interruptions
- Triggered recovery through Ignite's auto-recovery mechanisms

Recovery Metrics

- Recovery time following disruption: from interruption to normal service resumption
- Data consistency checking: comparison of checksums before and after interruption

– Recovery phase performance impact: observing throughput decline

To ensure data consistency and fault tolerance, we perform consistency checks upon each write operation. The operation verifies that the data that is being written to the Ignite Distributed File System (IDFS) is written and can be read without compromising data integrity. For fault tolerance testing, we shut down and restarted the operation intentionally to simulate real-life interruptions. The aim was to understand the resilience of Ignite's recovery systems in such interruptions without compromising data consistency. This is crucial to ensure reliability in scientific applications, wherein data loss or inconsistency can have serious consequences.

4 Preliminary Results Analysis and Discussions

In this section, we present the obtained performance metrics as shown in Tables 1, 2 and 3, beginning with read/write operations, followed by query performance and resource utilization metrics. Preliminary results indicate that Ignite's in-memory architecture significantly minimizes I/O latency, facilitating rapid data retrieval and real-time processing even with complex datasets as depicted in Fig. 1.

Table 1. Performance Metrics for 1H9T and 1FME Datasets

Metric	1H9T	1FME
Total Frames	151	26,284
Write Throughput (frames/second)	625	722
Average Write Time per Frame (seconds)	0.0015	0.0013
CPU Usage during Writes (%)	0.38	0.53
Memory Usage during Writes (%)	8.00	8.00
Read Throughput (frames/second)	1,311	1,354
Average Read Time per Frame (seconds)	0.0006	0.0007
CPU Usage during Reads (%)	0.45	0.53
Memory Usage during Reads (%)	8.00	7.50

4.1 Detailed Analysis of Performance Metrics

Figures 1 and 2 illustrates the key performance characteristics observed from our benchmarks using the 1H9T and 1FME molecular dynamics datasets. The top-left graph demonstrates that write throughput remains relatively stable across increasing frame counts, with a slight upward trend for the larger 1FME dataset. This indicates that Apache Ignite is capable of sustaining consistent data ingestion performance even as the data volume scales significantly. Such behavior

Table 2. I/O Performance in Standard Units

Metric	1H9T	1FME
Read Throughput (MB/s)	28.4	36.2
Write Throughput (MB/s)	13.5	19.5
Read IOPS	1,311	1,354
Write IOPS	625	722
Read Latency (ms)	0.762	0.738
Write Latency (ms)	1.6	1.38

Table 3. Resource Utilization During Peak Workloads

Metric	Read Operations	Write Operations
Peak CPU Usage (%)	0.65	0.78
Peak Memory Usage (%)	9.2	10.5
Java Heap Usage (GB)	28.4	32.7
Garbage Collection Time (ms)	124	186
Network I/O (MB/s)	0.8	1.2

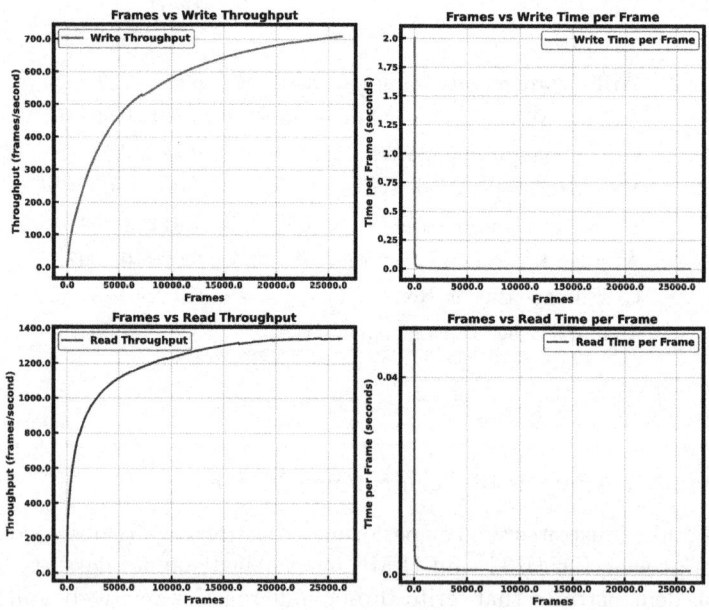

Fig. 1. Comparison of Write/Read Throughput vs. Time per Frame.

is critical for scientific applications that require high-throughput processing of time-series data, such as molecular simulations and environmental monitoring.

The top-right graph shows that the average write time per frame remains consistently low, under 2 s, for both datasets. This efficiency highlights the advantage of using an in-memory file system where the latency introduced by disk I/O operations is avoided. Apache Ignite's internal transactional mechanisms and efficient memory storage architecture help maintain low overhead even under concurrent data write operations. This makes it particularly suitable for real-time data logging and simulation workloads where minimal write delays are essential.

On the other hand, the graph at the bottom left reveals a significantly better read throughput compared with writes. For both datasets, read throughput is over 1300 frames per second, illustrating the performance benefits achieved by overcoming physical I/O limitations. One of the characteristics of in-memory computing systems is that operations on data access take place directly from RAM rather than from disk storage. Such fast access is valuable to applications that involve repeated retrievals of intermediate simulation states or metadata during the analysis process.

The bottom right plot also shows this advantage by showing that the read time per frame is still incredibly low, at or below 0.04 s. Low latency accelerates the speed of scientific analysis and allows for interactive visualization and real-time decision-making within simulation pipelines. For scientific applications such as molecular dynamics or protein folding simulations, where scientists need quick access to atomic structures at varying timesteps, this responsiveness can be transformative.

To ensure the accuracy of these results is not affected by caching artifacts or temporary performance fluctuations, a strict benchmarking approach was utilized. Between each test cycle, we explicitly cleared the in-memory caches using Apache Ignite's `cache.clear()` API to remove any leftover data that might influence performance evaluations. Each benchmark was performed five times, and the average figures were reported. The standard deviation across the evaluations remained within $\pm 5\%$, confirming that the results are reliable and reproducible.

Memory utilization was also continuously tracked throughout testing with both system-level tools and Ignite's internal metrics. This ensured that each dataset was freshly loaded from scratch for every test iteration and that Ignite did not retain any implicit memory state between tests. To manage any potential overhead related to the JVM, Java heap usage, and garbage collection (GC) metrics were also gathered. GC activity was minimal for read operations, indicating effective utilization of memory and minimal disruption at runtime.

To isolate the performance of Ignite I/O, all tests were run on a standalone node of the Perlmutter system that offered exclusive access to its resources. Thread affinity was set so that the Ignite processing threads were restrained to one CPU core, lowering context-switching overhead and ensuring a more accurate timing measurement.

In summary, the performance results provide sufficient evidence of the applicability of Apache Ignite's in-memory file system to I/O-bound scientific workloads. The high sustained throughput, low latency, and less resource utilization across operations validate Ignite's capabilities in mitigating I/O bottlenecks typical of conventional HPC workflows. The results also serve as the foundation for future multi-node scalability evaluation, where the effects of network communication and distributed caching policies will be explored.

4.2 Write Performance

The write performance result values show the effectiveness of Apache Ignite in handling large data under various dataset sizes. In both the small 1H9T and large 1FME datasets, Ignite has good write performance at all times, which is an indication of its scalability and flexibility. This is due to the in-memory nature of Ignite, which removes the latency involved in disk-based systems.

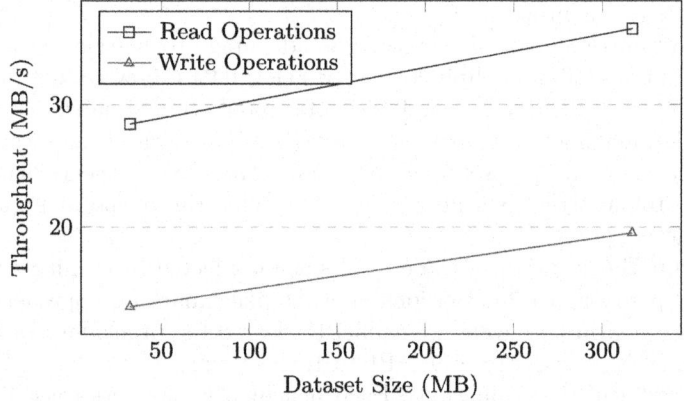

Fig. 2. Performance comparison of read and write operations in MB/s.

Ignite's low CPU usage during writes ensures that it can support streaming data, even on low-end systems. This feature positions it especially apt for HPC workloads, where efficiency in the use of resources is critical. The write latencies also show that Ignite can process enormous amounts of data at great speed, which keeps the latency that is typically found in traditional storage systems to a minimum. The combination of ACID-safe transactions and in-memory cache assures that the data is used quickly and safely.

4.3 Read Performance

Ignite's in-memory caching offers substantial advantages in read operations, particularly in minimizing data retrieval times. For both datasets, read performance is highly efficient, enabling rapid access to scientific data, even when dealing with complex atomic structures typical in molecular dynamics simulations.

Unlike disk-based systems that experience I/O bottlenecks during large-scale data retrieval, Ignite's in-memory processing ensures that frequently accessed data is available almost instantaneously.

The variations in read throughput between the two datasets are a function of their respective size and complexity. Nevertheless, Ignite always delivers low-latency data access, which is essential for real-time scientific workflows. This feature makes Ignite particularly useful for applications with fast iterative processing and analysis, such as simulations that involve repeated data access and decision-making in real-time results.

4.4 Resource Utilization

One of the most notable strengths of Apache Ignite is its resource efficiency. CPU and memory usage were minimal in both read and write operations, even with a large data set. This indicates that Ignite can efficiently handle data-intensive loads without a heavy burden on the system, thereby releasing resources for other computations. Memory usage is constant because Ignite has efficient in-memory data management, so the data accessed most often is cached without excessive memory overhead. This is especially crucial in scientific computations where there is large data because high memory usage would restrict the scalability of the simulation. Having low CPU usage, Ignite prevents data management activities from controlling the computational resources of HPC systems and assigning suboptimal use of the system to computationally expensive computations.

5 Conclusions and Future Work

5.1 Conclusions

The study of Apache Ignite on the NERSC Perlmutter supercomputer verifies that in-memory computing is extremely beneficial for processing and handling large-scale molecular dynamics data. In particular, Ignite's in-memory caching significantly reduces read and write latency, allowing real-time analysis of complex scientific data like 1H9T and 1FME.

Apache Ignite has proven to be a powerful solution for single-node data processing, effectively handling substantial workloads, including parallel operations and complex queries, even without multi-node deployment. The results suggest that scaling to multi-node setups could enhance performance, particularly for larger datasets and more demanding workflows.

However, due to time constraints, this study's primary limitation is the single-node setup, which does not fully leverage Apache Ignite's distributed capabilities. While the results indicate strong performance for in-memory processing on one node, it is crucial to evaluate scalability and potential bottlenecks in a multi-node configuration, especially when handling exponentially larger scientific computing datasets.

5.2 Future Work

Multi-node Evaluation Plan. Our future work will focus on expanding the evaluation to a multi-node Apache Ignite deployment with the following approach:

- Scaling strategy: Progressive testing with 2, 4, 8, and 16 nodes to analyze performance scaling
- Expected performance improvements: Linear or near-linear throughput increases with node count
- Potential bottlenecks to investigate: Network communication overhead, data partitioning effects, and memory utilization across nodes

Comparative Analysis Framework. We will conduct a comprehensive comparison with established HPC storage systems:

- Baseline systems: Lustre, HDFS, and Ceph deployed on equivalent hardware
- Common benchmarks: IOR, IO500, and custom molecular dynamics I/O patterns
- Performance metrics for comparison:
  - Read/write throughput (MB/s)
  - Latency (ms)
  - Resource utilization
  - Scalability with dataset size

Integration with Real-World Scientific Workflows. To validate practical benefits, we plan to integrate IDFS with scientific applications:

- Target workflows: NWChem, LAMMPS, and other molecular dynamics applications
- Application-specific performance metrics: Time-to-solution, checkpoint overhead reduction
- Expected benefits: Reduced simulation time, improved data analysis capabilities, and enhanced interactive visualization support

Future work should focus on expanding the study to a multi-node configuration to assess Ignite's scalability under more complex conditions. Additionally, conducting a comparative analysis with systems like Lustre and HDFS would provide valuable benchmarks and deeper insights into the trade-offs between in-memory and disk-based architectures for large-scale scientific computing.

Acknowledgments. This material is based upon work supported by the Advanced Scientific Computing Research Program in the U.S Department of Energy, Office of Science, under FAIR Award number DE-SC0026194. This manuscript has been authored by an author at Lawrence Berkeley National Laboratory under Contract No. DE-AC02-05CH11231 with the U.S. Department of Energy. This research used resources of the National Energy Research Scientific Computing Center, a DOE Office of Science User Facility using NERSC award ASCR-ERCAP0031060.

References

1. "Apache hadoop", 2019. http://hadoop.apache.org/. Accessed 10 Sept 2024
2. "Apache spark^{TM} - unified analytics engine for big data", 2019. http://spark.apache.org/. Accessed 1 Nov 2019
3. "Apache ignite", 2024. https://ignite.apache.org/. Accessed 6 Sept 2024
4. Braam, P.: "The lustre storage architecture," 2019. Accessed 5 Mar 2019
5. Dean, J., Ghemawat, S.: Mapreduce: simplified data processing on large clusters. Commun. ACM **51**(1), 107–113 (2008)
6. Khunjush, F., Dehghan, M., Afsharchi, M., Ghodsi, A.: Ignite-GPU: a GPU-enabled in-memory computing architecture. J. Supercomput. (2020)
7. Shvachko, K., Kuang, H., Radia, S., Chansler, R.: The hadoop distributed file system. In: IEEE 26th Symposium on Mass Storage Systems and Technologies (MSST). IEEE 2010, pp. 1–10 (2010)
8. Weil, S., Brandt, S.A., Miller, E.L., Long, D.D., Maltzahn, C.: Ceph: a scalable, high-performance distributed file system. In: Proceedings of the 7th Symposium on Operating Systems Design and Implementation (OSDI). USENIX Association, pp. 307–320, 2006
9. Dorier, M., Antoniu, G., Ross, R., Kimpe, D., Ibrahim, S.: CALCioM: mitigating I/O interference in HPC systems through cross-application coordination. In: 2014 IEEE International Parallel Distributed Processing Symposium, pp. 155–164. IEEE, 2014
10. Datacenter Dynamics. 2020. NERSC finalizes contract for Perlmutter supercomputer. Datacenter Dynamics. Accessed 15 Oct 2020
11. Valiev, M., et al.: NWChem: a comprehensive and scalable open-source solution for large scale molecular simulations. Comput. Phys. Commun. **181**, 1477 (2010)

HPC on Heterogeneous Hardware (H3)

H3 2025 Preface

Objectives/Topics

The 4th edition of the HPC on Heterogeneous Hardware (H3) Workshop provided a platform for pioneering work on algorithmic research, software library design, programming models, and workflow development for increasingly heterogeneous hardware, while identifying synergistic activities and connecting the dots in the software/hardware ecosystem. In the workshop context, such hardware spans from ARM and RISC-V processor variants featuring long-vector extensions through GPU-accelerated systems to architectures deploying special function units, FPGAs, or specialized deep learning processors.

The workshop was composed of a well-balanced mix of invited talks, peer-reviewed conference contributions (published here), and a panel bringing together worldwide experts in heterogeneous computing. The themes also included heterogeneity in programming approaches such as mixed-language solutions and DSL-friendly middleware libraries, heterogeneous workloads that rely on convergence of scientific ab-initio modeling, just-in-time data analytics, and assistive scientific AI/ML data models, heterogeneity in data representation including hierarchical, randomized, compressive, and mixed-precision methods, and finally mixing of hardware from novel chiplet designs, application-specific processing, and offload methods across the CPU-GPU-FPGA spectrum.

Workshop Organization

Piotr Luszczek	MIT Lincoln Lab, USA
Hartwig Anzt	Technical University of Munich, Germany
Bilel Hadri	KAUST, Saudi Arabia
Hatem Ltaief	KAUST, Saudi Arabia

Generation of Mixed-Precision Kernels for Quantized Transformer Encoders with Exo

Adrián Castelló[1(✉)], Héctor Martínez[2], Francisco D. Igual[3], and Enrique S. Quintana-Ortí[1]

[1] Universitat Politècnica de València, València, Spain
{adcastel,quintana}@disca.upv.es
[2] Universidad de Córdoba, Córdoba, Spain
el2mapeh@uco.es
[3] Universidad Complutense de Madrid, Madrid, Spain
figual@ucm.es

Abstract. The computing landscape has shifted from homogeneous x86 architectures to a heterogeneous mix including ARM and RISC-V, introducing challenges for high performance computing. Simultaneously, numerical formats have diversified, with modern deep learning workloads favoring low- and mixed-precision arithmetic to boost efficiency. This complexity demands advanced compiler frameworks and portable performance tools. This work explores using the Exo framework to automatically generate optimized, mixed-integer precision GEMM micro-kernels for ARM-NEON and RISC-V Vector, easing the burden of architecture-aware tuning for developers of transformer pipelines. Our experimental evaluation on state-of-the-art, low-power CPUs shows competitive performance for mixed-precision integer arithmetic using a representative quantized BERT model. The benefits can be expected to carry over to convolutional neural networks.

Keywords: Automatic code generation · High performance · Exo · Matrix multiplication · Mixed-precision · Quantization

1 Introduction

In recent years, the computing landscape has undergone a dramatic transformation from a relatively homogeneous ecosystem dominated by Intel x86 architectures to a diverse and rapidly evolving "zoo" of processor designs, including ARM-based systems and the open RISC-V architecture. This architectural heterogeneity introduces challenges in the domain of high performance computing, where maximizing computational efficiency is critical. Beyond hardware, the shift is further compounded by the diversification of numerical representations.

A. Castelló and H. Martínez—These authors contributed equally to this work.

Modern workloads in deep learning (DL) have embraced low-precision formats like FP16, BF16, FP8 or even integer arithmetic, to boost throughput and reduce memory footprint and energy consumption. Furthermore, mixed-precision computing, which combines different data types, has become a cornerstone for the acceleration of quantized DL pipelines while maintaining acceptable accuracy.

This growing complexity underscores the need for advanced compiler technologies, portable performance libraries, and domain-specific languages that can abstract hardware-specific optimizations while maintaining high performance. A promising solution in this space is to adopt user-schedulable languages (USLs), which are typically integrated into compiler frameworks. These tools promote a clean separation between the definition of an operation and its schedule, encompassing architecture-aware transformations such as tiling, unrolling, and vectorization. Notable examples include Halide, TVM, MLIR, and EXO.

Along this line, we address the automatic generation of highly tuned, mixed-integer precision (MIP) realizations of the general Matrix Multiplication (GEMM), a foundational operation in DL, particularly for transformers and convolutional neural networks [4,12]. Concretely, we leverage EXO [7] to implement our MIP GEMM, applying a range of optimization strategies tailored to the ARM-NEON and RISC-V Vector (RVV) extensions, to the type of multiplication kernels appearing in quantized transformer encoders. By automating this task we expect to partially relieve the developer from taking into account factors such as instruction set architecture (ISA), multithreading, and vectorization opportunities unique to each architecture. In addition, we adapt an analytical model [8] to a MIP scenario to address the presence of a multilevel cache hierarchy.

2 Transformer Encoders

Anatomy of the Encoder. Transformer encoders play a fundamental role in text classification, question answering, information retrieval, speech recognition, etc. In recognition of this relevance, our work targets transformer encoder inference on low-power, general-purpose CPUs such as those found in edge devices.

A transformer encoder is composed of an input embedding layer, followed by a stack of encoder blocks (layers), and an output classification layer. Since the initial and final stages contribute only marginally to the overall computational cost, our focus shifts to the intermediate encoder blocks. Each of these blocks consists of a multi-head attention (MHA) followed by a feed-forward network (FFN). Table 1 outlines the primary operations within the encoder block, highlighting the dimensions of the corresponding GEMM kernels, of dimensions given by the triplet (m, n, k). There, the MHA module comprises h attention heads; d denotes the embedding dimension; and f is the hidden dimension, typically set to $f = 4d$. Additionally, l is the number of tokens and b is the batch size.

High Performance GEMM. Modern, highly tuned instances of GEMM in scientific computing libraries are largely inspired by the design of GotoBLAS2 [5], which is tailored for CPUs featuring SIMD (single-instruction, multiple-data) units, deep memory hierarchies, and multiple cores. The reference algorithm,

Table 1. Operations in the MHA and FNN modules.

			m	n	k
MHA	M1-M3.	$(Q, K, V) = (W_Q, W_K, W_V) \cdot E_I$	d	lb	d
	M4.	$\mathsf{Split}(Q, K, V) \rightarrow$			
		$(Q^{i,j}, K^{i,j}, V^{i,j})_{i=1:h}^{j=1:b}$			
		for $j = 1 : b$			
		for $i = 1 : h$			
	M5.	$\bar{E}_1^{i,j} = ((K^{i,j})^T \cdot Q^{i,j})/\sqrt{d_k}$	l	l	d/h
	M6.	$E_1^{i,j} =\mathsf{Softmax}\,(\bar{E}_1^{i,j})$			
	M7.	$E_2^{i,j} = V^{i,j} \cdot E_1^{i,j}$	d/h	l	l
	M8.	$\mathsf{Concatenate}(E_2^{i,j})_{i=1:h}^{j=1:b} \rightarrow E_2$			
	M9.	$\bar{A}_O = W_O \cdot E_2$	d	lb	d
	M10.	$A_O =\mathsf{Lnorm}\,(\bar{A}_O + E_I)$			
FFN	F11.	$\bar{E}_3 = W_1 \cdot A_O$	f	lb	d
	F12.	$E_3 =\mathsf{GELU}\,(\bar{E}_3)$			
	F13.	$\bar{E}_O = W_2 \cdot E_3$	d	lb	f
	F14.	$E_O =\mathsf{Lnorm}\,(\bar{E}_O + A_O)$			

illustrated in Fig. 1 (left), expresses GEMM as five nested loops (labeled L1 through L5). It also includes two packing routines to copy blocks of A, B into contiguous buffers A_c, B_c (bottom-right in the figure). At the core of the computation lies a micro-kernel with an inner loop L6 (top-right in the figure).

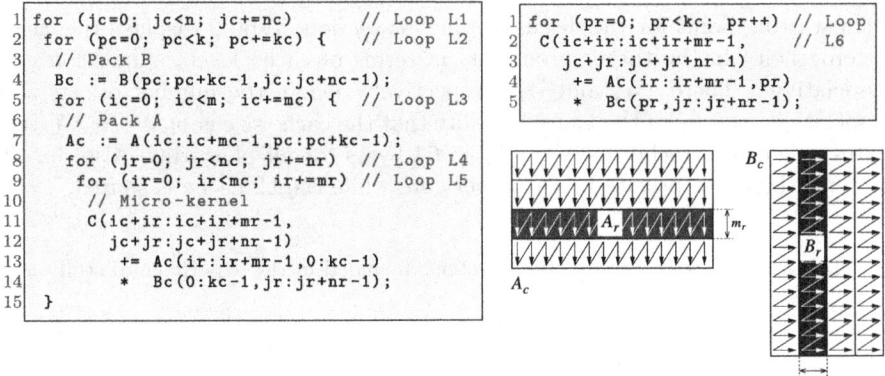

Fig. 1. Reference algorithm for GEMM in GotoBLAS2. Left: blocked algorithm; Top-right: micro-kernel; Bottom-Right: Packing of input operands.

Optimizing GEMM for modern CPUs involves three key challenges:

– Design a micro-kernel that fully utilizes the SIMD units.

- Tune the loop blocking parameters m_c, n_c, k_c to exploit the multi-level memory hierarchy [5,8].
- Expose ample parallelism in the iteration space to favor load balancing across cores and make an effective use of private/shared caches [10,11].

In the following two sections we focus on these three factors. With respect to the micro-kernel, this component must be carefully adapted to repurpose the traditional floating point-oriented GEMM into a variant suitable for quantized encoder inference on low-power CPUs. Notably, popular libraries like AMD AOCL, IBM ESSL, BLIS, and OpenBLAS only support floating point matrix operations in their GEMM implementations.

Quantized Encoders and MIP GEMM. Following the common practice in transformer models, we apply quantization exclusively to the linear layers – specifically, to the GEMM operations– within the encoder block. In contrast, we do not quantize the batched GEMM kernels (M5, M7) in the attention mechanism [3].

We consider a matrix multiplication where both input matrices, A^q and B^q, are quantized and consist of 8-bit signed integers (INT8). The output is a matrix $C^q = A^q B^q$ represented using 32-bit signed integers (INT32). The use of INT32 for the result is essential to prevent overflow during accumulation. For large language models (LLMs) with fewer than 6.7 billion parameters, like that considered in our work, this bitwidth is sufficient to maintain numerical stability [3].

3 Tackling the Cache Hierarchy

As a starting point for the discussion in this section, Table 2 displays the cache heterogeneity in the target processors in terms of cache levels, dimension and associativity. There, N_{Lx} and W_{Lx} respectively denote the number of sets and associativity degree of the Lx cache. Note that the cache size is $S_{Lx} = N_{Lx} C_{Lx} W_{Lx}$ bytes, where the cache line size $C_{Lx} = 64$ bytes for all platforms. Also, for all systems there is a private L1 cache per core while the L2 cache is shared.

Table 2. Cache hierarchy of the systems included in the experimental study.

Board	Processor	$N_{L1}\|W_{C1}$	$N_{L2}\|W_{C2}$
NVIDIA Jetson Nano	ARM Cortex-A57	256|2	2048|16
Raspeberry Pi	ARM Cortex-A72	256|2	1024|16
Sipeed LicheeRv	XuanTie C910	512|2	1024|16
Banana Pi F3	SpacemiT K1	512|4	1024|16

Assuming the micro-kernel is fixed, the analytical model in [8] considers the organization of the cache hierarchy to select the cache configuration parameters (CCPs) $k_c \rightarrow m_c \rightarrow n_c$, *in that order*, which respectively favor a high usage

Table 3. ISA of the systems included in the experimental study.

Processor	Freq. (GHz)	#Cores	ISA (SIMD)	vl (bits)
ARM Cortex-A57	1.43	4	ARMv8-A (NEON)	128
ARM Cortex-A72	1.80	4	ARMv8-A (NEON)	128
XuanTie C910	1.85	4	RISC-V (RVV 0.7.1)	128
SpacemiT K1	1.60	8	RISC-V (RVV 1.0)	256

of the L1→L2→L3 caches. Concretely, for the L1 cache, the original model sets the value for k_c by choosing the parameters that maximize the following expressions:

$$C_{A_r} \leq \left\lfloor \frac{W_{L1} - 1}{1 + \frac{n_r}{m_r}} \right\rfloor, \quad C_{B_r} = \max\left(W_{L1} - 1 - C_{A_r}, \left\lceil C_{A_r} \cdot \frac{n_r}{m_r} \right\rceil\right), \quad k_c = \frac{C_{B_r} \, N_{L1} \, C_{L1}}{n_r \, S_{\mathsf{DATA}}},$$

where $C_{A_r}|C_{B_r}$ denote the number of cache lines taken up by a micro-panel $A_r|B_r$ in each set of the L1 cache. This scheme reserves one line per set for C and distributes the remaining ones proportionally to the ratio m_r/n_r, which is linked to the number of entries retrieved from these operands in loop L6. In these expressions S_{DATA} refers to the number of bytes per element for the operands in the corresponding cache level: A_r, B_r for the L1 cache, with a pure FP32 GEMM, $S_{\mathsf{DATA}} = 4$; however, in the quantized INT8+INT32 counterpart $S_{\mathsf{DATA}} = 1$.

Next, given that loop L5 operates on an $m_c \times n_r$ block of C alongside the complete $m_c \times k_c$ buffer A_c, a line per set of the L2 cache is reserved for B_r, and the remaining ones are distributed between the matrix operands C_c and A_c proportionally to ratio defined by their dimensions $m_c n_r/(m_c k_c) = n_r/k_c$. Finally, the model determines n_c for the L3 cache by reserving one line per set for A_c, and distributing the rest between C_c and B_c proportionally to their respective dimensions: $m_c n_c/(k_c n_c) = m_c/k_c$. Note that in the MIP micro-kernel, S_{DATA} needs to be set to 4 bytes for the INT32 blocks of C and 1 byte for the INT8 blocks of A, B when adjusting the analytical model.

High-performance implementations of GEMM on a multi-core platform usually exploit loop parallelism while considering the underlying cache hierarchy [11]. Concretely, parallelizing loop L1 of the baseline algorithm for GEMM is the preferred option on multi-socket platforms. In contrast, loop L3 is better suited for systems with private L1/L2 cache and shared L3 cache. Moreover, parallelizing either loop L4 or loop L5 is a fair option for platforms with private L1 cache but shared L2/L3 cache. Finally, parallelizing loops L2, L6 should be avoided due to potential race conditions. As all target platforms present private L1 caches but a shared L2, we always extract parallelism from loop L4.

4 Micro-Kernel Generation with Exo

To motivate the automatic generation of the micro-kernel, Table 3 illustrates a variety of micro-architectures, with distinct ISA and/or vector lengths (vl) of the

SIMD units for the target processors considered in our work. This heterogeneity supports the generation of micro-kernels using the Exo framework.

In this seciton we evolve the base micro-kernel generator in [1,2,6] in order to produce a MIP micro-kernel. Concretely, the code commences with a definition of a *generic* micro-kernel following the ideas discussed in the previous section, which is then progressively refined using the Exo Python application programming interface (API). Figures 2, 3, 4, and 5 display the different parts of the entire generator code. Figure 2 presents the basic code definition in lines 2–10 and its specialization as follows:

BK1 receives the code to be transformed and fixes the sizes and types of the operands.
  1) Rename the final function label and sets the dimensions of the micro-kernel to $m_r = 8$ and $n_r = 16$.[1]
  2) Set the precision for the micro-kernel operands: A_c and B_c are both INT8 and C is INT32.

```
1  # Simplified micro-kernel definition
2  @proc
3  def intrinsic_ukernel( MR: size, NR: size, KC: size, Ac: f32[KC, MR] @ DRAM,
4                         Bc: f32[KC, NR] @ DRAM, C: f32[NR, MR] @ DRAM):
5
6    # C += Ac * Bc
7    for k in seq(0, KC):
8      for j in seq(0, NR):
9        for i in seq(0, MR):
10           C[j, i] += Ac[k,i] * Bc[k,j]
11
12 # BK1: BASIC CODE SETTINGS
13 #  1) Get and fix the micro-kernel dimensions
14 p = rename(intrinsic_ukernel, f"uk_{MR}x{NR}_i8_i32")
15 p = p.partial_eval(MR=8,NR=16)
16
17 #  2) Set the micro-kernel precisions
18 p = p.set_precision(p, 'Ac', "i8")
19 p = p.set_precision(p, 'Bc', "i8")
20 p = p.set_precision(p, 'C',  "i32")
```

Fig. 2. Part 1: GEMM structure and scheduling for C in the 8×16 MIP μkernel.

Figure 3 displays the loop partitioning and the handling of matrix C:

BK2 divides the structure of the loops into the desired schema. In this case, we distinguish between RVV and NEON. In the former, only one loop needs to be split; in the latter both are divided. The reason is the different characteristics of the ISAs. Both loops are split accordingly to *vl*.

BK3 orchestrates the scheduling of the load/store operations on C as follows:
  1) Map the elements of C to the vector registers. As the loop splitting affects the access to C, we utilize a distinct formula for each architecture.

---

[1] These sizes were chosen as illustrative examples because they fit the target hardware.

2) Resize the number (or dimensions) of vector registers used for C. Concretely, the C register is a 3D structure where the first dimension equals vl, the second equals m_r/vl, and the third one equal n_r.
3) Move the declaration of the variable to the top of the code.
4) Uncouple the loads and stores of matrix C from the computation loop.
5) Replace the loads and stores with the appropriate vector intrinsic.
6) Set the type of the vector registers.

```
22  # BK2: LOOP STRUCTURE DESIGN
23  # 1) Generate loop estructure
24  p = divide_loop(p,'i', vl, ['it','itt'])
25  if arch == "Neon":
26      p = divide_loop(p,'j', vl, ['jt','jtt'])
27
28  # BK3: C MANAGEMENT SCHEDULER
29  #   1) Map C buffer to vectorial register C_reg
30  if arch == "Neon":
31      Cp = f'C[jtt + {vl} * jt, {vl} * it + itt]'
32  else:
33      Cp = f'C[j, {vl} * it + itt]'
34  p = stage_mem(p, 'C[_] += _', Cp, 'C_reg')
35
36  #   2) Build a 3D structure of C_reg
37  p = expand_dim(p, 'C_reg', vl, 'itt', ...)
38  p = expand_dim(p, 'C_reg', MR//vl, 'it', ...)
39  if arch == "Neon":
40      p = expand_dim(p, 'C_reg', NR, f'jt * {vl} + jtt', ...)
41  else:
42      p = expand_dim(p, 'C_reg', NR, 'j', ...)
43
44  #   3) Move the register declaration to the top
45  p = lift_alloc(p, 'C_reg', n_lifts=4)
46  #   4) Extract the C load and store from the k-loop
47  p = autofission(p, p.find('C_reg[_] = _').after(), n_lifts=4)
48  p = autofission(p, p.find('C[_] = _').before(), n_lifts=4)
49
50  #   5) Replace the indicated loops by intrinsics
51  p = replace(p, 'for itt in _: _', vld_4xi32)
52  p = replace(p, 'for itt in _: _', vst_4xi32)
53
54  #   6) Set the C_reg memory to target
55  p = set_memory(p, 'C_reg', NEON if arch == 'Neon' else RVV)
```

Fig. 3. Part 2: GEMM structure and scheduling for C in the 8×16 MIP μkernel.

Figure 4 shows the load of A_c values into micro-kernel registers:

BK4 Manages the load and the data type conversion of the A_c values:
1) Bind the access to A_c to a temporary register (A_tmp) and this to the final register. This transforms the data type from INT8 to INT16.
2) Set the precision of each register structure.
3) Resize the number (or dimensions) of the registers for the A_c elements: The registers for A_c are organized into a 2D structure where the first dimension equals vl and the second one equals m_r/vl.
4) Move the declaration of the variables to the top of the code.

5) Uncouple the load of A_c from the computation loop. This movement generates a loop structure for moving data from A_c to A_{tmp} registers and another structure for moving and converting data from A_{tmp} to A_{reg} registers.
6) As the loop structure is divided (BLK2) to match that of C (INT32), the generator fuses the loops it and itt bound to the A_{tmp} register into one and then splits it by a factor of 8 (vl_ld that matches the INT8 size).
7) Replace the last loop with the intrinsic that loads 8 INT8 elements.
8) Convert the INT8 data into INT16 type. This is mandatory to unify the loops bound to the A_{reg} registers and split them again by factors that match the vl_{ld} and vl values. Then, each loop is replaced by the intrinsics to load the lower and higher half of the register.
9) Set the type of the vector registers.

```
57  # BK4: AC MANAGEMENT SCHEDULER
58  #   1) Map Ac buffer to vectorial register A_reg
59  p = bind_expr(p, 'Ac[_]','A_tmp')
60  p = bind_expr(p, 'A_tmp','A_reg')
61
62  #   2) Set the precision for each buffer
63  p = set_precision(p,'A_temp',"i8")
64  p = set_precision(p,'A_reg',"i16")
65
66  #   3) Build a 2D structure of A_reg
67  p = expand_dim(p, 'A_reg' , vl, 'itt', ...)
68  p = expand_dim(p, 'A_reg', MR//vl, 'it', ...)
69  p = expand_dim(p, 'A_tmp' , vl_ld, 'itt', ...)
70  p = expand_dim(p, 'A_tmp', MR//vl_ld, 'it', ...)
71
72  #   4) Move the register declaration to the top
73  p = lift_alloc(p, 'A_reg', n_lifts=5)
74  p = lift_alloc(p, 'A_tmp', n_lifts=5)
75
76  #   5) Move the Ac load to the k-loop
77  p = autofission(p, p.find('A_reg[_] = _').after(),n_lifts=4)
78  p = autofission(p, p.find('A_tmp[_] = _').after(),n_lifts=2)
79
80  #   6) Regenerate the loop structure for loading i8
81  p = mult_loops(p,p.find('for it in _:_ #1'),'ld8')
82  p = divide_loop(p,'ld8', vl_ld, ['ld8t','ld8tt'], perfect=True)
83  p = divide_dim(p,'A_temp',0,vl_ld)
84
85  #   7) Replace the loop by load intrinsics
86  p = replace_all(p, vld_8xi8)
87
88  #   8) Manage the conversion from i8 to i16
89  p = mult_loops(p,p.find('for it in _:_ #1'),'cast')
90  p = divide_loop(p,'cast', vl_ld, ['co','ci'], perfect=True)
91  p = divide_loop(p,'ci', vl, ['cio','cii'], perfect=True)
92  p = replace(p,p.find('for cii in _:_ '), get_low_8xi16)
93  p = replace(p,p.find('for cio in _:_'), get_high_8xi16)
94
95  #   9) Set the A_reg memory to target
96  p = set_memory(p, 'A_reg', NEON if arch == 'Neon' else RVV)
97  p = set_memory(p, 'A_tmp', NEON if arch == 'Neon' else RVV)
```

Fig. 4. Part 3: GEMM structure and schedule for A_c in the 8×16 MIP μkernel.

Finally, Fig. 5 comprises the last steps in the code generation:

BK5 loads the elements from B_C and converts them from INT8 to INT16 datatypes. This is omitted because, in the case of ARM NEON, the procedure is analogous to that described in BK4. When generating RVV code, this step is not necessary because the intrinsics load the data directly from memory.

BK6 replaces the loop that executes the update of the C values with the desired intrinsic.

BK7 applies loop-unrolling while avoiding unnecessary conditional jumps in the code. The only loop that cannot possibly be unrolled is k_c as the number of iterations is not known in advance.

BK8 applies buffer-unrolling optimizations to prevent compiler issues when dealing with pointer structures and avoid access to structures by accessing the register directly.

```
 99 # BK5: BC MANAGEMENT SCHEDULER
100 #   In the case of Neon, the scheduler for loading Bc values
101 #   is the same that the Ac loads using B-related arguments.
102
103 #   In the case of RISC-V, Bc values are accessed directly from
104 #   memory to the intrinsic instruction.
105
106 # BK6: COMPUTATION MANAGEMENT
107 p = replace_all(p, macc_8xi16_8xi16)
108
109 # BK7: UNROLL LOOP OPTIMIZATIONS
110 p = unroll_loop(p, list_of_loops)
111
112 # BK8: UNROLL BUFFER OPTIMIZATIONS
113 p = unroll_buffer(p, list_of_buffers)
```

Fig. 5. Part 4: GEMM structure and schedule for A_c in the 8×16 MIP μkernel.

Once the generation is complete, the `exocc` compiler produces the code for the micro-kernels. In particular, the compiler converts the Exo representation into a C code where the vector operations are translated into actual intrinsic functions. Table 4 lists the equivalence between the macros used in Exo and the architecture-specific intrinsic. It is noticeable that the `get_high` and `get_low` intrinsic are replaced with the same RVV function because the API does not offer the same functionality as ARM. Instead, the generator tackles this scenario with two loads and two widening, one for each half of the vector.

5 Performance Evaluation

Experimental Setup. We evaluate several optimized implementations of GEMM inspired by the high-performance matrix multiplication approach in GotoBLAS2 (see Sect. 2), yet differing in the data types and micro-kernel. They all set the CCPs m_c, n_c, k_c using the ideas for the analytical model presented in Sect. 3.

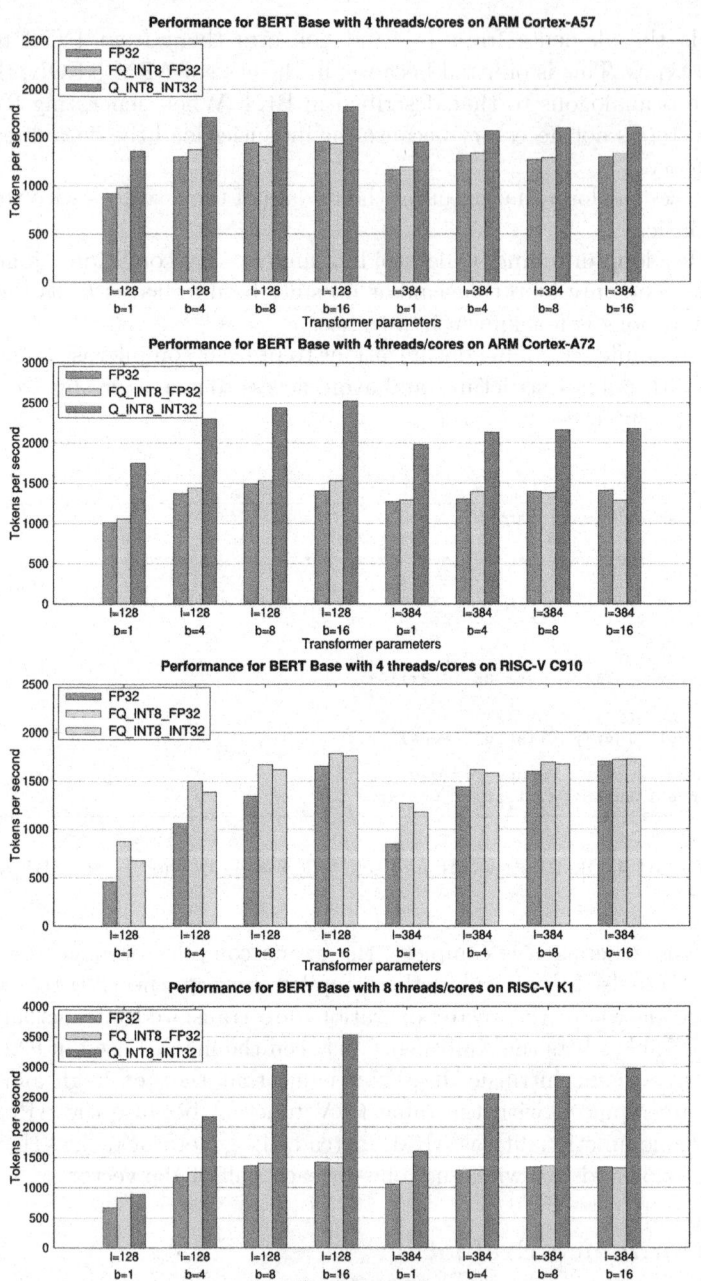

Fig. 6. Evaluation of the BERT Base model for different token lengths, batch sizes, and GEMM implementations for the linear layers.

Table 4. Macros for the intrinsics used in the generator codes.

Generator	ARM NEON	RISCV-V
vld_4xi32	vld1q_s32	__riscv_vle32_v_i32m1
vst_4xi32	vst1q_s32	__riscv_vse32_v_i32m1
vld_8xi8	vld1_s8	__riscv_vle8_v_i8mf4
get_low_8xi16	vget_low_s16	__riscv_vwadd_vx_i16mf2
get_high_8xi16	vget_high_s16	__riscv_vwadd_vx_i16mf2
macc_8xi16_8xi16	vmlal_lane_s16	__riscv_vwmacc_vx_i32m1

- FP32: This is our 32-bit floating-point implementation of GEMM. In earlier work [9], we showed that this implementation is competitive or even outperforms BLIS, OpenBLAS, and ARM PL on NVIDIA Jetson boards.
- FQ_INT8_FP32 and FQ_INT8_INT32: These variants take two INT8 input matrices, A^q, B^q which, during their packing into the buffers A_c, B_c, are converted to either FP32 or INT32. All subsequent arithmetic is then performed using FP32 or INT32, and the output is an FP32 or INT32 matrix. We refer to this option as "fake" quantization (FQ) because the inputs are in INT8 format yet the core arithmetic is entirely in extended precision.
- Q_INT8_INT32: This scheme computes the matrix product using a MIP microkernel generated with Exo, operating with two INT8 input matrices A^q, B^q to produce an INT32 result matrix using MIP vector instructions.

We next present the time savings for encoder inference achieved by replacing the standard FP32 GEMM kernels with inference-specific implementations that employ mixed-precision arithmetic. To assess performance, we focus on the BERT Base model, where the number of layers is 12, $d = 768$, $h = 12$, and $f = 3072$. We consider executions with $l = 128, 384$ tokens and latency-oriented scenarios with batch size (number of samples) $b = 1, 4, 8$. We measure throughput using tokens per second and report results obtained using all cores on each platform. Similar trends were observed in single-core executions. Each experiment was repeated 10 times and the average of the results was taken.

Results and Discussion. Figure 6 shows that, overall, on the three platforms that support MIP arithmetic, a consistently superior performance can be observed for the Q_INT8_INT32 configuration. In particular, on the ARM Cortex-A72 and RISC-V K1, the performance difference between Q_INT8_INT32 and the alternative kernels is significantly more pronounced than on the ARM Cortex-A57, reaching acceleration factors greater than 2× in some cases.

The RISC-V C910 platform implements RVV 0.7.1, which lacks native ISA support for MIP arithmetic. As a result, this platform could only be evaluated with the pure FP32 and the two fake quantization schemes. As shown in the figure, the performance across the three different configurations for this particular architecture is comparable. Similarly, for all architectures, the performance difference between FP32 and FQ_INT8_FP32 is small, providing no significant advantage in terms of execution speed but offering benefits in reduced memory usage-consistent with the observations on the RISC-V C910.

Across all evaluated platforms, a general trend can be identified: as the batch size increases, the number of tokens processed per second also rises, for both sequence lengths $l = 128$ and 384. This highlights the scalability of the model for large workloads and emphasizes the efficiency gains achievable through quantization when paired with increased parallelism.

6 Conclusions

In this paper, we have tackled the increasing demand for mixed-precision arithmetic in DL workloads, and hence in the underlying GEMM implementations, by means of automatic code generation frameworks. Specifically, we have employed a combination of EXO as the target compilation framework and a higher-level GEMM skeleton parametrized via an analytical model adapted to the underlying memory hierarchy. Together, both components dramatically alleviate the development effort for the library developer by (*i*) assisting on the automatic development of high-performance GEMM micro-kernels –the basic building block for high-performance GEMM realizations– that harness all the potential of the underlying compute units; and (*ii*) efficiently exploiting the cache hierarchy and multi-threading capabilities of modern architectures.

By developing high-performance GEMM realizations with mixed-integer precision arithmetic and after integrating them within a transformer encoder, we have demonstrated the benefits of this kind of compilation frameworks from two different perspectives. First, *programmability*, as a common code generator expressed in a high-level language can be seamlessly adapted to different architectures (ARM and RISC-V) with distinct vector processing ISAs (NEON and RVV, respectively); and second, *performance portability*, as the experimental results reveal consistent performance across dramatically different ISAs.

In addition, our results reveal the benefits, in terms of performance, of the use of mixed-integer precision across different architectures that, according to our observations, can yield up to 2× speedups compared with *classic* FP32 arithmetic, and also serve as a practical comparison the mixed-precision capabilities of different state-of-the-art ARM and RISC-V processors with SIMD units.

Acknowledgments. This work is supported by grants PID2021-126576NB-I00 and PID2023-146569NB-C2 of MCIN/AEI/10.13039/501100011033, by *"ERDF A way of making Europe"*, and by Ayuda a Primeros Proyectos de Investigación (PAID-06-24), Vicerrectorado de Investigación de la Universitat Politécnica de Valéncia. A. Castelló is supported by the CIAPOS/2023/431 grant, and Fondo Social Europeo Plus 2021–2027 from the Generalitat Valenciana.

References

1. Castelló, A., et al.: Tackling the matrix multiplication micro-kernel generation with Exo. In: 2024 IEEE/ACM CGO, pp. 182–193 (2024)

2. Castelló, A., et al.: Portable, high performance matrix multiplication micro-kernels for risc-v with exo. In: 2025 33rd Euromicro International Conference on Parallel, Distributed, and Network-Based Processing (PDP), pp. 25–32 (2025)
3. Dettmers, T., et al.: LLM.int8(): 8-bit matrix multiplication for transformers at scale. In: 36th NIPS. Curran Associates Inc., Red Hook, NY, USA (2024)
4. Goodfellow, I., Bengio, Y., Courville, A.: Deep Learning. MIT Press, Cambridge (2016)
5. Goto, K., van de Geijn, R.: Anatomy of high-performance matrix multiplication. ACM Trans. Math. Softw. **34**(3), 12:1–12:25 (2008)
6. Igual, F., et al.: Automatic generation of micro-kernels for performance portability of matrix multiplication on RISC-V vector processors. In: Proceedings of the SC '23 Workshops, pp. 1523–1532 (2023)
7. Ikarashi, Y., et al.: Exocompilation for productive programming of hardware accelerators. In: PLDI 2022, pp. 703–718, New York, NY, USA (2022)
8. Low, T.M., et al.: Analytical modeling is enough for high-performance BLIS. ACM Trans. Math. Softw. **43**(2), 12:1–12:18 (2016)
9. Martínez, H., et al.: Inference with transformer encoders on ARM and RISC-V multicore processors. In: Euro-Par 2024: Parallel Processing, pp. 377–392 (2024)
10. Smith, T.M., et al.: Anatomy of high-performance many-threaded matrix multiplication. In: Proceedings of the IEEE 28th IPDPS, pp. 1049–1059 (2014)
11. Van Zee, F.G., et al.: The BLIS framework: experiments in portability. ACM Trans. Math. Softw. **42**(2) (2016)
12. Vaswani, A., et al.: Attention is all you need. In: Advances in Neural Information Processing Systems, vol. 30 (2017)

Training an Image Classification Model on a Supercomputer with AMD Genoa Compute Nodes

Maram Hesham Badawi[1] and Mohsin Ahmed Shaikh[2](✉)

[1] Brightskies Inc., Alexandria, Egypt
maram.hesham@brightskiesinc.com
[2] King Abdullah University of Science and Technology,
Thuwal, Kingdom of Saudi Arabia
mohsin.shaikh@kaust.edu.sa

Abstract. For training a deep neural network (DNNs), GPUs are considered a *de facto* accelerator device. However, access to these devices is often limited due to high demand and cost, whether for procurement or on-demand usage in cloud environments. CPUs, on the other hand, are traditionally cheaper and are more accessible in data centers with HPC clusters, in academia or in enterprise. With recent advancements in CPU architectures, such as AMD Genoa, this paper investigates the feasibility of training an image classifier as an example workload on a representative public dataset called ImageNet1K and a smaller version of it, TinyImageNet. We evaluated the acceleration on one compute node with two AMD Genoa CPUs. We also scale it to multiple nodes to determine the number of nodes required to match the compute time of a single NVIDIA V100 or A100 GPU. Our findings set some expectations when running such workloads on a supercomputer like Shaheen III, a Cray EX system, and also provide guidelines around the choice of compiler and choice of software dependencies to make the most of the compute resources.

Keywords: Pre-training · Deep Learning · Distributed training

1 Introduction

Training DNNs is a popular workload in HPC clusters to obtain faster time to develop enough accurate models. With shorter time to train the models, users can fail fast and accelerate their research by accelerating their training. This trend is only going to exacerbate because the traditional science domains are finding ways to use AI as an alternative to large-scale simulations and most, if not all, have access to big datasets. Therefore, it is in the interest of an HPC center to find ways to increase both the performance and the availability of devices capable of training and fine-tuning DNNs of all sizes.

GPUs are considered a *de facto* device to train DNN models. Due to high demand, it is common to see congestion in the HPC cluster job scheduler queues.

One way to mitigate this is to buy new generation GPUs which are faster, but this puts pressure on the vendors' supply chains. The purchase of new-generation faster GPUs also increases the power requirements in a data center.

The HPC centers traditionally possess more CPU compute nodes than GPU nodes. It is therefore important to understand the feasibility of using CPU-only resources for a selection of AI workload. To this end, this paper investigates the training of an image classifier model as an example and assesses the feasibility of using CPU compute nodes of a supercomputer. We chose to train ResNet-50, a popular convolutional neural network (CNN) for the image classification task, on a large dataset of images, called ImageNet1K, which is a publicly available benchmark dataset for computer vision task.

2 Test System

Software Environment. For the model training we used PyTorch 2.2 which was compiled from source using three different compilers and the corresponding BLAS libraries. This was done to assess the best possible combination of dependencies in pursuit of the best computational performance. We label our compiled versions of PyTorch, as shown in Table 1. As Shaheen III is HPE Cray EX system, we leverage its proprietary Cray Programming Environment (CPE), which is a collection of compilers, the performance libraries, the debugging and profiling tools.

Table 1. Software Configurations for Different Compiler, Math Library, and Networking Library Setups.

	Compiler	Math Library	Networking Library
Setup A	Gcc	Intel MKL	libmpi gnu
Setup B	AOCC	Blis	libmpi aocc
Setup C	Cray	LibSci	libmpi cray

We also use Horovod [4] for distributed data parallel training of our model of choice. Building Horovod from source allows linking with the host MPICH library provided by the Cray programming environment from setups A, B, and C respectively. This enables us to train the model with large mini-batches and provides the basis of scaling out to multiple nodes.

Hardware Setup. Shaheen III Supercomputer was used for CPU-only experiments. It is an HPE Cray EX system built with AMD Genoa compute nodes interconnected via HPE's proprietary Slingshot 11 interconnect. Each node has one Cassini network interface card capable of 200 Gbps theoretical bandwidth. The dataset is read from a Lustre filesystem composed of SSD flash drives.

Every compute node of Shaheen III is a dual-socket AMD EPYC 9654 (Genoa family) with a total of 192 physical cores (or 384 hyperthreads) and 384 GB of DDR5 memory operating at 4800 MHz. Each socket is configured with four NUMA nodes (i.e. 8 NUMA nodes per compute node). Each compute node of Shaheen III has a total of 768 MB of coherent Last-Level Cache (L3 Cache). AMD Genoa's Core Chiplet Design (CCD) puts eight consecutive cores and serves as a building block of the CPUs architecture and scales to 12 CCDs per socket. Each CCD contains a 32 MB L3 cache unit, and with 24 CCDs on two sockets adds up to a total of a cache coherent 768MB. The default clock speed of the compute nodes is set to 2.4 GHz, but can boost up to 3.7 GHz, depending on the workload. Each compute node has a total of 12 memory channels, 6 per socket.

3 Test Case

3.1 Dataset

For our dataset, we used the ImageNet1K dataset, also known as ILSVRC2012 [2] (ImageNet Large Scale Visual Recognition Challenge 2012), which is one of the most influential and widely used datasets in computer vision. It consists of approximately 1.2 million images, categorized into 1,000 diverse object classes. These categories include a wide range of real-world items, from animals and plants to everyday objects and tools, allowing the dataset to represent a broad spectrum of visual concepts. Each image is labeled with one of these 1,000 classes and the images have varying resolutions and settings, offering a challenging variety of contexts. ImageNet1K was pivotal in advancing deep learning research, especially image classification, as it provides a standard benchmark for model evaluation. The dataset's large size and diversity have contributed to the development of CNNs.

In this study, we also used a smaller version of ImageNet called TinyImageNet [6]. It has 200 classes and has a total of 120,000 images. The training dataset has 100,000 images and the 10,000 each validation and testing datasets are composed on 10,000 images each. The running of scaling experiments was faster than using the full ImageNet dataset while still exhibiting the same scaling characteristics. The captions of the figures mention the dataset used for each experiment.

3.2 Model

In this test case, we focus on training the ImageNet1K (ILSVRC2012) dataset using the ResNet-50 model [3], a widely recognized deep learning architecture known for its effective use of residual connections to facilitate the training of deep neural networks. ResNet-50, with its 50-layer deep convolutional network, is particularly well-suited for this task due to its ability to learn rich hierarchical features from complex image data. In the following sections, we explore the experimental setup, training procedure, and performance results, including accuracy and computational efficiency. ResNet-50 is a variant of the popular ResNet architecture and comprises 50 layers, enabling it to learn much deeper architectures than previously possible without encountering the problem of vanishing gradients. The architecture of ResNet-50 is divided into four main components: the convolutional layers, the identity block, the convolutional block, and the fully connected layers. The convolutional layers are responsible for extracting features from the input image, the identity block and convolutional block process and transform these features, and the fully connected layers make the final classification. ResNet-50 has been trained on the large ImageNet dataset, achieving an error rate comparable to human performance, making it a powerful model for various image classification tasks such as object detection, facial recognition and medical image analysis. Additionally, it has been used as a feature extractor for other tasks, such as object detection and semantic segmentation.

3.3 Performance Metric

The metric used to compare performance in our experiments is epoch time. An epoch refers to presenting all the training samples in the training split of the dataset to the model once. We run the training for 5 epochs, keeping the hyperparameters as constant. At the end of the fifth epoch, the average epoch time is computed and used as the performance comparison metric.

4 Performance Results

4.1 Single Node Study

Varying Thread Count. We begin by evaluating performance on a single AMD Genoa node with a varying number of OpenMP threads. We evaluated the performance of a single AMD Genoa node with varying thread counts from 12 to 192. The PyTorch build was compiled using GCC 13, as it was linked to Intel MKL for accessing BLAS functions. Intel MKLDNN is an open-source library that provides highly vectorized and threaded implementations of convolution kernels and other building blocks of a CNN.

The results, as shown in Fig. 1, demonstrate a significant reduction in epoch time as the number of OpenMP threads increases. However, beyond 96 threads (i.e. a single socket of a Shaheen III compute node), performance degrades, and no further acceleration is observed. This test helps identify the optimal number of threads (96 in this case) for efficient resource utilization and maximum performance during training. Hardware threads or hyperthreads were disabled in this experiment.

Software Variants. We evaluate the performance impact of using different compilers to build PyTorch from source, as shown in Table 1. We experiment with GCC, Cray, and AOCC compilers along with their respective optimized BLAS and MPI libraries. The goal of this experiment is to identify performance benefits from the software environment.

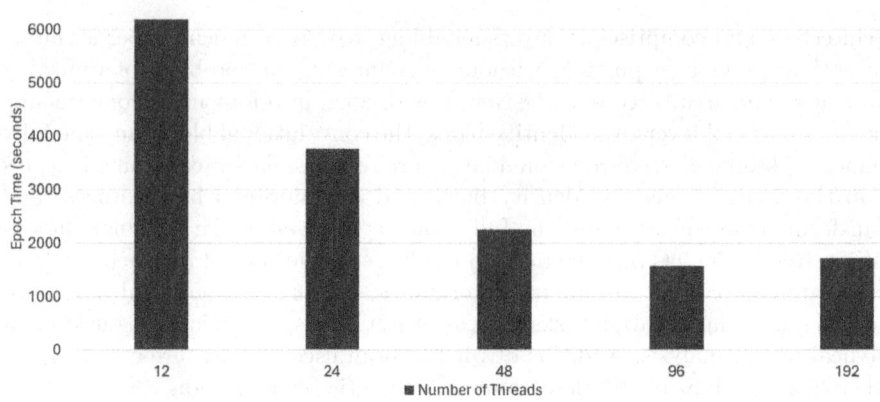

Fig. 1. Performance Analysis with Varying Thread Counts (12 to 192) Using a Single MPI Rank. Setup A was used as software environment in this experiment. TinyImageNet with batch size 256 was used as input.

Figure 2 shows a comparison of the epoch time with different software setups tabulated in Table 1, varying OpenMP thread count from 24 to 192. The strong scaling trend, where the number of threads is doubled, demonstrates consistent performance gains up to 96 threads, followed by significant diminishing returns at 192 threads. At 192 threads, we observe nontrivial overhead when using GCC and AOCC, while the impact is less severe with the Cray compiler. Nevertheless, 192 threads is an overkill when training with mini-batch size of 256 images.

Varying MPI Ranks. Next, we evaluate the impact of varying the number of MPI ranks on a single compute node. The testing configuration involves doubling the number of MPI ranks from 1 to 8, while halving the thread count, i.e. 1 MPI rank with 192 OpenMP threads versus 8 MPI ranks with 24 OpenMP threads. It is important to note that when doubling the MPI ranks, though we keep the mini-batch size constant for each MPI rank and the respective OpenMP threads, we double the global batch size, therefore traversing through the training dataset faster. As shown in Fig. 3, we achieve optimal performance at 8 MPI ranks with 24 OpenMP threads per rank. For the software environment we used setup A from Table 1. Using full ImageNet1K instead of TinyImageNet in this experiment was to increase the practicality of the benchmark given the global batch size is increasing with MPI ranks.

Effect of L3 Cache. AMD Genoa has large Last Level Cache (L3). We study the contribution of cache when processing the training samples. The hypothesis is that if the mini-batches, along with the model, fit into L3, it may show faster epoch time. To test this hypothesis, we compare runs on different generations of Intel and AMD CPUs to identify any inflection points with respect to mini-batch size. For the software environment we chose Setup A and recreated the equivalent

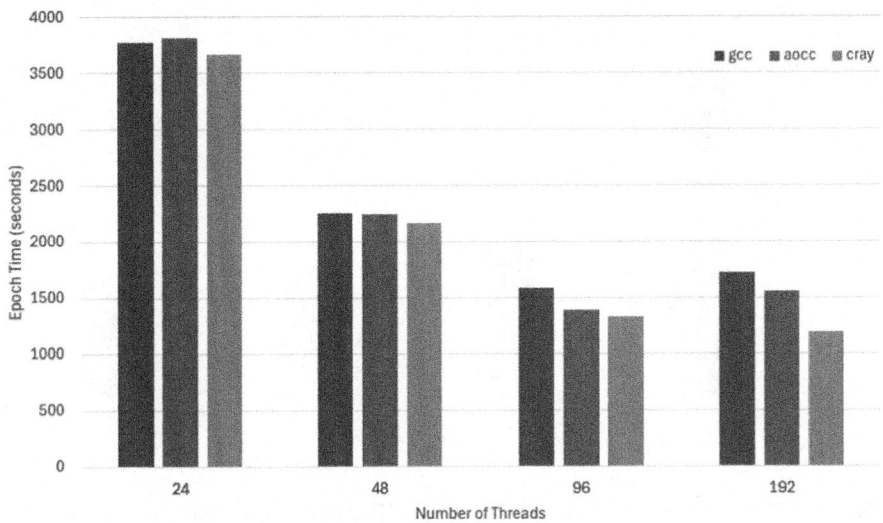

Fig. 2. Performance Comparison of Different PyTorch Builds with Varying Thread Counts (24 to 192). TinyImageNet with batch size 256 was used as input.

on a different cluster having compute nodes with AMD Rome and Intel Cascade Lake processors. We kept the model, dataset, and performance metric the same as in our previous experiments. The number of OpenMP threads is set to 96 for AMD Genoa, 128 for AMD Rome and 40 for Intel Cascade Lake. We chose 96 for AMD Genoa as it shows the best performance metric as seen in Fig. 1.

Figure 4 shows a noticeable advantage across the three CPU architectures when the samples fit in the L3 cache. AMD Genoa, having the largest L3 cache, extends this benefit to a mini-batch size of 512. Beyond the L3 saturation point, the performance metric plateaus, indicating that performance is dictated primarily by the type and speed of DRAM rather than L3 cache size. Additionally, doubling the mini-batch size does not result in a twofold speedup. However, this scaling behavior is more favorable in AMD Genoa, which may be attributed to the L3 cache layout on the chip, i.e., per CCD, as described in Sect. 2.

Comparison to Single GPUs. In this section, we analyze the performance gap between GPUs, which are considered the *de facto* compute device for this workload, and the CPU compute nodes of Shaheen III. To quantify this gap, we train the model on a single NVIDIA V100 and a single A100 GPU, respectively, and compare the results with the best performance metric obtained from a full Shaheen III compute node. As shown in Fig. 5, a Shaheen III node is six times slower than an A100 GPU for training ImageNet1K over five epochs. We treat this as a baseline to gauge any possible improvements offered when the training

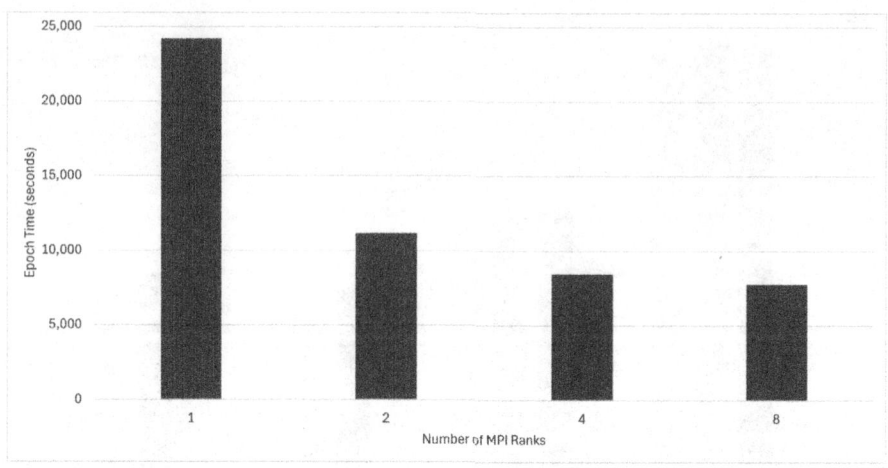

Fig. 3. Performance Evaluation with Varying MPI Ranks on a Single Node. OpenMP threads per MPI process half as MPI process double (i.e. 192 and 24 OpenMP threads for 1 MPI rank and 8 MPI ranks cases respectively). Setup A was used as the software environment. ImageNet1K dataset was used for this experiment with batch size 256 per MPI rank.

is scaled out on multiple Shaheen III CPU nodes. Note that V100's 32 GB GPU memory could accommodate a maximum of 256 training samples.

Power Scaling Tests. AMD Genoa CPUs can be power capped to limit the power drawn when running compute-intensive workloads. We investigate the impact of power capping on performance metric of the model training.

To set the power cap, a series of commands modify system parameters through the Host System Management Port (HSMP) interface, introduced in AMD Genoa [1]. HSMP grants OS level software access to system management. We use AMD/HPE provided proprietary BASH scripts to manipulate power cap between 100 Watts to 400 Watts. After setting the selected power limit, we rerun the workload on the same compute node to ensure minimum variability in the environment. This is repeated for all software environment setups listed in Table 1. All runs are configured with 8 MPI ranks and 24 OpenMP threads per MPI rank, using a mini-batch size of 256.

Figure 6 shows that the performance metric remains largely intact, even when capping the maximum power draw to 300 W, with only a 5% performance trade-off, depending on the software setup used. We confirmed that the loss and accuracy remained intact on all the power cap levels.

We also aimed to quantify the energy consumption during model training over five epochs. Since Shaheen III uses SLURM as its job scheduler, we utilize ConsumedEnergy metric reported by SLURM [7] (measured in joules) to assess the impact of increasing the mini-batch size on energy cost. This energy metric is

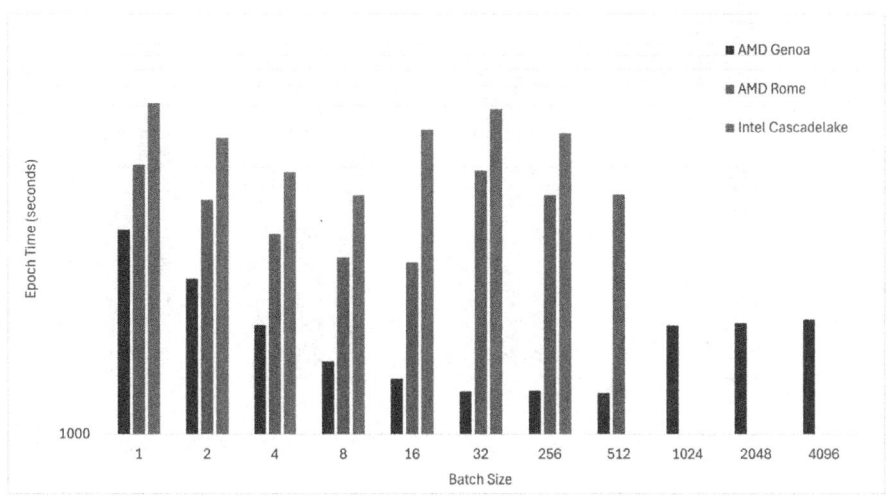

Fig. 4. Performance Analysis of Batch Size Scaling on Intel Cascade Lake (40 cores), AMD Rome (128 cores), and AMD Genoa (96 cores). TinyImageNet with batch size 256 was used as input.

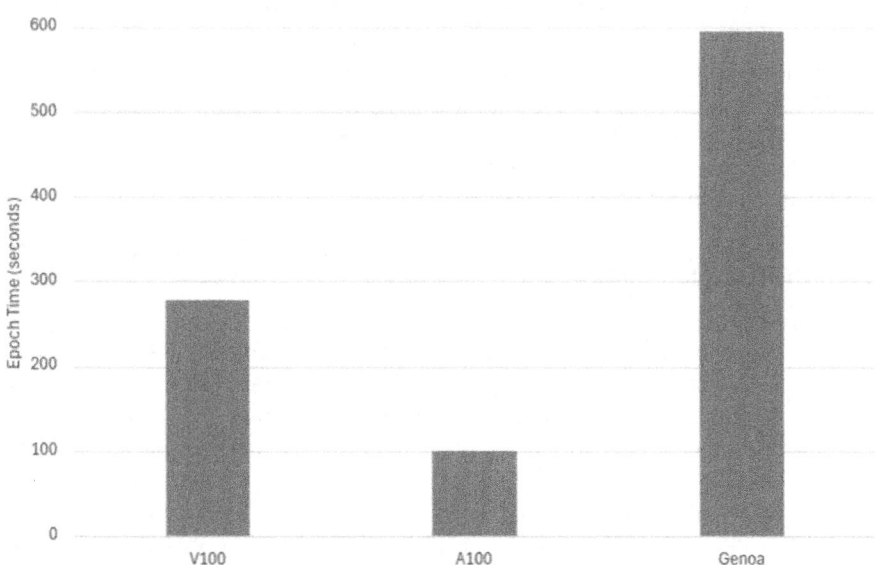

Fig. 5. Comparative Analysis of Training Performance on a Single Node of AMD Genoa Versus a Single Nvidia V100 and A100 GPU. TinyImageNet with batch size 256 was used as input. The graph compares the average epoch time achieved on each compute device.

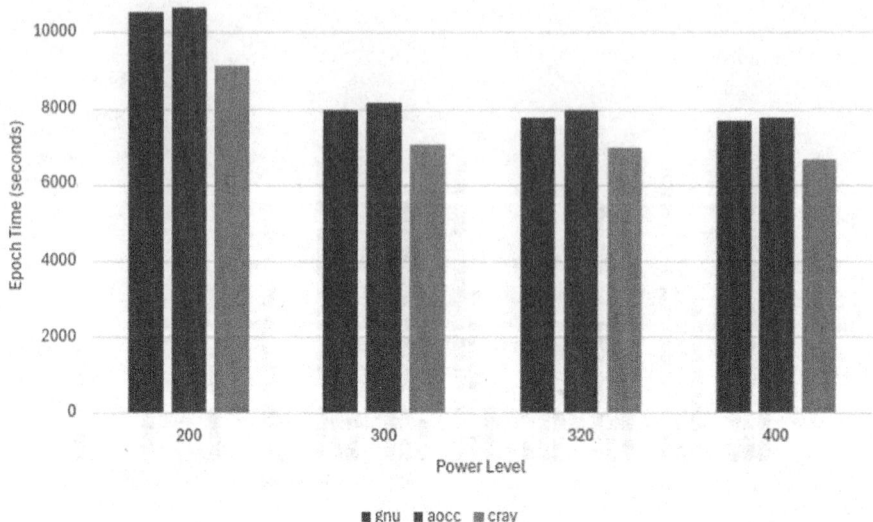

Fig. 6. Performance Comparison of Different Software Setups Across Varying Power Levels. ImageNet1K with batch size 256 was used as input.

representative of the base board energy cost which includes peripherals. Since Shaheen III compute nodes are exclusively allocated to a job, the measurement of consumed energy accurately reflects the workload in question, without interference from other energy-intensive processes. Again, all runs use 8 MPI ranks and 24 OpenMP threads per MPI rank.

Figure 7 illustrates the effect of increasing the mini-batch size on consumed energy. The trend follows the findings of Fig. 4 which is expected given the longer epoch times at larger mini-batch sizes.

4.2 Multi-node Study

Multi-node Distributed Training. To bridge the performance gap observed on a single node, we scale training across multiple nodes of Shaheen III. Figure 8 illustrates the impact of distributed training, increasing from 1 to 32 nodes on Shaheen III. For this experiment, we maintain the same MPI ranks per node and threads per MPI rank, while doubling the node count at each step. Also, we keep the mini-batch size per MPI rank the same. The global batch size increases as a multiple of MPI ranks, i.e. `batch size * Total MPI ranks`. For this experiment, we used all three Setups from Table 1. We include GPU baselines for comparison. The results demonstrate that the performance metric can be recovered when training on 8 nodes of Shaheen III, achieving a performance level comparable to a single NVIDIA V100 GPU, and on 32 nodes, achieving performance similar to a single NVIDIA A100 (80 GB) GPU. We also repeated the experiment with a mini-batch size of 1024, but it did not affect the performance metric or alter the overall trend shown in Fig. 8.

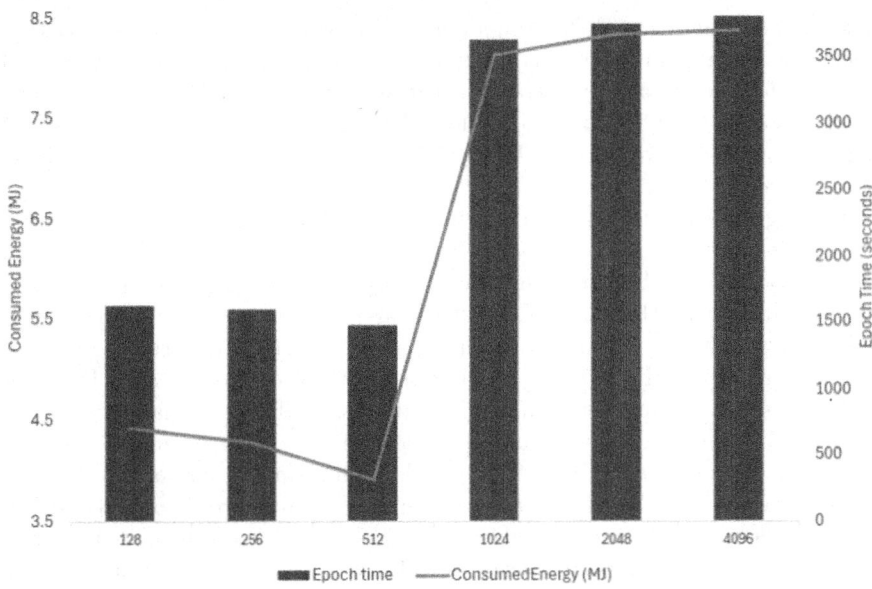

Fig. 7. Effect of increasing mini-batch size of a single node distributed training on Consumed Energy. TinyImageNet was used as input.

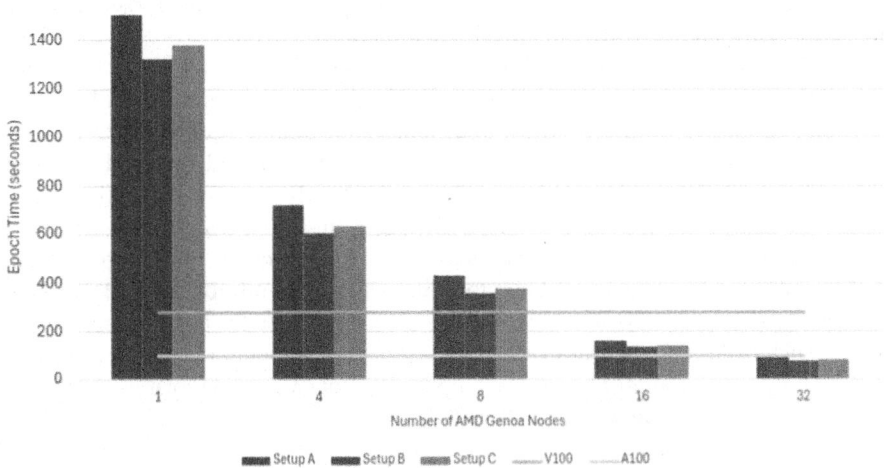

Fig. 8. Performance Scaling of AMD Genoa from 1 to 32 Nodes. TinyImageNet with batch size 256 was used as input.

5 Conclusion and Executive Summary

There is no contest that GPUs are more suitable to training deep learning models in general and specifically in the current case of a computer vision model. However, the abundance in the availability of CPUs and scarcity of GPUs due to their cost, availability and the compounding factor of export control restrictions together are compelling reasons for finding viable alternatives for some if not all model for pre-training and transfer learning/fine-tuning. Expanding selected workloads onto the CPU partition allows HPC clusters in academia to provide more opportunities to run workloads that are otherwise impractical except on new-generation GPUs.

Porting PyTorch-based model training to CPUs required minimal refactoring, thanks to its device recognition functionality. However, building PyTorch, Horovod and math libraries from source is a good starting point to allow compilers to align with the target CPU micro-architecture using appropriate flags and linking with host optimized math, OpenMP and MPI libraries.

Although OpenMP threading was important to accelerate the MKLDNN kernels for a set mini-batch size on single node, using all the available cores on a Shaheen III compute node demonstrated loss of scalability beyond 48 threads. Instead, using multiple MPI ranks per node with a smaller number of OpenMP threads per rank produced faster epoch times. This was pre-dominantly due to increased global batch size while also utilizing all the cores on the node resources. However, very large mini-batch sizes introduced additional limitations, particularly when they exceeded L3 cache capacity, suggesting that filling the DRAM of a compute node may not be advisable when aiming for optimal performance. Developers therefore should benchmark their model before running long training runs in pursuit of minimizing training loss. Therefore CPUs with larger L3 cache are more aminable to train our benchmark model.

Scaling out the pre-training process reduces epoch time, which was our chosen performance metric. A single V100 GPU's performance metric can be recovered on 8 nodes of Shaheen III and 32 nodes were found equivalent to a single A100. These equivalence numbers could be further improved if mixed precision is enabled on CPUs, as all experiments in this study were conducted in FP32 (single-precision). In general, distributed large mini-batch training requires tuning hyper-parameters to recover the loss of accuracy metrics of the pre-training and transfer learning process. Therefore, increasing the number of node and e.g. optimizing the learning rates may require more epoch to get to a target training metric such as loss or accuracy of a model. Model developers may need to budget for some hyper-parameter optimization experiments when exploring distributed training on multiple devices, CPUs or GPUs.

Lastly, it was comforting to find that we could reproduce the performance metric when the node was power capped at 300 W. Though the maximum allowable power draw is 400W, the improvement we witnessed was no more than 5%. Although more models can be investigated to this end, HPC centers may use this information to put a power cap on jobs using CPUs for training models and mitigate their operating power expense.

6 Future Work

The current study motivates us to explore additional avenues to optimize the training process, improve the performance metric, and reduce the number of compute nodes required to match the performance of the GPU. Future work may include results on NVIDIA H100 and AMD MI300 GPUs. Reducing the precision of training and/or improving the MPI scaling to larger number of compute nodes may help reduce the epoch time on CPUs even further.

Exploring the epoch times on CPUs with specialized matrix multiplication units such as Advanced Matrix Extensions (AMX) [5] in Intel Sapphire Rapids and Emerald Rapids will be an interesting extension of this study.

We also aim to extend our study in future to include training language models composed of transformer architecture. Subject to acceptable performance on Shaheen III CPUs, such investigation may encourage users to finetune language models on CPU only supercomputers. This can be a potential alternative to developers who do not have to state-of-the-art GPUs due to lack of availability or budgetary constraints.

References

1. AMD. Tuning guide amd epyc 9004, July 2024. https://docs.amd.com/v/u/en-US/58002_amd-epyc-9004-tg-hpc. Publication 58002, Version 1.7
2. Deng, J., Dong, W., Socher, R., Li, L.J., Li, K., Fei-Fei, L.: Imagenet: a large-scale hierarchical image database. In: 2009 IEEE Conference on Computer Vision and Pattern Recognition (CVPR), pp. 248–255, 2009. https://doi.org/10.1109/CVPR.2009.5206848
3. He, K., Zhang, X., Ren, S., Sun, J.: Deep residual learning for image recognition, 2015. https://arxiv.org/abs/1512.03385
4. Uber Horovod. Horovod: Distributed training framework for tensorflow, keras, pytorch, and apache mxnet. https://horovod.ai/
5. Intel. Intel amx. https://www.intel.com/content/www/us/en/products/docs/accelerator-engines/advanced-matrix-extensions/overview.html
6. Le, Y., Yang, X.S.: Tiny imagenet visual recognition challenge, 2015. https://api.semanticscholar.org/CorpusID:16664790
7. SchedMD. Slurm accounting. https://slurm.schedmd.com/sacct.html

Exploring QUBO on LPUs for Engineering

Johannes Gebert[1](✉), Dan Glück[2], Chene Tradonsky[2], and Jonathan Schäfer[1]

[1] High-Performance Computing Center Stuttgart, Nobelstraße 19, 70569 Stuttgart, Germany
{johannes.gebert,jonathan.schaefer}@hlrs.de
[2] LightSolver Ltd., Alon Tower 2, Yigal Alon 94, Tel Aviv, Israel
{dani,Chene}@lightsolver.com
https://www.hlrs.de/ , https://lightsolver.com/

Abstract. Increased computational performance benefits simulations run on high-performance computing systems. While Moore's law on integrated circuits weakens, specialized processors promise to accelerate certain mathematical operations in many common software stacks. However, emerging processing elements must significantly reduce the total time to solution, allow for an energy reduction, and come with readily available APIs to justify financial and development efforts. We focus on comparing mesh decomposition implementations of finite element analysis, a task for which we use a readily available biomechanical real-world application called Direct Tensor Computation. The data of the mesh decomposition step and the software's downstream behavior about the METIS serial graph partitioning for defining mesh parts is the ground truth of the study. We will compare this to the mesh decomposition's quadratic unconstrained binary optimization (QUBO) formulation run on the laser-based processing unit (LPU) from LightSolver to determine its characteristics in an exemplary and exploratory manner. First, we investigate offline and online comparisons of the METIS and the LPU implementation. Once these results are promising, we apply the QUBO LPU implementation to OpenFoam, a widely used computational fluid dynamics software for large-scale simulations in HPC. This paper suggests an approach to investigating recurring tasks in engineering applications sent to devices in heterogeneous computing platforms. Succeeding publications will show in-depth results, while this paper concentrates on the concept and discussion of our proposed methodology.

Keywords: Heterogeneous · LPU · hpc · photonic · laser · accelerator

1 Introduction

Engineering applications in high-performance computing (HPC) are well established but still benefit from increasingly performant computers and algorithms.

Personalized medical applications and computational fluid dynamics (CFD) with direct numerical simulations (DNS) of boundary layer flow are just two of many examples [7,8]. Research and engineering questions for mechanical systems approximate the physical fields describing the object's behavior of interest in 3-dimensional space. Field values, therefore, are distributed in a continuum and need a discretization and an interpolation between these discrete points in space. Such approaches result in meshes, e.g., in a finite element analysis (FEA) or for a CFD simulation. Meshes, consequently, are a recurring pattern for small and large systems. Moore's law is slowing down, among other things, due to the physically limitations of processing elements (PEs), e.g., CPUs or GPUs. We aim to investigate other hardware paradigms in computing to further accelerate mathematical operations, even if they only apply to certain tasks in common applications. These approaches can allow for significant speed-ups, e.g., based on lasers, light, or single photons [9]. In general, analog light-based representations of mathematical formulations promise to compute solutions faster than integrated circuits. LightSolver develops one of the first laser-based processing units (LPUs). We aim to cover several aspects of this new hardware architecture and its programming for HPC by investigating a common recurring task in engineering applications. First, we investigate the translation of an algorithm into a quadratic unconstrained binary optimization (QUBO) formulation as a proof-of-concept for mesh-decomposition algorithms. In addition, we outline the steps to call this proof-of-concept from a real-world application with which we will quantify different parameterizations of the algorithm, especially concerning the effects of the QUBO results downstream in the application runtime. With this general approach, we cover algorithmic research and demonstrate a prototyped workflow, emphasizing its real-world implications.

2 Motivation

Triggered by aforementioned physical limitations, a massive paralellization is observed in HPC systems. Parallelizing engineering applications can only increase efficiency if the load is distributed evenly, with the load primarily caused by large linear algebraic systems. Hence, a qualitatively and quantitatively efficient mesh decomposition as a pre-processing step is paramount in many engineering use cases. We define the qualitative mesh decomposition referring to the distribution of mesh elements and the surface of the cuts between mesh parts. Quantitative mesh decomposition characteristics essentially relate to the time to solution. However, time to solution needs a careful consideration as the mesh decomposition algorithm may be fast, but the data handling to implement it may negate potential speed-ups.

2.1 Direct Tensor Computation

Human trabecular bone is a calcified tissue with bone marrow stored in its cavities. Structurally, however, are the calcified structures of significant interest

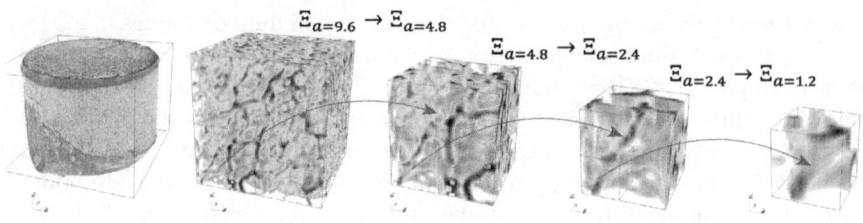

Fig. 1. The volume element sizes schematic to extract cuboid subsets of the CT scan [2] are introduced by Ralf Schneider [1].

for biomechanical research. Therefore, programming a software stack to solve FEAs based on human bone's high-resolution computed tomography (CT) data is justified. Ralf Schneider initialized its development [1], and the software's extension was done by Johannes Gebert, now called Direct Tensor Computation (DTC). Tensor in the context of the software refers to mechanical 4th rank stiffness tensors and does not refer to tensors as it may be in the context of tensor processing units. For investigating laser-based processing units with DTC, we benefit from

- simple and straightforward finite element (FE) meshes,
- exporting the data structures as required,
- different mesh decomposition characteristics,
- scalability from two cores up to many compute-node parameterizations,
- employing software that already represents a real-world use case,

and by understanding the software comparatively well. The latter point allows for modifications to accelerate iterative improvements of the implementation, e.g., bypassing the PETSc solver and post-processing if no such downstream investigations of the pre-processing step mesh decomposition are required. The software is written in Fortran and parallelized with the Message-Passing Interface (MPI) [3], the Portable, Extensible Toolkit for Scientific Computation (PETSc) [4] and METIS [5] for mesh decompositioning. METIS also provides the `PartMeshDual` library call, which we replace with the LightSolver QUBO algorithm. GPU support, parallel mesh decomposition, and parallel post-processing are not yet implemented due to the software stack's current legacy status.

Table 1. Parameters of the CT scan used.

Axes	x	y	z
Dimensions	2940	2940	2141
Voxel spacing (mm)	0,01495	0,01495	0,01495
Field of view (mm)	43,96	43,96	33,01
Number of Voxels	18 505 947 600		

2.2 Mesh Decomposition

DTC creates FE meshes by direct discretization of binary segmented CT scans. An entire CT scan provides a field of view as shown in Table 1. Biomechanical intrinsics require the computation of the intended mechanical parameters based on cuboid volume elements (VEs) as shown in Fig. 1. We defined fixed edge lengths Ξ_a as given in Table 2. Since the field of view is constant, the number of available VEs varies, as demonstrated by the number of VEs n_Ξ. It is essential to notice that the computation of these VEs is embarrassingly parallel as they do not share any computational relationship due to the biomechanical intrinsics of this engineering application. The biomechanical research question underlying this method leads to a 4th rank stiffness tensor per VE, resulting in a tensor field computed based on adjacent VEs. Stiffness tensors represent a transfer function between displacement and forces; strain and stress, respectively. However, this paper does not deal with such particular biomechanical intrinsics. The total volume of all VEs of a specific size Ξ_a does not add up to the field of view as

Table 2. VE sizes Ξ_a, numbers of grid-parallel VEs contained in the CT scan n_Ξ, and the number of x86 64-Bit cores suitable n_c. Cavities in human trabecular bone govern the smallest sensible VE size, with larger sizes following in increments.

Ξ_a (mm)	n_Ξ	n_c
0,6	191825	2 to 16
1,2	25865	2 to 32
2,4	3484	16 to 1024
4,8	455	64 to 2048
7,2	143	2048 to 4096
9,6	40	4096 to 8192

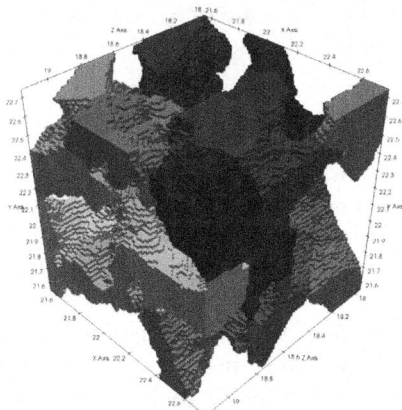

Fig. 2. The FE mesh and its decomposition for a VE size of 1.2 mm, a grid-parallel subset of the CT scan.

implied in Table 1 because the VEs are only considered valid by fulfilling distinct mechanical criteria that are not related to the paper's topic. However, the number of VEs influences the efficiency of calling mesh decomposition algorithms, as we expect significant differences when calling small mesh decompositions many times or large mesh decompositions only a few times during an application's execution.

The direct discretization of CT scans that are equidistant, isotropic voxel fields allows for a mesh consisting of gridparallel, ideally shaped hexahedral elements. The weight of all FEs during mesh decomposition initially is equal. Meshes after decomposition can look like in Fig. 2 that shows a medium sized VE split into 16 mesh parts, identified by colors.

3 Approach

We suggest three steps to increase the complexity of implementing mesh decompositions into the exemplary use cases of DTC and OpenFoam. First, we implement the QUBO mesh decomposition for DTC offline. If that succeeds, we will implement it online during DTC's runtime. In an additional step, we implement the LPU-based decomposition online in OpenFoam. Offline means calculating the result of the mesh decomposition of DTC by exporting the respective data structures. We then compute the result on the LightSolver LPU. Performance metrics evaluate the results compared to the call to METIS by DTC. Online means calculating the result of the mesh decomposition of DTC by calling the LPU-based computation during the software's runtime. We then evaluate the result alongside the conventional version of DTC.

4 Laser-Based Processing Technology Overview

LightSolver develops an all-optical HPC paradigm capable of solving complex computational problems with laser interference patterns, potentially circumventing the limits of silicon-based processors.

4.1 Laser Computing Paradigm

LPUs exploit laser dynamics, specifically the evolution of an electromagnetic field over time. By coupling multiple lasers in an optical cavity, we translate computational problems into laser electrical field physical properties such as the phases and amplitudes - the LPU leverages laser cavity structure for conducting complex, highly iterative computations. Unlike silicon-based architectures, the system capitalizes on the inherent parallelism of photonics and the rapid clock cycle defined by the photon's in-cavity round-trip time (typically on the nanosecond scale) making it particularly well-suited for iterative problems. Laser act as a persistent optical memory, where data is embedded in the physical states of laser modes (such as amplitude and phase). A suite of optical analog actuators that precisely manipulate interactions between these memory elements allows for general mathematical operations directly in memory. This configuration allows to solve computationally demanding problems, particularly in the realms of combinatorial optimization and physical simulation. In optimization applications, the system's capability for arbitrary connectivity and analog variable encoding efficiently handles complex constraints and diverse variable types. In simulation tasks, the combination of parallel processing and rapid iteration facilitates the execution of many computational steps much faster than classical hardware, bypassing common bottlenecks associated with data transfer and processing delays and achieving the steady-state solution quickly (Fig. 3).

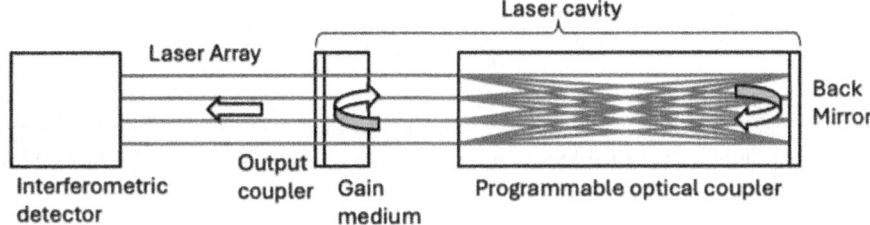

Fig. 3. Laser Processing Unit (LPU): coupled-laser array with interferometric readout. A uniformly pumped gain array and a programmable diffractive coupler form a coupled-laser array that embodies the optimization variables and their constraints. The light oscillates between the mirrors; on every round-trip the gain section amplifies each beam, while the coupler redistributes power and phase among the lasers according to a user-defined coupling matrix (red rays illustrate the fully reconfigurable all-to-all mixing). A small fraction of the intracavity field exits through an output coupler and is routed to an interferometric detector that records the intensity and phase of every laser. (Color figure online)

4.2 Problem Solving Flow

Problem solving on the LPU follows the below steps:

1. Encoding the Problem - a given computational problem is transformed into an optical representation using a spatial light modulator. This involves setting specific parameters such as coupling coefficients.
2. Laser Activation - the optical system is initialized, and lasers are activated. These lasers are configured to represent the constraints and objectives of the encoded problem.
3. Iterative Solution Process - the lasers interact dynamically within a closed cavity, undergoing multiple iterations in a feedback loop. During each iteration, the system evolves toward minimizing a defined objective function. This process mimics the behavior of classical iterative algorithms but leverages the speed of light for computation. Each iteration occurs in nanoseconds, reflecting the transit time of photons within the cavity.

4. Convergence - after several iterations, the laser system reaches a steady-state configuration that represents the optimal or near-optimal solution to the encoded problem.

5 QUBO Quadratic Unconstrained Binary Optimization

One of the modes in which the LPU can be operated is finding approximate solutions to QUBO (Quadratic Unconstrained Binary Optimization) problems. A QUBO problem is defined as the problem of finding a binary vector z (i.e., $z_i \in \{0, 1\}$ for $1 \leq i \leq N$) that minimizes:

$$\sum_{i,j=1}^{N} Q_{ij} z_i z_j \tag{1}$$

where Q is a given $N \times N$ matrix. Note that since the z_i-s are binary (rather than continuous), this problem is in general non-convex. Some QUBO problems are NP-hard.

6 Generalized Graph Partitioning Formulation

Let $G = (V, E)$ be a connected, undirected graph with vertices V and edges E. We assign weights to both edges and vertices. Let $v_1 \ldots v_N$ be the vertices; then w_i is the weight of v_i, and W_{ij} is the weight of the edge (v_i, v_j) (with $W_{ij} = 0$ if no such edge exists). The weight of a subgraph is defined as the sum of weights of its vertices. The weight of the cut of a graph is defined as the sum of weights of the edges in the cut. The weighted (k, f) balanced partition problem, with weights w and W, is the problem of finding a k-partition that minimizes the weight of the cut, under the constraint that the weight of each subgraph is at most f times the mean subgraph weight. We formulate the problem as follows: Let a k-cut be a cut $E_C \subseteq E$ so that there are exactly k connected components of $(V, E \backslash E_C)$. Denoting these connected components as $\{G_i = (V_i, E_i) \mid 1 \leq i \leq k\}$, the problem is to find a cut E_C that minimizes:

$$\sum_{(v_m, v_n) \in E_C = E \backslash \bigcup_{i=1}^{k} E_i} W_{mn} \tag{2}$$

under the constraint that for every $i \leq k$:

$$\sum_{v_j \in V_i} w_j \leq f \cdot M \qquad M \equiv \frac{1}{k} \sum_{j=1}^{N} w_j \tag{3}$$

Thus, M is the mean subgraph weight. The subgraph weights variance is:

$$Var = \sum_{i=1}^{k} \left(\sum_{v_j \in V_i} w_j - M \right)^2 \tag{4}$$

We also define the imbalance of the cut as:

$$Imb = \max_i \left(\sum_{v_j \in V_i} w_j \right) / \min_i \left(\sum_{v_j \in V_i} w_j \right) - 1 \qquad (5)$$

Note that for $f = 1$, all subgraphs have equal weights, and the cut is said to be fully balanced. Additionally, $Var = 0$ and $Imb = 0$. For $k = 2$, the constraint for the weighted $(2, f)$ balanced partition problem is the same as the condition $Var/M^2 \leq f$. Also, for $k = 2$, we have $Imb = \frac{2\sqrt{Var}}{M - \sqrt{Var}}$. Finally, note that if all weights are equal, we get the unweighted (k, f) balanced partition problem, where we minimize over the size of the cut, and the constraints are over the sizes of the subgraphs, rather than their weights.

7 Generalized Graph Partitioning and QUBO

In QUBO, constraints can only be implemented in a "soft" way, as a part of the cost function defined by the matrix Q. Therefore, we minimize over a combination of the cut and the subgraph weight variance, with a parameter $\lambda > 0$ over the latter. Thus, we seek to minimize the following:

$$\sum_{(v_m, v_n) \in E \setminus \bigcup_{i=1}^{k} E_i} W_{mn} + \lambda \sum_{i=1}^{k} \left(\sum_{v_j \in V_i} w_j - M \right)^2 \qquad (6)$$

The partitioning to k subgraphs need to be signified by the variables. It is natural to have a variable (or a set of variables) per vertex, determining to which subgraph this vertex belongs. One method is to partition the graph in several steps, in each of which the graph is partitioned to two parts; this method is natural for QUBO implementation, since QUBO uses binary variables. We thus henceforth assume $k = 2$, for a single step of partitioning. We assign a binary variable z_i per vertex v_i. The partition is then to the two subgraphs:

$$V_2 = \{v_i \mid z_i = 0\}, \qquad V_1 = \{v_i \mid z_i = 1\} \qquad (7)$$

Note that the total weight of the cut is:

$$\sum_{(v_m,v_n) \in E \setminus \bigcup_{i=1}^{2} E_i} W_{mn} = \sum_{z_m=1, z_n=0 \text{ or } z_m=0, z_n=1} W_{mn}$$

$$= \sum_{m,n=1}^{N} W_{mn}[(1 - z_m)z_n + z_m(1 - z_n)]$$

$$= \sum_{m,n=1}^{N} W_{mn}(z_n + z_m - 2 z_n z_m)$$

$$= 2 \sum_{n=1}^{N} z_n \sum_{m=1}^{N} W_{mn} - 2 \sum_{m,n=1}^{N} W_{mn} z_n z_m$$

where we have used the symmetry of W_{mn} in the last equality. Since z_n is either 0 or 1, we have $z_n = z_n^2$ and the total weight of the cut can also be written as:

$$2\sum_{n=1}^{N} z_n^2 \sum_{m=1}^{N} W_{mn} - 2\sum_{m,n=1}^{N} W_{mn} z_n z_m \tag{8}$$

As for the imbalance term, note that since $k = 2$ and $V_1 \cup V_2 = V = \{v_1 \ldots v_N\}$, we have:

$$\sum_{v_j \in V_1} w_j - \frac{1}{2}\sum_{j=1}^{N} w_j = -\left(\sum_{v_j \in V_2} w_j - \frac{1}{2}\sum_{j=1}^{N} w_j\right) \tag{9}$$

Therefore, the imbalance term can be written as:

$$\lambda \sum_{i=1}^{k}\left(\sum_{v_j \in V_i} w_j - \frac{1}{k}\sum_{j=1}^{N} w_j\right)^2 \tag{10a}$$

$$= 2\lambda \left(\sum_{v_j \in V_1} w_j - \frac{1}{2}\sum_{j=1}^{N} w_j\right)^2 \tag{10b}$$

$$= 2\lambda \left(\sum_{j=1}^{N} w_j(z_j - \frac{1}{2})\right)^2 \tag{10c}$$

$$= 2\lambda \sum_{m,n=1}^{N} w_m w_n \left(z_m z_n - \frac{1}{2}z_m - \frac{1}{2}z_n + \frac{1}{4}\right) \tag{10d}$$

$$= 2\lambda \sum_{m,n=1}^{N} w_m w_n z_m z_n - 2\lambda \sum_{n=1}^{N} z_n w_n \sum_{m=1}^{N} w_m + \frac{\lambda}{2}\left(\sum_{m=1}^{N} w_m\right)^2 \tag{10e}$$

$$= 2\lambda \sum_{m,n=1}^{N} w_m w_n z_m z_n - 2\lambda \sum_{n=1}^{N} z_n^2 w_n \sum_{m=1}^{N} w_m + \frac{\lambda}{2}\left(\sum_{m=1}^{N} w_m\right)^2 \tag{10f}$$

where in the last equality we have again used $z_n = z_n^2$. Note that the last term is constant and therefore does not affect the minimization.

Hence, we minimize the following expression:

$$2\sum_{n=1}^{N} z_n^2 \sum_{m=1}^{N} W_{mn} - 2\sum_{m,n=1}^{N} W_{mn} z_n z_m + 2\lambda \sum_{m,n=1}^{N} w_m w_n z_m z_n - 2\lambda \sum_{n=1}^{N} z_n^2 w_n \sum_{m=1}^{N} w_m \tag{11}$$

We define the following QUBO matrix:

$$Q_{mn} = 2\delta_{nm}\left(\sum_{l=1}^{N} W_{ln} - \lambda w_n \sum_{l=1}^{N} w_l\right) - 2W_{mn} + 2\lambda w_m w_n \tag{12}$$

The minimization problem is then equivalent to the QUBO problem of minimizing over:

$$\sum_{n,m=1}^{N} Q_{nm} z_n z_m \qquad (13)$$

A QUBO solution is a valid solution to a $(2, f)$ balanced partition problem if it satisfies the imbalance constraint. In order to get a solution to this problem, one solves the QUBO problem for different values of λ, and takes the solution with the minimal λ for which the solution is valid.

8 An Example

As an example for QUBO utilization in graph partitioning, we took an arbitrary graph of 5000 vertices, and solved the $(2, f)$-graph partitioning problem by the following steps, which for convenience we will call here the LightSolver (LS) method: The graph was coarsened to either 500 (option a) or 200 (option b) vertices. The corresponding QUBO problem for graph 2-partitioning was solved using the TABU algorithm, with different values of λ. The solution was refined. The solution for the minimal λ that was valid was taken. Steps 1 and 3 were performed using the coarsening and refinement steps of the METIS algorithm [6]. Figure 4 shows the Pareto front of the cut weight for the $(2, f)$-graph partitioning as a function of the allowed imbalance, both for the LS and METIS methods. As seen, for this particular problem, each option is superior in different imbalance values.

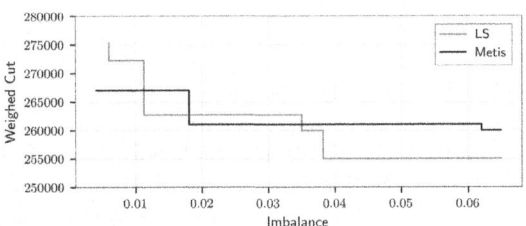

Fig. 4. Pareto front example plot.

9 Discussion

The state-of-the-art implementation by METIS might be surpassed by a QUBO implementation running on a single LPU. Furthermore, we distinguish between offline and online implementation on hosts or devices as illustrated in Fig. 5. The goal of using, e.g., LPUs in engineering applications is in accelerating the program's execution and in lowering an HPC system's energy use. Especially

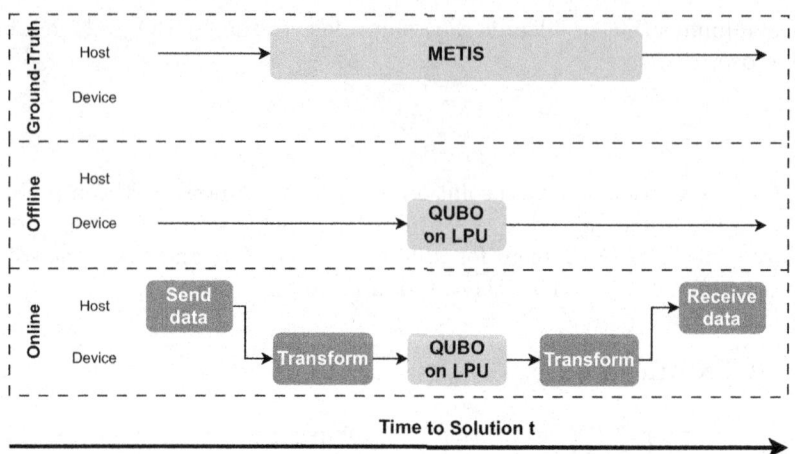

Fig. 5. Qualitatively expected times to readily decomposed meshes with the ground-truth, online, and offline mesh decompositions of DTC.

lowering the execution time of the application can only work if the overhead by sending raw data to the LPU and by sending mesh parts back is overcompensated by the LPUs acceleration of the decomposition itself. Probably, for the LPU to outperform traditional processing elements, there is a need for more complex QUBO tasks such as the ones found in, e.g., OpenFoam. If we prove or at least show probable performance gains, then the implementation can move forward to an application programming interface (API) to call the QUBO stack online while the application, in our case DTC, executes.

10 Conclusion and Outlook

We present a strategy to demonstrate the LightSolver LPU's capabilities in an exemplary real-world use case. It has to be shown if the results for mesh decompositioning both in runtime and in quality can surpass the ground-truth METIS. Downstream effects of mesh decomposition strategies, e.g., while solving the linear systems with PETSc, also are a research question since fast LPU's may allow for more specific parameterizations of mesh decompositions.

Acknowledgments. This study is funded by the Institute for High-Performance Computing (IHR) of the University of Stuttgart, the High-Performance Computing Center Stuttgart (HLRS) and LightSolver Ltd., Tel Aviv.

References

1. Schneider, R.: Analyse kontinuumsmechanischer, anisotroper Materialparameter mikrostrukturierter Volumina mit Hilfe direkter mechanischer Simulation, University of Stuttgart (2016)
2. Ruf, M., Steeb, H., Gebert, J., Schneider, R., Helwig, P.: Sample 1 of human femoral heads: micro-XRCT data sets. In: DaRUS (2021)
3. Message Passing Interface Forum: MPI: A Message-Passing Interface Standard Version 4.0 (2021)
4. Balay, S., et al.: PETSc/TAO Users Manual, Argonne National Laboratory (2023)
5. Karypis, G., Kumar, V.: METIS: a software package for partitioning unstructured graphs, partitioning meshes, and computing fill-reducing orderings of sparse matrices (1997)
6. Karypis, G., Kumar, V.: Multilevelk-way partitioning scheme for irregular graphs. J. Parallel Distrib. Comput. **48**, 96–129 (1998)
7. Keller, M., Kloker, M.: Effusion cooling and flow tripping in laminar supersonic boundary-layer flow. AIAA J. **53**, 902–919 (2015)
8. Keller, M., Kloker, M.: Direct numerical simulation of foreign-gas film cooling in supersonic boundary-layer flow. AIAA J. **55**, 99–111 (2017)
9. Maring, N., et al.: A versatile single-photon-based quantum computing platform. Nat. Photonics **18**, 603–609 (2024)

Investigating Matrix Repartitioning to Address the Over and Undersubscription Challenge for a GPU-Based CFD Solver

Gregor Olenik[1](✉)[iD], Marcel Koch[2][iD], and Hartwig Anzt[1][iD]

[1] Chair of Computational Mathematics, TUM School of Computation, Technical University of Munich, Heilbronn, Germany
{gregor.olenik,hartwig.anzt}@tum.de
[2] Scientific Computing Center, Karlsruhe Institute of Technology, Karlsruhe, Germany
marcel.koch@kit.edu

Abstract. Modern high-performance computing (HPC) increasingly relies on GPUs, but integrating GPU acceleration into complex scientific frameworks like OpenFOAM remains a challenge. Existing approaches either fully refactor the codebase or use plugin-based GPU solvers, each facing trade-offs between performance and development effort. In this work, we address the limitations of plugin-based GPU acceleration in OpenFOAM by proposing a repartitioning strategy that better balances CPU matrix assembly and GPU-based linear solves. We present a detailed computational model, describe a novel matrix repartitioning and update procedure, and evaluate its performance on large-scale CFD simulations. Our results show that the proposed method significantly mitigates oversubscription issues, improving solver performance and resource utilization in heterogeneous CPU-GPU environments.

Keywords: Linear solver · High-performance computing · Computational fluid dynamics · Heterogeneous computing

1 Introduction

Modern general-purpose GPUs have become an integral part of most HPC clusters. However, in many cases, adopting scientific research software to leverage GPU acceleration is an ongoing effort. One example is the widely used computational fluid dynamics (CFD) framework OpenFOAM [6]. To this date, despite multiple efforts, no official OpenFOAM version has been released that provides general GPU support. Currently, two orthogonal approaches are pursued in the wider community: (1) a general refactoring of the OpenFOAM code base and (2) plugin-based approaches providing access to GPU capable linear solver. Examples of the refactoring approach are OpenFOAM_HMM [9], or zeptoFOAM. Furthermore, examples of the plugin-based approach are OGL [8] and petsc4FOAM

[3]. For a more comprehensive overview of projects that target OpenFOAM, the interested reader is referred to [8]. The re-implementation/refactoring approach promises larger performance benefits because here the complete simulation workflow including matrix assembly can be offloaded to the GPU and thus reduces the inherent communication overhead between host and device present. However, the refactoring approach has considerable development costs. Compared to the refactoring approach, the plugin approach has two main drawbacks, first, due to the design of OpenFOAM plugins, it can only offload the linear solver; consequently, matrix assembly remains on the CPU. This limits performance benefits to cases where matrix assembly contributes only a small share of the total computational costs. Second, if distributed computations are performed, finding an optimal partitioning of the computational domain such that matrix assembly on the CPU and linear solver on the GPU costs are well-balanced, is challenging. The authors of [7] refer to this as the over- and under-subscription challenge. In the case of an OpenFOAM simulation with a GPU solver plugin, this can be illustrated as follows: consider a typical HPC node with two CPU sockets each with 64 cores per socket and four accelerators. Common decomposition strategies are to decompose the case into (i) $64 = N_{CPU}$ or (ii) $4 = N_{GPU}$ subdomains. Case (i) will ensure optimal performance for the matrix assembly portion of the computational cost, which generally benefits from more parallelism. However, with a naïve implementation, case (i) will also cause oversubscription of the GPUs with N_{CPU}/N_{GPU} ranks per GPU. Especially, OpenMPI is very sensitive to oversubscribing GPUs, which can cause serious performance degradation [2]. Additionally, an overhead is introduced from the additional communication required between ranks on the same device. Case (ii) avoids oversubscription of the GPUs by partitioning into N_{GPU} subdomains, which additionally reduces the unnecessary communication between inter-device ranks by reducing the number of cells at processor boundaries on the same GPU. The drawback, however, is that matrix assembly, which is performed on the CPU, can only utilize N_{GPU} CPU cores, leading to an under-subscription of the CPU. While an optimal partitioning can be found based on a computational costs model that considers the computational costs of the matrix assembly, the linear solve, and the expected speed-up when employing more parallelism, it is a substantial change from the typical "use all available cores" workflow. In this work, we investigate a repartitioning approach to mitigate the drawbacks of case (i) when utilizing as many CPU cores as possible. The rest of this manuscript is structured as follows: in Sect. 2 a brief discussion of the underlying computational procedure and a basic computational cost model is presented, Sect. 3 presents a detailed discussion of how matrices on the CPU (host) and GPU (device) side are generated and updated, and finally Sect. 4 presents performance data of the implemented repartitioning procedure for a common benchmark case.

2 Computational Cost Model

The OpenFOAM framework implements multiple finite volume method (FVM) based computational fluid dynamics (CFD) solvers, which typically are based on segregated projection methods like SIMPLE, PISO, or PIMPLE. As a consequence, linear systems of multiple partial differential equations, namely the momentum and the pressure equations, are assembled into separate linear equations and are usually solved in an iterative way. The computational procedure of OpenFOAM's icoFOAM solver is illustrated in Fig. 1. Within each time step, the set of linear equations for the momentum equation is assembled and solved. The result is used as a predictor of the velocity field and serves as an input for the PISO procedure, which assembles and solves the linear equations for a pressure corrector in an iterative way. After reaching the final iteration of the PISO loop, the velocity solution gets corrected by applying the effect of the pressure corrector to yield a conservative velocity field. It should be noted that the icoFOAM solver serves as a model solver in this work, neglecting, for example, other computational costs like non-orthogonal correctors, IO, or additional physical models. However, the proposed procedure can be beneficial to other solvers as well. Neglecting any additional costs, the time required to solve a single time step T is the sum of the total matrix assembly and total linear solver costs, written as

$$T(n) = T_{AS}(n) + T_{LS}(n), \qquad (1)$$

where n is the number of used MPI ranks. Each part of the RHS in Eq. (1) could be split further into individual equations depending on the OpenFOAM solver, e.g. the momentum and pressure for icoFOAM. In the following, we assume that the individual equations have the same speed-up regarding the number of used MPI ranks, thus splitting each part into equations is not considered further. The speed-up per part is defined as $S_{LS}(n) = T_{LS}(1)/T_{LS}(n)$, and $S_{AS}(n)$ accordingly. In the heterogeneous setting, i.e. employing a different number of MPI ranks for matrix assembly and the linear solver, the speed-ups behave differently, that is $S_{LS} \neq S_{AS}$. This could be the case, for example, if the assembly is done on CPUs, while the linear solver is offloaded to GPUs, which matches the OpenFOAM approach as discussed in Sect. 1.

The speed-ups attain their maximum at different inputs $N_{LS}^* < N_{AS}^*$ with $S_{LS}(n) \leq S_{LS}(N_{LS}^*)$, and $S_{AS}(n) \leq S_{AS}(N_{AS}^*)$. In the case of ideal scaling, the optimal number of MPI ranks N^* are the maximal available resources. Thus, $N_{AS}^* = N_{CPU}$ is the number of available CPUs, and $N_{LS}^* = N_{GPU}$ is the number of available GPUs. Considering the total runtime again

$$\begin{aligned} T(n) &= T_{AS}(n) + T_{LS}(n) \\ &= \frac{T_{AS}(1)}{S_{AS}(n)} + \frac{T_{LS}(1)}{S_{LS}(n)} \end{aligned} \qquad (2)$$

neither $n = N_{AS}^*$, nor $n = N_{LS}^*$ will achieve the minimum runtime. Instead, optimizing the runtime requires some value for n which achieves suboptimal speed-ups in both components. Thus, some computing resources must be left unused.

However, by choosing the number of MPI ranks for T_{AS} and T_{LS} independently, optimal utilization for both components can be achieved. Then the run-

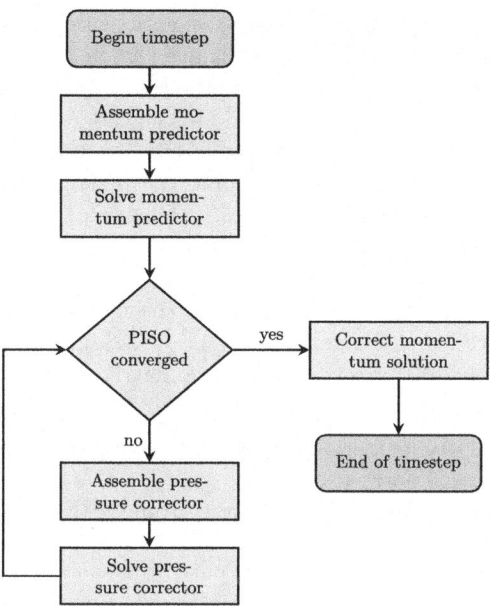

Fig. 1. Flow chart of the principal steps within a timestep in the icoFOAM solver.

time can be expressed as

$$T(n_{AS}, n_{LS}) = T_{AS}(n_{AS}) + T_{LS}(n_{LS}) + T_R(n_{AS}, n_{LS}) \quad (3)$$

where T_R contains the cost to communicate between the two different MPI groups. Now, it is clear that using the pair $(N_{AS}^*, N_{LS}*) = (N_{CPU}, N_{GPU})$ minimizes the cost for both the assembly and linear solver component. Only the cost for the T_R term has to be accounted for. Additionally, this approach can be easily integrated into existing workflows, as already existing decompositions into N_{CPU} can be reused.

3 The Repartitioning Procedure

In the following, we will use the term repartitioning for the process of mapping from a CPU partition, used for assembling the linear system, to a separate GPU partition, used to solve the linear system. Each partition consists of a number of parts, which are assigned an MPI rank r. The number of parts in the CPU partition n_{CPU} is determined by the domain decomposition procedure, which is applied as a preprocessing step by the utility decomposePar that is part of the OpenFOAM framework. In contrast, the number of parts in the GPU partition n_{GPU} depends on a repartitioning ratio $\alpha \geq 1$ and is determined at run time as $n_{GPU} = n_{CPU}/\alpha$, i.e. it defines the number of ranks per GPU. Thus, for the number of parts the following relationship holds: $n_{GPU} \leq n_{CPU}$. To facilitate the mapping between the two partitions, connections between ranks in the CPU partition and ranks in the GPU partition need to be defined. The connection defines which degrees of freedom (DOF) in the linear system are owned by which ranks. In this work, a blockwise distribution is considered, where the GPU rank k owns the same DOFs as the α CPU ranks $\{\alpha k, \alpha k + 1, \ldots, \alpha k + \alpha - 1\}$.

For both the CPU and GPU partitions, the matrix coefficients are stored according to their communication properties. That is, all matrix coefficients that are applied solely to local components are stored in a local matrix and coefficients requiring components from a different rank are stored separately in a non-local matrix. An additional constraint is given by the fact that in OpenFOAM, the host matrix is stored in LDU format. Thus, additionally, a mapping between LDU matrix entries and the entries of device matrix format is required.

The repartitioning procedure investigated for this work can be described as:

1. Extract the sparsity pattern from the host matrix, including all coupling terms with non-local entries.
2. Send local and non-local sparsity patterns from CPU ranks to their connected GPU ranks.
3. On the GPU ranks, all received local sparsity patterns are fused into a single local sparsity pattern, i.e. the GPU rank k fuses the sparsity pattern received from the CPU ranks $\{\alpha k, \alpha k + 1, \ldots, \alpha k + \alpha - 1\}$. The received non-local matrix elements are included in the new local sparsity pattern, if the former communication partner resides on the same part after repartitioning. Otherwise, they are fused in the non-local matrix.

To illustrate, Fig. 2 shows the initial structure of the distributed LDU matrix on the host (top) and the resulting matrix in COO format on the accelerator after repartitioning (bottom). By reducing the number of individual parts, the resulting repartitioned matrix also has fewer coefficients in the non-local interface matrix.

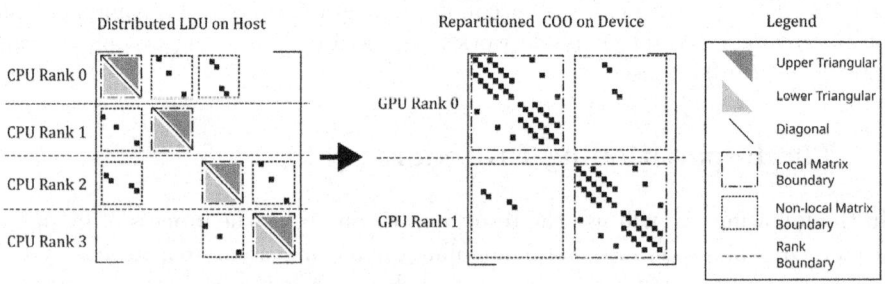

Fig. 2. Structure of the distributed matrix in LDU format on the host (top) and after repartitioning on the accelerator (bottom), with $\alpha = 2$.

The approach presented first applies the repartitioning procedure to the sparsity pattern of the matrix. Hence, it yields a repartitioned matrix without computing the repartitioned matrix coefficients. Thus, in a separate step, the matrix coefficients of the repartitioned matrix have to be set on the basis of the matrix values of the host matrix. From step (3) a mapping between the ordering of the host matrix in LDU format and the required ordering of the matrix on the destination rank, e.g. a row-major ordered COO matrix, is created. To update the matrix coefficients, each rank sends its matrix coefficients to the corresponding owner GPU rank into a continuous buffer array. The owning rank then orders the data according to the computed mapping into a view of repartitioned device matrix. The principal process of repartitioning the matrix coefficients is illustrated in Fig. 3. The repartitioner combines several CPU-based LDU blocks by gathering onto an owning GPU MPI rank. As mentioned before, the assignment from CPU-to-GPU rank follows block-wise. Other methods for distributing matrix elements among parts that might yield more optimal partitions, e.g. Metis, are possible but lie outside the scope of this work. Additionally, the repartitioner is responsible for localizing non-local blocks that have purely local communication after repartitioning. These can be identified as blocks in which global column index j is within the set of global row indices $I_{GPU}(r)$ of the fused sparsity pattern on the GPU with rank r i.e. $j \in I_{GPU}(r) = \bigcup_{l=0}^{\alpha-1} I_{CPU}(\alpha\ r + l)$.

The process of repartitioning yields three data structures:

1. The sparsity pattern, i.e. row and column indices, of the repartitioned matrix.
2. An update pattern U for the repartitioned coefficients. Here, the update pattern stores on each rank (a) the target ranks of its send operation, (b) send and receive pointers to the host data and the target data buffer respectively, and (c) the corresponding sizes for the MPI communication. This allows each rank to send its corresponding LDU matrix data to a designated buffer on the device on the receiving owner rank.
3. A permutation matrix which maps from the original LDU-based ordering to a row-major ordering of the resulting repartitioned device matrix.

To realize the different CPU and GPU partitions, a new MPI communicator is created by splitting the CPU MPI communicator C into active C_a and inactive C_i ranks, where C_a contains the active ranks in the GPU partition. The default communicator C is required for matrix coefficient updates. The communicator C_a is passed to the linear solver handling the distributed linear system, while the inactive ranks C_i just skip this step. The communicator C_a is then used exclusively on the GPUs. This process avoids creating any empty matrices on devices for non-owning ranks, since this can cause significant performance degradation.

To ensure optimal performance, creating and updating the system matrix are two distinct processes. This allows one to create the repartitioned, distributed matrix once and reuse it by updating its value through the course of a simulation. The update procedure for the matrix coefficients is illustrated in Fig. 3b. If GPU aware MPI is available, each host rank sends its local data directly to a memory location of a temporary buffer on the device. Otherwise, the data is gathered on the CPU ranks αk first and then copied to the GPU in a separate step. This results in an array that is consecutively ordered regarding the original LDU order and the originating ranks. Thus, in a second step, the coefficients are reordered

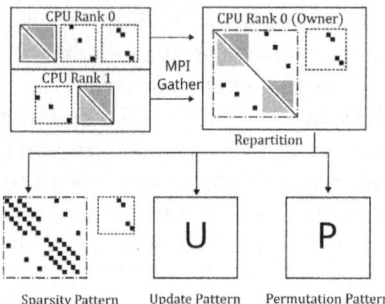
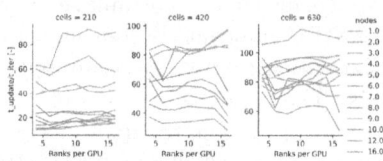

(a) Resulting data structures to for updating of the matrix coefficients.

(b) Update procedure of the distributed matrix coefficients.

Fig. 3. Illustration of the repartitioning procedure.

by the permutation matrix P to satisfy the row-major ordering expected by the linear solver library.

4 Performance Evaluation

For the performance evaluation, the GPU based linear solvers of the Ginkgo library [1] are employed. The Ginkgo library is made available to OpenFOAM via the OpenFOAM-Ginkgo Layer (OGL) [8] plugin. The repartition procedure discussed in Sect. 3 is fully implemented within OGL. The lidDrivenCavity3D case [3] is taken as a benchmark case. The computational grid is based on a uniform cubic grid with $2 \times 3 \times 5 \times 7 \times n_p$ cells along each axis, where n_p is the factor controlling the overall size of the problem. This ensures that the resulting computational domains are decomposable into equally sized subdomains by a wide range of factors. The value of n is 1, 2, or 3 for the small, medium, and large cases with approximately 9M, 74M, and 250M cells, respectively. The time steps of the corresponding runs are adapted to ensure a constant CFL number. The cases are decomposed into subdomains using the OpenFOAM multilevel decomposition strategy, with a simple decomposition on the outermost node level and Scotch for the GPU and CPU levels, with $n_{tot,domains} = n_{nodes} \times n_{GPUs} \times \alpha$. The pressure equation is solved by Ginkgos CG solver for the GPU runs and with OpenFOAMs PCG for the CPU reference case. For solving the momentum equation, which accounts only for a small portion of the total compute time, OpenFOAMs native BiCGStab solver is used. The cases are run for exactly 20 time steps to ensure a balance between reasonable computational costs and sufficient computational work to extract meaningful statistics. For statistical analysis, an average of all computational time steps is calculated, excluding the first time step. The setup, execution and post-processing of the parameter study conducted is handled by the OpenFOAM Benchmark Runner (OBR) [5]. The numerical experiments were conducted on the HoreKa HPC cluster, which is equipped with two Intel Xeon Platinum 8368 CPUs and four NVIDIA A100-40 GPUs per compute note. Furthermore, the software stack included the following software versions: OpenFOAM 2412, Ginkgo 1.9, OpenMPI 5.0.1, with UCX v1.18.0 and CUDA 12.2. Figure 4 shows the impact of different repartitioning ratios α on the linear solver performance (LSP), reported as TFLOP/s. It can be seen that the performance of the linear solver is mostly independent of the repartitioning ratio α and is mainly influenced by the problem size and the number of compute nodes used. However, in some cases, performance degradation was observed. This typically occurred when more than one, four, or six compute nodes were used for the small, medium, and large case, respectively. This indicates that a minimum number of DOFs per GPU device is required for a constant performance across all repartitioning ratios.

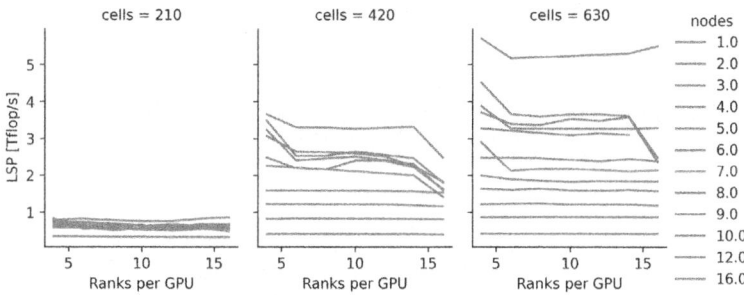

Fig. 4. Impact of the repartitioning ratio RPG on the linear solver performance in Tflop/s for a different number of compute nodes and problem sizes.

While the performance of linear solver is approximately constant for different repartitioning ratios, an increasing α allows employing more MPI-Ranks for computations residing on the host, e.g. the matrix assembly. Thus, employing more parallelism on the host side should speed up the host-side computations. The time spent on the host side computations is given in Fig. 5, which shows a clear trend of decreasing the time required on the CPU with increasing α. With a decreasing amount of time spent on the host side computations, the ratio $\phi = t_{GPU}/t_{CPU}$ between the time spent on the GPU device and the CPU increases as shown in Fig. 6. Thus, for a sufficiently large number of compute nodes and α, the time spent on the host side becomes almost negligible as *phi* approaches values between 15 and 30. After ensuring a reasonable behavior of the repartitioning strategy over a wide set of parameters and problem sizes, a limited number of cases were selected to study the impact of the repartitioning strategy compared to typical alternative partitioning strategies.

Thus, for further investigation of the impact of offloading and repartitioning on the performance PISO algorithm shown in Fig. 7 the following cases were selected for further investigation: (1) the reference case (blue line) without GPU acceleration using all available CPU cores, (2) a repartitioned case (red line) where 16 CPU MPI ranks were mapped to one GPU rank. (3) an unpartitioned

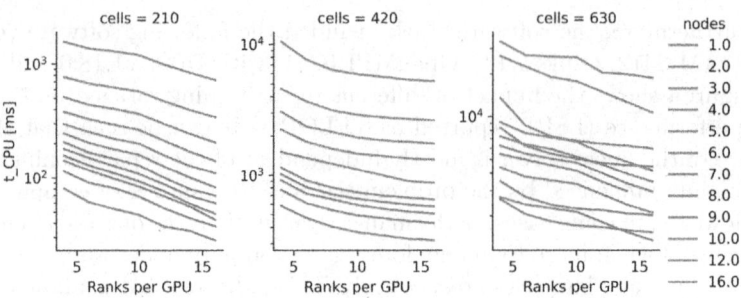

Fig. 5. Impact of the repartitioning ratio RPG on the time spent on host-side computations for different problem sizes and number of compute nodes.

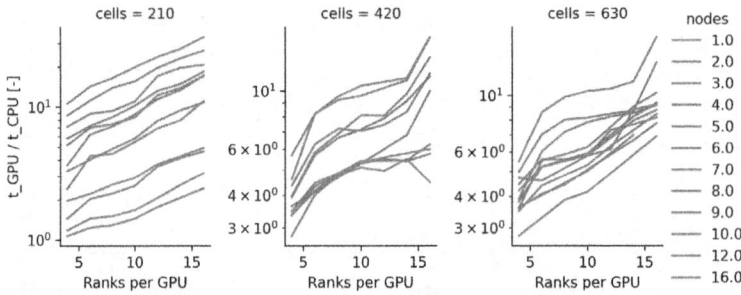

Fig. 6. Impact of the repartitioning ratio α on the ratio of time spent on the GPU to CPU for different problem sizes and number of compute nodes.

case (green line, GPUURR1) in which exactly n_{GPU} MPI ranks were used for linear solvers and matrix assembly and (4) an unrepartitioned case (orange line, GPUOSR1) that uses n_{CPU} ranks and thus overutilizes the GPUs. Figure 7 shows the strong scaling behavior performance $P = n_{cells}/t_{TS}$ in 10^6fvOps on up to 16 nodes with 64 GPUs. The following findings can be observed here; the compute performance increases with increasing problem size on the GPUs, from 420^3 compute cells both cases GPUURR1 and GPUOSR16 perform consistently better compared to the unaccelerated cases. The GPUOSR1 case, on the other hand, shows a significant reduction in performance of up to a factor 140. It is therefore not advisable to use unrepartitioned and overloaded cases in combination with OpenMPI. Figure 8 compares the speed-up of the different partitioning strategies of the accelerated version regarding the non-accelerated CPU code for the small, medium, and large computational grid over different number of compute nodes. In general, it can be observed that the speed-up of the accelerated cases increases for increasing problem sizes and decreases for increasing number of nodes. Which, suggests that the accelerated cases profit from a larger number of DOFs per GPU in contrast to the CPU case. This is in line with the findings of [4] which suggest that OpenFOAM cases can profit from optimal cache utilization when partitioning approx. 10000-30000 DOFs per CPU core.

In contrast, optimal utilization of the GPU is observed for more than 1M DOFs per GPU. This leads to better parallel efficiency of the CPU cases compared to the GPU cases when increasing the number of compute nodes and explains the decreasing speed-up with decreasing number of DOFs per compute unit. Of the tested cases, the repartitioned case with $\alpha = 16$ (GPUOSRR16) performed best over a wide range of nodes and cases with a maximum acceleration of up to a factor of 10, however, for a larger number of compute nodes, the results are converging towards the unrepartitioned case GPUUSR1. Of the accelerated cases tested, the oversubscription case without repartitioning (GPUOSR1) showed the worst performance with a speed-up of 0.007 in the worst case, which seems to be a consequence of the aforementioned oversubscription issue of OpenMPI [2]. In summary, the use of the newly developed repartitioning method succeeds in matching computing performance using a smaller number of computing nodes. Furthermore, for the presented repartitioning method, efficient communication among CPU-GPU and GPU-GPU is crucial. The former is required for an efficient update of the matrix coefficients, and the latter is required for distributed SpMVs in the distributed linear solver. Thus, the impact of enabling GPU-aware MPI and GPU-direct is shown in Fig. 9 for the repartitioning case GPUOSRR16 and the oversubscribing case GPUOSR1. Here, solid lines indicate cases that take advantage of GPU-aware MPI by directly sending data to buffers on the GPU device. For the cases without GPU aware MPI (dashed lines and HB suffix), the data were first copied from the device back to the host before communicating with other ranks. A substantial impact on the performance can be observed that ranged from 25% to 50%.

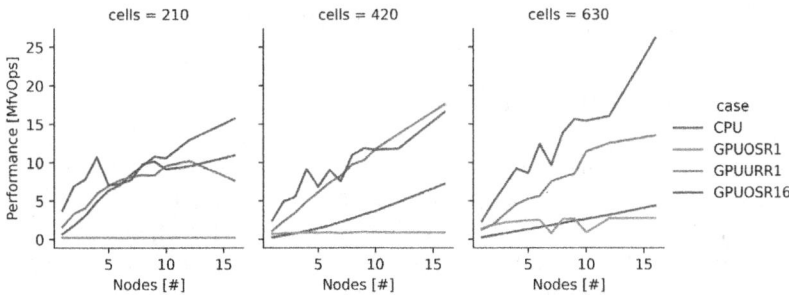

Fig. 7. Strong scaling performance for the different partitioning strategies, undersubscribing (GPUURR1), oversubscribing (GPUOSR1), repartitioning (GPUOSRR16) compared to the unaccelerated reference case (CPU).

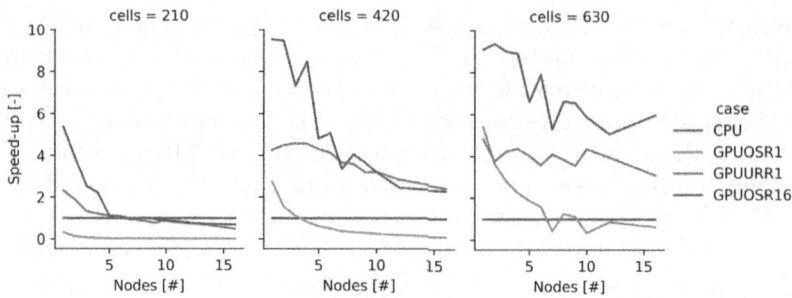

Fig. 8. Speedup of the tested partitioning strategies: undersubscribing (GPUURR1), oversubscribing (GPUOSR1), repartitioning (GPUOSRR16) wrt. to the reference case (CPU) for different problem sizes and number of compute nodes.

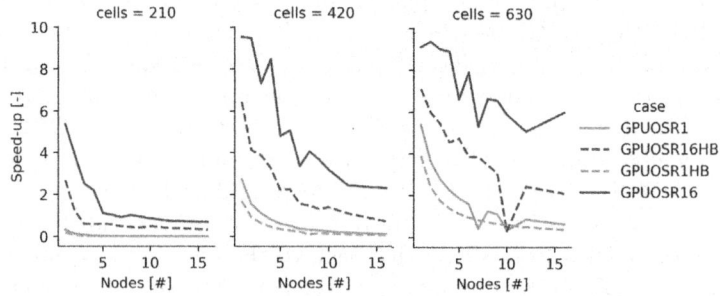

Fig. 9. Impact of GPU aware MPI functionalities (solid lines) compared to communication via a host-side buffer (dashed lines and HB suffix in the case name) for different partitioning strategies, problem sizes, and number of compute nodes.

5 Conclusion and Outlook

In this work, a repartitioning procedure was investigated to address the challenge of over- and undersubscription, which is a consequence of the heterogeneous computing approach of GPU offloading plugins for OpenFOAM. It was demonstrated that by repartitioning significant performance gains are achievable compared to the unaccelerated case. Additionally, it performed better against the accelerated cases with either undersubscribing or oversubscribing. The investigated lidDriven3D case spent the majority of the compute time for the linear solver. Thus, more complex test cases should be investigated, since for industrially relevant cases often an equal ratio between matrix assembly and linear solver costs is reported. Additionally, the impact of repartitioning on other solver like the distributed multigrid solvers and the convergence behavior of the preconditioner should be investigated.

Acknowledgments. This work was supported by the German Federal Ministry of Education and Research (grant number 16ME0676K). This work was performed on the HoreKa supercomputer funded by the Ministry of Science, Research and the Arts Baden-Württemberg and by the Federal Ministry of Education and Research.

References

1. Anzt, H., et al.: Ginkgo: a high performance numerical linear algebra library. J. Open Source Softw. **5**(52), 2260 (2020). https://doi.org/10.21105/joss.02260
2. Bierbaum, J., Planeta, M., Härtig, H.: Towards efficient oversubscription: on the cost and benefit of event-based communication in MPI. In: 2022 IEEE/ACM International Workshop on Runtime and Operating Systems for Supercomputers (ROSS), pp. 1–10. IEEE (2022)
3. Bn'a, S., Spisso, I., Olesen, M., Rossi, G.: PETSc4FOAM: A Library to plug-in PETSc into the OpenFOAM Framework. PRACE White paper (2020)
4. Galeazzo, F.C.C., Weiß, R.G., Lesnik, S., Rusche, H., Ruopp, A.: Understanding superlinear speedup in current HPC architectures. In: IOP Conference Series: Materials Science and Engineering, vol. 1312, p. 012009. IOP Publishing (2024)
5. Gärtner, J.W., et al.: Testing Strategies for OpenFOAM Projects. OpenFOAM® **5**, 115–130 (2025). https://doi.org/10.51560/ofj.v5.134
6. Jasak, H., Jemcov, A., Tukovic, Z., et al.: Openfoam: a C++ library for complex physics simulations. In: International Workshop on Coupled Methods in Numerical Dynamics, vol. 1000, pp. 1–20. Dubrovnik, Croatia) (2007)
7. Mills, R.T., et al.: Toward performance-portable PETSc for GPU-based exascale systems. Parallel Comput. **108**, 102831 (2021). https://doi.org/10.1016/j.parco.2021.102831, https://www.sciencedirect.com/science/article/pii/S016781912100079X
8. Olenik, G., Koch, M., Boutanios, Z., Anzt, H.: Towards a platform-portable linear algebra backend for OpenFOAM. Meccanica (2024). https://doi.org/10.1007/s11012-024-01806-1
9. Tandon, S., et al.: Porting HPC applications to AMD instinct™ MI300A using unified memory and OpenMP®. In: ISC High Performance 2024 Research Paper Proceedings (39th International Conference), pp. 1–9. Prometeus GmbH (2024)

Stream-K++: Adaptive GPU GEMM Kernel Selection and Scheduling for AI Using Bloom Filters

Harisankar Sadasivan[1], Muhammed Emin Ozturk[2](✉),
Muhammad Osama[2], Chris Millette[2], Astha Rai[2],
Maksim Podkorytov[2], John Afaganis[2], Carlus Huang[2], Jing Zhang[3],
and Jun Liu[3]

[1] University of Washington, Seattle, USA
hsadasiv@uw.edu
[2] Advanced Micro Devices, Inc., Santa Clara, USA
{muhammed.ozturk,muhammad.osama,chris.millette,astha.rai,
maksim.podkorytov,john.afaganis,carlus.huang}@amd.com
[3] Meta Platforms, Inc., Austin/Menlo Park, USA
{jizhan,junliume}@meta.com

Abstract. General matrix multiplication (GEMM) operations are the fundamental building blocks of computational domains including artificial intelligence (AI). As GPU architectures evolve and high-performance AI becomes increasingly important, optimizing GEMM performance becomes a fundamental problem that needs to be addressed. This paper introduces Stream-K++, an enhancement to the promising Stream-K GEMM scheduling algorithm for workload balancing. We expand Stream-K's scheduling policies from three to seven and implement an efficient solution selection mechanism using Bloom filters. Our approach rapidly eliminates up to ~95.8% of unsuitable configurations while maintaining a 100% true-negative rate.

Implemented using the AMD Composable Kernel library and evaluated on AMD Instinct™MI250X GPUs, Stream-K++ demonstrates significant performance gains (up to ~43%) in select scenarios. It remains competitive (within 20% of optimal) for ~60-97.6% of problem sizes. Our flexible framework, implemented in the Open-sieve C++ library, allows for easy adaptation to new problem sizes, scheduling policies, or additional tuning parameters, paving the way for future optimizations in GPU-based GEMM operations.

Keywords: Artificial Intelligence · Bloom filter · GEMMs · GPUs · Stream-K

H. Sadasivan, J. Zhang and J. Liu—Contributed to this work while they were employed full-time at AMD.

1 Introduction

General matrix multiplication (GEMM) operations are fundamental to a wide range of computational tasks, from machine learning [31] and scientific simulations [13] to computer graphics [25] and signal processing [30]. The importance of GEMMs in artificial intelligence (AI) has grown exponentially with the rise of transformer models [8,32] in natural language processing. For example, the BERT model [12], which revolutionized language understanding, relies heavily on matrix multiplications in its self-attention mechanism. Similarly, GPT-3 [19], with its 175 billion parameters, performs an enormous number of GEMM operations during both training and inference. Beyond transformers, GEMM is critical in convolutional neural networks for image recognition (e.g., ResNet) [31], in recommendation systems for e-commerce platforms [15], and in physics simulations for climate modeling [14]. As these applications become more complex and data-intensive, optimizing GEMM performance on modern hardware architectures has become increasingly crucial for achieving efficient and scalable computations.

Conventional GEMM implementations employ data-parallel tiling of the output matrix, dividing the computation into smaller, manageable blocks that can be processed independently. These approaches often use hierarchical implementations, where the problem is broken down into progressively smaller units to match the hardware's memory hierarchy and computational capabilities. For example, a large matrix multiplication might be divided into blocks that fit into shared memory, which are further subdivided into thread-level computations that use thread-local registers [1,3].

However, as GPU cores have grown in size and complexity, a new challenge has emerged: GPU utilization [23]. Traditional tiling methods can struggle when the workload cannot be easily broken down or quantized into waves that efficiently fit onto all compute units (CUs). This issue is particularly pronounced for matrix shapes that do not align well with the GPU's architecture, leading to underutilization of computational resources and suboptimal performance. When the last round of wavefronts scheduled on the GPU only fills some of the CUs, the unused CUs must wait for the active CUs to complete millions (if not billions) of multiply-accumulate (MAC) operations before they can execute any dependent work.

Stream-K [23] addresses this challenge by introducing a novel approach to workload distribution. Instead of rigidly dividing the output matrix across the CUs, Stream-K distributes the actual work (total MAC operations), instead of the output matrix, to the CUs. This method enables finer-grained load balancing, as the streaming nature of the algorithm allows it to adapt to the available resources more dynamically. The key innovation of Stream-K lies in its ability to maintain high GPU utilization across a wide range of matrix dimensions while keeping the overhead at a constant cost. By processing the input matrices in a continuous stream, it keeps all CUs busy even when the problem size is not divisible evenly among them. This is particularly beneficial for irregular or non-square matrix shapes that might leave significant portions of the GPU idle under conventional tiling schemes.

Despite its promise, the optimal utilization of Stream-K presents a significant challenge. The algorithm's performance is highly sensitive to the specific Stream-K configuration used, which must be tailored to the dimensions of the matrices being multiplied (M, N, and K) and the underlying hardware characteristics. This sensitivity creates a complex optimization problem: for each GEMM operation, an appropriate Stream-K configuration must be selected to maximize performance. A configuration that performs well for one set of matrix dimensions may be suboptimal for another, necessitating a dynamic approach to configuration selection. A naive solution proposed [23] picks one Stream-K configuration for a particular GPU architecture. However, this may not be optimal in every scenario.

This paper addresses the critical need for an efficient method to select the most suitable Stream-K configuration for arbitrary GEMM problem sizes and hardware architectures. We propose Stream-K++, which significantly expands upon the original Stream-K framework by introducing four additional work schedule configurations, bringing the total to seven distinct policies. This expansion offers a more nuanced approach to workload distribution, potentially catering to a wider array of GEMM scenarios and hardware configurations. To efficiently navigate this expanded configuration space, we introduce a novel bloom-filter-based methodology for dynamic kernel selection. Implemented in Opensieve, a new C++ header-only library, our approach utilizes a set of Bloom filters to rapidly filter out unsuitable Stream-K++ schedule configurations, narrowing down the search space for a particular GEMM problem size (M, N, K). This method successfully eliminates up to $\sim$95.8% of unnecessary configuration checks with a 100% true negative rate, significantly reducing selection overhead while maintaining both time and space efficiency.

Our comprehensive evaluation on AMD Instinct™MI250X GPUs demonstrates that while Stream-K configurations may not outperform traditional approaches in most cases, they offer substantial gains of up to 43% in specific scenarios and maintain competitive performance within a small margin of 20% of the optimal configuration's performance for $\sim$60-97.6% of problem sizes. These findings underscore the importance of adaptive, context-aware GEMM optimization strategies. By streamlining the configuration selection process and providing a flexible framework for future optimizations, Stream-K++ not only enhances immediate GEMM performance but also paves the way for continued advancements in GPU-based matrix multiplication. In the following sections, we detail our methodology, present our experimental results, and discuss the broader implications of this work for high-performance computing on modern GPU architectures.

2 Related Work

Larsen et al. [20] performed matrix-matrix multiplication on GPUs by repurposing the graphics pipeline to visualize the computation as a multi-texture multiplication and blending operation. Later GPU architectures enabled high-performance GEMMs with two levels of blocking (user-programmable cache and registers) where tile sizes are chosen from extensive micro-benchmarking [9,22,27,28], and auto-tuning [11,17,21]. MAGMA GPU math library [22] is one of the early works to optimize for different GEMM problem sizes. Size thresholds based on naive handwritten rules were used for kernel selection. Subsequent GPU math libraries rely on more sophisticated code-generation and kernel-selection techniques. For example, ISAAC [28] uses machine learning to predict optimal tiling parameters. Domain Specific Languages (DSLs) like Halide [26] and TVM [10] separate the definition of the algorithm from the scheduling logic. Fireiron [16] adds constructs for scheduling data movement. Triton [29] is another popular DSL that introduces a block-based instead of thread-based programming model that automatically performs low-level optimizations like memory coalescing, shared memory management, and scheduling within CUs, and leaves the high-level logic of the parallel code to the developer.

Optimal GEMM implementations on GPUs are often found in GPU vendor libraries. The NVIDIA cuBLAS [2] (closed-source) and the AMD rocBLAS [7] (open-source) support basic linear algebra subroutines (BLAS) that include GEMMs. NVIDIA also offers CUTLASS [3], an open-source collection of CUDA C++ templates for high-performance matrix multiplication. Similarly, the AMD Composable Kernel [1,18] library provides a flexible, open-source approach to building complex GPU operations from reusable components. These libraries use hierarchical implementations of GEMMs where grids of thread blocks or wavegroups are distributed across CUs to keep the GPU occupied. Additionally, each CU has multiple resident wavegroups or blocks and each wavegroup resident on a CU may consist of one or more wavefronts or warps that are groups of 32 or 64 threads. GPUs are designed to context-switch between wavefronts with zero overhead and having multiple resident wavefronts on each CU is important to hide the memory access latency for each wavefront on the GPU. Moreover, all of these GEMM libraries rely on the custom-designed and fast Matrix Fused Multiply and Accumulate (MFMA) hardware for efficient multiply-and-accumulate (MAC) operations.

Tiling is a strategy that the GEMM libraries have adopted to reduce bandwidth usage by exploiting spatial and temporal cache locality. Input and output matrices are divided into smaller tiles or sub-matrices. Each pair of input tiles required to compute an output tile is fetched and stored in user-programmable cache (shared memory or local data share) until all the MAC operations with it are performed. In scenarios where the K dimension is very large, libraries employ a strategy known as split-K [4] where the computation is split along the K dimension and spread across multiple blocks or wavegroups to better utilize the GPU hardware.

Stream-K [23] is a recent optimization strategy that builds upon the concept of split-K for better workload balancing and hardware utilization. Stream-K does a work-centric decomposition where the total MAC operations involved in a GEMM are uniformly spread across all the CUs.

3 Background

3.1 Stream-K Algorithm

Stream-K, introduced by Osama et al. [23], represents a significant advancement in GEMM optimization for modern GPUs. This innovative strategy fundamentally restructures workload distribution by uniformly dividing the total computational work (MAC operations) across CUs, as shown in Fig. 1. Stream-K surpasses the limitations of traditional approaches like split-K, which rigidly partitions output tile computations along the K dimension using a fixed factor. The core strength of Stream-K lies in its dynamic and flexible workload balancing mechanism, as illustrated in Algorithm 1. The algorithm initiates by calculating the total number of iterations required for the GEMM operation, considering the matrix dimensions and workgroup sizes (lines 2-3). It then evenly distributes these iterations among 'g' workgroups (line 4). Each workgroup processes its assigned range of iterations (lines 5-8), with each iteration potentially contributing to different output tiles. This approach allows for fine-grained load balancing, adapting to varying matrix sizes and hardware configurations.

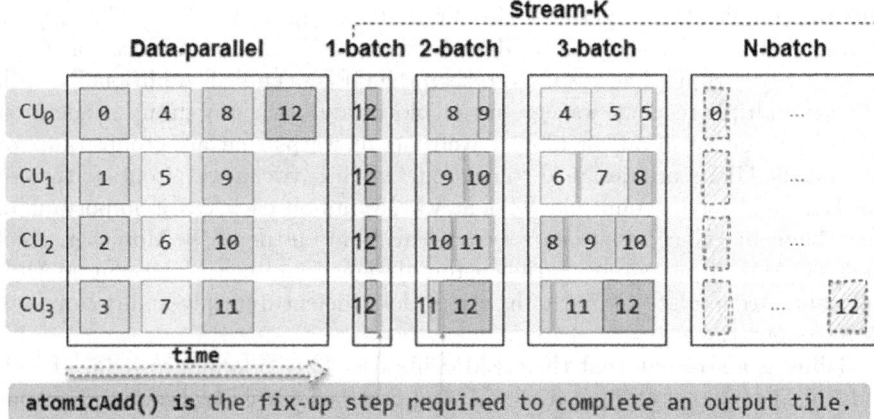

Fig. 1. Stream-K distributes batches of output tile computations uniformly across CUs, allowing multiple CUs to collaboratively complete tiles using atomic operations for fix-up, in contrast to traditional data-parallel GEMM approaches.

The core computation occurs in the MAC_loop function (line 14), which returns a local accumulator. Each workgroup directly updates the global output matrix C using atomic add operations (line 17). This implementation of Stream-K in Algorithm 1 using atomic adds for writing output to memory eliminates the need for explicit inter-workgroup synchronization and separate partial result accumulation steps. The algorithm iterates through the assigned work, computing portions of output tiles and atomically adding results to the corresponding positions in C.

Moreover, Stream-K's design inherently supports efficient deployment on modern multi-chiplet GPUs without necessitating additional tuning for parameters like grid size. This adaptability is particularly valuable in the context of evolving GPU architectures, where traditional optimization techniques may require significant adjustments for each new hardware configuration. By reimagining workload distribution and incorporating sophisticated synchronization mechanisms, Stream-K not only achieves superior load balancing but also enhances scalability and portability across diverse GPU architectures. For example, Stream-K's flexible workload distribution could be particularly advantageous when running kernels on virtual cloud instances that may be allocated to specific chiplets or CUs on a multi-chiplet GPU like AMD Instinct™MI300X. These characteristics position Stream-K as a pivotal advancement in the field of high-performance computing, particularly for large-scale matrix operations in machine learning and scientific computing applications.

Algorithm 1. Streamk-K GEMM (using atomic adds) with grid size g

1: __shared__ accum [BLK_M, BLK_N]
2: iters_per_tile = ceil (K / BLK_K)
3: total_iters = ceil (M / BLK_M) × ceil (N / BLK_N) × iters_per_tile
4: iters_per_wg = ceil (total_iters/g)
5: **for** WG[x] **in** [g] **do**   ▷ *Launch g workgroups*
6:      iter = x × iters_per_wg   ▷ *Initialize*
7:      iter_end = iter + iters_per_wg
8:      **while** iter < iter_end **do**   ▷ *Outer loop to process iteration*
9:          tile_idx = iter / iters_per_tile
10:         tile_iter = tile_idx × iters_per_tile
11:         tile_iter_end = tile_iter + iters_per_tile
12:         local_iter = iter - tile_iter
13:         local_iter_end = min(iter_end, tile_iter_end)- tile_iter
14:         accum = MAC_loop (tile_idx, local_iter, local_iter_end)   ▷ *MAC iterations for this tile*
15:         **for** i in 0 to BLK_M **do**
16:             **for** j in 0 to BLK_N **do**
17:                 atomic_add(C [tile_idx.m + i, tile_idx.n + j], accum [i, j])
18:             **end for**
19:         **end for**
20:         iter = tile_iter_end
21:     **end while**
22: **end for**
23: **join**

3.2 Challenges in Stream-K Configuration Selection

Osama et al. [23] introduce three different Stream-K schedules in their work: basic Stream-K, data-parallel followed by one-batch Stream-K, and two-batch

Stream-K followed by data-parallel. Each "batch" or "round" in this context represents a single iteration (as in line 8 on Algorithm 1 and in Fig. 1) for all GPU wavefronts, processing their allocated workload. In the basic or all-Stream-K configuration, as shown in Algorithm 1, the total workload is equally distributed among all the workgroups. Here, the workgroups do not perform the conventional output tile-based (data-parallel) work.

In the second configuration of data-parallel followed by one-batch Stream-k, all the workgroups perform multiple batches or rounds of the conventional data-parallel GEMM computation, followed by one batch of Stream-K computation on whatever work that remains. However, this fails to hide the latencies of atomic adds to the output. For instance, the atomic adds into the shared output tile can take thousands of clock cycles, potentially creating a performance bottleneck at the end of the computation. To address these limitations, the authors propose a third policy as an improvement over the second one. In this approach, two batches of Stream-K work precede the conventional data-parallel computation. Initiating with Stream-K batches facilitates the overlap of the atomic write latencies with the data-parallel computation.

However, the authors leave two critical areas unexplored: the potential benefits of extending the Stream-K methodology beyond two batches, and a systematic methodology for selecting optimal Stream-K configurations across various GEMM sizes and hardware architectures.

Stream-K++ significantly enhances and expands upon the original Stream-K framework, introducing a comprehensive suite of seven distinct scheduling policies. These policies range from the all-Stream-K approach to a series of hybrid configurations, systematically increasing the number of Stream-K batches (from zero to six) along with the configuration for the conventional data-parallel computation. This expanded set of policies offers a more nuanced and flexible approach to workload distribution, potentially catering to a wider array of GEMM scenarios and hardware configurations. Moreover, we introduce a novel bloom-filter-based methodology for dynamically selecting the optimal scheduling policy. This innovative selection mechanism efficiently chooses between the seven Stream-K++ policies, adapting to the specific characteristics of each GEMM operation and hardware environment. By combining an extended range of scheduling options with an intelligent selection mechanism, Stream-K++ represents a significant advancement in GPU-based matrix multiplication optimization, promising improved performance across diverse computational.

4 Our Approach

4.1 Stream-K++: Scheduling Policy

Our implementation of the Stream-K++'s scheduling policy begins with the launch of a persistent kernel. The grid size for this kernel is carefully optimized to maximize GPU utilization, taking into account both the compiler-determined occupancy and the number of CUs available on the target GPU. This initial step ensures efficient resource allocation from the outset. Following the kernel launch, we employ a dynamic workload distribution strategy based on user-defined Stream-K++ configurations. This approach allows for flexible partitioning of work across CUs, adapting to various problem sizes and GPU architectures.

The workload is then assigned to wavefronts in two distinct batch types: Stream-K batches (ranging from zero to six based on input from the user or ckProfiler) and data-parallel batches. This hybrid assignment leverages the load-balancing strengths of Stream-K while maintaining the high throughput capabilities of traditional data-parallel execution. A key feature of our implementation is the strategic overlap of execution, where the latencies inherent in the atomic adds of Stream-K batches are effectively masked by the concurrent processing of data-parallel batches. This technique minimizes idle time and maximizes computational efficiency, potentially leading to significant performance gains across a wide spectrum of matrix dimensions and shapes.

4.2 Bloom Filter Design for Efficient Stream-K++ Policy Selection

The integration of additional Stream-K++ policies into ckProfiler significantly expands the search space for optimal GEMM configurations, potentially leading to prohibitive increases in tuning time for our FP16 GEMM benchmark. To address this challenge, we have developed a novel approach utilizing space and time-efficient Bloom filters for each Stream-K++ policy. This innovative design ensures a 100% true negative rate when determining whether a specific GEMM size is associated with any of the seven filters corresponding to the Stream-K++ policies.

Bloom filters, renowned for their efficiency in set membership queries, form the cornerstone of our solution. We employ the popular Murmur hash implementation, mmh3 [6], to generate unique keys from the problem size parameters (M, N, K), which are then used to query the Bloom filters. Our implementation, Open-sieve, is a C++ header-only library that maps winning Stream-K++ configurations for GEMM problem sizes to their corresponding Bloom filters. We utilize 7 distinct hash functions, one for each filter, and configure the Bloom filters to accommodate 10,000 problem sizes each, minimizing false positives for our 923 GEMM sizes while maintaining scalability for future expansions.

As a one-time preprocessing step, Open-sieve analyzes all 923 problem sizes in our benchmark suite, encoding the winning configurations into a compact C++ header file. This file, containing approximately 1 byte of information per problem size, serves as a highly efficient lookup table. When queried with a new GEMM problem size, the system rapidly checks the Bloom filters to determine if (M, N, K) corresponds to any Stream-K++ policies. Our optimized implementation achieves a remarkably low query time of 0.4 microseconds per lookup on a single CPU thread.

Our experimental results demonstrate the exceptional efficiency of this approach. The Bloom filter-based checks eliminate up to ∼95.8% of the additional policy evaluations that would otherwise be required when using ckProfiler. This significant reduction in computational overhead not only accelerates the tuning process but also enhances scalability. Furthermore, our method readily accommodates additional GEMM problem sizes and Stream-K++ policies, and even extends to other tuning parameters beyond Stream-K++, all while maintaining exceptional space and time efficiency.

This solution represents a significant advancement in GEMM optimization techniques, offering a scalable and efficient approach to navigating the complex landscape of Stream-K++ policy selection.

5 Evaluation

5.1 Experiment Setup

Our experiments were conducted on an AMD Instinct™MI250X GPU operating in its default Single Process Execution (SPX) mode, utilizing all 104 CUs on a single chiplet for computation. We designed a comprehensive FP16 benchmark suite comprising 923 unique GEMM problem sizes, with dimensions varied in powers of 2 within the following ranges: M from 1 to 8192, N from 64 to 8192, and K from 16 to 65536. We chose FP16 because it has emerged as a de facto standard for many popular inference engines [5,8,24]. While the GEMM problem ranges are informed by industry trends, they were generalized to maintain confidentiality and ensure broad applicability.

To evaluate GEMM performance, we employed the AMD Composable Kernel library [1,18], specifically utilizing the ckProfiler tool. ckProfiler is a tool that systematically evaluates various GEMM instances, aiming to determine the GEMM instance with the optimal wavegroup configurations and Stream-K++ policy for maximizing performance. For benchmarking each configuration, we perform fifty GPU kernel launches to warm the GPU up to a steady state and then measure performance as an average of another fifty kernel launches.

For in-depth performance analysis of the optimal kernels identified by ckProfiler, we used rocProf v6.1, which is an AMD GPU profiler included in the AMD ROCm™6.1 software stack. This profiling tool provided detailed insights into kernel execution characteristics and resource utilization. We used a 64-core AMD EPYC™7713 processor for CPU-related tasks.

5.2 GEMM Performance Analysis

Our comprehensive analysis reveals nuanced insights into the performance dynamics of Stream-K++ policies compared to conventional data-parallel approaches. As illustrated in Fig. 2, the data-parallel policy emerges as the optimal configuration for ~87% of the GEMM problem sizes. However, this initial observation belies the more complex performance landscape of Stream-K-based schedules.

A key finding emerges when we examine performance within varying tolerance thresholds. As we expand the acceptable performance slow-down margin from 5% to 20% relative to the data-parallel or no-stream-K baseline, we observe

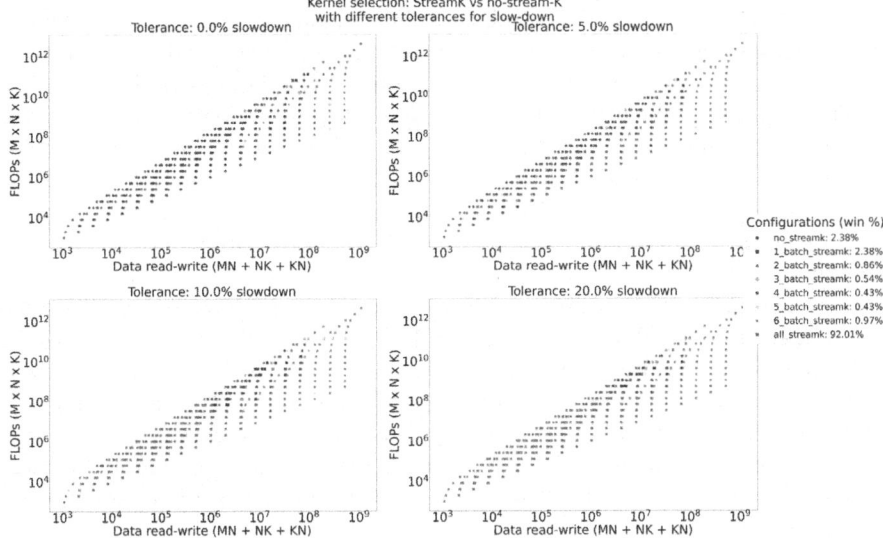

Fig. 2. A significant fraction of the winning kernel configurations in Stream-K++ are from Stream-K-based work schedules when we allow for some tolerance in slowdown with respect to the data-parallel schedule.

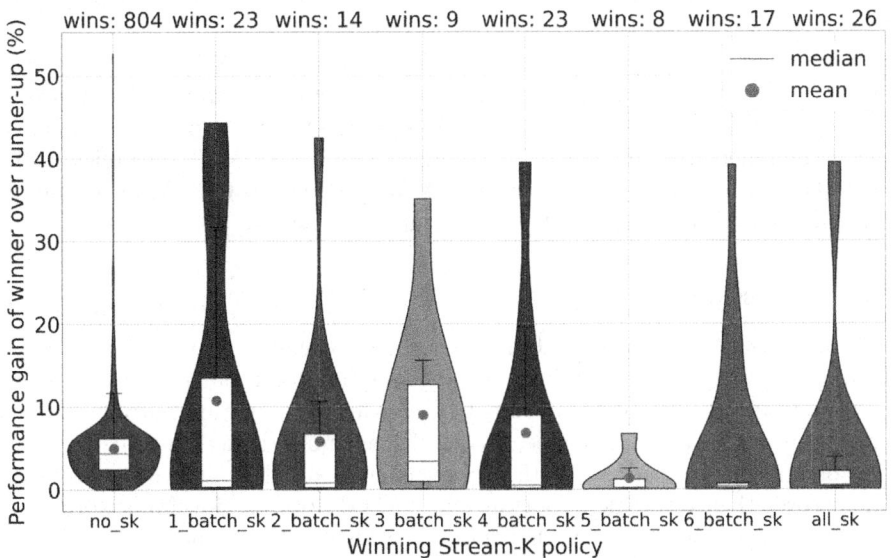

Fig. 3. Although just 13% of the winning kernel configurations are from Stream-K-based schedules, the gains are significant. The median performance gain for the Stream-k schedules over the runner-up configuration is significantly higher than the mean.

a dramatic increase in the prevalence of Stream-K-based winners—from approximately ~60% to ~97.6%. This significant shift underscores that while Stream-K configurations may not win most of the time, they consistently deliver competitive performance, often within a narrow margin of the data-parallel approach.

The apparent discrepancy between the ~13% optimal occurrence rate of Stream-K configurations and their broader competitiveness warrants further investigation. To this end, Fig. 3 provides crucial insights through a detailed violin plot analysis. This visualization contrasts the performance gains of winning configurations for both Stream-K and data-parallel approaches relative to their runners-up.

Stream-K schedules exhibit a distinctly asymmetric performance distribution. The mean gain (denoted by a green dot) substantially exceeds the median (indicated by a dashed line), revealing a right-skewed distribution characterized by several high-impact cases. This stands in stark contrast to the more symmetrical distribution observed for data-parallel configurations. Notably, the extended upper tail of the Stream-K violin plot highlights instances of exceptional performance enhancement, with some cases showing improvements of over ~40% compared to the runner-up.

These findings underscore the strategic importance of incorporating Stream-K schedules in GEMM optimization frameworks. Despite their less frequent occurrence as globally optimal solutions, Stream-K configurations demonstrate the potential for substantial performance improvements in specific scenarios. This potential for high-impact optimization, coupled with their broad competitiveness across problem sizes, reinforces the value of the expanded policy set introduced in Stream-K++.

Our results not only justify the inclusion of all Stream-K configurations but also emphasize the necessity of sophisticated selection mechanisms to leverage these policies effectively. The significant performance gains observed in select cases, combined with the overall competitiveness of Stream-K schedules, highlight the importance of a nuanced, adaptive approach to GEMM optimization that can identify and exploit these high-impact scenarios.

5.3 Discussion

Our analysis reveals important insights about Stream-K performance. While data-parallel policies are optimal for the majority of problem sizes, Stream-K configurations demonstrate competitive performance within narrow margins and exceptional gains in select scenarios. The asymmetric performance distribution of Stream-K schedules, with improvements exceeding 40% in some cases, underscores their strategic importance in GEMM optimization frameworks.

We identify two primary challenges in Stream-K implementation. Firstly, despite the multi-batch schedules in Stream-K++ helping to mitigate some latencies associated with atomic adds, this remains problematic for large K dimensions. While atomic adds simplify the algorithm by eliminating explicit inter-workgroup synchronization and separate partial result accumulation, an alternative approach using parallel reduction to combine partial results from wavegroups could potentially yield superior results. However, the effect of inter-workgroup synchronization for parallel reduction on performance would need to be investigated.

Secondly, we observed increased L1 cache misses as a limitation in certain cases, with Stream-K-based schedules suffering up to ~30% lower L1 cache hits compared to no-Stream-K in scenarios where the latter prevails. This finding emphasizes the need to incorporate cache locality considerations when allocating work to CUs, a factor that will become increasingly critical for multi-chiplet GPUs with disaggregated caches.

Our current study focuses on FP16 GEMMs on the MI250X GPU. Future work will expand to other precisions and mixed precision (FP32, FP16, FP6, FP4), profiling energy efficiency of Stream-K++, exploring additional tuning parameters beyond Stream-K policies, and diverse GPU architectures and form factors. This expansion will provide a more comprehensive understanding of Stream-K's applicability and performance across various computational contexts.

The flexibility of our Bloom filter approach in Open-sieve is a key strength, allowing for easy modification to accommodate new problem sizes, policies, or tuning parameters. New key-value entries corresponding to additional GEMM problem sizes can be swiftly integrated into the Bloom filters. Moreover, new policies or tuning parameters can be incorporated through the creation of new Bloom filters. This extensibility positions Stream-K++ as a versatile framework for ongoing GEMM optimization research, adaptable to evolving hardware landscapes and computational demands.

6 Conclusion

Stream-K++ represents a significant advancement in GPU-based matrix multiplication optimizations for domains including AI. By expanding Stream-K policies and introducing an efficient Bloom filter-based selection mechanism, we have enhanced the practicality and performance of Stream-K across diverse GEMM operations. Our results demonstrate that while Stream-K configurations may not outperform traditional approaches in most cases, they offer substantial gains in specific scenarios and maintain competitive performance overall.

The asymmetric performance distribution of Stream-K schedules reveals their potential for exceptional optimization in certain cases, justifying their inclusion in GEMM frameworks despite less frequent occurrences as globally optimal solutions. This research not only improves immediate GEMM performance but also establishes a flexible foundation for future optimizations, particularly as GPU architectures continue to evolve.

The insights gained from this study highlight the importance of nuanced, adaptive approaches to GEMM optimization that can identify and exploit high-impact scenarios. As we continue to refine these techniques, the potential for significant performance enhancements in critical computational tasks across AI, scientific computing, and beyond becomes increasingly apparent.

References

1. ck. https://github.com/ROCm/composable_kernel
2. cublas. https://docs.nvidia.com/cuda/cublas/
3. Cutlass. https://github.com/NVIDIA/cutlass
4. Efficient gemm in cuda. https://github.com/NVIDIA/cutlass/blob/main/media/docs/efficient_gemm.md
5. Nvidia tensorrt. https://docs.nvidia.com/deeplearning/tensorrt/developer-guide/index.html
6. Python implementation of murmur hash. https://github.com/hajimes/mmh3
7. rocblas. https://github.com/ROCm/rocBLAS
8. Aminabadi, R.Y., et al.: Deepspeed-inference: enabling efficient inference of transformer models at unprecedented scale. In: SC22: International Conference for High Performance Computing, Networking, Storage and Analysis, pp. 1–15. IEEE (2022)
9. Barrachina, S., Castillo, M., Igual, F.D., Mayo, R., Quintana-Orti, E.S.: Evaluation and tuning of the level 3 cublas for graphics processors. In: 2008 IEEE International Symposium on Parallel and Distributed Processing, pp. 1–8. IEEE (2008)
10. Chen, T., et al.: TVM: end-to-end optimization stack for deep learning. arXiv preprint arXiv:1802.04799 **11**(2018), 20 (2018)
11. Cui, X., Chen, Y., Zhang, C., Mei, H.: Auto-tuning dense matrix multiplication for GPGPU with cache. In: 2010 IEEE 16th International Conference on Parallel and Distributed Systems, pp. 237–242. IEEE (2010)
12. Devlin, J., Chang, M.W., Lee, K., Toutanova, K.: Bert: pre-training of deep bidirectional transformers for language understanding. arXiv preprint arXiv:1810.04805 (2018)
13. Dongarra, J., et al.: Accelerating numerical dense linear algebra calculations with GPUs. In: Numerical Computations with GPUs, pp. 3–28 (2014)
14. Fuhrer, O., et al.: Near-global climate simulation at 1 km resolution: establishing a performance baseline on 4888 GPUs with COSMO 5.0. Geoscientific Model Develop. **11**(4), 1665–1681 (2018)
15. Gupta, U., et al.: The architectural implications of Facebook's DNN-based personalized recommendation. In: 2020 IEEE International Symposium on High Performance Computer Architecture (HPCA), pp. 488–501. IEEE (2020)
16. Hagedorn, B., Elliott, A.S., Barthels, H., Bodik, R., Grover, V.: Fireiron: A data-movement-aware scheduling language for GPUs. In: Proceedings of the ACM International Conference on Parallel Architectures and Compilation Techniques, pp. 71–82 (2020)
17. Jiang, C., Snir, M.: Automatic tuning matrix multiplication performance on graphics hardware. In: 14th International Conference on Parallel Architectures and Compilation Techniques (PACT'05), pp. 185–194. IEEE (2005)
18. Khan, J., et al.: Miopen: an open source library for deep learning primitives. arXiv preprint arXiv:1910.00078 (2019)
19. Kublik, S., Saboo, S.: GPT-3. O'Reilly Media, Inc. (2022)
20. Larsen, E.S., McAllister, D.: Fast matrix multiplies using graphics hardware. In: Proceedings of the 2001 ACM/IEEE Conference on Supercomputing, p. 55 (2001)
21. Li, Y., Dongarra, J., Tomov, S.: A Note on Auto-tuning GEMM for GPUs. In: Allen, G., Nabrzyski, J., Seidel, E., van Albada, G.D., Dongarra, J., Sloot, P.M.A. (eds.) ICCS 2009. LNCS, vol. 5544, pp. 884–892. Springer, Heidelberg (2009). https://doi.org/10.1007/978-3-642-01970-8_89

22. Nath, R., Tomov, S., Dongarra, J.: An improved magma GEMM for fermi graphics processing units. Int. J. High Perform. Comput. Appl. **24**(4), 511–515 (2010)
23. Osama, M., Merrill, D., Cecka, C., Garland, M., Owens, J.D.: Stream-k: work-centric parallel decomposition for dense matrix-matrix multiplication on the GPU. In: Proceedings of the 28th ACM SIGPLAN Annual Symposium on Principles and Practice of Parallel Programming, pp. 429–431 (2023)
24. Paszke, A., et al.: Pytorch: an imperative style, high-performance deep learning library. In: Advances in Neural Information Processing Systems, vol. 32 (2019)
25. Pharr, M., Jakob, W., Humphreys, G.: Physically Based Rendering: From Theory to Implementation. MIT Press (2023)
26. Ragan-Kelley, J., Barnes, C., Adams, A., Paris, S., Durand, F., Amarasinghe, S.: Halide: a language and compiler for optimizing parallelism, locality, and recomputation in image processing pipelines. ACM Sigplan Notices **48**(6), 519–530 (2013)
27. Tan, G., Li, L., Triechle, S., Phillips, E., Bao, Y., Sun, N.: Fast implementation of DGEMM on fermi GPU. In: Proceedings of 2011 International Conference for High Performance Computing, Networking, Storage and Analysis, pp. 1–11 (2011)
28. Tillet, P., Cox, D.: Input-aware auto-tuning of compute-bound HPC kernels. In: Proceedings of the International Conference for High Performance Computing, Networking, Storage and Analysis, pp. 1–12 (2017)
29. Tillet, P., Kung, H.T., Cox, D.: Triton: an intermediate language and compiler for tiled neural network computations. In: Proceedings of the 3rd ACM SIGPLAN International Workshop on Machine Learning and Programming Languages, pp. 10–19 (2019)
30. Van Loan, C.: Computational frameworks for the fast Fourier transform. SIAM (1992)
31. Vasilache, N., et al.: Tensor comprehensions: Framework-agnostic high-performance machine learning abstractions. arXiv preprint arXiv:1802.04730 (2018)
32. Vaswani, A., et al.: Attention is all you need. In: Advances in Neural Information Processing Systems, vol. 30 (2017)

Accelerating Electrostatics Simulations with GPUs

Amir Bouslama[1(✉)], Pratik Nayak[1], Andreas Blaszczyk[1,3], Carsten Trinitis[1], and Hartwig Anzt[1,2]

[1] Technical University of Munich, Munich, Germany
{amir.bouslama,pratik.nayak,andreas.blaszczyk,
carsten.trinitis,hartwig.anzt}@tum.de
[2] The Innovative Computing Laboratory, The University of Tennessee, Knoxville, USA
[3] Andreas Blaszczyk Consulting, Zurich, Switzerland

Abstract. Electrostatics simulations often employ Boundary Element Methods (BEM) that result in fully populated (dense) matrices. Direct solvers are typically used for solving of these dense linear systems. But iterative solvers can also be very effective when tunable accuracy is required. In this paper, we investigate to which extent offloading the iterative solver to a GPU accelerator can speed up the overall simulation. We use the `Ginkgo` library [5] as a solver backend for the Fortran-based `CASOPT` [17] simulations. We consider three production-relevant test cases and demonstrate the superiority of the GPU-accelerated `CASOPT` version.

Keywords: Electrostatics · Boundary Element Method · GPU · GMRES

1 Introduction

A popular method for simulating electrostatic fields is the Boundary Element Method (BEM) [8]. BEM is a mesh reduction technique used in solving boundary value problems by discretizing the structure's contour with piecewise functions. As a result of using the BEM formulation, the coefficient matrices are fully populated, unlike the FEM [15] discretizations that generally result in sparse matrices. The use of dense matrices in BEM corresponds to a reduction of the size of the problem, as only the outer space boundary points of the geometry are meshed. While compression techniques like hierarchical matrices [7] can reduce the computational and memory complexity of the dense matrices, they usually come at the cost of reduced accuracy with the consequences for a specific application typically unknown beforehand. For this reason, in particular when targeting safety-critical components, many BEM simulations forgo compression and instead assemble complete dense system matrices. Traditionally, the dense linear systems are solved with direct solvers like the LU factorization and subsequent triangular solves. However, for diagonal-dominant problems, a sufficiently accurate solution may be found significantly faster with a robust iterative solver. For example, a preconditioned GMRES [14] iterative solver can be an attractive alternative to the direct solver (LU + trsv) if it converges to the required accuracy in less iterations than the problem size. In an effort to make electrostatics simulations faster, aside from algorithmic considerations, the hardware architecture needs to be taken into account. In this paper, we consider the CASOPT simulation software [17], popular for electrostatics simulations. CASOPT is written in Fortran77, and porting the complete CASOPT software stack to GPUs is a major undertaking that exceeds the resources of this project. Instead, to answer the question of whether executing the numerical solver on a state-of-the-art GPU accelerator reduces the overall CASOPT simulation runtime, we leverage the Ginkgo high performance linear algebra library and interface Ginkgo's GMRES solver directly from the CASOPT Fortran code. We acknowledge that the workflow outsourcing only the linear solver to the GPU incurs significant overhead in terms of GPU memory allocation and data transfers, and we include these aspects in our analysis.

The remainder of this paper is structured as follows: In Sect. 2 we introduce the CASOPT and Ginkgo software stacks, and the workflow used to offload the linear solver to Ginkgo's GPU backend. In Sect. 3, we analyze the performance benefits rendered by the GPU acceleration considering GPUs from AMD and NVIDIA. For this analysis, we focus on three representative test cases in different discretizations. We conclude in Sect. 4 with a summary of the findings and an outlook for future research.

2 Background

2.1 CASOPT

CASOPT [17] or *Controlled Component and Assembly-Level Optimization of Industrial Devices* was developed since 2009 and was funded by the European Union.

CASOPT is a derivative of the POLOPT [3], a BEM solver for electrostatic calculations [4], in addition to being a complete framework for the electrical field simulation. CASOPT features a sequential version, and an MPI [11] based parallel version [6] that runs on multiple CPU cores or on a distributed cluster. It has been utilized as a reliable simulation framework for the electrostatic simulation on compute clusters in both industry and academia for many decades [1] [16] [12].

For solving the electrostatic simulation matrices, CASOPT uses its own integrated GMRES solver implementation [10] written in the same FORTRAN77 interface of the complete program and utilizes simple arrays for storing the matrix and other data of the solver. The parallel solver in CASOPT [6], parallelizes only the matrix-vector multiplication step of GMRES and uses a master-slave approach and a mandelbrot algorithm for distributing the computation over the multiple cores.

2.2 Ginkgo

Ginkgo [5] is a software library focusing on efficient solution of linear systems (sparse and dense) on many-core architectures. It supports multiple backends in hardware-native languages: CUDA for NVIDIA GPUs, HIP for AMD GPUs, and SYCL for Intel GPUs in [9]. With software sustainability as a core design principle, comprehensive unit tests and continuous integration (CI) ensure the robustness of solvers, preconditioners and of the various functionality implemented in Ginkgo. In addition to optimized backends for different accelerators, Ginkgo also supports distributed multi-node solvers and preconditioners using MPI. Ginkgo has been integrated with various applications such as MFEM [2], deal.ii, OpenFOAM [13], and is publicly available through a permissive BSD-3 license.

2.3 Portability with an ANSI C Interface

Many popular simulation codes use traditional languages and frameworks which can be challenging to directly interface with C++. Ginkgo therefore provides a ANSI C interface for its API, which is known to be interoperable with languages such as Fortran. This ensures that applications can benefit from the high-performance of Ginkgo's functionalities, with a relatively low code maintenance overhead.

CASOPT is one such Fortran library, which can take advantage of Ginkgo's C API wrapper. The C API wrapper of Ginkgo exposes the important functionality of Ginkgo including creation of Ginkgo objects (arrays, vectors, matrices etc.), and generation and application of solvers and preconditioners.

In addition to the availability of a wide range of solvers and preconditioners, the mixed-precision functionality of Ginkgo is also available through the C interface. Users can explicitly create objects in the required precision (single, double, half) and pass the data to Ginkgo through views, thereby incurring to no additional overhead.

2.4 Using Ginkgo Inside CASOPT

The complete electrostatic simulation consists of 3 main steps as shown in Fig. 1. Once the system matrix has been assembled within CASOPT, the matrices and the vectors (right hand side and solution) are transferred to the GPU. The data for these objects is then wrapped into a gko::array_view<> and passed to Ginkgo's solvers. This ensures that no additional copies are created by Ginkgo. After solving the system matrix, the solution is copied back to the host and CASOPT proceeds with the rest of the computation and reassembling the complete electrostatics output from the solution. Ginkgo therefore enables offloading of one of the most expensive parts of the simulation to a GPU device.

While CASOPT uses a preconditioned GMRES solver, a different solver and preconditioner can be used in the C interface. Using Ginkgo as the solver within CASOPT enables the selection of a solver from a wide range of solver algorithms and preconditioners.

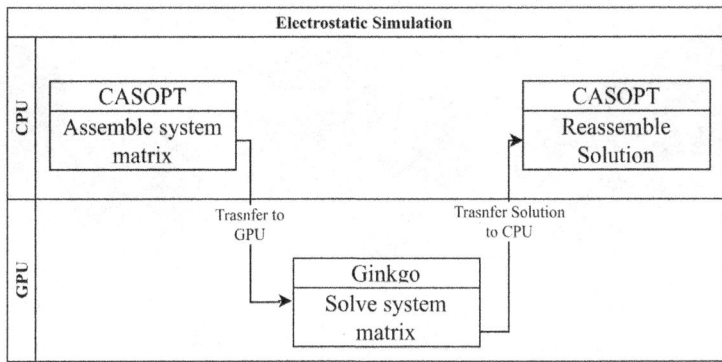

Fig. 1. Electrostatic Simulation Complete Flow

3 Experimental Results

Table 1. Hardware Specifications

Spec	CPU node	GPU-NVIDIA node	GPU-AMD node
CPU	2 AMD EPYC Milan 7713	2 Intel Xeon Gold 6548N	2 Intel Xeon Gold 6438Y
Num cores	2 × 64	2 × 32	2 × 32
GPU	-	4 NVIDIA H100 NVL (96 GB)	2 AMD MI210 (64 GB)
Main memory	512 GB	2 TB	256 GB

We now evaluate the effectiveness of using the Ginkgo library for the numerical computations within CASOPT simulations, and consider both solver runtime, and the auxiliary runtime (Initialization, memory allocation, memory transfer, etc.)

Table 1 shows the hardware configuration of the two nodes we use for our study. The CASOPT simulations are run on the CPU node consisting of 2 AMD EPYC CPUs with 64 cores each, while the simulations with the solver offloaded to the GPU (with Ginkgo) is run on the GPU node consisting of NVIDIA H100 GPU.

System matrices in CASOPT are assembled in IEEE single precision and all computations of the linear solver use IEEE single precision. We aim to solve to a relative residual goal of 1e-06 as deemed satisfactory for the electrostatic computation in CASOPT. We ensure that both Ginkgo and CASOPT solve the same problem by comparing the element wise residual of the electrostatic potential after the completion of the simulation.

3.1 Test Cases

We consider three applications, representative of CASOPT benchmark models. The applications are visualized in Fig. 2, the corresponding numerical solutions (the

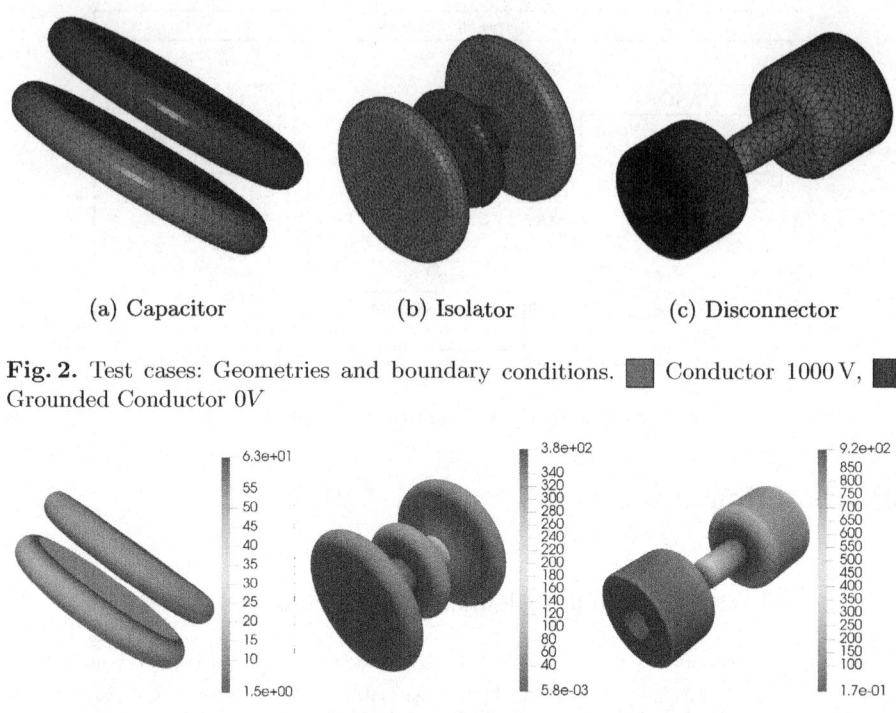

Fig. 2. Test cases: Geometries and boundary conditions. ■ Conductor 1000 V, ■ Grounded Conductor 0V

Fig. 3. Test cases: Solution visualization (Electrostatic Field Magnitude).

electrostatic field magnitude) in Fig. 3. The "Capacitor" application represents a capacitor with a layer of air between a grounded and a high voltage disk electrodes. The "Isolator" application includes similarly to "Capacitor" two disk electrodes both with applied 1000 V potential and a grounded electrode inserted between them. The Disconnector is a simplified representation of a medium voltage disconnector. We consider these test cases in different discretizations, listed along with some key properties in Table 2. Additionally, as the matrices are dense, even a moderate matrix with size 60,000 rows takes approximately 14 GB of memory for storage. For single node GPU tests on the NVIDIA H100 GPU with 96 GB GPU memory, a problem size can not exceed 155,000.

3.2 Iterative Solver Performance

For both CASOPT and Ginkgo, we first compare the GMRES Krylov solver. Though we don't show the visualizations, we ensure that an accuracy sufficient for engineering purposes has been achieved for all tested mesh variants with GMRES. Figure 4 shows the runtime of the CASOPT and Ginkgo GMRES for different discretizations of the Capacitor (top), Isolator (middle), and Disconnector (bottom) problems, respectively. For all test problems and dis-

Table 2. Key characteristics of test problems along with the memory volume that needs to be transferred. The matrix and the vectors are handled in IEEE single precision.

Problem	Matrix Size num_rows	Memory size [GB]	Condition est.
Capacitor (a)	3,318	4.30e−02	2.60e+02
Capacitor (b)	7,272	2.02e−01	3.69e+02
Capacitor (c)	16,827	1.10e+01	3.69e+02
Capacitor (d)	33,363	4.20e+00	8.44e+02
Capacitor (e)	53,586	1.10e+01	1.04e+03
Isolator (a)	4,239	6.90e−02	2.79e+02
Isolator (b)	14,014	7.50e−01	4.93e+02
Isolator (c)	147,702	8.20e+01	-
Disconnector (a)	15,165	8.78e−01	1.72e+03
Disconnector (b)	19,820	1.50e+00	1.19e+03
Disconnector (c)	26,639	2.70e+00	1.02e+03
Disconnector (d)	42,982	6.90e+00	9.48e+02
Disconnector (e)	87,001	2.90e+01	1.06e+03
Disconnector (f)	152,016	8.70e+01	-

cretization sizes, Ginkgo outperforms CASOPT, for some cases by more than an order of magnitude. Ginkgo also performs better for larger problem sizes, as the overhead of offloading the solver kernel can be better amortized for larger problem sizes.

In Fig. 5, in addition to the solve time, we consider the auxiliary runtimes: namely, memory allocation and data transfers. Within CASOPT, after assembling the matrix, the necessary memory is allocated and the matrix and the vectors are copied to the GPU. After the solution is computed with Ginkgo, we copy the solution back to the CPU and pass it to CASOPT. We analyze the three problem classes separately as they differ in their numerical properties. First, we notice that the GPU memory allocation and initialization overheads are constant, independent of the specific problem characteristics. This overhead of about 0.3 seconds is a one-time cost we pay for the first GPU solver invocation. This allocation overhead could be eliminated in case more than one solver run is needed. The data transfer to the GPU is dominated by the cost of transferring the dense system matrix; the memory size of the distinct test problems is listed in Table 2. The data transfer time is quadratically dependent on the problem size, and linearly dependent on the memory size. For the larger test cases, Ginkgo GMRES solver runtime is only a fraction of the data transfer time. From Fig. 5, we see that even after including the memory allocation and the data transfers times, the GPU-based Ginkgo solver is faster than the CASOPT GMRES for problems of size larger than 5,000 elements.

Finally, we analyze the overall performance improvement of the workflow using the GPU-based Ginkgo GMRES solver over the standard workflow using

Capacitor

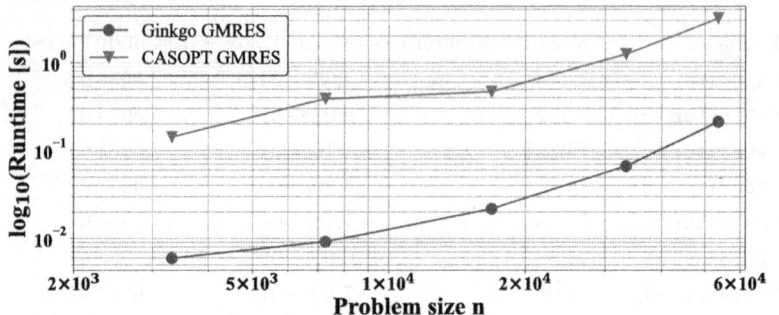

Isolator

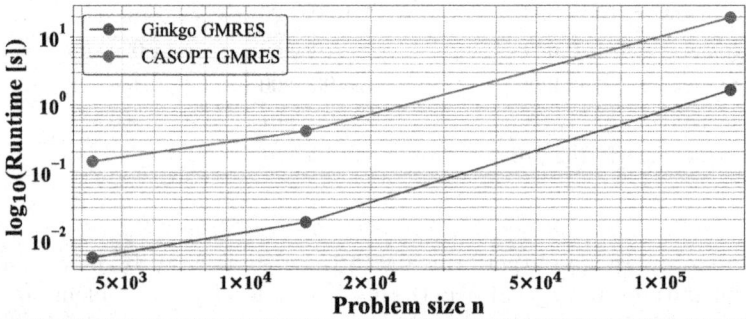

Disconnector

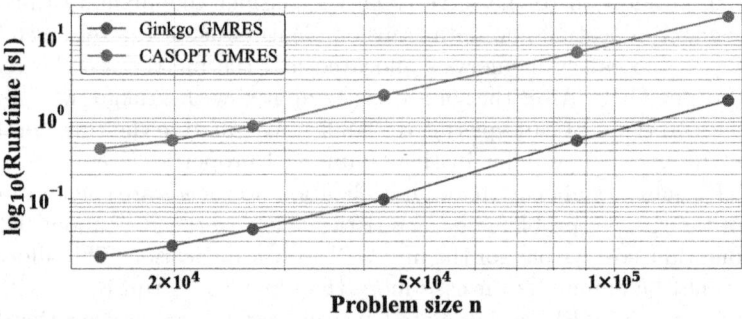

Fig. 4. Runtime of the GMRES iterative solver for different discretizations of the Capacitor, Isolator, and Disconnector problems.

the CASOPT-internal GMRES solver. In Fig. 6, we relate the speedup to the problem size. For all three use cases, we visualize the speedup trajectories for multiple applications increasing problem size. The dashed lines show the speedup of only the linear solver component, while the solid lines show the speedup with the memory transfer and GPU memory allocation included. For the solid lines, the speedup values are larger than one – which reflects the GPU-accelerated version being faster – for all problem sizes larger than 5,000. The dashed lines reflect the speedup of the solver and are more representative of a scenario where the complete CASOPT simulation is ported to the GPU or an architecture that combines CPU and GPU in one device.

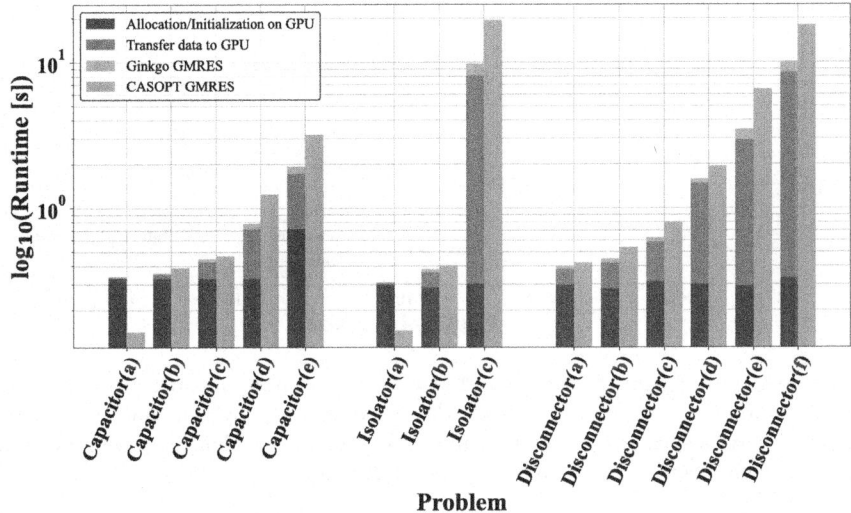

Fig. 5. Runtime Comparison between CASOPT and Ginkgo for the three test cases. Smaller problems have a larger overhead of data allocation and transfer to the GPU, but these are amortized for larger problems and using Ginkgo is faster for larger models, for all three test cases.

3.3 Convergence of GMRES on the GPU

We are interested whether offloading the solver to the GPU through Ginkgo affects the convergence of the GMRES algorithm. The number of iterations taken for GMRES between CASOPT and Ginkgo to achieve a satisfactory relative residual 1e-06 for each of the test cases is shown in Table 3. We observe that in most examples there is no difference in the number of iterations between both GMRES implementation and certain discretizations of the Disconnector test case show at most 2 iterations of difference. For the test cases, offloading the solver to the GPU and using Ginkgo kernels for GMRES does not have any significant effect on the convergence of GMRES and any numerical differences result in at most 1 or 2 iterations of difference between the GMRES implementation in CASOPT and that of Ginkgo

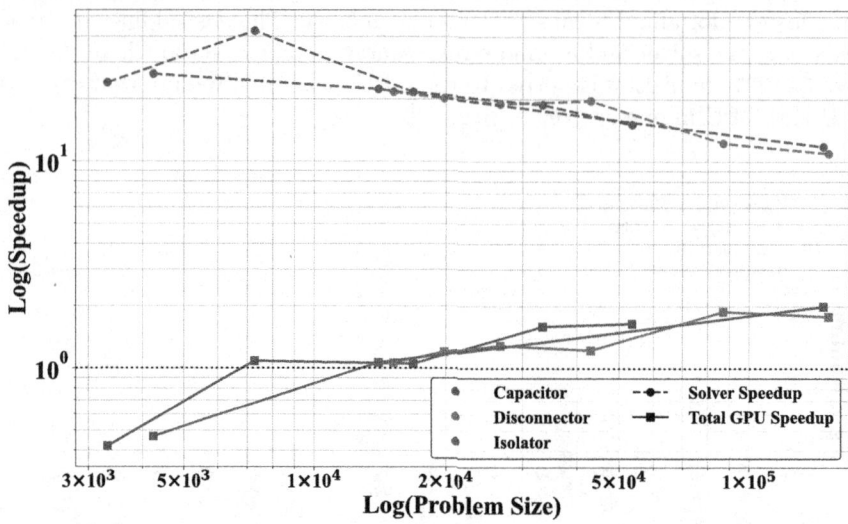

Fig. 6. Speedup of `Ginkgo` over `CASOPT`. Dashed lines show the speedup of only the solver component. The solid line shows the speedup of the overall simulation. Using `Ginkgo` we have a speedup of over 1 for medium and large problem sizes, while we have the solver component being always faster with `Ginkgo`.

Table 3. Comparison of GMRES number of iteration between `CASOPT` and `Ginkgo` for a given relative residual goal of 1e-06.

Problem	Ginkgo GMRES iterations	CASOPT GMRES iterations
Capacitor (a)	30	30
Capacitor (b)	33	33
Capacitor (c)	38	38
Capacitor (d)	42	42
Capacitor (e)	45	45
Isolator (a)	26	26
Isolator (b)	38	38
Isolator (c)	55	55
Disconnector (a)	37	35
Disconnector (b)	37	36
Disconnector (c)	39	38
Disconnector (d)	40	40
Disconnector (e)	45	45
Disconnector (f)	49	49

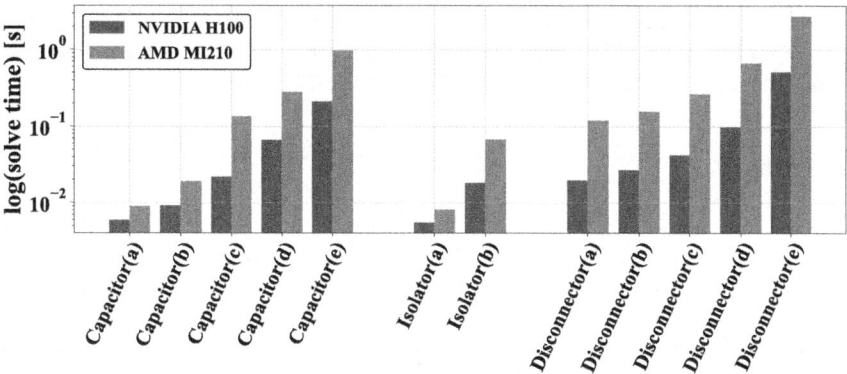

Fig. 7. Comparison of solve times on an NVIDIA H100 GPU and an AMD MI210 GPU. The AMD GPU, being an older generation of GPU is slower than the NVIDIA GPU, but both the GPUs perform better than the CASOPT multi-core CPU.

3.4 Portability to Other GPU Architectures

Ginkgo aims for performance portability and provides a uniform interface with the ability to run on different GPU architectures with minimal code changes. In Fig. 7, we showcase the runs of the solver on an AMD GPU, MI210. While the NVIDIA H100 performs better in this case, the AMD GPU remains competitive, given that it is an older generation of GPU with a performance of 45.3 FP32 TFLOPS against the H100's 60 FP32 TFLOPs. Additionally, the solution offloaded to either of the GPUs is faster than the multi-core CPU solution with CASOPT.

4 Conclusion

In this paper, we investigated the potential of outsourcing the linear solver of the Fortran-based electrostatics simulation framework CASOPT to GPU accelerators. We interface the Ginkgo high performance math library for three representative applications to handle the linear solve on server-grade GPUs from AMD and NVIDIA. The results demonstrate that for large problems, the introduced overheads stemming from GPU initialization, memory allocation and data transfers are easily compensated by faster solver execution. With hardware architectures increasingly designing CPUs and GPUs as unified devices, the cost of data movement is expected to be reduced, increasing the performance advantages of GPU acceleration. A key observation from this study is that porting the complete CASOPT simulation to GPUs, in particular the matrix assembly, is expected to bring significant performance advantages over the current state-of-the-art. Additionally, interfacing legacy Fortran codes with modern C++ codes can be performed with a relatively low cost, enabling Fortran codes to take advantage of newer hardware architectures.

Disclosure of Interests. Hartwig Anzt is a member of the steering committee of the HPC on Heterogeneous Hardware workshop. The other authors have no competing interests to declare that are relevant to the content of this article.

References

1. Amann, D., Blaszczyk, A., Of, G., Steinbach, O.: Simulation of floating potentials in industrial applications by boundary element methods. J. Math. Ind. **4**(1), 13 (2014). https://doi.org/10.1186/2190-5983-4-13, https://mathematicsinindustry.springeropen.com/articles/10.1186/2190-5983-4-13
2. Anderson, R.W., et al.: MFEM: a modular finite element methods library. Comput. Math. Appl. **81**, 42–74 (2021). https://doi.org/10.1016/j.camwa.2020.06.009
3. Andjelic, Z.: A contribution to the BEM for calculation and optimization of 3D electrostatic fields. Ph.D. thesis, Faculty of Electrical Engineering, University of Zagreb (1984)
4. Andjelic, Z., Krstajic, B., Milojkovic, S., Blaszczyk, A., Steinbigler, H., Wohlmuth, M.: Integral Methods for the Calculation of Electric Fields: For Application in High Voltage Engineering, Scientific Series of the International Bureau, vol. 10. Forschungszentrum Jülich GmbH, Jülich, Germany (1992)
5. Anzt, H., et al.: Ginkgo: a modern linear operator algebra framework for high performance computing. ACM Trans. Math. Softw. (TOMS) **48**(1), 1–33 (2022)
6. Blaszczyk, A., Andjelic, Z., Levin, P., Ustundag, A.: Parallel computation of electric fields in a heterogeneous workstation cluster. In: Hertzberger, B., Serazzi, G. (eds.) HPCN-Europe 1995. LNCS, vol. 919, pp. 606–611. Springer, Heidelberg (1995). https://doi.org/10.1007/BFb0046688
7. Börm, S., Grasedyck, L., Hackbusch, W.: Introduction to hierarchical matrices with applications. Eng. Anal. Boundary Elem. **27**(5), 405–422 (2003). https://doi.org/10.1016/S0955-7997(02)00152-2, https://people.math.ethz.ch/~hiptmair/Seminars/HMAT/Papers/BGH03.pdf
8. Brebbia, C.A., Telles, J.C.F., Wrobel, L.C.: Boundary Element Techniques: Theory and Applications in Engineering. Springer, Heidelberg (1984). https://doi.org/10.1007/978-3-642-48860-3
9. Cojean, T., Tsai, Y.H.M., Anzt, H.: Ginkgo—a math library designed for platform portability. Parallel Comput. **111**, 102902 (2022)
10. Levin, D., Meroth, P.L., Spasojevic, A., Michalson, W.R., Ustundag, A.: Iterative matrix solvers for large full systems. In: Eighth International Symposium on High Voltage Engineering, vol. 23, p. 27 (1993)
11. Message Passing Interface Forum: MPI: A Message-Passing Interface Standard, Version 3.1. Technical report, University of Tennessee (2015). https://www.mpi-forum.org/docs/mpi-3.1/mpi31-report.pdf
12. Münger, C.: Dielectric Breakdown Prediction with GPU-Accelerated BEM. Master's thesis, Department of Mathematics, ETH Zürich (2020)
13. OpenFOAM Foundation: OpenFOAM: The Open Source CFD Toolbox. OpenFOAM Foundation Ltd. (2023). https://openfoam.org, Version 11
14. Saad, Y., Schultz, M.H.: Gmres: a generalized minimal residual algorithm for solving nonsymmetric linear systems. SIAM J. Sci. Stat. Comput. **7**(3), 856–869 (1986)
15. Strang, G., Fix, G.J.: An Analysis of the Finite Element Method. Prentice-Hall, Englewood Cliffs (1973)

16. Szary, D., Blaszczyk, A., Ostrowski, J., Samul, B.: Dielectric and thermal design of power devices - simulation toolbox. ABB Rev. **3**, 16–21 (2013)
17. Trinitis, C.: The EU fp7 IAPP project casopt. In: Proceedings of the Conference. IEEE, Luton, United Kingdom/Munich, Germany (2012). https://doi.org/10.1109/XYZ.2012.123456, http://www.casopt.com/

International Workshop on RISC-V for HPC at ISC

RISK-V for HPC 2025 Preface

Objectives/Topics

RISC-V is an open standard Instruction Set Architecture (ISA) which enables the open development of CPUs and a shared common software ecosystem. There are already over 16 billion RISC-V cores, which is expected to accelerate rapidly as we progress further into the decade. Nonetheless, for all the successes that RISC-V has achieved, it is yet to become popular in HPC. Recent advances however, such as the vectorisation standard and HPC/AI-focused RISC-V-based CPUs, mean that this technology is becoming a more realistic proposition for our workloads.

This workshop connects those currently involved in RISC-V with the wider HPC community.

We bring together RISC-V experts with scientific software developers, vendors, and supercomputing center operators to explore the advantages, challenges, and opportunities that RISC-V can bring to HPC and AI.

Furthermore, we further expand the RISC-V HPC SIG, enabling interested attendees to participate in one of the most exciting open-source technological activities of our time.

Workshop Organization

Nick Brown	EPCC, UK
Teresa Cervero	Barcelona Supercomputing Center, Spain
Daniele Gregori	E4 Computer Engineering, Italy
David Donofrio	Tactical Computing Laboratories, USA
Matt Turner	Samsung, USA

Streamlining Fedora Linux Distributions for RISC-V: A Scalable and Automated Approach

Surendra Billa, Arif Badar, Rushikesh Jadhav, Yogeshwar Sonawane[✉],
and Sanjay Wandhekar

Centre for Development of Advanced Computing, Pune 411008, India
yogeshwars@cdac.in

Abstract. The RISC-V architecture, renowned for its open-source foundation and extensibility, drives innovation in custom processor development across diverse applications. However, this flexibility results in hardware straying from the standard. Bootstrapping tailored Linux distributions for specific RISC-V profiles that deviate from mandated standardized extensions is challenging [3]. This is particularly evident in embedded devices and proprietary server applications.

The issue is compounded by the absence of robust package management systems, making toolchain management and dependency resolution more complex. This paper highlights the limitations of existing approaches, such as Linux From Scratch (LFS), Buildroot and The Yocto Project. While these frameworks enable developing Linux distributions for unique RISC-V hardware configurations, their reliance on manual processes makes it time-consuming, difficult to maintain and scale poorly [1,4,5].

To address these challenges, we propose a novel methodology tailored to the RV64G extension set, subset of RISC-V RVI profile. The approach begins by leveraging existing RISC-V images and adapting core toolchains to meet target-specific requirements. It incorporates the Koji build system to facilitate systematic package rebuilding and dependency management. Furthermore, a Python-based automation tool is introduced to minimize manual intervention and streamline workflows [6].

This strategy reduces development effort, enhances organization, and enables scalable customization. It bridges software gaps, empowering developers to create tailored Linux distributions for specialized computing, fostering broader adoption in academia and industry.

Keywords: RISC-V (RV64G) Architecture · Fedora Linux Distribution · Dependency Resolution · Koji Build System

1 Introduction

RISC-V, an open-source instruction set architecture (ISA), transforms processor design by enabling flexible, versatile solutions. Unlike proprietary ISAs, it removes innovation barriers, allowing developers to tailor systems for diverse applications, from resource-limited embedded devices to high-performance computing servers. Its open ecosystem boosts cost efficiency and accelerates hardware/software advancements. One of RISC-V's key strengths is its modular design, which allows for the selective incorporation of standard extensions to meet application-specific requirements. This versatility aids in minimizing complexity, optimizing performance and aligning resource utilization with the unique demands of applications [2]. However, the rapid adoption of RISC-V has revealed significant gaps in software support, particularly for Linux distributions designed to cater to subsets of the RISC-V standard extensions.

1.1 Gaps in Linux Distribution Support for RISC-V

In the current landscape, major distributions including Debian, Ubuntu and Fedora, are designed for general-purpose RISC-V system [11–13]. Consequently, custom hardware solutions often receive limited attention, highlighting the need for dedicated software support. Developing Linux distributions for such bespoke hardware is a complex and resource-intensive task, with traditional methodologies, such as Linux From Scratch (LFS), offering limited scalability and maintainability [14]. Furthermore, distributions developed by OEMs (Original Equipment Manufacturers) frequently lead to vendor lock-in, constraining flexibility and innovation for independent developers and smaller players.

For smaller organizations, academic institutions and researchers, implementing a personalized RISC-V design may provide a practical way to balance performance and cost constraints. These solutions enable reduced die size, lower power consumption and simplified design, consistent with the aims of restricted budgets or application requirements. However, the lack of readily available Linux distributions optimized for these designs limits their adoption and usability.

1.2 Limitations of Custom Build Systems Compared to Standard Distributions

Distributions built with the likes of Buildroot and Yocto project, overcome the manual build processes of LFS by providing a framework [4,5]. However, these cater to specific hardware configurations and this can lead to challenges in binary compatibility between applications. This contrasts with standard distributions like Debian or Fedora, which ensure broader ABI compatibility within the same architecture.

1.3 Proposed Approach

This research proposes a comprehensive methodology to develop a Fedora-based Linux distribution adapted to the RV64G architecture. The approach focuses on:

– Patching Toolchains: Adapting essential tools, including GCC, Binutils and Rust, for RV64G-specific requirements.

– Systematic Builds: Leveraging the Koji build system and a Python-based application to automate the package rebuilding process, streamlining it and improving efficiency.
 – Maintaining Compatibility: Ensuring compatibility and maintainability through a localized repository and structured build pipelines.

2 Related Work

The adoption of RISC-V as an open-source instruction set architecture (ISA) has accelerated Linux distribution development for its ecosystem. While mainstream distributions like Alma Linux, Fedora and Ubuntu support RISC-V, they focus on widely adopted configurations like RV64GC [11,13]. This often overlooks specialized hardware needing customized software. The lack of prebuilt packages for variants like RV64G challenges developers, requiring cross-compilation, package rebuilding and build automation. Addressing these challenges is crucial for broader adoption and performance efficiency across diverse RISC-V hardware.

The Fedora-V Force team plays a pivotal role in the Fedora/RISC-V initiative by upstreaming patches, porting essential components and maintaining a robust compilation system tailored for RISC-V hardware. This team, led by RISC-V ambassador Wei Fu, ensures compatibility across various Fedora releases while leveraging the Koji build system to automate package builds and repository management [7]. Complementing these efforts, the RISC-V Special Interest Group (SIG) maintains key packages, creates bootable images and addresses upstream integration challenges [9].

In our previous work [1], we detailed the development of a Fedora Linux distribution for the RV64G architecture using a Linux From Scratch (LFS) methodology. This approach involved manually compiling essential packages and their dependencies to construct a minimal, bootable system. While effective, this iterative process was highly labor-intensive, requiring extensive time and effort to establish a working build infrastructure with tools like Mock and Koji. Once operational, the Koji build system improved package rebuilding and repository management, but the sequential nature of package builds still posed scalability challenges.

In this paper, we address these challenges by introducing an alternative to the LFS approach, leveraging automated RPM-based builds for large-scale package rebuilding on the RV64G architecture. This alternative significantly enhances efficiency and minimizes the manual effort of Fedora's build system for RISC-V.

3 Implementation

Developing a Fedora Linux distribution for RISC-V (RV64G) required a structured methodology to ensure optimization and flexibility. Initially, we followed the Linux From Scratch (LFS) approach to manually build the distribution, gaining insights into the bootstrapping process. However, this approach was time-consuming and challenging for large-scale deployment [1].

To accelerate development, we utilized existing Fedora RISC-V (RV64GC) images [10], modifying toolchain source RPMs with architecture-specific patches and rebuilding them for RV64G. This adaptation enabled seamless integration into Fedora's ecosystem while supporting the new architecture. For package management, we incorporated Koji, Fedora's tag-based build system [6], where builders prioritized locally compiled toolchain binaries and sourced additional dependencies from Fedora Rocks to ensure compatibility with RV64G.

A significant improvement was the development of a Python-based automation tool that reduced manual intervention in large-scale RPM rebuilding. By integrating with Koji, this tool streamlined package compilation and enhanced workflow efficiency.

While our earlier research examined Koji's RPM build automation at a broader level [1], this work provides a detailed implementation of the Python-based automation library. The following sections describe each stage of our process, illustrating how these enhancements created a more streamlined and structured development framework.

3.1 Patching Toolchains

Step 1: Patching GCC and Initial Toolchain Build. The GNU toolchain consists of three primary components: GCC, Binutils and Glibc. These components are interdependent, with GCC required to compile all three.

Patching GCC: We modified GCC's spec file to target RV64G as the default architecture using the -with-arch=rv64g option.

Re-building Binutils: We subsequently patched binutils, the package responsible for providing the GNU assembler and linker, as well as other vital binary utilities like objdump. Harnessing the previously patched GCC, we proceeded to rebuild binutils.

Glibc: Glibc supplies the GNU C standard library, which serves as an interface to the kernel. Although libc is a shared library linked at runtime, the glibc package also provides other crucial relocatable object files, including the entry point and C runtime.

Step 2: Pedantic Rebuilds. We conducted a second comprehensive rebuild of the toolchain to ensure that gcc and binutils now accurately incorporate the amended relocatable objects from glibc. This eliminated residual compressed instructions and ensured compatibility with RV64G.

The image in Fig. 1 compares the disassembly of an application binary built with the default GNU toolchain versus the patched one. Initially, the application was compiled using rpmbuild with the default toolchain. After updating to the patched toolchain, the RPM was rebuilt and the disassembly was examined using objdump. The binary compiled with the RV64GC toolchain includes 16-bit compressed instructions, evident from instructions at 2-byte length prefixed with c.

Disassembly of Application Banner

Default GNU toolchain(rv64gc)	Patched GNU toolchain(rv64g)
Disassembly of section .text:	Disassembly of section .text:
0000000000004130 <main@@Base>:	0000000000004130 <main@@Base>:
4130: 7115 c.addi16sp sp,-224	4130: f2010113 addi sp,sp,-224
4132: e9a2 c.sdsp s0,208(sp)	4134: 0c813823 sd s0,208(sp)
4134: e1ca c.sdsp s2,192(sp)	4138: 0d213023 sd s2,192(sp)
4136: 1180 c.addi4spn s0,sp,224	413c: 0e010413 addi s0,sp,224
4138: ed86 c.sdsp ra,216(sp)	4140: 0c113c23 sd ra,216(sp)
413a: e5a6 c.sdsp s1,200(sp)	4144: 0c913423 sd s1,200(sp)
413c: fd4e c.sdsp s3,184(sp)	4148: 0b313c23 sd s3,184(sp)
413e: f952 c.sdsp s4,176(sp)	414c: 0b413823 sd s4,176(sp)
4140: f556 c.sdsp s5,168(sp)	4150: 0b513423 sd s5,168(sp)
4142: f15a c.sdsp s6,160(sp)	4154: 0b613023 sd s6,160(sp)
4144: ed5e c.sdsp s7,152(sp)	4158: 09713c23 sd s7,152(sp)
4146: e962 c.sdsp s8,144(sp)	415c: 09813823 sd s8,144(sp)

Fig. 1. Disassembled Binary Comparison: RV64GC vs. Patched RV64G Toolchain.

3.2 Setting Up the Koji Build System

Deploying Koji Infrastructure: To facilitate RPM package compilation for the RV64G architecture, we implemented the Koji build system, utilizing its hierarchical, tag-based package management framework. This structured methodology enhanced the efficiency of large-scale package rebuilding and repository maintenance. Koji's design is centered around six fundamental components, each integral to coordinating the build environment, managing dependencies and ensuring seamless package deployment [6]. The image in Fig. 2 illustrates how the various Koji components are connected and interact with each other.

Koji Deployment Steps

Infrastructure Installation: We deployed the Fedora RISC-V Rocks image on QEMU and installed the Koji builder daemon (kojid).

Authentication Configuration: We utilized SSL certificate-based authentication, generating our own Certificate Authority (CA) key and signing certificates for users and builders to securely communicate with the hub.

3.3 Tag Creation and Repository Management

In the Koji build system [6], a tag is a collection of packages with metadata such as target architecture and repositories. Tags also feature inheritance. A target

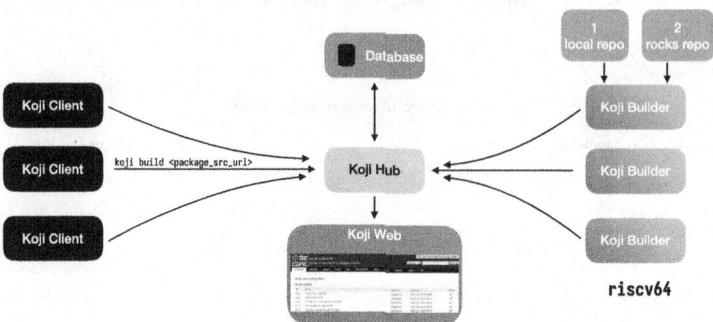

Fig. 2. Koji infrastructure

is a pair of tags the build tag and destination tag. It specifies where a package should be built and how it should be tagged afterward, allowing target names to remain consistent as tags change through releases. We created tags and targets for Fedora release version 38:

- Patched GNU toolchain packages (GCC, Binutils and Glibc) were imported into Koji and tagged. Subsequently, a local repository was created containing these packages.
- The Fedora Rocks repository was added to aid in resolving dependency packages, prioritizing the local repository to ensure the patched toolchains were used first during dependency resolution phase.
- This setup enabled systematic package rebuilding personalized for the RV64G architecture.

3.4 Deployment of Source Code Management (SCM) Server

The RPM package is composed of two components - the source-code archive and the spec file, the blueprint detailing package build. The source tarball is fetched from a lookaside-cache, while spec file is maintained on dist-git server, alongside other downstream and backport patches. This enables organization and control over the package builds. The image in Fig. 3 illustrates this architecture.

To manage patches for the package source tree and spec files, we deployed an SCM server using Forgejo, an open-source git server. Applying RV64G-specific patches ensured efficient version control and tracking. Builders were configured to fetch source files from this server. The image in Fig. 4 shows a diff view of applied patch to spec file, modifying the default target architecture for gcc.

3.5 Automating Package Builds

To simplify the package build process and minimize the need for manual intervention, we automated package builds. This increased efficiency, maximized resource

Dist-git server
Remote Git Server
Lookaside Cache
Spec file
Source Tarball

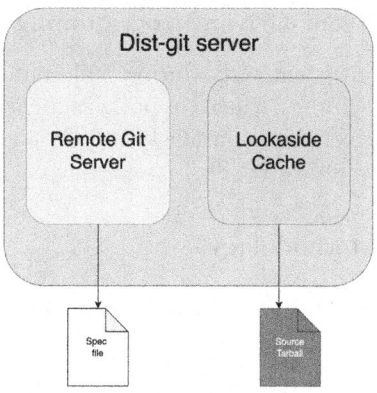

Fig. 3. dist-git architecture

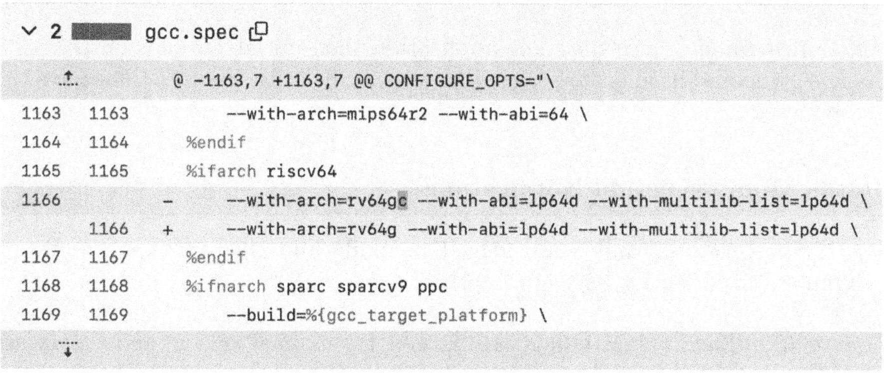

2 gcc.spec
@ -1163,7 +1163,7 @@ CONFIGURE_OPTS="\
1163 1163 --with-arch=mips64r2 --with-abi=64 \
1164 1164 %endif
1165 1165 %ifarch riscv64
1166 - --with-arch=rv64gc --with-abi=lp64d --with-multilib-list=lp64d \
1166 + --with-arch=rv64g --with-abi=lp64d --with-multilib-list=lp64d \
1167 1167 %endif
1168 1168 %ifnarch sparc sparcv9 ppc
1169 1169 --build=%{gcc_target_platform} \

Fig. 4. gcc git diff with applied patch

utilization and improved build management. While our previous research paper provided an overview of this process, the current paper presents a detailed implementation of the complete automation workflow [1].

Parallel Builds. Building packages is IO-bound and can take an indeterminate amount of time, varying with each package. However, waiting for successive builds to complete is inefficient when multiple builders are available. Koji can queue multiple builds simultaneously; however, monitoring build status remains crucial. Thread pools can manage and observe build tasks; however, waking and polling threads introduce overhead in such a setting. Furthermore, Python's GIL (Global Interpreter Lock) only allows one thread to execute code at a time.

3.6 Asynchronous Event-Driven Programming

To efficiently manage concurrent tasks during build automation, the application utilizes Python's asyncio library, which supports asynchronous, event-driven programming. This approach enables non-blocking I/O operations by using an event loop to schedule and execute tasks [8].

Build Management Methodology

Package Queue Creation: A list of packages is maintained in a text file. The application would fetch and queue tasks based on available builder resources.

Metadata Retrieval: Using Koji's Python APIs, the application queries Fedora's upstream Koji instance to retrieve the latest SCM URL and git commit for each package.

Automated Build Triggering: The application then initiates builds on the local instance. Successful builds are tagged under specified tag. Figure 5 illustrates the detailed workflow.

Status Monitoring and Notifications

Real-Time Updates: Builds are logged to a file and the status is monitored continuously to identify issues promptly.

Failure Handling: Failed builds are flagged for manual review and errors are logged for troubleshooting.

Email Notifications: Emails notifications that include the build logs and URLs, enable administrators to diagnose issues efficiently. Figure 6 shows email displaying the build status of packages.

Enhancements. Future enhancements include dynamic dependency resolution, integration with CI/CD pipelines and advanced notification mechanisms like dashboards and graphical reports.

This implementation successfully engineered a Fedora-based Linux distribution for RV64G. By leveraging Koji, automating RPM builds, and deploying a robust SCM server, we addressed inefficiencies, improved adaptability, and advanced RISC-V support within the Linux ecosystem.

4 Results and Testing

A comprehensive testing strategy was implemented to validate the efficiency, scalability and compatibility of the Fedora-based Linux distribution for RV64G. The evaluation focused on four key aspects:

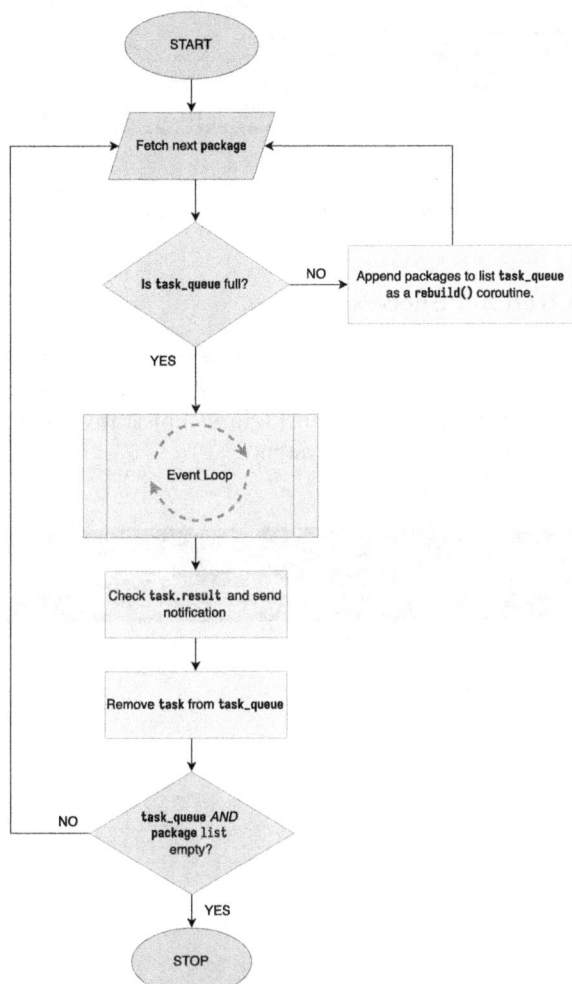

Fig. 5. Workflow for package queuing, metadata retrieval, and automated builds via Koji.

4.1 Toolchain Robustness

The robustness of the RV64G native GCC compiler was assessed by compiling and rebuilding multiple software packages, followed by execution on RV64G hardware. The compatibility of these compiled binaries with the GNU toolchain was verified, ensuring seamless interoperability with existing RV64GC binaries, as both conform to the LP64D ABI standard.

Fig. 6. Email notifications showing the build status of a package

4.2 Package Rebuild Success Rates

Core system components, development libraries and essential user-space applications were rebuilt. The strong success rates and rigorous testing established a stable and resilient software ecosystem. Figure 7 illustrates the rebuild status of packages in our personal Koji build system.

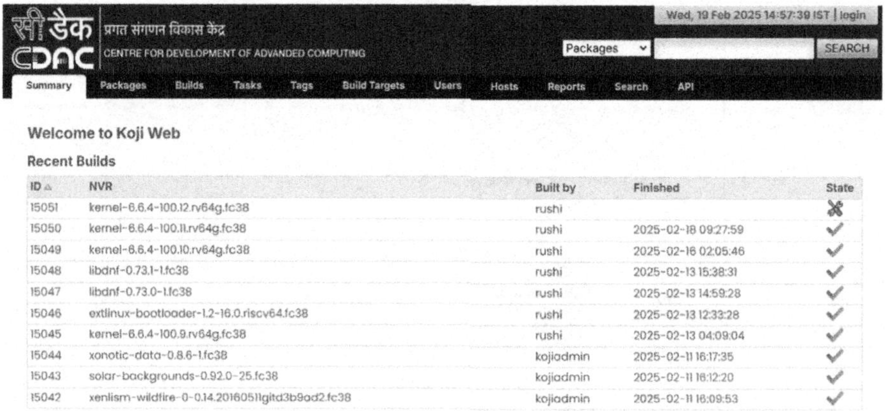

Fig. 7. Package build status on Koji Web

4.3 System Stability

System reliability was evaluated using stress tests, memory diagnostics, and process assessments. The execution of HPC benchmarks such as HPL, along with general-purpose applications, demonstrated stable performance with no crashes observed.

4.4 Bootability on RV64G Hardware

Bootloader configurations and kernel parameters were thoroughly validated across multiple RV64G platforms, including the StarFive board, Vega board, and QEMU emulator [15]. Successful initialization using both U-Boot and GRUB confirmed robust compatibility with diverse storage media.

These results demonstrate that a Fedora-based Linux distribution can be effectively adapted for RV64G, providing high rebuild success rates, stable performance, and seamless booting, laying a foundation for broader RISC-V adoption.

5 Conclusion

The rising prominence of the RISC-V architecture has highlighted the need for flexible and modular Linux distributions tailored to its specialized profiles, particularly RV64G. This paper presents a systematic strategy to address essential software support deficiencies by utilizing existing resources and enhancing automation in distribution development. By adapting essential toolchains, implementing the Koji build system and deploying Python-based automation tools, this methodology significantly reduces manual effort and ensures compatibility with specialized hardware requirements.

The results validate the feasibility and effectiveness of this approach, demonstrating a robust framework for building and maintaining customized Linux distributions that cater to lesser-known RISC-V subsets. This vendor-neutral, modular solution not only enhances the RISC-V ecosystem but also empowers developers, researchers and organizations to meet diverse computing demands.

6 Future Work

Our present approach enables creating Linux distributions for RISC-V architecture targeting any subset of the RV64GC extensions. Moving forward, we aim to enhance this approach to develop distributions that combine the base RV64GC architecture with additional extensions, allowing for tailored solutions to meet specific application needs.

To enhance the package build process, we plan to introduce an optimized dependency management system that improves efficiency and reliability during rebuilds. Additionally, we will revamp the email notification system by implementing a configurable, consolidated mechanism. This will be further enhanced by leveraging large language models (LLMs) to generate concise, user-friendly summaries, simplifying package monitoring and build tracking.

A key focus of our future research is the development of a specialized Fedora-based RISC-V server distribution optimized for high-performance computing (HPC). This effort will involve refining the Fedora Koji build system and employing Python-driven automation to streamline the rebuilding of HPC-centric packages for diverse RISC-V hardware configurations.

These developments will significantly enhance adaptability, performance, and usability of Fedora-based RISC-V distributions for Linux and HPC communities.

Acknowledgments. This work is supported by the Microprocessor Development Program (MDP), funded by the Ministry of Electronics and Information Technology, Government of India. We express our sincere gratitude for their support.

References

1. Billa, S., Badar, A., Jadhav, R., Sonawane, Y., Wandhekar, S.: Development of fedora linux distribution for RISC-V (RV64G) architecture. In: SC24-W: Workshops of the International Conference for High Performance Computing, Networking, Storage and Analysis, pp. 1685–1689 (2024). https://doi.org/10.1109/SCW63240.2024.00210
2. Brown, N., Jamieson, M., Lee, J., Wang, P.: Is RISC-V ready for HPC primetime: evaluating the 64-core Sophon SG2042 RISC-V CPU. In: Proceedings of the SC '23 Workshops of the International Conference on High Performance Computing, Network, Storage, and Analysis, pp. 1566–1574. Association for Computing Machinery, New York, NY, USA (2023). https://doi.org/10.1145/3624062.3624234
3. RISC-V Technical Specifications. https://lf-riscv.atlassian.net/wiki/spaces/HOME/pages/16154769/RISC-V+Technical+Specifications. Accessed 12 Mar 2025
4. Buildroot. https://buildroot.org/. Accessed 12 Dec 2024
5. RISC-V Yocto. https://github.com/riscv/meta-riscv. Accessed 25 May 2024
6. Koji Infrastructure. https://docs.fedoraproject.org/en-US/koji/. Accessed 02 Jan 2025
7. Fedora-V Force. https://www.fedoravforce.org/. Accessed 21 Feb 2024
8. Python asynchronous frameworks. https://docs.python.org/3/library/asyncio.html. Accessed 28 Apr 2024
9. RISC-V SIGs. https://fedoraproject.org/wiki/SIGs/RISC-V. Accessed 02 May 2024
10. RISC-V Fedora Rocks. http://fedora.riscv.rocks/koji/. Accessed 30 Jan 2025
11. RISC-V/Fedora. https://fedoraproject.org/wiki/Architectures/RISC-V. Accessed 05 Feb 2024
12. RISC-V/Debian. https://wiki.debian.org/RISC-V. Accessed 25 July 2024
13. RISC-V/ubuntu. https://ubuntu.com/download/risc-v. Accessed 07 June 2024
14. LFS. https://www.linuxfromscratch.org/lfs/. Accessed 08 Apr 2024
15. C-DAC Vega Board. https://vegaprocessors.in/. Accessed 08 May 2025

Evaluating RISC-V Processor as an Alternative for High Performance Computing

Aniket P. Garade[(✉)], Ashish Bisht, H. V. Deepika, P. Haribabu, S. A. Kumar, and S. D. Sudarsan

Centre for Development of Advanced Computing (CDAC), Bengaluru, India
{aniketpg,ashishbisht,deepikahv,hari,sakumar,sds}@cdac.in

Abstract. The current landscape of High-Performance Computing (HPC) systems is predominantly dominated by x86-based processors, as reflected by the Top 500 list, which showcases their processing power and software ecosystem maturity. However, ARM architectures are steadily gaining traction, driven by their energy efficiency and increasing support in the software ecosystem. Recently, the open-source RISC-V architecture has emerged as a potential alternative, offering flexibility. As RISC-V gains momentum, it is essential to assess its performance. This paper presents an in-depth evaluation of the performance of the RISC-V-based SOPHGO SG2042 processor, comparing it against prominent high-performance processors, including Intel Sapphire Rapids (SPR) and other widely used architectures, through a series of applications based on the Berkeley dwarfs. We assess the processor's performance across a diverse range of computational tasks, covering areas such as dense and sparse linear algebra, spectral methods, graph traversal, and more. We also compare performance in terms of memory & network bandwidth. Our results reveal that while the SG2042 demonstrates strong performance in specific tasks such as Combination Logic and Dynamic Programming, it lags behind in most other applications along with network and memory bandwidth efficiency. However, it shows notable improvements in scalability for some of the benchmarks. The paper provides valuable insights into the potential of RISC-V-based systems for high-performance computing, highlighting both their strengths and limitations. As RISC-V continues to mature, this research provides an objective analysis of the architecture's current performance and its potential for future competitiveness in the high-performance processor landscape.

Keywords: RISC-V · High performance Computing · Berkeley Dwarfs · Performance evaluation

1 Introduction

High-Performance Computing (HPC) is evolving rapidly due to the increasing demands of complex scientific simulations, data-intensive applications, and the growing need for computational power across various domains, including artificial intelligence, machine learning, weather forecasting, and large-scale simulations. HPC systems are specifically designed to handle these resource-intensive tasks, offering the necessary computational capabilities to process massive datasets and complex algorithms efficiently. The x86 architecture remains dominant in the Top500 due to its broad adoption, high performance, and well-established software ecosystem [1]. Processors from Intel and AMD are widely recognized for their computational power, scalability, and extensive software compatibility [2]. However, despite the dominance of x86 based processors, ARM-based systems are gaining traction in HPC, driven by their energy efficiency and competitive performance in specific workloads [3]. ARM processors offer a strong power-to-performance ratio, making them particularly attractive for power-sensitive applications, and are increasingly being considered as viable alternatives in the HPC ecosystem [4].

Alongside ARM, RISC-V is also being looked at as one of the contenders for power efficiency in the HPC landscape. As an open-source, royalty-free Instruction Set Architecture (ISA) [5], RISC-V was initially favored for low-power and embedded systems. However, its flexibility and open nature enable hardware designers to customize the ISA for specific application needs, making it particularly useful in areas such as embedded systems, automotive applications, and microcontrollers. More recently, RISC-V has demonstrated potential in reshaping HPC by supporting diverse processor implementations that provide customized solutions for high-performance workloads [6].

While the industry is still in the early stages of integrating RISC-V into HPC, its growing ecosystem and adaptability are making it an increasingly viable option [7,8]. A decade after its inception at UC Berkeley, RISC-V is no longer confined to academia; its ISA specification has gained widespread industry adoption, further solidifying its position as a flexible and competitive alternative to proprietary architectures [9]. As RISC-V designs continue to mature, the architecture has the potential to become a key player alongside x86 and ARM in the HPC sector, offering a customizable and open-source alternative to traditional architectures.

As RISC-V gains traction in High-Performance Computing (HPC), understanding its ability to handle computationally intensive workloads is crucial. Our motivation stems from the need to assess whether RISC-V can serve as a viable alternative to established architectures such as x86 and ARM for scientific computing and data-intensive applications. In this paper, we evaluate the application performance based on Berkeley Dwarfs [10], network performance and memory bandwidth efficiency. The ultimate goal of this study is to identify the strengths and limitations of RISC-V in HPC environments, offering insights into its potential for future adoption in large-scale computing.

The following sections of the document are organized as follows: Sect. 2 reviews related work, while Sect. 3 presents the experimentation and analysis. Finally, Sect. 4 concludes the paper by summarizing key findings and suggesting potential directions for future research.

2 Related Works

Nick Brown et al. [11] investigate the performance of the Sophon SG2042, the world's first 64-core RISC-V CPU designed for high-performance computing workloads, in this paper. Previous studies have explored the evolving capabilities of RISC-V processors in comparison to dominant x86 architectures, highlighting significant progress in RISC-V hardware. Specifically, the SG2042 demonstrates a substantial performance boost over earlier RISC-V models, achieving up to ten times better performance in single-precision computations. However, when compared to high-performance x86 processors such as AMD Rome and Intel Ice Lake, the SG2042 still falls behind, particularly in multi-threaded and double-precision workloads. The paper underscores the importance of performance optimization strategies, including efficient thread-to-core mapping, to fully leverage the SG2042's parallel processing potential. Additionally, related work suggests that future iterations of RISC-V processors could close the performance gap with x86 through improvements such as wider vector registers, larger L1 cache, and additional memory controllers per NUMA region, thereby significantly enhancing their capabilities for large-scale HPC applications.

Christian Fibich et al. [12] conducted a comprehensive evaluation of various open-source BLAS libraries optimized for ARM and RISC-V architectures on Linux-compatible embedded platforms. Their study underscores the critical role of BLAS as a fundamental standard for efficient linear algebra operations, particularly in the context of the growing reliance of IoT devices on powerful processors capable of handling demanding computational tasks. They emphasized that, as the capabilities of embedded systems continue to advance, the optimization of libraries like BLAS becomes increasingly important. Their results demonstrate that optimized BLAS implementations deliver significant performance improvements over standard C alternatives, making them an essential tool for achieving high computational efficiency. In their testing, ARM platforms consistently outperformed RISC-V platforms, highlighting the current performance disparity between the two architectures. This study not only demonstrates the power of optimized libraries in enhancing the performance of embedded systems but also suggests potential areas for future optimizations within the RISC-V architecture, particularly as it continues to evolve and gain traction in the embedded systems community.

Nick Brown et al. [13] conducted a performance characterization of the 64-core SG2042 RISC-V CPU for high-performance computing by benchmarking it against various other CPU architectures, including RISC-V, x86-64, and AArch64. Their results, using NASA's NAS Parallel Benchmark (NPB) suite, demonstrate that the SG2042 significantly outperforms other RISC-V solutions, offering a 2.6 to 16.7-fold performance improvement at the single-core level. While the SG2042 performs competitively in computationally bound algorithms, it faces limitations in memory-bound workloads due to a bottleneck in its memory subsystem. The authors suggest that Sophon's upcoming SG2044, with its improved memory bandwidth and RVV v1.0 support, could address these challenges and enhance the SG2042's performance, making the SG family a promising candidate for HPC applications.

3 Experimentation and Analysis

3.1 Hardware Setup and Benchmarks Used

In order to evaluate the performance of the RISC-V based processor SOPHGO SG2042 [14], a comparative analysis is conducted alongside several other high-performance processors. The processors and their respective specifications utilized in the experiments are outlined in Table 1. Table 2 provides a summary of the applications employed, along with the computational dwarfs they represent. GCC v12.2 is used as the base compiler for all the processors/applications with -O3 flag used for compilation. All the applications are parallel in nature using OpenMP as the threading mechanism. For evaluating the performance of network we use MPI programs compiled using OpenMPI v5.0.6.

Table 1. Hardware details

Category	Processors			
	Fujitsu A64FX	Intel SPR	AMD Genoa	SOPHGO SG2042
Architecture	ARM	X86	X86	RISC-V
Number of cores	48	64	192	64
Frequency	2 GHz	3.4 GHz	2.4GHz	2 GHz

As all processors have different number of cores, in order to have a fair comparison between the processors, the applications are executed using two different thread count. Since A64FX has the least amount of cores i.e. 48, we choose it as one of the thread count to be evaluated on. The other thread count is chosen based on the total number of cores present in the processor. So if the processor has x cores we use x number of threads for the application. Execution in this manner gives the full potential of a processor. In order to avoid context switching we bind the threads to cores using OMP_PROC_BIND environment variable.

3.2 Experimentation and Observation

Figure 1 presents the performance data for Dense Linear Algebra, focusing on the Double-precision General Matrix Multiply (DGEMM) [15] operation executed with the OpenBLAS [16] math library on a 32k × 32k square matrix. Intel's Sapphire Rapids processor leads in DGEMM performance, outperforming all other processors. In contrast, the SOPHGO SG2042 shows significant underperformance, falling behind by a factor of 48.62x when utilizing 48 threads and 49.50x when running with its maximum thread count, compared to the top-performing HPC processor. Furthermore, when compared to the A64FX, the

Table 2. Applications used

Sr No.	Berkeley Dwarf	Application
1	Dense Linear Algebra	DGEMM
2	Sparse Linear Algebra	SpMM
3	Spectral Methods	FFT
4	Structured Grids	Convolution
5	Unstructured Grids	Laplace Equation
6	N-body Simulations	Bruteforce n-body
7	Map Reduce	Monte Carlo-based Pi Calculation
8	Combination Logic	Encryption
9	Dynamic Programming	Knapsack
10	Graph Traversal	BFS
11	Backtracking & Branch and Bound	Knapsack
12	Construct Graphical Models	Hidden Markov Models

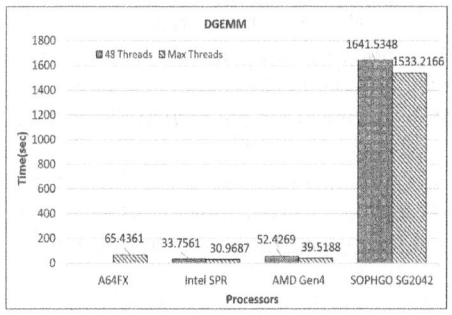

Fig. 1. Performance for Dense Linear Algebra (DGEMM)

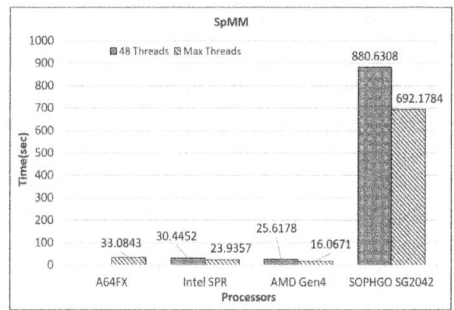

Fig. 2. Performance for Sparse Linear Algebra (SpMM)

lowest-performing HPC processor, the SG2042 still lags considerably, showing performance deficits of 25.08x with 48 threads and 23.43x at full thread capacity.

Figure 2 showcases the results for sparse linear algebra, specifically for the Sparse Matrix Multiplication (SpMM) benchmark on a square matrix with 2 million rows. AMD's Genoa processor stands out as the best performer in this benchmark. On the other hand, the SOPHGO SG2042 trails far behind, performing 34.37× slower with 48 threads and 43.08× slower when using its maximum thread count. Even in comparison to the A64FX, the least efficient HPC processor in this test, the SG2042 still demonstrates a considerable performance gap, trailing by 28× with both 48 threads and the maximum thread count.

Figure 3 provides performance results for the Spectral Method, utilizing the Cooley-Tukey Radix-2 Decimation in Time FFT application with a problem size of 2^{25}. AMD's Genoa once again leads in performance among all proces-

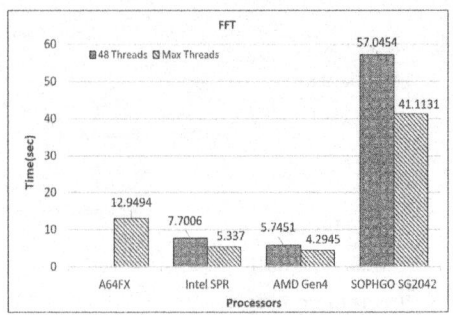
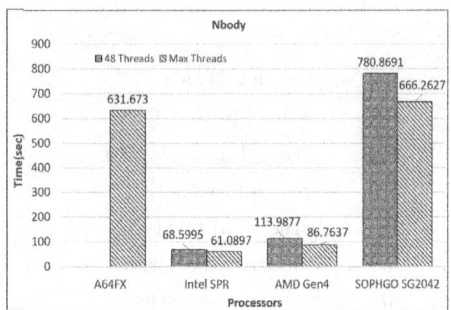

Fig. 3. Performance for Spectral Methods (FFT)

Fig. 4. Performance for N-Body simulations (Bruteforce n-body)

sors tested. The SOPHGO SG2042, however, lags significantly, showing a 9.92× slower performance with 48 threads and 9.57× slower when utilizing the maximum number of threads. In comparison to the A64FX, the lowest-performing HPC processor, the SG2042 still demonstrates a noticeable performance gap, being 4.40× slower with 48 threads and 3.17× slower at full thread capacity.

Figure 4 illustrates the performance of N-body simulations, specifically using the Nbody application with a sample size of 40,000 particles. Intel Sapphire Rapids again takes the lead in this evaluation. In contrast, the SOPHGO SG2042 underperforms significantly, showing a 11.38× slower result with 48 threads and 10.90× slower at its maximum thread count. When compared to the A64FX, the lowest-performing HPC processor, the SG2042 exhibits a more modest performance gap, trailing by 1.23× with 48 threads and nearly matching performance at full thread capacity.

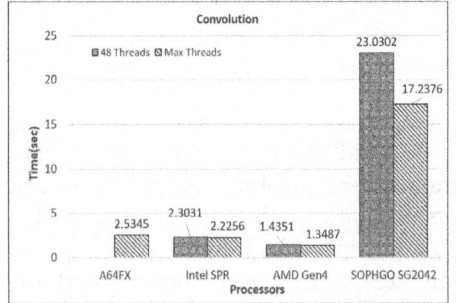
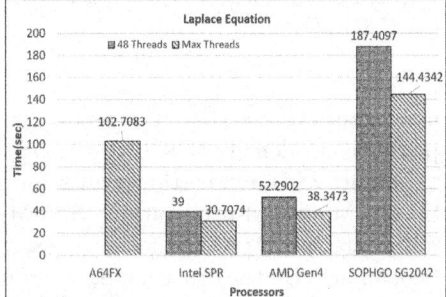

Fig. 5. Performance for Structured Grids (Convolution)

Fig. 6. Performance for Unstructured Grids (Laplace Equation)

Figure 5 presents the performance outcomes for structured grids, utilizing the Convolution benchmark on a 32k × 32k sample size. AMD's Genoa achieves the highest performance in this test. Meanwhile, the SOPHGO SG2042 lags behind considerably, showing performance deficits of 16.04× with 48 threads and 12.78× at the maximum thread count. Compared to the A64FX, the lowest-performing HPC processor, the SG2042's performance gap is moderate, trailing by 9.08× with 48 threads and 6.80× slower at full thread capacity.

Figure 6 presents performance results for unstructured grids, focusing on the Laplace Equation with a sample size of 102400 × 204800. Intel Sapphire Rapids again emerges as the top performer in this benchmark. The SOPHGO SG2042, however, performs 4.8× slower with both 48 threads and the maximum thread count. In comparison to the A64FX, the least efficient HPC processor, the SG2042 shows a more moderate performance gap, being 1.82× slower with 48 threads and 1.40× slower at full thread capacity.

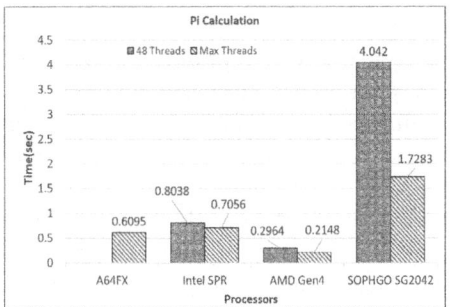
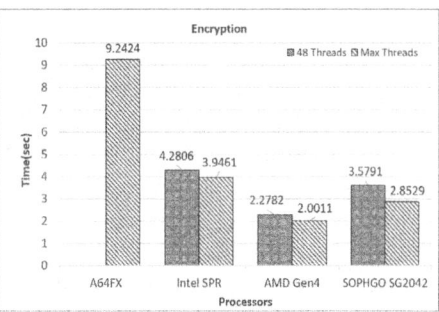

Fig. 7. Performance for Map Reduce (Monte-Carlo based Pi calculation)

Fig. 8. Performance for Combinational Logic(Encryption)

Figure 7 presents the performance analysis of Map Reduce, using a Monte Carlo-based Pi Calculation on a dataset of 1 billion samples. In this benchmark, AMD Genova outperforms all other processors, achieving the best performance. On the other hand, the SOPHGO SG2042 significantly trails behind, with performance degradation of 13.63× slower using 48 threads and 8.04× slower when operating at its maximum thread count. When compared to the least efficient HPC processor, the A64FX, the SG2042 demonstrates a moderate performance gap, performing 6.63× slower with 48 threads and 2.83× slower at full thread capacity.

Figure 8 shows the performance results for Combinational Logic, specifically in Encryption tasks, using a message size of 163MB. In this evaluation, AMD Genova leads in terms of performance. In contrast, the SOPHGO SG2042 is considerably slower, showing a 1.57× performance gap with 48 threads and 1.42× slower at its maximum thread count. However, the SOPHGO SG2042 outperforms both Intel Sapphire Rapids and the A64FX. It achieves a 2.58× performance gain over the A64FX with 48 threads and 3.23× at full thread capacity, as well as a 1.20× gain over Intel Sapphire Rapids with 48 threads and 1.38× at maximum threads.

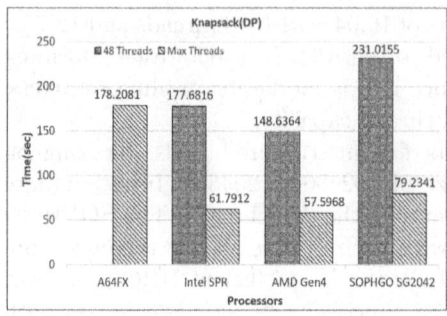
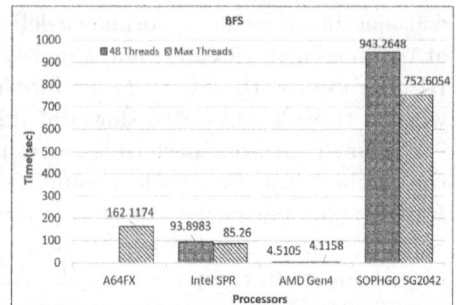

Fig. 9. Performance for Dynamic Programming(Knapsack)

Fig. 10. Performance for Graph Traversal(BFS)

Figure 9 illustrates the performance of Dynamic Programming, utilizing the Knapsack algorithm with a problem size of 500k items and a maximum weight capacity equal to 500k. AMD Genova again achieves the best performance in this benchmark. Meanwhile, the SOPHGO SG2042 lags significantly behind, performing 1.55× slower with 48 threads and 1.37× slower at its maximum thread count. When compared to the A64FX with 48 threads, the SOPHGO SG2042 is 1.30× slower. However, at its maximum thread count, the SG2042 surpasses the A64FX, demonstrating a 2.25× performance improvement.

Figure 10 presents the performance results for Graph Traversal using Breadth-First Search (BFS) on a graph of 50 million nodes and edges. Among all the processors evaluated, AMD Genoa leads with the highest performance. In contrast, the SOPHGO SG2042 falls far behind, being 209× slower with 48 threads and 183× slower when utilizing its maximum thread count. Even when compared to the least performing HPC processor, the A64FX, the SG2042 still exhibits a notable performance gap, trailing by 5.81× with 48 threads and 4.64× slower at full thread capacity.

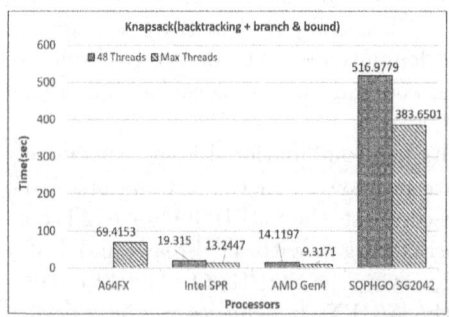
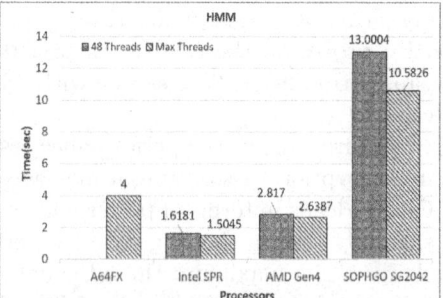

Fig. 11. Performance for Backtracking, Branch and Bound (Knapsack)

Fig. 12. Performance for Construct Graphical Models (HMM)

Figure 11 shows the performance results for Backtracking and Branch-and-Bound techniques applied to the Knapsack problem with size of 64 items and a maximum weight capacity equal to 64. In this test, AMD Genova outperforms all other processors. The SOPHGO SG2042, however, shows a significant performance deficit, being 36.61× slower with 48 threads and 41.17× slower at its maximum thread count. When compared to the A64FX, the least efficient HPC processor, the SG2042 still demonstrates a substantial performance gap, being 7.44× slower with 48 threads and 5.52× slower at full thread capacity.

Figure 12 presents the performance outcomes for constructing graphical models using Hidden Markov Models (HMM), with 2048 observations. Intel Sapphire Rapids delivers the best performance in this evaluation. On the other hand, the SOPHGO SG2042 exhibits a significant performance shortfall, performing 8× slower with 48 threads and 7× slower at its maximum thread count. When compared to the lowest-performing HPC processor, the A64FX, the SG2042 still shows a notable performance difference, being 3.25× slower with 48 threads and 2.64× slower at full thread capacity.

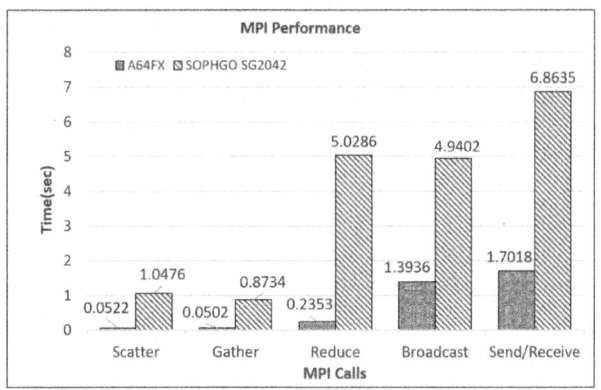

Fig. 13. Performance for MPI across 2 nodes

Figure 13 illustrates the performance of basic MPI calls across two nodes with a data size of 100 MB. All collective operations are performed between two nodes, each with four processes, while the point-to-point communication involves one process per node. Both the A64FX and SG2042 use a 10 Gbps Ethernet connection for communication. The results show that A64FX outperforms the SG2042 by a factor of 20 for *MPI_Scatter*, 17.39 for *MPI_Gather*, 21.37 for *MPI_Reduce*, 3.54 for *MPI_Bcast*, and 4.03 for *MPI_Send* & *MPI_Recv*.

3.3 Analysis

The SOPHGO SG2042 outperforms both the Intel Sapphire Rapids (SPR) and Fujitsu A64FX processors in the combination logic benchmark and exceeds the

A64FX in dynamic programming using the knapsack problem when utilizing the maximum thread count. This demonstrates its strength in handling logical operations, computational tasks involving complex encryption and decision-making processes, as well as dynamic programming. However, despite its impressive performance in combination logic and dynamic programming, the SG2042 lags significantly behind the other processors in all other evaluated Berkeley dwarfs. This performance gap indicates that while the SG2042 excels in specific areas, it struggles to deliver comparable results across a broader range of computational tasks. The results highlight the potential for specialized optimization in certain domains, but also point to limitations when considering general-purpose performance across diverse computational workloads. The disparity in performance across these benchmarks suggests that the SG2042 may be more narrowly tailored for certain applications, rather than being a broadly high-performing processor in all use cases.

In terms of scalability, we examined the performance gains resulting from increasing the thread count from 48 to 64. Our analysis reveals that the SOPHGO SG2042 experiences a noticeable improvement in performance, outperforming the Intel Sapphire Rapids in certain applications when the thread count is increased. This indicates that the SG2042 benefits from higher thread utilization in specific workloads. Table 3 provides a detailed comparison of the performance gains for both the Intel Sapphire Rapids (SPR) and SOPHGO SG2042 processors, each having a core count of 64, which allows for a direct comparison of how the processors handle scaling with an increase in thread count.

Table 3. Performance gains after increasing thread count

Berkeley Dwarf	Intel SPR	SOPHGO SG2042
Dense Linear Algebra	1.09x	1.07x
Sparse Linear Algebra	1.271x	1.272x
Spectral Methods	1.44x	1.38x
Structured Grids	1.03x	1.34x
Unstructured Grids	1.27x	1.29x
N-body Simulations	1.12x	1.17x
Map Reduce	1.13x	2.33x
Combination Logic	1.08x	1.25x
Dynamic Programming	2.87x	2.91x
Graph Traversal	1.10x	1.25x
Backtracking & Branch and Bound	1.45x	1.34x
Construct Graphical Models	1.07x	1.22x

A comparison of network performance reveals that the A64FX outperforms the SG2042 significantly. This performance gap may be addressed through the vectorization support provided by the RISC-V architecture, a solution that has been applied to similar performance bottlenecks in OpenMPI for ARM processors [17]. Additionally, we run the STREAM benchmark [18] with a 2 GB data size to assess memory bandwidth performance. The results show that the memory bandwidth efficiency of the SG2042 is 42.9%. Typically, for optimized HPC systems, the STREAM benchmark yields efficiencies between 50–80%. This lower efficiency may be attributed to various factors, including suboptimal memory interleaving, inefficient memory access patterns that fail to utilize all controllers, limited core-memory bandwidth, or the absence of necessary compiler or system software optimizations.

RISC-V-based high performance systems are still in the early stages of their development, with much of the ecosystem for these processors still emerging. In contrast, processors built on more established architectures have long benefited from mature and extensive software ecosystems, enabling developers to leverage a wide range of optimized tools and libraries. As a result, RISC-V faces certain challenges in gaining widespread adoption, particularly in the realm of software development. At the time of writing this paper, LLVM [19], one of the leading open-source compilers widely used in both academic and industrial settings, does not yet offer support for OpenMP on RISC-V-based systems. This lack of support for such a critical parallel programming model highlights the ongoing need for further development and optimization in the RISC-V software ecosystem to enable efficient parallel computing on these processors.

4 Conclusion

In this paper, we evaluated the performance of the RISC-V-based SOPHGO SG2042 processor using the Berkeley dwarfs, comparing it with other high-performance processors based on ARM and X86 architectures. Our findings show that while the SG2042 excels in combination logic and dynamic programming, it performs relatively lower in all other dwarfs evaluated. However, it is worth noting that the SG2042 demonstrates superior scaling performance compared to the Intel Sapphire Rapids in nearly half of the evaluated dwarfs, indicating the promising potential of RISC-V architecture for specific workloads. We also evaluate the network and memory bandwidth performance of the SG2042 in comparison to the A64FX. Our analysis reveals a significant performance deficiency in both memory bandwidth efficiency and network bandwidth for the SG2042. Despite being in the early stages of development, RISC-V-based systems show considerable promise, with ongoing improvements in performance and scalability. The RISC-V ecosystem is still evolving, and as the software support matures and optimization efforts progress, it is expected that the architecture will become a competitive player in the high-performance processor landscape.

Acknowledgment. We gratefully acknowledge the University of Oregon for providing access to its infrastructure, including the Intel Sapphire Rapids and AMD Genoa CPUs of the Frank System. Additionally, we acknowledge the use of the ExCALIBUR H&ES

RISC-V testbed. We extend our sincere gratitude to Mr. Sushil Pratap Singh, Mr. Ram Bajgire and Mr. Sourav Ravindran for their invaluable support, without which this work would not have been possible.

References

1. TOP500. TOP500: The List of the World s Most Powerful Computers. https://top500.org/. Accessed 12 Mar 2025
2. Blem, E., Menon, J., Sankaralingam, K.: Power struggles: revisiting the RISC vs. CISC debate on contemporary ARM and x86 architectures. In: 2013 IEEE 19th International Symposium on High Performance Computer Architecture (HPCA), pp. 1–12. IEEE (2013)
3. Jackson, A., et al.: Evaluating the arm ecosystem for high performance computing. In: Proceedings of the Platform for Advanced Scientific Computing Conference, pp. 1–11 (2019)
4. Ouro, P., Lopez-Novoa, U., Guest, M.F.: On the performance of a highly-scalable Computational Fluid Dynamics code on AMD, ARM and Intel processor-based HPC systems. Comput. Phys. Commun. **269**, 108105 (2021)
5. Waterman, A., et al.: The RISC-V instruction set manual, volume I: user-level ISA, version 2.0. Technical report, UCB/EECS-2014-54, p. 4, EECS Department, University of California, Berkeley (2014)
6. Diehl, P., et al.: Preparing for HPC on RISC-V: examining vectorization and distributed performance of an astrophysics application with HPX and Kokkos. In: SC24-W: Workshops of the International Conference for High Performance Computing, Networking, Storage and Analysis, pp. 1656–1665. IEEE (2024)
7. Mantovani, F., et al.: Software development vehicles to enable extended and early co-design: a RISC-V and HPC case of study. In: Bienz, A., Weiland, M., Baboulin, M., Kruse, C. (eds.) ISC High Performance 2023. LNCS, vol. 13999, pp. 526–537. Springer, Cham (2023). https://doi.org/10.1007/978-3-031-40843-4_39
8. Perez, B., Fell, A., Davis, J.D.: Coyote: an open source simulation tool to enable RISC-V in HPC. In: 2021 Design, Automation and Test in Europe Conference and Exhibition (DATE), pp. 130–135. IEEE (2021)
9. Semico Research & Consulting Group: RISC-V Market Analysis: The New Kid on the Block (2019). https://semico.com/content/risc-v-market-analysis-new-kid-block
10. Asanovic, K., et al.: The landscape of parallel computing research: a view from Berkeley (2006)
11. Brown, N., et al.: Is RISC-V ready for HPC prime-time: Evaluating the 64-core Sophon SG2042 RISC-V CPU. In: Proceedings of the SC 23 Workshops of the International Conference on High Performance Computing, Network, Storage, and Analysis, pp. 1566–1574 (2023)
12. Fibich, C., et al.: Evaluation of open-source linear algebra libraries targeting arm and RISC-V architectures. In: 2020 15th Conference on Computer Science and Information Systems (FedCSIS), pp. 663–672. IEEE (2020)
13. Brown, N., Jamieson, M.: Performance characterisation of the 64-core SG2042 RISC-V CPU for HPC. In: Weiland, M., Neuwirth, S., Kruse, C., Weinzierl, T. (eds.) ISC High Performance 2023. LNCS, vol. 15058, pp. 354–367. Springer, Cham (2025). https://doi.org/10.1007/978-3-031-73716-9_25

14. EPCC: RISC-V Hardware Documentation. https://riscv.epcc.ed.ac.uk/documentation/hardware/. Accessed 12 Mar 2025
15. Wei, Y., et al.: DGEMM Optimization Oriented to ARM SVE Instruction Set Architecture. In: 2022 IEEE 28th International Conference on Parallel and Distributed Systems (ICPADS), pp. 514–521. IEEE (2023)
16. OpenMathLib: OpenBLAS v0.3.29 Release. https://github.com/OpenMathLib/OpenBLAS/releases/tag/v0.3.29. Accessed 12 Mar 2025
17. Zhong, D., et al.: Using arm scalable vector extension to optimize open MPI. In: 2020 20th IEEE/ACM International Symposium on Cluster, Cloud and Internet Computing (CCGRID), pp. 222–231. IEEE (2020)
18. Hammond, J.: STREAM: A High Performance STREAM Benchmark (2025). https://github.com/jeffhammond/STREAM. Accessed 19 Apr 2025
19. LVM Project. LLVM. https://llvm.org/. Accessed 12 Mar 2025

Evaluation of RVV-Enabled COTS Platforms with Matrix Multiplication and Exo

Adrián Castelló[1], Héctor Martínez[2], Sandra Catalán[3], Francisco D. Igual[4(✉)], and Enrique S. Quintana-Ortí[1]

[1] Universitat Politècnica de València, Valencia, Spain
{adcastel,quintana}@disca.upv.es
[2] Universidad de Córdoba, Córdoba, Spain
el2mapeh@uco.es
[3] Universitat Jaume I, Castellón de la Plana, Spain
catalans@uji.es
[4] Universidad Complutense de Madrid, Madrid, Spain
figual@ucm.es

Abstract. We conduct a detailed performance comparison of state-of-the-art commercial-off-the-shelf (COTS) RISC-V processors, equipped with single-instruction multiple-data (SIMD) units, using the general matrix-matrix multiplication (GEMM). To address the differences in the implementation of the RISC-V ISA (instruction set architecture) in general, and its RVV vector extension in particular, we use Exo as a tool to accelerate the development of a complete family of micro-kernels that take into account the different characteristics of the architectures and facilitate the generation of highly optimized realizations of GEMM. We show that, since the specific optimizations differ between targets (even if they are under the same RVV umbrella), automatic generation and analytical models are essential tools to identify the optimal realizations.

Keywords: Multicore processors · Matrix-matrix multiplication · RISC-V processors · RISC-V vector extension (RVV) · Exo

1 Introduction

In response to the recent standardization of the RISC-V vector extension (RVV) [12], a number of *commercial-off-the-shelf* (COTS) *single-board computers* (SBCs) have recently integrated RISC-V cores with floating point SIMD capabilities. These products advance the democratization of RISC-V platforms for high performance computing (HPC) and artificial intelligence (AI), and pave the interest for adapting the software stack (mainly at the application and library level) to take advantage of vectorization for RISC-V. Although there have been some preliminary studies of the potential of RVV-enabled processors in terms of performance for operations where vectorization is key [2,10], their actual arithmetic capabilities have not yet been compared in detail.

Historically, the general matrix-matrix multiplication (GEMM) has served as a popular benchmark to evaluate the arithmetic performance of any new architecture. In fact, although open source implementations of the Basic Linear Algebra Subprograms (BLAS) typically cover a wide variety of processors, vendors such as Intel, AMD, NVIDIA, ARM, or IBM put considerable effort into their proprietary instances of BLAS in order to demonstrate the sustainable peak performance of their new processor designs.

Almost all high-performance implementations of GEMM follow the ideas introduced in GotoBLAS [5], which aims to build the functionality in the form of a small (but highly tuned) piece of code known as a *micro-kernel*, constructed under a set of loops and a couple of ad hoc packing routines. Despite its regularity, the development of a highly tuned micro-kernel and the correct parameterization of the tiling within GEMM ultimately determine the fraction of peak performance that is actually extracted from the underlying architecture. This process can be not only a daunting task for the open-source BLAS developer, but close to impossible in cases where microarchitectural details are not fully disclosed. Thus, open-source BLAS realizations (e.g., BLIS or OpenBLAS) only include implementations for large processor families or vectorization technologies, ignoring fine-grained adaptations to different microarchitectural details or cache specifications, and thus losing the battle for the *"last mile"* in performance.

To reduce this effort, automatic code generation has proven to be useful for building both vectorized micro-kernels and complete GEMM realizations that are portable across architectures, starting from high-level code that abstracts away the details of the underlying architecture [1,3,6]. *User-schedulable* languages (USLs) bundled with compiler frameworks propose a clear separation of concerns between the *definition* of the logic of an operation (e.g., a matrix multiplication) and its *schedule*, that is, the set of general and architecture-aware optimizations that can be applied to the operation, such as unrolling, tiling, or vectorization. Examples of such USLs and frameworks are Halide [11], TVM [4], MLIR [8], and Exo [7]. USLs can fill the productivity gap by providing a convenient tool to accelerate the development of GEMM code in general and the micro-kernel in particular. Together with analytical models [9] that guide the selection of the tiling parameters, USLs can reduce the need to know the details of the underlying architecture and cut the development time to virtually zero.

In this paper, we use Exo to develop a complete family of micro-kernel realizations that apply a collection of optimization techniques targeting RVV, evaluating their performance on state-of-the-art vector-enabled COTS platforms. The goal of this paper is threefold: First, to demonstrate that while GEMM is a valid benchmark to illustrate the sustainable peak performance of an architecture, the actual arithmetic throughput differs significantly depending on the kernel realization; second, to prove that USLs (specifically Exo) are a valid solution to gain useful insight in this regard; and third, to provide a comparative analysis of the performance of state-of-the-art COTS platforms equipped with RVV capabilities available in the market.

The contributions of this paper can be summarized as follows:

- We use the USL Exo to generate a comprehensive family of GEMM micro-kernels for RISC-V processors, including a full range of dimensions and different optimization strategies to cover virtually all architecture-aware optimizations that can be leveraged in RVV.
- We provide a thorough evaluation of the generated micro-kernels on four RVV-enabled COTS boards, highlighting the type of optimizations that are better suited to each.
- We integrate the best-performing micro-kernel into a higher level GEMM routine, using analytical models to select the parameters of the loop-tiling strategy to exploit the cache hierarchy of each platform. In addition, we provide a comparative analysis of the potential performance that can be extracted for each platform.
- We evaluate the parallelization capabilities of GEMM and illustrate the scalability of the multi-core platforms (when available), providing a detailed overview of the potential of each in a comparative manner.

The rest of the paper is structured as follows: Sect. 2 dissects the general anatomy of a high-performance GEMM implementation and illustrates different strategies for the micro-kernel implementation; Sect. 3 introduces the EXO fundamentals and user code necessary to generate a family of GEMM micro-kernels; Sect. 4 reports the observed results for the aforementioned micro-kernels on four different COTS platforms; Finally, Sect. 5 closes the paper with some general remarks.

2 High-Performance GEMM for SIMD Architectures

2.1 General Structure

GEMM realizations targeting SIMD architectures with a hierarchical cache system encode GEMM as three nested loops around two *packing routines*. This structure is known as the *macro-kernel*, and its code as well as organization is usually shared across different hardware architectures. The macro-kernel is further decomposed into two additional loops around a small piece of code, called the *micro-kernel*, that consists of a single loop which performs an *outer product* per iteration. In the following, we consider the GEMM $C = C + AB$, where A, B, and C are matrix operands with dimensions $m \times k$, $k \times n$, and $m \times n$, respectively. Figure 1a depicts the structure of the baseline GEMM algorithm with the six loops, the two packing routines that copy certain blocks of A, B into the buffers A_c, B_c, and the micro-kernel.

The three outermost loops of the baseline algorithm traverse the $n-$, $k-$, and m–dimensions of the operands with strides dictated by the cache configuration parameters (CCPs) n_c, k_c, and m_c. A careful selection of these parameters via experimentation [14,15], or more interestingly via an analytical model [9], favors that the buffer B_c stays in the L3 cache and the buffer A_c remains in the L2 cache during the execution of the micro-kernel, while C is streamed from the main memory into the processor registers. In addition, the packing routines ensure

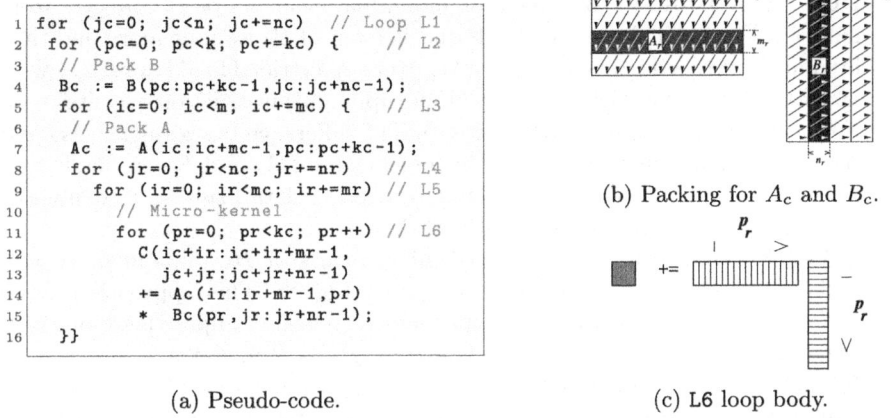

```
1  for (jc=0; jc<n; jc+=nc)       // Loop L1
2    for (pc=0; pc<k; pc+=kc) {   // L2
3      // Pack B
4      Bc := B(pc:pc+kc-1,jc:jc+nc-1);
5      for (ic=0; ic<m; ic+=mc) { // L3
6        // Pack A
7        Ac := A(ic:ic+mc-1,pc:pc+kc-1);
8        for (jr=0; jr<nc; jr+=nr)     // L4
9          for (ir=0; ir<mc; ir+=mr)   // L5
10           // Micro-kernel
11           for (pr=0; pr<kc; pr++)   // L6
12             C(ic+ir:ic+ir+mr-1,
13                jc+jr:jc+jr+nr-1)
14             += Ac(ir:ir+mr-1,pr)
15              * Bc(pr,jr:jr+nr-1);
16 }}
```

(a) Pseudo-code.

(b) Packing for A_c and B_c.

(c) L6 loop body.

Fig. 1. Baseline GEMM algorithm.

that the data in A_c, B_c are accessed with unit stride from the micro-kernel, favoring SIMD load/stores from/to memory; see Fig. 1b. The micro-kernel, usually written in assembly or in C using vector intrinsics, updates an $m_r \times n_r$ micro-tile of C inside the innermost loop; see Fig. 1c. The values of m_r and n_r are commonly used to name the micro-kernel. Finally, the operands involved in the micro-tile update are portions of the buffers A_c, B_c, more specifically the micro-panels A_r, B_r, with dimensions $m_r \times k_c$ and $k_c \times n_r$, respectively. The entries of the buffers are carefully packed to ensure unit-stride access from the micro-kernel and proper cache exploitation.

Open-source libraries like BLIS or OpenBLAS provide specialized micro-kernels for many processors from AMD, Intel, ARM, and IBM. However, developing a hardware-optimized micro-kernel for each new architecture is a complex and costly effort, and, as a result, in general these libraries provide a single micro-kernel per architecture only, and a few selections for the CCPs targeting different realizations of the architecture with distinct cache specifications.

2.2 Micro-kernel Flavors

The outer product of a column of A_r and a row of B_r during an iteration of loop L6 of the micro-kernel can be lowered to different low-level codes (RVV instructions) which offer distinct performance [2,10] depending on the target architecture. Excerpts of the RVV assembly code compiled with gcc-13.1.0 -O3 -march=rv64imafdcv for the loop L6 body are given in Fig. 2 and cover several options, mainly differing in the way and order in which elements of A_r and B_r are loaded from memory to vector registers, as detailed next. We note that, in all cases, the elements of A_r are loaded via a scalar load instruction (vle32.v).

1. **BCAST-AB and -BA** broadcast individual elements of B_r directly from memory, Fig. 2a. This scheme loads one element of B_r from memory and then broadcasts it to a destination vector register via a strided load (vlse32.v with *stride* 0). After that, the FMA (fused-multiply-add) instruction executes with two vector register inputs (vfmacc.vv). The difference between the -AB and the -BA variants is the order in which elements of A_r and B_r are loaded. In some scenarios, this swap contributes to overlap data loads and arithmetic, resulting in an additional burst of performance [6].

2. **GATHER-AB and -BA** vector-load elements of B_r from memory and gather individual lanes to vector registers, Fig. 2b. This approach is used in devices where data transfers from cache to registers impose a serious bottleneck. Here, the row of the micro-panel B_r is loaded via a vector load (vle32.v), and individual lanes are then gathered and replicated to individual vector registers. After that, the FMA instruction operates with two vector registers as inputs (vfmacc.vv). As in the previous case, we consider two orders to load the elements of A_r and B_r.

3. **DIRECT** performs individual loads of elements of B_r, Fig. 2c. This approach avoids the intermediate loading of the elements from B_r into vector registers. Instead, single elements of the micro-panel row are loaded by means of a scalar load (flw), and the update is performed via an FMA intrinsic involving a vector register (column of A_r) and the scalar register that stores a single element of B_r (vfmacc.vf).

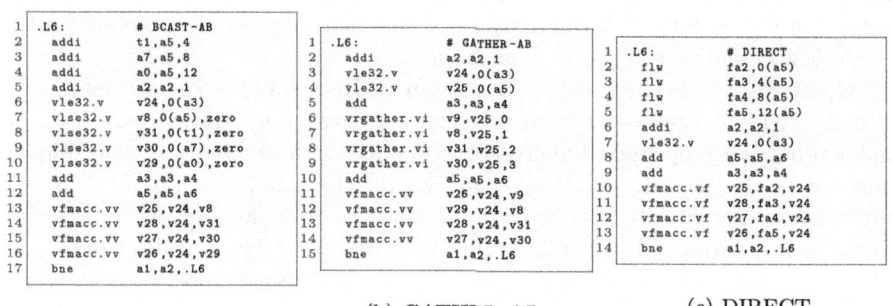

(a) BCAST-AB.   (b) GATHER-AB.   (c) DIRECT.

Fig. 2. Excerpts of the assembly code for different realizations of loop L6.

3 Automatic Micro-kernel Generation with Exo

In this section, we describe the changes to the baseline micro-kernel generation already presented in detail in [3] for the ARM ISA with NEON vector instructions *(i)* in order to adapt it to the RVV extension and *(ii)* to accommodate the micro-kernel variants described in the previous section.

The code to build an Exo generator commences with a definition of a *generic* micro-kernel following the ideas discussed in the previous section, which is then progressively refined using the EXO Python application programming interface (API). Figure 3 displays the transformed generator. The invocation to the Exo Python API to carry out the transformations proceeds in several stages, marked with the comment BK in the code. We briefly describe these stages next, making two assumptions: *(i)* the reader is familiar with [2,3] for an explanation of the details of code generation; and *(ii)* we only emphasize the relevant changes to accommodate RVV and different micro-kernel variants in the generator.

BK1: First, we generate the function to schedule and specialize the generated code by specifying (in this particular example) $m_r = 8, n_r = 6$, via the partial_eval Exo function.

BK2: Loops i and j are split to match the vector length of the architecture, in our case $vl = 4$, via the divide_loop Exo function. This results in the creation of the nested loops *it*, *itt*, *jt* and *jtt*. Exo automatically tiles the access to C, A_c and B_c to match the new loop structure.

BK3: Operations related to the management of the operand C are issued. This includes binding C to vector registers (stage_mem); resizing the vector register to a 3D structure that corresponds to the iteration of each loop (expand_dim); moving the declaration of the registers for C to the top of the generated code (lift_alloc); moving the store and load of C out of the computation loop (autofission); replacing the *itt* loop iterations of the load and store with RVV intrinsics (replace with rvv_vld_4xf32 for loads, and rvv_vst_4xf32 for stores); and setting the register variables for C to type RVV (set_memory). Given the complexity of this stage and for the sake of simplicity, we refer the reader to [3] for further details.

BK4: Generate the loads from A_c to registers. First, we map A_c to a RVV vector register (set_memory); resize the vector register to a 2D structure where the first dimension is the vector length (vl) and the second dimension is the outermost loop (expand_dim); move the declaration of the registers outside the k-loop (lift_alloc); move the loading of the operand to the k-loop (autofission); replace the *itt* loop with an RVV vector load intrinsic (replace with rvv_vld_4xf32); and set the register variable to RVV.

BK5: A similar approach applies to the loading of B_c, but in this case the operation differs depending on the specific micro-kernel variant. In the listing, we illustrate the case for the GATHER option. First, this case loads B_c in a two-step process performing a vector load from B_c to *Btmp* and then, from *Btmp* to *B_reg* registers. This data movement involves the size modification of both mappings, the *Btmp* register to the vl value, and the *B_reg* first to the vl value and then to the NR-loop. Once the data movement is defined, we replace the *jtt* loop with a vector load intrinsic (replace with rvv_vld_4xf32) for *Btmp* and we replace the *itt* loop with a gather intrinsic (replace with rvv_gather_4xf32); finally, both register variables are set to RVV. For the BCAST variant, instead of loading the data to *Btmp* and from there to *B_reg*, we load the data from B_c to *B_reg* using the broadcast intrinsic (`rvv_bcast_4xf32`) in the replacement. For the DIRECT case, no B_c data management is needed.

BK6: Loops it and jt, which load A_c, B_c into registers, are unrolled (`unroll_loop`).

Generating the flavors where B_c is loaded before A_c is as simple as swapping the order of BK4 and BK5. With this change, the B_c loads are located prior to the management of A_c.

```
1  # Simplified micro-kernel definition
2  @proc
3  def rvv_ukernel_f32( MR: size, NR: size, KC: size,
4      alpha: f32[1], Ac: f32[KC, MR] @ DRAM,
5      Bc: f32[KC, NR] @ DRAM, beta: f32[1],
6      C: f32[NR, MR] @ DRAM,):
7
8      # C += Ac * Bc
9      for k in seq(0, KC):
10         for j in seq(0, NR):
11             for i in seq(0, MR):
12                 C[j, i] += Ac[k,i] * Bc[k,j]
13
14 # BK1
15 p = rename(rvv_ukernel_f32, f"rvv_ukernel_8x6_f32")
16 p = p.partial_eval(MR=8,NR=6)
17
18 # BK2
19 p = divide_loop(p,'i', vl, ['it','itt'])
20 p = divide_loop(p,'j', vl, ['jt','jtt'])
21
22 # BK3
23 # 1) Map C buffer to vectorial register C_reg
24 Cp = 'C[j, 4 * it + itt]'
25 p = stage_mem(p, 'C[_] += _', Cp, 'C_reg')
26 # 2) Build a 3D structure of C_reg
27 p = expand_dim(p, 'C_reg', vl, 'itt', ...)
28 p = expand_dim(p, 'C_reg', MR//vl, 'it', ...)
29 p = expand_dim(p, 'C_reg', NR, 'j', ...)
30 # 3) Move the register declaration to the top
31 p = lift_alloc(p, 'C_reg', n_lifts=4)
32 # 4) Extract the C load and store from the k-loop
33 p = autofission(p, p.find('C_reg[_] = _').after(),
34     n_lifts=4)
35 p = autofission(p, p.find('C[_] = _').before(),
36     n_lifts=4)
37 # 5) Replace the indicated loops by RVV intrinsics
38 p = replace(p, 'for itt in _: _', rvv_vld_4xf32)
39 p = replace(p, 'for itt in _: _', rvv_vst_4xf32)
40 # 6) Set the C_reg memory to RVV
41 p = set_memory(p, 'C_reg', RVV)
42
43 # BK4
44 # 1) Map Ac buffer to vectorial register A_reg

43 # BK4
44 # 1) Map Ac buffer to vectorial register A_reg
45 p = bind_expr(p, 'Ac[_]','A_reg')
46 # 2) Build a 2D structure of A_reg
47 p = expand_dim(p, 'A_reg', vl, 'itt', ...)
48 p = expand_dim(p, 'A_reg', MR//vl, 'it', ...)
49 # 3) Move the register declaration to the top
50 p = lift_alloc(p, 'A_reg', n_lifts=4)
51 # 4) Move the Ac load to the k-loop
52 p = autofission(p, p.find('A_reg[_] = _').after(),
53     n_lifts=3)
54 # 5) Replace the itt loop by RVV intrinsics
55 p = replace(p, 'for itt in _: _', rvv_vld_4xf32)
56 # 6) Set the A_reg memory to RVV
57 p = set_memory(p, 'A_reg', RVV)
58
59 # BK5
60 # 1) Divide the j loop by a factor vl
61 p = divide_loop(p,'j', vl, ['jt','jtt'])
62 # 2) Map Bc buffer to vectorial register Btmp
63 p = bind_expr(p, 'Bc[_]','Btmp')
64 # 3) Map Btmp to vectorial register B_reg
65 p = bind_expr(p, 'Btmp','B_reg')
66 # 4) Build a 2D structure of B_reg and Btmp
67 p = expand_dim(p, 'Btmp', vl, 'jtt', ...)
68 p = expand_dim(p, 'B_reg', vl, 'itt', ...)
69 p = expand_dim(p, 'B_reg', NR, 'jt * 4 + jtt', ...)
70 # 5) Move the register declaration to the top
71 p = lift_alloc(p, 'B_reg', n_lifts=5)
72 p = lift_alloc(p, 'Btmp', n_lifts=5)
73 # 6) Move the Bc load to the k-loop
74 p = autofission(p, p.find('B_reg[_] = _').after(),
75     n_lifts=4)
76 p = autofission(p, p.find('Btmp[_] = _').after(),
77     n_lifts=2)
78 # 7) Replace the itt loop by RVV intrinsics
79 p = replace(p, 'for jtt in _: _', rvv_vld_4xf32)
80 p = replace(p, 'for itt in _: _', rvv_gather_4xf32)
81 # 8) Set the A_reg memory to RVV
82 p = set_memory(p, 'B_reg', RVV)
83 p = set_memory(p, 'Btmp', RVV)
84
85 # BK6
86 p = unroll_loop(p,'it')
87 p = unroll_loop(p,'jt')
```

Fig. 3. Example of Exo user code to generate an 8×6 micro-kernel for RVV.

4 Experimental Evaluation

Armed with the generator described in the previous section, we have instructed Exo to produce a collection of micro-kernels for a range of pairs $m_r \times n_r$. This produces C code with the appropriate intrinsics, which is then passed to an RVV-compliant compiler (in our case gcc 13.1.0) to obtain the assembly,[1] and from there to lower it to binary vectorized code ready to run in the target architecture.

---

[1] The assembly codes in Fig. 2 were automatically generated with Exo.

Table 1. Summary of the target RVV platforms.

Name	SBC	Processor	Freq. (GHz)	#Cores	RVV version	Vector units	Vector length	RAM GBytes	L1 KBytes	L2 MBytes
C906	LicheeRV	XuanTie C906	1.00	1	0.7.1	1	128	2 DDR3	32	1
C908	CanMV-K230	XuanTie C908	1.60	1	1.0	1	128	2 LPDDR3	32	1
C910	LicheePi 4a	XuanTie C910	1.85	4	0.7.1	2	128	8 LPDDR4	64	1
K1	BananaPi F3	SpaceMiT K1	1.60	8	1.0	1	256	4 LPDDR4	32	1

We have integrated the micro-kernel codes inside our own GEMM macro-kernel following the ideas from GotoBLAS. We have enhanced the macro-kernel with an analytical model to determine the values of CCPs for each target architectures (m_c, n_c and k_c) following the ideas of [9]. Finally, we have manually vectorized the packing routines for A_c, B_c.

In this section, we evaluate both the performance of each member of the generated micro-kernel family in an isolated manner for the distinct target RVV architectures (Sect. 4.2) and the final performance of GEMM in both sequential and parallel implementations using our macro-kernel combined with the best micro-kernel for each target (Sect. 4.3). All the experiments were carried out using single-precision floating point arithmetic, yet the effort of generating micro-kernels for other precisions is minimal with Exo.

4.1 Target COTS Platforms

We have employed the following list of RISC-V processors (see also Table 1):

C906. A LicheeRV SBC, that integrates an Allwinner D1 SoC, with a single C906 core running at 1 GHz, a low-power core targeting IoT applications in severely power-restricted scenarios, yet supporting RVV version 0.7.1. The core implements a 5-stage single-issue in-order execution pipeline, with support for a 128-bit vector unit. The core includes a 32-KByte, 4-way associative L1 cache.

C908. A CanMV-K230 SBC integrating a K230 system-on-chip (SoC). We employed the only RVV-capable C908 core in the *"big-LITTLE"* dual-core, working at 1.6 GHz. The core supports the RVV version 1.0 on a 128-bit vector unit, with 32 KBytes of L1 and 256 KBytes of L2 data caches.

C910. A Sipeed LicheePi 4a SBC that embeds an Alibaba T-HEAD 1520 with four XuanTie C910 cores running at 1.85 GHz. The core supports RVV version 0.7.1. Each core utilises a deep 12-stage pipeline, out-of-order, multi-issue superscalar architecture. It integrates a 64-KByte, 2-way associative L1 data cache; plus a 1-MByte, 16-way associative L2 data cache (shared with the remaining cores). Two vector slices (pipelines) with 128-bit vector length are in place.

K1. The BananaPi F3 SBC integrates an 8-core SpaceMiT K1 processor running at 1.6 GHz, 32 Kbytes L1 4-way associative data cache and 512 Kbytes of L2 16-way associative cache shared across cores in a cluster (group of 4 cores). Vector length is 256-bit, with two 128-bit vector units (RVV 1.0 compliant).

4.2 Micro-kernel Performance

The first round of experiments evaluates the performance of the family of micro-kernels automatically generated by Exo in the four target platforms. The objective is two-fold. From a quantitative perspective, to illustrate the arithmetic performance that can be extracted from each architecture, establishing a comparative baseline among platforms. From a qualitative perspective, to justify the need to offer specific micro-kernel options (i.e., micro-kernel variants and values for $m_r \times n_r$) that specifically target the characteristics of each platform.

The performance obtained for each platform, in terms of GFLOPS, is reported in Figs. 4 (for C906 and C908) and 5 (for C910 and K1). The results are summarized by means of heatmaps, with the color reflecting the performance observed for each pair $m_r \times n_r$. The plot rows correspond to different micro-kernel variants. The coordinates in white in the plots correspond to combinations of

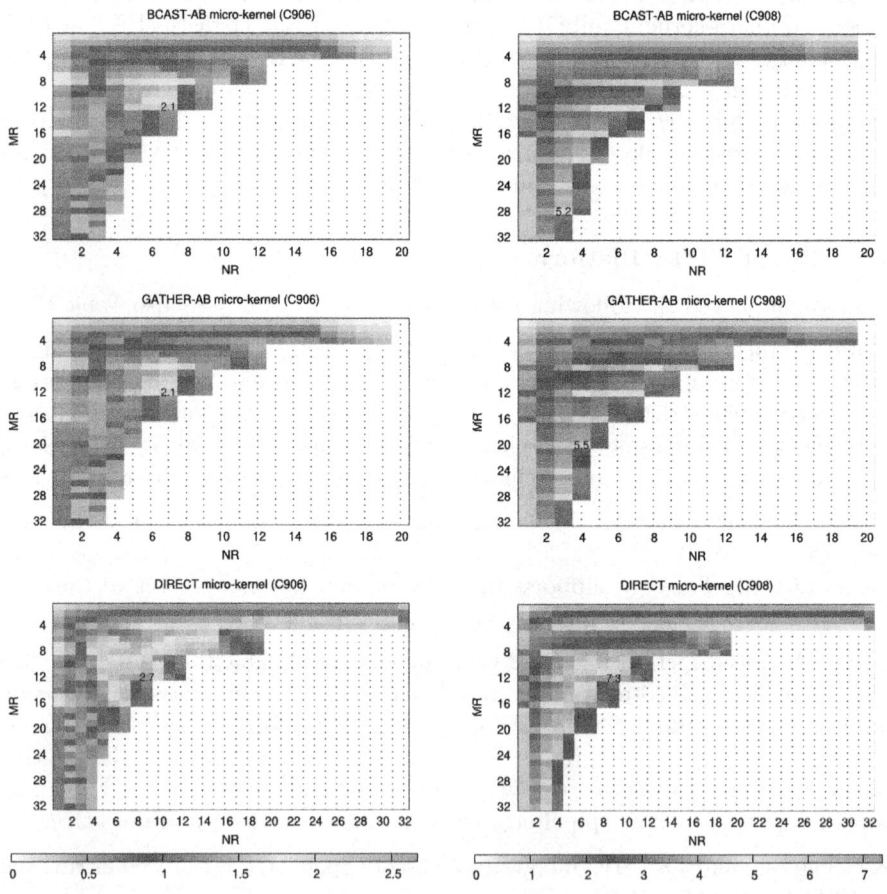

Fig. 4. Detailed performance for different micro-kernel variants and dimensions ($m_r \times n_r$) generated by Exo for C906 (left) and C908 (right).

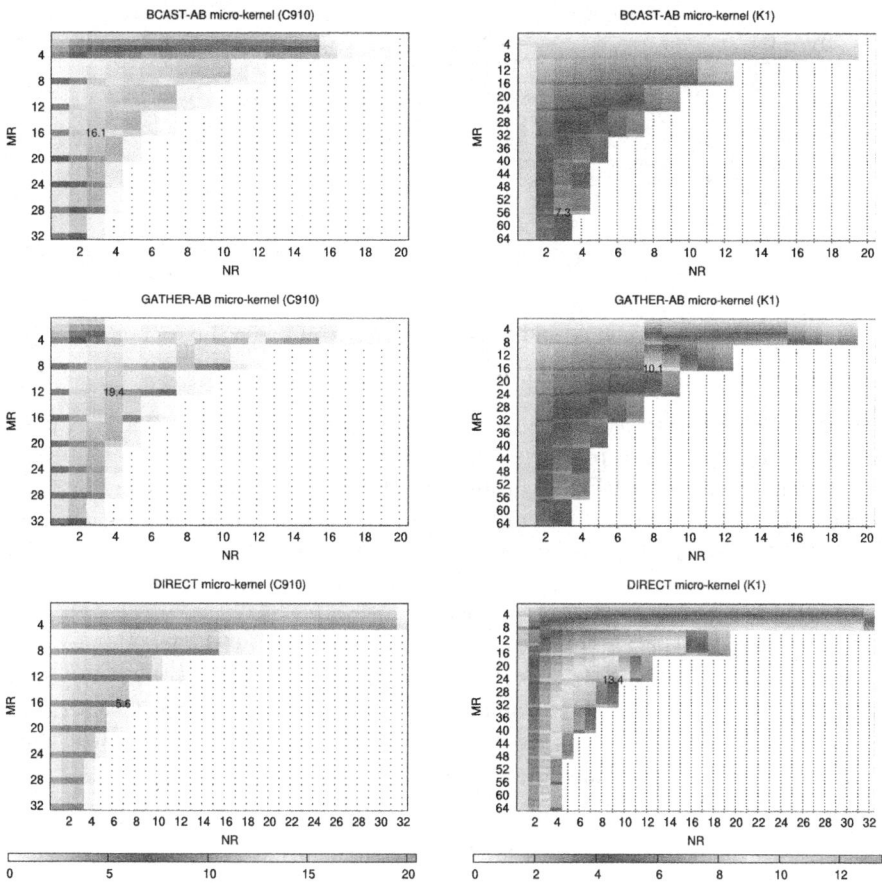

Fig. 5. Detailed performance for different micro-kernel variants and dimensions ($m_r \times n_r$) generated by Exo for C910 (left) and K1 (right).

$m_r \times n_r$ whose micro-kernel would exceed the number of available vector registers. The number highlighted in each heatmap displays the highest observed performance; and its coordinates identify the optimal pair $m_r \times n_r$.

Quantitatively, the maximum performance numbers reflect the arithmetic capabilities of each platform, and divide them into two groups: low-performing cores (C906 and C908, yielding 2.7 and 7.3 GFLOPS, respectively), and HPC cores (K1 and C910, yielding 13.4 and 20.5 GFLOPS, respectively). This exposes the scenarios which are more appropriate for each type of platform.

Qualitatively, the selection of the optimal pair $m_r \times n_r$ differs across architectures. While C906 and C908 share a common optimal micro-kernel of dimension $m_r \times n_r = 12 \times 9$, C910 favors a 16×7 micro-kernel, and K1 a 24×9 micro-kernel. This supports the vision of providing specific micro-kernel dimensions for each core type, which in many cases is not available in current BLAS distribu-

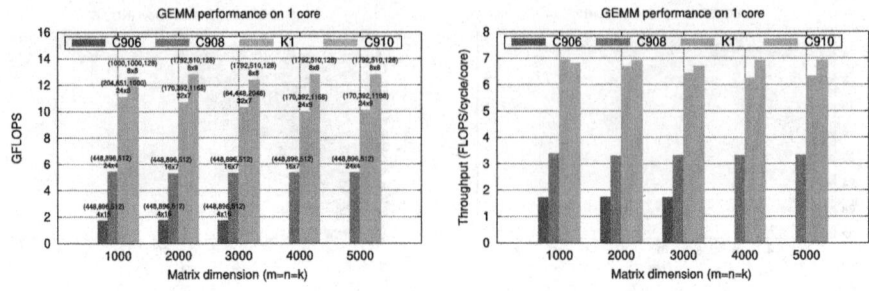

Fig. 6. Performance and throughput of GEMM on a single core.

tions for RVV. The type of optimization (micro-kernel variant) that yields the best performance across platforms differs. Specifically, while C906, C908 and K1 benefit from the DIRECT variant, the difference in performance for C910 between DIRECT and the remaining variants is remarkable; in this case, the GATHER variant is, by far, the best-performing micro-kernel. Also, note that the order in which elements of A_c and B_c are loaded in the k-loop is also key in some architectures from the perspective of performance.

In general, the heatmaps also reveal the tolerance of the architecture for a suboptimal selection of $m_r \times n_r$ and the specific micro-kernel variant. Some architectures reveal few *green* points (e.g. C910), hence a correct selection is of capital importance. Others reveal larger *green* areas in the heatmaps, hence exhibiting extended tolerance to an incorrect micro-kernel selection.

4.3 Sequential and Parallel GEMM Performance

Figure 6 reports the absolute performance in GFLOPS (left) and the throughput in terms of FLOPS/cycle (right) when the best performing micro-kernel is integrated within a complete GEMM routine on a single core of all architectures, for a range of square matrices. The plot also specifies the selected values for $m_r \times n_r$ and the CCP triplet (m_c, n_c, k_c) considering the cache hierarchy of each platform. For both metrics, we observe again a clear division of the four architectures into two groups: C906 and C908, with a throughput of around 1.5 and 3.2 FLOPS/cycle, respectively; and K1 and C910, with a throughput ranging from 6.7 to 7 FLOPS/cycle. Regarding the performance degradation due to the integration of the micro-kernels into the GEMM macro-kernel, taking the performance of the isolated micro-kernel in Figs. 4 and 5, we note that this is relatively small for the lowest-performing architectures (C906 and C908), but very relevant for the remaining two (34.6 % and 18 %) for C910 and K1, respectively; for the latter, the cache hierarchy performance seems to introduce a very relevant penalty in performance.

We also highlight the dependence of the optimal micro-kernel and the CCPs on the target architecture. This reinforces the benefits of adapting the configurations and micro-kernel variants to each RVV target, an extreme that is usually not pursued in high-performance instances of BLAS.

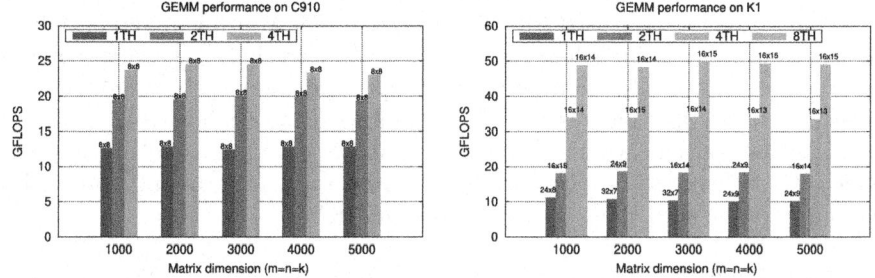

Fig. 7. Parallel GEMM performance on C910 (left) and K1 (right).

Figure 7 extends the study for a parallel implementation of the complete GEMM on C910 and K1. In this case, we proceed by parallelizing Loop 5 (ir) in the baseline GEMM implementation via OpenMP `pragmas` [13]. The plot also includes the optimal values for $m_r \times n_r$, which do not match in all cases those observed in the sequential executions. For both architectures, the use of the maximum number of available cores (4 for C910, 8 for K1) reveals a severe drop of the speed-up: for $m = n = k = 3000$, 1.56×, and 1.91× for 2 and 4 cores in C910; 1.76×, 3.29×, and 4.86× for 2, 4, and 8 cores in K1.

Figure 8 summarizes many of the aforementioned observations by reporting the raw performance (in terms of GFLOPS) and normalized throughput (FLOPS/cycle/core) for GEMM on the four architectures. As said, the SBCs are clearly divided into two different categories (low- and high-performance cores); throughput follows this trend too for sequential implementations, but the lack of scalability severely penalizes the throughput when multiple cores are in use.

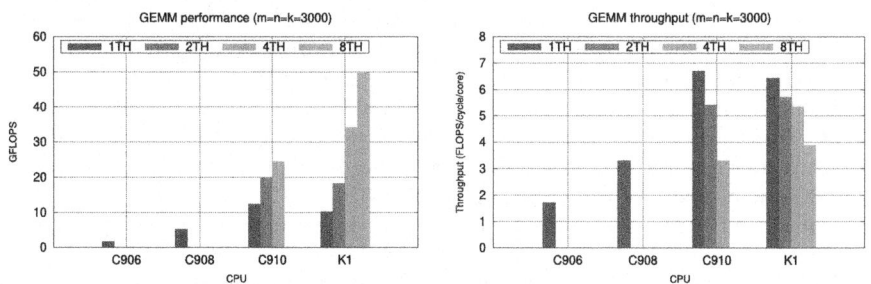

Fig. 8. Performance and throughput comparison across RVV architectures.

5 Concluding Remarks

We have provided a detailed evaluation of the arithmetic capabilities of four different COTS platforms that implement the RVV vector extension. To conduct our study, we have used EXO to generate a family of micro-kernels following the GotoBLAS approach for GEMM, and evaluated both the isolated micro-kernels, and the overall performance and (sequential and parallel) throughput of the complete GEMM. The results offer quantitative and qualitative insights and highlight the convenience of leveraging automatic generation tools to obtain a sufficiently rich variety of micro-kernels in order to extract the full potential of the target cores, even those sharing a common ISA.

Acknowledgments. Research funded by projects PID2023-146569NB, PID2021-126576NB-I00, PPID2023-146569NB-C22, TED2021-129334B-I00, TED2021-130123B-I00 (MCIN/AEI/10.13 039/501100011033), GVA CIPROM/2022/20, UJI-2023-04. A. C. is supported by the CIAPOS/2023/431 grant, Fondo Social Europeo Plus 2021–2027 from the GVA, and PAID_06_2024 from Universitat Politcnica de Valncia. H. M. is a POSTDOC_21_00025 fellow supported by Junta de Andalucía. S. C. is supported by grant RYC2021-033973-I, funded by MCIN/AEI/10.13 039/501100011033 and the EU "NextGenerationEU"/PRTR.

References

1. Alaejos, G., et al.: Algorithm 1039: automatic generators for a family of matrix multiplication routines with apache TVM. ACM Trans. Math. Softw. **50**(1) (2024)
2. Castelló, A., et al.: Portable, high performance matrix multiplication micro-kernels for RISC-V with EXO. In: 2025 33th Euromicro International Conference on Parallel, Distributed and Network-Based Processing (PDP) (2022, to appear)
3. Castelló, A., et al.: Tackling the matrix multiplication micro-kernel generation with Exo. In: Proceedings of 2024 IEEE/ACM International Symposium on Code Generation and Optimization. CGO '24, pp. 182–192 (2024)
4. Chen, T., et al.: TVM: end-to-end optimization stack for deep learning. CoRR abs/1802.04799 (2018). http://arxiv.org/abs/1802.04799
5. Goto, K., Geijn, R.A.v.d.: Anatomy of high-performance matrix multiplication. ACM Trans. Math. Softw. **34**(3), 12:1–12:25 (2008)
6. Igual, F., et al.: Automatic generation of micro-kernels for performance portability of matrix multiplication on risc-v vector processors. In: Proceedings of the SC '23 Workshops of the International Conference on High Performance Computing, Network, Storage, and Analysis, pp. 1523–1532 (2023)
7. Ikarashi, Y., et al.: Exocompilation for productive programming of hardware accelerators. PLDI 2022, New York, NY, USA, pp. 703–718 (2022)
8. Lattner, C., et al.: MLIR: scaling compiler infrastructure for domain specific computation. In: 2021 IEEE/ACM International Symposium Code Generation and Optimization (CGO), pp. 2–14. IEEE (2021)
9. Low, T.M., et al.: Analytical modeling is enough for high-performance BLIS. ACM Trans. Math. Softw. **43**(2), 12:1–12:18 (2016)

10. Martínez, H., et al.: Performance analysis of BERT on RISC-V processors with simd units. In: Weiland, M., Neuwirth, S., Kruse, C., Weinzierl, T. (eds.) ISC High Performance 2023. LNCS, vol. 15058, pp. 325–338. Springer, Cham (2025). https://doi.org/10.1007/978-3-031-73716-9_23
11. Ragan-Kelley, J., et al.: Halide: a language and compiler for optimizing parallelism, locality, and recomputation in image processing pipelines. In: Conference on Programming Language Design and Implementation. PLDI '13, pp. 519–530 (2013)
12. RISC-V V Vector extension. https://github.com/riscv/riscv-v-spec/releases/download/v1.0/riscv-v-spec-1.0.pdf
13. Smith, T.M., et al.: Anatomy of high-performance many-threaded matrix multiplication. In: Proceedings of IEEE 28th International Parallel and Distributed Processing Symposium. IPDPS'14, pp. 1049–1059 (2014)
14. Van Zee, F.G., van de Geijn, R.A.: BLIS: a framework for rapidly instantiating BLAS functionality. ACM Trans. Math. Softw. **41**(3), 14:1–14:33 (2015)
15. Van Zee, F.G., et al.: The BLIS framework: experiments in portability. ACM Trans. Math. Softw. **42**(2) (2016)

Advancing the RISC-V Performance Simulation Ecosystem with Data Prefetching

Luís Crespo[✉], Nuno Neves, Pedro Tomas, and Nuno Roma

INESC-ID, Instituto Superior Técnico, Universidade de Lisboa, Lisbon, Portugal
{luis.miguel.crespo,nuno.neves,
pedro.z.tomas,nuno.roma}@tecnico.ulisboa.pt

Abstract. As processor speeds continue to outpace memory access times, memory latency remains a critical bottleneck in modern computing systems. Addressing this challenge requires effective memory access optimizations, such as data prefetching, which can anticipate memory requests and reduce stalls. Meanwhile, RISC-V has emerged as a compelling open-source alternative to proprietary ISAs with increasing adoption in domains ranging from embedded systems to high-performance computing. However, as RISC-V systems scale in complexity, there is a growing need for accurate and efficient performance modeling to guide architectural optimizations. Accordingly, this paper enhances the RISC-V Olympia trace-based performance simulator by extending it to support prefetching mechanisms. Additional contributions include modifications to the Spike simulator and the development of a complementary parser for generating an open-source simulation trace format. The effectiveness of these prefetching strategies is evaluated, demonstrating their potential to reduce memory access latency and enhance RISC-V system performance.

Keywords: RISC-V · Performance Modeling · Data Prefetching · Processor Simulation · High-Performance Computing

1 Introduction

The emergence of RISC-V as a royalty-free and versatile instruction set architecture (ISA) has significantly influenced processor design, offering an open-source alternative to proprietary ISAs like x86 and ARM [5,24–26]. With growing adoption in academia and industry, performance optimization is increasingly critical. To address this, the RISC-V Performance Modelling (and Simulation) Special Interest Group (SIG) was established to coordinate efforts toward a unified performance modelling and cycle-accurate simulation framework[1]. One key outcome is *Olympia*[2], a trace-driven simulator under development for evaluating RISC-V

---

[1] https://lists.riscv.org/g/sig-perf-modeling.
[2] https://github.com/riscv-software-src/riscv-perf-model.

architectural optimizations, including branch prediction, caching, and prefetching.

However, *Olympia*'s current trace generation relies on an emulator limited to the RV64GC ISA subset, excluding extensions relevant to performance modelling. A more suitable approach is leveraging *Spike*[3], the golden reference RISC-V simulator, given its broad adoption and role in validating new instructions and features. Additionally, *Olympia* lacks support for modelling data prefetching, a crucial technique for mitigating the "memory wall" [22]—the growing disparity between processor speed and memory latency. Prefetching improves memory efficiency, making its integration vital for modern performance models [14,21].

This paper extends *Olympia* with data prefetching mechanisms and introduces a complementary parser to generate traces from *Spike*. These enhancements strengthen RISC-V's performance modelling capabilities, advancing its competitiveness for high-performance computing. The contributions of this work include: (i) the integration of data prefetching mechanisms into *Olympia*; (ii) the development of a parser to convert *Spike*-generated traces into *Olympia*'s format; (iii) the implementation of multiple prefetching algorithms within *Olympia*; (iv) the evaluation of prefetching strategies based on performance impact; and (v) the identification of memory hierarchy bottlenecks and guidelines for future improvements.

2 Background and Related Work

Architectural simulation is essential for evaluating processor designs and optimizing performance. This section reviews key performance modelling approaches, introduces *Olympia*, a RISC-V out-of-order (OoO) CPU performance model, and discusses data prefetching as a way to mitigate memory access latency.

2.1 Performance Modeling

Processor simulation is the standard method for evaluating design choices, testing research ideas, and analyzing performance and power consumption [2,18]. Timing simulators, which capture microarchitectural behaviour to generate performance statistics such as Instructions Per Cycle (IPC), are commonly used to identify bottlenecks.

Timing simulators fall into three main categories [2]: (1) *Cycle-level simulators* [6,17] model every processor cycle with high accuracy but significant computational cost. (2) *Event-driven simulators* [9,10] improve efficiency by focusing on discrete events rather than every cycle. (3) *Interval simulators* [8] increase simulation speed by processing instruction flow in intervals based on key miss events (e.g., cache misses, branch mispredictions).

Among widely used simulators, *gem5* [6] supports RISC-V [16,20] and offers full-system functional simulation. Other RISC-V-compatible simulators include

---
[3] https://github.com/riscv-software-src/riscv-isa-sim

Spike, the official functional simulator, Sniper [12], and *Olympia*, developed within the RISC-V foundation. While *gem5* is well-suited for functional simulation, *Olympia* provides a more precise framework for performance modeling and design space exploration, making it particularly relevant for RISC-V.

2.2 Olympia

Olympia is a recent RISC-V OoO CPU performance model built on the Sparta Modeling Framework[4]. It functions as a trace-driven simulator, processing instruction streams in JavaScript Object Notation (JSON) or Simulation Trace Format (STF)[5]. While JSON is human-readable but limited in scope, STF is a more efficient binary format for full application traces. Currently, STF traces in *Olympia* are generated using an instrumented version of *Dromajo*[6], an emulator restricted to RV64GC, limiting flexibility.

Olympia models an OoO superscalar CPU with five pipeline stages: Fetch, Decode, Rename, Issue/Execute/Write Back, and Commit. It includes an L1 instruction and data cache and a shared L2 cache. Each component communicates through latency-defined ports, enabling modular design and ease of extension.

2.3 Data Prefetching

Prefetching in particular is a widely studied technique [3,4,13,14,21,23] that proactively anticipates and loads data into caches before it is requested by the processor, thereby reducing stall cycles and improving system throughput [7,14]. This helps reducing cache misses and improves the overall performance, since it minimizes the time the processor spends waiting for data, by overlapping the memory accesses with instruction execution. This latency-hiding effect makes prefetching an essential optimization mechanism for modern memory hierarchies.

Prefetching can be implemented in two primary ways: software prefetching [1, 11] and hardware prefetching [3,4,13,23]. In software prefetching, the compiler (or a programmer) inserts explicit instructions to anticipate the load of data into the cache before it is accessed by the program. On the other hand, hardware prefetching is dynamically managed by a dedicated hardware component that predicts memory access patterns and issues prefetch requests based on run-time information. Because of its larger adoption, this work will be focused on hardware prefetching, although it could be later extended to support software prefetching.

Independently of the prefetcher type, prefetching can be applied at various cache levels, each with its own tradeoffs, resulting in different prefetching mechanisms [13]. Specifically, an L1 prefetcher makes use of information that would be costly to propagate to the L2-Cache, such as the Program Counter (PC) [3]. In contrast, lower-level caches (e.g., L2 and L3) are characterized by a larger

---

[4] https://github.com/sparcians/map.
[5] https://github.com/sparcians/stf_spec.
[6] https://github.com/chipsalliance/dromajo.

capacity and bandwidth, making them more tolerant to inaccurate and aggressive prefetching.

Several parameters and metrics are essential for a convenient characterization of prefetchers. Particular parameters include *prefetch distance* and *prefetch degree*, which control the *aggressiveness* of the prefetching strategy. *Prefetch distance* refers to the number of instructions or memory accesses anticipated ahead of the current instruction. Conversely, *prefetch degree* denotes the number of data blocks fetched into the cache. Although aggressive prefetching can help cover cache misses, it can also lead to reduced accuracy and inefficient memory bandwidth utilization.

The most relevant metrics related to prefetching are: (i) the *Issued prefetches*, i.e., the number of prefetch requests issued to the memory hierarchy after being filtered by the cache and the Miss Status Holding Registers (MSHR); (ii) the *Demand misses* which evaluates the number of cache accesses that result in misses not solved by the prefetcher (cache misses that are in the MSHR do not count as demand misses); (iii) *Useful prefetches*, corresponding to the number of issued prefetches that eliminate original misses and whose data (fetched by the prefetcher) is completed and placed in the cache before it is accessed; (iv) *Useless prefetches* indicating the number of prefetch requests whose fetched data (in the cache) is replaced before being used; (v) *Late prefetches* corresponding to the number of prefetch requests that are already in the cache or MSHR; (vi) *Accuracy* that measures how effectively a prefetcher predicts memory access patterns of applications and is calculated as the ratio of the number of useful prefetches to the total number of issued prefetches; and (vii) *Coverage*, indicating how prefetches can mitigate cache misses, and is calculated as the ratio of useful prefetches to the sum of useful prefetches and demand misses.

3 Proposed Simulation Flow

This section details the integration of prefetching mechanisms into the *Olympia* RISC-V performance simulator, ensuring the completion of the simulation flow entirely within the RISC-V environment (as summarized in Fig. 1). Specifically, it describes *i)* the adopted methodology for trace generation using *Spike*; *ii)* the implementation of prefetching in the *Olympia* simulator as a module and its integration within the simulator memory hierarchy.

3.1 Trace Generation

Trace files serve as inputs for trace-driven simulators. These files contain prerecorded instruction streams from executed applications, capturing details such as PC, instruction opcodes, data memory addresses, and branch target addresses.

As mentioned above (see Sect. 2.2), the current trace generation method used by Olympia involves instrumenting the *Dromajo* functional model, which is not ideal, as it implements a specific configuration (RV64GC), leaving out extensions that would benefit from performance modeling. Accordingly, a new STF

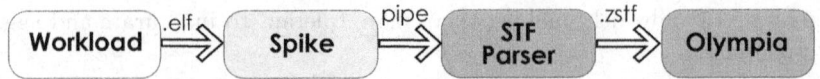

Fig. 1. Overview of the proposed simulation pipeline. A workload with the capture zone inserted in the code (using predefined MACROs) is compiled with a RISC-V-compatible compiler. It is then executed in *Spike* with the `--log-commits` flag. The output of *Spike* is parsed using the proposed STF parser through a pipe, capturing the intended code section and generating a trace binary file following the STF specification. The traces can then be fed into *Olympia* for performance modeling.

parser (see Algorithm 1) was specifically developed that receives the execution log produced by *Spike* (`--log-commits`) and outputs the required STF trace file (`.zstf`) (see Fig. 1). Following a similar approach used by the *Dromajo* implementation, the parser only captures the delimited code section of the application under consideration through a START and END macro. The `--log-commits` flag must be used in *Spike* (instead of the default log (`-l`)) since the STF specification requires the memory access addresses that are only made available within this specific log. Furthermore, it was necessary to extend it to include the data size. The instruction parameters are also obtained from the commit log using pattern matching with *regular expressions*. The required parameters to produce the STF log include: *i)* PC, which is directly exposed; *ii)* next PC (in case of a branch) – a buffer of one instruction is maintained to keep track of non-sequential PCs; *iii)* instruction encoding, which is also directly exposed; *iv)* instruction type (load/store), obtainable with a simple analysis; *v)* data size, directly exposed after instrument spike; and *vi)* instruction width, obtainable with a simple analysis of the instruction binary.

3.2 Prefetcher Module

As mentioned earlier (Sect. 2.2), the simulator features a two-level cache. Prefetchers can be deployed at different (or multiple) cache levels [14]. Accordingly, the implemented data prefetcher operates as a single module (see Fig. 2D) that is instantiated in two distinct units: L1D-Cache and L2-Cache (see Fig. 2A). Each prefetcher monitors its corresponding cache requests and fill responses, generating prefetch requests for the subsequent lower-level cache. Before being issued, these requests pass through the associated cache to squash unnecessary prefetches – either because the requested cache line is already in the cache or allocated in the MSHR.

The internal prefetching engine (`Pf engine`) is the component that handles the demand and fill requests to generate the prefetch requests according to the prefetch algorithm under evaluation. Leveraging a prefetch engine allows the model to rapidly customize the prefetchers by selecting a given prefetch algorithm, being only necessary to implement each prefetcher algorithm once as an independent module. As a consequence, the latency of the engine in generating prefetch requests depends on the selected algorithm. The requests are stored in

Algorithm 1. STF Parser

```
1:  Initialize STF writer
2:  current_line = getline(pipe)
3:  while next_line = getline(pipe) do            ▷ Go one inst. ahead to detect jumps
4:      if trace_regex = regex(current_line, PATTERN) then
5:          Extract PC, instruction (and width), and operation type from trace_regex
6:          if Instruction == END then            ▷ Trace until finding the END macro
7:              Exit loop
8:          end if
9:          if Setup then                         ▷ STF needs the starting PC for the header
10:             Write to STF the Setup Header with the starting PC
11:         end if
12:         if Tracing enabled then
13:             Extract next PC from next_line
14:             if next PC not expected PC then   ▷ Checked with the inst. width
15:                 Write to STF the next PC target
16:             end if
17:             if Memory operation detected then
18:                 Extract and log memory details in STF
19:             end if
20:             Write instruction record in STF   ▷ Depends on inst. width
21:         end if
22:         if Instruction is START then ▷ Ensure START is excluded from the trace
23:             Enable tracing
24:         end if
25:     end if
26:     current_line = next_line
27: end while
28: Close STF writer and exit
```

a prefetch queue (`Pf Queue`), and later sent to the cache. To prevent redundant requests, addresses already present in the queue are dropped.

In addition to the set of parameters specific to each prefetcher, they are configurable with *degree* and *distance* parameters to control the prefetch *aggressiveness*. Each prefetcher can also be set to generate prefetch requests triggered by store operations (turned off by default). Additionally, as a design decision, to maintain security while avoiding the extension of the Memory Management Unit (MMU), prefetch requests that would cross page boundaries are discarded.

By default, both the L1 and L2 prefetchers are disabled. Users can activate a prefetcher by modifying the architecture configuration file or passing it as an argument when running the simulator. In this work, three prefetch algorithms were implemented:

- Next-Line [19]: Assumes that accessing a memory location will likely lead to an access to the next one. It always fetches the next sequential memory block and can be applied at any cache level.
- Stride [3]: Predicts future data requests based on stride access patterns, like R[i], R[i+Q], R[i+2Q], R[i+3Q], where Q is the stride. It tracks these patterns for memory accesses triggered by the same PC and is best suited for implementation at the L1 data cache level.
- Best-Offset [13]: Dynamically selects the prefetch offset based on the application behavior. It has a learning phase, where it tests multiple offsets to determine the most effective. By recording the base addresses of completed

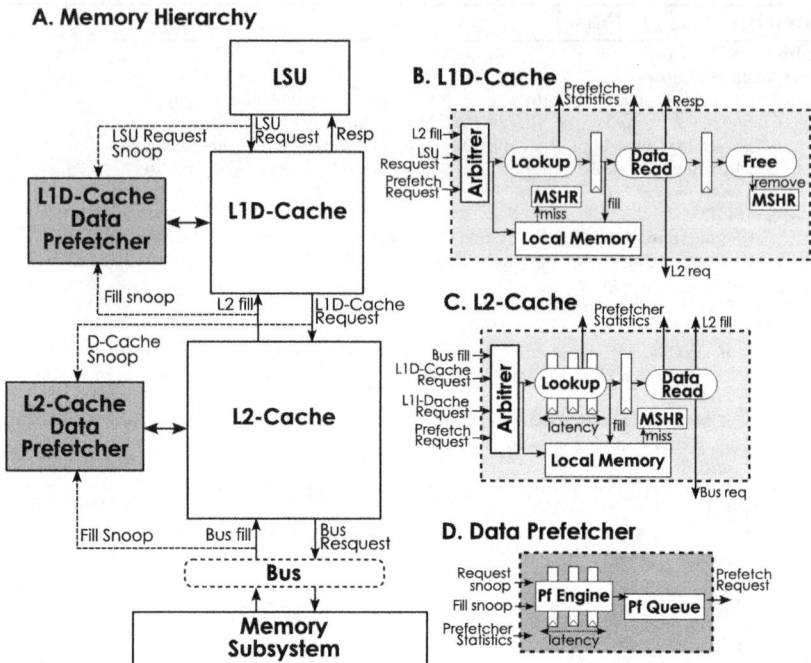

Fig. 2. Integration of prefetchers in the *Olympia* simulator: (A) High-level view of the memory hierarchy with data prefetchers; (B) D-Cache, (C) L2-Cache, and (C) Data Prefetcher architectures.

prefetch requests in a *recent requests table*, it infers the optimal timeliness for prefetch candidates. After the learning phase, it generates one request for each demand. This algorithm is usually more suited for L2 Caches and is the only implemented prefetcher that snoops both demand and refill requests.

Prefetch Statistics: The developed prefetcher module includes the gathering infrastructure to collect all the metrics described in Sect. 2.3, which are incremented as the corresponding events occur in the respective cache. In particular, an *issued prefetch* is counted when the cache issues it, a *demand access* is counted when a request is not found in the cache or the MSHR, and a *late prefetch* is recorded when a requested prefetch is found in the cache or MSHR. To identify *useful* and *useless prefetches*, a prefetch request is sent with the prefetch flag set, such that when the request arrives at the issuing cache, the corresponding cache line is marked as prefetched. If a subsequent memory request accesses that line, the cache notifies the prefetcher, which then increments the *useful prefetches* counter. The prefetch flag is subsequently disabled. Additionally, if a cache refill evicts a cache line with the prefetch flag set, the cache notifies the prefetcher to increment the *useless prefetches* counter.

3.3 Prefetcher Integration in the Olympia Simulator

Since *Olympia* is a trace-based simulator, it accepts as input the trace generated by a functional simulator. In the proposed solution, the *Spike* simulator is adopted (see Fig. 1). The following paragraphs outline the architecture of the *Olympia* L1D-Cache and L2-Cache, highlighting the required modifications for the prefetcher integration. Both caches transmit the statistical data to the respective prefetcher according to the events described above.

L1D-Cache: The L1D-Cache aggregated to the OoO processor model simulated by the *Olympia* simulator was implemented as a 3-stage pipelined unit, capable of accepting one request per cycle (see Fig. 2B):

i) In the first stage (`Lookup`), the pipeline arbitrates between refill requests from L2 (`L2 fill`) and LoadStore Unit (LSU) requests (`LSU Request`), giving priority to refill requests. This stage also performs a memory lookup, allocating a new entry in the MSHR on a cache miss.
ii) In the second stage (`Data Read`), the L1D-Cache acts based on the lookup result: on a hit, it forwards data to the LSU; on a miss, it sends a request to the L2. If processing a refill request occurs, it updates the cache memory.
iii) The third stage (`Free`) deallocates the MSHR entries upon cache refills.

Required Modifications: The current implementation of the LSU keeps making requests to the L1D-Cache until it receives a hit. While it manages the arbitration among memory accesses within the LSU, it frequently repeats requests to the same memory access (that are still being serviced by the L2-Cache in case of a miss). This repetition floods the L1D-Cache with redundant memory requests. In a simulation system without prefetchers, this behavior is less problematic, as the L1D-Cache can simply drop the repeated LSU requests. However, since the L1D-Cache must prioritize memory requests over prefetch requests, the latter may not be serviced effectively. Accordingly, the L1D-Cache was adapted so that it notifies the prefetcher when it can accept prefetch requests. This is performed by the L1D-Cache at the data read stage (see Fig. 2B). Then, prefetch requests are issued to the L2-Cache if its address is not in the cache or the MSHR.

Another limitation arises from the fact that, despite featuring a MSHR, the L1D-Cache could only support one outstanding request at a time, stalling until the L2-Cache responded. This effectively nullified the benefits of the prefetcher. To address this issue, the existing (but unused) credit-based communication system between the L1D-Cache and L2 was used to make the L1D-Cache non-blocking. In this scheme, the L2-Cache signals the L1D-Cache when it is ready to receive new requests, similar to a hardware *ready* signal. This mechanism allows the L1D-Cache to issue new requests as long as it has available credits, blocking further requests when credits are exhausted.

L2-Cache: The L2-Cache is implemented within the simulator with a configurable size pipeline unit, capable of accepting one request per cycle, either from the Bus (`Bus fill`), the L1D-Cache (`L1D-Cache Request`), or the I-Cache

(I-Cache Request) (see Fig. 2C). Requests from the Bus have the highest priority, while L1D-Cache and I-Cache requests are arbitrated using a round-robin approach. During the first stage (Lookup), which spans several cycles (latency), the cache memory is accessed. In case of a cache refill, the respective cache line is updated. In the second stage (Data Read), the L2-Cache responds based on the lookup result: on a hit, it forwards data to the respective cache; on a miss, it sends a request to the Bus and allocates an entry on the MSHR. Misses already present in the MSHR are squashed, and the entry is deallocated upon a refill.

The integration of the prefetcher in the L2-Cache is slightly different from the L1D-Cache as it is not flooded with repeated requests. It sends an *acknowledge* signal to the prefetcher when it can receive prefetch requests. These requests are then arbitrated alongside the other requests, having the least priority. They follow the normal pipeline (see Fig. 2C), being issued to the Bus if their addresses are not in the memory or the MSHR, being squashed otherwise. Prefetch requests generated by the L2-Cache prefetcher are not sent to the L1D-Cache when refilled.

4 Evaluation

The following paragraphs evaluate the proposed prefetching features introduced in the *Olympia* simulation ecosystem.

The experimental setup includes a selection of 8 applications from the Mach-Suite [15] benchmark suite, providing a diverse collection of computational kernels. These benchmarks were compiled using Clang with the following optimization and architecture-specific flags: -O3, and -march=rv64imafdc. The corresponding binaries were then executed in *Spike*, and the execution traces were generated using the proposed STF parser. The obtained traces were then used as inputs for the *Olympia* simulator, configured with its reference architectural parameterization for an out-of-order RISC-V processor (big_arch), publicly available in the *Olympia* repository. Table 1 summarizes the parameters of the modeled baseline architecture. Finally, the three implemented prefetcher models are validated by considering different prefetching setups, mixing the utilization of the next-line, stride, and best-offset prefetchers in the L1 and L2 caches.

4.1 L1 Data Prefetcher Validation

Figure 3 presents the obtained metrics for the implemented next-line and stride prefetchers in the L1 data cache, across the considered benchmarks, including speedup (over the baseline), accuracy, and coverage of the prefetching algorithm. A perfect cache scenario is also included, representing the theoretical upper bound where every request results in a cache hit. To adjust the prefetcher *aggressiveness*, we select the prefetch *degree* to its best configuration for each benchmark (obtained experimentally), with values ranging from 1 to 8.

As could be expected, the performance impact for each model varies significantly across different workloads and prefetching methods. The highest speedups

Table 1. CPU Architecture Specifications

CPU	Functional Units	Caches
RV64GC 1 OoO core 8-wide fetch/issue/commit 8 LSQ, 30 ROB	5 Int ALU (1 cycle) 2 Int Mult (3 cycles) 1 Int Div (23 cycles) 2 FP ALU (2 cycles) 2 FP MUL/DIV (4/63 cycles)	**L1-I:** - 16KB / 2-way - 8 MSHRs / 2-cycle latency **L1-D:** - 64KB / 2-way - 8 MSHRs / 2-cycle latency **L2:** - 512KB / 16-way - 16 MSHRs / 10-cycle latency

are observed in bfs_bulk, followed closely by bfs_queue, spmv_ellpack, and spmv_crs. These algorithms exhibit sparse memory access patterns, meaning they do not access data sequentially in the cache and therefore do not naturally benefit from its spatial locality. As a result, they experience the largest improvements with prefetching. Conversely, gemm_ncubed is an algorithm where both next-line and stride prefetchers should perform well. The accuracy results confirm this expectation. However, the low coverage values indicate that the *Olympia* memory hierarchy is overloaded with requests spanning multiple cache lines, limiting the overall benefits (discussed in Sect. 4.3). This is further verified with the coverage in another benchmark that saturates the cache (i.e., gemm_ncubed), having high accuracy but lower coverage. The gemm_blocked on the other hand, implements a version of gemm with tiling dimensioned to the cache configuration. As would be expected, a next-line prefetcher cannot accurately predict such a pattern, which is successfully identified by the stride prefetcher.

Overall, both prefetching algorithms exhibit comparable performance to that reported in the literature [3,19], validating the implemented prefetcher models.

4.2 L2 Data Prefetcher Validation

To validate the integration of the implemented prefetcher in the L2 cache, four different setups are considered: *i)* L2 next-line; *ii)* L2 best-offset; *iii)* L1 next-line + L2 best-offset; and *iv)* L1 stride + L2 best-offset. Similarly to the previous validation, a perfect cache scenario is also considered as a baseline reference. Figure 4 presents the obtained evaluation metrics for the four setups.

As expected, contrarily to its deployment on the L1 data cache, it can be observed that coupling a next-line prefetcher in the L2 is insufficient to predict the memory access patterns given the lower amount of cache requests reaching the L2, hence showing inferior performance improvements. Nonetheless, it accurately predicts the patterns of the considered benchmarks. On the other hand, given the long training latency necessary to start up the best-offset prefetcher, its effects are only visible on benchmarks with large datasets (i.e.,

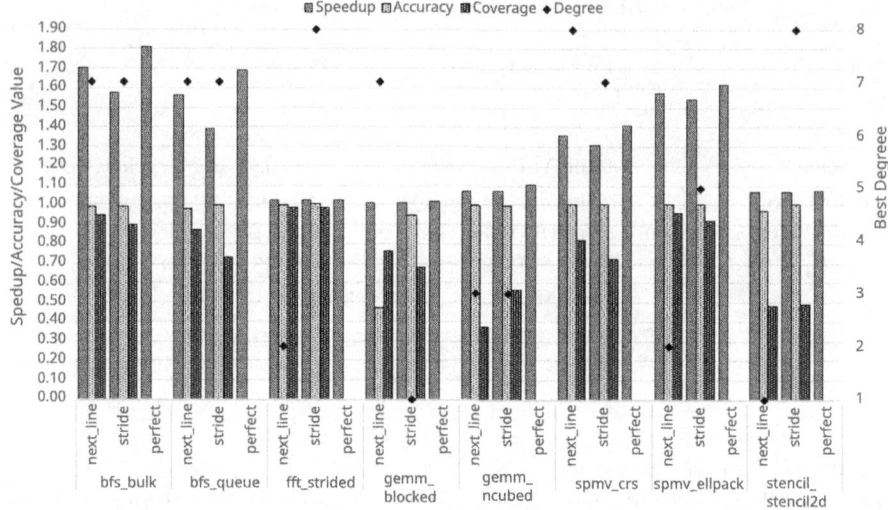

Fig. 3. Evaluation results for the next-line and stride prefetchers, deployed in the L1 data cache, for the considered benchmarks. Metrics include speedup, accuracy, and coverage. A perfect cache scenario is included as a theoretical upper bound. The prefetching degree is tuned per benchmark (within the range of 18).

gemm_blocked and gemm_ncubed). In these cases, once the best-offset prefetcher has acquired sufficient history it issues more prefetch requests. To further validate this behavior, all benchmarks were executed in the gem5 [6] simulator (which also deploys an equivalent model for the best-offset prefetcher). As expected, the gem5 version also only generated prefetch requests for the gemm benchmarks (i.e., gemm_blocked and gemm_ncubed).

Overall, the considered setups for the L2 cache further validate the implemented prefetcher models and allow the identification of bottlenecks and limitations in the *Olympia* simulator, which are discussed in the next section.

4.3 Limitations and Future Development Guidelines

While the integration of data prefetching mechanisms in *Olympia* enhances its modeling capabilities, several limitations can still be found in the underlying processor and memory hierarchy models.

One key challenge is the limited flexibility of the memory hierarchy model in handling aggressive prefetching strategies. As observed in the experimental results, certain workloads expose bottlenecks in the cache and bus structures, as they cannot handle multiple outstanding requests, reducing the effectiveness of the prefetching strategy. In particular, the bus model that handles the communication of the L2 with the memory is blocking, causing the L2 to stop sending memory requests, eventually causing several pipeline bubbles in the processor.

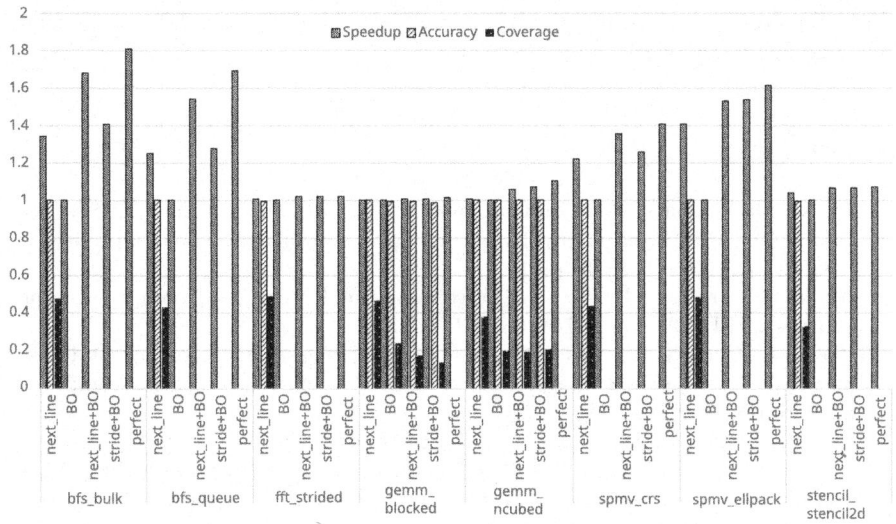

Fig. 4. Evaluation of prefetchers in the L2 cache.

Another significant bottleneck in *Olympia* is its load-store unit, which continuously generates memory requests (even for outstanding ones already sent to the memory hierarchy), contributing to increased congestion in the memory system. Also, since store operations must be processed immediately, they may delay or block demand loads and prefetches, leading to suboptimal performance. Addressing this issue requires implementing a store queue to decouple store operations from the LSU, allowing more efficient handling of memory requests and reducing pressure on the cache hierarchy.

5 Conclusion

This work extends the RISC-V *Olympia* simulator with data prefetching mechanisms and a new trace generation process using *Spike*, improving simulation flexibility and robustness. Experimental results confirm performance gains across workloads, validating the next-line, stride, and best-offset prefetchers. Future work will address the identified bottlenecks, explore software prefetching, refine page boundary handling, and integrate additional prefetching techniques to further enhance accuracy and efficiency.

Acknowledgments. Work supported by national funds through Fundação para a Ciência e a Tecnologia (FCT) under project 2022.06780.PTDC (DOI: 10.54499/2022.06780.PTDC). We also acknowledge the contributions from projects UIDB/50021/2020 (DOI: 10.54499/UIDB/50021/2020), 2022.11626.BD, and from the European High Performance Computing Joint Undertaking (JU) under Framework Partnership Agreement No 800928 and Specific Grant Agreement No 101036168 (EPI SGA2). The JU receives support from the European Union's Horizon 2020 research and innovation programme and from Croatia, France, Germany, Greece, Italy, Netherlands, Portugal, Spain, Sweden, and Switzerland.

References

1. Ainsworth, S., Jones, T.M.: Software prefetching for indirect memory accesses. In: 2017 IEEE/ACM International Symposium on Code Generation and Optimization (CGO), pp. 305–317. IEEE (2017)
2. Akram, A., Sawalha, L.: A survey of computer architecture simulation techniques and tools. IEEE Access **7**, 78120–78145 (2019)
3. Baer, J.L., Chen, T.F.: An effective on-chip preloading scheme to reduce data access penalty. In: Proceedings of the 1991 ACM/IEEE Conference on Supercomputing, pp. 176–186 (1991)
4. Bakhshalipour, M., Shakerinava, M., Lotfi-Kamran, P., Sarbazi-Azad, H.: Bingo spatial data prefetcher. In: 2019 IEEE International Symposium on High Performance Computer Architecture (HPCA), pp. 399–411. IEEE (2019)
5. Balkind, J., et al.: Openpiton: an open source manycore research framework. ACM SIGPLAN Not. **51**(4), 217–232 (2016)
6. Binkert, N., et al.: The gem5 simulator. ACM SIGARCH Comput. Archit. News **39**(2), 1–7 (2011)
7. Falsafi, B., Wenisch, T.F.: A Primer on Hardware Prefetching. Springer, Cham (2022)
8. Genbrugge, D., Eyerman, S., Eeckhout, L.: Interval simulation: Raising the level of abstraction in architectural simulation. In: HPCA-16 2010 The Sixteenth International Symposium on High-Performance Computer Architecture, pp. 1–12. IEEE (2010)
9. Hardavellas, N., et al.: Simflex: a fast, accurate, flexible full-system simulation framework for performance evaluation of server architecture. ACM SIGMETRICS Perform. Eval. Rev. **31**(4), 31–34 (2004)
10. Hughes, C.J., Pai, V.S., Ranganathan, P., Adve, S.V.: RSIM: simulating shared-memory multiprocessors with ILP processors. Computer **35**(2), 40–49 (2002)
11. Khan, M., Sandberg, A., Hagersten, E.: A case for resource efficient prefetching in multicores. In: 2014 43rd International Conference on Parallel Processing, pp. 101–110. IEEE (2014)
12. Mallya, N.B., Gonzalez-Alvarez, C., Carlson, T.E.: Flexible timing simulation of RISC-V processors with sniper. Simulation **4**(1) (2018)
13. Michaud, P.: Best-offset hardware prefetching. In: 2016 IEEE International Symposium on High Performance Computer Architecture (HPCA), pp. 469–480. IEEE (2016)
14. Mittal, S.: A survey of recent prefetching techniques for processor caches. ACM Comput. Surv. (CSUR) **49**(2), 1–35 (2016)
15. Reagen, B., Adolf, R., Shao, Y.S., Wei, G.Y., Brooks, D.: Machsuite: benchmarks for accelerator design and customized architectures. In: 2014 IEEE International Symposium on Workload Characterization (IISWC), pp. 110–119. IEEE (2014)
16. Roelke, A., Stan, M.R.: Risc5: implementing the RISC-V ISA in gem5. In: First Workshop on Computer Architecture Research with RISC-V (CARRV) (2017)
17. Sharkey, J., Ponomarev, D., Ghose, K.: M-sim: a flexible, multithreaded architectural simulation environment. Technical report, Department of Computer Science, State University of New York at Binghamton (2005)

18. Skadron, K., Martonosi, M., August, D.I., Hill, M.D., Lilja, D.J., Pai, V.S.: Challenges in computer architecture evaluation. Computer **36**(8), 30–36 (2003)
19. Smith, A.J.: Sequential program prefetching in memory hierarchies. Computer **11**(12), 7–21 (1978)
20. Ta, T., Cheng, L., Batten, C.: Simulating multi-core RISC-V systems in gem5. In: Workshop on Computer Architecture Research with RISC-V (2018)
21. Vanderwiel, S.P., Lilja, D.J.: Data prefetch mechanisms. ACM Comput. Surv. (CSUR) **32**(2), 174–199 (2000)
22. Wulf, W.A., McKee, S.A.: Hitting the memory wall: implications of the obvious. ACM SIGARCH Comput. Archit. News **23**(1), 20–24 (1995)
23. Yu, X., Hughes, C.J., Satish, N., Devadas, S.: IMP: indirect memory prefetcher. In: Proceedings of the 48th International Symposium on Microarchitecture, pp. 178 190 (2015)
24. Zaruba, F., Benini, L.: The cost of application-class processing: energy and performance analysis of a Linux-ready 1.7-GHz 64-bit RISC-V core in 22-nm FDSOI technology. IEEE Trans. Very Large Scale Integr. (VLSI) Syst. **27**(11), 2629–2640 (2019)
25. Zaruba, F., Schuiki, F., Benini, L.: Manticore: a 4096-core RISC-V chiplet architecture for ultraefficient floating-point computing. IEEE Micro **41**(2), 36–42 (2020)
26. Zhao, J., Korpan, B., Gonzalez, A., Asanovic, K.: SonicBOOM: the 3rd generation berkeley out-of-order machine. In: Fourth Workshop on Computer Architecture Research with RISC-V, vol. 5, pp. 1–7 (2020)

RISC-V in HPC: a Look Into Tools for Performance Monitoring

Fabio Banchelli[1(✉)], Rafel Albert Bros Esqueu[1], Tiago Rocha[2], Nuno Roma[2], Pedro Tomás[2], Nuno Neves[2], and Filippo Mantovani[1]

[1] Barcelona Supercomputing Center, Plaça Eusebi Güell, 1–3, 08034 Barcelona, Spain
{fabio.banchelli,rafel.bros,filippo.mantovani@bsc.es

[2] INESC-ID, Instituto Superior Técnico, University of Lisbon, Lisbon, Portugal
{tiagolopesrocha,nuno.roma,pedro.tomas,nuno.neves}@inesc-id.pt

Abstract. This paper explores the current state of performance monitoring on RISC-V based high-performance computing systems. We analyse hardware counters support across several commercial and experimental RISC-V platforms, highlighting the challenges and advancements in utilising tools like perf and PAPI. We propose modifications to the Linux kernel to enable user-level access to hardware counters and evaluate the overhead of different instrumentation methods compared to x86. It is a work-in-progress contribution that aims to enhance performance analysis capabilities within the growing RISC-V ecosystem for HPC.

Keywords: RISC-V · HPC · Hardware Counters

1 Introduction and Related Work

RISC-V is increasingly gaining popularity in the high-performance computing (HPC) domain, notably due to its vector extension [14] that enables highly flexible exploitation of data-level parallelism. In HPC systems, precise performance measurement at various levels of granularity is critical. Hardware performance counters, which track diverse architectural and micro-architectural events, play an essential role in these measurements. However, their implementation depends on the underlying instruction set and the specific chip manufacturer.

Over the years, several software methods have been developed to access the data stored in hardware counters [7,8,13,17]. Among them, the Linux kernel tool perf [16] and the libpfm4 [4] library, in which PAPI [9] relies upon, have become de facto standards for abstracting hardware counter information from chip-specific implementations. These tools simplify the development of performance analysis applications and provide software developers with easier access to performance metrics. As such, to promote the adoption of the RISC-V ecosystem in the HPC context, it is imperative that it continues to support these tools.

In this article, we present an overview of the current state of hardware counter support in RISC-V-based HPC systems. Our study analyses three commercial platforms – Banana Pi, Pioneer, and Unmatched – as well as an experimental platform – EPAC, a RISC-V vector central processing unit (CPU) developed as part of the European Processor Initiative (EPI) project. The technical contributions of this work include: *i)* proposing a modification to the Linux kernel to enable user-space reading of Control and Status Registers (CSRs), *ii)* extending PAPI support for the Banana Pi and Pioneer systems (building on previous work for Unmatched systems [3]), and *iii)* evaluating the overhead introduced by three different methods for accessing hardware counters.

The document is organized as follows. Section 2 explains the instrumentation methodology for accessing hardware counters in RISC-V. Section 3 introduces the hardware platforms considered in our study. Section 4 presents two additional methods, alongside `perf`, for accessing hardware counters and a preliminary quantification of the overhead introduced by each of the three methods on the different hardware platforms.

2 Performance Monitoring in RISC-V

This section describes how performance monitoring is implemented in RISC-V systems, synthesizing information from diverse sources, including the latest RISC-V Privileged Architecture specification (version 20241101) [15], the OpenSBI repository [6], and the SBI Performance Monitoring Unit (PMU) extension [5]. Additionally, we compare the RISC-V specification to the x86_64 architecture (hereafter referred to as x86) to illustrate common practices in HPC performance monitoring and highlight the typical options available to users.

The Hardware Performance Monitor (HPM) serves as the RISC-V counterpart to the PMU found in x86 and ARMv8 architectures. It is responsible for monitoring hardware events that occur during application execution.

The RISC-V standard mandates a minimal set of performance monitoring events that all implementations must support[1]. These essential events include the total number of cycles executed by the processor core and the number of retired instructions. These two metrics are stored in the machine-mode CSRs `mcycle` and `minstret`, respectively. Beyond these mandatory counters, the RISC-V specification allows for up to 29 additional configurable machine-mode counters and corresponding event selectors, represented by CSRs `mhpmcounter[3,31]` and `mhpmevent[3,31]`, respectively. The mapping of specific events to these counters is implementation-dependent, where a value of zero in an `mhpmevent` CSRs indicates that no event is being monitored.

Figure 1 shows an example with three micro-architectural events (X, Y, and Z) that are readable from `hpmcounter3` and `hpmcounter4`. In this particular case, event X can only be read from counter 3, event Y can be read from both counters, and event Z can only be read from counter 4. Registers `hpmevent3` and `hpmevent4` select which event should be monitored by the associated `hpmcounter`.

---

[1] Additionally, RISC-V defines the `mtime` memory-mapped register, which tracks cycles at a fixed frequency; however, it is not formally a part of the RISC-V HPM.

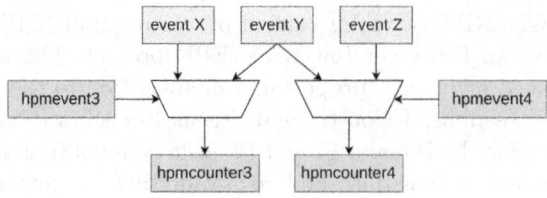

Fig. 1. Example of `hpmevent` event selectors for the `hpmcounter` registers

The RISC-V specification includes additional CSRs for managing the HPM. Specifically, the `mcountinhibit` register controls whether a given `hpmcounter` is actively counting or paused. If a specific bit in `mcountinhibit` is set, the corresponding `hpmcounter` pauses counting, and repeated reads of that counter return the same value. Consequently, as user-level libraries that access hardware counters typically report the difference between two successive reads rather than absolute counter values, if the corresponding bit in `mcountinhibit` is set, the reported difference will always be zero, as the counter remains unchanged between consecutive reads.

Since all of the aforementioned counters operate in machine mode, direct access would normally result in an illegal instruction. However, RISC-V defines a hierarchy of `counteren` registers that allow a lower privilege level to read the corresponding `hpmcounter`. Specifically, the `mcounteren` register controls access to counters for the next privilege level (hypervisor mode, if supported, or supervisor mode otherwise). The `hcounteren` register governs access in supervisor mode and the `scounteren` register manages access in user mode.

For instance, in a system where mcounteren=0x07 and mcountinhibit=0x1A: *i)* any attempt by a user program to direcly read from `hpmcounter[3-7]` triggers an exception; *ii)* multiple reads from the `cycle` and `instret` counters always return the same value[2].

2.1 Bridge Between Privilege Levels

To facilitate communication between supervisor mode (S-mode) and machine mode (M-mode), RISC-V defines the Supervisor Binary Interface (SBI), a standard interface that enables operating systems to access machine-mode services in a portable manner. SBI provides essential functionality such as performance monitoring, timer management, interprocessor interrupts, and power control. Since registers like `mhpmcounter[3-31]`, `mhpmevent[3-31]`, and `mcounteren` are restricted to M-mode access, SBI ensures controlled access to these resources from lower privilege levels. One widely used implementation of SBI is OpenSBI [6], which serves as the reference firmware for many platforms, including several RISC-V-based.

On the other hand, performance monitoring in RISC-V systems primarily relies on `perf`, a Linux kernel tool that provides access to hardware performance

---

[2] For brevity, we only discuss the first eight counters and corresponding register bits.

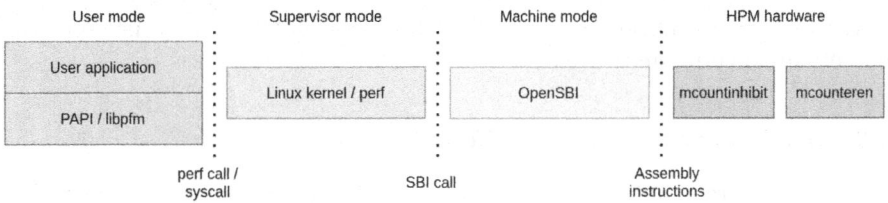

Fig. 2. Schematic view of software components and privilege levels involved in the RISC-V performance monitoring stack.

counters. The `perf` driver operates at the kernel level in supervisor mode, which, while having higher privileges than user mode, still requires SBI calls to configure hardware performance monitoring (HPM) registers. The Linux kernel has progressively improved its RISC-V support, with `perf` integration first introduced in version 5.4, albeit without specific CPU performance monitoring unit (PMU) support. Kernel 6.2 added support for the first PMU (SiFive FU740-C000 – Unmatched), and as of kernel 6.8, `perf` officially includes broader RISC-V functionality, currently supporting four PMUs (SiFive FU740-C000, StarFive Dubhe-80, Andes AX45, and T-Head C900).

By default, the `mcounteren` and `mcountinhibit` registers are not accessible from user mode and must be configured by the `perf` driver. Consequently, without modifications, `perf` remains the only mechanism for users to read performance counters and obtain meaningful insights. Another widely used tool for performance monitoring is PAPI [9], which provides a platform-independent API. PAPI's support for RISC-V is discussed in Sect. 4.2.

Figure 2 illustrates the hierarchical structure of software components and privilege levels involved in performance monitoring. User applications must rely on `perf` or an OS-provided system call to access privileged performance counter information. The kernel, in turn, invokes SBI calls to interact with the underlying hardware, such as configuring `mcounteren` and `mcountinhibit` registers.

2.2 Mode Filtering

The RISC-V privileged specification [15] defines the `Sscofpmf` extension, which introduces mode-based filtering for hardware performance counters. This feature allows counters to be selectively inhibited based on the current privilege mode of the system, enabling more precise performance measurements. It is particularly useful for user applications that need to exclude performance events triggered by the operating system, such as those occurring during a context switch.

Mode-based filtering can be configured on a per-event basis by setting or clearing specific bits in the `hpmevent` registers, allowing fine-grained control over which privilege levels contribute to each counter. However, not all RISC-V hardware supports this feature, as it was recently added to the RISC-V specification. In platforms lacking mode-based filtering, events such as cycle counts and retired instructions will continue to be recorded even during OS-induced preemptions, potentially affecting measurement accuracy.

2.3 Availability of Hardware Counters

Which hardware counters are available depends on the core's implementation. Ideally, the hardware designer should provide a list of events with their respective identifier. These lists can later be used to set the hpmevent[3,31] registers, associating an event identifier to a specific counter. Furthermore, these lists also need to include which events can be mapped to which hpmcounter event counter. For example, an implementation may count the number of cache accesses but only allow this event to be mapped to hpmcounter[3,4].

By itself, perf does not know which counters and events are available and to which hpmcounter those events can be mapped. Part of this information is given to perf in a description of the HPM included with the device tree. The format of this description depends on the SBI implementation, such as the OpenSBI PMU extension [5].

The PAPI library provides a layer of abstraction over the hardware counters of supported platforms. It does so by defining a list of platform-independent events called *preset*. These preset events are mapped to one or more *native* events. Native events are platform-dependent and how to operate them to build preset events is decided by the team extending PAPI. For example, for the Intel Sapphire Rapids CPU, the preset event PAPI_VEC_DP is defined as "Single precision vector/SIMD instructions" and implemented as the sum of three native events of type FP_ARITH_INST_RETIRED: 128B_PACKED_DOUBLE, 256B_PACKED_DOUBLE, and 512B_PACKED_DOUBLE. Native events have a one-to-one match with the actual hardware counters and this mapping is done through a library bundled with PAPI, called libpfm4.

2.4 Comparison to Other Architectures

On x86 architectures, user code can read a timestamp counter using the instructions rdtsc[3] and rdtscp[4]. This counter tracks CPU cycles at the nominal frequency of the processor, making it a common tool for scientific applications that require precise timing measurements.

In addition to the timestamp counter, user code can access other performance counters using the rdpmc instruction[5]. However, on x86, the Performance Counter Enable (PCE) bit must be set to allow user-level access. The specific counter being read depends on an input operand, and since the list of available counters is implementation-dependent and not widely documented, direct usage of rdpmc is complex. As a result, most applications rely on higher-level tools like perf to access performance counters.

---

[3] https://www.felixcloutier.com/x86/rdtsc.
[4] https://www.felixcloutier.com/x86/rdtscp.
[5] https://www.felixcloutier.com/x86/rdpmc.

At a low-level abstraction, the RISC-V specification is more flexible than x86, allowing user-level access and selective pausing of individual counters. Contrarily, x86 only permits enabling or disabling user access for all counters simultaneously.

Comparing timestamp counters (`rdtscp` for x86 and `time` for RISC-V), both architectures provide similar functionality. However, in the current Linux kernel, user access to `time` is disabled, preventing RISC-V applications from measuring time directly. As discussed in Sect. 2.4, this limitation is problematic for scientific workloads that rely on precise timing data.

Additionally, the RISC-V standard mandates two other counters for CPU cycles and retired instructions, but access to these counters is also disabled by default in the Linux kernel.

We believe that restricting user access to these fundamental counters is a missed opportunity. To address this, we propose a kernel patch for Linux 6.10 that introduces the `perf_user_access` kernel parameter, allowing users to switch between `perf` and direct `csrr` access. More details on this approach are provided in Sect. 4.1.

3 Hardware Platforms

This section describes the hardware platforms under study. Table 1 summarizes hardware and corresponding system software configuration. We categorize these platforms loosely following the concept of Technology Readiness Level (TRL) [1] to indicate the maturity of the systems.

High TRL corresponds to systems based on well-established technology, with extensive usage across the HPC space. Systems based on the x86_64 or aarch64 architecture that have been dominating the Top500 list for years are thus examples of high TRL.

Medium TRL corresponds to commercially available systems that lack wide adoption by the HPC community (e.g., development boards). Examples include the HiFive Unmatched board, which has been available for many years and has boosted the RISC-V user base.

Low TRL corresponds to systems that are still in development and not widely available to the public. The maturity of these platforms ranges from hardware simulation at the scale of thousands of cycles, to physical chips capable of booting a Linux operating system.

3.1 High TRL MareNostrum 5

MareNostrum 5 [2] is the flagship tier-0 supercomputer hosted at the Barcelona Supercomputing Center (BSC). It is composed of multiple partitions which are based on different CPU architectures. For the purpose of this work, we will always refer to the General Purpose Partition (GPP), which is based on Intel Sapphire Rapids CPUs.

Nodes of the GPP partition house two 56 core CPUs running at a nominal frequency of 2 GHz (can be boosted up to 3 GHz). Access to hardware counters

Table 1. Summary of RISC-V platforms under study.

System	Extensions		OpenSBI		Linux		CPU		
	rvv	Sscofpmf	Version	PMU	Kernel	Rootfs	Model	Cores	MHz
Unmatched	–	×	v0.3	✓	5.13.19	Ubuntu 22.04	SiFive FU740-C000	4	1200
Pioneer	0.7	×	v1.0	✓	6.1.80	Ubuntu 22.04	SOPHON SG2042	64	2000
Banana Pi	1.0	✓	v1.0	✓	6.1.15	Armbian 24.11.1	SpacemiT K1	8	1600
EPAC-5.7	0.7	×	v0.2	×	5.7	Ubuntu 22.04	EPAC	1	50
EPAC-6.10	0.7	×	v2.0	✓	6.1	Ubuntu 22.04	EPAC	1	50

is possible via `perf` or the PAPI library, which has extensive support for the Sapphire Rapids CPU. In MareNostrum 5, PAPI reports up to 117 available native counters. Additionally, user code can access the timestamp counter `rdtsc`, which is a cycle counter that runs at the nominal frequency of the CPU (does not take into account boosted frequency). This can be done with inline assembly or intrinsics and it is a common practice for scientific applications to do so.

3.2 Medium TRL RISC-V Commercial Platforms

Unmatched, Pioneer, and Banana Pi are commercial RISC-V platforms that have become available in recent years. In terms of hardware implementation, Unmatched does not support vector instructions, Pioneer supports the RISC-V "V" Vector Extension, version 0.7 (rvv0.7, for short), and Banana Pi supports version 1.0 (rvv1.0). In terms of system software, each board comes with a different kernel and Linux distribution containing vendor-specific modifications.

Unmatched runs a kernel based on release public 5.13, with specific modifications [3] to enable access to hardware counters. This is required because, at the time of release, the Linux kernel did not have specific support for RISC-V and the OpenSBI PMU extension was not yet available. Furthermore, at the time, PAPI support needed to be extended both to recognize RISC-V as a whole and to target the CPU in Unmatched specifically.

Pioneer runs a modified version of the 6.1 kernel provided by the vendor. By default, the `mcounteren` is configured to forbid user access to hardware counters. Furthermore, there is no official PAPI support for the CPU powering the Pioneer.

Similarly to Pioneer, the Banana Pi runs a vendor-provided kernel. In this case, `mcounteren` is configured to allow user access, but `mcountinhibit` is configured to pause all hardware counters unless `perf` is used.

3.3 Low TRL - EPAC

One of the outcomes of the European Processor Initiative project is a RISC-V-based accelerator called EPAC. EPAC houses an in-order scalar core tightly coupled with a vector unit that implements the RISC-V V extension (rvv0.7), The design of EPAC is emulated in an FPGA running at 50 MHz that is capable of booting a standard Ubuntu image.

The first iteration of EPAC runs a heavily modified version of the Linux kernel 5.7 that implements a custom system call connecting user code with OpenSBI. At the time, the `perf` driver did not have any support for RISC-V PMUs and the registers `mcounteren` and `mcountinhibit` are always configured to allow user code to read `mcycle`, `mtime`, `minstret`, and `mhpmcounter[3,4]`. This means that the only way of reading hardware counters in EPAC-5.7 is with raw assembly instructions.

At the time of writing, a new setup in which EPAC runs the 6.10 kernel has been developed. The kernel still requires some minor patches but it now relies on the upstream `perf` stack to access the PMU. In this configuration, the user code has lost the ability to access hardware counters directly. To overcome this limitation we propose in Sect. 4.1 a small modification of `perf`. On top of that, we also extend PAPI to support EPAC-6.10 (see Sect. 4.2).

4 Evaluation

In this section, we present two methods of accessing hardware counters in the systems presented in Sect. 3. We only consider the platforms that run a kernel version in which the `perf` driver supports the underlying PMU (all but EPAC-5.7). Taking `perf` as a reference, we propose two alternative ways in which the user can access hardware counters: *i)* low-level abstraction with direct assembly instructions in user mode; and *ii)* high-level abstraction with the PAPI library. Lastly, we present a comparison between the overheads of the three measurement methods and also compare them to similar methods on an x86-based system.

4.1 Low-Level Instrumentation

In this section, we propose the use of a kernel parameter called `perf_user_access` to toggle user access to the hardware counters via raw assembly. Listing 1.1 shows a typical user code reading the counters for cycles and instructions. As discussed earlier, this code will not always measure correctly either metric because it depends on the configuration of the `counteren` and `countinhibit` registers.

```
uint64_t cycles_start, instret_start;
uint64_t cycles_end, instret_end;

__asm__ __volatile__("rdcycle    %0" : "=r" (cycles_start ));
__asm__ __volatile__("rdinstret  %0" : "=r" (instret_start));
// do some work...
__asm__ __volatile__("rdcycle    %0" : "=r" (cycles_end ));
__asm__ __volatile__("rdinstret  %0" : "=r" (instret_end));
```

Listing 1.1. User code reading counters with raw assembly.

The `perf` driver within the Linux kernel 6.10 already contains functionality to react to system configuration changes such as modifying the `perf_user_access` parameter. In particular, the code already configures the `counteren` register. The only missing piece is to pause and resume the counters depending on the value of this parameter (i.e., modifying the `countinhibit` register through SBI). Listing 1.2 contains the full implementation of this functionality. When setting `perf_user_access` to `SYSCTL_LEGACY` the code resumes the counters, while setting any other value pauses them.

```
static void riscv_pmu_update_counter_access(void *info) {
  if (sysctl_perf_user_access == SYSCTL_LEGACY) {
    // Enable access with inline assembly (breaks perf measurements)
    csr_write(CSR_SCOUNTEREN, 0x7);
    sbi_ecall(SBI_EXT_PMU, SBI_EXT_PMU_COUNTER_START, 0, 0x7, 0, 0, 0, 0);
  } else {
    // Enable access with perf (removes access with inline assembly)
    csr_write(CSR_SCOUNTEREN, 0x2);
    sbi_ecall(SBI_EXT_PMU, SBI_EXT_PMU_COUNTER_STOP, 0, 0x7, 0, 0, 0, 0);
  }
}
```

Listing 1.2. Toggle user access to counters depending on `perf_user_access`.

Naturally, our implementation conflicts with `perf`, which pauses and resumes the counters by itself when user code invokes the `perf` API or tools such as `perf stat`. This means that both measurement methods, raw assembly and `perf`, cannot coexist and require changing the `perf_user_access` parameter.

We also note that one of the reasons behind disabling assembly reads with user code is to prevent misinterpretation of the counters due to process migration. In a multi-core system, the OS might transparently migrate the user process to a different CPU. The user code is oblivious to this change and naively reads the hardware counters that are connected to the core it is running on. This situation might cause the user code to read from counters that changed the monitored event across execution, resulting in useless measurements. Users can prevent process migration by pinning their processes with standard tools such as `cpubind`. Furthermore, single-core systems are completely unaffected by this issue.

We consider that allowing user code to directly access hardware counters supersedes the limitations of our proposed implementation, which can be easily circumvented. This is of special importance in low TRL systems such as EPAC because it enables performance analysis while support for high-level abstractions such as PAPI are in development. We also acknowledge the security concerns, such as information side-channel leaks [10], that arise from our proposal, but argue that these are not a priority in a platform where the main focus is to explore architectural design parameters.

Version 20241101 of the RISC-V privileged specification introduced the "Smcsrind/Sscsrind Indirect CSR Access" extension, which would allow for the delegation of HPM control all the way down to the user level. Future work might consider making the proposed low-level implementation compatible with this specification when the first implementations are available in hardware.

4.2 High-Level Instrumentation

In this section, we present our work extending PAPI support for RISC-V-based systems, building upon previous work [3]. Following previous efforts to support

SiFive Unmatched board, we add both the Milk-V Pioneer and Banana Pi-F3 boards. In general, extending support to a new RISC-V processor requires two steps: *i)* recognize the CPU by looking at system information such as /proc/cpuinfo, and *ii)* providing a list of all the available hardware counters.

As of the time of writing, there is no standardized format for /proc/cpuinfo, meaning that different vendors provide different information regarding their products. The only solution is to query specific keywords depending on the target board. For example, mvendorid=0x5b7 for Pioneer.

Regarding the list of available counters, one must search through the documentation provided by the hardware vendor and add this information to libpfm4, which is the library that PAPI uses to match the name of a native event (string of characters) to its ID in the hardware (hexadecimal value). In the case of Pioneer, the board features a SOPHON SG2042 processor and the vendor provides documentation on how to access counters via perf [11]. Events are divided into three different groups: Cache, Instruction and Microarchitecture. In the case of Banana Pi, the board features a SpacemiT K1 processor and there is also information provided by the vendor [12].

On top of adding the native events of Pioneer and Banana Pi to libpfm4 we also add some preset events such as PAPI_L1_DCA and PAPI_FP_INS which are a one-to-one match to a native event. It is important to add support to preset events since these are the ones that HPC users tend to query when instrumenting their code. Future work includes adding more complex preset events which are the result of combining multiple native events. The code for our extension of PAPI is available upon request, while we plan to open a merge request with previous efforts to the repository owned by IST.

4.3 Instrumentation Overhead

To compare the overhead of our three selected performance monitoring methods (assembly inline CSR, perf, and PAPI), we use a simple assembly code. Each iteration performs 16 add operations, while the remaining two instructions handle the iteration counter and jump to the next iteration. To prevent interference between methods, each method is implemented in a separate program with a single instrumentation technique. For each program, the instruction counter is measured before and after the assembly code fragment of interest. By managing the loop within the assembly code, we minimize potential compiler interference that could alter the actual number of instructions executed. This way, we can deterministically predict the exact number of instructions executed and compare them with the measurements performed with the three methods.

In Fig. 3, the first column reports i_e, the number of expected instructions executed, while the remaining columns show $\Delta_i = i_m - i_e$, i.e., the difference between i_m, the number of actual instructions measured by perf on each platform listed in the header, and i_e, the number of expected instructions. Ideally, one would like $\Delta \to 0$. The color code indicates how far are the measured values from the expected ones (green=accurate, red=inaccurate). We observe that on x86, the overhead introduced by perf is more than two orders of magnitude lower

Exp. Instructions	Banana Pi	EPAC	Pioneer	Unmatched	x86
1,80E+01	2719	2321	2613	1784	12
1,80E+02	2719	2321	2613	1784	12
1,80E+03	2719	2321	2613	1784	12
1,80E+04	2719	2321	2613	1784	12
1,80E+05	2719	11514	2613	1784	12
1,80E+06	2719	71820	2613	1784	12
1,80E+07	15176	594111	13387	27330	17
1,80E+08	178615	5992007	164422	273632	65
1,80E+09	1551683	60269205	1220320	2724128	546

Fig. 3. Expected instructions executed (first column) and overheads (measured difference to expected instructions) on different platforms using `perf`. (Color figure online)

than on all RISC-V platforms. This significant gap is not completely understood so far and is under study. Additionally, regardless of the architecture, once the number of executed instructions exceeds a certain threshold (which varies across machines), the discrepancy between the expected and measured values begins to diverge and increases significantly.

Exp. Instructions	EPAC	Unmatched
1,80E+01	6	5
1,80E+02	6	6
1,80E+03	6	6
1,80E+04	6	6
1,80E+05	15974	6
1,80E+06	67850	6
1,80E+07	619599	30961
1,80E+08	6031365	268276
1,80E+09	61171912	2723433

Exp. Instructions	Banana Pi	Pioneer	Unmatched	x86
1,80E+01	4126	3899	4051	806
1,80E+02	4126	3899	4051	806
1,80E+03	4126	3899	4051	806
1,80E+04	4126	3899	4051	806
1,80E+05	4126	3899	4051	806
1,80E+06	4126	3899	4051	806
1,80E+07	24225	14845	24615	811
1,80E+08	207973	169415	276478	860
1,80E+09	1862211	1237343	2565450	1343

Fig. 4. Expected instructions executed (columns 1 and 4) and overheads (measured difference to expected instructions) on different platforms using CSR (left) and PAPI (right).

In Fig. 4-left, the first column reports i_e, the number of expected instructions executed, while the remaining columns show $\Delta_i = i_m - i_e$, i.e., the difference between i_m, the actual instructions measured with CSR on Unmatched and EPAC, and i_e, the number of expected instructions. To enable the measurements in EPAC we used a kernel patched as explained in Sect. 4.1. The color code follows the same scheme as in Fig. 3. Measurements for Banana Pi and Pioneer are not included, as CSR cannot be used on these platforms. As expected, the overhead introduced by the CSR method is lower than that of `perf` (shown in Fig. 3). However, the same divergence observed with `perf` is also present here. In the case of CSR, we suspect that the increasing inaccuracy at higher instruction counts is caused by the impact of context switching, which statistically affects longer executions. This highlights the importance of the virtualization of hardware counters. This comes as a surprise for Banana Pi, since its hardware implements the mode filtering extension and should not be affected by OS code. It is possible that some layer of the software stack (OpenSBI, perf, or PAPI) is still not mature enough to leverage mode filtering.

In Fig. 4-right, the first column reports the number of expected instructions executed, while the remaining columns show the instructions measured with PAPI on Unmatched, Banana Pi, x86, and Pioneer. To enable measurements in Banana Pi and Pioneer we used the extended PAPI library introduced in Sect. 4.2. The color code is consistent with Fig. 3. Measurements for EPAC are not included, as PAPI cannot be used on this platform so far. We observe that the overhead introduced by PAPI is higher across all platforms. Additionally, beyond a certain threshold (consistent with that identified using perf and CSR) measurement accuracy degrades, which comes as a surprise for Banana Pi, given that while supporting mode filtering, it should not be affected by OS code.

5 Conclusions

This study presents an in-depth evaluation of hardware counter support across various RISC-V platforms, including three commercial systems (Banana Pi, Pioneer, and Unmatched) and an experimental platform (EPAC). The proposed modification to the Linux kernel enables user-space reading of Control and Status Registers (CSRs) to provide low-level access to performance counters. Furthermore, the extension of support for the PAPI library to the Banana Pi and Pioneer platforms builds upon earlier work with Unmatched, thereby offering a higher-level, platform-independent interface for performance monitoring.

An evaluation of three instrumentation methods raw assembly via CSR, perf, and PAPI revealed notable differences in overhead. In particular, perf exhibited significantly higher overhead on RISC-V platforms compared to x86 systems, the CSR method achieved lower overhead yet was prone to inaccuracies due to context switching, and PAPI demonstrated the highest overhead among the methods tested. The analysis also highlighted that, unlike x86, user access to basic hardware counters (cycles, time, instructions) is disabled by default in the current Linux kernel for RISC-V, which is a missed opportunity that the proposed patch aims to address.

The case of Banana Pi is especially noteworthy, since its hardware implements the mode filtering extension that should allow to minimize OS interference in performance measurements. However, the current software stack implementation does not leverage this functionality. Future work includes studying how to take advantage of mode filtering in RISC-V platforms that support it.

In summary, this work underscores the ongoing efforts to enhance performance monitoring capabilities on RISC-V platforms for high-performance computing. It identifies current limitations in software support and quantifies the overhead associated with different instrumentation methods. Future work could explore compatibility with the "Smcsrind/Sscsrind Indirect CSR Access" extension, which may enable user-level delegation of HPM control and further bridge the performance monitoring gap with mature architectures such as x86.

Acknowledgments. Supported by the EuroHPC Joint Undertaking (JU): FPA 800928 (EPI), SGA 101036168 (EPI-SGA2). The JU receives support from the EU Horizon 2020 programme and from Croatia, France, Germany, Greece, Italy, Netherlands, Portugal, Spain, Sweden, Denmark and Switzerland. The EPI-SGA2 project, PCI2022-132935 is also co-funded by MCIN/AEI/10.13039/501100011033 and by the UE NextGenerationEU/PRTR. F. Banchelli has been supported by the predoctoral program AGAUR-FI ajuts (2024 FI-200424) Joan Oró. We also acknowledge the contributions from project UIDB/50021/2020 (DOI: 10.54499/UIDB/50021/2020), supported by Portuguese national funds through Fundação para a Ciência e a Tecnologia (FCT).

References

1. Technology readiness level definitions. https://www.nasa.gov/pdf/458490main_TRL_Definitions.pdf Accessed Jun 2021
2. Banchelli, F., et al.: Introducing marenostrum5: a European pre-exascale energy-efficient system designed to serve a broad spectrum of scientific workloads (2025), https://arxiv.org/abs/2503.09917
3. Domingos, J.M., Rocha, T., Neves, N., Roma, N., Tomás, P., Sousa, L.: Supporting risc-v performance counters through linux performance analysis tools. In: 2023 IEEE 34th International Conference on Application-specific Systems, Architectures and Processors (ASAP), pp. 94–101 (2023). https://doi.org/10.1109/ASAP57973.2023.00027
4. Eranian, S.: libpfm4, https://sourceforge.net/p/perfmon2/libpfm4/ci/master/tree/
5. International, R.V.: Opensbi sbi pmu extension support (2025), https://github.com/riscv-software-src/opensbi/blob/master/docs/pmu_support.md
6. International, R.V.: Risc-v open source supervisor binary interface (opensbi) (2025), https://github.com/riscv-software-src/opensbi
7. Kleen, A., Strong, B.: Intel ® processor trace on linux. Tracing Summit (2015), https://citeseerx.ist.psu.edu/viewdoc/download?doi=10.1.1.735.3516&rep=rep1&type=pdf
8. Lee, Y., et al.: Using CoreSight PTM to integrate CRA monitoring IPs in an ARM-based SoC. ACM Trans. Des. Autom. Electron. Syst. **22**(3), 52:1–52:25 (2017). https://doi.org/10.1145/3035965, https://doi.org/10.1145/3035965
9. Mucci, P.J., Browne, S., Deane, C., Ho, G.: Papi: a portable interface to hardware performance counters. In: Proceedings of the Department of Defense HPCMP Users Group Conference, vol. 710 (1999)
10. Segev, R., Mendelson, A.: The use of performance-counters to perform side-channel attacks. In: International Symposium on Cyber Security, Cryptology, and Machine Learning, pp. 216–233. Springer (2023)
11. SOPHGO: how to use perf with the sg2042 core (2025), https://github.com/sophgo/sophgo-doc/blob/main/SG2042/HowTo/How%20to%20use%20perf%20on%20SG2042.rst

12. Spacemit: counter listing for spacemit k1 processor (2025), https://developer.spacemit.com/documentation?token=ZZrhw4xvHiIVa7kTHlycxrmXn6d#part999
13. Su, A.P., et al.: Multi-core software/hardware co-debug platform with ARM CoreSight^{TM}, on-chip test architecture and AXI/AHB bus monitor. In: International Symposium on VLSI Design, Automation and Test, pp. 1–6, April 2011. https://doi.org/10.1109/VDAT.2011.5783594
14. Waterman, A., Asanovic, K.: RISC-V "V" vector extension - version 1.0. Technical Report, RISC-V Foundation (2021), https://github.com/riscvarchive/riscv-v-spec/releases/download/v1.0/riscv-v-spec-1.0.pdf
15. Waterman, A., Lee, Y., Avižienis, R., Patterson, D., Asanović, K.: The risc-v instruction set manual: Volume ii: privileged architecture (2024), https://riscv.github.io/riscv-isa-manual/snapshot/privileged
16. Weaver, V.M.: Linux perf_event features and overhead. In: The 2nd International Workshop on Performance Analysis of Workload Optimized Systems, FastPath, vol. 13, p. 5 (2013)
17. Zeinolabedin, S.M.A., Partzsch, J., Mayr, C.: Real-time hardware implementation of ARM CoreSight trace decoder. IEEE Des. Test **38**(1), 69–77 (2021). https://doi.org/10.1109/MDAT.2020.3002145

Monte Cimone v2: HPC RISC-V Cluster Evaluation and Optimization

Emanuele Venieri[1(✉)], Simone Manoni[1], Gabriele Ceccolini[1],
Giacomo Madella[1], Federico Ficarelli[3], Daniele Gregori[4], Andrea Acquaviva[1],
Luca Benini[1,2], and Andrea Bartolini[1]

[1] University of Bologna, Bologna, Italy
`emanuele.venieri2@unibo.it`
[2] ETH Zürich, Zürich, Switzerland
[3] CINECA, Casalecchio di Reno, Italy
[4] E4 Computer Engineering Spa, Viale Martiri della Libertà 66, 42019 Scandiano, Italy

Abstract. Many RISC-V (RV) platforms and SoCs have been announced in recent years targeting the HPC sector, but only a few of them are commercially available and engineered to fit the HPC requirements. The Monte Cimone project targeted assessing their capabilities and maturity, aiming to make RISC-V a competitive choice when building a datacenter. Nowadays, Systems-on-chip (SoCs) featuring RV cores with vector extension, form factor and memory capacity suitable for HPC applications are available in the market, but it is unclear how compilers and open-source libraries can take advantage of its performance. In this paper, we describe the performance assessment of the upgrade of the Monte Cimone (MCv2) cluster with the Sophgo SG2042 processor on HPC workloads. Also adding an exploration of BLAS libraries optimization. The upgrade increases the attained node's performance by 127x on HPL DP FLOP/s and 69x on Stream Memory Bandwidth.

Keywords: RISC-V · HPC · HPL · STREAM · OpenBLAS · BLIS · Milk-V · SG2042

1 Introduction

In recent years, RISC-V has gained significant traction as an open-standard Instruction Set Architecture (ISA) with its open-source, modular, and extensible design. Early academic and commercial implementation of RISC-V platforms targeted mainly low-power embedded systems and microcontrollers [1]. This initial focus served as a natural starting point, as embedded platforms are inherently simpler from an architectural design perspective and allowed for the incremental development of the RISC-V ecosystem, ensuring the gradual maturation of compilers, software toolchains, and system-level optimizations.

In the last few years, advancements in RISC-V hardware and software ecosystems have driven its evolution toward higher-performance platforms. The introduction of 64-bit processors [2], vector extensions (RVV) [3,4], and improved memory subsystems has enabled RISC-V to scale beyond embedded computing, making it increasingly viable for high-performance computing (HPC) workloads.

As the push for RISC-V in HPC gained momentum, early efforts focused on validating the potential of this open ISA for highly demanding computational tasks. As part of this exploration, Monte Cimone (MCv1) [5] was developed as the first pioneering multi-node computing platform to assess the maturity of RISC-V HPC system software. Designed to address the challenges of integrating multi-node RISC-V clusters, MCv1 serves as a testbed for building a comprehensive HPC stack, including interconnects, storage and power monitoring, all using RISC-V hardware.

In this paper, we propose a major upgrade of Monte Cimone named MCv2 to assess the maturity of software libraries and compilers in leveraging novel, more compute-capable RISC-V many-core processors featuring vector extensions and larger memory capacity. The key contributions include:

- The description of the hardware architecture of the new MCv2 nodes and the hardware-software infrastructure we developed for performance analysis.
- The enhancement of the software stack with compilation toolchains and optimized BLAS libraries both from the community and produced in this work.
- An extensive benchmarking campaign leveraging HPC-class tools to evaluate performance, efficiency, and scalability, which provides a comprehensive insight into the state-of-the-art in RISC-V HPC architectures.

2 Background

Monte Cimone is a multi-node compute cluster built on RISC-V architecture, designed as a validation platform for HPC systems. The first iteration of the Monte Cimone (MCv1) [5] compute cluster utilized four E4 RV007 Server Blades, based on two boards SiFive HiFive Unmatched featuring the SiFive Freedom U740 SoC. The peak theoretical performance was 4.0 Gflop/s per node. The Monte Cimone software stack is built with Spack and accessible via shared modules. Nodes run Ubuntu 21.04, and mount a shared NFS, the job scheduler is SLURM and the system monitor is ExaMon [6]. The system achieves 12.65 Gflop/s for full-machine HPL [7] and of 1.1 GB/s for STREAM DDR bandwidth [8] benchmarks.

Since the first iteration of the Monte Cimone cluster, new and enhanced hardware has become available. Notably, a new processor has emerged in high-performance RISC-V-based platforms: the Sophgo Sophon SG2042 System-on-Chip (SoC) [9], the first RISC-V processor specifically designed for server applications. The SG2042 features a 64-core RISC-V CPU based on the Xuantie C920 architecture. Each core includes a 128-bit wide vector unit supporting RVV 0.7.1 for vector execution. The SoC provides 64 KB of L1 instruction and data caches per core, a 1 MB L2 cache shared among four-core clusters, and a 64 MB system-wide L3 cache. It supports four channels of 3200MHz ECC DDR4 memory and provides 32 PCIe Gen4 lanes. The Sophgo processor has been made commercially available for software development and prototyping with the Pioneer Milk-V board [10].

3 Methods

3.1 Monte Cimone v2 Hardware and Software Setup

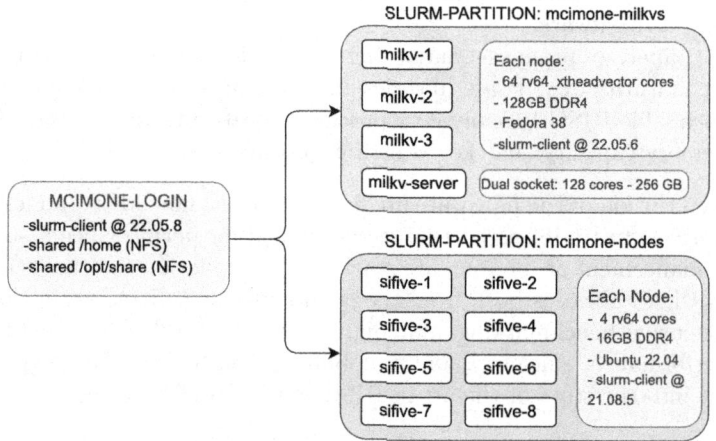

Fig. 1. Monte Cimone v1 (green) + v2 (blue) view (Color figure online)

The first enhancement we introduced to the MCv2 setup is a hardware scale-out, expanding the original configuration with four additional nodes, each powered by the Sophgo Sophon SG2042. Three of the nodes are Milk-V Pioneer Box systems, each featuring an SG2042 processor and 128 GB of memory. The fourth node is a dual-socket system with two SG2042 processors, providing a total of 128 cores and 256 GB of system memory, built on the Sophgo SR1-2208A0 platform. The SG2042-based blades are integrated into the Monte Cimone system (i) using the existing 1Gb/s network and (ii) as an additional SLURM partition. Similarly, the MCv2 nodes have been configured using Spack and integrated into the ExaMon monitoring infrastructure.

The MCv2 nodes run Fedora 38 as the operating system, along with the upstream GCC 13 toolchain. To enhance compatibility with the Xuantie C920 core and its vector unit, we built and made available as shared modules two additional toolchains. The first one is the Xuantie GNU Toolchain [11], a customized GCC 10-based toolchain specifically designed by the Xuantie core developer for compiling code targeting the RVV 0.7.1 vector extension. The second one is the

GNU GCC 14 toolchain, which introduces support for the theadvector compilation target, as GNU GCC identifies the vector extension of the C920 core. The overall structure of the system can be seen in Fig. 1.

3.2 MCv2 Performance Analysis Tools

To assess MCv2, we carried out a series of tests focusing on memory performance and FP64 scalar and vector execution. For these evaluations, we employed the STREAM benchmark to measure memory bandwidth and the HPL benchmark to assess high-performance computing capabilities. STREAM and HPL were compiled with GCC 13 with the latter linked against two different sets of OpenBLAS libraries [12]. The first configuration used OpenBLAS built for the generic RV64 target, serving as a baseline that does not leverage the processor's vector unit. The second configuration utilized an optimized version of OpenBLAS, incorporating assembly kernels specifically designed for the C920 core and its vector unit. These optimized kernels, available in the official OpenBLAS repository, were compiled with the appropriate architectural target using the Xuantie GNU Toolchain.

3.3 MCv2 Software Stack Enhancement: BLIS Optimization

In addition to the initial setup and characterization of MCv2, our efforts were dedicated to expanding its software stack. A key focus of our work was integrating an alternative set of BLAS libraries known as BLIS [15]. BLIS is an open-source BLAS implementation designed to enhance portability across emerging microarchitectures, offering an alternative to other open-source libraries like OpenBLAS. Its framework contains small computational units called microkernels that, wrapped in different ways called macro-kernels, implement different BLAS functions. This blocking is exposed to the programmer facilitating efficient cache utilization and micro-kernel optimization. In our work, we leverage these features to develop a viable alternative to OpenBLAS for MCv2 and, more broadly, for the SG2042 processor.

3.3.1 Retrofitting from RVV 1.0 to RVV 0.7.1

By default, BLIS includes assembly micro-kernels written for RVV 1.0, enabled via the rv64iv target. However, by adapting the microkernels to RVV 0.7.1, following our translation process, these libraries can be built for the theadvector machine architecture supported by GCC 14. This process involved adapting *load* and *store* instructions, as well as *vsetvl* operations to the older syntax. Additionally, a *th.* prefix was added to each vector instruction, enabling the compiler to recognize them as theadvector. The adapted and compiled microkernels were evaluated using the same HPL benchmark, with results obtained from OpenBLAS serving as the baseline. As discussed in Sect. 4.3, there was still room for improvement, prompting the start of the optimization process.

3.3.2 BLIS Optimization

The first step in our optimization process was to assess the primary bottleneck, which could stem from either inefficient cache utilization or suboptimal microkernel code. As discussed in Sect. 4.3 the main performance bottleneck of BLIS is the second.

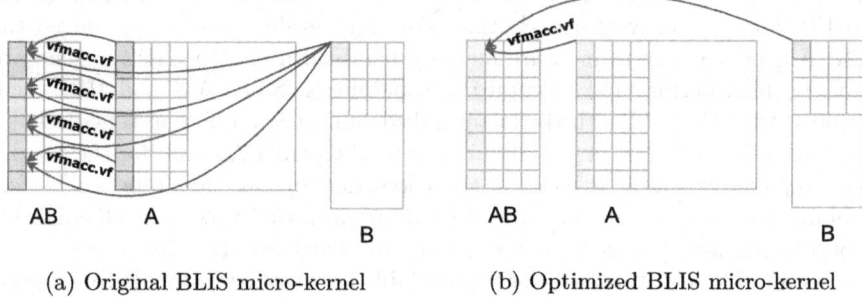

(a) Original BLIS micro-kernel   (b) Optimized BLIS micro-kernel

Fig. 2. Focus point of our micro-kernel optimization

The micro-kernel targeted for optimization serves as the foundation for level-3 BLAS functions, such as GEMM, and is primarily composed of rank-1 updates. The original implementation, illustrated in Fig. 2a, operates on single vector registers, repeatedly invoking the *vfmacc.vf* instruction on contiguous data. This design choice was likely intended to maintain microarchitecture agnosticism and ensure a reusable RVV-based micro-kernel.

We optimized this implementation by reducing the number of fetched instructions while preserving the existing data blocking and algorithm. On the SG2042 processor, each vector register holds two FP64 values. Consequently, updating an eight-element column of AB requires four *vfmacc.vf* calls and four load operations to populate four vector registers with a column of A. To enhance efficiency, we leveraged register grouping by increasing the RVV LMUL parameter from one to four, with a subsequent remap of data across vector registers. This adjustment allows a single load operation to populate four vector registers with an entire column of A, and a single *vfmacc.vf* instruction to update a column of AB, as illustrated in Fig. 2b.

4 Experimental Results

In this section, we summarize the achieved performance in memory bandwidth using the STREAM benchmark and in FP64 execution using HPL. The latter is analyzed from two perspectives. First, we present a system-wide characterization of MCv2 using HPL linked to OpenBLAS libraries. Second, we evaluate the impact of our BLIS porting and optimization efforts.

4.1 MCv2 Memory Performance

The MCv2 single socket node saturates its memory bandwidth with 64 OpenMP threads, achieving a bandwidth of 41.9 GB/s. Interestingly, the MCv2 dual socket node achieves a memory bandwidth of 82.9 GB/s, still using 64 OpenMP threads but pinned symmetrically in the two sockets - increasing the number of OpenMP threads reduces the attained bandwidth. In contrast, an MCv1 node achieves a memory bandwidth of 1.1 GB/s with 4 OpenMP threads. A comprehensive view of this data is visible in Fig. 3.

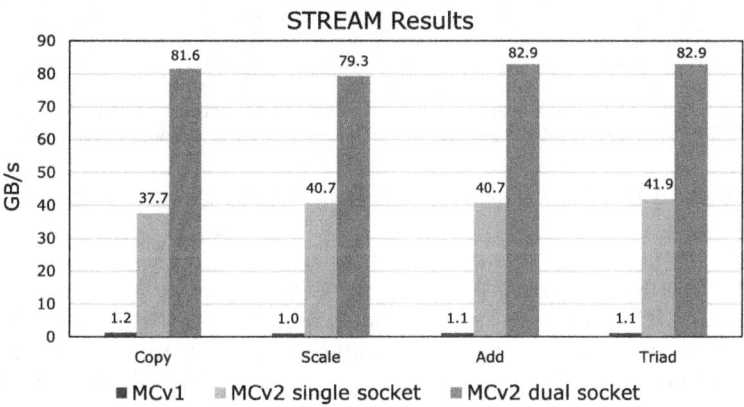

Fig. 3. STREAM benchmark on a MCv2 node with 64 OpenMP threads compared to a MCv1 node

4.2 MCv2 FP64 Performance

Figure 4 reports the performance characterization for the HPL benchmark for the MCv2 compute node while scaling the number of cores and for different BLAS libraries. From the Figure, we can see that the vanilla OpenBLAS libraries are still lagging behind the SG2042-optimized ones, with a relative efficiency of 68% with one core, which increases to 89% of the optimized one. Both of them experience a degradation in relative performance when all the cores are used. This suggests that the optimized OpenBLAS suffers from SoC's bottlenecks as the unoptimized one.

These results confirm previous work comparison between the SiFive Freedom U740 SoC and the Sophgo Sophon SG2042 [13], though obtained using a different software stack. Furthermore, we extend previous works to a multi-node cluster and dual-socket nodes, providing further insights into performance scaling across multiple MCv2 nodes.

Figure 5 shows the performance results from HPL runs with different node configurations. The MCv1 32-cores case refers to the HPL executed in parallel on

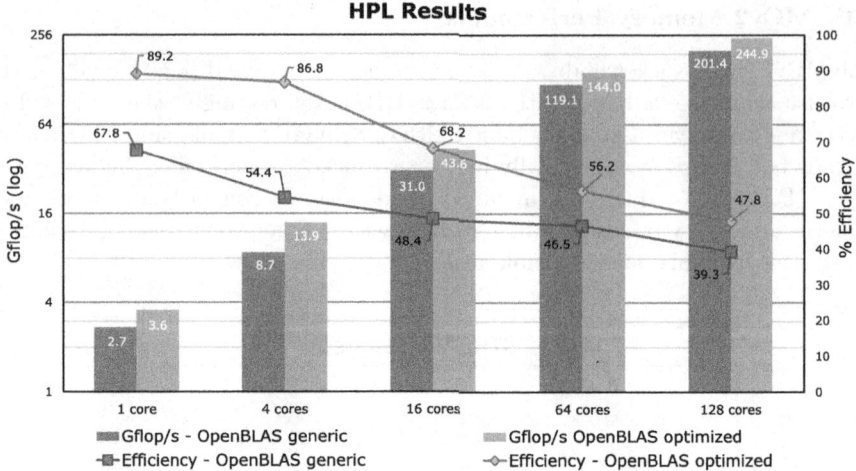

Fig. 4. MCv2 HPL w. OpenBLAS (generic & optimized compiling target)

all 8 MCv1 compute nodes, which achieves 13 Gflop/s. The MCv2 64-cores case refers to the MCv2 single-socket HPL run, while the MCv2 128-cores case refers to both (i) a dual MCv2 single socket nodes configuration and (ii) a single MCv2 dual socket node configuration. From it, we can notice that while in MCv1, the 1 Gb/s network was sufficient for obtaining almost an HPL linear scaling, in the case of the performance of the MCv2 nodes, it is no longer sufficient and increasing the number of parallel processes reduces the HPL efficiency (only the 1.33× w.r.t single node performance). The MCv2 dual-socket compute node, in contrast, achieves almost 1.76× of the performance of the MCv2 single-socket node and 127× more performance of an MCv1 compute node.

4.3 BLIS Porting and Optimization Evaluation

With a performance baseline for MCv2 established using HPL and OpenBLAS, we can now evaluate the impact of our work on the BLIS library. Figure 7 provides a comprehensive view of HPL benchmark results across different libraries and core counts. The first column for each core count represents our baseline, obtained from HPL linked to the optimized OpenBLAS, while the second column illustrates the performance of HPL using BLIS with the provided vector microkernels. The third column of each core count group contains the final results of HPL linked to our optimized version of BLIS. The first two served as the foundation for our optimization process, with the goal of developing a BLIS version that achieves performance on par with, or exceeding, that of OpenBLAS. After obtaining the initial performance results for BLIS, our first objective was to identify and address the primary performance bottleneck. Since BLIS optimization primarily follows two approaches–cache blocking adjustments and micro-kernel optimization–we conducted a comparative analysis of cache misses to determine

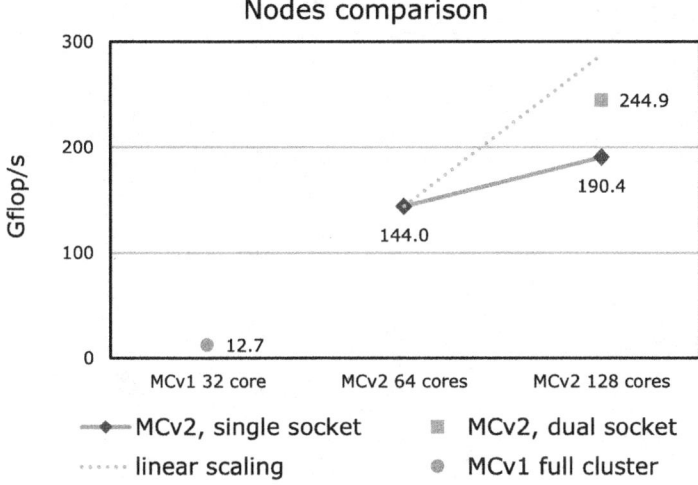

Fig. 5. HPL on different node's configurations

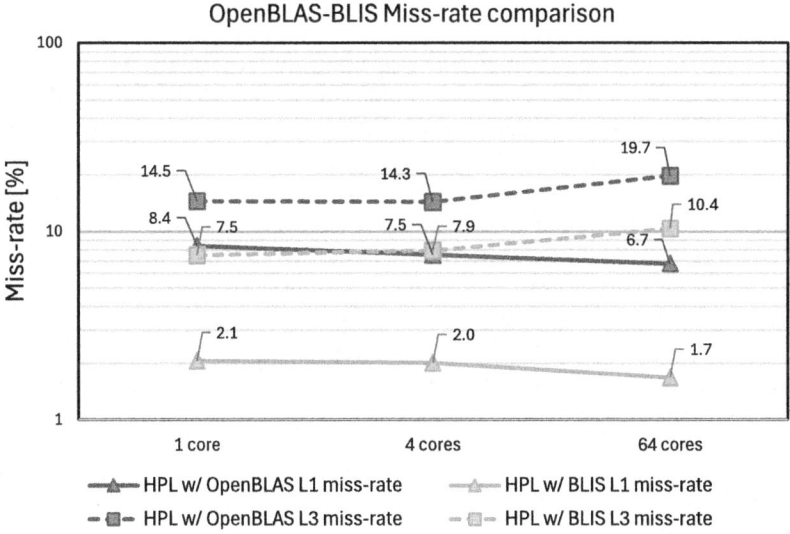

Fig. 6. MCv2 cache Miss-rate: HPL+OpenBLAS vs HPL+BLIS.

the most effective path forward. This analysis involved running HPL and measuring cache miss data using Linux perf [16].

Figure 6 presents the results that guided our decision to focus on micro-kernel refinement. The horizontal axis represents various core counts, while the vertical axis shows the cache miss rate for L1 and L3 caches during HPL runs linked to both optimized OpenBLAS and non-optimized BLIS. The data clearly indicate that non-optimized BLIS already exhibits superior cache performance (L1-to-L1

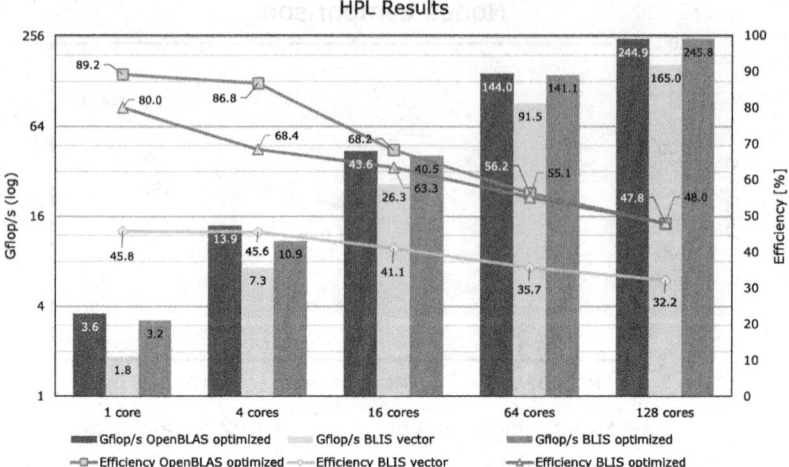

Fig. 7. MCv2 attained performance comparison between HPL+OpenBLAS vs HPL+BLIS pre/post-optimization.

and L3-to-L3 comparison) compared to optimized OpenBLAS. This observation led us to conclude that the FP64 performance of BLIS is hindered by inefficiencies in the provided vector micro-kernels. With the reduction in the instruction count of the micro-kernel described in Sect. 3.3.2, we conducted tests to evaluate its impact. As shown by the third column of each core count group in Fig. 7, there is a significant improvement in attainable performance compared to the original BLIS micro-kernel. The results are now comparable to those of OpenBLAS and, in some cases, even superior. For example, the most noticeable case occurs when running HPL on 128 cores. In these tests, the baseline performance with HPL linked to optimized OpenBLAS is 244.9 Gflop/s, while the non-optimized BLIS implementation achieves only 165.0 Gflop/s. Through our optimizations, BLIS surpasses OpenBLAS, reaching 245.8 Gflop/s, representing a 49% improvement over the baseline BLIS implementation.

5 Conclusions

This work presents a comparative analysis of MCv1 and MCv2 using standard HPC evaluation tools. Our findings highlight the rapid evolution of the RISC-V ecosystem within just two years. For context, the Top500 list reports an average 127× in performance improvement over eight years [14], underscoring the accelerated development of RISC-V hardware as a viable platform for HPC systems. Furthermore, our efforts in porting and optimizing BLAS libraries, specifically BLIS, demonstrate the feasibility of enhancing the RISC-V software ecosystem, ultimately benefiting the broader HPC community.

Acknowledgments. This activity has been supported by the HE EU Graph-Massivizer (g.a. 101093202), DECICE (g.a. 101092582), and DARE (g.a. 101143421) projects, as well as the Italian Research Center on High Performance Computing, Big Data, and Quantum Computing.

References

1. Flamand, E., et al.: GAP-8: a RISC-V SoC for AI at the edge of the IoT. In: 2018 IEEE 29th International Conference on Application-specific Systems, Architectures and Processors (ASAP), pp. 1–4 (2018). https://doi.org/10.1109/ASAP.2018.8445101
2. Zaruba, F., Benini, L.: The cost of application-class processing: energy and performance analysis of a Linux-ready 1.7-GHz 64-bit RISC-V core in 22-nm FDSOI technology. IEEE Trans. Very Large Scale Integr. (VLSI) Syst. **27**(11), 2629–2640 (2019). https://doi.org/10.1109/TVLSI.2019.2926114
3. Perotti, M., Cavalcante, M., Wistoff, N., Andri, R., Cavigelli, L., Benini, L.: A 'New Ara' for vector computing: an open source highly efficient RISC-V V 1.0 vector processor design. In: 2022 IEEE 33rd International Conference on Application-specific Systems, Architectures and Processors (ASAP), Los Alamitos, CA, USA, pp. 43–51 (2022). https://doi.org/10.1109/ASAP54787.2022.00017
4. Minervini, F., et al.: Vitruvius+: an area-efficient RISC-V decoupled vector coprocessor for high performance computing applications. ACM Trans. Archit. Code Optim. **20**(2), Article no. 28 (2023). https://doi.org/10.1145/3575861
5. Bartolini, A., et al.: Monte Cimone: paving the road for the first generation of RISC-V high-performance computers. In: Proceedings of the 2022 System-on-Chip Conference (SOCC), pp. 1–6 (2022). https://doi.org/10.1109/SOCC56010.2022.9908096
6. ExaMon. https://examonhpc.github.io/examon/latest/
7. HPL. www.netlib.org/benchmark/hpl/
8. STREAM. www.cs.virginia.edu/stream/
9. SG2042 Technical Reference Manual. https://github.com/milkv-pioneer/pioneer-files/blob/main/hardware/SG2042-TRM.pdf
10. Milk-V Pioneer. https://milkv.io/pioneer
11. Xuantie GNU Toolchain repository. http://github.com/XUANTIE-RV/xuantie-gnu-toolchain
12. OpenBLAS repository. https://github.com/OpenMathLib/OpenBLAS
13. Brown, N., Jamieson, M.: Performance characterisation of the 64-core SG2042 RISC-V CPU for HPC. In: Weiland, M., Neuwirth, S., Kruse, C., Weinzierl, T. (eds.) High Performance Computing. ISC High Performance 2024 International Workshops. ISC High Performance 2023. LNCS, vol. 15058. Springer, Cham (2025). https://doi.org/10.1007/978-3-031-73716-9_25
14. Top500 projections. https://top500.org/statistics/perfdevel/
15. Van Zee, F.G., van de Geijn, R.A.: BLIS: a framework for rapidly instantiating BLAS functionality. ACM Trans. Math. Softw. **41**(3), 1–33, Article no. 14 (2015). https://doi.org/10.1145/2764454
16. perf Linux. https://perfwiki.github.io/main/

Parallel FFTW on RISC-V: A Comparative Study Including OpenMP, MPI, and HPX

Alexander Strack[1](✉)[iD], Christopher Taylor[2][iD], and Dirk Pflüger[1][iD]

[1] Institute of Parallel and Distributed Systems, University of Stuttgart, 70569 Stuttgart, Germany
{alexander.strack,dirk.pflueger}@ipvs.uni-stuttgart.de
[2] Tactical Computing Labs LLC, 1001 Pecan St, Lindsay, TX, USA
ctaylor@tactcomplabs.com

Abstract. Rapid advancements in RISC-V hardware development shift the focus from low-level optimizations to higher-level parallelization. Recent RISC-V processors, such as the SOPHON SG2042, have 64 cores. RISC-V processors with core counts comparable to the SG2042, make efficient parallelization as crucial for RISC-V as the more established processors such as x86-64.

In this work, we evaluate the parallel scaling of the widely used FFTW library on RISC-V for MPI and OpenMP. We compare it to a 64-core AMD EPYC 7742 CPU side by side for different types of FFTW planning. Additionally, we investigate the effect of memory optimization on RISC-V in HPX-FFT, a parallel FFT library based on the asynchronous many-task runtime HPX using an FFTW backend.

We generally observe a performance delta between the x86-64 and RISC-V chips of factor eight for double-precision 2D FFT. Effective memory optimizations in HPX-FFT on x86-64 do not translate to the RISC-V chip. FFTW with MPI shows good scaling up to 64 cores on x86-64 and RISC-V regardless of planning. In contrast, FFTW with OpenMP requires measured planning on both architectures to achieve good scaling up to 64 cores.

The results of our study mark an early step on the journey to large-scale parallel applications running on RISC-V.

Keywords: FFTW · RISC-V · OpenMP · MPI · HPX · FFT

1 Introduction

The RISC-V [22] hardware architecture emerges as a promising alternative to established architectures such as x86-64 or ARM, both of which are locked behind license. This trend is supported by the EuroHPC[1] that actively promotes the development of new RISC-V hardware. As a result, new projects like

---
[1] https://eurohpc-ju.europa.eu/index_en on 05/16/2025.

© The Author(s), under exclusive license to Springer Nature Switzerland AG 2026
S. Neuwirth et al. (Eds.): ISC High Performance 2025 Workshops, LNCS 16091, pp. 586–597, 2026.
https://doi.org/10.1007/978-3-032-07612-0_45

the *European Processor initiative*[2] or the *Digital Autonomy with RISC-V in Europe* project were created. Their objective extends beyond the development of RISC-V hardware, to support the complete software stack of existing high-performance computing (HPC) applications such as large-scale simulations or artificial intelligence workloads.

One of the essential HPC software building blocks is the fast Fourier transform (FFT). The Fourier transform is a fundamental tool for converting data from the spatial domain into the frequency domain. FFTs accelerate convolution operations and serve as an integral part of many scientific applications such as in molecular dynamics [6]. Undoubtedly, the most popular FFT library is the open source project *Fastest Fourier Transform in the West* (FFTW). More recent libraries show minor improvements in parallel performance [1]. However, FFTW serves as a base for many of these newer parallel FFT libraries.

In this work, we evaluate the performance of parallel FFTW on the SG2042 64-core RISC-V chip recently developed by SOPHGO[3]. We compare the performance of different parallelization approaches side-by-side with a 64-core AMD EPYC 7742[4] chip based on the x86-64 architecture. Based on our previous work [20], we also benchmark the HPX-FFT tool and investigate the impact of different memory access optimizations. Furthermore, we also compare HPX-FFT with parallel FFTW for different planning types.

Our main contributions in this work include, to the best of our knowledge:

- The first side-by-side comparison of parallel FFT on x86-64 and RISC-V hardware.
- The first evaluation of multidimensional FFTW planning on up to 64 RISC-V cores.
- The first comparison of asynchronous tasking with HPX and MPI+OpenMP on RISC-V.

The remainder of this work has the following structure: In Sect. 2, we review related work on FFT and HPX on RISC-V. Then in Sect. 3, we introduce the FFTW library and give an overview of the different parallelization approaches used in FFTW and HPX-FFT. In Sect. 4, we explain the basics of parallel multi-dimensional FFT and describe our benchmark setup. The results of our side-by-side comparison of RISC-V and x86-64 are discussed in Sect. 5. Lastly, in Sect. 6 we conclude our work and give an outlook on future work regarding FFTW on RISC-V and other architectures.

2 Related Work

Several studies focused on FFT implementations targeting RISC-V. The studies assess FFTW as a reference point for performance comparison. In [21], the

---

[2] https://www.european-processor-initiative.eu/project/epi/ on 05/16/2025).
[3] https://en.sophgo.com/sophon-u/product/introduce/sg2042.html on 05/16/2025).
[4] https://www.amd.com/en/support/downloads/drivers.html/processors/epyc/epyc-7002-series/amd-epyc-7742.html (accessed on 05/16/2025).

authors use a scalar FFTW to compare performance against their vectorized approaches on a RISC-V core prototype. The authors of [15], benchmark their FFTASI framework against FFTW on a C910MP chip. In [24], the authors benchmark their PerfMPL-FFT library against FFTW in single and double precision on a C910MP chip. Those works are motivated by FFTW's singular support for the ratified RVV1.0 specification.

Many of the current RISC-V chips only support the unratified RVV0.7.1 specification. The author of [3] implemented RVV0.7.1 support for FFTW and compared the performance on several RISC-V chips. All these works on FFTW with RISC-V have one thing in common: FFTW is always used sequentially to compute a 1D FFT. In contrast, we investigate parallel 2D FFT with FFTW.

The first efforts to port the HPX runtime to RISC-V were made in [7]. The authors evaluated the parallel performance and energy consumption of different hardware architectures using the Octo-Tiger astrophysics library [16]. In [8] their RISC-V work is extended to benchmark vectorization with Octo-Tiger on the SG2042 chip. A detailed performance analysis and comparison of the SG2042 chip against x86-64 is given in [2]. Their comparison includes the two chips used in our work. When applied to a double-precision workload, the EPYC 7742 chip out performed the SG2042 chip by a factor of five. The authors use the RAJA performance suite [13] to benchmark the system for different workloads. However, the RAJA performance suite does not include the FFT algorithm and MPI-based parallelization.

3 Software Stack

In the following subsections, we discuss the idea behind the FFTW [9] library and its different parallelization approaches. Furthermore, we introduce HPX-FFT and the asynchronous many-task runtime HPX.

3.1 FFTW

FFTW is the de facto standard for FFT in HPC. To date, its hardware adaptivity and vectorization make FFTW one of the fastest libraries to compute multidimensional FFT. Although in distributed memory environments, libraries like P3DFFT [18], exhibit a slight performance advantage due to a more advanced data distribution strategy. One major drawback of FFTW is its lack of accelerator support. Developers seeking to benefit from accelerators are required to incorporate hybrid solutions themselves or rely on libraries such as AccFFT [11] that combine FFTW with GPU FFT libraries.

The compilation of FFTW is tedious and not recommended for end-users. Inside this tedious process lies the secret of FFTW's performance. FFTW uses code generation to produce highly optimized FFT codelets that serve as a basis for large-scale transformations. The best-performing combination of these codelets is different from system to system. In FFTW, the art of finding the optimal combination is called *planning*. For planning, FFTW performs an offline test on a set of combinations for a FFT of given size and dimension. The result is called a *plan* and can be reused multiple times. This makes it perfect for iterative workloads typically found in scientific computing applications. FFTW can rely on precomputed FFT plans in the form of *wisdom*. FFTW's *wisdom* is a cache of optimal performance parameters used in an FFT execution plan. The FFTW library supports multiple types of planning. We focus on *estimated* and *measured* planning. Estimated planning uses an exclusive heuristic to approximate the best combination of codelets. In contrast, measured planning uses a reduced subset of parameter combinations.

FFTW supports three different parallelization variants out-of-the-box: MPI, OpenMP, and POSIX threads. We omit the HPX backend developed in [20] from this list as it is not yet part of an official FFTW release. The HPX backend requires compiling FFTW from source. In the following subsections, we discuss the MPI and OpenMP backends in more detail. The POSIX backend is not considered in this work because of implementation and performance similarities with the OpenMP backend.

3.2 OpenMP

The Open Multiprocessing Standard [5] was added to C/C++ in 1999. It contains a set of compiler directives that allow for easy-to-implement shared memory parallelization. The main parallelization concept of OpenMP is built on the fork-join principle. As an example, when the compiler encounters `#pragma omp parallel for` to schedule an embarrassingly parallel for loop, the iteration range of the loop is partitioned. Each partition forks threads. Each thread works on a different part of the loop. After all threads have finished their work, they are joined back together. The remaining portions of the application are executed sequentially until the next directive. Note that since OpenMP 3.0 tasking is also supported.

In FFTW, the OpenMP backend optimizes the critical path and number of threads for minimal parallelization overhead. The OpenMP backend can be easily incorporated into existing sequential FFTW code. Threading is initialized by calling the `fftw_init_threads()` function. For multithreading-aware planning invoke `fftw_plan_with_threads(n_threads)`. Here `n_threads` resembles the number of OpenMP threads.

3.3 MPI

Since its release in 1994, the Message Passing Interface [17] has evolved into the standard for communication between distributed physical or logical memory entities, referred to as ranks in MPI terminology. As the name suggests, MPI is based on sending and receiving data packed into messages. MPI supports both synchronous (blocking) and asynchronous (non-blocking) point-to-point communication. For complex parallel algorithms, point-to-point communication quickly becomes tedious and error-prone. MPI tackles the complexity by providing a set of pre-defined communication patterns in the form of collective operations. Collectives operate on participating ranks grouped within a communicator. MPI only serves as a standard that defines syntax and functionalities. There exist multiple implementations of this standard such as OpenMPI [10] and MPICH [12].

Parallel multidimensional FFT communication follows a clear pattern. It perfectly matches the all-to-all collective pattern. FFTW uses `MPI_all_to_all` to handle communication between ranks. Using the MPI backend in FFTW requires including the MPI-specific header file. The MPI backend is initialized with a call to `fftw_mpi_init()`. Dimension-specific `fftw_mpi_local_size_<dim>d` functions then determine the local data size on each rank in an MPI communicator. Special `fftw_mpi_plan_<type>_<dim>d` functions enable planning on data distributed across multiple ranks. It is also possible to combine the MPI with the OpenMP backend. As a result, we can run FFTW with MPI+OpenMP. Note that `MPI_THREAD_FUNNELED` has to be set for this combination to work correctly. For a more detailed explanation of how to run FFTW in parallel, we refer to the FFTW3 documentation for shared[5] and distributed[6] tutorials.

3.4 HPX-FFT

HPX-FFT is a software tool developed to compute 2D FFTs utilizing the asynchronous many-task runtime HPX. It is targeted towards shared-memory and distributed environments of arbitrary scale. HPX-FFT is built on HPX [14], the standard C++ library for concurrency and parallelism, to enable the parallelization of 1D FFTs. FFTW is used as the backend for computing the 1D FFTs. For a more detailed explanation of the parallelization approach, see Sect. 4.1.

HPX facilitates asynchronous parallelization through the use of futures to define task dependencies. Task dependencies can be chained together creating a task graph. Task graphs are efficiently scheduled by work-stealing schedulers and executed via lightweight HPX threads. HPX provides an Active Global Address Space (AGAS) for communication. The AGAS enables both implicit and explicit communication via active messages. These active messages, named *parcels*, are sent over a so-called *parcelport*. At the time of writing, HPX supports three parcelports: TCP, MPI, and LCI [23]. A performance comparison of these parcelports using HPX-FFT is given in [19].

In this work, we use HPX-FFT as a reference point to assess the quality of parallel 2D FFTW plans. Furthermore, we use HPX-FFT as an example of parallel memory access pattern optimization.

---

[5] https://www.fftw.org/fftw3_doc/Multi_002dthreaded-FFTW.html#Multi_002dthreaded-FFTW (accessed on 05/16/2025).

[6] https://www.fftw.org/fftw3_doc/Distributed_002dmemory-FFTW-with-MPI.html#Distributed_002dmemory-FFTW-with-MPI (accessed on 05/16/2025).

4 Methods

In this section, we briefly introduce the Fourier transform and its extension to multiple dimensions. Furthermore, we present a robust parallelization scheme. In the end, we state the different implementations of HPX-FFT and FFTW used in our benchmarks.

4.1 Parallel FFT

For a real-valued discrete 1D signal $f = [f_0, ..., f_{N-1}]$, the discrete Fourier transform is given by

$$\hat{f}_k = \sum_{n=0}^{N-1} f_n \cdot \phi_k(n) \qquad (1)$$

for $k = 0, ..., \frac{N}{2}$. With different basis functions $\phi_k(n)$ we can perform Fourier, sine, and cosine transforms. To expand the Fourier transform into multiple dimensions, a 1D transform is performed sequentially in every dimension. For a multidimensional signal containing real values, this means that the first transform changes from real to complex space (r2c). All subsequent transforms remain in the complex space (c2c). Assuming the signal is stored in row-major storage format, only the first dimension is stored contiguously in matrix rows. Thus, for a 2D Fourier transform, there are two options to handle the second 1D transform. Either the transform is computed with index offsets or the matrix is transposed to compute the second dimension in contiguous memory. If the signal is small, the first approach is typically faster. However, as soon as the matrix rows do not fit in the cache anymore, the second approach is favorable.

The naive Fourier transform has a computational complexity of $\mathcal{O}(N^{d+1})$ for d dimensions. In 1965, Cooley and Turkey proposed the FFT algorithm [4]. FFT reduces the complexity of the multidimensional Fourier transform to $\mathcal{O}(N^d \cdot \log(N))$. The resulting parallel algorithm using FFT and data transposition consists of four sequential steps for two dimensions (see Fig. 1). In the next subsection, we introduce different HPX-FFT implementations that all perform these four steps but differ in synchronization.

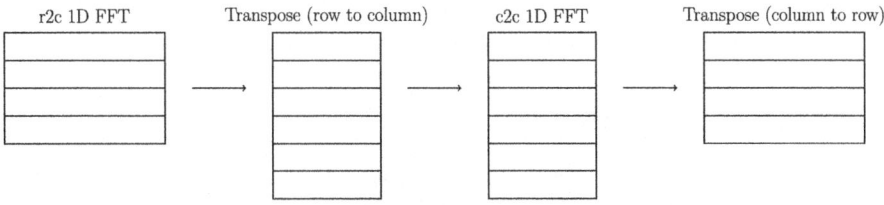

Fig. 1. Four steps of parallel 2D FFT

4.2 Implementations

In this work, we benchmark several different implementations that perform a 2D FFT in parallel. To investigate the effect of memory optimization on RISC-V, we consider the following implementations:

- HPX-FFT *naive*: Future-based with minimal synchronization.
- HPX-FFT *opt*: Future-based with memory access optimization.
- HPX-FFT *sync*: Future-based with maximal synchronization.
- HPX-FFT *for_loop*: Fork-join-based implementation using `hpx::experimental::for_loop`.

To compare the FFTW backends, we consider the following implementations:

- FFTW MPI: Parallelization with MPI ranks.
- FFTW OpenMP: Parallelization with OpenMP threads.
- FFTW MPI+OpenMP: Parallelization with a combination of OpenMP threads and MPI ranks.

5 Results

We divide the results into three different parts. First, we compare the different HPX-FFT implementations to investigate the impact of memory access optimizations on RISC-V. Then, we perform a scaling test of parallel FFTW using estimated planning. Followed by a scaling test using measured planning.

As a uniform benchmark, we choose a 2D FFT of size $2^{14} \times 2^{14}$ in FP64 precision and perform strong scaling benchmarks from 1 to 64 cores on both chips. All runtimes presented in this section are the median of ten runs. The error bars visualize the minimum and maximum of these runs. The results of our previous work are not reused. Instead, we rerun the benchmarks on the x86-64 system with software versions that match the RISC-V system.

The specifications of the systems used in this work are presented in Table 1. Note that the 64 cores on the EPYC 7742 chip are organized in eight clusters with eight Zen2 cores each. Each core has 96KB of L1 cache and 512KB of L2 cache. In contrast, the 64 cores on the SG2042 chip are organized into 16 clusters of 4 RISC-V cores per cluster. Each cluster has 64KB of data cache and 64KB of instruction cache. Additionally, each cluster has 1MB of L2 cache.

5.1 Memory Access Optimization

Accordingly to [20], we observe a significant performance difference between the different optimization levels. In Fig. 2, the naive implementation shows a nearly constant multiplicative overhead compared to the best implementation from one core to 64 cores. This overhead is not significant on the RISC-V machine (see Fig. 3). In general, the optimizations have little impact on the RISC-V machine. Up to 16 cores, the performance delta between RISC-V and x86-64 is

Table 1. Hardware specification of the x86-64 and RISC-V chips

Architecture	x86-64	RISC-V
CPU	AMD EPYC 7742	SOPHON SG2042
Cores	64	64
Base clock	2.25GHz	2.00GHz
L3 Cache	256MB	64MB
SIMD	AVX2	RVV0.7.1
TDP	225W	120W

around factor 5.6 for the naive implementation and around factor 10.7 for the remaining three implementations. For more than 32 cores, the performance of all implementations is significantly reduced.

Upon closer analysis of the HPX-FFT *for_loop* variant, performance bottlenecks become evident (see Figs. 4 and 5). On x86-64, the runtime distribution between FFT computation and data transposition is approximately 60% to 40% up to 32 cores and reaches 50% to 50% at 64 cores. The RISC-V processor contrasts as the ratios change significantly: 30% to 70% up to 16 cores, 20% to 80% at 32 cores, and 10% to 90% at 64 cores. This suggests less efficient memory access and cache utilization on the SG2042 chip.

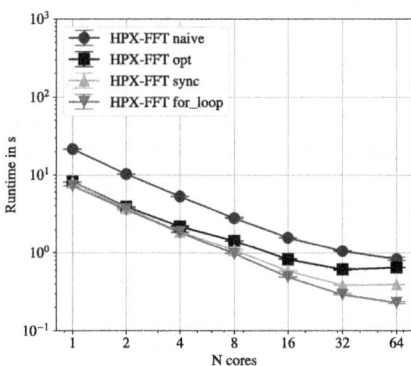

Fig. 2. Strong scaling runtimes of different optimizations on up to 64 x86-64 cores for a $2^{14} \times 2^{14}$ FFT using HPX-FFT.

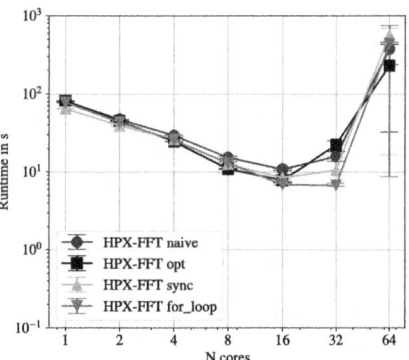

Fig. 3. Strong scaling runtimes of different optimizations on up to 64 RISC-V cores for a $2^{14} \times 2^{14}$ FFT using HPX-FFT.

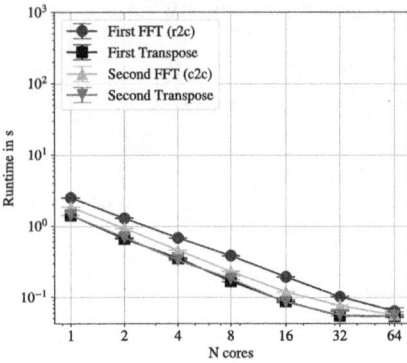 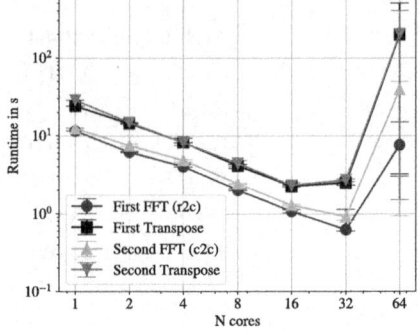

Fig. 4. Partial runtimes of HPX-FFT *for_loop* on up to 64 x86-64 cores for a $2^{14} \times 2^{14}$ FFT.

Fig. 5. Partial runtimes of HPX-FFT *for_loop* on up to 64 RISC-V cores for a $2^{14} \times 2^{14}$ FFT.

5.2 Estimated Planning

RISC-V support for FFTW is currently under active development. We use the most recent release on GitHub[7] available at the time of writing. Since the release supports RVV1.0 and the SG2042 chip only supports RVV0.7.1, we do not consider vectorization for better comparability.

The performance of the FFTW backends on the x86-64 machine is visualized in Fig. 6. For 64 cores, OpenMP performance significantly drops, while MPI scales as expected. The HPX-FFT tool shows the best performance and scaling. These observations change when we run the same code on the SG2042 RISC-V machine (see Fig. 7). Depending on the backend, we observe an overall performance delta of factor 4.0 to 8.0 for parallel FFTW. Note that FFTW with OpenMP suffers from the same performance drop for 64 cores on RISC-V.

5.3 Measured Planning

With measured planning, specifically through the creation of a sophisticated parallel plan, the performance of FFTW improves on the x86-64 system (see Fig. 6). Compared to estimated planning, HPX-FFT and the MPI backend of FFTW show an average speedup of 1.15 and 1.27 respectively. The OpenMP backend shows an average speedup of 3.12, including superior scaling for 64 cores. Since HPX-FFT and the MPI backend employ similar parallelization strategies, performance gains are limited to improvements in the underlying 1D FFTs. In contrast, the OpenMP backend allows FFTW to optimize the entire 2D FFT, resulting in greater overall performance improvements.

On the RISC-V machine, efficient planning utilizing a cycle counter requires the FFTW RISC-V release. Although the standard FFTW release can be used on

---

[7] https://github.com/rdolbeau/fftw3/releases/tag/r5v-test-release-005 (accessed on 05/16/2025).

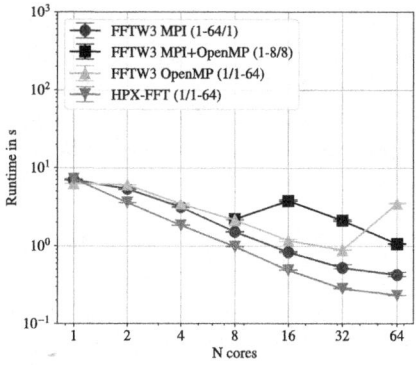

Fig. 6. Strong scaling runtimes on up to 64 x86-64 cores for a $2^{14} \times 2^{14}$ FFT using FFTW with estimated planning. The execution configuration is represented as (#processes/#threads).

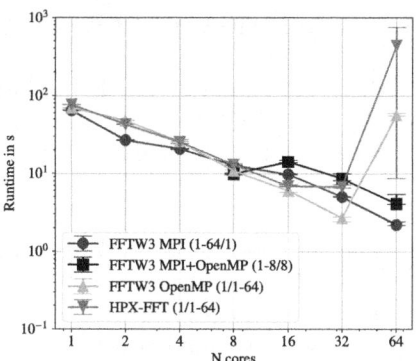

Fig. 7. Strong scaling runtimes on up to 64 RISC-V cores for a $2^{14} \times 2^{14}$ FFT using FFTW with estimated planning. The execution configuration is represented as (#processes/#threads).

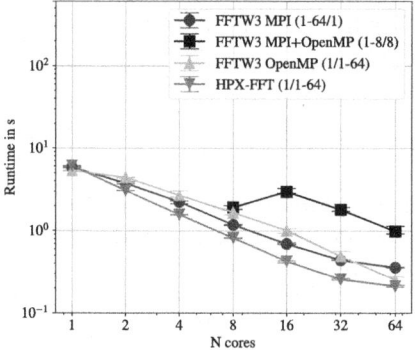

Fig. 8. Strong scaling runtimes on up to 64 x86-64 cores for a $2^{14} \times 2^{14}$ FFT using FFTW with measured planning. The execution configuration is represented as (#processes/#threads).

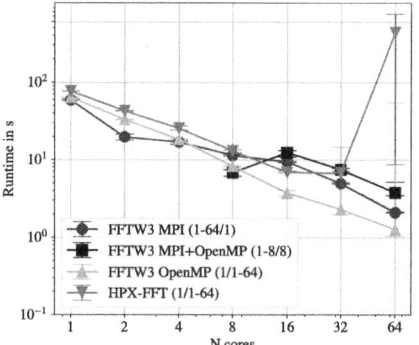

Fig. 9. Strong scaling runtimes on up to 64 RISC-V cores for a $2^{14} \times 2^{14}$ FFT using FFTW with measured planning. The execution configuration is represented as (#processes/#threads).

the SG2042 chip, the lack of a cycle counter makes efficient planning impossible. Alternatively, FFTW can use software timers instead of the cycle counter at the cost of significantly increasing the planning time.

See the performance for FFTW with measured planning on RISC-V in Fig. 9. Similarly to the x86-64 machine, measured planning resolves the performance drop of the OpenMP backend. The MPI backend shows an average speedup of 1.13, while for OpenMP the speedup is 7.51 on average (Fig. 8).

6 Conclusion and Outlook

In this work, we evaluate the performance of parallel FFT on a recent RISC-V chip using FFTW. In a side-by-side comparison of 64 RISC-V cores against 64 x86-64 cores, we highlight the current performance gap between the two architectures. We measure a performance delta of around factor eight averaged over all FFT benchmarks conducted in this work.

Furthermore, we show that optimizing the memory access pattern has significantly less impact on the performance on the SG2042 RISC-V processor. Measured planning results in a significant performance boost for the OpenMP backend of FFTW on both chips. The MPI backend profits only marginally from planning, but shows consistent scaling. The performance advantage of HPX-FFT observed on x86-64 does not translate to RISC-V, as HPX-FFT does not scale beyond 16 cores. Based on these findings, we recommend using FFTW with MPI for parallel FFT on currently available many-core RISC-V systems.

In future work, we plan to consider the power efficiency of the different architectures and compare the performance per watt. Additionally, we plan to evaluate a broader set of FFT benchmarks, including different problem sizes and configurations with vectorization enabled. Furthermore, we want to extend the FFT benchmark to ARM-based systems.

Supplementary Materials

The source code, including installation and benchmark scripts, is available at DaRUS[8]. Details on the software and compiler versions used are provided in the README.md file included with the source code.

References

1. Ayala, A., et al.: FFT benchmark performance experiments on systems targeting exascale. Technical report, University of Tennessee (2022)
2. Brown, N., Jamieson, M., Lee, J., Wang, P.: Is RISC-V ready for HPC prime-time: evaluating the 64-core Sophon SG2042 RISC-V CPU. In: SC-W 2023, pp. 1566–1574. SC-W 2023. ACM (2023)
3. Cai, J.: Performance evaluation of numerical libraries on RISC-V architectures with SIMD extensions. Master's thesis, Universidad Complutense de Madrid, Madrid (2024)
4. Cooley, J., Tukey, J.: An algorithm for the machine calculation of complex Fourier series. Math. Comput. **19**(90), 297–301 (1965)
5. Dagum, L., Menon, R.: OpenMP: an industry standard API for shared-memory programming. IEEE Comput. Sci. Eng. **5**(1), 46–55 (1998)
6. Deserno, M., Holm, C.: How to mesh up Ewald sums. I. A theoretical and numerical comparison of various particle mesh routines. J. Chem. Phys. **109**(18), 7678–7693 (1998)

---

[8] https://doi.org/10.18419/DARUS-5056 (accessed on 05/16/2025)

7. Diehl, P., et al.: Evaluating HPX and Kokkos on RISC-V using an astrophysics application octo-tiger. In: SC-W 2023, pp. 1533–1542. Association for Computing Machinery, New York (2023)
8. Diehl, P., et al.: Preparing for HPC on RISC-V: examining vectorization and distributed performance of an astrophysics application with HPX and Kokkos. In: SC-W 2024, pp. 1656–1665. IEEE (2024)
9. Frigo, M., Johnson, S.: The design and implementation of FFTW3. Proc. IEEE **93**(2), 216–231 (2005)
10. Gabriel, E., et al.: Open MPI: goals, concept, and design of a next generation MPI implementation. In: Proceedings of the 11th European PVM/MPI Users' Group Meeting, Budapest, Hungary, pp. 97–104 (2004)
11. Gholami, A., et al.: Accfft: a library for distributed-memory FFT on CPU and GPU architectures. CoRR (2015)
12. Gropp, W., Lusk, E., Skjellum, A.: Using MPI: Portable Parallel Programming with the Message Passing Interface, 2nd edn. MIT Press, Cambridge (1999)
13. Hornung, R.D., Jones, H.E.: RAJA performance suite. Technical report, Lawrence Livermore National Laboratory (LLNL), Livermore, CA, United States (2017)
14. Kaiser, H., et al.: HPX - the C++ standard library for parallelism and concurrency. J. Open Source Softw. **5**(53), 2352 (2020)
15. Li, Z., et al.: Generating fast FFT kernels on CPUS via FFT-specific intrinsics. In: PPoPP 2023, p. 427–428. Association for Computing Machinery, New York (2023)
16. Marcello, D.C., et al.: Octo-tiger: a new, 3D hydrodynamic code for stellar mergers that uses HPX parallelization. Mon. Notices Royal Astron. Soc. **504**(4), 5345–5382 (2021)
17. Message Passing Interface Forum: MPI: A Message-Passing Interface Standard Version 3.0 (2021)
18. Pekurovsky, D.: P3dfft: a framework for parallel computations of Fourier transforms in three dimensions. SISC **34**(4), C192–C209 (2012)
19. Strack, A., Pflüger, D.: A HPX communication benchmark: distributed FFT using collectives. In: Euro-Par 2024: Parallel Processing Workshops. LNCS. Springer, Cham (2025)
20. Strack, A., Taylor, C., Diehl, P., Pflüger, D.: Experiences Porting Shared and Distributed Applications to Asynchronous Tasks: A Multidimensional FFT Case-Study, pp. 111–122. Springer, Cham (2024)
21. Vizcaino, P., et al.: Acceleration with long vector architectures: Implementation and evaluation of the FFT kernel on NEC SX-aurora and RISC-V vector extension. Concurr. Comput. Pract. Exp. **35** (2022)
22. Waterman, A., et al.: The RISC-V Instruction Set Manual, Volume I: User-Level ISA. Technical report 2, University of California, Berkeley (2014)
23. Yan, J., Kaiser, H., Snir, M.: Design and analysis of the network software stack of an asynchronous many-task system – the LCI parcelport of HPX. In: Proceedings of the SC 2023 Workshops, pp. 1151–1161. ACM, New York (2023)
24. Zhao, X., Zhang, X., Zhang, Y.: Optimization of the FFT algorithm on RISC-V CPUs. In: ISC HP 2023 Workshops, pp. 515–525. Springer, Heidelberg (2023)

Exploring Fast Fourier Transforms on the Tenstorrent Wormhole

Nick Brown[1], Jake Davies[1], and Felix Le Clair[2]

[1] Bayes Centre, EPCC, 47 Potterrow, Edinburgh, UK
n.brown@epcc.ed.ac.uk
[2] Tenstorrent, 2600 Great America Way, Santa Clara, CA, USA

Abstract. Whilst numerous areas of computing have adopted the RISC-V Instruction Set Architecture (ISA) wholesale in recent years, it is yet to become widespread in HPC. RISC-V accelerators offer a compelling option where the HPC community can benefit from the specialisation offered by the open nature of the standard but without the extensive ecosystem changes required when adopting RISC-V CPUs. In this paper we explore porting the Cooley-Tukey Fast Fourier Transform (FFT) algorithm to the Tenstorrent Wormhole PCIe RISC-V based accelerator. Built upon Tenstorrent's Tensix architecture, this technology decouples the movement of data from compute, potentially offering increased control to the programmer. Exploring different optimisation techniques to address the bottlenecks inherent in data movement, we demonstrate that for a 2D FFT whilst the Wormhole n300 is slower than a server-grade 24-core Xeon Platinum CPU, the Wormhole draws around 8 times less power and consumes around 2.8 times less energy than the CPU when computing the Fourier transform.

Keywords: RISC-V · Tenstorrent Wormhole · Fourier Transforms · FFTs · Cooley-Tukey · Accelerator

1 Introduction

The recent availability of high core count commodity available RISC-V CPUs [2] is driving increased interest in the role of RISC-V for HPC [3]. However, there is still some way to go for the ecosystem to fully support CPU based RISC-V supercomputers, and instead a more gradual short term adoption route is likely to be in RISC-V based PCIe accelerator cards. The major benefit of these is that they fit into existing, x86 or AArch64, systems as an add-ons. Several vendors are developing such accelerator cards, often aimed at Artificial Intelligence (AI) and Machine Learning (ML) workloads, driven by the current boom in AI. Indeed, each vendor is taking a different approach to the design of their technology based upon a set of principals that they consider important, and this demonstrates the flexibility provided by RISC-V where hardware designers can use the standard in the manner most suitable to them.

Whether initially designed for ML or HPC, RISC-V accelerator hardware fundamentally provides the building blocks to accelerate mathematical operations. Consequently, there is a role for these accelerator technologies to be leveraged by the HPC community, and one such RISC-V based accelerator card is the Wormhole developed by Tenstorrent. Available for purchase at a modest price, this commodity card is, as of 2025, one of the few RISC-V based accelerators that are publicly available. The availability and moderate price-point not only means that these can be leveraged in best-of-class supercomputers, but furthermore that they are also suitable for smaller HPC machines and even workstations. Indeed, Tenstorrent have opened up their entire software stack and work in the open, in collaboration with the wider community.

In this paper we calculate the Discrete Fourier Transform (DFT) by porting the CooleyâĂŞTukey Fast Fourier Transform (FFT) algorithm to the Tenstorrent Wormhole accelerator. An algorithm that is ubiquitous, not only in scientific computing but also far more generally such as signal processing, our hypothesis was that the decoupling of data movement from compute provided by the Tenstorrent architecture has the potential to deliver performance and energy efficiency improvements compared to running on a CPU. The paper is structured as follows; in Sect. 2 we survey the Tenstorrent Tensix architecture and describe the FFT algorithm, before reporting the experimental setup in Sect. 3 used throughout this paper. Section 4 describes the design of the FFT algorithm for the Tenstorrent architecture and then explores the efficacy of optimisation techniques that aim at reducing the overhead of data movement. We then compare all 24-cores of a Xeon Platinum Cascade Lake CPU against 64 Tensix cores on the n300 for a 2D FFT in Sect. 5, before drawing conclusions and discussing further work in Sect. 6.

The novel contributions of this paper are:

- We undertake, to the best of our knowledge, the first study of porting the FFT algorithm to a RISC-V PCIe accelerator.
- An exploration of optimisation strategies for data reordering on the Tenstorrent Tensix architecture.
- A performance and energy efficiency analysis of an FFT solver on the Tenstorrent Wormhole against a server grade CPU.

2 Background

2.1 The Tenstorrent Architecture

The Grayskull, Wormhole and Blackhole PCIe accelerator cards, developed by Tenstorrent, are built around the Tensix architecture. As sketched in Fig. 1, each Tensix core contains five RISC-V CPUs, known as *baby cores*, 1.3MB of local SRAM, two routers each of which are connected to separate Networks on Chip (NoCs), and compute engine. Out of the five RISC-V baby cores, one of these is for moving data into the Tensix core, one for moving data out, and three drive the compute engine. The compute engine itself provides scalar (ThCon), vector (SFPU) and matrix (FPU) units that support a range of precisions up to FP32, which we use throughout this paper, although the matrix unit relaxes IEEE compliance. Out of the three RISC-V baby cores driving the compute engine, one called *UNPACK* issues instructions to the unpacker in the compute engine, which copies data from SRAM into the source registers, *srcA* and *srcB*. The *MATH* RISC-V baby compute core issues instructions to the ThCon, SFPU and FPU units, directing them to undertake operations on source registers. The third RISC-V baby compute core, *PACK*, packs (or copies) result data from the *dst* register to SRAM. The *srcA* and *srcB* registers are 4KiB in size, holding a maximum of 1024 single precision floating point numbers, and the *dst* register is of size 32KiB and segmented into 16 chunks [4]. To avoid being a bottleneck, input and result values are never transferred through the RISC-V compute baby cores, but instead instruct the unpacker and packer in the compute unit to accesses SRAM directly.

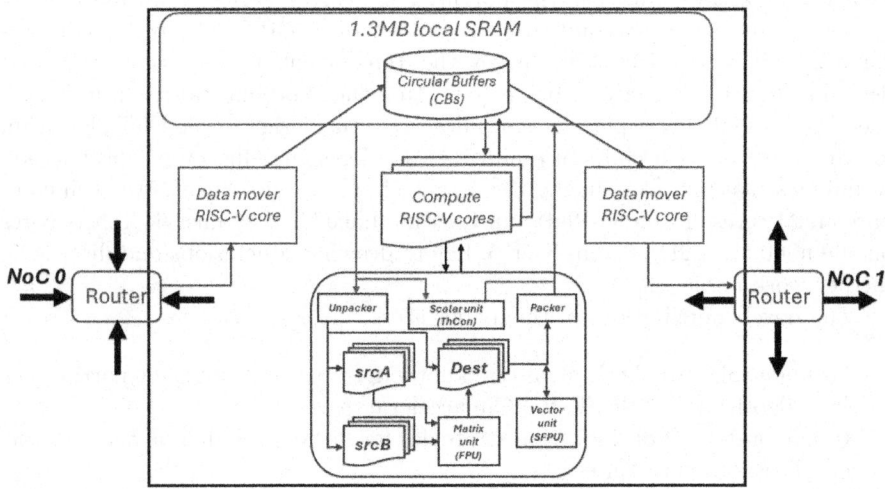

Fig. 1. A single Tensix core in the Wormhole accelerator, containing five RISC-V *baby cores*, 1.3MB of local SRAM memory, a compute engine and two routers to the Network on Chip (NoC).

The *dst* register is used as both an input to, and output from, the vector unit and this is why it is split into 16 segments. Consequently, compute can undertaken by the matrix unit and results can then be provided to the vector unit for further processing. Indeed, the matrix unit only supports a restricted set of operations including matrix multiplication, addition, subtraction, multiplication, transposition and reduction. By contrast, the vector unit is more general and in addition to binary arithmetic also provides support for operations including squares, square root, cos, tan, sin, and conditionals. In-fact, the programmer can write their own code directly for the SFPU and the compiler will then vectorise this. The matrix unit can perform 2048 floating point multiplications and 2048 floating point additions per cycle. The vector unit comprises eight registers, each with thirty two 32-bit lanes and consequently is capable of operating on up to 256 FP32 numbers per cycle.

The abstraction of *Circular Buffers* (CBs) represents data held in local SRAM. These are First In First Out (FIFO) queues and follow a producer-consumer model, where a page of data is requested in the CB by the producer, populated and pushed to be made available. The consumer blocks on the availability of a page, and once it is, then consumes the data before freeing the memory so that this can be reused. CBs combine semantics around memory and synchronisation, enabling coordination between the RISC-V baby cores. An example is the common situation where a data mover core requests a CB page, then fills this with data read from external DRAM and pushes this. The RISC-V compute cores then consume this CB, with the *UNPACK* core instructing the *unpacker* in the compute engine to copy data from this page in the CB into a target register.

In this work we focus on a Wormhole n300 which contains 120 Tensix cores that are provided as two, 60-core, chips running at 1 GHz. There is a total of 24GB of GDDR6, external, memory on the board which is split across twenty four banks each of 1GB, with twelve banks directly connected to each chip [6]. Whilst, at the time of writing, Tenstorrent have recently released their next generation accelerator, the Blackhole, the Wormhole is currently by far the more common technology and due to the same underlying architecture, lessons learnt on this generation will apply to the next.

The TT-Metalium framework, *tt-metal*, is Tenstorrent's direct programming SDK which exposes access to the hardware, providing an API for kernel development. The SDK provides an API that programmers can use to undertake a range of low level activities such as the movement of data, driving the compute engine, and interacting with Circular Buffers (CBs). The programmer develops three kernels, one for each data movement RISC-V baby core and one for the compute cores.

Previous work [1] explored stencil applications on the first generation, Grayskull e150, Tenstorrent accelerator. This work demonstrated that it was possible for the architecture to perform comparatively to a server-grade CPU but at five times less energy. However, a major challenge was in reworking the algorithm to suit the architecture, with the final version of the code around 160 times faster on the Grayskull than the initial, naive, kernel implementation.

2.2 Fast Fourier Transforms (FFTs)

The calculation of the Discrete Fourier Transform (DFT) is of critical importance to a wide variety of applications ranging from digital signal processing to solving systems of partial differential equations. Converting between the spatial and frequency domains, the former represents a collection of values and the later describes the rate at which these values are changing. Fast Fourier Transforms

(FFTs) are a class of fast algorithms that compute the DFT, with the Cooley–Tukey algorithm [5] being the most common and the focus in this work. Indeed, the FFT algorithm was described as *the most important numerical algorithm of our lifetime* [5] as it reduces the computational complexity to O(N log N). Cooley-Tukey follows a divide-and-conquer approach and simple implementations adopt a recursive form, however for performance this is expressed iteratively with an outer loop of log N steps.

Figure 2 illustrates an FFT operating on eight input values, requiring three steps. We follow a 2-radix approach, were in the first step calculations involving neighbouring values are undertaken, in the second step intermediate results are then calculated between neighbour plus (or minus) 2, and in the third step intermediates with neighbour plus (or minus) four.

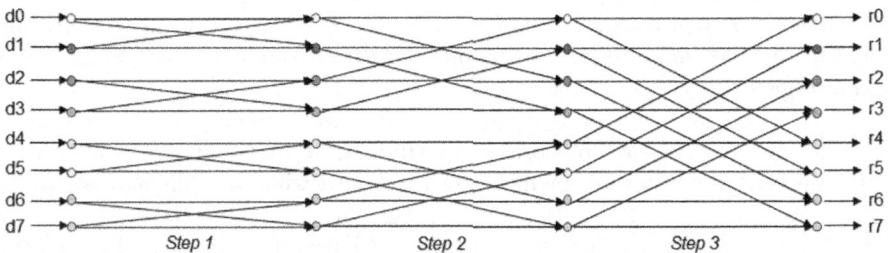

Fig. 2. Illustration of the steps involved and data dependencies with a radix-2 Cooley-Tukey FFT on eight values

Consequently, in addition to the calculation itself, the movement of data is an important consideration as from one step to the next the compute requires different pairs of numbers. This is illustrated in Listing 1.1 where, for each step, individual *points* in groups of *spectra* are processed. There are two data elements per point, and it can be seen that the indices of these, *d0_data_index* and *d1_data_index*, are calculated at lines 6 and 7, with *matching_second_point* providing the offset for the second element, for instance 1, 2, 4 for steps 1, 2 and 3 in Fig. 2. Values *f0* and *f1* are then calculated based upon twiddle factors and the second element of data at lines 9 and 10, before these values are applied to the real and imaginary components of the two data elements at lines 12 to 15. Twiddle factors are trigonometric constants that are multiplied by the data during execution of the algorithm.

```
1   for (int step=0; step <= num_steps; step++) {
2     int matching_second_point=...
3     for (int spectra=0; spectra < num_spectra_in_step; spectra++) {
4       int twiddle_index=spectra << (num_steps−step);
5       for (int point=0; point < domain_size; point+=
              increment_next_point_in_step) {
6         int d0_data_index=(spectra + point);
```

```
7           int d1_data_index=(spectra + point + matching_second_point
                );
8
9           float f0=(data[d1_data_index].r * twiddle_factors[
                twiddle_index].r) - (data[d1_data_index].i *
                twiddle_factors[twiddle_index].i);
10          float f1=(data[d1_data_index].r * twiddle_factors[
                twiddle_index].i) + (data[d1_data_index].i *
                twiddle_factors[twiddle_index].r);
11
12          data[d1_data_index].r=data[d0_data_index].r - f0;
13          data[d1_data_index].i=data[d0_data_index].i - f1;
14          data[d0_data_index].r=data[d0_data_index].r + f0;
15          data[d0_data_index].i=data[d0_data_index].i + f1;
16        }
17     }
18  }
```

Listing 1.1. Sketch of FFT algorithm which is computing using real and imaginary components

3 Experimental Setup

Results reported from the experiments run throughout this paper are averaged over five runs. All Tenstorrent runs were undertaken on a Wormhole n300 connected to the host system by PCIe Gen 3. The host machine contains a 26-core 8170 Skylake Intel Xeon Platinum CPU and 128 GB of DRAM. All experiments are built using version 0.56 of the tt-metal framework, and Clang 17 is used to compile host codes. CPU runs are undertaken on a 24-core 8260M Cascade Lake Xeon Platinum CPU, which is equipped with 512GB of DRAM and codes are compiled using GCC version 11.2. All codes are compiled at optimisation level three. Multi-core runs on the CPU are multi threaded using OpenMP. Energy usage on the CPU is based upon values reported by RAPL, and on the n300 from the Tenstorrent System Management Interface (TT-SMI).

All results reported in this paper are running single precision, FP32, which is the maximum precision supported by the n300. Unless otherwise stated, performance numbers reported for the Wormhole are execution time only.

4 Porting Fourier Transforms to the Wormhole

In this section we focus on porting FFTs to the Wormhole and optimising for a single Tensix core. Whilst complex numbers are not directly supported by the Tensix's compute engine, it is possible to work with the real and imaginary components individually as illustrated in Listing 1.1 and this is the approach adopted here.

Figure 3 illustrates the design that we initially leveraged when porting the FFT algorithm to the Tensix core. For each step, the in data mover core will read the input data for that step. This is read either from external on-card DDR for the first step or from local SRAM for subsequent ones, and a page in four CBs is populated with the data correctly ordered for that specific step. These CBs are the computation's Left Hand Side (LHS) and Right Hand Side (RHS) for both real and imaginary components. These are then used as an input to the compute core which provides these to the compute unit to undertake the calculations. The output of these calculations is stored in real and imaginary CBs which are consumed by the out data mover core which then reorders the data into the original order and will either store this in SRAM, ready to be consumed by the next step, or external DDR for the final results. Consequently, for each step we undertake two reorderings of data, from the original data order to the order required for pair wise operations by that current step, and then results are ordered from this stepwise ordering back to the original orientation.

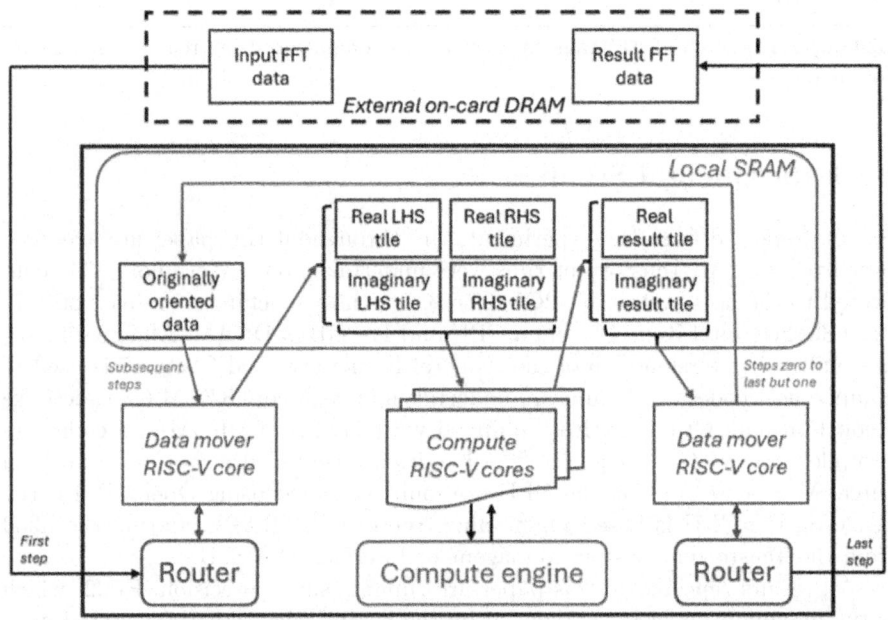

Fig. 3. Basic design approach of running FFTs on a Tensix core

Figure 3 is simplified somewhat, for instance twiddle factors are calculated by the compute engine on initialisation and stored in SRAM but these do not change from step to step. Listing 1.2 sketches the FFT compute kernel, at line 1 operating in steps, and lines 2 and 3 waiting for pages of real and imaginary data to be available in these CBs for the second element of data. Lines 5 to 13 then use the SFPU to compute *f0* and *f1* before the real and imaginary pages of the first element of data in the CBs are waited on at lines 15 and 16. Lines 21 to 28 then applying *f0* and *f1* to the real and imaginary components of the two data values before popping the input data CBs at lines 27 to 30, which will enable the pages of memory to be reused by the next step. The *cb_int0* and *cb_int1* CBs are circular buffers used to hold intermediate calculation data, and the *cb_twiddle_r* and *cb_twiddle_i* hold twiddle values.

```
1   for (int step=0; step <= num_steps; step++) {
2       cb_wait_front(cb_data1_r, 1);
3       cb_wait_front(cb_data1_i, 1);
4
5       // Calculate f0
6       maths_sfpu_op<MUL>(cb_data1_r, cb_twiddle_r, cb_int0);
7       maths_sfpu_op<MUL>(cb_data1_i, cb_twiddle_i, cb_int1);
8       maths_sfpu_op<SUB, true, true>(cb_int0, cb_int1, cb_f0);
9
10      // Calculate f1
11      maths_sfpu_op<MUL>(cb_data1_r, cb_twiddle_i, cb_int0);
12      maths_sfpu_op<MUL>(cb_data1_i, cb_twiddle_r, cb_int1);
13      maths_sfpu_op<ADD, true, true>(cb_int0, cb_int1, cb_f1);
14
15      cb_wait_front(cb_data0_r, 1);
16      cb_wait_front(cb_data0_i, 1);
17
18      // Calculate data_1 real
19      maths_sfpu_op<SUB>(cb_data0_r, cb_f0, cb_out_data1_r);
20      // Calculate data_1 imaginary
21      maths_sfpu_op<SUB>(cb_data0_i, cb_f1, cb_out_data1_i);
22      // Calculate data_0 real
23      maths_sfpu_op<ADD>(cb_data0_r, cb_f0, cb_out_data0_r);
24      // Calculate data_0 imaginary
25      maths_sfpu_op<ADD>(cb_data0_i, cb_f1, cb_out_data0_i);
26
27      cb_pop_front(cb_data0_r, 1);
28      cb_pop_front(cb_data0_i, 1);
29      cb_pop_front(cb_data1_r, 1);
30      cb_pop_front(cb_data1_i, 1);
31  }
```

Listing 1.2. Sketch of FFT compute kernel code

The *maths_sfpu_op* function that is called in Listing 1.2 is sketched in Listing 1.3. We developed this as a helper function due to the boilerplate code that is required for each operation, where a lock on the *dst* register must first be acquired by the *MATH* RISC-V compute core, tiles are then copied in from page location 0 in CBs *cb_in_1* and *cb_in_2* to segments 0 and 1 of the *dst* register at lines 7 and 8, before the compute operation is performed on *dst* register segments 0 and 1 at lines 9 to 17 and results written to the 0 segment. The *MATH* RISC-V compute core then releases its lock on the *dst* register at line 18, before a page in the *cb_tgt* CB is waited on at line 22, and then the *PACK* RISC-V compute core acquires a lock on the *dst* register, packs values from the 0 segment of the *dst* register to a page in the CB, and releases the lock at lines 23 to 25, before making the page in *cb_tgt* CB available. Optionally, this function will also wait for pages in input CBs and free these up, and it can be see in Listing 1.2 that this is used when working with intermediate values. Whilst we focus here on the vector unit, SFPU, we also provide versions of this maths operation function for computing with matrix unit, FPU, which is similar to Listing 1.3 but somewhat simplified because the Metalium API call performs copying of input data into the *srcA* and *srcB* registers itself.

```
1   template <int OPERATION, bool CB_OP_IN1=false, bool
        CB_OP_IN2=false>
2   void maths_sfpu_op(uint32_t cb_in_1, uint32_t cb_in_2, uint32_t
        cb_tgt) {
3     // Copy from input CBs into index 0 and 1 of DST regs
4     if constexpr(CB_OP_IN1) cb_wait_front(cb_in_1, 1);
5     if constexpr(CB_OP_IN2) cb_wait_front(cb_in_2, 1);
6     tile_regs_acquire();
7     copy_tile(cb_in_1, 0, 0);
8     copy_tile(cb_in_2, 0, 1);
9     if (OPERATION == ADD) {
10        add_binary_tile(0, 1);
11    } else if (OPERATION == SUB) {
12        sub_binary_tile(0, 1);
13    } else if (OPERATION == MUL) {
14        mul_binary_tile(0, 1);
15    } else if (OPERATION == DIV) {
16        div_binary_tile(0, 1);
17    }
18    tile_regs_commit();
19    if constexpr(CB_OP_IN1) cb_pop_front(cb_in_1, 1);
20    if constexpr(CB_OP_IN2) cb_pop_front(cb_in_2, 1);
21    // Result is in 0 index of DST regs, extract
22    cb_reserve_back(cb_tgt, 1);
23    tile_regs_wait();
24    pack_tile(0, cb_tgt);
25    tile_regs_release();
26    cb_push_back(cb_tgt, 1);
27  }
```

Listing 1.3. Sketch of SFPU maths helper function

Table 1 reports performance of an FFT implementation for a problem size of 16384 elements on a single Xeon Platinum (Cascade Lake) CPU core, along with different versions on a single Tensix core in the Wormhole. The first version on the Wormhole is as illustrated in Fig. 3 and Listing 1.2, using the SFPU for the calculation. It can be seen that it is around eight times slower than a single core is on the Xeon Platinum CPU.

Table 1. Runtime on Tenstorrent Tensix and CPU core executing FFT algorithm for problem size 16384 of elements.

Version	Runtime (ms)
Xeon Platinum CPU single core	1.85
Initial	14.39
Chunked	9.38
Data copy by ThCon	7.56
128-bit copies	6.61
Single data copy	5.31

To explore the underlying reasons for this performance on the Tensix we experimented with disabling certain components in the algorithm and the performance that these individual components delivered is reported in Table 2. The major overhead is in the reordering of data, for instance when disabling data reordering for reading the runtime halves, and when also disabling write reordering the runtime is around a sixteenth of the original. Clearly data reordering is a significant bottleneck, and by comparing the performance when only read or write reordering is enabled in Table 2 it can be observed that read reordering is the more expensive of the two operations. Incidently, compute-only performance was comparable regardless of whether we used the FPU (matrix unit) or SFPU (vector unit) to undertake mathematical operations.

Table 2. Performance on a single Tensix core executing FFT algorithm for 16384 elements when specific components are enabled (Y) or disabled (N).

External read	Read reorder	Compute	Write reorder	External write	Runtime (ms)
Y	Y	Y	Y	Y	14.4
Y	N	Y	Y	Y	7.3
N	N	Y	Y	Y	7.3
N	Y	Y	N	N	10.5
Y	Y	Y	N	N	10.6
N	N	Y	N	Y	0.9
N	N	Y	N	N	0.9

Our initial approach placed the entire domain into single CB pages step by step, for instance loading and reordering all the data, then computing with this, and lastly reordering and writing this all out. Whilst placing the entire domain in a single page was the simplest approach, it meant that different components of the Tensix core could not run concurrently, for instance whilst data loading was occurring by the data mover RISC-V core, the compute engine and data writing kernels were idle. Consequently, we enhanced the code to operate in chunks, *chunked* in Table 1, where the entire domain is split into segments and consequently the components of the Tensix core can run in parallel on different chunks.

When reordering the data, this data is loaded into the data mover cores from SRAM and then written out to a new location. The cores themselves are fairly limited and designed more for driving components such as the routers, compute engine and marshalling control with the CBs rather than undertaking extensive data loads and stores. Instead, the compute engine contains a scalar unit, ThCon, which itself can load and write data and the hypothesis [4] was that this could reduce the runtime due to improved performance of compute engine to SRAM data transfers. Whilst there are no API calls to ThCon exposed directly by Metalium, it is possible to program this via intrinsics provided by the Tenstorrent Low Level Kernels (llk) underlying library. The code for this is sketched in Listing 1.4 which loads 32-bit data from SRAM. The address *from_addr* is decomposed into a base address and offset and then stored into registers *0* and *1* via the *TT_SETDMAREG* intrinsic. These registers are then provided to the *TT_LOADIND* intrinsic, with register *2* provided as the destination to hold the loaded value. There are four tiles of data being reordered, the LHS and RHS for both real and imaginary components, and we found the most effective approach was to distribute these across all three RISC-V compute cores; *UNPACK*, *MATH* and *PACK* which individually issue instructions to ThCon for their respective pages.

```
1   uint32_t base_addr=from_addr / 16;
2   uint32_t addr_offset=from_addr-(base_address*16);
3
4   TT_SETDMAREG(0,LOWER_HALFWORD(addr_offset),0,LO_16(0));
5   TT_SETDMAREG(0,UPPER_HALFWORD(addr_offset),0,HI_16(0));
6   TT_SETDMAREG(0,LOWER_HALFWORD(base_addr),0,LO_16(1));
7   TT_SETDMAREG(0,UPPER_HALFWORD(base_addr),0,HI_16(1));
8
9   TT_LOADIND(p_ind::LD_32bit, LO_16(0), p_ind::INC_4B, 2, 1);
```

Listing 1.4. Sketch of loading data from SRAM via ThCon using LLK intrinsics

The result of this optimisation is reported as *Data copy by ThCon* in Table 1 where it can be seen that it reduced the runtime by around a millisecond. It is possible for ThCon to read and write data of size 8, 16, 32 or 128 bits, and due to us working with FP32 up until this point all data accesses were 32 bit. However, when the kernel reorders input data, stores are all contiguous and when reordering results for writing the loads are all contiguous. The kernel was therefore modified to unroll the reordering loop by four and to use 128-bit wide data accesses for contiguous data. This is reported as *128-bit copies* in Table 1 and it can be seen that this further reduced the runtime.

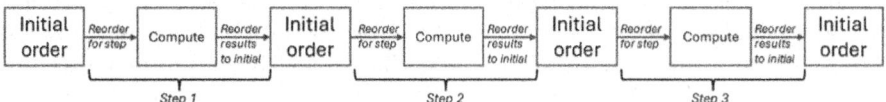

Fig. 4. Two data reordering stages per step, converting back to the original data order between steps

To this point, as per Fig. 4, there were two data reorderings per step. This is because, at the end of a step, the data is reordered back to the original data order. Whilst this was the simplest approach from a code perspective, the reordering of data is expensive and we therefore modified this to instead reorder data to the arrangement required by the next step. This is illustrated in Fig. 5, and it reduces the number of reorderings per step to one, apart from the initial and last step. However, this increases the complexity of the code which resulted in link errors where the compiler reported *.bss will not fit in region `TRISC2_LOCAL_DATA_MEM`*. The bss section holds uninitialized data and this was overflowing, likely due to too many variables. To address this we edited the *kernel_trisc2.ld* linker script to increase the *TRISC2_LOCAL_DATA_MEM* from 1280 to 3328 bytes.

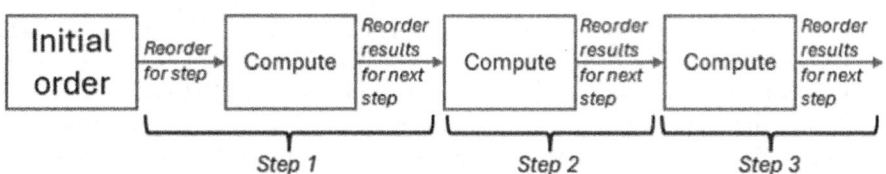

Fig. 5. One data reordering stage per step, converting to the next step's data order directly to reduce the overall number of expensive data reorderings required.

Performance of the one-copy optimisation is reported as *Single data copy* in Table 1 and, whilst it resulted in a performance improvement, the limited nature of this surprised us as we had expected a more considerable reduction in runtime. When investigating we found that this was due to all data accesses now being non-contiguous and therefore 32 rather than 128 bits wide. Effectively we had increased the number of individual memory accesses with a larger number of narrow accesses, whereas before we had fewer wider accesses.

5 Scaling up with a 2D FFT

Thus far we have concentrated on running over a single Tensix core and in this section we scale up by studying a 2D FFT. Figure 6 illustrates the data orientation required by such an operation, where rows of data are distributed across the Tensix cores, here $t0$ to $t7$, and one dimensional FFTs are first executed across each row. The data is then globally transposed so that each Tensix core receives a column of data comprising parts made up from across each Tensix core. Each core then undertakes another FFT on its newly transposed local data. Ultimately, an FFT has been performed across each global row and down each global column to produce the overall result.

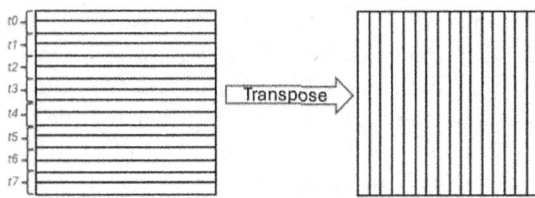

Fig. 6. Illustration of data movement involved in a 2D FFT

We enhanced our FFT implementation to work across a several locally held rows and leveraged the *transpose* routine from Tenstorrent's tt-nn library to undertake transposition across the Tensix cores. For simplicity we assume an even decomposition of rows across Tensix cores, and with a problem size of 1024 by 1024 this limits us to 64 Tensix cores, each holding 16 local rows. Table @reftab:2dfftspsperf reports performance and power of a 2D FFT of size 1024 by 1024 elements parallelised via OpenMP on all 24 cores of the Xeon Platinum Cascade Lake CPU against 64 Tensix cores of the n300. It can be seen that whilst the CPU is faster than the n300, it draws over eight times more power, ultimately resulting in the n300 being 3.6 times more energy efficient.

Table 3. Runtime of Wormhole n300 and entire Xeon Platinum Cascade Lake CPU executing 2D FFT for problem size 1024 by 1024 elements.

Version	Number of cores	Runtime (ms)	Average Power (Watts)	Energy usage (J)
Xeon Platinum CPU	24	10.24	353	3.62
Wormhole n300	64	23.56	42	0.99

6 Conclusions and Future Work

In this paper we have explored calculating the DFT by porting the Cooley-Tukey FFT algorithm to the Tensix architecture. We explored our general design approach of building up tiles of real and imaginary data which are then used as inputs to the compute engine, and abstracting the boilerplate around Metalium mathematical operators via C++ templated functions. We found data reordering was a significant bottleneck and explored optimisation techniques to address this, with the use of ThCon and 128-bit wide memory accesses especially effective.

Whilst the performance of a single Tensix core was around 2.8 times lower than a Xeon Platinum Cascade Lake CPU core, the Wormhole n300 contains many more energy efficient Tensix cores. Consequently we scaled up our approach and explored 2D FFT demonstrating that, whilst 64 Tensix cores in the n300 were slower than the Xeon Platinum CPU, they also drew around eight times less power, ultimately with the Wormhole being 3.6 times more energy efficient.

This paper has highlighted that there is great potential for Tenstorrent technology to benefit HPC workloads, especially due to its energy efficiency nature. However, given that these accelerators have been designed for ML workloads a challenge is to understand how to adapt the algorithms and tooling to best suit general purpose HPC. To this end, more integrated control of ThCon in Metalium would be beneficial, especially if this better abstracted the reordering of data. Furthermore, the ability to load in, and store, data from the matrix and vector registers based upon a user defined mapping directly would likely improve performance as it would avoid additional data copying.

In this paper we limited ourselves to holding the entirety of the domain in local SRAM and, with other data structures required for reordering and tiling, this resulted in a maximum problem size of 16384 FP32 elements. When scaling to 2D, our problem size was 1 million elements, and this is also small. The next step will be to support larger domains by reordering from external, on-card, DRAM, using SRAM as a temporary staging area. Furthermore, we might be able to obtain improved performance within a single Tensix core by reworking the one-copy data reordering scheme to work across contiguous memory, thus resulting in single 128-bit rather than four 32-bit memory accesses. Moreover, expanding the transposition to support an uneven distribution of rows across Tensix cores will enable us to leverage all 120 cores on the n300, likely closing the gap significantly with the Xeon Platinum CPU. Whilst in this paper we focussed on a single Wormhole card, a major bottleneck for multi-dimensional FFTs is the all-to-all communications required during transposition. This work acts as a foundation that can be built upon in the future to explore how the high performance network connecting multiple n300 cards can remove this bottleneck.

Acknowledgement. The CPU runs in this paper ran on NextGenIO which funding from the EU Horizon 2020 research and innovation programme under grant agreement No 671591. This research was supported by an RSE personal research fellowship. We thank Tenstorrent, especially Pete Cawley, for their technical assistance. For the purpose of open access, the author has applied a Creative Commons Attribution (CC BY) licence to any Author Accepted Manuscript version arising from this submission.

References

1. Brown, N., Barton, R.: Accelerating stencils on the Tenstorrent Grayskull RISC-V accelerator. In: SC24-W: Workshops of the International Conference for High Performance Computing, Networking, Storage and Analysis, pp. 1690–1700. IEEE (2024)
2. Brown, N., Jamieson, M.: Performance characterisation of the 64-core SG2042 RISC-V CPU for HPC. In: International Conference on High Performance Computing, pp. 354–367. Springer (2025)
3. Brown, N., Jamieson, M., Lee, J., Wang, P.: Is RISC-V ready for HPC prime-time: evaluating the 64-core Sophon SG2042 RISC-V CPU. In: Proceedings of the SC'23 Workshops of The International Conference on High Performance Computing, Network, Storage, and Analysis, pp. 1566–1574 (2023)
4. Cawley, P.: Tenstorrent Wormhole Series (2025). https://www.corsix.org/
5. Strang, G.: Linear algebra and its applications (2000)
6. Tenstorrent: Wormhole Tensix Processor (2025). https://cdn.sanity.io/files/jpb4ed5r/production/6217a901d675d37ccb3cf1e8ba74f91a9f992577.pdf

The First International Workshop on Foundational Large Language Models Advances for HPC (LLM4HPC)

LLM4HPC 2025 Preface

Objectives/Topics

Since their development and release, modern Large Language Models (LLMs), such as the Generative Pre-trained Transformer (GPT) model and the Large Language Model Meta AI (LLaMA), have come to signify a revolution in human-computer interaction spurred on by their high-quality results. LLMs have repaved this landscape thanks to unprecedented investments and enormous training models (hundreds of billions of parameters). The availability of LLMs has led to increasing interest in how they could be applied to a large variety of applications. The HPC community made recent research efforts to evaluate current LLM capabilities for some HPC tasks, including code generation, auto parallelization, performance portability, and correctness, among others. All these studies concluded that state-of-the-art LLM capabilities have proven so far insufficient for these targets. Hence, it is necessary to explore novel techniques to further empower LLMs to enrich the HPC mission and its impact.

This workshop's objectives are focused on LLMs' advances for any HPC major priority and challenge with the aims to define and discuss the fundamentals of LLMs for HPC-specific tasks, including but not limited to hardware design, compilation, parallel programming models and runtimes, and application development, enabling LLM technologies to have more autonomous decision-making about the efficient use of HPC.

This workshop provides a forum to discuss new and emerging solutions to address these important challenges towards an AI-assisted HPC era.

Papers cover many aspects of LLM for HPC targets including (but not limited to):

- LLMs for Programming Environments and Runtime Systems
- LLMs for HPC and Scientific Applications
- LLMs for Hardware Design (including non-von Neumann Architectures)
- Reliability/Benchmarking/Measurements for LLMs

Workshop Organization

Pedro Valero-Lara	Oak Ridge National Laboratory, USA
Harshitha Menon	Lawrence Livermore National Laboratory, USA
Konstantinos Parasyris	Lawrence Livermore National Laboratory, USA
Daniel Nichols	University of Maryland, USA

Leveraging AI for Productive and Trustworthy HPC Software: Challenges and Research Directions

Keita Teranishi[1], Harshitha Menon[2], William F. Godoy[1(✉)], Prasanna Balaprakash[1], David Bau[5], Tal Ben-Nun[2], Abhinav Bhatele[6], Franz Franchetti[4], Michael Franusich[7], Todd Gamblin[2], Giorgis Georgakoudis[2], Tom Goldstein[6], Arjun Guha[5], Steven E. Hahn[1], Costin Iancu[3], Zheming Jin[1], Terry Jones[1], Tze-Meng Low[4], Het Mankad[1], Narasinga Rao Miniskar[1], Mohammad Alaul Haque Monil[1], Daniel Nichols[6], Konstantinos Parasyris[2], Swaroop Pophale[1], Pedro Valero-Lara[1], Jeffrey S. Vetter[1], Samuel Williams[3], and Aaron Young[1]

[1] Oak Ridge National Laboratory, Oak Ridge, TN, USA
godoywf@ornl.gov
[2] Lawrence Livermore National Laboratory, Livermore, CA, USA
[3] Lawrence Berkeley National Laboratory, Berkeley, CA, USA
[4] Carnegie Mellon University, Pittsburgh, PA, USA
[5] Northeastern University, Boston, MA, USA
[6] University of Maryland, College Park, MD, USA
[7] SpiralGen Inc., Pittsburgh, PA, USA

Abstract. We discuss the challenges and propose research directions for using AI to revolutionize the development of high-performance computing (HPC) software. AI technologies, in particular large language models, have transformed every aspect of software development. For its part, HPC software is recognized as a highly specialized scientific field of its own. We discuss the challenges associated with leveraging state-of-the-art AI technologies to develop such a unique and niche class of software and outline our research directions in the two US Department of Energy–funded projects for advancing HPC Software via AI: Ellora and Durban.

Keywords: AI · HPC Software · Performance portability · Large language models · Parallel code

1 Introduction

As a key government investment, high-performance computing (HPC) has enabled unprecedented advances in science and engineering in recent decades. However, the future of HPC in the post-Moore era faces new challenges, including record-breaking costs in semiconductor manufacturing, an unprecedented number of AI workloads, tighter energy requirements and ever-increasing operational costs [10, 35].

To fully leverage the capabilities of the latest generation of exascale systems, the US Department of Energy (DOE) made significant investments in a large, interoperable, and performance-portable HPC software ecosystem as part of the Exascale Computing Project (ECP, 2016–2023) [26]. These efforts included the Extreme-Scale Scientific Software Stack (E4S),[1] which is now being supported by the DOE's Advanced Scientific Computing Research (ASCR) program as it continues the development of the exascale software ecosystem. Nevertheless, programming, developing, and deploying robust, trustworthy, and verifiable HPC software has become a complex endeavor, with ever-increasing advancement costs required to meet the science-application needs on new heterogeneous systems and architectures [42].

AI technologies, in particular state-of-the-art large language models (LLMs), have shown incredible potential in a variety of software tasks [6,11,31,36] and can significantly improve programmer productivity [2,13,27,30]. For example, Meta reports that 99% of their developers use an internal LLM to discover APIs, accelerate their work, and generate 9%–17% of all code that they write [13]. However, advancements in state-of-the-art foundational LLMs, such as the Generative Pre-trained Transformer (GPT-3/4) [3], Claude 3 [8], and Llama-3 [1], are driven mainly by industry needs. As a result, despite the popularity of general-purpose LLMs for writing code, our team's pioneering research in this area showed that LLMs are far less effective at HPC programming tasks [15,17,32–34,41] because the data used to train the LLMs contains far fewer HPC-specific codes (i.e., there are simply fewer HPC codes vs. general software from which the LLMs can learn) [5,23]. This means that other runtime dimensions (e.g., parallel performance, portability, reproducibility of scientific results) are also not reflected in code/text sources or other AI training corpora.

Integrating AI into HPC software development presents a transformative opportunity to enhance the efficiency, performance, and productivity of the entire software development life cycle. Fortunately, DOE's ASCR program has recognized the need to explore the use of AI in advancing the next generation of HPC codes and launched the Advancements in Artificial Intelligence for Science program in 2024 by awarding $68 million to proposed research projects that leverage AI for scientific innovation. One key area is the "AI Innovations for Scientific Knowledge Synthesis and Software Development." In this paper, we provide an overview of the characteristics of HPC software (Sect. 2), describe the challenges at the intersection of AI and coding for HPC (Sect. 3), and propose research directions for an impactful application of AI in the HPC software ecosystem (Sect. 4). We mainly focus on two important areas in which AI can revolutionize HPC software: productivity and performance portability.

2 Background on HPC Software

HPC software has been the cornerstone of scientific discovery at scale for decades [12]. This history is built upon a rich legacy of advances in algorithms, math

---

[1] https://e4s.io/.

libraries, programming languages, and systems and standards that enable the actual utility provided by the fastest supercomputers in the world. In fact, given their niche nature, HPC codes are closer to scientific instruments than they are to general-purpose software, with their clear goals of advancing the state of the art in computational and computer sciences.

Characteristics: Below are some of the unique characteristics of HPC software that must be understood before anyone can replicate—for HPC—the impact that AI has had in other software domains:

- Massively parallel and scalable up to the largest supercomputers in the world
- Vendor neutral/portable to new architectures
- The vast majority is written in C, C++, and Fortran with ecosystem components in high-level languages (e.g., Python, R, Julia, Matlab)
- Deep reliance on vendor software stacks such as CUDA and HIP for accelerator platforms
- Low developers-to-users ratio (i.e., few developers, many users)
- Complex and diverse ecosystem that includes algorithms, programming systems, runtime systems, compilers, tools, applications, libraries, workflows, network, I/O, packaging, and more
- Requires knowledge of hardware specifications to balance compute, communication, memory, I/O
- Correctness includes runtime characteristics such as performance, portability, scalability, reliability, and scientific accuracy
- Driven by impact on scientific discovery, thus not necessarily prioritizing resources for general software use (e.g., documentation, training)
- Developed by highly specialized individuals with multidisciplinary scientific backgrounds
- Cutting-edge HPC software evolves significantly with every supercomputing architecture (e.g., distributed, many-core, GPU/hybrid)
- HPC software has benefited from advancements in open-source technologies, although much of the mission-critical software is still classified or not publicly available
- The vast majority is government funded (e.g., DOE) and does not have for-profit goals

Requirements for Modern Software: HPC software relies on the broader software landscape (e.g., programming languages, vendor tools, runtimes). Hence, the HPC stack must evolve accordingly and alongside the broader software ecosystem to meet the post-Moore era's requirements—including trustworthiness (e.g., memory-safety, robustness) [20], reproducibility, maintainability, and energy-efficiency—and to align with national interests. Not meeting these requirements puts the field at risk in mission-critical scenarios, and the clearest example of vulnerability is the overwhelming reliance on Fortran [25,37] in legacy HPC codes.

3 AI Challenges for HPC Software

State-of-the-art AI advancements present numerous opportunities to enhance HPC software. However, bridging HPC and AI requires a concerted effort from the community because it faces several well-documented challenges in scientific computing [4]. This section explores key challenges in leveraging AI across various aspects of HPC software.

Code Generation, Translation, and Optimization: State-of-the-art foundational LLMs are not trained to generate, translate, and optimize HPC code. The low-level features and software characteristics of even the most widely used libraries (e.g., math kernels, programming models) make the training and fine-tuning cumbersome to understand and reason with for *science corner cases*. Heterogeneity adds more complexity owing to the multitude of vendors and runtime options that AI can be trained on. Additionally, because AI is statistical in nature, it adds its own bias, hallucinations, poor reproducibility, and errors. HPC software requires significant experimentation, and the data currently available from public sources (e.g., software repositories such as GitHub and GitLab, published literature) is not sufficient to train LLMs on the more important aspects beyond simple coding.

Engineering the Software Ecosystem: The DOE's ECP made significant investments that enabled the strategic application of software engineering practices [16,19,28]. These efforts included customized approaches such as continuous integration, performance testing on CPUs and GPUs, unified packaging and deployment via Spack [14], memory sanitizers, SLURM scripts, workflow composition, and more. Hence, the cost of these tasks must be commensurate with post-ECP funding levels. Current AI technologies are not trained on custom HPC solutions that target specific hardware and use cases for validation and verification [29]. For example, we might have to adapt current testing knowledge to future architectures, and we might have to increase the coverage and capabilities of existing test programs and frameworks to match the evolution of the software.

Ethics: Several ethical challenges are associated with LLMs, including intellectual property and copyright, security and privacy, bias and fairness, and impact on software developer and skill degradation.

Training and Workforce Development: State-of-the-art AI provides incredible opportunities in the broader landscape of science education [9]. The handful of core developers and advanced users are typically the *educators* of HPC software. Like any specialized field, AI-generated educational resources need the critical oversight of those HPC software educators. Foregoing that oversight could actually increase the costs of training future HPC software developers because relying on unsupervised multimodality resources could lead to misuse of the software and a steeper learning curve in an already highly experimental field.

4 Research Directions

Below, we outline future research directions for a more productive HPC software ecosystem to advance scientific discovery. These efforts are part of two ASCR AI4Science funded projects with two clear goals:

(1) Durban: AI for performance-portable programming systems and libraries
(2) Ellora: LLMs for a highly productive, AI-assisted HPC software ecosystem that targets E4S products

These efforts aim to be cross-cutting and cover different aspects of the complex HPC software life cycle. As with the broader software landscape, state-of-the-art AI offers many opportunities for deployment at low (e.g., compilers, runtimes), intermediate (e.g., code generation, models), and high (e.g., software engineering, packaging, documentation) levels of the software development stack.

We have identified several research directions to advance DOE's computing mission and to ensure that these innovations are mutually beneficial for the HPC and broader software development communities. Figure 1 shows the different research thrust areas that each project targets and their clear complementary efforts.

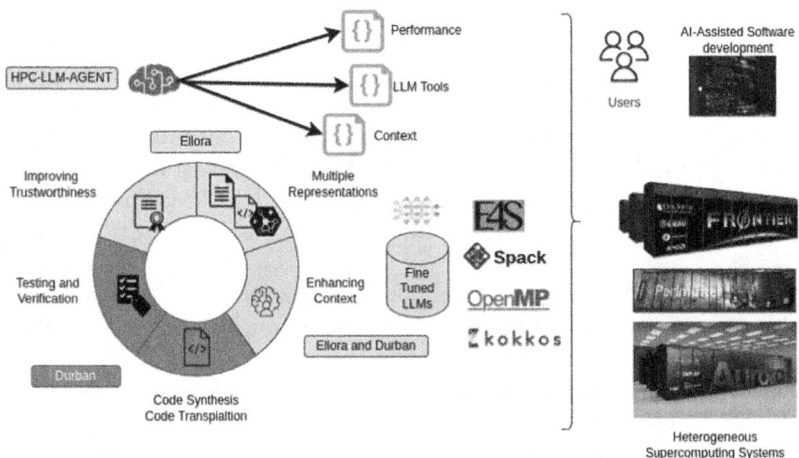

Fig. 1. Research thrusts for Durban and Ellora, which target ASCR's focus on AI Innovations for Scientific Knowledge Synthesis and Software Development.

Fine-Tuning LLMs: To leverage state-of-the-art LLMs such as Llama and GPT, much effort is needed to introduce expert-in-the-loop knowledge. Specialized LLMs for coding such as CodeLlama and Deepseek-Coder [18] demonstrate the potential for fine-tuning LLMs for a specific area. Applying techniques from libraries such as LoRA (low-rank adaptation of LLMs) [21] has shown on-par or better success in fine-tuned LLMs versus the 175-billion parameter GPT models. LoRA requires fewer resources (i.e., trainable parameters) while displaying a higher throughput and no additional inference latency. Preliminary work has also been done for the popular level-1 BLAS subroutines [40], and this ChatBLAS effort showcases the path forward to integrating fine-tuning with HPC software. This direction requires targeted efforts to train foundational LLMs to understand patterns in HPC software APIs and contracts. Exploration of fine-tuning capabilities is a key research direction for an effective cost-benefit option.

Enhance Context Window: A context window, measured with "tokens," is the limited text or memory that an LLM can process at a time. This limitation impacts HPC software largely because individual components are rarely used in isolation, and composing very specialized parallel simulation and analysis codes can be incredibly complex. To overcome the constraints imposed by a model's context window size, we must explore efficient solutions for large-context inference to reduce the likelihood of LLM hallucinations and increasing the likelihood of producing authoritative and relevant information.

Leverage Multimodality: Current coding LLMs are trained on code as text and thus lack information on program behavior (e.g., data flow, control flow) and are limited in associating additional metadata (e.g., performance characteristics) with the code structure, and this limits their ability to generate efficient HPC programs. Being able to learn across multiple code modalities will improve the ability of coding LLMs to reason about code properties by giving them access to more data. We need to curate large-scale, multimodal code datasets that include code as text, LLVM Intermediate Representation (IR), performance counters etc. We also need to develop new, fine-tuned, multimodal LLMs that comprehend different code modalities to improve the performance on HPC coding tasks.

Enhance Existing Program Source Synthesis and Compiler Optimization Methods, Auto-tuning, and Source-to-Source Transpilation: The primary goal of program source synthesis is to enhance the correctness of the generated source code based on the given prompt description. In other words, the generated code should align semantically with the prompt, thereby ensuring a strong correspondence between them. This alignment is often evaluated subjectively and requires some external processing for training to establish the context and most common patterns specific to the applications of interest. One good example is using a specific set of prompt keywords to navigate compiler optimization [22] incrementally to verify individual optimization techniques through differential testing. This approach can be extended to different programming languages and parallel programming frameworks to clarify their context and common patterns for training.

Compared to prompt-based code synthesis, source-to-source transpilation involves less ambiguity. However, it has broad applications in the HPC and scientific computing communities, in which many scientific simulations still rely on large legacy code bases such as Fortran 77. Modernizing these code bases is essential for adapting to contemporary HPC architectures and system features, including massive parallelism, accelerators, asynchronous task execution, and the integration of modern HPC libraries for I/O and visualization. Additionally, an important goal of transpilation is optimizing application performance for modern HPC systems.

For both modernization and performance optimization, LLM-based code transpilation must generate semantically equivalent programs while maintaining good code readability. Efforts to develop foundation models [39] for translating between HPC-relevant programming languages have successfully leveraged compiler abstract syntax trees to recognize patterns and apply language-specific keywords before the conventional training process. These preprocessing techniques can be extended to other source code analysis methods (e.g., semantic lifting [43] and lowering) to create training datasets at different levels of granularity. Formal methods would help ensure the semantic equivalence of two program sources [7], but these techniques are still immature in parallel computing, and the scalability of formal checking needs special attention to make it feasible for large program sources.

Improve Dynamic Mapping, Scheduling, and Data Orchestration: In heterogeneous computing architectures, performance and energy consumption often depend on the mapping of kernels to the most appropriate compute device(s) and on the orchestration of the data necessary for that kernel's execution. To that end, AI could be used to explore a variety of techniques for auto-tuning, scheduling, and performance modeling. Reinforcement learning and graph neural network methods are excellent candidates for task and task-graph levels for code optimizations. Optimization of truly heterogeneous systems could be explored by leveraging AI and task-based HPC runtime frameworks (e.g., IRIS [24]).

Trustworthiness and Verifiability: We must explore techniques that can characterize correct behaviors and also react to potential errors in the ever-evolving HPC software targets. Testing efforts that verify model correctness and ensure proper understanding of errors will reduce hallucinations and false positives in an AI-assisted software ecosystem. Research directions should focus on improving prediction and explanation of model errors on coding tasks, including robust testing frameworks for verification and validation of AI-generated HPC software, and addressing other key challenges in this domain.

Integration and High-Level Interfaces: Parallel code development in HPC software is inherently an iterative process that requires a developer to break down tasks into a sequence of steps and use various tools to complete them. LLM agents have shown their potential in software development practices [38], and developing and using HPC-LLM agents could reduce the manual effort required to deliver an entire workflow if the LLM-based system can orchestrate and execute complex, multistep tasks with the support of tools and developer feedback.

Ethics: Ethical challenges associated with LLMs range from intellectual property and copyright to biases and fairness. Developing ethical guidelines for using LLMs is important if we want to ensure responsible use. Robust testing and validation are essential to ensuring the security and reliability of the generated code, and making LLMs more explainable can help identify potential biases. By considering all these aspects, we can work toward developing and using coding LLMs in a responsible fashion.

5 Conclusions

Although today's unprecedented investments in AI have not yet inundated the HPC software ecosystem, which is characterized by low-data resources and high-specialization, we have provided our view for leveraging state-of-the-art AI technologies to advance current and future HPC software efforts. We outlined the nuances of HPC software and the challenges and research directions needed to capitalize on the investments in AI. These key research directions require multidisciplinary collaboration between HPC and AI experts in the larger software development community. Although productivity is an important goal, any advancements must be accompanied with trustworthiness in the AI-assisted activities. Therefore, it is crucial that the community be involved in the research directions of a future AI-powered HPC software ecosystem.

Acknowledgments. This material is based upon work supported by the U.S. Department of Energy, Office of Science, Office of Advanced Scientific Computing Research, through solicitation DE-FOA-0003264, "Advancements in Artificial Intelligence for Science," under Award Numbers DE-SC0025598 and DE-SC0025645. This manuscript has been authored by UT-Battelle, LLC, under contract DE-AC05-00OR22725 with the US Department of Energy (DOE). The US government retains and the publisher, by accepting the article for publication, acknowledges that the US government retains a nonexclusive, paid-up, irrevocable, worldwide license to publish or reproduce the published form of this manuscript, or allow others to do so, for US government purposes. DOE will provide public access to these results of federally sponsored research in accordance with the DOE Public Access Plan (https://www.energy.gov/doe-public-access-plan). This work performed under the auspices of the U.S. Department of Energy by Lawrence Livermore National Laboratory under Contract DE-AC52-07NA27344 (LLNL-CONF-2005811). This manuscript has been authored by an author at Lawrence Berkeley National Laboratory under Contract No. DE-AC02-05CH11231 with the U.S. Department of Energy. The U.S. Government retains, and the publisher, by accepting the article for publication, acknowledges, that the U.S. Government retains a nonexclusive, paid-up, irrevocable, world-wide license to publish or reproduce the published form of this manuscript, or allow others to do so, for U.S. Government purposes.

References

1. AI@Meta: Llama 3 model card (2024). https://github.com/meta-llama/llama3/blob/main/MODEL_CARD.md
2. Bird, C., et al.: Taking flight with copilot: early insights and opportunities of AI-powered pair-programming tools. Queue **20**(6), 10:35-10:57 (2023). https://doi.org/10.1145/3582083
3. Brown, T., et al.: Language models are few-shot learners. In: Advances in Neural Information Processing Systems, vol. 33. Curran Associates, Inc. (2020)
4. Carter, J., et al.: Advanced research directions on AI for science, energy, and security: Report on summer 2022 workshops. Tech. rep., Argonne National Laboratory (ANL), Argonne, IL (United States) (2023). https://doi.org/10.2172/1986455, https://www.osti.gov/biblio/1986455
5. Chen, L., et al.: The landscape and challenges of HPC research and LLMs. arXiv preprint arXiv:2402.02018 (2024)
6. Chen, M., et al.: Evaluating large language models trained on code. arXiv preprint arXiv:2107.03374 (2021)
7. Churchill, B., Padon, O., Sharma, R., Aiken, A.: Semantic program alignment for equivalence checking. In: Proceedings of the 40th ACM SIGPLAN Conference on Programming Language Design and Implementation, pp. 1027–1040. PLDI 2019, Association for Computing Machinery, New York (2019). https://doi.org/10.1145/3314221.3314596
8. Claude Team: Introducing the next generation of Claude. https://www.anthropic.com/news/claude-3-family
9. Cooper, G.: Examining science education in chatGPT: an exploratory study of generative artificial intelligence. J. Sci. Educ. Technol. **32**(3), 444–452 (2023)
10. Deelman, E., et al.: High-performance computing at a crossroads. Science **387**(6736), 829–831 (2025)
11. Dehaerne, E., Dey, B., Halder, S., De Gendt, S., Meert, W.: Code generation using machine learning: a systematic review. IEEE Access **10**, 82434–82455 (2022). https://doi.org/10.1109/ACCESS.2022.3196347
12. Dongarra, J., Keyes, D.: The co-evolution of computational physics and high-performance computing. Nature Rev. Phys. **6**(10), 621–627 (2024)
13. Dunay, O., et al.: Multi-line AI-assisted code authoring. In: ACM International Conference on the Foundations of Software Engineering (FSE) (2024)
14. Gamblin, T., et al.: The Spack package manager: bringing order to HPC software chaos. In: Proceedings of the International Conference for High Performance Computing, Networking, Storage and Analysis, pp. 1–12 (2015)
15. Godoy, W., Valero-Lara, P., Teranishi, K., Balaprakash, P., Vetter, J.: Evaluation of OpenAI codex for HPC parallel programming models kernel generation. In: Proceedings of the 52nd International Conference on Parallel Processing Workshops, pp. 136–144. ICPP Workshops '23, Association for Computing Machinery, New York (2023). https://doi.org/10.1145/3605731.3605886
16. Godoy, W.F., et al.: Software stewardship and advancement of a high-performance computing scientific application: QMCPACK. Futur. Gener. Comput. Syst. **163**, 107502 (2025). https://doi.org/10.1016/j.future.2024.107502
17. Godoy, W.F., Valero-Lara, P., Teranishi, K., Balaprakash, P., Vetter, J.S.: Large language model evaluation for high-performance computing software development. Concurrency Comput. Pract. Exp. **36**(26), e8269 (2024)

18. Guo, D., et al.: Deepseek-coder: when the large language model meets programming–the rise of code intelligence. arXiv preprint arXiv:2401.14196 (2024)
19. Heroux, M.A.: Scalable delivery of scalable libraries and tools: how ECP delivered a software ecosystem for Exascale and beyond. Comput. Sci. Eng. **26**(1), 9–18 (2024)
20. House, T.W.: Back to the building blocks: a path toward secure and measurable software (2024)
21. Hu, E.J., et al.: LoRA: low-rank adaptation of large language models. ICLR **1**(2), 3 (2022)
22. Italiano, D., Cummins, C.: Finding missed code size optimizations in compilers using large language models. In: Proceedings of the 34th ACM SIGPLAN International Conference on Compiler Construction, pp. 81–91. CC '25. Association for Computing Machinery, New York (2025). https://doi.org/10.1145/3708493.3712686
23. Joel, S., Wu, J.J., Fard, F.H.: A survey on LLM-based code generation for low-resource and domain-specific programming languages (2024). arXiv:2410.03981
24. Johnston, B., Miniskar, N.R., Young, A., Monil, M.A.H., Lee, S., Vetter, J.S.: Iris: exploring performance scaling of the intelligent runtime system and its dynamic scheduling policies. In: 2024 IEEE International Parallel and Distributed Processing Symposium Workshops (IPDPSW), pp. 58–67 (2024). https://doi.org/10.1109/IPDPSW63119.2024.00017
25. Kedward, L.J., et al.: The State of Fortran. Comput. Sci. Eng. **24**(2), 63–72 (2022). https://doi.org/10.1109/MCSE.2022.3159862
26. Kothe, D., Lee, S., Qualters, I.: Exascale computing in the United States. Comput. Sci. Eng. **21**(1), 17–29 (2018)
27. Liang, J.T., Yang, C., Myers, B.A.: A large-scale survey on the usability of AI programming assistants: successes and challenges. In: IEEE/ACM International Conference on Software Engineering (ICSE), pp. 1–13. Association for Computing Machinery, New York (2024). https://doi.org/10.1145/3597503.3608128
28. McInnes, L.C., et al.: A cast of thousands: how the ideas productivity project has advanced software productivity and sustainability. Comput. Sci. Eng. **26**(1), 48–60 (2024). https://doi.org/10.1109/MCSE.2024.3383799
29. Munley, C., Jarmusch, A., Chandrasekaran, S.: LLM4VV: developing LLM-driven testsuite for compiler validation. Futur. Gener. Comput. Syst. **160**, 1–13 (2024). https://doi.org/10.1016/j.future.2024.05.034
30. Murali, V., et al.: AI-assisted code authoring at scale: fine-tuning, deploying, and mixed methods evaluation. In: ACM International Conference on the Foundations of Software Engineering (FSE) (2024)
31. Nguyen, N., Nadi, S.: An empirical evaluation of github copilot's code suggestions. In: Proceedings of the 19th International Conference on Mining Software Repositories. p. 1–5. MSR '22. Association for Computing Machinery, New York (2022). https://doi.org/10.1145/3524842.3528470
32. Nichols, D., Davis, J.H., Xie, Z., Rajaram, A., Bhatele, A.: Can large language models write parallel code? (2024)
33. Nichols, D., Marathe, A., Menon, H., Gamblin, T., Bhatele, A.: HPC-coder: modeling parallel programs using large language models (2023)
34. Nichols, D., Polasam, P., Menon, H., Marathe, A., Gamblin, T., Bhatele, A.: Performance-aligned LLMs for generating fast code (2024)
35. Reed, D., Gannon, D., Dongarra, J.: Reinventing high performance computing: challenges and opportunities (2022). arXiv:2203.02544

36. Sarsa, S., Denny, P., Hellas, A., Leinonen, J.: Automatic generation of programming exercises and code explanations using large language models, pp. 27–43. ICER '22. Association for Computing Machinery, New York (2022). https://doi.org/10.1145/3501385.3543957
37. Shipman, G.M., Randles, T.C.: An evaluation of risks associated with relying on Fortran for mission critical codes for the next 15 years. Tech. rep., Los Alamos National Laboratory (LANL), Los Alamos, NM (United States) (2023)
38. Talebirad, Y., Nadiri, A.: Multi-agent collaboration: harnessing the power of intelligent LLM agents. arXiv preprint arXiv:2306.03314 (2023)
39. TehraniJamsaz, A., Bhattacharjee, A., Chen, L., Ahmed, N.K., Yazdanbakhsh, A., Jannesari, A.: CodeRosetta: pushing the boundaries of unsupervised code translation for parallel programming (2024). https://doi.org/10.48550/arXiv.2410.20527, arXiv:2410.20527 [cs]
40. Valero-Lara, P., Godoy, W.F., Teranishi, K., Balaprakash, P., Vetter, J.S.: ChatBLAS: the first AI-generated and portable BLAS library. In: SC24-W: Workshops of the International Conference for High Performance Computing, Networking, Storage and Analysis, pp. 19–24 (2024). https://doi.org/10.1109/SCW63240.2024.00010
41. Valero-Lara, P., et al.: Comparing Llama-2 and GPT-3 LLMs for HPC kernels generation (2023)
42. Vetter, J.S., et al.: Extreme Heterogeneity 2018 - Productive Computational Science in the Era of Extreme Heterogeneity: Report for DOE ASCR Workshop on Extreme Heterogeneity (2018). https://doi.org/10.2172/1473756
43. Zhang, N., Rao, S., Franusich, M., Franchetti, F.: Towards semantics lifting for scientific computing: a case study on FFT (2025). arXiv:2501.09201

LLM & HPC: Benchmarking DeepSeek's Performance in High-Performance Computing Tasks

Noujoud Nader[1]([✉]) [iD], Patrick Diehl[1,2] [iD], Steve Brandt[1] [iD], and Hartmut Kaiser[1] [iD]

[1] Louisiana State University, Baton Rouge, LA 70803, USA
{nnader,sbrandt,hkaiser}@lsu.edu
[2] Los Alamos National Laboratory, Los Alamos, NM 87544, USA
diehlpk@lanl.gov

Abstract. Large Language Models (LLMs), such as GPT-4 and DeepSeek, have been applied to a wide range of domains in software engineering. However, their potential in the context of High-Performance Computing (HPC) much remains to be explored. This paper evaluates how well DeepSeek, a recent LLM, performs in generating a set of HPC benchmark codes: a conjugate gradient solver, the parallel heat equation, parallel matrix multiplication, DGEMM, and the STREAM triad operation. We analyze DeepSeek's code generation capabilities for traditional HPC languages like C++, Fortran, Julia and Python. The evaluation includes testing for code correctness, performance, and scaling across different configurations and matrix sizes. We also provide a detailed comparison between DeepSeek and another widely used tool: GPT-4. Our results demonstrate that while DeepSeek generates functional code for HPC tasks, it lags behind GPT-4, in terms of scalability and execution efficiency of the generated code.

Keywords: LLM · DeepSeek · GPT-4 · HPC · Code Performance · Programming language processing

1 Introduction

Large Language Models (LLMs) have rapidly advanced, potentially approaching Artificial General Intelligence (AGI). Trained on vast textual data, LLMs have shown remarkable capabilities in natural language processing and visualization tasks [1,15,25]. This trend has accelerated with the release of the DeepSeek models by the Chinese company DeepSeek [7]. Their DeepSeek-V3 [17,20] was trained in two months at a cost of $5.6 million, significantly cheaper than similar models. In contrast, the development cost of ChatGPT-4 ranged between $41 million and $78 million [3]. On January 20th 2025, they launched DeepSeek-R1 [16], a reasoning model exhibiting performance comparable to OpenAI's O1 model, available for open research [12]. DeepSeek-R1 is trained through large-scale reinforcement learning (RL) without supervised fine-tuning, demonstrating powerful reasoning behaviors [16].

In the high-performance computing (HPC) domain, LLMs are being explored for tasks such as code analysis, generation, and optimization. However, there is a lack of standardized, reproducible evaluation processes for LLMs in HPC-specific tasks. For this reason, this paper explores the performance of the open-source LLM DeepSeek for simple code generation tasks in HPC. We evaluate code generation using four programming languages (PLs) selected for their prominence in HPC and based on the *TIOBE index* [27]. The PLs are C++ for performance and simulation, Fortran for numerical and array optimizations, Python for flexibility and integration with other HPC languages, and Julia for scientific computing performance with a Python-like syntax.

We present five examples to assess the performance of the model. The first example in this study features a conjugate gradient solver that incorporates matrix and vector operations. The second example is a parallel 1D stencil-based heat equation solver [10], chosen for its relevance in testing parallel computational workflows and its widespread use in scientific computing. The third example is parallel matrix multiplication, a fundamental operation in scientific computing and machine learning, often accelerated by using HPC systems to enhance computational speed. The fourth example is parallel double-precision general matrix multiply (DGEMM), a widely used operation in numerical linear algebra that is essential for many scientific and engineering applications, testing the system's computational efficiency for large-scale matrix operations. The final example is the STREAM triad operation, a key benchmark for testing memory bandwidth and data movement between CPU and memory, commonly used to evaluate the memory subsystem's performance in HPC systems. We summarize the main contributions of this paper as follows:

- A comparison of DeepSeek and GPT-4 for HPC code generation, specifically targeting five simple tasks.
- A systematic evaluation of the performance and quality of code generated by DeepSeek in when writing code for four widely used HPC programming languages: C++, Fortran, Python, and Julia.
- A comprehensive analysis of the models' ability to generate optimized code for common HPC operations, offering insights into the potential of LLMs for high-performance computing tasks.

2 Related Work

LLMs have been widely used across various domains, including natural language processing (NLP) and visualization. Multiple efforts have also been made to benchmark LLMs for tasks such as code generation [6,8,9]. However, their application in analyzing and optimizing HPC tasks remains challenging. In Table 1, we present the related works that use LLMs for HPC tasks. LLM4HPC [5]

Table 1. Summary of LLM-based HPC related work

Paper	Main Focus	LLM Model Used
LLM4HPC [5]	HPC Adaptation	LLaMa-2
LLM4VV [23]	OpenACC Testing	GPT-4, CodeLlama
HPC-GPT [11]	AI Model Management	LLaMa-13B
Tokompiler LLM [18]	Code Completion	GPT-3
HPC-Coder [24]	OpenMP & MPI Handling	DeepSpeed
Dataset for OpenMP Translation [19]	Code Translation	LLaMa-2
LLMs in HPC [4]	LLM-HPC Challenges	Various LLMs
Godoy et al. (2023) [13]	Kernel Code Generation	LLaMa-2
Valero-Lara et al. (2023) [28]	LLaMa-2 Comparison	LLaMa-2
Godoy et al. (2024) [14]	Code Parallelization	GPT-3
chatHPC [29]	HPC Chatbot	GPT-like (based on StarCoder)

represents the first effort to adapt an LLM specifically to the HPC domain. The LLM4HPC framework is specifically designed for HPC, showing success in code similarity analysis, parallelism detection, and OpenMP question-answering tasks. LLM4VV [23] is a fine-tuned model that uses the capabilities of GPT-4 and CodeLlama (based on Llama-2) to successfully generate OpenACC directives. HPC-GPT introduced by Ding et al. [11], was built on LLaMa-13B. HPC-GPT has been successfully applied to managing AI models and datasets, as well as detecting data races. Kadosh et al. [18] introduced the domain-specific Tokompiler LLM, which outperforms a GPT-3-based model in code completion and semantics for Fortran, C, and C++ code. Nichols et al. [24] present HPC-Coder. Their work demonstrated varying success in code completion, including handling OpenMP pragmas and MPI calls. Lei et al. [19] introduced a dataset designed for fine-tuning models on OpenMP Fortran and C++ code translation. Their fine-tuned model yielded more accurate results compared to GPT-4. Chen et al. [4] provide an insightful overview of the challenges and opportunities at the intersection of LLMs and HPC, extending beyond code generation. Notably, the works by Godoy et al. [13] and Valero-Lara et al. [28], which evaluate HPC kernel code generation and results for LLaMa-2, are among the first to apply LLM-based code generation to the domain of HPC software development. Additionally, Godoy et al. [14] apply LLM capabilities of GPT-3 targeting HPC kernels for code generation, and auto-parallelization of serial code in C++, Fortran, Python and Julia. Yin et al. [29] proposed chatHPC, a chatbot for HPC question answering and script generation.

3 Methodology

We used five examples: *(1)* a conjugate gradient solver, *(2)* a parallel one-dimensional heat equation solver using finite differencing, *(3)* parallel matrix multiplication, *(4)* parallel DGEMM, and *(5)* the STREAM triad operation. The complexity of the code increases with each example. We generated the code for these examples using DeepSeek-R1 and compared it with our previous results [9] obtained using GPT 4.0 for the first two examples. The code was generated on 02/03/2025. The queries used for code generation are shown in Table 2.

Table 2. Queries for HPC tasks code generation, whether the language was C++, Fortran, Julia, Python

Ex.	Problem	Prompt
1	Conjugate Gradient Solver	Write a **language** code to solve the linear equation system using the conjugate gradient solver and validate it.
2	Parallel 1D Stencil-Based Heat Equation Solver	Write a parallel **language** code to solve the one-dimensional heat equation using a finite difference scheme for the discretization in space and the Euler method for time integration, validate it and plot the solution.
3	Parallel Matrix Multiplication	Write a parallel **language** code for matrix multiplication and validate it.
4	Double-Precision General Matrix Multiplication	Write a parallel **language** code to perform DGEMM on large matrices, optimize the implementation for performance using parallel computing techniques, validate the results, and compare the performance with different matrix sizes and parallelization strategies.
5	STREAM	Write a parallel **language** code to perform the STREAM triad operation on large arrays.

Example 1. An advanced example from numerical methods textbooks is using a conjugate gradient solver to solve a system of linear equations [26].

$$A^{n \times n} \cdot x^n = b^n \quad \text{with} \quad n \in \mathbb{Z}^+, A = A^t, \text{ and } x^t A x > 0, \forall X \in \mathbb{R}^n. \quad (1)$$

To evaluate the code, we asked DeepSeek to use the following equation system $M \cdot x = b$ with

$$M = \begin{pmatrix} 4 & -1 & 0 \\ -1 & 4 & -1 \\ 0 & -1 & 4 \end{pmatrix}, b = \begin{pmatrix} 1.0 \\ 2.0 \\ 3.0 \end{pmatrix} \quad (2)$$

And the correct result is $x_{\text{exact}} = \begin{pmatrix} 13.0/28.0 \\ 6.0/7.0 \\ 27.0/28.0 \end{pmatrix}$.

Example 2. Here, we want to evaluate whether DeepSeek can write the code that can solve:

$$\frac{\partial u}{\partial t} = \alpha \frac{\partial^2 u}{\partial x^2}, \quad 0 \leq x < L, t > 0 \tag{3}$$

where α is the material's diffusivity. For the discretization in space, a finite difference scheme was used

$$u(t+1, x_i) = u(t, x_i) + dt\, \alpha \frac{u(t, x_{i-1}) - 2u(t, x_i) + u(t, x_{i+1})}{h^2} \tag{4}$$

We did not specify how to generate the grid, *i.e.* equidistant nodal spacing with n grid points $x = \{x_i = i \cdot h \in \mathbb{R} | i = 0, \ldots, n-1\}$, nor what time integration method to use, *e.g.* the Euler method.

Example 3. In this example, we evaluate DeepSeek's ability to generate parallel code for **matrix multiplication**, a general benchmarking task used to evaluate the basic performance and scalability of parallel code. It is also a fundamental operation in numerical simulations and machine learning. The task involves writing efficient parallel code that runs across multiple threads or processors, optimizing for memory usage and computational speed. The generated code is supposed to compute the following:

$$C(i,j) = C(i,j) + A(i,k) * B(k,j), \quad A, B, C \in \mathbb{R}^{n \times n}. \tag{5}$$

Example 4. The fourth example is more general and focuses on **DGEMM**, which targets a more specialized application within the HPC domain. The objective here is to analyze the ability of DeepSeek to generate parallel code for performing DGEMM on large-scale matrices, with a particular focus on optimizing for performance using parallel computing techniques. The generated code is supposed to compute the following:

$$C = \alpha \cdot A \cdot B + \beta \cdot C, \quad A, B, C \in \mathbb{R}^{n \times n}, \alpha, \beta \in \mathbf{R}. \tag{6}$$

While Example 3 is useful for assessing general parallel performance, DGEMM provides a deeper evaluation of optimized performance for large-scale, high-precision operations.

Example 5. The final example evaluates DeepSeek's ability to implement the **STREAM** triad operation, which is commonly used in HPC benchmarks to measure memory bandwidth and data throughput. The task requires writing parallel code that performs the STREAM triad operation:

$$A[i] = B[i] + scalar \cdot C[i], \quad A, B, C \in \mathbb{R}^n, scalar \in \mathbb{R}. \tag{7}$$

The performance of the implementation is evaluated based on its ability to efficiently utilize memory bandwidth, especially in multi-core or distributed HPC systems. The goal is to assess how well the code is generated, how well it scales as the array sizes grow, and how effectively it can handle large data sets while maintaining high computational throughput.

Table 3. Results for the generated code performance across two examples (Conjugate Gradient and Parallel Heat Equation). We verify that the code compiled successfully for C++ and FORTRAN. We verified that the codes executed without any runtime errors, and that the code produced correct results for all languages. A comparison was made between DeepSeek and our previous results with GPT [9].

Model	Deep Seek				ChatGPT [9]			
Language	C++	Fortran	Python	Julia	C++	Fortran	Python	Julia
Conjugate gradient								
Compile	✓	x	–	–	✓	✓	–	–
Execution	✓	✓	✓	✓	✓	✓	✓	x
Correctness	✓	✓	✓	✓	✓	✓	✓	✓
Parallel heat equation								
Compile	✓	x	–	–	x	✓	–	–
Execution	✓	✓	✓	x	✓	✓	x	x
Correctness	✓	✓	✓	✓	✓	x	✓	✓

We copied the generated code to the paper's GitHub repository[1]. For some of the generated codes, DeepSeek provided instructions on how to compile the code and some examples of expected output. These instructions were added to the Github repository.

4 Quality of the Generated Code

All of the generated codes were checked for compilation errors, runtime errors, and correctness. Table 3 summarizes the evaluation of all examples. For the conjugate gradient and parallel heat equation solver, the generated code with the Deep Seek model is compared with the generated code with ChatGPT 4.0 from the author's previous work [9].

4.1 Conjugate Gradient

For Python, the generated code executed and produced the correct results. The C++ code compiled, executed, and produced the correct result. The Fortran code did not compile due to the following `Error: Unexpected data declaration statement at (1)` since the exact result was declared in the third last line. Moving the declaration to the top fixed the issue. After that the code compiled, executed, and produced the correct results. In Python, the exact solution was computed using np.linalg.solve from the NumPy package, and in the Julia code used x_exact = A b. In the other codes the exact solution was hard-coded. The Deep Seek model had one compilation issue in the Fortran code and GPT had

---

[1] https://github.com/NoujoudNader/AiCode_DeepSeek.

no compilation issues. The Julia code had runtime issues for GPT but not for Deep Seek. To summarize, for the conjugate gradient method, each model had one issue with the generated code.

4.2 Parallel Heat Equation Solver

The C++ and Python code worked without issue. The Fortran code did not compile since the variable pi was used but not declared. After declaring the variable the code worked. The Julia code had the following error `ERROR: LoadError: UndefVarError: '@printf' not defined in 'Main'`. After adding using Printf the code worked. The C++ and Fortran code used OpenMP for parallelism. The Python code used *numba* and Julia used *Base.Threads* for parallelism. The Fortran code did not compile for DeepSeek but did compile for ChatGPT. The Fortran code produced the correct result for Deep Seek but not for ChatGPT. For both models, the Julia code had runtime errors. The Python code had runtime errors for ChatGPT but no errors for DeepSeek. The model added the following parameters: heat coefficient $\alpha = 0.1$, length of the bar $L = 1$, nodal spacing $h = 0.1$, final time $T = 1$, and time step width $dt = 10^{-3}$.

4.3 Parallel Matrix Multiplication

The matrices were filled with random numbers and the serial and parallel computation were compared. The C++, Fortran, and Python codes worked and had correct results with respect to the serial execution. The Julia code had one error while printing the results. The C++ and Fortran code used OpenMP, the Python code used the *multiprocessing* package, and the Julia code used *Base.Threads* package.

4.4 DGEMM

The Fortran code did not compile due to `passed REAL(4) to REAL(8)` and the result for the parallel implementation was incorrect. The Python code stopped execution with numba.core.errors.UnsupportedRewriteError. After investigating the error, we discovered that the model generated the code using `nb.prange(0, n, block_size)`, however, the Python package *numba* does not provide these arguments. To fix the code, we needed to edit the *numba* API calls. The C++ and Fortran code used OpenMP and Julia used the package *Base.Threads*.

4.5 STREAM

The C++ code did not compile due to SIMD errors `error: 'c' in 'aligned' clause is neither a pointer nor an array nor a reference to pointer or array`. The Fortran code did not compile due to `Error: Unclassifiable statement at (1)`. The Python code stopped with the error `AttributeError: 'c_double_Array_100000000' object has no attribute` 'get_obj'. The Julia code had the following error ERROR: LoadError: UndefVarError: 'nthreads' not defined in local scope. The C++ code used OpenMP, the Fortran code used coarray, the Python code used the *multiprocessing* package, and Julia used the *Base.Threads* package.

Table 4. Results for the performance of the generated code across three HPC examples (Matrix Multiplication, DGEMM, and Stream). We verified that the code compiled successfully for C++ and FORTRAN. We verified that the codes executed without any runtime errors, and that the code produced correct results for all codes.

Language	C++	Fortran	Python	Julia	C++	Fortran	Python	Julia	C++	Fortran	Python	Julia
Example	Matrix Multiplication				DGEMM				Stream			
Compilation	✓	✓	–	–	✓	x	–	–	x	x	–	–
Execution	✓	✓	✓	x	✓	✓	x	x	✓	✓	x	x
Correctness	✓	✓	✓	✓	✓	x	?	✓	✓	✓	✓	✓

4.6 Programming Efforts

Similar to the quality, the effort to write the code generated by a programmer is investigated. One way to estimate that effort is by using the **Co**nstructive **Co**st **Mo**del (COCOMO) [2,22]. The COCOMO model does not take parallelism into account and ignores features like synchronization. Starting in the 90 s, the HPC community discussed the development of a similar model for parallel and distributed applications. No such model has been proposed as of the time of this writing. One attempt was made to add parallel programming to the COCOMO II model [21].

We used the tool scc[2] to estimate the human effort to produce the code. We use Tables 3 and 4 to quantify the quality of the software from **poor** to **good**. Figure 1 shows the estimated programming efforts and quality of the code. For the conjugate gradient the C++ code needed more effort. For the heat equation the effort was more balanced. For the matrix multiplication the C++ code required the most effort. For DGEMM and STREAM Triad the effort was more balanced.

5 Performance Evaluation

For the performance evaluation, the following versions were used: g++/gfortran 13/14, Julia 1.11.3 and Python 3.11. Recall that we just fixed compilation and runtime errors in the code, but did not improve the parallel implementations.

---
[2] https://github.com/boyter/scc

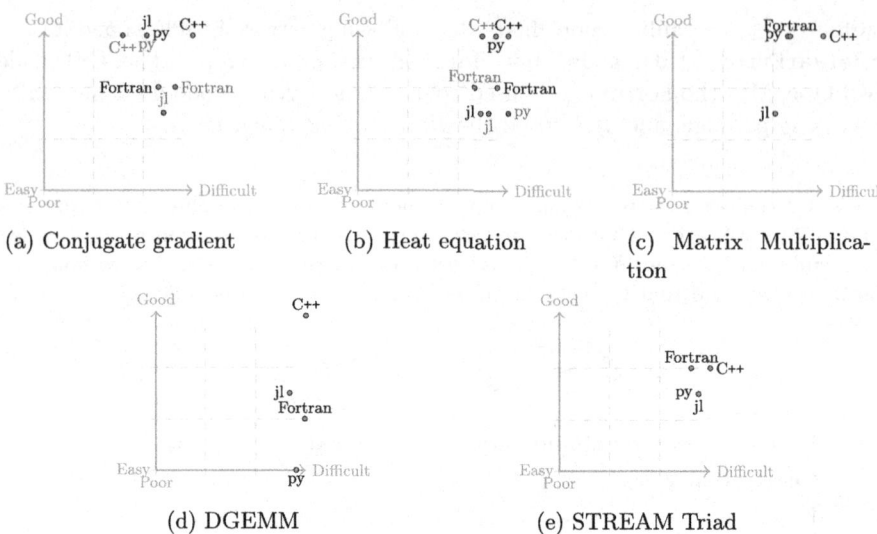

Fig. 1. Two-dimensional classification using the estimated schedule effort of the COCOMO model (**easy** vs **difficult**) and the quality of the code using compilation, execution, and correctness (**poor** vs **good**). The blue values show the results from ChatGPT [9] and the black values the results for Deep Seek. The Python and Julia data points are tagged with the common file endings py and jl, respectively. (Color figure online)

Figure 2a shows the scaling for the generated codes on *AMD EPYC 7763* (x86) from one thread to 64 cores. We used 10,000,000 nodes and changed the length of the domain L to 100,000. The C++ code and Python code scaled with the number of cores. The Fortran and Julia code showed some speedup from a single core to five cores. After that, the code did not benefit from additional cores. Figure 2b shows the scaling from one core to 64 cores on *Intel Xeon Platinum 8358* (x86). The matrix size was $10,000 \times 10,000$ with 100,000,000 elements. Here, only the Julia, code scaled. Python, C++ and Fortran showed strange behavior. Figure 2c shows the DGEMM benchmark for matrices with 512, 1024, and 2048 rows and columns and a block width of 64 on Arm A64FX. These numbers were generated by the LLM. The Fortran code was very slow and the GFLOP/s were in the range of 0.02. The Python code reported around the same values for all sizes. The C++ and Julia code had increasing numbers. However, the Julia codes reported GFLOP/s for a BLAS implementation and these values were hundreds times bigger. Thus, all of the codes had a very poor performance. Figure 2d shows the performance for stream triad for 10^4, 10^5, and 10^6 elements on ARM Grace using 72 cores. Here, all code increased performance with the array size. For the Fortran code, we used opencoarrays with openmpi 4.1 as the coarray implementation. Table 5 shows the peak performance for the parallel heat equation and matrix multiplication.

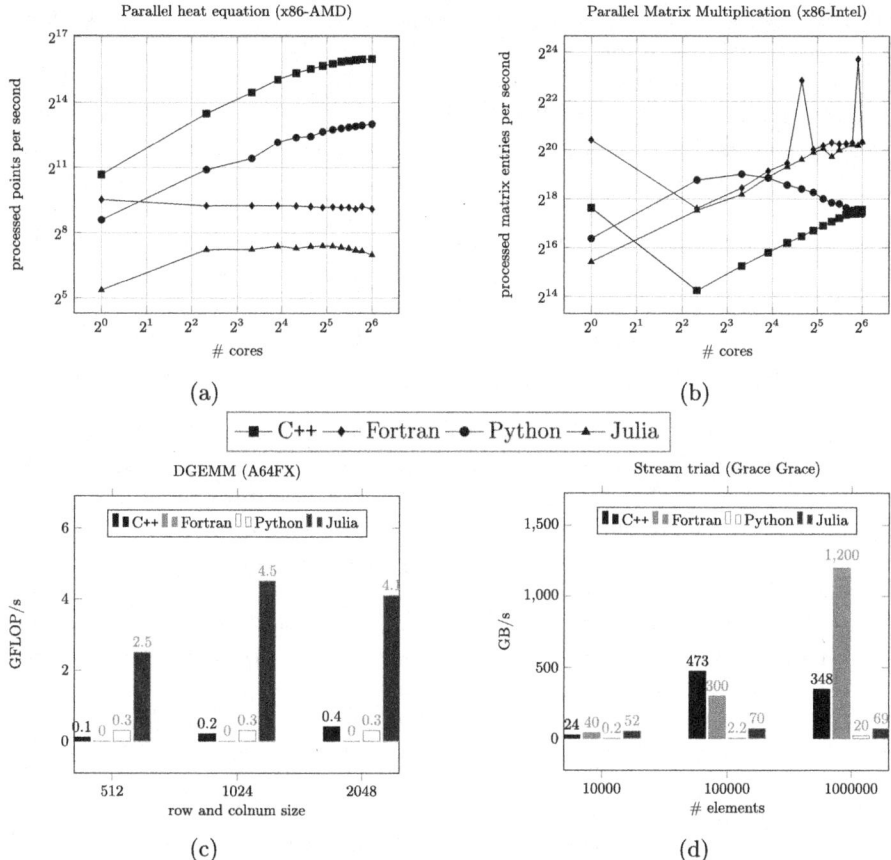

Fig. 2. Performance measurements: (a) parallel heat equation solver on x86-AMD, (b) parallel matrix multiplication on x86-Intel, (c) DGEMM on Arm A64FX, and (d) stream triad on Arm Grace Hopper.

Table 5. Peak performance for the parallel heat equation and parallel matrix multiplication as points processed per second and matrix entries processed per second, respectively. The number in parentheses are the number of cores at the peak performance.

Example	C++	Fortran	Python	Julia
Heat equation	6.5×10^7 (64)	6.0×10^5 (15)	8.1×10^6 (64)	1.7×10^5 (15)
Matrix multiplication	1.9×10^5 (60)	7.5×10^6 (25)	1.7×10^5 (60)	1.2×10^6 (55)

6 Discussion and Conclusion

The results of this study reveal both the potential and limitations the LLM model DeepSeek in HPC. By evaluating the performance of generated code across different benchmarks, we identified key insights regarding code quality, scalability, and parallel execution.

One important observation is that LLMs struggle to write scalable codes. In first two examples, both the C++ and Python codes showed consistent scaling with the increase in the number of cores, while the Fortran and Julia implementations showed limited scalability. This is consistent with prior research on HPC applications, which highlights the challenges of parallelism in certain programming languages. In example three, both Python and Fortran did not scale. The Stream Triad clearly improved in performance with increasing array sizes for the all generated codes. Using COCOMO analysis, the C++ code required more effort in the conjugate gradient and matrix multiplication examples. While the effort was more balanced between all the languages for the heat equation solver and STREAM Triad tasks.

DeepSeek shows promise in generating code across several HPC benchmarks, however the performance of the generated code needs more improvement for HPC tasks. The results also highlight the difficulties in optimizing for parallel execution and memory efficiency when generating code with LLMs. Future work should focus on improving the parallelization and performance of the generated code for HPC tasks like DGEMM and Stream Triad. To conclude, when used alongside traditional programming methods, LLMs can significantly reduce the effort required for code generation, but there is still work to be done to reach the performance levels expected for high-performance applications.

In a future work we will study the performance for distributed applications, like MPI, acceleration cards, and abstraction layers (like Kokkos or SYCL).

Acknowledgments. This work was supported by the U.S. Department of Energy through the Los Alamos National Laboratory. Los Alamos National Laboratory is operated by Triad National Security, LLC, for the National Nuclear Security Administration of U.S. Department of Energy (Contract No. 12345) LA-UR-25-22174

Supplementary Materials. The generated source code is available on GitHub (https://github.com/NoujoudNader/AiCode_DeepSeek) or Zenodo(https://doi.org/10.5281/zenodo.14968599), respectively.

References

1. Anthropic: Claude 3.5 Sonnet — anthropic.com. https://www.anthropic.com/claude/sonnet?ref=oncely.com. Accessed 11 Feb 2025
2. Boehm, B.W.: Software engineering economics. IEEE Trans. Software Eng. **SE–10**(1), 4–21 (1984). https://doi.org/10.1109/TSE.1984.5010193
3. Buchholz, K.: The extreme cost of training AI models like ChatGPT and Gemini — forbes.com. https://www.forbes.com/sites/katharinabuchholz/2024/08/23/the-extreme-cost-of-training-ai-models/. Accessed 08 Apr 2025
4. Chen, L., et al.: The landscape and challenges of HPC research and LLMs. CoRR (2024)

5. Chen, L., Lin, P.H., Vanderbruggen, T., Liao, C., Emani, M., De Supinski, B.: LM4HPC: towards effective language model application in high-performance computing. In: International Workshop on OpenMP, pp. 18–33. Springer (2023). https://doi.org/10.1007/978-3-031-40744-4_2
6. Chen, M., et al.: Evaluating large language models trained on code. arXiv preprint arXiv:2107.03374 (2021)
7. DeepSeek: DeepSeek Homepage (2025). https://www.deepseek.com/. Accessed 11 Feb 2025
8. Diehl, P., Nader, N., Moraru, M., Brandt, S.R.: LLM benchmarking with LLaMA2: evaluating code development performance across multiple programming languages. arXiv preprint arXiv:2503.19217 (2025)
9. Diehl, P., Nader, N., Brandt, S., Kaiser, H.: Evaluating AI-generated code for C++, Fortran, Go, Java, Julia, Matlab, Python, R, and Rust. arXiv preprint arXiv:2405.13101 (2024)
10. Diehl, P., et al.: Benchmarking the parallel 1D heat equation solver in Chapel, Charm++, C++, HPX, Go, Julia, Python, Rust, Swift, and Java. In: European Conference on Parallel Processing, pp. 127–138. Springer (2023). https://doi.org/10.1007/978-3-031-48803-0_11
11. Ding, X., et al.: HPC-GPT: integrating large language model for high-performance computing. In: Proceedings of the SC 2023 Workshops of The International Conference on High Performance Computing, Network, Storage, and Analysis, pp. 951–960 (2023)
12. Gibney, E.: China's cheap, open AI model DeepSeek thrills scientists. Nature **638**(8049), 13–14 (2025)
13. Godoy, W., Valero-Lara, P., Teranishi, K., Balaprakash, P., Vetter, J.: Evaluation of OpenAI codex for HPC parallel programming models kernel generation. In: Proceedings of the 52nd International Conference on Parallel Processing Workshops, pp. 136–144 (2023)
14. Godoy, W.F., Valero-Lara, P., Teranishi, K., Balaprakash, P., Vetter, J.S.: Large language model evaluation for high-performance computing software development. Concurrency Comput. Pract. Experience **36**(26), e8269 (2024)
15. Google: Our next-generation model: Gemini 1.5 — blog.google. https://blog.google/technology/ai/google-gemini-next-generation-model-february-2024/. Accessed 11 Feb 2025
16. Guo, D., et al.: Deepseek-r1: incentivizing reasoning capability in LLMs via reinforcement learning. arXiv preprint arXiv:2501.12948 (2025)
17. Guo, D., et al.: DeepSeek-coder: when the large language model meets programming–the rise of code intelligence. arXiv preprint arXiv:2401.14196 (2024)
18. Kadosh, T., et al.: Scope is all you need: transforming LLMs for HPC code. arXiv preprint arXiv:2308.09440 (2023)
19. Lei, B., Ding, C., Chen, L., Lin, P.H., Liao, C.: Creating a dataset for high-performance computing code translation using LLMs: a bridge between OpenMP Fortran and C++. In: 2023 IEEE High Performance Extreme Computing Conference (HPEC), pp. 1–7. IEEE (2023)
20. Liu, A., et al.: Deepseek-v3 technical report. arXiv preprint arXiv:2412.19437 (2024)
21. Miller, J., et al.: Applicability of the software cost model COCOMO II to HPC projects. Int. J. Comput. Sci. Eng. **17**(3), 283–296 (2018)

22. Molokken, K., Jorgensen, M.: A review of software surveys on software effort estimation. In: 2003 International Symposium on Empirical Software Engineering, 2003. ISESE 2003. Proceedings, pp. 223–230 (2003). https://doi.org/10.1109/ISESE.2003.1237981
23. Munley, C., Jarmusch, A., Chandrasekaran, S.: LLM4VV: developing LLM-driven testsuite for compiler validation. Future Gener. Comput. Syst. (2024)
24. Nichols, D., Marathe, A., Menon, H., Gamblin, T., Bhatele, A.: HPC-coder: modeling parallel programs using large language models. In: ISC High Performance 2024 Research Paper Proceedings (39th International Conference), pp. 1–12. Prometeus GmbH (2024)
25. OpenAi: Hello GPT-4o (2024). https://openai.com/chatgpt/overview/. Accessed 11 Feb 2025
26. Shewchuk, J.R., et al.: An introduction to the conjugate gradient method without the agonizing pain (1994)
27. Tiobe: TIOBE Index - TIOBE — tiobe.com (2024). https://www.tiobe.com/tiobe-index/. Accessed 04 Oct 2024
28. Valero-Lara, P., et al.: Comparing Llama-2 and GPT-3 LLMs for HPC kernels generation. arXiv preprint arXiv:2309.07103 (2023)
29. Yin, J., et al.: chatHPC: empowering HPC users with large language models. J. Supercomput. **81**(1), 194 (2025)

Analysis of MPI Parallel Code Generated by GPT-4o

Rin Tanaka[✉] [iD], Hayato Yamaki [iD], Shinobu Miwa [iD], and Hiroki Honda [iD]

The University of Electro-Communications, Tokyo 182-8585, Japan
tanaka@hpc.is.uec.ac.jp, {yamaki,shinobu.miwa,h.honda}@uec.ac.jp

Abstract. Developing efficient parallel programs is very tough even for experts. Advanced AI technology, such as large language models (LLMs), is expected to help with this. In this context, a state-of-the-art study has evaluated the ability to write parallel codes for various LLMs. However, the previous study does not provide a detailed analysis of the codes generated by LLM. Moreover, due to the rapid advancement of LLMs, the LLMs used in the previous study are becoming stale. In this paper, we provide the first detailed analysis of the MPI parallel codes generated by GPT-4o, the latest accessible LLM when we started this study. More specifically, we collect 1,200 MPI codes by executing the ParEval benchmark suite on GPT-4o and then classify the generated codes into four categories (pass, and logical, runtime, and compile errors) based on the types of errors. We further analyze the codes in each category to identify the sources of errors. Our analysis observed many cases where generated codes were parallelized incorrectly but passed given unit tests. This suggests that a new metric is needed to assess the correctness of parallel codes generated by LLMs.

Keywords: MPI · Large Language Model · LLM · Code Generation · GPT-4o

1 Introduction

Large language models (LLMs) are increasingly used in modern software development. For example, GitHub Copilot uses LLMs to make suggestions to complete code under development [7]. Another example is CodeRabbit, which automatically provides feedback on pull requests with the help of LLMs [2]. In extreme cases, software developers use some prominent LLMs such as ChatGPT [14] and Gemini [8] to obtain an initial implementation of a targeted code from the corresponding natural-language description [6]. These examples suggest that LLMs are becoming indispensable for rapid software development.

This trend is spreading to the development of parallel software. Recently, ParEval, the first benchmark suite that evaluates the ability of LLMs to generate parallel code, has been developed [13]. At the same time, the authors evaluated various LLMs with this benchmark and showed that generating parallel code is more difficult for LLMs than generating sequential code. This previous study is an important first step in benchmarking LLMs for parallel code generation; however, it has not reported what types of errors LLMs tend to make when generating parallel code. In addition, the previous study benchmarked various LLMs, including the latest model (the gpt-4-1106-preview model) at that time, but the rapid advancement of LLMs somewhat stales these models.

This paper provides the first detailed analysis of the parallel code generated by GPT-4o, the latest accessible LLM when we started this study, while focusing on MPI, the programming model most used in the field of HPC. More specifically, we collect 1,200 MPI codes by executing the ParEval benchmark suite on GPT-4o and then classify the generated codes into four categories (*pass, logical error, runtime error, and compile error*) based on the types of errors. We further analyze the codes in each category to identify the sources of errors.

Our main findings are summarized as follows.

- We observed many cases where generated codes were parallelized incorrectly but passed given unit tests. This suggests that the metric widely used to assess the correctness of generated code (i.e. pass@k) is inappropriate, and a new metric is needed for parallel code generation.
- We found that many generated codes cause logical errors due to forgetting the parallelization of loop bodies. Giving more instructions to the LLM may alleviate this issue.
- We revealed that many runtime errors occurred when generated codes called MPI functions such as MPI_Gather().

The remainder of this paper is organized as follows. We describe our research background in Sect. 2. Sections 3 and 4 show our analysis methodology and results, respectively. Finally, we conclude this paper in Sect. 5.

2 Background

2.1 LLM

LLMs are generative AIs specialized in natural language processing. An input text provided to an LLM is called a prompt. LLMs consist of many parameters trained with a large amount of data. The performance of LLMs has improved dramatically in recent years. The accuracy of the state-of-the-art LLM is reported to exceed 80% for various tasks [17]. In contrast, since approximately 20% of the LLM output still contains errors, the output must be carefully verified. The development of LLMs is primarily driven by industries such as OpenAI and Google, and various services utilizing LLMs are offered online.

It is important to note that the output of an LLM is probabilistic. This means that an LLM produces various outputs for an identical input. Incorporating this diversity into given tasks is preferable to increase the effectiveness of LLMs. For this purpose, sampling is widely used, which randomly selects tokens based on their predicted probabilities [1,4,5,9,12]. The level of randomness is typically controlled by a hyperparameter called *temperature* [1]. A higher temperature

Table 1. Node Configuration of Wisteria-A

Name	Remarks
CPU	2x Intel Xeon Platinum 8360Y (36 cores, 2.4 GHz, 54 MB LLC)
Memory	512 GB, 409.6 GB/s

produces a more uniform probability distribution, resulting in more diverse (i.e. creative) outputs, while a lower temperature increases the probability of selecting specific tokens, resulting in more consistent (i.e. predictable) outputs.

2.2 GPT-4o

GPT-4o is the flagship LLM operated by OpenAI as of May 2024 [15]. GPT-4o has over 200 billion parameters, which were trained on approximately 25,000 NVIDIA A100 GPUs for about 100 days [18]. GPT-4o can be accessed with a dedicated API. The usage fee is $2.5 per 1M tokens at the time of writing this paper. Due to its notable performance, GPT-4o is used in many fields, such as document translation, summarization, and text and code generation.

2.3 Related Work

D. Nichols et al. evaluated the ability of seven LLMs to generate parallel code for seven programming models (sequential, OpenMP, Kokkos, CUDA, HIP, MPI, and MPI+OpenMP) [13]. In this previous study, the correctness of the generated parallel code is evaluated by comparing the execution results with those of the reference sequential code. The authors also evaluated the speed of the generated parallel code against the reference sequential code. They reported that many LLMs generated the highest number of incorrect codes for MPI in the seven programming models. However, they did not show how the generated parallel code was incorrect.

Z. Liu et al. evaluated the capability of ChatGPT in generating sequential code [11]. They gave GPT-3.5 various tasks to generate five sequential codes (C, Java, Python, C++, and JavaScript), which are listed on the competitive programming site called LeetCode [10]. Based on the status of the code submitted to LeetCode, the authors classified the generated codes into five classes: *accepted, wrong answer, time limit exceeded, and runtime and compile error*. *Accepted* means the generated code passes a given unit test. Their analysis provided valuable insights into sequential codes generated by an LLM, but no analysis of parallel codes generated by LLMs has been performed.

Table 2. ParEval benckmark

Problem types	Problems
Dense Linear Algebra	LU decomposition, linear system solver, GEMM, AXPY, GEMV
Fourier Transform	inverse FFT, DFT, conjugate, split FFT, FFT
Geometry	convex hull, perimeter of convex hull, smallest triangle, 2D closest pair, 1D closest pair
Graph	edge counting, counting the number of vertices in the largest component, highest node degree, counting connected components, shortening path
Histogram	pixel counting, histogram 0–100, counting the number of cartesian points in each quadrant, counting first letter, quartile counting
Reduce	XOR, the product of the vector x with every odd indexed element inverted, mean, smallest odd number, the sum of the minimum value at each index of vectors x and y
Scan	prefix sum, scan min and replace, sum of prefix sum, reverse prefix sum, largest contiguous subarray sum
Search	search last struct by key, search value, find the closest number to pi, search first even number, search xor
Sort	complex number sort, finding k-th element, sorted vector's index, sort by key, sort but ignore zero
Sparse Algebra	linear system solver, SpMM, SpMV, AXPY, ludecomp
Stencil	xor, grayscale image convolution with the edge kernel, 3-point 1D Jacobi stencil, 3-point 2D Jacobi stencil, game of life
Transform	ReLU, odd value division by 2, x to 1/x, squared value, map

3 Methodology

3.1 Experimental System

We used the supercomputer Wisteria-A, which is operated by the Information Technology Center at the University of Tokyo. Table 1 shows the configuration of a compute node in Wisteria-A. Each node is equipped with 8 NVIDIA A100 GPUs, but we used only the CPU for our experiment. We executed each generated code with four MPI processes on a single node. All generated codes were compiled with the OpenMPI-4.1.6 compiler. The options `-std=c++20 -ltbb -O3` was used.

3.2 Benchmarks

We used the ParEval benchmark suite [13], which is designed to evaluate the ability of LLMs to generate parallel code. ParEval consists of 12 problem types, each corresponding to a fundamental computational pattern (e.g., Fourier transformation) generally seen in HPC applications. Each problem type has five problems, so ParEval includes a total of 60 (= 12 × 5) problems. The details of ParEval are summarized in Table 2.

Each problem includes one prompt as an input to an LLM. A prompt contains several instructions on a used programming model, a description of a targeted function, and the first line of the function body. In this paper, we used the prompts that specify MPI to be used.

A prompt included in ParEval contains the instruction "Only write the body of the function," but it often allows GPT-4o to generate a code without the closing curly brace of the function. Therefore, we removed this instruction from the prompt.

Furthermore, we found several bugs of reference sequential codes in ParEval. We fixed these bugs and then used this bug-fixed version for our experiment.

3.3 Evaluation Metrics

Two types of metrics have been used to evaluate the correctness of the code generated by an LLM.

The first type is metrics that evaluate the similarity of the generated code with the reference code. An example is the BLEU score, which was originally designed to evaluate the ability of LLMs in the generation of natural-language text. CodeBLEU [16] is a metric extended from BLEU to code generation tasks. It uses abstract syntax trees, enabling the evaluation of the semantic similarity between two codes independent of the variable and function names.

The second type is metrics that evaluate the functional correctness of the generated code. Lately, many studies have used this type of metric. For example, the HumanEval benchmark [3], which aims to evaluate the ability of LLMs to generate Python functions, includes a unit test for each problem, and a generated function is considered correct when it passes the test.

The functional correctness of generated codes is typically evaluated with pass@k [3]. The definition of pass@k is given in the following formula.

$$\text{pass@k} = \mathbb{E}[1 - \frac{\binom{n-c}{k}}{\binom{n}{k}}] \tag{1}$$

where n represents the number of samples (i.e. generated codes) per prompt, k ($n \geq k$) is the number of samples used for the test, and c is the number of samples that pass the test. For a single prompt, if any of the k generated codes passes the test, pass@k is 1. In this paper, we also used pass@k to evaluate the correctness of generated codes.

3.4 Analysis Methods

Based on the previous study [11], we classified the generated codes into the following four categories, which combine *time limit exceeded* with *runtime error*.

Pass represents the case where the generated code passes a given unit test. In other words, the execution of the generated code is completed and the final output matches the output of the reference code.

Logical error represents the case where the generated code fails the unit test due to the mismatch between the final and reference outputs. The execution of the generated code is completed.

Runtime error represents the case where the generated code fails the unit test due to incomplete execution. Incomplete execution means that the execution of the generated code is aborted or exceeds a given time limit. The compilation of the generated code finishes successfully.

Compile error represents the case where the compilation of the generated code fails.

We further subdivided the generated codes into finer groups according to the source of errors. For this, we carefully analyzed each generated code within the categories, except for *pass*.

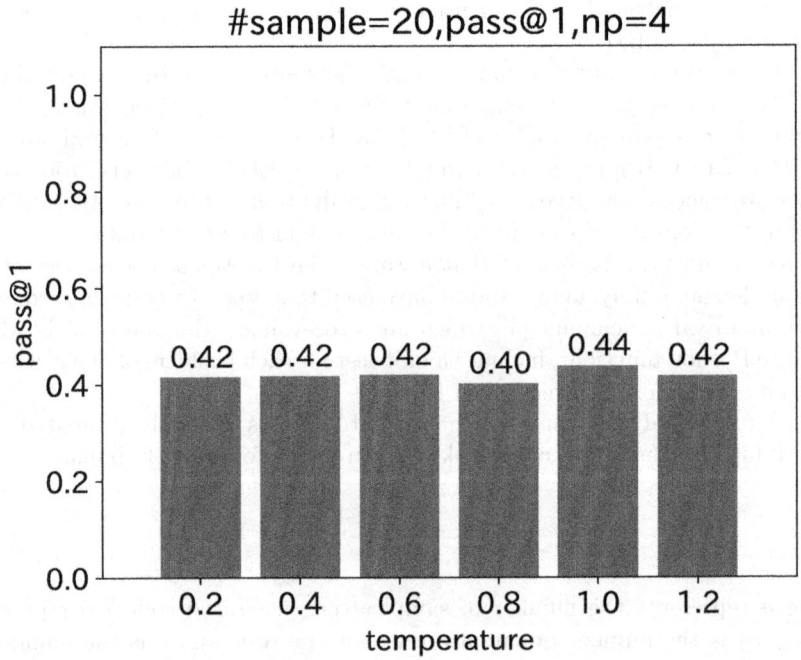

Fig. 1. Pass@1 of MPI codes generated by GPT-4o at different temperatures.

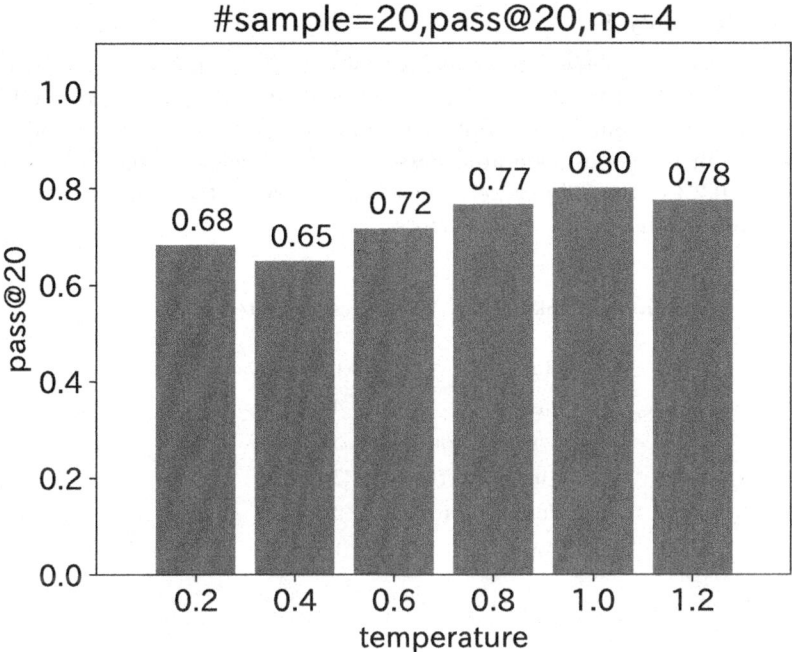

Fig. 2. Pass@20 of MPI codes generated by GPT-4o at different temperatures.

4 Results

4.1 Impact of Temperature

To evaluate the impact of temperature on GPT-4o, we conducted the experiment where GPT-4o generated 20 MPI parallel code per prompt while varying the temperature from 0.2 to 1.2.

Figure 1 shows pass@1 for GPT-4o when $n = k = 1$. The figure shows that pass@1 is almost constant (0.40–0.42) at different temperatures. This number is significantly higher than the value (about 0.20 for the gpt-4-1106-preview model) reported in previous work [13], and may be affected by a lack of samples (i.e., $n = 1$). An increase in the number of samples may be close to the previous result.

In contrast, pass@20 can be improved as the temperature increases, as shown in Fig. 2. This is because a higher temperature facilitates the generation of a more diverse code, thus increasing the probability that one of the generated codes passes the tests. We note that pass@20 is computed at $n = k = 20$ and reaches the maximum value at a temperature of 1.0. Consequently, the following sections focus on analyzing the MPI parallel codes generated at a temperature of 1.0.

4.2 Code Analysis

Overview. Table 3 shows the breakdown of the MPI codes generated by GPT-4o. Because ParEval has 60 problems, as described in Sect. 3.2, asking GPT-4o to generate 20 outputs per problem results in 1,200 codes. The table shows that 43.8% of the codes generated passed the tests, whereas the rest failed. In addition, 70.2% of the failures were due to logical errors. Only 16.8% of the codes encountered runtime and compile errors.

Table 3. Breakdown of MPI codes generated by GPT-4o

Status	Count	Percentage
Pass	526	43.8%
Logical error	473	39.4%
Runtime error	85	7.1%
Compile error	116	9.7%
Total	1,200	100.0%

Pass. A passed code produces a correct output for a given input but is not guaranteed to be parallelized correctly. To confirm the correctness of the passed code, we focus on the usage of the variable corresponding to my MPI rank (referred to as a *rank variable*). If the rank variable is not used to divide the problem into multiple processes, the parallelization applied to the code is incorrect. We can check this by simply counting the number of occurrences of the rank variable (referred to as the *rank variable count*) in the code. When computing the rank variable count, we excluded the case where the variable was defined or used to call an MPI function. If the rank variable count is 0, the rank variable is not used for problem division (i.e. each MPI process computes the whole problem).

Our analysis showed that 124 of 526 passed codes showed a rank variable count of 0. This means that 23.6% of the passed codes are incorrectly parallelized. Furthermore, our analysis showed that all passed codes showed a rank variable count of 0 for 11 problems. They are 22.9% (= 11/48) of the problems in which any of the 20 generated codes passed the test.

These results suggest that the use of only the conventional metric that evaluates the correctness of the generated sequential codes is insufficient to evaluate the correctness of the generated parallel code. A new metric is needed for the evaluation of the generated parallel codes.[1]

Some incorrectly parallelized codes can be detected by measuring their performance scalability. MPI codes that do not divide the problems show almost

---

[1] The previous study [13] uses $speedup_n$@k and $efficiency_n$@k as performance metrics, in addition to pass@k, but these performance metrics also do not guarantee that a code is parallelized correctly. We elaborate on this in Sect. 4.3.

constant performance as the number of MPI processes increases, as shown in Sect. 4.3. We note that the low performance scalability does not directly mean incorrect parallelization. Some correctly parallelized codes have low scalability due to the lack of parallelism. We need some static analysis, such as an AST-level code analysis, to precisely detect incorrectly parallelized code.

Logical Error. Like the passed codes, for 473 codes that encountered logical errors, we checked whether the problems were divided into multiple processes. Our experimental results showed that 336 (71.0%) of 473 codes showed a rank variable count of 0. Furthermore, 256 of the 336 codes passed the tests when each code was executed on a single process. In these codes, as shown in Code 1.1, the problems were not divided at all, but MPI_Reduce() was inserted at the end of the code to aggregate the results produced by multiple processes. As a result, the outputs of these codes matched the reference outputs on a single node, while they did not match the reference outputs on multiple nodes.

Code 1.1: Pseudocode that lacks problem division

```
function() {
    // Each process executes the same computation to obtain a local
        output.
    local_output;

    // Use MPI_Reduce to aggregate outputs from multiple processes.
    // However, because the computation is not parallelized, a logical
        error occurs.
    MPI_Reduce(..., local_output, ..., global_output, ..., MPI_SUM);

    return global_output;
}
```

Table 4. Source of logical errors

Source	# of codes	# of problems
Misuse of MPI_IN_PLACE	45	16
Improper problem division	27	6
Lack of synchronization	10	1
Gather improper data	4	1
Confusion of gathering with reduction	2	2
Misimplementation of workers	2	1
Perform reduction for improper data	2	2
Misuse of identifiers	2	1
Unknown, but few-shot works	5	2
Others	5	5
Unknown	33	11

We investigated the sources of logical errors for the rest of the 437 codes (137 codes). The results are shown in Table 4. The table shows that 45 of the 137 codes used MPI_IN_PLACE incorrectly. Code 1.2 exemplifies this error. Since this error occurred in multiple problems, GPT-4o may lack knowledge of MPI_IN_PLACE. Furthermore, 27 of the 137 codes divided the problems improperly, as shown in the table. For example, in the case of the problem that finds the largest contiguous value in a given array, the array was evenly divided among processes without duplication, destroying the continuity between subarrays. GPT-4o generated 19 of the 137 codes for two problems. These problems are particularly challenging for GPT-4o in generating MPI code.

Code 1.2: Pseudocode that incorrectly uses MPI_IN_PLACE

```
1 function( ){
2   // compute local output
3   local_output
4
5   // Logical error occurs because local_output is not copied to
        global_output at rank 0
6   if (rank==0)
7       MPI_Reduce(MPI_IN_PLACE, global_output, ...);
8   else
9       MPI_Reduce(&local_output,...);
10 }
```

Logical errors occurred in 10 of 12 problems for which all generated codes failed the tests. We observed that multiple codes generated for a problem often caused the same logical error. Since adding instructions to the prompts may be effective for some logical errors, we will evaluate the impact of this approach.

Runtime Error. We analyzed the 85 codes that encountered runtime errors. The results of our analysis are summarized in Table 5. The table shows that many runtime errors were related to MPI functions. For example, 14 of the 85 errors are due to the receive buffer shortage. In addition, 6 of the 85 errors are due to the use of incorrect types for message buffers. Furthermore, 26 of the 85 codes caused runtime errors related to MPI_Gather() and MPI_Gatherv().

Compile Error. 116 codes generated by GPT-4o encountered compile errors. Table 6 summarizes the first errors that appeared during the compiling processes of these codes. We were unable to find any specific errors for MPI.

4.3 Performance Analysis

We examined the speedup of the passed codes compared to the sequential codes. We executed each passed code with 4 MPI processes 20 times and then selected the code exhibiting the shortest execution time for each problem to compute the speedup against the sequential code.

Table 5. Source of runtime errors

Source	# of codes	# of problems
Receive buffer shortage	14	7
Access to unallocated data	6	4
Misuse of MPI_Datatype	6	5
Mismatch between send and receive message sizes	4	4
Misuse of identifiers	3	2
Synchronization failure	3	1
Incorrect initialization	2	1
Unexpected data size	2	1
Deadlock	2	1
Array index out-of-range	2	1
Invalid message size	2	2
Unknown, but few-shot works	17	4
Others	10	7
Unknown	12	4

Figure 3 shows the results. Surprisingly, even though the body of the computation was not parallelized in some passed codes (i.e., the purple bars), they showed a significant speedup compared to the reference codes. This is because these passed codes use more efficient sequential algorithms than the reference codes. For example, in Problem 34, which computes the largest sum of any contiguous subarray in a given vector, the reference code is written with an $\mathcal{O}(N^2)$ algorithm, whereas the generated MPI code uses an $\mathcal{O}(N)$ algorithm. This difference in computational complexity brings a speedup of 9,050x. This means that speedup against the reference code is not helpful in assessing the correctness of generated parallel codes.

To filter out the above situation, we can use *the performance difference between the generated and reference codes when executing each of them in a single process*. The performance difference becomes small if both codes use an identical algorithm, while it becomes large if the two codes use different algorithms. However, because a small performance difference does not ensure the equivalence between two given algorithms, some static analysis, such as an AST-level code analysis, will be needed to precisely detect the algorithmic difference between the generated and the reference codes.

Table 6. Source of compile errors

Source	# of codes	# of problems
Redefinition	23	9
Use of deleted function	21	2
Unexpected definition	14	5
Invalid initialization	12	1
Undefined function call	10	6
Assignment of read-only location	7	2
No member	9	5
No declaration within scope	6	4
No match	6	3
Invalid conversion	3	2
Use a variable before deduction of 'auto'	1	1
Invalid lambda expression	1	1
No declaration	1	1
Misuse of return value	1	1
Invalid operator	1	1

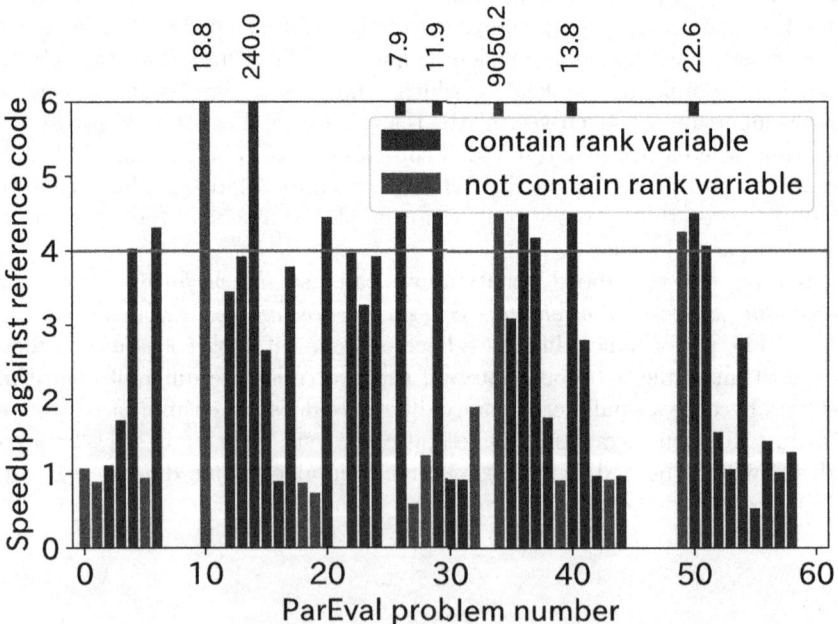

Fig. 3. Speedup of passed codes against sequential codes in the case that generated codes. Each MPI code is executed with 4 processes.

5 Conclusion

In this paper, we analyzed the MPI parallel codes generated by GPT-4o. Our analysis found that a significant number of the generated codes were parallelized incorrectly, even though they passed the given unit tests. Our finding suggests that a new method that replaces unit tests is required to assess the correctness of generated parallel codes.

Our future work will develop a method to evaluate the correctness of parallel codes generated by LLMs. In addition, we will improve the correctness of the generated parallel codes by using LLMs iteratively. Many problems included in ParEval are relatively simple compared to those encountered in the development of real HPC applications. We, therefore, will develop a more practical benchmark that evaluates the capability of LLMs in generating parallel code.

Acknowledgements. This work was partially supported by JST, PRESTO Grant Number JPMJPR22P9.

References

1. Ackley, D.H., Hinton, G.E., Sejnowski, T.J.: A learning algorithm for Boltzmann machines. Cogn. Sci. **9**(1), 147–169 (1985)
2. CodeRabbit: AI code review. https://coderabbit.ai/. Accessed 5 Mar 2025
3. Du, X., et al.: Evaluating large language models in class-level code generation. In: Proceedings of the IEEE/ACM 46th International Conference on Software Engineering, ICSE 2024 (2024)
4. Fan, A., Lewis, M., Dauphin, Y.: Hierarchical neural story generation. In: Gurevych, I., Miyao, Y. (eds.) Proceedings of the 56th Annual Meeting of the Association for Computational Linguistics (Volume 1: Long Papers), pp. 889–898 (2018). https://aclanthology.org/P18-1082/
5. Freitag, M., Al-Onaizan, Y.: Beam search strategies for neural machine translation. CoRR arXiv:1702.01806 (2017)
6. Gewirtz, D.: How to use ChatGPT to write code: what it does well and what it doesn't (2024). https://www.zdnet.com/article/how-to-use-chatgpt-to-write-code-what-it-does-well-and-what-it-doesnt/
7. GitHub Copilot: The AI editor for everyone. https://github.com/features/copilot. Accessed 5 Mar 2025
8. Google DeepMind: Gemini 2.0. https://deepmind.google/technologies/gemini/. Accessed 5 Mar 2025
9. Holtzman, A., Buys, J., Du, L., Forbes, M., Choi, Y.: The curious case of neural text degeneration. In: 8th International Conference on Learning Representations, ICLR 2020, Addis Ababa, Ethiopia, 26–30 April 2020 (2020). https://openreview.net/forum?id=rygGQyrFvH
10. LeetCode: LeetCode. https://leetcode.com/. Accessed 17 Feb 2025
11. Liu, Z., Tang, Y., Luo, X., Zhou, Y., Zhang, L.F.: No need to lift a finger anymore? Assessing the quality of code generation by ChatGPT. IEEE Trans. Softw. Eng. (2024)

12. Nguyen, M., Baker, A., Neo, C., Roush, A., Kirsch, A., Shwartz-Ziv, R.: Turning up the heat: min-p sampling for creative and coherent LLM outputs (2024). arXiv:2407.01082
13. Nichols, D., Davis, J.H., Xie, Z., Rajaram, A., Bhatele, A.: Can large language models write parallel code? In: Proceedings of the 33rd International Symposium on High-Performance Parallel and Distributed Computing, pp. 281–294 (2024)
14. OpenAI: ChatGPT. https://openai.com/chatgpt/overview/. Accessed 5 Mar 2025
15. OpenAI, et al.: GPT-4o system card (2024). arXiv:2410.21276
16. Ren, S., et al.: CodeBLEU: a method for automatic evaluation of code synthesis. CoRR arXiv:2009.10297 (2020)
17. Vellum: LLM benchmarks: Overview, limits and model comparison (2024). https://www.vellum.ai/blog/llm-benchmarks-overview-limits-and-model-comparison
18. Walker II, S.M.: Everything we know about GPT-4 (2023). https://klu.ai/blog/gpt-4-llm

Workshop Review Contributions

Summary Papers of ISC Workshops Without Proceedings

ISC-HPC traditionally features workshops with proceedings as collected in this volume, as well as workshops without a proceedings track. In 2025, we decided to invite the organisers of workshops without proceedings to summarise their workshop outcomes in brief overview state-of-the-art papers. Five colleagues took the opportunity and contributed their insights from the event to this book.

QRUCH Workshop Summary

Philippe Deniel[1(✉)], Suzanne Talon[2], Venkatesh Kannan[3], and Ariana Torres[4]

[1] CEA/DIF, Chemin du Ru, 91680 Bruyères-le-Châtel, France
philippe.deniel@cea.fr
[2] Calcul Québec, 2375 Chemin de la Côte-Sainte-Catherine, bureau 5070, Montréal, Québec H3T 1A8, Canada
, suzanne.talon@calculquebec.ca
[3] 7th Floor, Tower Building Technology & Enterprise Campus Grand Canal Quay, Dublin 2 D02 HP83, Ireland
venkatesh.kannan@ichec.ie
[4] Offices Hoog Overborch (Hoog Catharijne), Moreelsepark 48, 3511 EP Utrecht, The Netherlands
ariana.torres@surf.nl

1 About the QRUCH Workshop

QRUCH is the acronym for **Q**uantum **R**esources for **U**nified **C**omputing **H**ub.

QRUCH is a ISC'25 Workshop focused on middleware dedicated in integrating actual Quantum Computer into HPC compute centers. It's a"half a day" workshop addresses some of these topics as it aims to depict the available pieces of software that will help in integrating an actual quantum computer inside a machine room, making it available to end users.

This workshop is a follow-up to the BoF "Towards Hardware Agnostic Standards in Hybrid HPC/Quantum Computing" at ISCâĂŹ24. It took place on the afternoon of June 13, from 2:00 pm to 6:00 pm, during ISC'25 in Hamburg.

2 About QRUCH 1st Edition

Quantum Computing is not a completely new topic: it was introduced in 1981 during a conference at MIT, but it really came into the spotlight as Peter Shor released his famous algorithm capable of breaking RSA encryption with tremendous acceleration. The domain remained a bit theoretical, studied in mathematical computer science, until a few years ago when actual Quantum Computers arrived on the market, providing real (but yet limited) quantum computing resources. In the very last years, Quantum Computers gained more computing power, and they started to be deployed inside HPC centers while also becoming available on cloud-based platforms.

As Quantum Computers leave the laboratories where they were designed and enter the HPC machine room, it becomes necessary to consider how they can be used to perform actual computation on real-life use cases. As we are still in

---

© The Author(s), under exclusive license to Springer Nature Switzerland AG 2026
S. Neuwirth et al. (Eds.): ISC High Performance 2025 Workshops, LNCS 16091, pp. 655–659, 2026.
https://doi.org/10.1007/978-3-032-07612-0_50

the NISQ era, and because HPC resources may help in using quantum computers efficiently, the hybrid HPC/QC naturally appeared, providing acceleration similar to GPUs previously.

This is not as easy as it seems. As the hardware becomes ready to be installed in computer rooms, the software stack has not evolved as fast. In particular, the required software stack to "glue" HPC and QC is not fully defined. Solutions exist and are provided by both research institutes and vendors, but they obey no standard.

Current Quantum Computers are provided with a very simple software stack, usually a Python based framework, providing native access to the computing resources as well as a "mock device" providing emulation on standard CPU (and sometimes GPU) compute power. As we consider the integration inside the computer center, many topics, related to system integration as well as application integration are to be considered, such as:

- authentication and accounting;
- job scheduling;
- bench-marking;
- programming interfaces beyond Python
- mixing HPC and QC steps to perform actual HPC/QC hybridization

3 Content of the Workshop

The workshop followed this agenda

Time	Topic
14h00 - 1405	Participants Welcoming
15h05 - 15h00	Keynote Speakers
15h00 - 16h00	Lightning Talks (1st round)
16h00 - 16h30	Coffee Break
16h30 - 17h00	Lightning Talks (2nd round)
17h00 - 17h55	Expert Panel
18h00	End of Workshop

3.1 Keynote Speakers

This first session of the workshop included three keynote speakers, each depicting how compute centers integrated quantum computer technologies in their environment and the kind of software that they are using to make it possible for their users to use the available quantum resources.

Three keynote speakers shared the time for this first session:

1. **Quantum @ SURF:** Arianas Torress, lead of Quantum Computing at SURF, in the Netherlands
2. **RIKEN Quantum HPC Hybrid Platform:** Miwako Tsuji, lead of Quantum-HPC Hybrid Software Environment Unit in RIKEN Center for Computational Science
3. **Calcul Québec's HPC and Quantum Computing Infrastructures:** Suzanne Talon, CEO of Calcul Quebec

3.2 Lightning Talks

The second session consisted of small topics, or *Lightning talks*. Each topic presented an approach of middleware dedicated to exploiting quantum computers.

Connecting Hardware and Software in Quantum Computing: The Quantum Device Management Interface (QDMI). (Lukas Burgholzer (TUM)).

This lightning talk will showcase an interface, called the Quantum Device Management Interface (QDMI), that addresses this problem by explicitly connecting the software and hardware developers, mediating between their competing interests. QDMI allows hardware platforms to provide their physical characteristics in a standardized way, and software tools to query that data to guide the compilation process accordingly. QDMI is publicly available as open source at https://github.com/Munich-Quantum-Software-Stack/QDMI.

SmartHPC.QC: evaluating the impact of malleability for HPC-QC integration. (Gabriella Bettonte (E4))

Today, HPC centers and quantum computers, as the number of quantum machines is dramatically lower than that of classical nodes. As jobs execute quantum kernels (or wait for their turn in a time-partitioned quantum resource), HPC nodes may be idle, thus occupying resources without performing anything. This phenomenon introduces inefficiencies in the overall HPC center performance. We suggest tackling the issue by adopting a more dynamic method to handle resource assignments, i.e., through malleability properties. With the SmartHPC.QC project (a collaboration between E4 Computer Engineering, Links Foundation, Università di Torino and CINECA), we aim to develop a malleable solution for allocating quantum resources in an HPC-QC pipeline.

Qunicorn: A Middleware for Unified Execution Across Heterogeneous Quantum Cloud Offerings. (Lavinia Stiliadou (IAAS / University of Stuttgart))

Quantum computers are available via a variety of different quantum cloud offerings, and quantum circuits can be implemented using different quantum programming languages. As a consequence, using a specific quantum programming language for implementing the application at hand can limit the set of compatible quantum cloud offerings and cause a vendor lock-in. Therefore, we introduce the architecture for a unification middleware that facilitates accessing quantum computers available via different quantum cloud offerings by automatically translating between various quantum circuits and result formats.

Programming models for hybrid HPC-QPU applications. (Santiago Nunez-Corrales (NCSA))
Programming quantum computers today still requires substantial knowledge of the physical basis of these devices. This creates a tall barrier for non-physicists to benefit from the additional computational resources QPUs provide and constrains the growth in the number of successful final applications. When put in the perspective of integrating HPC and QPU resources, hybrid classical-quantum programming today seems not to be poised to scale up alongside qubit counts, fault tolerance, and utility-scale devices within the following decade. We will discuss new directions for quantum-only programming models inspired by four decades of parallel computing (including MPI, OpenMP, and CUDA), where the main objective is to provide a uniform programming surface with much lower difficulty for newcomers.

A critical look at the state of quantum software stack. (Vlad Stirbu (University of Jyväskalä))
The talk will take a critical look at the current state of the quantum software stack and what we can learn from 70 years of classical computing when designing the integration of quantum computing into classical infrastructures.

Heterogeneous quantum computing in C++ with Q-Pragma. (Océane Koska (EVIDEN)) Quantum computing offers a promising approach to solving complex computational problems. However, integrating quantum computing into existing high-performance computing (HPC) environments remains a significant challenge. The Q-Pragma programming framework aims to facilitate this integration by embedding quantum directives within C++ code, enabling the development of hybrid quantum-classical applications. This presentation will explore the architecture of Q-Pragma, its role in optimizing quantum-classical interactions, and its potential for enhancing computational performance.

3.3 Expert Panel

The last session was based on a set of questions asked to a panel of experts:

- Suzanne Talon, CEO of Calcul QUébec
- Patrick Carribault, Fellow Expert and Research Director at CEA
- Lukas Burgholzer from Technische Universität München (TUM)
- Daniele Grigori, Chief Science Officer at E4

The set of questions included the following ones

1. From your perspectives, what are the most relevant HPC/QC use cases? Are we limited to QAOA and VQE, or even QML, or do you foresee other tracks to be followed?
2. What should be the best programming languages for HPC/QC? Should we stay with Python or move to different languages (C++, Julia, Rust, or even something else)?

3. Is QC to be considered only as an accelerator to address NP complex steps in a HPC-based computation, or should we see things from a different perspective?
4. How do you handle hybrid HPC/QC scheduling? Should the QC resources be considered as "exclusive", with no time sharing, or should we envisage "quantum time sharing" by introducing new models such as an "embarrassingly quantum" usage of the QPU?
5. If we succeed in having a quantum network link, making parallel or distributed QC devices, how would you handle them?
6. Imagine that an efficient Quantum Memory technology is available on the market, how would it handle your HPC/QC frameworks?

4 Future Work

The QRUCH workshop occurred for the first time at ISC'25. The workshop will be resubmitted next year at ISC'26, in order to become a recurring workshop.

State of the Art in High-Performance Containerization: Insights from the 11th HPC Container Workshop at ISC 2025

Abdulrahman Azab[1], Christian Kniep[2(✉)], Barbara Krašovec[3], Holger Gantikow[4], and David Brayford[5]

[1] Sigma2 AS and University of Oslo, Oslo, Norway
abdulrahman.azab@sigma2.no
[2] QNIB Solutions, Eschweiler, Germany
christian@qnib.org
[3] Jožef Stefan Institute and EGI CSIRT, Ljubljana, Slovenia
barbara.krasovec@ijs.si
[4] Eviden Science + Computing, Munich, Germany
[5] HPE, Hamburg, Germany

Abstract. The 11th High Performance Container Workshop at the ISC 2025 (HPCW'25) brought together stakeholders from the global HPC community to address the rapid evolution of container technologies in High Performance Computing environments. As containers become a fundamental part of AI/ML workflows and simulation workloads, their seamless integration with HPC infrastructure is a growing priority. This paper captures the key discussions, technological advancements, and future challenges presented during the workshop. Topics include hot-swapping of GPU-based AI jobs, transparent checkpointing, confidential computing, secure multi-tenancy, orchestration of hybrid workloads, and best practices for scalable container environments. These developments reflect the community's convergence around secure, portable, and performant HPC software delivery models.

1 Introduction

The convergence of high-performance computing (HPC), cloud-native technologies, and artificial intelligence (AI) is reshaping scientific computing. Containers, once regarded as tools for ease of packaging, are now critical enablers of workload portability, reproducibility, and agile deployment on diverse compute infrastructures.

The High Performance Container Workshop (HPCW), held annually at International Supercomputing Conference (ISC), serves as a key gathering point for researchers and practitioners to explore the evolving role of containerization

---

A. Azab, C. Kniep, B. Krašovec, H. Gantikow and D. Brayford—These authors contributed equally to this work.

© The Author(s), under exclusive license to Springer Nature Switzerland AG 2026
S. Neuwirth et al. (Eds.): ISC High Performance 2025 Workshops, LNCS 16091, pp. 660–667, 2026.
https://doi.org/10.1007/978-3-032-07612-0_51

in high-performance computing workflows. The 2025 edition showcased significant advances in container runtime support, orchestration systems, GPU and accelerator resource management, and AI-driven applications. In addition, the workshop tackled pressing topics in security and confidential containers, addressing the growing need for data protection and secure execution environments in different HPC scenarios.

This paper presents the scientific contributions of HPCW'25, with a focus on the implications for next-generation HPC systems. It integrates workshop presentations and discussion highlights to outline the state-of-the-art and identify directions for research and production deployments.

2   AI and HPC Convergence

The convergence of artificial intelligence (AI) and high-performance computing (HPC) is rapidly transforming the computing infrastructure and software practices in science and industry. At the HPCW'25 workshop, critical advancements in supporting containerized AI workloads within HPC systems were showcased, revealing a shared goal of making AI workflows more portable, resource-efficient, and accessible on supercomputers. The presentations at the workshop addressed this intersection from architectural, operational, and usability perspectives, with solutions ranging from runtime innovations to federated platforms.

Stoyanov introduced his work on hot-swapping LLMs by migrating inference jobs from active GPU memory to CPU memory to free up the GPU to run a different model. This allows us to serve different models without the complete lifecycle of stopping and starting the process from scratch. Applied within inference serving clusters, it will enable better utilization and faster startup time of LLM inference services [15].

Kniep introduced a GPU-aware checkpointing and live migration system using CRIU and CUDA plugins, allowing inference workloads to be transparently paused, relocated, and restored across compute nodes. This method targets inefficient GPU usage typical of large language model (LLM) inference jobs and enables resource reallocation in shared environments. Their Kubernetes Checkpoint Operator manages life-cycle events for containerized workloads, demonstrating how preemptive AI inference can increase system utilization without compromising correctness [8].

Mansouri shared how LuxProvide restructured the MeluXina supercomputer into a flexible AI platform by layering Kubernetes atop traditional Slurm scheduling. The system supports concurrent use cases, including generative models and bioinformatics pipelines, while providing user-friendly interfaces and curated software stacks for AI practitioners. Operational lessons emphasized the importance of hybrid orchestration, GPU scheduling, and accessible observability tools to effectively support diverse workloads [2].

Azab presented the LUMI AI Factory (LAIF), a federated EuroHPC initiative that integrates LUMI with national OpenStack-based cloud regions to create an AI-optimized supercomputing platform. LAIF exposes GPU resources through containerized workflows and APIs using tools such as Apptainer, MLflow, and Nextflow. This co-designed architecture supports reproducibility and modularity, providing scalable access to foundation model training and inference across user communities [3,5].

Taken together, these contributions show that integrating AI into HPC systems is not solely a hardware challenge, but one of systems co-design, orchestration, and user engagement. Transparent migration techniques, hybrid batch-service scheduling, and federated container-native platforms represent the direction of travel. Containers are no longer just packaging tools; they are becoming central to platform abstraction, workload resilience, and accessibility in AI-driven HPC environments.

3 Runtime and Scheduling Advances

As container-based workloads become commonplace in AI and HPC environments, the capabilities of runtimes and scheduling must evolve to support the execution of dynamic, accelerator-driven jobs. At HPCW 2025, several presentations addressed the need for fine-grained resource allocation, multi-framework orchestration, and compatibility with evolving runtime ecosystems.

CJ Newburn introduced NVIDIA's Dynamic Resource Allocation (DRA), a Kubernetes native interface for precise allocation of GPUs, FPGAs, NICs and other devices to containerized workloads. By pairing DRA with Node Feature Discovery (NFD), the system enables pods to request devices based on hardware characteristics, capabilities, and workload profiles. This granular control enables AI applications to share accelerator resources more efficiently, paving the way for topology-aware scheduling and device-level telemetry integration [13]. The work reflects a growing shift in HPC centers toward composable infrastructure and runtime specialization for accelerator-bound tasks.

Alberto Madonna from CSCS presented the evolution of Sarus, a container runtime tailored for HPC environments, and its integration with Podman. This work brings Open Container Initiative (OCI) compatibility to HPC systems while preserving essential capabilities such as shared MPI environments, parallel file system access, and site-specific security policies. The combination of Sarus and Podman allows users to benefit from container standards and toolchains without sacrificing performance or system integration, thus bridging traditional HPC workflows with modern development ecosystems [11].

Jonathan Sparks explored the orchestration challenges posed by the increasing diversity of container-aware schedulers in HPC. His analysis of the "scheduler soup" highlighted the overlapping roles of Slurm, Flux, Kubernetes, and Nomad, often coexisting within the same system. While this flexibility supports specialized workloads, it creates operational complexity, requiring careful coordination and service segregation. The talk emphasized the need for unified resource views, policy-driven job placement, and standardized APIs to reduce friction and improve maintainability in hybrid scheduler environments.

Collectively, these efforts underscore a pivotal transition in HPC scheduling: from coarse-grained, job-centric models to dynamic, device-aware orchestration frameworks that accommodate containers, accelerators, and multi-tenant workloads. Runtime advances such as DRA and Sarus point toward systems that are not only performance-optimized, but also modular, portable, and developer-friendly.

4 Security and Confidential Computing

Security remains a central concern when deploying containerized workloads in multi-tenant HPC environments, where strong isolation, data confidentiality, and policy enforcement are often mandated by both research and industrial stakeholders. At HPCW 2025, the presenters addressed both system-level hardening and emerging technologies that address these requirements while preserving performance and usability. Industry and SMEs are used to public cloud environments that offer a wide range of versatile tools to improve security, as public clouds - being frequent targets of cyberattacks - have evolved into highly secure platforms. This familiarity has led to expectations that HPC environments provide similar protections, including robust access control and encryption. Importantly, security extends beyond the protection of confidential or sensitive data; it also includes safeguarding proprietary software and innovation. At HPCW'25, the presenters examined how to secure the HPC environment from potentially malicious containers, as well as how to protect containerized workloads from other users of the system, including those with elevated privileges such as administrators. These efforts reflect a comprehensive approach to workload isolation and system integrity, underscoring the critical role of confidential computing in enabling trusted execution and robust security in multi-tenant HPC infrastructure.

In collaboration with Holger Gantikow, Barbara Krašovec presented an overview of the best practices for securing containers in shared HPC clusters. Their analysis emphasized the trade-offs between flexibility and enforcement, particularly when users run arbitrary workloads on privileged systems. Their recommendations included using kernel-level confinement with AppArmor, Linux kernel capabilities and seccomp profiles, secure image provisioning, automated CI/CD deployment, signing and encrypting containers, security monitoring, and using runtime sandboxing techniques that align with organizational policies. With regards to security monitoring, they also suggested considering approaches that take greater consideration of the actual behaviour of the workload, for example at system call level [6,7] GPU usage [16] or communication patterns. The talk also highlighted gaps in existing tools when scaled to HPC environments. These include possible performance regressions from overzealous security profiles and hardware encryption, as well as the lack of fine-grained user namespaces. Their findings support a layered security model that can be selectively tuned depending on workload trust and risk profiles [9,10].

CJ Newburn continued with updates regarding NVIDIA's confidential containers (CoCo). NVIDIA is pushing the boundaries of confidential computing with deep integration of Kata Containers, enabling secure MicroVM-based isolation for GPU workloads in Kubernetes. Its Hopper (H100) and Blackwell (B100)

GPUs feature encrypted memory, attested boot, and hardware root of trust, but B100 takes it further by adopting the TDISP/IDE PCI standard, offloading encryption to the PCIe bus, eliminating performance overhead during intense CPUGPU communication. NVIDIA is also working on expanding support for multi-GPU and virtual GPU (vGPU) setups. Its strategy involves a lift-and-shift approach that enables the seamless migration of existing AI/ML workloads into confidential computing environments. This integration combines LLMs and GPU-accelerated computing, orchestrated via Kubernetes, to strike an effective balance between computational power and data privacy.

Lukáš Hejtmánek and Viktória Spišaková presented practical deployments of confidential computing using Intel SGX and AMD SEV, enabling secure enclave execution of containerized applications on bare-metal systems. Using Kata Containers and gVisor, they demonstrated integration with Kubernetes clusters and showed how trusted execution environments (TEEs) can isolate sensitive code from the host OS and other tenants. Their work within e-INFRA CZ showcased use cases including secure model inference and privacy-preserving analytics. Although TEEs currently impose limitations on memory size and hardware availability, the presenters argued that these constraints are rapidly diminishing with new processor generations. Their experience demonstrates the feasibility of zero-trust execution in scientific computing environments where data sovereignty and auditability are critical [1].

Together, these contributions reveal a maturing landscape for secure container operations in a HPC environment. Kernel hardening techniques offer baseline protections for general workloads, while confidential computing introduces new security guarantees for highly sensitive use cases. A common theme was the need for better tooling integration, both for platform operators and end users, and for community-driven standards that align with the performance and operational needs of large-scale systems.

5 Use Cases and Industry

Insights into the use of containers by industry HPC users were provided by the The Containers in Automotive Engineering segment which was held by Gunter Mayer (Volkswagen AG) and Holger Gantikow (Eviden science + computing).

Gunther Mayer presented the reasons behind the growing use of containers in Volkswagen and the current state of adoption. They rely on Podman as a container engine and use containers to run the applications on its HPC resources for several reasons. Key reasons include a stronger decoupling of the release cycles of the diverse Computer Aided Engineering (CAE) applications and the operating system and an easier opening of HPC resources for AI/ML workloads with a Bring Your Own Container approach. Other valuable benefits include synergies within the broader VW Group and the realization of security improvements through containerized HPC operations.

Holger Gantikow supplemented this with a broader market perspective, in which he introduced the reasons why a broader body of CAE Enterprise users favors containers. This includes standardization of application releases, use of off-premises resources, operation of legacy applications, security benefits, and increased transparency, e.g. through software bills of materials. He also reported on typical barriers to adaptation, such as a lack of images directly from software suppliers, fear of effort and complexity, and hesitation to change established processes. However, an accelerated adaptation of containers is increasingly taking place here, driven by non-traditional workloads such as Advanced Driver Assistance Systems (ADAS) and the rapid increase in the use of AI/ML, both in combination with traditional workloads and Large Language Models (LLMs). A key challenge in the coming years will be the convergence of different environments and the standardization on software controlling the resources.

A report on work in progress was provided by Gunther Meyer and Daniel Stone, which presented their work on using OpenGL and Vulcan streams to enable visual applications to run within the container, but stream the output to the Window manager of the host system. This novel approach is a step up on brittle X11 socket mappings from the past and allows a clean decoupling of the host and container. With OpenGL and Vulcan the separation is stable across multiple OS versions and GPUs [12].

6 Best Practices and Portability

The sustainability and portability of HPC container workflows depend on the adherence to best practices in image design, dependency management, and metadata standardization. The presenters at HPCW 2025 addressed the challenges of long-term maintenance, cross-environment compatibility, and transparent provenance for containerized software stacks used in research and industry.

Brayford presented a set of pragmatic best practices derived from community experience across supercomputing centers and container deployments. His guidance focused on modular image layering, strict version pinning, and reproducible builds using declarative approaches. The emphasis was placed on separating base images from application-specific artefacts to facilitate caching and auditability, as well as adopting tools like Apptainer and ORAS for image signing, verification, and registry integration. These practices enable environments where users can trace lineage, rebuild containers from source, and avoid 'black-box' software artifacts, the key to scientific reproducibility and compliance [4].

Harmen Stoppels presented an automated pipeline for generating container images from Spack-based software definitions, integrated with GitLab CI and metadata annotation. The system builds application stacks into OCI-compliant images with embedded provenance and dependency graphs, facilitating their reuse in diverse environments. This approach addresses the reproducibility and modularity gaps common in manually built containers and supports continuous integration of evolving scientific codes. The pipeline also supports hybrid deployment models, where Spack-generated containers can run, both in Kubernetes clusters and via traditional MPI launchers in batch environments. By combining automation, metadata, and standards compliance, this work demonstrates a path toward a scalable, maintainable, and portable software distribution in HPC [14].

These contributions highlight the increasing maturity of container engineering practices in HPC. As containers shift from prototype enablers to production infrastructure, traceability, automation, and community standards become essential. Toolchains such as Spack, Apptainer, and ORAS are evolving to meet these needs, allowing scientific software to be packaged, verified, and deployed across heterogeneous systems with minimal friction.

7 Conclusion and Outlook

The 11th High Performance Container Workshop at ISC 2025 demonstrated the increasing technical maturity and strategic relevance of container technologies within the HPC and AI infrastructure. The workshop highlighted that containers are no longer treated merely as a mechanism to package software, but are rapidly becoming integral components of scalable, reproducible, and secure scientific computing platforms. As AI workloads continue to grow in complexity and demand flexible, cloud-alike environments, HPC systems will need to evolve, adopting more agile infrastructure that blends classical supercomputing with containerization and cloud capabilities. This transformation not only broadens the appeal of HPC to AI users, but also amplifies the strategic importance of containers as a unifying layer across diverse computational ecosystems. Across a wide range of topics, from GPU hot-swapping and hybrid scheduling frameworks to confidential computing and provenance-aware image pipelines, the presentations collectively revealed a decisive shift toward co-designed, policy-aware, and automation-driven execution environments that embrace containers at their core.

A key insight emerging from the workshop is the necessity of dynamic, fine-grained runtime management to accommodate the non-traditional workload patterns introduced by AI and data-intensive applications. Technologies such as CRIU-based container migration, Kubernetes-native device schedulers like DRA, and hybrid orchestration models reflect a broader architectural transition toward elastic, accelerator-optimized systems. Simultaneously, contributions from security and infrastructure teams underscored that robust container adoption at scale must be underpinned by reproducibility, isolation, and trust—achievable through layered hardening, confidential computing, and signed image registries.

Portability and sustainability were framed not as afterthoughts but as foundational design principles, enabled through declarative software stacks, metadata-rich images, and automated build workflows. The convergence of community-driven standards, tooling maturity, and institutional adoption signals the emergence of containers as a unifying abstraction across traditional HPC, cloud-native AI, and hybrid research platforms.

Looking ahead, the workshop identified several research and operational challenges: intelligent cross-scheduler coordination, scalable support for preemptible inference, standardization of security postures, and seamless integration of provenance metadata into user workflows. Addressing these will require tighter collaboration between HPC centers, software developers, and domain scientists. As the line between HPC and AI continues to blur, container platforms will be instrumental in enabling flexible, trustworthy, and performant infrastructure at the exascale and beyond.

Acknowledgements. We thank the ISC program team, presenters, and attendees. This work is informed by community efforts across EuroHPC, Red Hat, NVIDIA, VW, HPE, MemVerge, and academic institutions.

References

1. Confidential containers on bare metal: Challenges and practices. https://docs.cerit-sc.cz (2025)
2. From HPC clusters to AI platforms: 5 use cases side by side. https://www.lxp.lu/en/about/meluxina (2025)
3. The LUMI AI factory: AI-optimized supercomputing and services. https://www.lumi-supercomputer.eu/ai-factory (2025)
4. Brayford, D.: HPC containers: Best practices and pitfalls. https://container-in-hpc.org/isc/2025/hpcw/index.html (2025)
5. Foundation, E.: AI interoperability and federation blueprint. https://www.egi.eu/projects/ai-blueprint (2024)
6. Gantikow, H., Reich, C., Knahl, M., Clarke, N.: Rule-based security monitoring of containerized environments. In: Ferguson, D., Méndez Muñoz, V., Pahl, C., Helfert, M. (eds.) Cloud Computing and Services Science, pp. 66–86. Springer International Publishing, Cham (2020)
7. Gantikow, H., Zöhner, T., Reich, C.: Container anomaly detection using neural networks analyzing system calls. In: 2020 28th Euromicro International Conference on Parallel, Distributed and Network-Based Processing (PDP), pp. 408–412 (2020). https://doi.org/10.1109/PDP50117.2020.00069
8. Kniep, C.: K8s snapshot/restore operator. https://memverge.com/memverge-ai/transparent-checkpointing/ (2025)
9. Krasovec B., L.D.: Confidential containers in multi-tenant HPC environments. https://ashpc.eu/event/25/attachments/151/300/ashpc25_booklet.pdf (2025)
10. Krasovec B., P.T.: Secure usage of containers in the HPC environment. https://doi.org/10.1007/978-3-031-86240-3_7 (2025)
11. Madonna, A.: Evolving sarus to augment podman for HPC. https://user.cscs.ch/tools/containers/sarus/ (2025)
12. Meyer, G., Stone, D.: Graphicontainer for HPC and workstations. https://container-in-hpc.org/isc/2025/hpcw/index.html (2025)
13. Newburn, C.: Dynamic resource allocation and node feature discovery. https://github.com/NVIDIA/k8s-device-plugin (2025)
14. Stoppels, H.: Spack container images: Sharing and running HPC software. https://spack.io (2025)
15. Stoyanov, R., Spišaková, V., Reber, A.: Transparent hot-swapping of containerized AI/ML workloads. https://arxiv.org/abs/2502.16631 (2025)
16. Zou, P., Li, A., Barker, K., Ge, R.: Detecting anomalous computation with RNNS on GPU-accelerated HPC machines. In: Proceedings of the 49th International Conference on Parallel Processing. ICPP '20, Association for Computing Machinery, New York, NY, USA (2020). https://doi.org/10.1145/3404397.3404435

A2SD: Accelerating Scientific Innovation Through Autonomous Discovery Systems

Michela Taufer[1](✉), Rafael Ferreira da Silva[2], Benjamin Mintz[2], Milad Abolhasani[3], Rosa M. Badia[4], Ewa Deelman[5], Robert G. Moore[2], and John Shalf[6]

[1] University of Tennessee, Knoxville, TN, USA
mtaufer@utk.edu
[2] Oak Ridge National Laboratory, Oak Ridge, TN, USA
[3] North Carolina State University, Raleigh, NC, USA
[4] Barcelona Supercomputing Center, Barcelona, Spain
[5] University of Southern California, Marina del Rey, CA, USA
[6] Lawrence Berkeley National Laboratory, Berkeley, CA, USA

Abstract. The 2025 Advancing Autonomous Scientific Discovery (A2SD) workshop convened researchers from academia, national laboratories, and industry to explore the transformative role of autonomy in scientific discovery. The workshop highlighted a convergence of artificial intelligence, robotics, and computational workflows into autonomous systems capable of accelerating the scientific process. Presentations and discussions spanned autonomous experimentation, intelligent workflow orchestration, digital twins, and agent-based systems for managing complex research ecosystems. Key challenges discussed included interoperability across heterogeneous infrastructures, near real-time data management under FAIR principles, reproducibility, and the integration of human oversight. The workshop also emphasized the need for modular software interfaces, federated learning models, and education initiatives to support a next-generation scientific workforce.

Keywords: Autonomous Scientific Discovery · AI-Driven Workflows · Cyberinfrastructure Interoperability

1 Introduction

The first Workshop on Advancing Autonomous Scientific Discovery (A2SD-2025) [1], held at the ISC High Performance Conference, marked a critical mile-

---

This manuscript has been authored in part by UT-Battelle, LLC, under contract DEAC05-00OR22725 with the US Department of Energy (DOE). The US government retains and the publisher, by accepting the article for publication, acknowledges that the US government retains a nonexclusive, paid-up, irrevocable, worldwide license to publish or reproduce the published form of this manuscript, or allow others to do so, for US government purposes. DOE will provide public access to these results of federally sponsored research in accordance with the DOE Public Access Plan (http://energy.gov/downloads/doe-public-access-plan).

stone in the evolution of scientific research. Against the backdrop of increasing complexity in modern scientific challenges and the growing volume of data from advanced instruments, the workshop brought together leaders from academia, national laboratories, and industry to explore how autonomous systems are reshaping the landscape of discovery. The aim was to assess the state of the art, identify common challenges, and foster cross-disciplinary dialogue toward the development of scalable, interoperable, and intelligent autonomous infrastructures.

Autonomous science [7] represents a paradigm shift that blends artificial intelligence (AI), robotics, and computational workflows into a cohesive framework capable of accelerating scientific cycles. This transformation promises to shorten the path from hypothesis to validation by enabling systems that can reason, adapt, and act with minimal human intervention. Participants at A2SD-2025 emphasized the value of tightly coupled loops between theory, experiment, and computation, where autonomous agents can drive discovery by optimizing experimental parameters, orchestrating workflows across facilities, and learning from previous results. The workshop demonstrated that, while progress has been substantial, realizing the full potential of autonomous discovery requires addressing persistent challenges in integration, reproducibility, and human-AI collaboration.

A2SD-2025 presentations highlighted a broad range of use cases, ranging from edge-to-cloud computational workflows to autonomous synthesis platforms and digital twin-enhanced experimentation. Discussions emphasized how experimental and computational domains, often seen as distinct, are increasingly converging. Common technical themes such as scheduling, fault tolerance, and resource elasticity now span both domains. Several discussions underscored the need for systems that can operate across heterogeneous infrastructures, from local instruments and edge devices to high-performance computing (HPC) and cloud environments. Portability, abstraction, and co-design emerged as foundational principles for building resilient and scalable autonomy.

In addition to technical depth, the workshop also emphasized broader ecosystem-level considerations. These include standardization of agent interfaces, mechanisms for federated learning and model sharing, and protocols for handling sensitive data and intellectual property. The discussions expanded into education, workforce development, and policy, recognizing that building an autonomous science infrastructure is not only a technical endeavor but also a cultural and organizational transformation. The need to democratize access to advanced experimentation and foster fair participation across institutions was framed as essential to the future of autonomous discovery.

This paper synthesizes the key insights, findings, and community-driven recommendations from A2SD-2025. It draws upon the workshop presentations, panel discussions, and shared notes to provide a brief state-of-the-art review.

2 Technological Foundations and Advances in Autonomous Scientific Discovery

Several presentations showcased how autonomous experimentation is rapidly transforming the pace and scale of scientific discovery. Speakers emphasized the transition from domain-specific automation to modular, experiment-agnostic platforms. These systems incorporate digital twins, virtual representations of physical experiments, to enable near real-time monitoring, simulation, and optimization. Prof. Milad Abolhasani highlighted how digital twins are used not only to guide decision-making in microfluidics and chemical synthesis but also to reduce the reliance on trial and error by simulating outcomes before physical execution [6]. Reinforcement learning was presented as a key technique for rapidly identifying optimal experimental policies, with AI agents generating their training data to fine-tune decision strategies. The integration of miniaturized systems and robotic platforms further accelerates iteration cycles and reduces material waste.

In parallel with experimental advances, the workshop featured multiple contributions focused on the automation of computational workflows. Dr. Rosa M. Badia outlined how workflow engines, such as PyCOMPSs [2], enable autonomous execution in heterogeneous environments, including HPC clusters, cloud services, and edge devices [4]. These systems support runtime decisions for scheduling, failure handling, and resource reallocation, key capabilities for scalable and resilient scientific computing. Features such as fault tolerance policies, dynamic resource elasticity, task checkpointing, and hardware-aware task constraints enable workflows to adapt to changing execution contexts without requiring human intervention. The ability to orchestrate computations across an edge-to-cloud continuum was seen to be highly synergistic with experimental autonomy, creating opportunities for seamless integration of data acquisition, processing, and interpretation.

Several talks advanced a vision of AI agents that go beyond automation to actively contribute to scientific reasoning. Dr. Rob Moore and Dr. John Shalf emphasized the role of agentic AI in managing complex and distributed research ecosystems. These agents act as digital scientific assistants, helping to automate hypothesis testing, monitor experimental states, and recommend next steps based on historical data and learned models. They operate in physical labs, edge devices, and supercomputers, acting as intelligent intermediaries that can coordinate workflows and adapt strategies based on near real-time data. Real-world applications presented at the workshop illustrated how intelligent agents are being used to coordinate multi-stage scientific processes, manage resources across facilities, and support adaptive experimentation in various domains. This agent-based paradigm requires deep co-design that spans software, hardware, data, and experimental protocols to enable interoperability, reuse, and reproducibility across institutions.

An emerging theme across the presentations was the tight coupling of experimental and computational workflows to form autonomous discovery loops. Prof. Ewa Deelman and Prof. Michela Taufer presented compelling examples where high-level workflow abstractions are compiled into executable pipelines that span multiple facilities, ensuring provenance and reproducibility throughout the process. These workflows must navigate challenges such as asynchronous data flows, heterogeneous instrumentation, and policy-based access constraints. Abstraction layers, such as those implemented in Pegasus [3] and PyCOMPSs, have been shown to facilitate the integration of diverse components, allowing scientists to focus on domain-specific questions. National initiatives, such as the National Science Data Fabric (NSDF) [8] [5], aim to provide a shared cyberinfrastructure that connects distributed instruments, storage, and compute environments. NSDF is an example of a software ecosystem that enables live autonomous steering of a neutron diffraction experiment by integrating near real-time data streaming, persistent storage, and interactive dashboards with Bayesian active learning methods to dynamically adjust measurement parameters and optimize scientific discovery. These capabilities align with the goals of autonomous science by enabling near real-time data curation, metadata enrichment, and federated access to AI-ready datasets across institutions.

A shared emphasis on reproducibility in both computational and experimental domains highlighted the need for standardized metadata, robust fault handling strategies, and transparent decision making to ensure the credibility and transferability of results from autonomous science. The workshop also raised concerns about reproducibility challenges across geographic and institutional boundaries, where differences in data formats, experimental setups, and regulatory constraints can hinder consistent replication of results.

3 Cross-Cutting Challenges and Collaborative Opportunities in Autonomous Science

During the discussion sessions, the participants explored the tension between the desire for standardization and the variety of experimental and computational environments. Although universal standards could facilitate broader integration, institutional constraints and unique hardware-software combinations often require flexible and layered approaches. Several speakers noted that full standardization may be unrealistic, but shared abstractions and modular interfaces could offer a practical path forward. Abstraction layers were proposed as a way to enable interoperability across heterogeneous systems without imposing rigid constraints. Participants also reflected on past efforts to generalize software across domains, recognizing that although full generalization was often not achievable, many underlying patterns and design principles could still be reused and adapted to new settings. The discussions acknowledged that many laboratories rely on custom-built instruments with proprietary interfaces, underscoring the need for adaptable middleware that can abstract hardware-specific details while facilitating workflow interoperability.

Data management has emerged as one of the most pressing and complex issues facing autonomous science. The discussions emphasized the importance of applying the FAIR principles [9] in near real-time, from data collection to long-term storage and reuse. The participants discussed the value of federated data architectures, which allow each institution to maintain control while enabling cross-facility collaboration. There was strong support for tools that can automatically capture metadata and assess data quality, especially given the scale and velocity of modern experimental systems. The topic of model sharing also featured prominently, with federated learning identified as a promising technique to move models instead of data. This approach not only enhances privacy and security but also supports scalable collaboration and decentralized innovation. Participants also emphasized the importance of publishing negative results and retaining rich metadata from autonomous workflows, recognizing that failed experiments can provide valuable training data and help prevent redundant exploration.

The role of human oversight in autonomous workflows was a recurring theme throughout the discussions. While autonomy can reduce manual workload and improve efficiency, participants stressed the need for well-defined protocols to determine when and where human input should remain essential. Examples from both experimental and computational workflows illustrated the risks of removing human judgment too early, especially when safety, credibility, or ethics are involved. Ethical considerations included the risk of indoctrinated science driven solely by data, without adequate theoretical grounding, and the potential propagation of bias in AI models trained on unbalanced or simulated datasets. There was also concern about overreliance on AI systems without a clear understanding of their limitations. To address these concerns, the group emphasized the need for transparent decision-making processes, validation mechanisms, and frameworks that allow scientists to inspect and override automated actions when necessary.

Participants agreed that technological progress must be accompanied by thoughtful investment in education and community development. Training the next generation of scientists to work alongside autonomous systems will require rethinking traditional curricula. Suggestions included integrating AI and data literacy into scientific education, developing hands-on training with virtual or simulated laboratories, and creating interdisciplinary programs that blend physical sciences, computing, and ethics. Beyond education, there was a strong call to democratize access to autonomous laboratory capabilities. This involves creating infrastructure that supports collaboration across institutions with varying resources and ensuring that scientific contributions across communities are recognized and valued. Community-driven initiatives and open platforms were identified as crucial tools for promoting equitable participation and advancing shared progress.

> **KEY RECOMMENDATIONS:**
>
> - Develop modular and interoperable software interfaces that support integration across heterogeneous experimental and computational systems.
> - Implement federated data management and model sharing frameworks that enforce the FAIR principles and protect data privacy.
> - Establish clear human-in-the-loop protocols to ensure scientific oversight and accountability in autonomous workflows.
> - Redesign scientific education to include AI, data management, and ethics as core components of training for future researchers.
> - Promote an open and collaborative infrastructure to democratize access to autonomous research tools and broaden community participation.

4 Conclusion

The A2SD-2025 workshop highlighted both the promise and complexity of building autonomous scientific discovery systems that can operate in various experimental and computational environments. Through a series of presentations and in-depth discussions, participants identified critical opportunities to advance autonomy in science, including the integration of intelligent agents, the coupling of digital twins with near real-time decision-making, and the development of resilient and reproducible workflows. Equally important were the cross-cutting challenges related to data management, system interoperability, human oversight, and fair access. As this field continues to evolve, long-term collaboration will require collaboration between disciplines, institutions, and communities. The insights and recommendations of this workshop offer a foundation for shaping a future in which autonomous systems accelerate discovery while preserving scientific rigor, open access, and trust.

Acknowledgments. We gratefully acknowledge all A2SD-2025 workshop participants for their valuable presentations, insights, and discussions. This research used resources of the Oak Ridge Leadership Computing Facility, and is sponsored by the INTERSECT Initiative as part of the Laboratory Directed Research and Development Program of Oak Ridge National Laboratory, supported by the Office of Science of the U.S. Department of Energy under Contract No. DE-AC05-00OR22725 and Lawrence Berkeley National Laboratory under Contract No. DE-AC02-05CH11231 with the U.S. Department of Energy. The material presented in the workshop is based on work supported by the National Science Foundation under Grant No. #2449103, #2513101, #2331152, #2223704, #2138811, #2103845. BSC authors acknowledge the partial support of projects PID2019-107255GB, CEX2021-001148-S, and PID2023-147979NB-C21 from the MCIN/AEI and MICIU/AEI /10.13039/501100011033 and by FEDER, UE, and by the Departament de Recerca i Universitats de la Generalitat de Catalunya, research group MPiEDist (2021 SGR 00412).

References

1. 1st Advancing Autonomous Scientific Discovery (A2SD-2025) Workshop. https://autonomousscience.org/workshops/a2sd-2025/ (2025)
2. Badia, R.M., Conejero, J., Ejarque, J., Lezzi, D., Lordan, F.: Pycompss as an instrument for translational computer science. Comput. Sci. Eng. **24**(2), 79–84 (2022)
3. Deelman, E., et al.: Pegasus, a workflow management system for science automation. Futur. Gener. Comput. Syst. **46**, 17–35 (2015)
4. Lordan, F., Casas-Moreno, X., Cummins, P., Conejero, J., Badia, R.M., Sirvent, R.: Taming the swarm: a role-based approach for autonomous agents. In: European Conference on Parallel Processing, pp. 15–25. Springer (2025)
5. Luettgau, J., et al.: Nsdf-services: integrating networking, storage, and computing services into a testbed for democratization of data delivery. In: Proceedings of the IEEE/ACM 16th International Conference on Utility and Cloud Computing, pp. 1–10 (2023)
6. Sadeghi, S., et al.: A self-driving fluidic lab for data-driven synthesis of lead-free perovskite nanocrystals. Digital Discovery (2025)
7. Ferreira da Silva, R., et al.: A grassroots network and community roadmap for interconnected autonomous science laboratories for accelerated discovery. arXiv preprint arXiv:2506.17510 (2025)
8. Taufer, M., et al.: Enhancing scientific research with fair digital objects in the national science data fabric. IEEE Comput. Sci. Eng. (CiSE) **25**(5), 39–47 (2023). https://doi.org/10.1109/MCSE.2024.3363828
9. Wilkinson, M.D., et al.: The fair guiding principles for scientific data management and stewardship. Sci. Data **3**(1), 1–9 (2016)

The Future of Benchmarks in Supercomputing

Sreenivas Rangan Sukumar[1(✉)], Jack C. Wells[2], and Roy Varghese[3]

[1] Hewlett Packard Enterprise (HPE), Spring, Texas, USA
ssrangan@hpe.com
[2] NVDIA, Santa Clara, California, USA
[3] Microsoft, Redmond, Washington, USA

Abstract. The advent of the Exascale era is transforming supercomputing, integrating new workflows that encompass simulations, data science, and artificial intelligence. This evolution necessitates a critical re-evaluation of how the supercomputing community assesses performance. To address this, a dedicated workshop was convened with the central aim of exploring and debating the future of performance benchmarks. The workshop featured presentations and interactive panel discussions, drawing expertise from prominent benchmarking communities. Key figures and stakeholders from industry, academia, and government participated, fostering a comprehensive dialogue on the necessity and desirability of developing a benchmark suite that accurately reflects and accommodates these emerging applications. This paper summarizes the insights and discussions from this pivotal workshop, offering a state-of-the-art overview of the ongoing efforts to evolve supercomputing benchmarks.

Keywords: Benchmarking · High performance computing (HPC) · Artificial Intelligence (AI) · Scientific Workflows

1 Introduction

1.1 Workshop Purpose

As supercomputing welcomes new workflows of simulations, data science and artificial intelligence in the Exascale era, the goal of this workshop was to pose, engage, debate, and address the question - "How should the supercomputing community evolve performance benchmarks?". The workshop was organized as presentations and panel discussions with audience participation that invited active members of the TOP500 [4], MilaBench [5], JUPITER [6] benchmark community and key personnel from industry (HPE, NVIDIA, Microsoft, etc.), academia (University of Southern California and

---

Workshop Speakers and Contributors: Horst Simon (ADIA Lab, UAE), Kalyan Kumaran (Argonne National Lab, USA), Andreas Herten (Juelich Supercomputing Center, Germany), Xavier Bouthillier (University of Montreal, Canada), Ewa Deelman (University of Southern California, USA), Michael Ringenburg (Microsoft, USA), Harun Bayraktar and John Gunnels (NVIDIA, USA)

University of Montreal), and government (Argonne National Lab) to discuss the value, need and desire for evolving a benchmark suite that is inclusive and accommodative of emerging applications to guide future supercomputing system design and architecture.

This document summarizes the key discussions and presentations from the "Future of Benchmarking in Supercomputing" workshop [1] held at ISC 2025 in Hamburg, Germany, on June 13, 2025.

1.2 Workshop Organization

The workshop session was organized to get community feedback on the following themes:

- How can we ensure that the next generation of supercomputers are well-designed and architected to meet the needs of the community?
- How can we design benchmarks that challenge and inspire computational and computer scientists and engineers like HPL did with TOP500 [4]?
- What applications and metrics are the most relevant to scientists? How can these metrics be captured for purchase/procurement decisions?

More specifically, the invited speakers and panelists were asked to provide their viewpoints on one or more of the following questions:

- How could benchmarks encourage creativity to counter the end of Dennard scaling and slowing down of Moore's Law for a post-Exascale future?
- Do you see the benchmarks of the future introducing sustainability and responsible use of HPC?
- Benchmarks have traditionally been artifacts of research. Who should own the benchmarks? Community? Industry? A consortium?
- Recent draft RFPs have emphasized on workflow creativity. Do existing benchmarks capture" workflow" elements?
- Benchmarks play a pivotal role in the cost of innovation for chips, network, and software towards national competitiveness. How can we as a community drive innovation with benchmarks? Any Ideas?
- Limited to no cross-leverage between supercomputing and cloud-computing practices are contributing to duplicated efforts (at times reinventing concepts). How can this be bridged with benchmarks?
- We will need the simplicity of TOP500, the inclusivity of MLPerf and openness of MLCommons. Please share your thoughts on best-practices to bring the best of these worlds and evolve at the pace of technology.

2 Workshop Proceedings

2.1 Workshop Keynote

Keynote Presented by Horst Simon, ADIA Lab

Horst Simon's keynote presentation defined "benchmarking in supercomputing" as evaluating system performance using standardized tests to measure metrics like processing speed, memory bandwidth, I/O throughput, scalability, and energy efficiency that serves several purposes such as.

- Comparing different high-performance computing (HPC) systems objectively.
- Tracking progress in computational capabilities over time.
- Guiding system design and procurement.
- Communicating community priorities to sponsors and the broader society.

The presentation showcased the seminal TOP500 list [4] used in HPC over the last three decades, which ranks the 500 most powerful computers worldwide using the R_{max} of LINPACK (solving $Ax = b$, a matrix-matrix multiplication dense linear algebra problem). Over the three decades, different missions and motivating applications have used the world's supercomputers for extracting scientific and strategic insights. The drive to build faster systems motivated by the race to top the list is what has created the inseparable relationship between HPC and artificial intelligence (AI) today. Horst's presentation posited that HPC has become a transformative force in AI and machine learning by handling massive datasets and complex algorithms with unparalleled speed and efficiency. HPC accelerates deep learning through massive parallel computations and enables the training of large language models and computer vision applications, as well as advancements in AI algorithms like reinforcement learning and generative AI.

After framing AI as the new "HPC killer app", the presentation highlighted that traditional HPC has expanded to include AI workloads, leading to the rise of "Enterprise AI" (new organizations acquiring HPC for AI) and "Hyperscale AI" (large organizations with AI-focused cloud infrastructure). This convergence necessitates a reevaluation of benchmarking – one that is motivated by new algorithms in practice, the business model of margins associated with efficiency of the compute cycles accessed on cloud infrastructure, responsible energy use in data centers, market-driven needs, investment budgets and desire for HPC from mega-cap hyperscale companies rivalling open government-funded academic innovation. In other words, HPC was historically motivated by computational physics applications, driving innovation with the Von Neumann architecture for large-scale, floating-point intense, 2D or 3D grid-based computations. However, this same architecture is now used for social networking, web searches, music, photography, and AI, indicating potential architectural and algorithmic gaps and challenges for future AI and HPC growth and innovation.

2.2 Emerging Benchmarks

Benchmarks for Leadership Class Systems by Kalyan Kumaran, Argonne National Lab

The Argonne Leadership Computing Facility (ALCF) has a well-established practice of creating tailored benchmark suites for each of its system procurements. These benchmarks are designed to represent the range of scientific applications typically run on ALCF systems, while also aligning with the goals and priorities of upcoming use-cases. At this workshop, Kalyan shared recent progress on defining a benchmark suite for ALCF-4 (looking 2–5 years ahead into the post-Exascale era) [7]. This set of benchmarks reflects key areas of interest for the system—artificial intelligence, modeling and simulation, and scientific workflows. The presentation listed scientific applications anticipated during the ALCF-4 timeframe, spanning science domains such as Computational Fluid Dynamics, Cosmology, Earth Sciences, Quantum Monte Carlo, Material Sciences, Biological Sciences, and Molecular Dynamics with a mapping of performance expectations of compute, memory capacity, memory bandwidth, point-to-point communication, collective communication and storage sub-systems. Recent additions to traditional simulation benchmarks like HACC and QMCPACK include AI-specific tests like LLM Training (AuroraGPT) and Inference (Llama-405B), Vision Transformers (ViT), and DBSCAN, and workflow benchmarks such as nekRS-GNN. Kalyan communicated that micro-benchmarks like ALCF AI-Communication Benchmarks [8], DLIO, OSU MPI Benchmarks, HPL, HPL-MxP, IOR/mdTest, STREAM, HPCG, and GEMM (across data types) along with functionality and reliability tests will also be included in the suite.

Benchmarks for the first Exascale System in Europe by Andreas Herten, Juelich Supercomputing Centre.

To procure the first exascale supercomputer in Europe, JUPITER, a comprehensive benchmark suite was developed to incorporate a diverse set of real-world applications and synthetic benchmarks. Designed on the principles of replicability, reproducibility and reusability, the JUPITER Benchmark Suite was published [9], released as open-source software [6] and used to evaluate systems based on total-cost-of-ownership/value-for-money and scalability as key figures of merit during the procurement process. Andreas Herten presented an overview of the benchmark suite, design decisions and reference results and shared experiences of the creation process that are influencing the plans of benchmarking the future HPC systems at Juelich Supercomputing Centre.

Benchmarking Suite for GPU-Intensive AI Pipelines Presented by Xavier Bouthillier, Mila at University of Montreal.

Xavier Bouthillier introduced Milabench [5], a benchmarking suite specifically designed for GPU-intensive AI pipelines. The motivation for Milabench was that AI workloads, particularly those driven by deep learning, are introducing novel usage patterns to HPC systems that are not comprehensively captured by standard HPC benchmarks. The presentation specifically attributed the following limitations in current benchmarking practices around AI pipelines:

- Snapshot Analysis: Publications are often based on projects completed a year prior, making it difficult to project future trends without analyzing further into the past and combining with surveys to account for new events.
- Model Anatomies: Models share many common parts, which are hard to account for by simply looking at model names. A way to represent models with computational graphs, based on paper descriptions or associated codebases, is needed. Furthermore, model complexity (and size) doubled every 6 months on state-of-the-art models until 2024.
- Training and Evaluation Procedures: There is often a mix of training and inference in real-world AI workflows, making it difficult to pinpoint the exact balance based solely on published papers.

As one of the largest academic research centers dedicated to deep learning, Mila identified the need to develop, maintain and evolve a custom benchmarking suite to address the diverse requirements of the fast-paced AI research community. Last year, the benchmarking suite was updated using a novel methodology [10] leveraging large language models (LLMs) to analyze the whole corpus of 867 papers published in 2023. This semi-automated analysis provided the Mila team with a better understanding of the research landscape (state-of-the-art AI models, libraries, kernels) and representative coverage from actual practice. The talk walked through the design process behind the

The Future of Benchmarks in Supercomputing   679

latest version of Milabench and the resulting 42 benchmarks (interestingly 26 of them are used for procurement decisions and 16 for in-depth analysis and research). This clever and creative approach using LLMs to evolve benchmarks could be used in practice to evolve HPC benchmarks in the future.

2.3 Benchmarking the End-To-End Workflow

Benchmarking with Workflows and Workflow Management Systems Presented by Ewa Deelman, University of Southern California, Information Sciences Institute.

Ewa Deelman's presentation highlighted the increasing complexity of supercomputing workloads, moving beyond single HPC applications to intricate workflows (single-site, multi-site, federated, instrument-in-the-loop, etc.). The presentation emphasized that data flow, interconnect performance, and file system interactions significantly influence overall performance and argued that benchmarks must capture end-to-end workflow performance and not just singular applications. Workflows often involve numerous small files and a high job count, necessitating intelligent scheduling capabilities for time-critical computations compared to single application runs.

One key example among several presented was the CyberShake workflow [11], which demonstrated substantial computational and data requirements. This workflow combined large-scale parallel CPU and GPU jobs with high-throughput computing (HTC) tasks, requiring a high degree of automation for continuous execution. The CyberShake workflow for a single site, including small jobs, involved 77,020 tasks, 2090 node-hours, and generates 2025 GB of output data. For the full region, it scaled to 25.8 million tasks, 700,000 node-hours, and 680 TB of data. The successful execution of CyberShake on ORNL's Summit supercomputer for 108 days, utilizing the Pegasus Workflow Management System, underscored the need for benchmarks that capture the nuances of real-world scientific long-duration workflows. The presentation stressed the importance of workflow management systems towards understanding workflow execution (job, task, resource usage, data transfer, provenance, system reliability etc.) and deriving additional performance statistics.

Benchmarking the Whole Workflow Presented by Mike Ringenburg, Microsoft Azure HPC & AI.

Michael Ringenburg from Microsoft Azure HPC & AI posed critical questions regarding the current state and future of benchmarking, particularly emphasizing the need to benchmark the "whole workflow". The talk highlighted a significant gap between traditional benchmarks and how systems are used in practice in a cloud-native world.

Ringenburg provided a real-world example of this gap: large AI models are data-hungry, consuming diverse formats and types of data (structured vs. unstructured), often requiring extensive preprocessing steps like deduplication, clustering, filtering, and image/video transformation. The presentation argued that data acquisition and ingestion are also non-trivial and involve significant compute spend with characteristics very different from model training. The gap in practice versus reality is that benchmarks chase the computationally intensive elements of the workflow ignoring these crucial early stages of interactive and iterative experimentation. These early iterative stages consume over 70% of the time-to-solution on most workflows – and speeding-up the compute-heavy parts of the workflow by 10× does not translate to a similar speed up for the end-to-end workflow.

The presentation questioned the current approach of relying on proxy applications or Mini-apps, which are considered "close enough" but may not accurately predict future usage of large systems over five or more years. To address this gap, several avenues were suggested:

- *Extend the Mini-app concept*: Potentially developing "mini-workflows" or "interactive mini-apps" that include latency of responses to queries/requests.
- *Diversify benchmarks*: Including all stages of the workflow, such as data ingestion and preprocessing, and emerging application areas.
- *Move away from a single performance score*: Instead, consider a score based on system balance, penalizing systems strong in some areas but weak in others. This requires balancing complexity and utility.

Evolving Benchmarks in an Era of Rapid AI & HPC Innovations Presented by Harun Bayraktar and John Gunnels, NVIDIA.

Harun Bayraktar and John Gunnels from NVIDIA also addressed the profound impact of AI on HPC and the consequent need for benchmarks to evolve. They highlighted the exponential growth in computation used to train notable AI systems across various domains like biology, games, image generation, language, robotics, speech, and vision. This growth, spanning from 2015 to 2024, showed training computation reaching billions of petaflops.

The presentation detailed the advancements in single GPU matrix multiplication performance and Tensor Core throughput across NVIDIA GPU generations, from Volta (V100) to Blackwell (B200). Significant improvements have been made in reduced and mixed precision support, including FP64, FP32, TF32, FP16, BF16, FP8 (E4M3, E5M2), and INT8. These developments in chip design, manufacturing, and algorithms have created a virtuous cycle driving performance.

The presentation put forth a provocative proposal to define representative benchmarks for the future:

- Leverage Gordon Bell Finalists/Winners to define scientifically relevant benchmarks.
- Focus on whole applications or key computational kernels.
- Encourage reproducibility of artifacts.
- Annually review and replace/delete benchmarks based on relevance to ensure they survive the test of time.
- Propose outcome-based metrics beyond FLOP/s or OP/s, such as time-to-solution, energy-saved etc.

This approach calls for an international committee to establish rules, processes, and ensure community buy-in for longevity.

2.4 Audience and Community Engagement Panels

During the workshop, the presentations were followed by two community-engagement panels (with our speakers as panelists) as a forum for debate and brainstorming future directions for benchmarks. Some of the key ideas raised during the panel discussions are summarized below:

- Recent procurements in HPC are beginning to incorporate a wider variety of applications (e.g. NERSC-10 [12], JSC [6], OLCF-6 [13], ATS-5 [14] etc.) with innovative scoring metrics (TOP500, Sustained system improvement -SSI, workflow-SSI, node-level SSI, etc.) that is inclusive of diverse figures-of-merit (speed-up, throughput, etc.).
- Expansion of lists like TOP500 to include Green500, HPCG, HPL-MxP, and MLPerf to cover edge, mobile, and datacenter scenarios, including storage, safety, and algorithmic benchmarks.
- "Comprehensive benchmarking" – to capture performance challenges of the end-to-end workflow and not just single applications.
- Introducing new benchmarks regularly via working groups to address evolving needs and keeping benchmarks relevant and fertile for innovation.

3 Conclusions

The presentations, panels and the audience [2, 3] collectively observed that the traditional benchmarking approach to engineer performance by design, i.e., building supercomputers within power and cost budgets to perform "as many" floating point operations a second has served as a directional compass for many years. The workshop participants concluded that it is indeed time to rethink this approach because existing benchmarks are:

- Not as inclusive/representative/comprehensive of the emerging use-cases in data-science and artificial intelligence (that need more data throughput, bandwidth, memory capacity, carbon-awareness etc.)
- Driving vendors and architects to design bespoke compute architectures that do not address a broader community interest in end-to-end workflows.
- Leading to proliferation of community-specific benchmarks (HPL, HPCG, MLPerf, etc.)
- Curbing creativity for better processor architectures (mixed precision arithmetic, data, model and tensor parallelism, etc.)
- Losing relevance that they are no-more considered competitive or worthwhile (e.g., organizations choosing not to submit results for Top500 or MLPerf)

The workshop underscored a collective recognition that traditional benchmarking methodologies, while valuable, are no longer sufficient to capture the complexities and diverse demands of modern supercomputing, particularly with the explosive growth of AI. The discussions highlighted the need for immediate and clear shift towards evaluating "whole workflows" rather than isolated components, emphasizing real-world use-cases, data processing, and the multifaceted nature of AI-driven computations. Proposals for future benchmarks include leveraging real-world scientific achievements, focusing on complete workflows, enhancing reproducibility, and developing new metrics beyond raw computational power to reflect system balance, carbon awareness and time-to-solution emerged. The ongoing efforts by various organizations to diversify benchmarks and incorporate all stages of computational workflows signal a promising direction for more relevant and representative evaluations of supercomputing systems. Enthused by the participation and audience engagement, the organizers look forward to engaging the community and re-imagining benchmarks based on these inputs at future meetings.

References

1. The Future of Benchmarks in Supercomputing Workshop Website, https://sites.google.com/view/thefutureofbenchmarks, last accessed July 4, 2025
2. Workshop Slides from ISC 2025, https://sites.google.com/view/thefutureofbenchmarks/agenda-at-isc-25/abstractsslides, last accessed July 4, 2025
3. Audience participation and social media engagement, https://www.linkedin.com/posts/torsten-hoefler_hpc-ai-activity-7340660242537492481-gGHl/ , last accessed July 4, 2025
4. TOP500 Benchmark, https://top500.org/ , last accessed July 4, 2025
5. Milabench benchmark source code, https://github.com/mila-iqia/milabench, last accessed July 4, 2025
6. JUPITER benchmark source code, https://github.com/FZJ-JSC/jubench, last accessed July 4, 2025
7. ALCF-4 benchmark source code, https://github.com/argonne-lcf/alcf4_benchmarks, last accessed July 4, 2025
8. ALCF AI-Communication benchmark source code, https://github.com/argonne-lcf/alcf4_aibenchmarks/tree/main/AICommsBench , last accessed July 4, 2025
9. JUPITER benchmark suite description, https://arxiv.org/abs/2408.17211, last accessed July 4, 2025
10. Milabench benchmark suite description, https://arxiv.org/abs/2411.11940, last accessed July 4, 2025
11. Callaghan, Scott, et al. "Using open-science workflow tools to produce SCEC CyberShake physics-based probabilistic seismic hazard models." *Frontiers in High Performance Computing* 2 (2024): 1360720
12. NERSC-10 Benchmark Suite, https://gitlab.com/NERSC/N10-benchmarks/run-rules-and-ssi/-/blob/main/N10_Benchmark_RunRules.pdf, last accessed July 4, 2025
13. OLCF-6 Benchmark Suite - https://www.olcf.ornl.gov/draft-olcf-6-technical-requirements/benchmarks/, last accessed July 4, 2025
14. ATS-5 Benchmark Suite - https://lanl.github.io/benchmarks/, last accessed July 4, 2025

RSEHPC@ISC25: Tools and Techniques for Continuous Integration and Benchmarking

René Caspart[1]( ), Robert Speck[2], and Michele Mesiti[1]

[1] Scientific Computing Center, Karlsruhe Institute of Technology,
Karlsruhe, Germany
{rene.caspart,michele.mesiti}@kit.edu
[2] Jülich Supercomputing Centre, Forschungszentrum Jülich GmbH, Jülich, Germany
r.speck@fz-juelich.de

Abstract. This summary paper presents the outcomes of the RSEHPC workshop at ISC25, which convened experts from the Research Software Engineering and High-Performance Computing communities to examine the integration of Continuous Integration and Continuous Benchmarking (CI/CB) throughout the HPC system life cycle. Through keynote and lightning talks as well as through lively discussions, participants explored the use of CI/CB from system design and procurement to deployment and production use. The paper highlights three case studies: KIT's CI/CB services in production for flexible HPC benchmarking; JSC's deployment of exaCB for system-wide benchmarking during the JUPITER exascale system preparations; and RIKEN R-CCS's integration of CI/CB in the early design phase of the FugakuNEXT project. User perspectives from software developers of projects like OpenFOAM, PIConGPU, and libNEGF underscore both the growing importance and the practical challenges of implementing CI/CB in diverse and complex HPC environments. A recurring theme is the tension between the need for customized solutions and the drawbacks of fragmentation, which hinder reproducibility, portability, and collaboration. The paper concludes with a call to action for the HPC community to establish common standards for CI/CB workflows and data formats. By making benchmarking practices more FAIR (Findable, Accessible, Interoperable, Reproducible), the community can enhance software sustainability and operational excellence in HPC ecosystems.

Keywords: Research Software Engineering · High-Performance Computing · Continuous Integration · Continuous Benchmarking

1 Introduction and Motivation

When developing research software, it is often relevant to track its performance over time. It is even vital when targeting HPC architectures. Changes in the

© The Author(s), under exclusive license to Springer Nature Switzerland AG 2026
S. Neuwirth et al. (Eds.): ISC High Performance 2025 Workshops, LNCS 16091, pp. 683–692, 2026.
https://doi.org/10.1007/978-3-032-07612-0_54

software itself, the tool chains used, or the system setup should not compromise how fast users obtain their results. Ideally, performance or scalability should only ever increase. Hence, benchmarking need to be an integral part of testing, in particular for HPC codes. At the same time, up-to-date benchmarks that are publicly available can advertise the code and the machines running them, informing users how to set up the software in the most ideal way or whether they are achieving the expected performance. To limit the burden on developers, the aforementioned steps should be automated within continuous integration (CI) practices, introducing continuous benchmarking (CB) to it. For HPC, an added complexity is the requirement of more than the usual CI backends, with access to longer running steps, more resources than available on a single node, and a diverse range of architectures on which the software needs to be tested.

This summary paper presents key discussions and insights from an ISC25 workshop that brought together experts from the Research Software Engineering (RSE) and High-Performance Computing (HPC) communities to explore the role of Continuous Integration and Continuous Benchmarking (CI/CB) across the full spectrum of HPC activities. The workshop was framed by keynote talks that addressed how CI/CB practices can be applied throughout the life cycle of HPC systems, from the early planning and procurement phases to the operational deployment and long-term maintenance. Central to the discussions were two distinct but complementary perspectives: that of the users, concerned with software development, performance tracking, and reproducibility; and that of system operators, focused on infrastructure management, reliability, and automation. Through shared experiences, the workshop surfaced both success stories and cautionary tales, offering a nuanced view of CI/CB adoption in practice. This paper summarizes those contributions and outlines potential paths forward for integrating CI/CB more deeply and effectively within the HPC ecosystem.

2 CI/CB Throughout the Life Cycle of HPC Systems

CI/CB plays a key role throughout the entire life cycle of an HPC system. In production environments, it offers valuable information and feedback to users and research software engineers. However, this needs to be paired with reliable and easily accessible services for CI/CB. Even earlier, CI/CB plays an important role when commissioning a cluster and supporting users with transitioning to a new cluster as well as in the designing phase. This section presents the key findings from three HPC centers, offering and leveraging CI/CB at various stages of the life cycle.

2.1 The Past, the Present and the Future of CI/CB at NHR@KIT

Since 2021, NHR@KIT has actively developed and promoted a flexible and user-friendly CI/CB service tailored to the needs of the HPC community [1]. One key ingredient is KIT's Future Technology Platform - allowing users to "future-proof" their software by ensuring early compatibility and performance optimization for emerging hardware architectures. With this, the service has evolved into a scalable and adaptable platform, enabling users to test and benchmark their codes directly on cutting-edge HPC resources.

Built upon the widely adopted GitLab CI/CD framework and supporting containerized workflows, the service is structured around a tiered model of increasing complexity and capability, ranging from basic build-and-test routines to advanced configurations involving full HPC job integration, as documented in the public CI guidelines [1]. Performance monitoring is further enhanced through the integration of JobMon [2], a web-based performance service visualizing selected performance metrics collected on the cluster nodes during runtime of a job.

While the de facto standard approach via Jacamar-CI [3] requires a dedicated GitLab instance, NHR@KIT offers a more flexible solution: users can register their own runners for any GitLab instance using a well-documented template and setup scripts. This approach was inspired by the Ginkgo RSE team [4], who initially developed a bespoke CI/CB workflow. Based on this offer, some users implemented sophisticated pipelines, while many continue to rely on GitLab's default shell executor, which suffices for simpler use cases. Prominent projects such as Ginkgo [4], Heat [5], and openCARP [6] have adopted NHR@KIT's CI/CB service successfully or are evaluating it, serving as reference cases for others.

Looking ahead, NHR@KIT plans to extend its training portfolio, simplify tooling, and lower entry barriers. Although the runner infrastructure is openly shared as infrastructure-as-code, questions around cross-institutional coordination—e.g., within the Helmholtz association—remain open. Given the diverse cluster environments and user expectations, a unified solution may not be feasible; rather, modular and interoperable approaches appear more promising for future development.

2.2 The Impact of CI/CB During JUPITER's Ascension

While CI/CB as a production service for users of HPC systems illustrates the clear value, and yet also challenges, for users and developers, the next sections goes one more step back in time, showing how CI/CB is an important ingredient for procuring a new system.

During the preparatory phase for the JUPITER exascale supercomputer [7], the integration of Continuous Benchmarking (CB) emerged as a critical strategy. As part of the JUPITER early access program JUREAP, the in-house developed exaCB system [8] was deployed to automate benchmarking across 50 key applications. Building on the JuBE benchmarking framework [13,14] and incorporating Jacamar-CI for SLURM integration, exaCB was embedded as a GitLab CI component capable of generating structured performance reports, including plots and tables, and supporting both strong and weak scaling tests. This automation replaced previously manual benchmarking methods, which were prone to inconsistency and latency in anomaly detection. The early adoption of CB—even before JUPITER became operational—enabled reproducible, large-scale application performance studies, and highlighted system-level issues such as faulty SLURM updates and workflow inconsistencies on the JEDI machine.

The JUPITER procurement process presented a unique opportunity to embed robust performance monitoring mechanisms "right from the start," especially given the anticipated operational challenges such as low mean time between failures (MTBF) and diverse user workloads. CB proved invaluable not only for system administrators—who leveraged it to track machine health and performance variability across applications—but also for users, who used it to benchmark and validate their codes during onboarding. The process, however, was not without challenges: diverse workflows, a tight procurement timeline, and significant person-month investments were required to design and maintain the system. Additional components such as energy monitoring were integrated into the workflow to support energy efficiency evaluations. With procurement finalized, the development of exaCB has now resumed, focusing on improved SLURM integration and enhanced user experience through the GitLab interface. The tool has also become instrumental in compute time reviews and is actively being improved with feedback from JUREAP users who contributed directly to its refinement. Overall, the structured approach offered by exaCB demonstrates how CI/CB frameworks can bridge the needs of HPC operations and software development, and highlights the potential of standardized, component-based benchmarking workflows in future exascale environments.

2.3 Utilization of CI/CB in Fugaku and FugakuNEXT

While the previous sections highlighted how CI/CB can be offered to users as part of a productive service or used in the tendering, setup and commissioning of a supercomputer, it can also be leveraged at an even earlier stage as part of designing a new system.

The FugakuNEXT project, launched in April 2025 by RIKEN R-CCS, represents Japan's next-generation supercomputing initiative, with a shift toward supporting both high-performance computing (HPC) and AI workloads through a GPU-accelerated architecture. As part of the co-design methodology driving FugakuNEXT, CI/CB approaches are positioned as central tools for application and system software evaluation. Building on lessons learned from the supercomputer Fugaku, R-CCS incorporates CI/CB technologies to systematically test and optimize software throughout the development life cycle. CI/CB capabilities are currently offered to a limited group of R-CCS developers on login nodes, including the ability to register custom GitLab runners. Initial efforts required significant adaptation of Jacamar-CI to support the Fugaku architecture, which did not function out-of-the-box. While these modifications form the foundation of the R-CCS CI/CB stack, they have not yet been merged upstream due to merge request conflicts.

An early and practical example of CI/CB in action is the integration of Spack-based package builds on Fugaku. Given that builds on this system have proven less stable than on comparable platforms, automated CI pipelines have been established to monitor and remediate package build failures. These workflows also require synchronization between GitHub and internal GitLab repositories—an ongoing challenge when using Jacamar-CI. As FugakuNEXT moves from feasibility study to basic design phase (ongoing through 2025), a more open and extensible CI/CB platform is being developed. This includes benchmarking pipelines for both applications and system software, enabling quantitative evaluation of the system design and early prototypes. Historical performance data will be recorded and shared with the broader community to inform both system architects and application developers. Furthermore, R-CCS is collaborating with the U.S. Department of Energy on the BenchPark initiative [9], which aims to create a standardized benchmarking framework across diverse architectures. These efforts collectively underscore the role of CI/CB in bridging system design, application readiness, and reproducibility in the path toward exascale and AI-capable HPC systems.

These three examples from KIT, JSC and R-CCS illustrate different approaches for the usage of CI/CB at different stages of the life cycle of an HPC system. They illustrate the importance of the contribution CI/CB can have for the usage, commissioning and design of a modern HPC cluster. Among other aspects, all three examples show that CI/CB is a crucial aspect that in itself depends on the availability of a sustainable, reliable, and ideally standardized tool chain for setting up, running and evaluating the runs.

3 User Perspectives

In addition to the findings for leveraging CI/CB in the different stages of the life cycle of an HPC system presented in the previous section, key players for providing insights into the state-of-the-art usage of and demand for CI/CB services and setups are the users and developers of software for HPC systems. This section highlights some of their perspectives raised at the workshop, both as part of the presentations as well as during the discussions.

While CI/CB is becoming increasingly important in HPC software development, research software engineers and users of simulation codes report significant challenges when adopting those techniques for the software. For instance, OpenFOAM [10], a widely used CFD toolkit, has established an extensive, fully automated validation database with over 700 test cases, enabling robust quality assurance. The diversity and size of both OpenFOAM's code and user base necessitate collaborative and flexible tooling, also because the software does not adhere to standard build systems, opting instead for a custom approach. Managing CI/CD workflows under these circumstances across heterogeneous HPC environments adds to this complexity and require treating this infrastructure with great care and dedicated, very much like the original research software. The developers underscore that while software sustainability is important for a code of this size and impact, it does require high and enforced standards of code quality (e.g., through CI pipelines), which in turn increases the complexity and overhead for contributors.

For libNEGF [11], a component of the larger DFTB+ package [12], the developers implemented end-to-end health checks using the JuBE framework. Continuous integration and benchmarking workflows are executed on dedicated, self-operated hosts via Docker containers, ensuring a controlled and reproducible testing environment. This setup balances flexibility and reproducibility, though it does imply ongoing effort in maintaining both the hardware and software components of the CI/CB environment in addition to the actual research software.

PIConGPU [15], a highly parallel particle-in-cell simulation framework targeting exascale performance, faces particularly intense testing demands. As new HPC architectures emerged—from Intel Xeon Phi to GPUs from NVIDIA, AMD, and Intel—the developers were driven to adopt a hardware-agnostic programming model using the alpaka abstraction library [16]. This facilitates the separation of application-level physics validation from lower-level math- and implementation-specific tests. However, the combinatorial explosion of test parameters (up to 2.5 million combinations per release, 30+ years for running the whole set) poses a critical challenge. To address this, the team uses pairwise testing to strategically sample the configuration space, implemented using automated job generation within GitLab CI. They further optimize test coverage by focusing on key versions of dependencies—typically the newest and oldest—to detect regressions while maintaining a manageable testing burden.

During this workshop, a recurring theme emerged: while automated testing, integration and benchmarking are indispensable for software reliability and sustainability, in particular in HPC, they require substantial engineering effort, system knowledge, and thoughtful reduction of complexity to remain tractable. This is further complicated by different solutions and interfaces employed by different centers. Often these differences emerge due to the need to address specific use-cases, operational models and security concerns.

4 Impending Split and a Call to Action

A severe threat this community is facing is an impending or even already ongoing split: there are multiple tool chains available to enable continuous benchmarking workflows for both users and operators of HPC systems. Many of these tool chains require entirely different configurations from users and provide incompatible interfaces and sometimes even very different output formats, data and granularity. Many of these are also in constant development (using the same CI practices we recommend for scientific codes), which adds a temporal depth to the problem and stresses the need for maintenance of the tool chains.

There are 3 levels of infrastructure where diversity can be seen:

1. At the version control platform level (limiting ourselves to git-based technologies), where different platforms offer different workflows and tools to implement CI/CB workflows. The community is mainly split between GitHub and GitLab, and many projects have spent considerable effort to bridge the two platforms, often with hand-crafted API calls.

2. At the software build/delivery system level, where different solutions such as spack [19], easybuild [20] as well as containerization frameworks like Apptainer/Singularity [21], Podman [22] or Enroot [23] cover different use cases with different trade-offs in terms of performance and control vs. portability and convenience. This level of infrastructure is typically managed by the HPC system administrators since it is either more difficult or outright impossible (because of user permissions) for users and developers to set these systems up and integrate into the environment of the HPC system;
3. At the end of the tool chain, different tools are acting as benchmarking drivers, collection and management systems for data and metadata or data visualization tools. Examples for tools typically employed for this step by different groups and centers are ReFrame [24], JuBE [13], Ramble [25] and JobMon [2], among others.

While diversity in solutions is generally favorable and something the scientific community has always been doing, the lack of common standards and interoperability is a major problem, for both users and operators. Operators are not able to compare their benchmark results properly with other hosting sites if the raw data cannot be accessed or processed or the metadata schema is not sufficiently clear. Users have to rely on the tool chain provided by the operators of the HPC system they are working with and may have to implement their continuous benchmarking workflows for different systems from scratch, impeding portability. Both drawbacks severely limit the acceptance and spreading of continuous benchmarking (and also integration to a certain extend) as a valuable service for users and operations on the one hand, but also as good scientific practice when working with HPC software on the other hand.

Hence, we end this summary paper with a call to action: the users, operators, research software engineers, researchers who code, they all need common standards for doing CI/CB on large HPC infrastructures. Benchmark workflows and data need to be FAIR: findable, accessible, interoperable, reusable (the latter only goes so far, admittedly). We explicitly value diversity in the field, in terms of point of origin, supporting institutions, technical approaches taken, complexity, target group, and so on. Science thrives also through competition and this niche is not an exception. Yet, joining forces by using common standards, at least for interfaces and output format and information, will bring this whole field much further than any single player alone could ever hope to get. Platforms like the workshop this paper summarizes or the High-Performance Software Foundation (HPSF, [17]) benchmarking working group are great places to continue this discussion and to initiate first steps. Let us not wait longer.

Acknowledgments. The authors thank all the speakers at the workshop, who contributed their valuable expertise, ideas and approaches:
- Jayesh Badwaik, Jülich Supercomputing Centre, Forschungszentrum Jülich GmbH, Germany
- Hitoshi Murai, RIKEN Center for Computational Science, Japan
- Fabian Schlegel, Helmholtz-Zentrum Dresden-Rossendorf, Germany
- Olga Pearce, Lawrence Livermore National Laboratory, USA

- Christoph Conrads, Jülich Supercomputing Centre, Forschungszentrum Jülich GmbH, Germany
- Michele Martone, Arjun Parab, Amir Raoofy, Leibniz Supercomputing Centre, Germany
- Thomas Breuer, Jülich Supercomputing Centre, Forschungszentrum Jülich GmbH, Germany
- Andy Turner, EPCC - The University of Edinburgh, United Kingdom
- Marcel Koch, Karlsruhe Institute of Technology, Germany
- Varun Sudharshnam, Helmholtz-Zentrum Dresden-Rossendorf, Germany
- Simeon Ehrig, Center for Advanced Systems Understanding, Germany.

In addition, the authors thank everyone participating in the Workshop and contributing to the lively discussion with their expertise, experiences and point of views.

A special recognition goes to the organization team of the workshop, who together with the authors helped in bringing together, spreading the word and evaluating the submission for the lightning talks:

- Stefanie Reuter, ECMWF
- Matthew Archer, University of Cambridge
- Andy Turner, EPCC - The University of Edinburgh
- Daniel S. Katz, National Center for Supercomputing Applications, University of Illinois Urbana-Champaign
- Jayesh Badwaik, Jülich Supercomputing Centre, Forschungszentrum Jülich GmbH
- Weronika Filinger, EPCC - The University of Edinburgh
- Sarah Neuwirth, Johannes Gutenberg University of Mainz.

Finally, this work and the three authors were supported by the Joint Lab HiRSE [18], funded by the Helmholtz Association.

Disclosure of Interests. The authors have no competing interests to declare that are relevant to the content of this article.

References

1. Scientific Computing Center at KIT. NHR@KIT User Documentation: Continuous Integration. https://www.nhr.kit.edu/userdocs/ci/. Accessed 4 July 2025
2. Scientific Computing Center at KIT. JobMon - Job Performance Metrics. https://www.nhr.kit.edu/userdocs/horeka/jobmon/. Accessed 4 July 2025
3. Jacamar-CI website and software. https://gitlab.com/ecp-ci/jacamar-ci. Accessed 4 July 2025
4. Ginkgo Website. https://ginkgo-project.github.io/. Accessed 4 July 2025
5. Götz, M., et al.: HeAT - a Distributed and GPU-accelerated tensor framework for data analytics. In 2020 IEEE International Conference on Big Data (Big Data), pp. 276–287. IEEE (2020). https://doi.org/10.1109/BigData50022.2020.9378050
6. Plank, G., et al.: The openCARP Simulation environment for cardiac electrophysiology. Comput. Methods Programs Biomed. **208**, 106223 (2021). https://doi.org/10.1016/j.cmpb.2021.106223
7. Jülich Supercomputing Centre at Forschungszentrum Jülich GmbH. JUPITER Website. https://www.fz-juelich.de/jupiter. Accessed 4 July 2025
8. ExaCB website and software. https://exacb.pages.jsc.fz-juelich.de/. Accessed 4 July 2025

9. Pearce, O., et al.: Towards collaborative continuous benchmarking for HPC. In Proceedings of the SC 2023 Workshops of the International Conference on High Performance Computing, Network, Storage, and Analysis (SC-W 2023), pp. 627–635. Association for Computing Machinery, New York, NY, USA (2023). https://doi.org/10.1145/3624062.3624135
10. OpenFOAM website and software. https://openfoam.org/. Accessed 4 July 2025
11. Pecchia, A., Salvucci, L., Penazzi, G., Di Carlo, A.: Non-equilibrium Green's functions in density functional tight binding: method and applications. New J. Phys. **10**, 065022 (2008). https://doi.org/10.1088/1367-2630/10/6/065022
12. Hourahine, B., et al.: DFTB+, a software package for efficient approximate density functional theory based atomistic simulations. J. Chem. Phys. **152**(12), 124101 (2020). https://doi.org/10.1063/1.5143190
13. Breuer, T., Wellmann, J., Souza Mendes Guimarães, F., Himmels, C., Luehrs, S.: JUBE (REL-2.7.1). Zenodo (2024). https://doi.org/10.5281/zenodo.11394333
14. Lührs, S., Rohe, D., Schnurpfeil, A., Thust, K., Frings, W.: Flexible and generic workflow management. In: Parallel Computing: On the Road to Exascale, vol. 27. Advances in Parallel Computing. International Conference on Parallel Computing 2015, Edinburgh (United Kingdom), 1 Sep 2015 – 4 Sep 2015 (2016). https://doi.org/10.3233/978-1-61499-621-7-431
15. Bussmann, M., et al.: Radiative signatures of the relativistic Kelvin-Helmholtz instability. In: Proceedings of the International Conference on High Performance Computing, Networking, Storage and Analysis (SC 2013), pp. 1–12. Association for Computing Machinery, New York, NY, USA (2013). https://doi.org/10.1145/2503210.2504564
16. Matthes, A., Widera, R., Zenker, E., Worpitz, B., Huebl, A., Bussmann, M.: Tuning and optimization for a variety of many-core architectures without changing a single line of implementation code using the Alpaka library. In: Kunkel, J., Yokota, R., Taufer, M., Shalf, J. (eds.) High Performance Computing. ISC High Performance 2017. Lecture Notes in Computer Science, vol. 10524. Springer, Cham (2017). https://doi.org/10.1007/978-3-319-67630-2_36
17. High Performance Software Foundation website. https://hpsf.io/. Accessed 4 July 2025
18. Joint Lab HiRSE (Helmholtz Information - Research Software Engineering) website. https://www.helmholtz-hirse.de/. Accessed 4 July 2025
19. Gamblin, T., et al.: The Spack package manager: bringing order to HPC software chaos. In: Supercomputing 2015 (SC 2015), Austin, Texas, November 15–20 2015. LLNL-CONF-669890 (2015). https://spack.io/. Accessed 4 July 2025
20. The High-Performance Computing team at Ghent University and the Easybuild community. EasyBuild - building software with ease. https://easybuild.io/. Accessed 4 July 2025
21. Singularity Developers: Singularity (2021). https://doi.org/10.5281/zenodo.1310023
22. Podman: A tool for managing OCI containers and pods. https://github.com/containers/podman. Accessed 4 July 2025
23. Enroot: A simple yet powerful tool to turn traditional container/OS images into unprivileged sandboxes. https://github.com/NVIDIA/enroot. Accessed 4 July 2025

24. Karakasis, V., et al.: Enabling continuous testing of HPC systems using ReFrame. In: Juckeland, G., Chandrasekaran, S. (eds.)Tools and Techniques for High Performance Computing. HUST - Annual Workshop on HPC User Support Tools (Denver, Colorado, USA, Nov. 17–18, 2019), vol. 1190. Communications in Computer and Information Science, pp. 49–68. Springer International Publishing, Cham, Switzerland (2020). https://doi.org/10.1007/978-3-030-44728-1_3
25. Jacobsen, D., et al.: Ramble: a multi-platform experimentation framework written in python. https://github.com/GoogleCloudPlatform/ramble. Accessed 4 July 2025

Author Index

A

Aach, Marcel 148
Abolhasani, Milad 668
Abt, Jordan M. 191
Abu Saleh, Muhammad 401
Acquaviva, Andrea 576
Adamson, Ryan 363
Aderholdt, Ferrol 401
Afaganis, John 480
Amati, Giorgio 245
Anzt, Hartwig 468, 494
Arzt, Peter 287, 300
Asifuzzaman, Kazi 177
Assmann, Greta 376
Azab, Abdulrahman 660

B

Bacciu, Davide 111
Badar, Arif 509
Badawi, Maram Hesham 444
Badia, Rosa M. 668
Bai, Zhe 135
Balaprakash, Prasanna 615
Banchelli, Fabio 562
Bartolini, Andrea 123, 576
Bau, David 615
Benini, Luca 576
Ben-Nun, Tal 615
Bhatele, Abhinav 615
Billa, Surendra 509
Bischof, Christian 287, 300
Bisht, Ashish 521
Blanc, Cyril 148
Blaszczyk, Andreas 494
Bloch, Gil 401
Boella, Elisabetta 245
Bonachea, Dan 135
Borghesi, Andrea 3
Bouslama, Amir 494
Brandoni, Domitilla 162
Brandt, Steve 626

Brayford, David 660
Brim, Michael J. 363
Brown, Nick 598
Bruce, Bobby R. 177

C

Calder, Alan 52
Carlson, David 52
Carretero, Jesus 387
Caspart, René 683
Castelló, Adrián 431, 534
Catalán, Sandra 534
Cavalli, Laura 162
Ceccolini, Gabriele 576
Ceni, Andrea 111
Cesarini, Daniele 123
Clair, Felix Le 598
Cossu, Andrea 111
Crespo, Luís 548
Croce, Danilo 245
Curtis, Anthony 52

D

da Silva, Rafael Ferreira 363
Davies, Jake 598
De Grave, Kurt 148
Deelman, Ewa 668
Deepika, H. V. 521
Deniel, Philippe 655
Diehl, Patrick 626
Dini, Paolo 219
Dorigo, Alvise 376

E

Eisenbach, Markus 231
Elwasif, Wael 231
Ergawy, Kareem 135
Esqueu, Rafel Albert Bros 562
Etz, Brian D. 363

F

Favre, Jean M. 95
Ferreira da Silva, Rafael 668
Ficarelli, Federico 576
Folchini, Sara 111
Franchetti, Franz 615
Franusich, Michael 615
Frings, Wolfgang 40

G

Gallicchio, Claudio 111
Gamblin, Todd 615
Gantikow, Holger 660
Garade, Aniket P. 521
Garcia-Blas, Javier 387
Garcia-Gasulla, Dario 311
Gebert, Johannes 456
Georgakoudis, Giorgis 615
Gerrits, Tim 67
Glück, Dan 456
Godoy, William F. 177, 615
Godoy, William 231
Goldstein, Tom 615
Gonzalez-Mallo, Marta 311
Gorentla Venkata, Manjunath 401
Grant, Ryan E. 191
Gregori, Daniele 245, 576
Guha, Arjun 615
Guimarães, Filipe Souza Mendes 40
Gutierrez, Cristian 311
Gutmann, Ethan 135

H

Hahn, Steven E. 615
Hanawa, Toshihiro 271
Haribabu, P. 521
Harrison, Robert J. 52
Hautreux, Gabriel 258
Heldmann, Tim 287, 300
Hernandez, Oscar 177, 231
Honda, Hiroki 639
Huang, Carlus 480

I

Iancu, Costin 615
Ibrahim, Khaled 416
Igual, Francisco D. 431, 534
Ilsche, Thomas 205
Ionkov, Latchesar 339

J

Jadhav, Rushikesh 509
Jin, Zheming 615
Jones, Terry 615

K

Kaiser, Hartmut 626
Kannan, Venkatesh 655
Kent, Paul R. C. 177
Kestor, Gokcen 311
Klemm, Michael 135
Kniep, Christian 660
Koch, Marcel 468
Krašovec, Barbara 660
Kress, James 81
Kreutzer, Sebastian 287
Krüger, Marcel 67
Kuhlen, Torsten W. 67
Kumar, S. A. 521

L

Lange, Jack 363
Leland, Kellen 363
Leone, Davide 3
Leonelli, Caterina 219
Liao, Chunhua 325
Lintermann, Andreas 148
Liu, Jun 480
Lomonaco, Vincenzo 111
Loreti, Daniela 3
Low, Tze-Meng 615
Lowe-Power, Jason 177

M

Madella, Giacomo 576
Maheshwari, Ketan 363
Mankad, Het 615
Manoni, Simone 576
Mantovani, Filippo 562
Martens, Silas 287
Martínez, Héctor 431, 534
Melesse Vergara, Verónica G. 363
Mendula, Matteo 219
Menon, Harshitha 615
Mesiti, Michele 683
Miller, Ross 231
Millette, Chris 480
Miniskar, Narasinga Rao 177, 615
Mintz, Benjamin 668

Author Index

Miozzo, Marco 219
Miwa, Shinobu 639
Monil, Mohammad Alaul Haque 615
Monterubbiano, Andrea 245
Moore, Robert G. 668
Morselli, Laura 162

N

Nader, Noujoud 626
Navuluru, Sai Karthik 416
Nayak, Pratik 494
Neves, Nuno 548, 562
Nichols, Daniel 615
Noor Mohamed, Mohamed Husain 339

O

Ohara, Ryoma 271
Olenik, Gregor 468
Oral, Sarp 363
Osama, Muhammad 480
Ozturk, Muhammed Emin 480

P

Paipuri, Mahendra 28
Paladino, Mattia 245
Parab, Arjun 351
Parasyris, Konstantinos 615
Patil, Adarsh 339
Patrou, Maria 177, 231
Pelfrey, Daniel 363
Pflüger, Dirk 586
Piccinali, Jean-Guillaume 95
Pirkelbauer, Peter 325
Pizzini Cavagna, Hiari 123
Podkorytov, Maksim 480
Pophale, Swaroop 615
Prica, Teo 15

Q

Quintana-Ortí, Enrique S. 431, 534

R

Rai, Astha 480
Raoofy, Amir 351
Rasmussen, Katherine 135
Richardson, Brad 135
Rocha, Tiago 562
Rogers, David M. 363
Roma, Nuno 548, 562

Rouson, Damian 135
Royuela, Sara 311

S

Sadasivan, Harisankar 480
Sala, Leonardo 376
Sanchez-Checa, Paula 387
Sankaran, Aravind 40
Saravanan, Vijayalakshmi 416
Schäfer, Jonathan 456
Scheda, Riccardo 162
Schirmeier, Horst 205
Schöne, Robert 205
Shaikh, Mohsin Ahmed 444
Shalf, John 668
Shankar, Mallikarjun 363
Sharapov, Borys 376
Shatsman, Yuri 401
Shende, Sameer 135
Siegmann, Eva 52
Simakov, Nikolay A. 52
Sinclair, Matthew D. 177
Singh, David E. 387
Skluzacek, Tyler J. 363
Smejkal, Till 205
Smith, Shaina 191
Sonawane, Yogeshwar 509
Speck, Robert 683
Strack, Alexander 586
Sudarsan, S. D. 521
Sukumar, Sreenivas Rangan 675

T

Talamo, Ivano 376
Talon, Suzanne 655
Tamil, Lakshman 416
Tanaka, Rin 639
Taufer, Michela 668
Taylor, Christopher 586
Teranishi, Keita 615
Theußl, Thomas 81
Tiffany, Zach 401
Tomas, Pedro 548
Tomás, Pedro 562
Torres, Ariana 655
Torres, David 135
Tradonsky, Chene 456
Trinitis, Carsten 494

Tröpgen, Hannes 205
Turisini, Matteo 245

V

Valenzuela, Andrea 311
Valero-Lara, Pedro 177, 615
Van Hensbergen, Eric 339
Varghese, Roy 675
Venieri, Emanuele 576
Vet, Jean-Yves 258
Vetter, Jeffrey S. 177, 615

W

Wandhekar, Sanjay 509
Wang, Thomas 231
Webb, Jordan 363
Weidendorfer, Josef 351

Wells, Jack C. 675
Widener, Patrick 363
Williams, Samuel 615

Y

Yamaki, Hayato 639
Yamamoto, Keiji 271
Young, Aaron 615

Z

Zambre, Rohit 401
Zamuda, Aleš 15
Zhang, Jing 480
Zhang, Yunhao 135
Ziegler, Tim 300
Zimmer, Christopher 363

Made in the USA
Monee, IL
03 May 2026

49438660R00391

PRAISE FOR LILI ST. GERMAIN
AND THE CARTEL TRILOGY

'Good lord, this series ... this book ... these characters ...
they are seriously playing all sorts of havoc with my emotions,
my feelings, my nerves and my anxiety levels'
THE HOPELESS ROMANTICS BOOK BLOG

'Possibly the best series I've ever read. Powerful, emotional,
entertaining, confronting yet clever storyline with plots, twists
and shocks – I could not put these books down.'
NAT COOLS FROM OZ, IBOOKS

'Had me on a tight grip for the entire ride ...
I was completely immersed' THE READING ESCAPADE

'Finally, a book that grabbed and kept my attention from
start to finish!' BOOK VIGILANTE REVIEWS

'Awesome job Lili ... I am ready to hop on the back of a bike
and join the club!' THE LITERARYGOSSIP BOOK BLOG

'Sensational, shocking, compelling and totally addictive ...
the best when it comes to dark, brooding and bloody romance'
KELLY, PERUSING PRINCESSES

Lili takes you for a walk on the dark and dirty side of life. She makes
you question how far you'd be willing to go to save those you loved
and what lengths you'd go to to survive. What happens when the lines
of right and wrong blur and when the lines of hate and love
are crossed ...' OBSESSED BY BOOKS

'Fast-paced. Thrilling. Violent. Dark. Raw. Ruthless'
WICKED READS

'Cartel is just the beginning to what promises to be an erotic,
twisted journey' THE ROMANCE REVIEWS